Elements of Criticism

Elements of Criticism
Henry Home, Lord Kames

MINT EDITIONS

Elements of Criticism was first published in 1762.

This edition published by Mint Editions 2021.

ISBN 9781513218267 | E-ISBN 9781513217260

Published by Mint Editions®

minteditionbooks.com

Publishing Director: Jennifer Newens
Design & Production: Rachel Lopez Metzger
Project Manager: Micaela Clark
Typesetting: Westchester Publishing Services

Contents

Volume I

Introduction	9
I. Perceptions and ideas in a train	17
II. Emotions and Passions	26
III. Beauty	116
IV. Grandeur and Sublimity	126
V. Motion and Force	148
VI. Novelty, and the unexpected appearance of objects	153
VII. Risible Objects	161
VIII. Resemblance and Contrast	165
IX. Of Uniformity and Variety	182

Volume II

X. Congruity and Propriety	201
XI. Of Dignity and Meanness	211
XII. Ridicule	217
XIII. Wit	227
XIV. Custom and Habit	242

XV. External Signs of Emotions and Passions	257
XVI. Sentiments	271
XVII. Language of Passion	303
XVIII. Beauty of Language	320

Volume III

XIX. Comparisons	437
XX. Figures	468
XXI. Narration and Description	534
XXII. Epic and Dramatic Compositions	563
XXIII. The three Unities	580
XXIV. Gardening and Architecture	595
XXV. Standard of Taste	619
Appendix	629

VOLUME I

Introduction

The five senses agree in the following particular, that nothing external is perceived till it first make an impression upon the organ of sense; the impression, for example, made upon the hand by a stone, upon the palate by sugar, and upon the nostrils by a rose. But there is a difference as to our consciousness of that impression. In touching, tasting, and smelling, we are conscious of the impression. Not so in seeing and hearing. When I behold a tree, I am not sensible of the impression made upon my eye; nor of the impression made upon my ear, when I listen to a song[1]. This difference in the manner of perception, distinguishes remarkably hearing and seeing from the other senses; and distinguishes still more remarkably the feelings of the former from those of the latter. A feeling pleasant or painful cannot exist but in the mind; and yet because in tasting, touching, and smelling, we are conscious of the impression made upon the organ, we naturally place there also, the pleasant or painful feeling caused by that impression. And because such feelings seem to be placed externally at the organ of sense, we, for that reason, conceive them to be merely corporeal. We have a different apprehension of the pleasant and painful feelings derived from seeing and hearing. Being insensible here of the organic impression, we are not misled to assign a wrong place to these feelings; and therefore we naturally place them in the mind, where they really exist. Upon that account, they are conceived to be more refined and spiritual, than what are derived from tasting, touching, and smelling.

The pleasures of the eye and ear being thus elevated above those of the other external senses, acquire so much dignity as to make them a laudable entertainment. They are not, however, set upon a level with those that are purely intellectual; being not less inferior in dignity to intellectual pleasures, than superior to the organic or corporeal. They indeed resemble the latter, being like them produced by external objects: but they also resemble the former, being like them produced without any sensible organic impression. Their mixt nature and middle place betwixt organic and intellectual pleasures, qualify them to associate with either. Beauty heightens all the organic feelings, as well as those

---

1. See the Appendix, § 13.

that are intellectual. Harmony, though it aspires to inflame devotion, disdains not to improve the relish of a banquet.

The pleasures of the eye and ear have other valuable properties beside those of dignity and elevation. Being sweet and moderately exhilerating, they are in their tone equally distant from the turbulence of passion, and languor of inaction; and by that tone are perfectly well qualified, not only to revive the spirits when sunk by sensual gratification, but also to relax them when overstrained in any violent pursuit. Here is a remedy provided for many distresses. And to be convinced of its salutary effects, it will be sufficient to run over the following particulars. Organic pleasures have naturally a short duration: when continued too long, or indulged to excess, they lose their relish, and beget satiety and disgust. To relieve us from that uneasiness, nothing can be more happily contrived than the exhilerating pleasures of the eye and ear, which take place imperceptibly, without much varying the tone of mind. On the other hand, any intense exercise of the intellectual powers, becomes painful by overstraining the mind. Cessation from such exercise gives not instant relief: it is necessary that the void be filled with some amusement, gently relaxing the spirits[2]. Organic pleasure, which hath no relish but while we are in vigour, is ill qualified for that office: but the finer pleasures of sense, which occupy without exhausting the mind, are excellently well qualified to restore its usual tone after severe application to study or business, as well as after satiety from sensual gratification.

Our first perceptions are of external objects, and our first attachments are to them. Organic pleasures take the lead. But the mind, gradually ripening, relisheth more and more the pleasures of the eye and ear; which approach the purely mental, without exhausting the spirits; and exceed the purely sensual, without danger of satiety. The pleasures of the eye and ear have accordingly a natural aptitude to attract us from the immoderate gratification of sensual appetite. For the mind, once accustomed to enjoy a variety of external objects without being conscious of the organic impression, is prepared for enjoying internal objects where there cannot be an organic impression. Thus the author of nature, by qualifying the human mind for a succession of enjoyments from the lowest to the highest, leads it by gentle steps from the most groveling

---

2. Du Bos judiciously observes, that silence doth not tend to calm an agitated mind; but that soft and slow music hath a fine effect.

corporeal pleasures, for which solely it is fitted in the beginning of life, to those refined and sublime pleasures which are suited to its maturity.

This succession, however, is not governed by unavoidable necessity. The God of nature offers it to us, in order to advance our happiness; and it is sufficient, that he hath enabled us to complete the succession. Nor has he made our task disagreeable or difficult. On the contrary, the transition is sweet and easy, from corporeal pleasures to the more refined pleasures of sense; and not less so, from these to the exalted pleasures of morality and religion. We stand therefore engaged in honour, as well as interest, to second the purposes of nature, by cultivating the pleasures of the eye and ear, those especially that require extraordinary culture[3], such as are inspired by poetry, painting, sculpture, music, gardening, and architecture. This chiefly is the duty of the opulent, who have leisure to improve their minds and their feelings. The fine arts are contrived to give pleasure to the eye and the ear, disregarding the inferior senses. A taste for these arts is a plant that grows naturally in many soils; but, without culture, scarce to perfection in any soil. It is susceptible of much refinement; and is, by proper care, greatly improved. In this respect, a taste in the fine arts goes hand in hand with the moral sense, to which indeed it is nearly allied. Both of them discover what is right and what is wrong. Fashion, temper, and education, have an influence upon both, to vitiate them, or to preserve them pure and untainted. Neither of them are arbitrary or local. They are rooted in human nature, and are governed by principles common to all men. The principles of morality belong not to the present undertaking. But as to the principles of the fine arts, they are evolved, by studying the sensitive part of human nature, and by learning what objects are naturally agreeable, and what are naturally disagreeable. The man who aspires to be a critic in these arts, must pierce still deeper. He must clearly perceive what objects are lofty, what low, what are proper or improper, what are manly, and what are mean or trivial. Hence a foundation for judging of taste, and for reasoning upon it. Where it is conformable to principles, we can pronounce with certainty, that it is correct; otherwise, that it is incorrect, and perhaps

---

3. A taste for natural objects is born with us in perfection; for relishing a fine countenance, a rich landscape, or a vivid colour, culture is unnecessary. The observation holds equally in natural sounds, such as the singing of birds, or the murmuring of a brook. Nature here, the artificer of the object as well as of the percipient, hath accurately suited them to each other. But of a poem, a cantata, a picture, or other artificial production, a true relish is not commonly attained, without some study and much practice.

whimsical. Thus the fine arts, like morals, become a rational science; and, like morals, may be cultivated to a high degree of refinement.

Manifold are the advantages of criticism, when thus studied as a rational science. In the first place, a thorough acquaintance with the principles of the fine arts, redoubles the entertainment these arts afford. To the man who resigns himself entirely to sentiment or feeling, without interposing any sort of judgment, poetry, music, painting, are mere pastime. In the prime of life, indeed, they are delightful, being supported by the force of novelty, and the heat of imagination. But they lose their relish gradually with their novelty; and are generally neglected in the maturity of life, which disposes to more serious and more important occupations. To those who deal in criticism as a regular science, governed by just principles, and giving scope to judgment as well as to fancy, the fine arts are a favourite entertainment; and in old age maintain that relish which they produce in the morning of life[4].

In the next place, a philosophic inquiry into the principles of the fine arts, inures the reflecting mind to the most enticing sort of logic. Reasoning upon subjects so agreeable tends to a habit; and a habit, strengthening the reasoning faculties, prepares the mind for entering into subjects more difficult and abstract. To have, in this respect, a just conception of the importance of criticism, we need but reflect upon the common method of education; which, after some years spent in acquiring languages, hurries us, without the least preparatory discipline, into the most profound philosophy. A more effectual method to alienate the tender mind from abstract science, is beyond the reach of invention. With respect to such speculations, the bulk of our youth contrast a sort of hobgoblin terror, which is seldom, if ever, subdued. Those who apply to the arts, are trained in a very different manner. They are led, step by step, from the easier parts of the operation, to what are more difficult; and are not permitted to make a new motion, till they be perfected in those which regularly precede it. The science of criticism appears then to be an intermediate link, finely qualified for connecting the different parts of education into a regular chain. This science furnisheth an inviting opportunity to exercise the judgement: we delight to reason upon subjects that are equally pleasant and familiar:

---

4. "Though logic may subsist without rhetoric or poetry, yet so necessary to these last is a sound and correct logic, that without it they are no better than warbling trifles."

—HERMES, p. 6

we proceed gradually from the simpler to the more involved cases: and in a due course of discipline, custom, which improves all our faculties, bestows acuteness upon those of reason, sufficient to unravel all the intricacies of philosophy.

Nor ought it to be overlooked, that the reasonings employed upon the fine arts are of the same kind with those which regulate our conduct. Mathematical and metaphysical reasonings have no tendency to improve social intercourse: nor are they applicable to the common affairs of life. But a just taste in the fine arts, derived from rational principles, is a fine preparation for acting in the social state with dignity and propriety.

The science of criticism tends to improve the heart not less than the understanding. I observe, in the first place, that it hath a fine effect in moderating the selfish affections. A just taste in the fine arts, by sweetening and harmonizing the temper, is a strong antidote to the turbulence of passion and violence of pursuit. Elegance of taste procures to a man so much enjoyment at home, or easily within reach, that in order to be occupied, he is, in youth, under no temptation to precipitate into hunting, gaming, drinking; nor, in middle age, to deliver himself over to ambition; nor, in old age, to avarice. Pride, a disgustful selfish passion, exerts itself without control, when accompanied with a bad taste. A man of this stamp, upon whom the most striking beauty makes but a faint impression, feels no joy but in gratifying his ruling passion by the discovery of errors and blemishes. Pride, on the other hand, finds in the constitution no enemy more formidable than a delicate and discerning taste. The man upon whom nature and culture have bestowed this blessing, feels great delight in the virtuous dispositions and actions of others. He loves to cherish them, and to publish them to the world. Faults and failings, it is true, are to him not less obvious: but these he avoids, or removes out of sight, because they give him pain. In a word, there may be other passions, which, for a season, disturb the peace of society more than pride: but no other passion is so unwearied an antagonist to the sweets of social intercourse. Pride, tending assiduously to its gratification, puts a man perpetually in opposition to others; and disposes him more to relish bad than good qualities, even in a bosom friend. How different that disposition of mind, where every virtue in a companion or neighbour, is, by refinement of taste, set in its strongest light; and defects or blemishes, natural to all, are suppressed, or kept out of view?

In the next place, delicacy of taste tends not less to invigorate the social affections, than to moderate those that are selfish. To be convinced of this tendency, we need only reflect, that delicacy of taste necessarily heightens our sensibility of pain and pleasure, and of course our sympathy, which is the capital branch of every social passion. Sympathy in particular invites a communication of joys and sorrows, hopes and fears. Such exercise, soothing and satisfactory in itself, is productive necessarily of mutual good-will and affection.

One other advantage of criticism is reserved to the last place, being of all the most important, that it is a great support to morality. I insist on it with entire satisfaction, that no occupation attaches a man more to his duty than that of cultivating a taste in the fine arts. A just relish of what is beautiful, proper, elegant, and ornamental, in writing or painting, in architecture or gardening, is a fine preparation for discerning what is beautiful, just, elegant, or magnanimous, in character and behaviour. To the man who has acquired a taste so acute and accomplished, every action, wrong or improper, must be highly disgustful. If, in any instance, the overbearing power of passion sway him from his duty, he returns to it upon the first reflection, with redoubled resolution never to be swayed a second time. He has now an additional motive to virtue, a conviction derived from experience, that happiness depends on regularity and order, and that a disregard to justice or propriety never fails to be punished with shame and remorse[5].

Rude ages exhibit the triumph of authority over reason. Philosophers anciently were divided into sects: they were either Epicureans, Platonists, Stoics, Pythagoreans, or Sceptics. Men relied no farther upon their own judgement than to chuse a leader, whom they implicitly followed. In later times, happily, reason hath obtained the ascendant. Men now assert their native privilege of thinking for themselves, and disdain to be ranked in any sect, whatever be the science. I must except criticism, which, by what fatality I know not, continues to be not less slavish in its principles, nor less submissive to authority, than it was originally. Bossu, a celebrated French critic, gives many rules; but can discover no better

---

5. Genius is allied to a warm and inflammable constitution; delicacy of taste to calmness and sedateness. Hence it is common to find genius in one who is a prey to every passion; but seldom delicacy of taste. Upon a man possessed of that blessing, the moral duties, no less than the fine arts, make a deep impression, and counterbalance every irregular desire at the same time, a temper calm and sedate is not easily moved, even by a strong temptation.

foundation for any of them, than the practice merely of Homer and Virgil, supported by the authority of Aristotle. Strange, that in so long a work, the concordance or discordance of these rules with human nature, should never once have entered his thoughts! It could not surely be his opinion, that these poets, however eminent for genius, were intitled to give laws to mankind, and that nothing now remains but blind obedience to their arbitrary will. If in writing they followed no rule, why should they be imitated? If they studied nature, and were obsequious to rational principles, why should these be concealed from us?

With respect to the present undertaking, it is not the author's intention to give a regular treatise upon each of the fine arts in particular; but only, in general, to apply to them some remarks and observations drawn from human nature, the true source of criticism. The fine arts are calculated for our entertainment, or for making agreeable impressions; and, by that circumstance, are distinguished from the useful arts. In order then to be a critic in the fine arts, it is necessary, as above hinted, to know what objects are naturally agreeable, and what naturally disagreeable. A complete treatise on that subject would be a field by far too extensive to be thoroughly cultivated by anyone hand. The author pretends only to have entered upon the subject so far as necessary for supporting his critical remarks. And he assumes no merit from his performance, but that of evincing, perhaps more distinctly than hitherto has been done, that the genuine rules of criticism are all of them derived from the human heart. The sensitive part of our nature is a delightful speculation. What the author hath discovered or collected upon that subject, he chuses to impart in the gay and agreeable form of criticism; because he imagines, that this form will be more relished, and perhaps be not less instructive, than a regular and laboured disquisition. His plan is, to ascend gradually to principles, from facts and experiments, instead of beginning with the former, handled abstractly, and descending to the latter. But though criticism be thus his only declared aim, he will not disown, that all along he had it in view, to explain the nature of man, considered as a sensitive being, capable of pleasure and pain. And though he flatters himself with having made some progress in that important science, he is however too sensible of its extent and difficulty, to undertake it professedly, or to avow it as the chief purpose of the present work.

To censure works, not men, is the just prerogative of criticism; and accordingly all personal censure is here avoided, unless where necessary to illustrate some general proposition. No praise is claimed on that account; because censuring with a view merely to find fault, is an entertainment that humanity never relishes. Writers, one would imagine, should, above all others, be reserved upon that article, when they lie so open to retaliation. The author of this treatise, far from being confident of meriting no censure, entertains not even the slightest hope of such perfection. Amusement was at first the sole aim of his inquiries. Proceeding from one particular to another, the subject grew under his hand; and he was far advanced before the thought struck him, that his private meditations might be publicly useful. In public, however, he would not appear in a slovenly dress; and therefore he pretends not otherwise to apologise for his errors, than by observing, that, in a new subject, not less nice than extensive, errors are in some measure unavoidable. Neither pretends he to justify his taste in every particular. That point must be extremely clear, which admits not variety of opinion; and in some matters susceptible of great refinement, time is perhaps the only infallible touch-stone of taste. To this he appeals, and to this he chearfully submits.

N. B. THE ELEMENTS OF CRITICISM, meaning the whole, is a title too assuming for this work. A number of these elements or principles are here evolved: but as the author is far from imagining, that he has completed the list, a more humble title is proper, such as may express any undetermined number of parts less than the whole. This he thinks is signified by the title he has chosen, *viz.* ELEMENTS OF CRITICISM.

I

Perceptions and ideas in a train

A man while awake is sensible of a continued train of objects passing in his mind. It requires no activity on his part to carry on the train: nor has he power to vary it by calling up an object at will[1]. At the same time we learn from daily experience, that a train of thought is not merely casual. And if it depend not upon will, nor upon chance, we must try to evolve by what law it is governed. The subject is of importance in the science of human nature; and I promise beforehand, that it will be found of great importance in the fine arts.

It appears that the relations by which things are linked together, have a great influence in directing the train of thought; and we find by experience, that objects are connected in the mind precisely as they are externally. Beginning then with things external, we find that they are not more remarkable by their inherent properties than by their various relations. We cannot any where extend our view without perceiving things connected together by certain relations. One thing perceived to be a cause, is connected with its several effects; somethings are connected by contiguity in time, others by contiguity in place; some are connected by resemblance, some by contrast; some go before, some follow. Not a single thing appears solitary, and altogether devoid of connection. The only difference is, that some are intimately connected, some more slightly; some near, some at a distance.

Experience as well as reason may satisfy us, that the train of mental perceptions is in a great measure regulated by the foregoing relations. Where a number of things are linked together, the idea of anyone suggests the rest; and in this manner is a train of thoughts composed. Such is the law of succession; whether an original law, or whether directed by some

---

1. For how should this be done? what idea is it that we are to add? If we can specify the idea, that idea is already in the mind, and there is no occasion for any act of the will. If we cannot specify any idea, I next demand, how can a person will, or to what purpose, if there be nothing in view? We cannot form a conception of such a thing. If this argument need confirmation, I urge experience: whoever makes a trial will find, that ideas are linked together in the mind, forming a connected chain; and that we have not the command of any idea independent of the chain.

latent principle, is doubtful; and probably will forever remain so. This law, however, is not inviolable. It sometimes happens, though rarely, that an idea presents itself to the mind without any connection, so far at least as can be discovered.

But though we have not the absolute command of ideas, yet the Will hath a considerable influence in directing the order of connected ideas. There are few things but what are connected with many others. By this means, when anything becomes an object, whether in a direct survey, or ideally only, it generally suggests many of its connections. Among these a choice is afforded. We can insist upon one, rejecting others; and we can even insist upon what has the slightest connection. Where ideas are left to their natural course, they are generally continued through the strongest connections. The mind extends its view to a son more readily than to a servant, and more readily to a neighbour than to one living at a distance. This order may be varied by Will, but still within the limits of connected objects. In short, every train of ideas must be a chain, in which the particular ideas are linked to each other. We may vary the order of a natural train; but not so as to dissolve it altogether, by carrying on our thoughts in a loose manner without any connection. So far doth our power extend; and that power is sufficient for all useful purposes. To give us more power, would probably be detrimental instead of being salutary.

Will is not the only cause that prevents a train of thought from being continued through the strongest connections. Much depends on the present tone of mind; for a subject that accords with this tone is always welcome. Thus, in good spirits, a chearful subject will be introduced by the slightest connection; and one that is melancholy, not less readily in low spirits. Again, an interesting subject is recalled, from time to time, by any connection indifferently, strong or weak. This is finely touched by Shakespear, with relation to a rich cargo at sea.

> *My wind, cooling my broth,*
> *Would blow me to an ague, when I thought*
> *What harm a wind too great might do at sea.*
> *I should not see the sandy hour-glass run,*
> *But I should think of shallows and of flats;*
> *And see my wealthy Andrew dock'd in sand,*
> *Vailing her high top lower than her ribs,*
> *To kiss her burial. Should I go to church,*

> *And see the holy edifice of stone,*
> *And not bethink me strait of dangerous rocks?*
> *Which touching but my gentle vessel's side,*
> *Would scatter all the spices on the stream,*
> *Enrobe the roaring waters with my silks,*
> *And, in a word, but now worth this,*
> *And now worth nothing.*

—*Merchant of Venice*, act 1. sc. 1

Another cause clearly distinguishable from that now mentioned, hath also a considerable influence over the train of ideas. In some minds of a singular frame, thoughts and circumstances crowd upon each other by the slightest connection. I ascribe this to a defect in the faculty of discernment. A person who cannot accurately distinguish betwixt a slight connection and one that is more solid, is equally affected with both. Such a person must necessarily have a great command of ideas, because they are introduced by any relation indifferently; and the slighter relations, being without number, must furnish ideas without end. This doctrine is, in a lively manner, illustrated by Shakespear.

FALSTAFF: What is the gross sum that I owe thee?
HOSTESS: Marry, if thou wert an honest man, thyself and thy money too. Thou didst swear to me on a parcel-gilt goblet, sitting in my Dolphin chamber, at the round table, by a sea-coal fire, on Wednesday in Whitsun-week, when the Prince broke thy head for likening him to a singing man of Windsor, thou didst swear to me then, as I was washing thy wound, to marry me, and make me my Lady thy wife. Canst thou deny it? Did not Goodwife Keech, the butcher's wife, come in then, and call me Gossip Quickly? Coming in to borrow a mess of vinegar; telling us she had a good dish of prawns; whereby thou didst desire to eat some; whereby I told thee they were ill for a green wound? And didst not thou, when she was gone down stairs, desire me to be no more so familiarity with such poor people, saying, that ere long they should call me Madam? And didst thou not kiss me, and bid me fetch thee thirty shillings? I put thee now to thy book-oath, deny it if thou canst.

—*Second part*, *Henry* IV. *act* 2. *sc.* 2

On the other hand, a man, of accurate judgement cannot have a great flow of ideas. The slighter relations making no figure in his mind, have no power to introduce ideas. And hence it is, that accurate judgement is not friendly to declamation or copious eloquence. This reasoning is confirmed by experience; for it is a noted observation, That a great or comprehensive memory is seldom connected with a good judgement.

As an additional confirmation, I appeal to another noted observation, That wit and judgement are seldom united. Wit consists chiefly in joining things by distant and fanciful relations, which surprise because they are unexpected. Such relations being of the slightest kind, readily occur to that person only who makes every relation equally welcome. Wit, upon that account, is, in a good measure, incompatible with solid judgement; which, neglecting trivial relations, adheres to what are substantial and permanent. Thus memory and wit are often conjoined: solid judgement seldom with either.

The train of thought depends not entirely upon relations: another cause comes in for a share; and that is the sense of order and arrangement. To things of equal rank, where there is no room for a preference, order cannot be applied; and it must be indifferent in what manner they be surveyed; witness the sheep that make a flock, or the trees in a wood. But in things of unequal rank, order is a governing principle. Thus our tendency is, to view the principal subject before we descend to its accessories or ornaments, and the superior before the inferior or dependent. We are equally averse to enter into a minute consideration of constituent parts, till the thing be first surveyed as a whole. In passing from a part to the whole, and from an accessory to its principal, the connection is the same as in the opposite direction. But a sense of order aids the transition in the latter case, and a sense of disorder obstructs it in the former. It needs scarce be added, that in thinking or reflecting on any of these particulars, and in passing from one to another ideally, we are sensible of easiness or difficulty precisely as when they are set before our eyes.

Our sense of order is conspicuous with respect to natural operations; for it always coincides with the order of nature. Thinking upon a body in motion, we follow its natural course. The mind falls with a heavy body, descends with a river, and ascends with flame and smoke. In tracing out a family, we incline to begin at the founder, and to descend gradually to his latest posterity. On the contrary, musing on a lofty oak, we begin at the trunk, and mount from it to the branches. As to historical facts, we love to proceed in the order of time; or, which comes to the same, to proceed along the chain of causes and effects.

But though, in following out a historical chain, our bent is to proceed orderly from causes to their effects, we find not the same bent in matters of science. There we seem rather disposed to proceed from effects to their causes, and from particular propositions to those which are more general. Why this difference in matters that appear so nearly related? The cases are similar in appearance only, not in reality. In a historical chain, every event is particular, the effect of some former event, and the cause of others that follow. In such a chain, there is nothing to bias the mind from the order of nature. Widely different is the case of science, when we endeavour to trace out causes and their effects. Many experiments are commonly reduced under one cause; and again, many of these under someone still more general and comprehensive. In our progress from particular effects to general causes, and from particular propositions to the more comprehensive, we feel a gradual dilatation or expansion of mind, like what is felt in proceeding along an ascending series, which is extremely delightful. The pleasure here exceeds what arises from following the course of nature; and it is this pleasure which regulates our train of thought in the case now mentioned, and in others that are similar. These observations, by the way, furnish materials for instituting a comparison betwixt the synthetic and analytic methods of reasoning. The synthetic method descending regularly from principles to their consequences, is more agreeable to the strictness of order. But in following the opposite course in the analytic method, we have a sensible pleasure, like mounting upward, which is not felt in the other. The analytic method is more agreeable to the imagination. The other method will be preferred by those only who with rigidity adhere to order, and give no indulgence to natural emotions[2].

It appears then that we are framed by nature to relish order and connection. When an object is introduced by a proper connection, we are conscious of a certain pleasure arising from that circumstance. Among objects of equal rank, the pleasure is proportioned to the degree of connection; but among unequal objects, where we require a certain order, the pleasure arises chiefly from an orderly arrangement. Of this one may be made sensible, in tracing objects contrary to the course

---

[2]. A train of perceptions or ideas, with respect to its uniformity and variety, is handled afterwards, chap. 9.

of nature, or contrary to our sense of order. The mind proceeds with alacrity from a whole to its parts, and from a principal to its accessories; but in the contrary direction, it is sensible of a sort of retrograde motion, which is unpleasant. And here may be remarked the great influence of order upon the mind of man. Grandeur, which makes a deep impression, inclines us, in running over any series, to proceed from small to great, rather than from great to small. But order prevails over this tendency; and in parting from the whole to its parts, and from a subject to its ornaments, affords pleasure as well as facility, which are not felt in the opposite course. Elevation touches the mind not less than grandeur doth; and in raising the mind to elevated objects, there is a sensible pleasure. But the course of nature hath still a greater influence than elevation; and therefore the pleasure of falling with rain, and descending gradually with a river, prevails over that of mounting upward. Hence the agreeableness of smoke ascending in a calm morning. Elevation concurs with the course of nature, to make this object delightful.

I am extremely sensible of the disgust men generally have at abstract speculation; and for that reason I would avoid it altogether, were it possible in a work which professes to draw the rules of criticism from human nature, their true source. There is indeed no choice, other than to continue for sometime in the same track, or to abandon the undertaking altogether. Candor obliges me to notify this to my readers, that such of them whose aversion to abstract speculation is invincible, may stop short here; for till principles be explained, I can promise no entertainment to those who shun thinking. But I flatter myself with a different taste in the bulk of readers. Some few, I imagine, will relish the abstract part for its own sake; and many for the useful purposes to which it may be applied. For encouraging the latter to proceed with alacrity, I assure them beforehand that the foregoing speculation leads to many important rules of criticism, which shall be unfolded in the course of this work. In the mean time, for instant satisfaction in part, they will be pleased to accept the following specimen.

It is required in every work of art, that, like an organic system, the constituent parts be mutually connected, and bear each of them a relation to the whole, some more intimate, some less, according to their destination. Order is not less essential than connection; and when due regard is paid to these, we have a sense of just composition, and so far are pleased with the performance. Homer is defective in order and connection; and Pindar more remarkably. Regularity, order, and connection, are painful restraints on a bold and fertile imagination; and are not patiently submitted to, but after much culture and discipline. In Horace there is no fault more eminent than want of connection. Instances are without number. In the first fourteen lines of ode 7. lib. 1. he mentions several towns and districts which by some were relished more than by others. In the remainder of the ode, Plancus is exhorted to drown his cares in wine. Having narrowly escaped death by the fall of a tree, this poet[3] takes occasion properly to observe, that while we guard against some dangers, we are exposed to others we cannot foresee. He ends with displaying the power of music. The parts of ode 16. lib. 2. are so loosely connected as to disfigure a poem otherwise extremely beautiful. The 1st, 2d, 3d, 4th, 11th, 24th, 27th odes of the 3d book, lie open all of them to the same censure. The 1st satire, book 1. is so deformed by want of unity and connection of parts, as upon the whole to be scarce agreeable. It commences with an important question, How it happens that persons who are so much satisfied with themselves, are generally so little with their condition? After illustrating the observation in a sprightly manner by several examples, the author, forgetting his subject, enters upon a declamation against avarice, which he pursues till the line 108. There he makes an apology for wandering, and promises to return to his subject. But avarice having got possession of his mind, he follows out that theme to the end, and never returns to the question proposed in the beginning.

In the Georgics of Virgil, though esteemed the most finished work of that author, the parts are ill connected, and the transitions far from being sweet and easy. In the first book[4] he deviates from his subject to give a description of the five zones. The want of connection here is remarkable, as well as in the description of the prodigies that accompanied the death of Cæsar, with which the same book is concluded. A digression upon the praises of Italy in the second book[5], is not more happily introduced. And in the midst of a declamation upon the pleasures of husbandry, that makes part of the same book[6], the author appears personally upon the stage without the slightest connection. The two prefaces of Sallust look as if they had been prefixed by some blunder to his two histories. They will suit any other history as well, or any subject as well as history.

---

3. Lib. 2. ode 13.
4. Lin. 231.
5. Lin. 136.
6. Lin. 475.

Even the members of these prefaces are but loosely connected. They look more like a number of maxims or observations than a connected discourse.

An episode in a narrative poem being in effect an accessory, demands not that strict union with the principal subject which is requisite betwixt a whole and its constituent parts. The relation however of principal and accessory being pretty intimate, an episode loosely connected with the principal subject will never be graceful. I give for an example the descent of Æneas into hell, which employs the sixth book of the Æneid. The reader is not prepared for this important event. No cause is assigned, that can make it appear necessary or even natural, to suspend, for so long a time, the principal action in its most interesting period. To engage Æneas to wander from his course in search of an adventure so extraordinary, the poet can find no better pretext, than the hero's longing to visit the ghost of his father recently dead. In the mean time the story is interrupted, and the reader loses his ardor. An episode so extremely beautiful is not at any rate to be dispensed with. It is pity however, that it doth not arise more naturally from the subject. I must observe at the same time, that full justice is done to this incident, by considering it to be an episode; for if it be a constituent part of the principal action, the connection ought to be still more intimate. The same objection lies against that elaborate description of Fame in the Æneid[7]. Any other book of that heroic poem, or of any heroic poem, has as good a title to that description as the book where it is placed.

In a natural landscape, we everyday perceive a multitude of objects connected by contiguity solely. Objects of sight make an impression so lively, as that a relation, even of the slightest kind, is relished. This however ought not to be imitated in description. Words are so far short of the eye in liveliness of impression, that in a description the connection of objects ought to be carefully studied, in order to make the deeper impression. For it is a known fact, the reason of which is suggested above, that it is easier by words to introduce into the mind a related object, than one which is not connected with the preceding train. In the following passage, different things are brought together without the slightest connection, if it be not what may be called verbal, *i. e.* taking the same word in different meanings.

---

[7]. Lib. 4. lin. 173.

> *Surgamus: solet esse gravis cantantibus umbra.*
> *Juniperi gravis umbra: nocent et frugibus umbræ.*
> *Ite domum saturæ, venit Hesperus, ite capellæ.*
>
> —*Virg. Buc.* 10. 75

The metaphorical or figurative appearance of an object, is no good cause for introducing that object in its real and natural appearance. A relation so slight can never be relished.

> *Distrust in lovers is too warm a sun;*
> *But yet 'tis night in love when that is gone.*
> *And in those climes which most his scorching know,*
> *He makes the noblest fruits and metals grow.*
>
> —Part 2. *Conquest of Granada*, act 3

The relations among objects have a considerable influence in the gratification of our passions, and even in their production. But this subject is reserved to be treated in the chapter of emotions and passions[8].

There is perhaps not another instance of a building so great erected upon a foundation so slight in appearance, as that which is erected upon the relations of objects and their arrangement. Relations make no capital figure in the mind: the bulk of them are transitory, and some extremely trivial. They are however the links that, uniting our perceptions into one connected chain, produce connection of action, because perceptions and actions have an intimate correspondence. But it is not sufficient for the conduct of life that our actions be linked together, however intimately: it is beside necessary that they proceed in a certain order; and this also is provided for by an original propensity. Thus order and connection, while they admit sufficient variety, introduce a method in the management of affairs. Without them our conduct would be fluctuating and desultory; and we would be hurried from thought to thought, and from action to action, entirely at the mercy of chance.

---

8. Chap. 2. part 1. sect. 4.

II

Emotions and Passions

The fine arts, as observed above, are all of them calculated to give pleasure to the eye or the ear; and they never descend to gratify the taste, touch, or smell. At the same time, the feelings of the eye and ear, are of all the feelings of external sense, those only which are honoured with the name of *emotions* or *passions*. It is also observed above, that the principles of the fine arts are unfolded by studying the sensitive part of human nature, in order to know what objects of the eye and ear are agreeable, what disagreeable. These observations show the use of the present chapter. We evidently must be acquainted with the nature and causes of emotions and passions, before we can judge with any accuracy how far they are under the power of the fine arts. The critical art is thus set in a fine point of view. The inquisitive mind beginning with criticism the most agreeable of all amusements, and finding no obstruction in its progress, advances far into the sensitive part of our nature; and gains insensibly a thorough knowledge of the human heart, of its desires, and of every motive to action; a science which of all that can be reached by man, is to him of the greatest importance.

Upon a subject so extensive, all that can be expected here, is a general or slight survey. Some emotions indeed more peculiarly connected with the fine arts, I propose to handle in separate chapters; a method that will shorten the general survey considerably. And yet, after this circumscription, so much matter comes under even a general view of the passions and emotions, that, to avoid confusion, I find it necessary to divide this chapter into many parts: in the first of which are handled the causes of those emotions and passions that are the most common and familiar; for to explain every passion and emotion, however singular, would be an endless work. And though I could not well take up less ground, without separating things intimately connected; yet, upon examination, I find the causes of our emotions and passions to be so numerous and various, as to make a subdivision also necessary by splitting this first part into several sections. Human nature is a complicated machine, and must be so to answer all its purposes. There have indeed been published to the world, many a system of human nature, that flatter the mind by their simplicity. But these, unluckily, deviate far from truth and reality. According to some writers, man is entirely a selfish being: according to others, universal benevolence is his duty. One founds morality upon sympathy solely, and one upon utility. If any of these systems were of nature's production, the present subject might be soon discussed. But the variety of nature is not so easily reached; and for confuting such Utopian systems without the intricacy of reasoning, it appears the best method to enter into human nature, and to set before the eye, plainly and candidly, facts as they really exist.

Part I

Causes evolved of the emotions and passions.

Section. I

Difference betwixt emotion and passion.—Causes that are the most common and the most extensive.—Passion considered as productive of action.

These branches are so interwoven, as to make it necessary that they be handled together. It is a fact universally admitted, that no emotion nor passion ever starts up in the mind, without a known cause. If I love a person, it is for good qualities or good offices: if I have resentment against a man, it must be for some injury he has done me; and I cannot pity anyone, who is under no distress of body or of mind.

The circumstances now mentioned, if they cause or occasion a passion, cannot be entirely indifferent: if they were, they could not move us in any degree. And we find upon examination, that they are not indifferent. Looking back upon the foregoing examples, the good qualities or good offices that attract my love, are antecedently agreeable. If an injury were not disagreeable, it would not occasion any resentment against the author; nor would the passion of pity be raised by an object in distress, if that object did not give us pain. These feelings antecedent to passion, and which seem to be the causes of passion, shall be distinguished by the name of *emotions*.

What is now said about the production of passion, resolves into a very simple proposition, That we love what is pleasant, and hate what is painful. And indeed it is evident, that without antecedent emotions we could not have any passions; for a thing must be pleasant or painful, before it can be the object either of love or of hatred.

As it appears from this short sketch, that passions are generated by means of prior emotions, it will be necessary to take first under consideration emotions and their causes.

Such is the constitution of our nature, that upon perceiving certain external objects, we are instantaneously conscious of pleasure or pain. A flowing river, a smooth extended plain, a spreading oak, a towering hill, are objects of sight that raise pleasant emotions. A barren heath, a dirty marsh, a rotten carcass, raise painful emotions. Of the emotions thus produced, we inquire for no other cause but merely the presence of the object.

It must further be observed, that the things now mentioned, raise emotions by means of their properties and qualities. To the emotion raised by a large river, its size, its force, and its fluency, contribute each a share. The pleasures of regularity, propriety, convenience, compose the emotion raised by a fine building.

If external properties make a being or thing agreeable, we have reason to expect the same effect from those which are internal; and accordingly power, discernment, wit, mildness, sympathy, courage, benevolence, render the possessor agreeable in a high degree. So soon as these qualities are perceived in any person, we instantaneously feel pleasant emotions, without the slightest act of reflection or of attention to consequences. It is almost unnecessary to add, that certain qualities opposite to the former, such as dullness, peevishness, inhumanity, cowardice, occasion in the same manner painful emotions.

Sensible beings affect us remarkably by their actions. Some actions so soon as perceived, raise pleasant emotions in the spectator, without the least reflection; such as graceful motion and genteel behaviour. But as the intention of the agent is a capital circumstance in the bulk of human actions, it requires reflection to discover their true character. If I see one delivering a purse of money to another, I can make nothing of this action, till I discover with what intention the money is given. If it be given to extinguish a debt, the action is agreeable in a slight degree. If it be a grateful return, I feel a stronger emotion; and the pleasurable emotion rises to a great height when it is the intention of the giver to relieve a virtuous family from want. Actions are thus qualified by the intention of the agent. But they are not qualified by the event; for an action well intended is agreeable, whatever be the consequence. The pleasant or painful emotion that ariseth from contemplating human actions, is of a peculiar kind. Human actions are perceived to be *right* or *wrong*; and this perception qualifies the pleasure or pain that results from them[1].

Not only are emotions raised in us by the qualities and actions of others, but also by their feelings. I cannot behold a man in distress, without partaking of his pain; nor in joy, without partaking of his pleasure.

The beings or things above described, occasion emotions in us, not only in the original survey, but when they are recalled to the memory in idea. A field laid out with taste, is pleasant in the recollection, as well as when under our eye. A generous action described in words or colours, occasions a sensible emotion, as well as when we see it performed. And when we reflect upon the distress of any person, our pain is of the same kind with what we felt when eye-witnesses. In a word, an agreeable or disagreeable object recalled to the mind in idea, is the occasion of a pleasant or painful emotion, of the same kind with that produced when the object was present. The only difference is, that an idea being fainter than an original perception, the pleasure or pain produced by the former, is proportionably fainter than that produced by the latter.

Having explained the nature of an emotion and mentioned several causes by which it is produced, we proceed to an observation of

---

1. In tracing our emotions and passions to their origin, my first thought was, that qualities and actions are the primary causes of emotions; and that these emotions are afterward expanded upon the being to which these qualities and actions belong. But I am now convinced that this opinion is erroneous. An attribute is not, even in imagination, separable from the being to which it belongs; and, for that reason, cannot of itself be the cause of any emotion. We have, it is true, no knowledge of any being or substance but by means of its attributes; and therefore no being can be agreeable to us otherwise than by their means. But still, when an emotion is raised, it is the being itself, as we apprehend the matter, that raises the emotion; and it raises it by means of one or other of its attributes. If it be urged, That we can in idea abstract a quality from the thing to which it belongs; it might be answered, that such abstraction may serve the purposes of reasoning, but is too faint to produce any sort of emotion. But it is sufficient for the present purpose to answer, That the eye never abstracts; by that organ we perceive things as they really exist, and never perceive a quality as separated from the subject. Hence it must be evident, that emotions are raised, not by qualities abstractly considered, but by the substance or body so and so qualified. Thus, a spreading oak raises a pleasant emotion, by means of its colour, figure, umbrage, &c.: it is not the colour, strictly speaking, that produces the emotion, but the tree coloured; it is not the figure abstractedly considered, that produces the emotion, but the tree of a certain figure. And hence, by the way, it appears, that the beauty of such an object is complex, resolvable into several beauties more simple.

considerable importance in the science of human nature, that some emotions are accompanied with desire, and that others, after a short existence, pass away without producing desire of any sort. The emotion raised by a fine landscape or a magnificent building, vanisheth generally without attaching our hearts to the object; which also happens with relation to a number of fine faces in a crowded assembly. But the bulk of emotions are accompanied with desire of one sort or other, provided only a fit object for desire be suggested. This is remarkably the case of emotions raised by human actions and qualities. A virtuous action raiseth in every spectator a pleasant emotion, which is generally attended with a desire to do good to the author of the action. A vicious action, on the other hand, produceth a painful emotion; and of consequence a desire to have the author punished. Even things inanimate often raise desire. The goods of fortune are objects of desire almost universally; and the desire, when more than commonly vigorous, obtains the name of *avarice*. The pleasant emotion produced in a spectator by a capital picture in the possession of a prince, seldom raiseth desire. But if such a picture be exposed to sale, desire of having or possessing is the natural consequence of the emotion.

If now an emotion be sometimes productive of desire, somtimes not, it comes to be a material inquiry, in what respect a passion differs from an emotion. Is passion in its nature or feeling distinguishable from emotion? I have been apt to think that there must be a distinction, when the emotion seems in all cases to precede the passion, and to be the cause or occasion of it. But after the strictest examination, I cannot perceive any such distinction betwixt emotion and passion. What is love to a mistress, for example, but a pleasant emotion raised by a sight or idea of the person beloved, joined with desire of enjoyment? In what else consists the passion of resentment, but in a painful emotion occasioned by the injury, accompanied with desire to chastise the author of the injury? In general, as to every sort of passion, we find no more in the composition, but the particulars now mentioned, an emotion pleasant or painful accompanied with desire. What then shall we say upon this subject? Are *passion* and *emotion* synonymous terms? This cannot be averred. No feeling nor agitation of the mind void of desire, is termed a passion; and we have discovered that there are many emotions which pass away without raising desire of any kind. How is the difficulty to be solved? There appears to me but one solution, which I relish the more, as it renders the doctrine of the passions and emotions simple and perspicuous. The solution follows. An internal motion or agitation of the mind, when it passeth away without raising desire, is denominated *an emotion*: when desire is raised, the motion or agitation is denominated *a passion*. A fine face, for example, raiseth in me a pleasant feeling. If this feeling vanish without producing any effect, it is in proper language an emotion. But if such feeling, by reiterated views of the object, become sufficiently strong to raise desire, it is no longer termed an emotion, but a passion. The same holds in all the other passions. The painful feeling raised in a spectator by a slight injury done to a stranger, being accompanied with no desire of revenge, is termed an emotion. But this injury raiseth in the stranger a stronger emotion, which being accompanied with desire of revenge, is a passion. Again, external expressions of distress, produce in the spectator a painful feeling. This feeling is sometimes so slight as to pass away without any effect, in which case it is an emotion. But if the feeling be so strong as to prompt desire of affording relief, it is a passion, and is termed *pity*. Envy is emulation in excess. If the exaltation of a competitor be barely disagreeable, the painful feeling is reckoned an emotion. If it produce desire to depress him, it is reckoned a passion.

To prevent mistakes, it must be observed, that desire here is taken in its proper sense, *viz.* that internal impulse which makes us proceed to action. Desire in a lax sense respects also actions and events that depend not on us, as when I desire that my friend may have a son to represent him, or that my country may flourish in arts and sciences. But such internal act is more properly termed a *wish* than a *desire*.

Having distinguished passion from emotion, we proceed to consider passion more at large, with respect especially to its power of producing action.

We have daily and constant experience for our authority, that no man ever proceeds to action but through the impulse of some antecedent desire. So well established is this observation, and so deeply rooted in the mind, that we can scarce imagine a different system of action. Even a child will say familiarly, What should make me do this or that when I have no inclination to it? Taking it then for granted, that the existence of action depends on antecedent desire; it follows, that where there is no desire there can be no action. This opens another shining distinction betwixt emotions and passions. The former, being without desire, are in their nature quiescent: the latter, involving desire, have a tendency to action, and always produce action where they meet with no obstruction.

Hence it follows, that every passion must have an object, *viz.* that being or thing to which our desire is directed, and with a view to which every action prompted by that desire is performed. The object of every passion is that being or thing which produced it. This will be evident from induction. A fine woman, by her beauty, causes in me the passion of love, which is directed upon her as its object. A man by injuring me, raises my resentment; and becomes thereby the object of my resentment. Thus the cause of a passion, and its object, are the same in different views. An emotion, on the other hand, being in its nature quiescent and merely a passive feeling, must have a cause; but cannot be said properly speaking to have an object.

As the desire involved in every passion leads to action, this action is either ultimate, or it is done as a means to some end. Where the action is ultimate, reason and reflection bear no part. The action is performed blindly by the impulse of passion, without any view. Thus one in extreme hunger snatches at food, without the slightest reflection whether it be salutary or not: Avarice prompts to accumulate wealth without the least view of use; and thereby absurdly converts means into an end: Fear often makes us fly before we reflect whether we really be in danger: and animal love not less often hurries to fruition, without a single thought of gratification. But for the most part, actions are performed as means to some end; and in these actions reason and reflection always bear a part. The end is that event which is desired; and the action is deliberately performed in order to bring about that end. Thus affection to my friend involves a desire to make him happy; and the desire to accomplish that end, prompts me to perform what I judge will contribute to it.

Where the action is ultimate, it hath a cause, *viz.* the impulse of the passion. But we cannot properly say it hath a motive. This term is appropriated to actions that are performed as means to some end; and the conviction that the action will tend to bring about the end desired, is termed a motive. Thus passions considered as causes of action, are distinguished into two kinds; instinctive, and deliberative. The first operating blindly and by mere impulse, depend entirely upon the sensitive part of our nature. The other operating by reflection and by motives, are connected with the rational part.

The foregoing difference among the passions, is the work of nature. Experience brings on some variations. By all actions performed through the impulse of passion, desire is gratified, and the gratification is pleasant. This lesson we have from experience. And hence it is, that after an action has often been performed by the impulse merely of passion, the pleasure resulting from performance, considered beforehand, becomes a motive, which joins its force with the original impulse in determining us to act. Thus a child eats by the mere impulse of hunger: a young man thinks of the pleasure of gratification, which is a motive for him to eat: and a man farther advanced in life, hath the additional motive that it will contribute to his health.

Instinctive passions are distinguished into two kinds. Where the cause is internal, they are denominated *appetites*: where external, they retain the common name of *passions*. Thus hunger, thirst, animal love, are termed *appetites*; while fear and anger, even when they operate blindly and by mere impulse, are termed *passions*.

From the definition of a motive above given, it is easy to determine, with the greatest accuracy, what passions are selfish, what social. No passion can properly be termed selfish, but what prompts me to exert actions in order for my own good; nor social, but what prompts me to exert actions in order for the good of another. The motive is that which determines a passion to be social or selfish. Hence it follows, that our appetites, which make us act blindly and by mere impulse, cannot be reckoned either social or selfish; and as little the actions they produce. Thus eating, when prompted by an impulse merely of nature, is neither social nor selfish. But add a motive, That it will contribute to my pleasure or my health, and it becomes in a measure selfish. On the other hand, when affection moves me to exert actions to the end solely of advancing my friend's happiness, without the slightest regard to my own gratification, such actions are justly denominated *social*; and so is the affection, that is their cause. If another motive be added, That gratifying the affection will contribute to my own happiness, the actions I perform become partly selfish. Animal love when exerted into action by natural impulse singly, is neither social nor selfish: when exerted with a view to gratification and in order to make me happy, it is selfish. When the motive of giving pleasure to its object is superadded, it is partly social, partly selfish. A just action when prompted by the love of justice solely, is neither social nor selfish. When I perform an act of justice with a view to the pleasure of gratification, the action is selfish. I pay my debt for my own sake, not with a view to benefit my creditor. But let me suppose the money has been advanced by a friend without interest, purely to oblige me. In this case, together with the inclination to do justice, there arises a motive of gratitude, which respects the creditor solely, and prompts me to act in order to do him good. Here the action is partly social, partly selfish. Suppose again I meet with a surprising and unexpected act of generosity, that inspires me with love to my benefactor and the utmost gratitude. I burn to do him good: he is the sole object of my desire; and my own pleasure in gratifying the desire, vanisheth out of sight. In this case, the action I perform is purely social. Thus it happens, that when a social motive becomes strong, the action is exerted with a view singly to the object of the passion; and the selfish pleasure arising from gratification is never once considered. The same effect of stifling selfish motives, is equally remarkable in other passions that are in no view social. Ambition, for example, when confined to exaltation as its ultimate end, is neither social nor selfish. Let exaltation be considered as a means to make me happy, and the passion becomes so far selfish. But if the desire of exaltation wax strong and inflame my mind, the selfish motive now mentioned is no longer felt. A slight degree of resentment, where my chief view in acting is the pleasure arising to myself from gratifying the passion, is justly denominated *selfish*. Where revenge flames so high as to have no other aim but the destruction of its object, it is no longer selfish. In opposition to a social passion, it maybe termed *dissocial*[2].

Of self, everyone hath a direct perception: of other things, we have no knowledge but by means of their attributes. Hence it is, that of self, the perception is more lively than of any other thing. Self is an agreeable object; and, for the reason now given, must be more agreeable than any other object. Is not this sufficient to account for the prevalence of self-love?

In the foregoing part of this chapter, it is suggested, that some circumstances make beings or things fit objects for desire, others not. This hint must be pursued. It is a truth ascertained by universal experience, that a thing which in our apprehension is beyond reach, never is the object of desire. No man, in his right senses, desires to walk in the air, or to descend to the centre of the earth. We may amuse ourselves in a reverie, with building castles in the air, and wishing for what can never happen. But such things never move desire. And indeed

---

2. This word, hitherto not in use, seems to fulfil all that is required by Demetrius Phalereus (*Of Elocution, sect.* 96.) in coining a new word; first that it be perspicuous; and next, that it be in the tone of the language; that we may not, says our author, introduce among the Grecian vocables, words that sound like those of Phrygia or Scythia.

a desire to act would be altogether absurd, when we are conscious that the action is beyond our power. In the next place, though the difficulty of attainment with respect to things within reach, often inflames desire; yet where the prospect of attainment is faint and the event extremely uncertain, the object, however agreeable, seldom raiseth any strong desire. Thus beauty or other good qualities in a woman of rank, seldom raises love in any man greatly her inferior. In the third place, different objects, equally within reach, raise emotions in different degrees; and when desire accompanies any of these emotions, its strength, as is natural, is proportioned to that of its cause. Hence the remarkable difference among desires directed upon beings inanimate, animate, and rational. The emotion caused by a rational being, is out of measure stronger than any caused by an animal without reason; and an emotion raised by such an animal, is stronger than what is caused by anything inanimate. There is a separate reason why desire of which a rational being is the object should be the strongest. Desire directed upon such a being, is gratified many ways, by loving, serving, benefiting, the object; and it is a well known truth, that our desires naturally swell by exercise. Desire directed upon an inanimate being, susceptible neither of pleasure nor pain, is not capable of a higher gratification than that of acquiring the property. Hence it is, that though every feeling which raiseth desire, is strictly speaking a passion; yet commonly those feelings only are denominated passions of which sensible beings capable of pleasure and pain are the objects.

Section. II

Causes of the emotions of joy and sorrow.

This subject was purposely reserved for a separate section, because it could not, with perspicuity, be handled under the general head. An emotion involving desire is termed *a passion*; and when the desire is fulfilled, the passion is said to be gratified. The gratification of every passion must be pleasant, or in other words produce a pleasant emotion; for nothing can be more natural, than that the accomplishment of any wish or desire should affect us with joy. I cannot even except the case, where a man, through remorse, is desirous to chastise and punish himself. The joy of gratification is properly called an emotion; because it makes us happy in our present situation, and is ultimate in its nature, not having a tendency to anything beyond. On the other hand, sorrow must be the result of an event contrary to what we desire; for if the accomplishment of desire produce joy, it is equally natural that disappointment should produce sorrow.

An event fortunate or unfortunate, that falls out by accident without being foreseen or thought of, and which therefore could not be the object of desire, raiseth an emotion of the same kind with that now mentioned. But the cause must be different; for there can be no gratification where there is no desire. We have not however far to seek for a cause. A man cannot be indifferent to an event that affects him or any of his connections. If it be fortunate, it gives him joy; if unfortunate, it gives him sorrow.

In no situation doth joy rise to a greater height, than upon the removal of any violent distress of mind or body; and in no situation doth sorrow rise to a greater height, than upon the removal of what makes us happy. The sensibility of our nature serves in part to account for these effects. Other causes also concur. We can be under no violent distress without an anxious desire to be free from it; and therefore its removal is a high gratification. We cannot be possessed of anything that makes us happy, without wishing its continuance; and therefore its removal by crossing our wishes must create sorrow. Nor is this all. The principle of contrast comes in for its share. An emotion of joy arising upon the removal of pain, is increased by contrast when we reflect upon our former distress. An emotion of sorrow upon being deprived of any good, is increased by contrast when we reflect upon our former happiness.

> JAFFIER: There's not a wretch that lives on common charity,
>   But's happier than me. For I have known
>   The luscious sweets of plenty: every night
>   Have slept with soft content about my head,
>   And never wak'd but to a joyful morning.
>   Yet now must fall like a full ear of corn,
>   Whose blossom 'scap'd, yet's wither'd in the ripening.
>
>   —*Venice preserv'd*, act 1. sc. 1

It hath always been reckoned difficult to account for the extreme pleasure that follows a cessation of bodily pain; as when one is relieved from the rack, or from a violent fit of the stone. What is said, explains this difficulty in the easiest and simplest manner. Cessation of bodily pain is not of itself a pleasure; for a *non-ens* or a negative can neither give pleasure nor pain. But man is so framed by nature as to rejoice when he is eased of pain, as well as to be sorrowful when deprived of any good. This branch of our constitution, is chiefly the cause of the pleasure. The gratification of desire comes in as an accessory cause; and contrast joins its force, by increasing the sense of our present happiness. In the case of an acute pain, a peculiar circumstance contributes its part. The brisk circulation of the animal spirits occasioned by acute pain, continues after the pain is vanished, and produceth a very pleasant feeling. Sickness hath not that effect, because it is always attended with a depression of spirits.

Hence it is, that the gradual diminution of acute pain, occasions a mixt emotion, partly pleasant, partly painful. The partial diminution produceth joy in proportion; but the remaining pain balanceth our joy. This mixt feeling, however, hath no long endurance. For the joy that ariseth upon the diminution of pain, soon vanisheth; and leaveth in the undisturbed possession, that degree of pain which remains.

What is above observed about bodily pain, is equally applicable to the distresses of the mind; and accordingly it is a common artifice, to prepare us for the reception of good news by alarming our fears.

Section. III

Sympathetic emotion of virtue, and its cause.

One feeling there is, that merits a deliberate view, for its singularity, as well as utility. Whether to call it an emotion or a passion, seems uncertain. The former it can scarce be, because it involves desire; and the latter it can scarce be, because it has no object. But this feeling and its nature will be best understood from examples. A signal act of gratitude, produceth in the spectator love or esteem for the author. The spectator hath at the same time a separate feeling; which, being mixed with love or esteem, the capital emotion, hath not been much adverted to. It is a vague feeling of gratitude, which hath no object; but which, however, disposes the spectator to acts of gratitude, more than upon ordinary occasions. Let any man attentively consider his own heart when he thinks warmly of any signal act of gratitude, and he will be conscious of this feeling, as distinct from the esteem or admiration he has for the grateful person. It merits our utmost attention, by unfolding a curious piece of mechanism in the nature of man. The feeling is singular in the following respect, that it involves a desire to perform acts of gratitude, without having any particular object; though in this state the mind, wonderfully disposed toward an object, neglects no object upon which it can vent itself. Any act of kindness or good-will that would not be regarded upon another occasion, is greedily seized; and the vague feeling is converted into a real passion of gratitude. In such a state, favours are returned double.

Again, a courageous action produceth in a spectator the passion of admiration directed upon the author. But beside this well-known passion, a separate feeling is raised in the spectator; which may be called *an emotion of courage*, because while under its influence he is conscious of a boldness and intrepidity beyond ordinary, and longs for proper objects upon which to exert this emotion.

> *Spumantemque dari, pecora inter inertia, votis*
> *Optat aprum, aut fulvum descendere monte leonem.*
>
> —*Æneid.* iv. 158

> *Non altramente 'il tauro, oue l' irriti*
> *Geloso amor con stimoli pungenti*
> *Horribilmente mugge, e co' muggiti*
> *Gli spirti in se risueglia, e l'ire ardenti:*
> *E'l corno aguzza a i tronchi, e par ch'inuiti*
> *Con vani colpi a' la battaglia i venti.*
>
> —*Tasso, canto 7. st. 55*

> *So full of valour that they smote the air*
> *For breathing in their faces.*
>
> —*Tempest, act. 4. sc. 4*

For another example, let us figure some grand and heroic action, highly agreeable to the spectator. Beside a singular veneration for the author, the spectator feels in himself an unusual dignity of character, which disposeth him to great and noble actions. And herein principally consists the extreme delight everyone hath in the histories of conquerors and heroes.

This singular feeling, which may be termed *the sympathetic emotion of virtue*, resembles, in one respect, the well-known appetites that lead to the propagation and preservation of the species. The appetites of hunger, thirst, and animal love, arise in the mind without being directed upon any particular object; and in no case whatever is the mind more solicitous for a proper object, than when under the influence of any of these appetites.

The feeling I have endeavoured to evolve, may well be termed *the sympathetic emotion of virtue*; for it is raised in a spectator by virtuous actions of every kind, and by no other sort. When we contemplate a virtuous action, which never fails to delight us and to prompt our love for the author, the mind is warmed and put into a tone similar to what inspired the virtuous action. The propensity we have to such actions is so much enlivened, as to become for a time an actual emotion. But no man hath a propensity to vice as such. On the contrary, a wicked deed disgusts him, and makes him abhor the author. This abhorrence is a strong antidote so long as any impression remains of the wicked action.

In a rough road, a halt to view a fine country is refreshing; and here a delightful prospect opens upon us. It is indeed wonderful to see what incitements there are to virtue in the human frame. Justice is perceived to be our duty, and it is guarded by natural punishments, from which the guilty never escape. To perform noble and generous actions, a warm sense of dignity and superior excellence is a most efficacious incitement[3]. And to leave virtue in no quarter unsupported, here is unfolded an admirable contrivance, by which good example commands the heart and adds to virtue the force of habit. Did our moral feelings extend no farther than to approve the action and to bestow our affection on the author, good example would not have great influence. But to give it the utmost force, nothing can be better contrived than the sympathetic emotion under consideration, which prompts us to imitate what we admire. This singular emotion will readily find an object to exert itself upon; and at any rate, it never exists without producing some effect. Virtuous emotions of this sort, are in some degree an exercise of virtue. They are a mental exercise at least, if they show not externally. And every exercise of virtue, internal and external, leads to habit; for a

---

3. See Essays on morality and natural religion, part 1. ess. 2. ch. 4.

disposition or propensity of the mind, like a limb of the body, becomes stronger by exercise. Proper means, at the same time, being ever at hand to raise this sympathetic emotion, its frequent reiteration may, in a good measure, supply the want of a more complete exercise. Thus, by proper discipline, every person may acquire a settled habit of virtue. Intercourse with men of worth, histories of generous and disinterested actions, and frequent meditation upon them, keep the sympathetic emotion in constant exercise, which by degrees introduceth a habit, and confirms the authority of virtue. With respect to education in particular, what a spacious and commodious avenue to the heart of a young person, is here opened?

Section. IV

In many instances one emotion is productive of another. The same of passions.

In the first chapter it is observed, that the relations by which things are mutually connected, have a remarkable influence in regulating the train of our ideas. I here add, that they have an influence not less remarkable, in generating emotions and passions. Beginning with the former, it holds in fact, that an agreeable object makes everything connected with it appear agreeable. The mind gliding sweetly and easily through related objects, carries along the beauty of objects that made a figure, and blends that beauty with the idea of the present object, which thereby appears more agreeable than when considered apart[4]. This reason may appear obscure and metaphysical, but it must be relished when we attend to the following examples, which establish

---

4. Such proneness has the mind to this communication of properties, that we often find a property ascribed to a related object, of which naturally it is not susceptible. Sir Richard Grenville in a single ship, being surprised by the Spanish fleet, was advised to retire. He utterly refused to turn from the enemy; declaring, "he would rather die, than dishonour himself, his country, and her Majesty's ship." *Hakluyt, vol. 2. part 2. p.* 169. To aid the communication, of properties in instances like the present, there always must be a momentary personification: a ship must be imagined a sensible being to make it susceptible of honour or dishonour. In the battle of Mantinea, Epaminondas, being mortally wounded, was carried to his tent in a manner dead; recovering his senses, the first thing he enquired about was his shield; which being brought, he kissed it as the companion of his valour and glory. It must be remarked, that among the Greeks and Romans it was deemed infamous for a soldier to return from battle without his shield.

the fact beyond all dispute. No relation is more intimate than that betwixt a being and its qualities; and accordingly, the affection I bear a man expands itself readily upon all his qualities, which by that means make a greater figure in my mind than more substantial qualities in others. The talent of speaking in a friend, is more regarded than that of acting in a person with whom I have no connection; and graceful motion in a mistress, gives more delight than consummate prudence in any other woman. Affection sometimes rises so high, as to convert defects into properties. The wry neck of Alexander was imitated by his courtiers as a real beauty, without intention to flatter. Thus Lady Piercy, speaking of her husband Hotspur,

———— By his light
Did all the chivalry of England move,
To do brave acts. He was indeed the glass,
Wherein the noble youth did dress themselves.
He had no legs that practis'd not his gait:
And speaking thick, which Nature made his blemish,
Became the accents of the valiant:
For those who could speak low and tardily,
Would turn their own perfection to abuse,
To seem like him.

—*Second part, Henry IV. act 2. sc. 6*

When the passion of love has ended its course, its object becomes quite a different creature.—Nothing left of that genteel motion, that gaiety, that sprightly conversation, those numberless graces, that formerly, in the lover's opinion, charmed all hearts.

The same communication of passion obtains in the relation of principal and accessory. Pride, of which self is the object, expands itself upon a house, a garden, servants, equipage, and everything of that nature. A lover addresseth his mistress's glove in the following terms:

Sweet ornament that decks a thing divine.

A temple is in a proper sense an accessory of the deity to which it is dedicated. Diana is chaste, and not only her temple, but the very isicle which hangs on it, must partake of that property:

> *The noble sister of Poplicola,*
> *The moon of Rome; chasle as the isicle*
> *That's curdled by the frost from purest snow,*
> *And hangs on Dian's temple.*
>
> —*Coriolanus, act 5. sc. 3*

Thus it is, that the respect and esteem, which the great, the powerful, the opulent naturally command, are in some measure communicated to their dress, to their manners, and to all their connections. It is this principle, which in matters left to our own choice prevails over the natural taste of beauty and propriety, and gives currency to what is called *the fashion*.

By means of the same easiness of transition, the bad qualities of an object are carried along, and grafted upon related objects. Every good quality in a person is extinguished by hatred; and every bad quality is spread upon all his connections. A relation more slight and transitory than that of hatred, may have the same effect. Thus the bearer of bad tidings becomes an object of aversion:

> *Fellow begone, I cannot brook thy sight,*
> *This news hath made thee a most ugly man.*
>
> —*King John, act 3. sc. 1*

> *Yet the first bringer of unwelcome news*
> *Hath but a losing office: and his tongue*
> *Sounds ever after, as a sullen bell*
> *Remember'd, tolling a departing friend.*
>
> —*Second part, Henry IV. act 1. sc. 3*

This disposition of the mind to communicate the properties of one object to another, is not always proportioned to the intimacy of their connection. The order of the transition from object to object, hath also an influence. The sense of order operates not less powerfully in this case, than in the succession of ideas. If a thing be agreeable in itself, all its accessories appear agreeable. But the agreeableness of an accessory, extends not itself so readily to the principal. Any dress upon a fine woman is becoming; but the most elegant ornaments upon one that is homely, have scarce any effect to mend her appearance. The reason will be obvious, from what is said in the chapter above cited. The mind passes more easily from the principal to its accessories, than in the opposite direction.

The emotions produced as above may properly be termed *secondary*, being occasioned either by antecedent emotions or antecedent passions, which in this respect may be termed *primary*. And to complete the present theory, I must now remark a difference betwixt a primary emotion and a primary passion in the production of secondary emotions. A secondary emotion cannot but be more faint than the primary; and therefore, if the chief or principal object have not the power to raise a passion, the accessory object will have still less power. But if a passion be raised by the principal object, the secondary emotion may readily swell into a passion for the accessory, provided the accessory be a proper object for desire. And thus it happens that one passion is often productive of another. Examples are without number: the sole difficulty is a proper choice. I begin with self-love, and the power it hath to generate other passions. The love which parents bear their children, is an illustrious example of the foregoing doctrine. Every man, beside making part of a greater system, like a comet, a planet, or satellite only; hath a less system of his own, in the centre of which he represents the sun dispersing his fire and heat all around. The connection between a man and his children, fundamentally that of cause and effect, becomes, by the addition of other circumstances, the completest that can be among individuals; and therefore, self-love, the most vigorous of all passions, is readily expanded upon children. The secondary emotion they at first produce by means of their connection, is, generally speaking, sufficiently strong to move desire even from the beginning; and the new passion swells by degrees, till it rival in some measure self-love, the primary passion. The following case will demonstrate the truth of this theory. Remorse for betraying a friend, or murdering an enemy in cold blood, makes a man even hate himself. In this state, it is a matter of experience, that he is scarce conscious of any affection to his children, but rather of disgust or ill-will. What cause can be assigned for this change, other than the hatred which beginning at himself, is expanded upon his children? And if so, may we not with equal reason derive from self-love the affection a man for ordinary has to them?

The affection a man bears to his blood-relations, depends on the same principle. Self-love is also expanded upon them; and the communicated passion, is more or less vigorous in proportion to the connection. Nor doth self-love rest here: it is, by the force of connection, communicated even to things inanimate. And hence the affection a man bears to his property, and to everything he calls his own.

Friendship, less vigorous than self-love, is, for that reason, less apt to communicate itself to children or other relations. Instances however are not wanting, of such communicated passion arising from friendship when it is strong. Friendship may go higher in the matrimonial state than in any other condition: and Otway, in *Venice preserv'd*, shows a fine taste in taking advantage of that circumstance. In the scene where Belvidera sues to her father for pardon, she is represented as pleading her mother's merit, and the resemblance she bore to her mother.

> PRIULI: My daughter!
> BELVIDERA: Yes, your daughter, by a mother
> Virtuous and noble, faithful to your honour,
> Obedient to your will, kind to your wishes,
> Dear to your arms. By all the joys she gave you,
> When in her blooming years she was your treasure,
> Look kindly on me; in my face behold
> The lineaments of hers y' have kiss'd so often,
> Pleading the cause of your poor cast-off child.

And again,

> BELVIDERA: Lay me, I beg you, lay me
> By the dear ashes of my tender mother.
> She would have pitied me, had fate yet spar'd her.

—Act 5. sc. 1

This explains why any meritorious action or any illustrious qualification in my son or my friend, is apt to make me overvalue myself. If I value my friend's wife or his son upon account of their connection with him, it is still more natural that I should value myself upon account of my own connection with him.

Friendship, or any other social affection, may produce opposite effects. Pity, by interesting us strongly for the person in distress, must of consequence inflame our resentment against the author of the distress. For, in general, the affection we have for any man, generates in us good-will to his friends and ill-will to his enemies. Shakespear shows great art in the funeral oration pronounced by Antony over the body of Cæsar. He first endeavours to excite grief in the hearers, by dwelling upon the deplorable loss of so great a man. This passion raised to a pitch, interesting them strongly in Cæsar's fate, could not fail to produce a lively sense of the treachery and cruelty of the conspirators; an infallible method to inflame the resentment of the multitude beyond all bounds.

> ANTONY: If you have tears, prepare to shed them now.
> You all do know this mantle; I remember
> The first time ever Cæsar put it on,
> 'Twas on a summer's evening in his tent,
> That day he overcame the Nervii—
> Look! in this place ran Cassius' dagger through;—
> See what a rent the envious Casca made.—
> Through this the well-beloved Brutus stabb'd;
> And as he pluck'd his cursed steel away,
> Mark how the blood of Cæsar follow'd it!
> As rushing out of doors, to be resolv'd,
> If Brutus so unkindly knock'd, or no:
> For Brutus, as you know, was Cæsar's angel.
> Judge, oh you gods! how dearly Cæsar lov'd him;
> This, this, was the unkindest cut of all;
> For when the noble Cæsar saw him stab,
> Ingratitude, more strong than traitors' arms,
> Quite vanquish'd him; then burst his mighty heart:
> And, in his mantle muffling up his face,
> Which all the while ran blood, great Cæsar fell,
> Even at the base of Pompey's statue.
> O what a fall was there, my countrymen!
> Then I and you, and all of us fell down,
> Whilst bloody treason flourish'd over us.
> O, now you weep; and I perceive you feel
> The dint of pity; these are gracious drops.
> Kind souls! what, weep you when you but behold
> Our Cæsar's vesture wounded? look you here!
> Here is himself, marr'd, as you see, by traitors.
>
> —*Julius Cæsar*, act 3. sc. 6

Had Antony directed upon the conspirators the thoughts of his audience, without paving the way by raising their grief, his speech perhaps might have failed of success.

Hatred and other dissocial passions, produce effects directly opposite to those above mentioned. If I hate a man, his children, his relations, nay his property, become to me objects of aversion. His enemies, on the other hand, I am disposed to esteem.

The more slight and transitory connections, have generally no power to produce a communicated passion. Anger, when sudden and violent, is one exception; for if the person who did the injury be removed out of reach, this passion will vent itself upon any related object, however slight the relation be. Another exception makes a greater figure. A group of beings or things, becomes often the object of a communicated passion, even where the relation of the individuals to the principal object is but faint. Thus though I put no value upon a single man for living in the same town with myself; my townsmen however, considered in a body, are preferred before others. This is still more remarkable with respect to my countrymen in general. The grandeur of the complex object, swells the passion of self-love by the relation I have to my native country; and every passion, when it swells beyond its ordinary bounds, hath, in that circumstance, a peculiar tendency to expand itself along related objects. In fact, instances are not rare, of persons, who, upon all occasions, are willing to sacrifice their lives and fortunes for their country. Such influence upon the mind of man, hath a complex object, or, more properly speaking, a general term[5].

The sense of order hath, in the communication of passion, an influence not less remarkable than in the communication of emotions. It is a common observation, that a man's affection to his parents is less vigorous than to his children. The order of nature in descending to children, aids the transition of the affection. The ascent to a parent, contrary to this order, makes the transition more difficult. Gratitude to a benefactor is readily extended to his children; but not so readily to his parents. The difference however betwixt the natural and inverted order, is not so considerable, but that it may be balanced by other circumstances. Pliny[6] gives an account of a woman of rank condemned to die for a crime; and, to avoid public shame, detained in prison to

---

5. See Essays on morality and natural religion, part 1. ess. 2. ch. 5.
6. Lib. 7. cap. 36.

die of hunger. Her life being prolonged beyond expectation, it was discovered, that she was nourished by sucking milk from the breasts of her daughter. This instance of filial piety, which aided the transition and made ascent not less easy than descent is for ordinary, procured a pardon to the mother, and a pension to both. The story of Androcles and the lion[7] may be accounted for in the same manner. The admiration, of which the lion was the cause, for his kindness and gratitude to Androcles, produced good-will to Androcles, and pardon of his crime.

And this leads to other observations upon communicated passions. I love my daughter less after she is married, and my mother less after a second marriage. The marriage of my son or my father diminishes not my affection so remarkably. The same observation holds with respect to friendship, gratitude, and other passions. The love I bear my friend, is but faintly extended to his married daughter. The resentment I have against a man, is readily extended against children who make part of his family: not so readily against children who are forisfamiliated, especially by marriage. This difference is also more remarkable in daughters than in sons. These are curious facts; and to evolve the cause we must examine minutely, that operation of the mind by which a passion is extended to a related object. In considering two things as related, the mind is not stationary, but passeth and repasseth from the one to the other, viewing the relation from each of them perhaps oftener than once. This holds more especially in considering a relation betwixt things of unequal rank, as betwixt the cause and the effect, or betwixt a principal and an accessory. In contemplating the relation betwixt a building and its ornaments, the mind is not satisfied with a single transition from the former to the latter. It must also view the relation, beginning at the latter, and passing from it to the former. This vibration of the mind in passing and repassing betwixt things that are related, explains the facts above mentioned. The mind passeth easily from the father to the daughter; but where the daughter is married, this new relation attracts the mind, and obstructs, in some measure, the return from the daughter to the father. Any obstruction the mind meets with in passing and repassing betwixt its objects, occasions a like obstruction in the communication of passion. The marriage of a male obstructs less the easiness of transition; because a male is less sunk by the relation of marriage than a female.

---

7. Aulus Gellius, lib. 5. cap. 14.

The foregoing instances, are of passion communicated from one object to another. But one passion may be generated by another, without change of object. It may in general be observed, that a passion paves the way to others, similar in their tone, whether directed upon the same or upon a different object. For the mind heated by any passion, is, in that state, more susceptible of a new impression in a similar tone, than when cool and quiescent. It is a common observation, that pity generally produceth friendship for a person in distress. Pity interests us in its object, and recommends all its virtuous qualities. For this reason, female beauty shows best in distress; and is more apt to inspire love, than upon ordinary occasions. But it is chiefly to be remarked, that pity, warming and melting the spectator, prepares him for the reception of other tender affections; and pity is readily improved into love or friendship, by a certain tenderness and concern for the object, which is the tone of both passions. The aptitude of pity to produce love is beautifully illustrated by Shakespear.

> OTHELLO: Her father lov'd me, oft invited me;
>   Still question'd me the story of my life,
> From year to year; the battles, sieges, fortunes,
> That I have past.
> I ran it through, e'en from my boyish days,
> To th' very moment that he bad me tell it:
> Wherein I spoke of most disast'rous chances,
> Of moving accidents by flood and field;
> Of hair-breadth 'scapes in th' imminent deadly breach;
> Of being taken by the insolent foe,
> And sold to slavery; of my redemption thence,
> And with it, all my travel's history.
> —— All these to hear
> Would Desdemona seriously incline;
> But still the house-affairs would draw her thence,
> Which ever as she could with haste dispatch,
> She'd come again, and with a greedy ear
> Devour up my discourse: which I observing,
> Took once a pliant hour, and found good means
> To draw from her a prayer of earnest heart,
> That I would all my pilgrimage dilate,
> Whereof by parcels she had something heard,

> But not distinctively. I did consent,
> And often did beguile her of her tears,
> When I did speak of some distressful stroke
> That my youth suffer'd. My story being done,
> She gave me for my pains a world of sighs:
> She swore, in faith, 'twas strange, 'twas passing strange—
> 'Twas pitiful, 'twas wondrous pitiful—
> She wish'd she had not heard it:—yet she wish'd,
> That heav'n had made her such a man:—she thank'd me,
> And bad me, if I had a friend that lov'd her,
> I should but teach him how to tell my story,
> And that would woo her. On this hint I spake,
> She lov'd me for the dangers I had past,
> And I lov'd her, that she did pity them:
> This only is the witchcraft I have us'd.
>
> *—Othello, act 1. sc. 8*

In this instance it will be observed that admiration concurred with pity to produce love.

Section. V

Causes of the passions of fear and anger.

Fear and anger, to answer the purposes of nature, are happily so contrived as to operate either instinctively or deliberately. So far as they prompt actions considered as means leading to a certain end, they fall in with the general system, and require no particular explanation. If any object have a threatening appearance, reason suggests means to avoid the danger. If I am injured, the first thing I think of, is in what manner I shall be revenged, and what means I shall employ. These particulars are not less obvious than natural. But as the passions of fear and anger, so far as instinctive, are less familiar to us, and their nature generally not understood; I thought it would not be unacceptable to the reader to have them accurately delineated. He may also possibly relish the opportunity of this specimen, to have the nature of instinctive passions more fully explained than there was formerly occasion to do. I begin with fear.

Self-preservation is to individuals a matter of too great importance to be left entirely under the guardianship of self-love, which cannot be put in exercise otherwise than by the intervention of reason and reflection. Nature hath acted here with her usual precaution and foresight. Fear and anger are passions common to all men; and by operating instinctively, they frequently afford security when the slower operations of deliberative reason would be too late. We take nourishment commonly, not by the direction of reason, but by the incitement of hunger and thirst. In the same manner, we avoid danger by the incitement of fear, which often, before there is time for reflection, placeth us in safety. This matter then is ordered with consummate wisdom. It is not within the reach of fancy, to conceive anything better fitted to answer its purpose, than this instinctive passion of fear, which, upon the first surmise of danger, operates instantaneously without reflection. So little doth the passion, in such instances, depend on reason, that we often find it exerted even in contradiction to reason, and when we are conscious that there is no hazard. A man who is not much upon his guard, cannot avoid shrinking at a blow, though he knows it to be aimed in sport; nor closing his eyes at the approach of what may hurt them, though he is confident it will not come their length. Influenced by the same instinctive passion of fear, infants are much affected with a stern look, a menacing tone, or other expression of anger; though, being incapable of reflection, they cannot form the slightest judgement about the import of these signs. This is all that is necessary to be said in general. The natural connection betwixt fear and the external signs of anger, will be handled in the chapter of the external signs of emotions and passions.

Fear provides for self-preservation by flying from harm; anger, by repelling it. Nothing indeed can be better contrived to repel or prevent injury, than anger or resentment. Destitute of this passion, men, like defenceless lambs, would lie constantly open to mischief[8]. Deliberate anger caused by a voluntary injury, is too well known to require any explanation. If my desire be in general to resent an afront, I must use means, and these means must be discovered by reflection. Deliberation is here requisite; and in this, which is the ordinary case, the passion seldom exceeds just bounds. But where anger suddenly inflames me to

---

8. Brasidas being bit by a mouse he had catched, let it slip out of his fingers: "No creature (says he) is so contemptible, but what may provide for its own safety, if it have courage."—*Ptutarch, Apothegmata.*

return a blow, the passion is instinctive, and the action ultimate; and it is chiefly in such cases that the passion is rash and ungovernable, because it operates blindly, without affording time for reason or deliberation.

Instinctive anger is frequently raised by bodily pain, which, when sudden and excessive as by a stroke on a tender part, ruffling the temper and unhinging the mind, is in its tone similar to anger. Bodily pain by this means disposes to anger, which is as suddenly raised, provided an object be found to vent it upon. Anger commonly is not provoked otherwise than by a voluntary injury. But when a man is thus beforehand disposed to anger, he is not nice nor scrupulous about an object. The man who gave the stroke, however accidentally, is by an inflammable temper held a proper object, merely because he was the occasion of the pain. It is still a stronger example of the kind, that a stock or a stone, by which I am hurt, becomes an object for my resentment. I am violently incited to bray it to atoms. The passion indeed in this case is but momentary. It vanisheth with the first reflection, being attended with no circumstance that can excuse it in any degree. Nor is this irrational effect confined to bodily pain. Inward distress, when excessive, may be the occasion of effects equally irrational. When a friend is danger and the event uncertain, the perturbation of mind occasioned thereby, will, in a fiery temper, produce momentary fits of anger against this very friend, however innocent. Thus Shakespear, in the *Tempest*,

> ALONZO:—— Sit down and rest.
> Ev'n here I will put off my hope, and keep it
> No longer for my flatterer: he is drown'd
> Whom thus we stray to find, and the sea mocks
> Our frustrate search on land. Well, let him go.
>
> —*Act 3. sc. 3*

The final words, *Well, let him go*, are an expression of impatience and anger at Ferdinand, whose absence greatly distressed his father, dreading that he was lost in the storm. This nice operation of the human mind, is by Shakespear exhibited upon another occasion, and finely painted. In the tragedy of *Othello*, Iago, by dark hints and suspicious circumstances, had roused Othello's jealousy; which, however, appeared too slightly founded to be vented upon Desdemona, its proper object. The perturbation and distress of mind thereby occasioned, produced a momentary resentment against Iago, considered as occasioning the jealousy though innocent.

> OTHELLO: Villain, be sure thou prove my love a whore;
>   Be sure of it: give me the ocular proof.
>   Or by the wrath of man's eternal soul
>   Thou hadst been better have been born a dog,
>   Than answer my wak'd wrath.
> IAGO: Is't come to this?
> OTHELLO: Make me see't; or, at the least, so prove it,
>   That the probation bear no hinge or loop
>   To hang a doubt on: or woe upon thy life!
> IAGO: My Noble Lord—
> OTHELLO: If thou dost slander her and torture me,
>   Never pray more; abandon all remorse;
>   On horrors head horrors accumulate;
>   Do deeds to make heav'n weep, all earth amaz'd:
>   For nothing canst thou to damnation add
>   Greater than that.
>
>   —*Othello, act 3. sc. 8*

This blind and absurd effect of anger, is more gaily illustrated by Addison, in a story, the *dramatis personæ* of which are a cardinal, and a spy retained in pay for intelligence. The cardinal is represented as minuting down everything that is told him. The spy begins with a low voice, "Such an one the advocate whispered to one of his friends within my hearing, that your Eminence was a very great poltron"; and after having given his patron time to take it down, adds, "That another called him a mercenary rascal in a public conversation." The cardinal replies, "Very well," and bids him go on. The spy proceeds, and loads him with reports of the same nature, till the cardinal rises in great wrath, calls him an impudent scoundrel, and kicks him out of the room[9].

We meet with instances everyday of resentment raised by loss at play, and wreaked on the cards or dice. But anger, a furious passion, is satisfied with a connection still slighter than that of cause and effect, of which Congreve, in the *Mourning Bride*, gives one beautiful example.

---

9. Spectator, No. 439.

GONSALEZ: Have comfort.
ALMERIA: Curs'd be that tongue that bids me be of comfort,
Curs'd my own tongue that could not move his pity,
Curs'd these weak hands that could not hold him here,
For he is gone to doom Alphonso's death.

—Act 4. sc. 8

I have chosen to exhibit anger in its more rare appearances, for in these we can best trace its nature and extent. In the examples above given, it appears to be an absurd passion and altogether irrational. But we ought to consider, that it is not the intention of nature to subject this passion, in every instance, to reason and reflection. It was given us to prevent or to repel injuries; and, like fear, it often operates blindly and instinctively, without the least view to consequences. The very first sensation of harm, sets it in motion to repel injury by punishment. Were it more cool and deliberate, it would lose its threatening appearance, and be insufficient to guard us against violence and mischief. When such is and ought to be the nature of the passion, it is not wonderful to find it exerted irregularly and capriciously, as it sometimes is where the mischief is sudden and unforeseen. All the harm that can be done by the passion in this case, is instantaneous; for the shortest delay sets all to rights; and circumstances are seldom so unlucky as to put it in the power of a passionate man to do much harm in an instant.

SECTION. VI

Emotions caused by fiction.

The attentive reader will observe, that in accounting for passions and emotions, no cause hitherto has been assigned but what hath a real existence. Whether it be a being, action, or quality, that moveth us, it is supposed to be an object of our knowledge, or at least of our belief. This observation discovers to us that the subject is not yet exhausted; because our passions, as all the world know, are moved by fiction as well as by truth. In judging beforehand of man, so remarkably addicted to truth and reality, one should little dream that fiction could have any effect upon him. But man's intellectual faculties are too imperfect to dive far even into his own nature. I shall take occasion afterward to show, that this branch of the human constitution, is contrived with admirable wisdom and is subservient to excellent purposes. In the mean time, I must endeavour to unfold, by what means fiction hath such influence on the mind.

That the objects of our senses really exist in the way and manner we perceive, is a branch of intuitive knowledge. When I see a man walking, a tree growing, or cattle grazing, I have a conviction that these things are precisely as they appear. If I be a spectator of any transaction or event, I have a conviction of the real existence of the persons engaged, of their words, and of their actions. Nature determines us to rely on the veracity of our senses. And indeed, if our senses did not convince us of the reality of their objects, they could not in any degree answer their end.

By the power of memory, a thing formerly seen may be recalled to the mind with different degrees of accuracy. We commonly are satisfied with a slight recollection of the chief circumstances; and, in such recollection, the thing is not figured as present nor any image formed. I retain the consciousness of my present situation, and barely remember that formerly I was a spectator. But with respect to an interesting object or event which made a strong impression, the mind sometimes, not satisfied with a cursory review, chutes to revolve every circumstance. In this case, I conceive myself to be a spectator as I was originally; and I perceive every particular passing in my presence, in the same manner as when I was in reality a spectator. For example, I saw yesterday a beautiful woman in tears for the loss of an only child, and was greatly moved with her distress. Not satisfied with a slight recollection or bare remembrance, I insist on the melancholy scene. Conceiving myself to be in the place where I was an eye-witness, every circumstance appears to me as at first. I think I see the woman in tears and hear her moans. Hence it may be justly said, that in a complete idea of memory there is no past nor future. A thing recalled to the mind with the accuracy I have been describing, is perceived as in our view, and consequently as presently existing. Past time makes a part of an incomplete idea only: I remember or reflect, that some years ago I was at Oxford, and saw the first stone laid of the Ratcliff library; and I remember that at a still greater distance of time, I heard a debate in the house of Commons about a standing army.

Lamentable is the imperfection of language, almost in every particular that falls not under external sense. I am talking of a matter exceeding clear in itself, and of which every person must be conscious; and yet I find no small difficulty to express it clearly in words; for it is not accurate to talk of incidents long past as passing in our sight, nor of hearing at present what we really heard yesterday or perhaps a year ago. To this necessity I am reduced, by want of proper words to describe ideal presence and to distinguish it from real presence. And thus in the description, a plain subject becomes obscure and intricate. When I recall anything in the distinctest manner, so as to form an idea or image of it as present; I have not words to describe this act, other than that I perceive the thing as a spectator, and as existing in my presence. This means not that I am really a spectator; but only that I conceive myself to be a spectator, and have a consciousness of presence similar to what a real spectator hath.

As many rules of criticism depend on ideal presence, the reader, it is expected, will take some pains to form an exact notion of it, as distinguished on the one hand from real presence, and on the other from a superficial or reflective remembrance. It is distinguished from the former by the following circumstance. Ideal presence arising from an act of memory, may properly be termed *a waking dream*; because, like a dream, it vanisheth upon the first reflection of our present situation. Real presence, on the contrary, vouched by eye-sight, commands our belief, not only during the direct perception, but in reflecting afterward upon the object. And to distinguish ideal presence from the latter, I give the following illustration. Two internal acts, both of them exertions of memory, are clearly distinguishable. When I think of an event as past, without forming any image, it is barely reflecting or remembering that I was an eye-witness. But when I recall the event so distinctly as to form a complete image of it, I perceive it ideally as passing in my presence; and this ideal perception is an act of intuition, into which reflection enters not more than into an act of sight.

Though ideal presence be distinguished from real presence on the one side and from reflective remembrance on the other, it is however variable without any precise limits; rising sometimes toward the former, and often sinking toward the latter. In a vigorous exertion of memory, ideal presence is extremely distinct. When a man, as in a reverie, drops himself out of his thoughts, he perceives everything as passing before him, and hath a consciousness of presence similar to that of a spectator. There is no other difference, but that in the former the consciousness of presence is less firm and clear than in the latter. But this is seldom the case. Ideal presence is often faint, and the image so obscure as not to differ widely from reflective remembrance.

Hitherto of an idea of memory. I proceed to consider the idea of a thing I never saw, raised in me by speech, by writing, or by painting. This idea, with respect to the present matter, is of the same nature with an idea of memory, being either complete or incomplete. An important event, by a lively and accurate description, rouses my attention and insensibly transforms me into a spectator: I perceive ideally every incident as passing in my presence. On the other hand, a slight or superficial narrative produceth only a faint and incomplete idea, precisely similar to a reflective recollection of memory. Of such idea, ideal presence makes no part. Past time is a circumstance that enters into this idea, as it doth into a reflective idea of memory. I believe that Scipio existed about 2000 years ago, and that he overcame Hannibal in the famous battle of Zama. When I revolve in so cursory a manner that memorable event, I consider it as long past. But supposing me to be warmed with the story, perhaps by a beautiful description, I am insensibly transformed to a spectator. I perceive these two heroes in act to engage; I perceive them brandishing their swords, and exhorting their troops; and in this manner I attend them through every circumstance of the battle. This event being present to my mind during the whole progress of my thoughts, admits not anytime but the present.

I have had occasion to observe[10], that ideas both of memory and of speech, produce emotions of the same kind with what are produced by an immediate view of the object; only fainter, in proportion as an idea is fainter than an original perception. The insight we have now got, unfolds the means by which this effect is produced. Ideal presence supplies the want of real presence; and in idea we perceive persons acting and suffering, precisely as in an original survey. If our sympathy be engaged by the latter, it must also in some measure be engaged by the former. The distinctness of ideal presence, as above mentioned, approacheth sometimes to the distinctness of real presence; and the consciousness of presence is the same in both. This is the cause of the pleasure that is felt in a reverie, where a man, losing sight of himself, is totally occupied with the objets passing in his mind, which he conceives to be really existing in his presence. The power of speech to raise emotions, depends entirely on the artifice of raising such lively and distinct images as are

---

10. Part 1. sect. 1. of the present chapter.

here described. The reader's passions are never sensibly moved, till he be thrown into a kind of reverie; in which state, losing the consciousness of self, and of reading, his present occupation, he conceives every incident as passing in his presence, precisely as if he were an eyewitness. A general or reflective remembrance hath not this effect. It may be agreeable in some slight degree; but the ideas suggested by it, are too faint and obscure to raise anything like a sympathetic emotion. And were they ever so lively, they pass with too much precipitation to have this effect. Our emotions are never instantaneous: even those that come the soonest to perfection, have different periods of birth, growth, and maturity; and to give opportunity for these different periods, it is necessary that the cause of every emotion be present to the mind a due time. The emotion is completed by reiterated impressions. We know this to be the case of objects of sight: we are scarce sensible of any emotion in a quick succession even of the most beautiful objects. And if this hold in the succession of original perceptions, how much more in the succession of ideas?

Though all this while, I have been only describing what passeth in the mind of everyone and what everyone must be conscious of, it was necessary to enlarge upon it; because, however clear in the internal conception, it is far from being so when described in words. Ideal presence, though of general importance, hath scarce ever been touched by any writer; and at any rate it could not be overlooked in accounting for the effects produced by fiction. Upon this point, the reader I guess has prevented me. It already must have occurred to him, that if, in reading, ideal presence be the means by which our passions are moved, it makes no difference whether the subject be a fable or a reality. When ideal presence is complete, we perceive every object as in our sight; and the mind, totally occupied with an interesting event, finds no leisure for reflection of any sort. This reasoning, if anyone hesitate, is confirmed by constant and universal experience. Let us take under consideration the meeting of Hector and Andromache in the sixth book of the Iliad, or some of the passionate scenes in King Lear. These pictures of human life, when we are sufficiently engaged, give an impression of reality not less distinct than that given by the death of Otho in the beautiful description of Tacitus. We never once reflect whether the story be true or feigned. Reflection comes afterward, when we have the scene no longer before our eyes. This reasoning will appear in a still clearer light, by opposing ideal presence to ideas raised by a cursory narrative; which ideas being faint, obscure, and imperfect, occupy the mind so little as to solicit reflection. And accordingly, a curt narrative of feigned incidents is never relished. Any slight pleasure it affords, is more than counterbalanced by the disgust it inspires for want of truth.

In support of the foregoing theory, I add what I reckon a decisive argument. Upon examination it will be found, that genuine history commands our passions by means of ideal presence solely; and therefore that with respect to this effect, genuine history stands upon the same footing with fable. To me it appears clear, that our sympathy must vanish so soon as we begin to reflect upon the incidents related in either. The reflection that a story is a pure fiction, will indeed prevent our sympathy; but so will equally the reflection that the persons described are no longer existing. It is present distress only that moves my pity. My concern vanishes with the distress; for I cannot pity any person who at present is happy. According to this theory, founded clearly on human nature, a man long dead and insensible now of past misfortunes, cannot move our pity more than if he had never existed. The misfortunes described in a genuine history command our belief: but then we believe also, that these misfortunes are at an end, and that the persons described are at present under no distress. What effect, for example, can the belief of the rape of Lucretia have to raise our sympathy, when she died above 2000 years ago, and hath at present no painful feeling of the injury done her? The effect of history in point of instruction, depends in some measure upon its veracity. But history cannot reach the heart, while we indulge any reflection upon the facts. Such reflection, if it engage our belief, never fails at the same time to poison our pleasure, by convincing us that our sympathy for those who are dead and gone is absurd. And if reflection be laid aside, history stands upon the same footing with fable. What effect either of them may have to raise our sympathy, depends on the vivacity of the ideas they raise; and with respect to that circumstance, fable is generally more successful than history.

Of all the means for making an impression of ideal presence, theatrical representation is the most powerful. That words independent of action have the same power in a less degree, everyone of sensibility must have felt: A good tragedy will extort tears in private, though not so forcibly as upon the stage. This power belongs also to painting. A good historical picture makes a deeper impression than can be made by words, though not equal to what is made by theatrical action. And as ideal presence depends on a lively impression, painting seems to possess a middle place betwixt reading and acting. In making an impression of ideal presence, it is not less superior to the former than inferior to the latter.

It must not however be thought, that our passions can be raised by painting to such a height as can be done by words. Of all the successive incidents that concur to produce a great event, a picture has the choice but of one, because it is confined to a single instant of time. And though the impression it makes, is the deepest that can be made instantaneously; yet seldom can a passion be raised to any height in an instant, or by a single impression. It was observed above, that our passions, those especially of the sympathetic kind, require a succession of impressions; and for that reason, reading and still more acting have greatly the advantage, by the opportunity of reiterating impressions without end.

Upon the whole, it is by means of ideal presence that our passions are excited; and till words produce that charm they avail nothing. Even real events intitled to our belief, must be conceived present and passing in our sight before they can move us. And this theory serves to explain several phenomena otherwise unaccountable. A misfortune happening to a stranger, makes a less impression than happening to a man we know, even where we are no way interested in him: our acquaintance with this man, however slight, aids the conception of his suffering in our presence. For the same reason, we are little moved with any distant event; because we have more difficulty to conceive it present, than an event that happened in our neighbourhood.

Everyone is sensible, that describing a past event as present, has a fine effect in language. For what other reason than that it aids the conception of ideal presence? Take the following example.

> *And now with shouts the shocking armies clos'd,*
> *To lances lances, shields to shields oppos'd;*
> *Host against host the shadowy legions drew,*
> *The sounding darts an iron tempest flew;*
> *Victors and vanquish'd join promiscuous cries,*
> *Triumphing shouts and dying groans arise,*
> *With streaming blood the slipp'ry field is dy'd,*
> *And slaughter'd heroes swell the dreadful tide.*

In this passage we may observe how the writer inflamed with the subject, insensibly slips from the past time to the present; led to this form of narration by conceiving every circumstance as passing in his own sight. And this at the same time has a fine effect upon the reader, by advancing him to be as it were a spectator. But this change from the past to the present requires some preparation; and is not graceful in the same sentence where there is no stop in the sense; witness the following passage.

> *Thy fate was next, O Phæstus! doom'd to feel*
> *The great Idomeneus' protended steel;*
> *Whom Borus sent his son and only joy*
> *From fruitful Tarne to the fields of Troy.*
> *The Cretan jav'lin reach'd him from afar,*
> *And pierc'd his shoulder as he mounts his car.*
>
> —*Iliad*, v. 57

It is still worse to fall back to the past in the same period; for this is an anticlimax in description:

> *Through breaking ranks his furious course he bends,*
> *And at the goddess his broad lance extends;*
> *Through her bright veil the daring weapon drove,*
> *Th' ambrosial veil, which all the graces wove:*
> *Her snowy hand the razing steel profan'd,*
> *And the transparent skin with crimson stain'd.*
>
> —*Iliad*, v. 415

Again, describing the shield of Jupiter,

> *Here all the terrors of grim War appear,*
> *Here rages Force, here tremble Flight and Fear,*
> *Here storm'd Contention, and here Fury frown'd,*
> *And the dire orb portentous Gorgon crown'd.*
>
> —*Iliad*, v. 914

Nor is it pleasant to be carried backward and forward alternately in a rapid succession:

> *Then dy'd Seamandrius, expert in the chace,*
> *In woods and wilds to wound the savage race;*
> *Diana taught him all her sylvan arts,*
> *To bend the bow and aim unerring darts:*
> *But vainly here Diana's arts he tries,*
> *The fatal lance arrests him as he flies;*
> *From Menelaus' arm the weapon sent,*
> *Through his broad back and heaving bosom went:*
> *Down sinks the warrior with a thund'ring sound,*
> *His brazen armor rings against the ground.*
>
> —*Iliad*, v. 65

It is wonderful to observe, upon what slender foundations nature, sometimes, erects her most solid and magnificent works. In appearance at least, what can be more slight than ideal presence of objects? And yet upon it entirely is superstructed, that extensive influence which language hath over the heart; an influence, which, more than any other means, strengthens the bond of society, and attracts individuals from their private system to exert themselves in acts of generosity and benevolence. Matters of fact, it is true, and truth in general, may be inculcated without taking advantage of ideal presence. But without it, the finest speaker or writer would in vain attempt to move any of our passion: our sympathy would be confined to objects that are really present: and language would lose entirely that signal power it possesseth, of making us sympathize with beings removed at the greatest distance of time as well as of place. Nor is the influence of language, by means of this ideal presence, confined to the heart. It reaches also in some measure the understanding, and contributes to belief. When events are related in a lively manner and every circumstance appears as passing before us, it is with difficulty that we suffer the truth of the facts to be questioned. A historian accordingly who hath a genius for narration, seldom fails to engage our belief. The same facts related in a manner cold and indistinct, are not suffered to pass without examination. A thing ill described, is like an object seen at a distance or through a mist: we doubt whether it be a reality or a fiction. For this reason, a poet who can warm and animate his reader, may employ bolder fictions than ought to be ventured by an inferior genius. The reader, once thoroughly engaged, is in that situation susceptible of the strongest impressions:

> *Veraque constituunt, quæ bellè tangere possunt*
> *Aureis, et lepido quæ sunt fucata sonore.*
>
> —*Lucretius, lib. 1. l. 644*

A masterly painting has the same effect. Le Brun is no small support to Quintus Curtius; and among the vulgar in Italy, the belief of scripture-history is perhaps founded as much upon the authority of Raphael, Michael Angelo, and other celebrated painters, as upon that of the sacred writers[11].

In establishing the foregoing theory, the reader has had the fatigue of much dry reasoning. But his labour will not be fruitless. From this theory are derived many useful rules in criticism, which shall be mentioned in their proper places. One specimen, being a fine illustration, I chuse to give at present. In a historical poem representing human actions, it is a rule, that no improbable incident ought to be admitted. A circumstance, an incident, or an event, may be singular, may surprise by being unexpected, and yet be extremely natural. The improbability I talk of, is that of an irregular fact, contrary to the order and course of nature, and therefore unaccountable. A chain of imagined facts linked together according to the order of nature, find easy entrance into the mind; and if described with warmth of fancy, they produce complete images, including ideal presence. But it is with great difficulty that we admit any irregular fact; for an irregular fact always puzzles the judgement. Doubtful of its reality we immediately enter upon reflection, and discovering the cheat, lose all relish and concern. This is an unhappy effect; for thereafter it requires more than an ordinary effort, to restore the waking dream, and to make the reader conceive even the more probable incidents as passing in his presence.

I never was an admirer of machinery in an epic poem; and I now find my taste justified by reason; the foregoing argument concluding still more strongly against imaginary beings, than against improbable facts. Fictions of this nature may amuse by their novelty and singularity: but

---

11. At quæ Polycleto defuerunt. Phidiæ atque Alcameni dantur. Phidias tamen diis quam hominibus efficiendis melior artifex traditur: in ebore vero longe citra æmulum. vel si nihil nisi Minervam Athenis, aut Olympium in Elide Jovem fecisset, cujus pulcritudo adjecisse aliquid etiam receptæ religioni videtur; adeo majestas opens Deum æquavit.—*Quintilian, lib. 12. cap. 10. sec. 1.*

they never move the sympathetic passions, because they cannot impose on the mind any perception of reality. I appeal to the discerning reader, whether this be not precisely the case of the machinery introduced by Tasso and by Voltaire. This machinery is not only in itself cold and uninteresting, but is remarkably hurtful, by giving an air of fiction to the whole composition. A burlesque poem, such as the Lutrin or the Dispensary, may employ machinery with success; for these poems, though they assume the air of history, give entertainment chiefly by their pleasant and ludicrous pictures, to which machinery contributes in a singular manner. It is not the aim of such a poem, to raise our sympathy in any considerable degree; and for that reason, a strict imitation of nature is not required. A poem professedly ludicrous, may employ machinery to great advantage; and the more extravagant the better. A just representation of nature, would indeed be incongruous in a composition intended to give entertainment by the means chiefly of singularity and surprise.

For accomplishing the task undertaken in the beginning of the present section, what only remains is, to show the final cause of the power that fiction hath over the mind of man. I have already mentioned, that language, by means of fiction, has the command of our sympathy for the good of others. By the same means, our sympathy may be also raised for our own good. In the third section it is observed, that examples both of virtue and of vice raise virtuous emotions; which becoming stronger by exercise, tend to make us virtuous by habit as well as by principle. I now further observe, that examples drawn from real events, are not so frequent as to contribute much to a habit of virtue. If they be, they are not recorded by historians. It therefore shows great wisdom, to form us in such a manner, as to be susceptible of the same improvement from fable that we receive from genuine history. By this admirable contrivance, examples to improve us in virtue may be multiplied without end. No other sort of discipline contributes more to make virtue habitual; and no other sort is so agreeable in the application. I add another final cause with thorough satisfaction; because it shows, that the author of our nature is not less kindly provident for the happiness of his creatures, than for the regularity of their conduct. The power that fiction hath over the mind of man, is the source of an endless variety of refined amusement, always ready to employ a vacant hour. Such amusement is a fine resource in solitude; and by sweetening the temper, improves society.

Part II

Emotions and passions as pleasant and painful, agreeable and disagreeable. Modifications of these qualities.

It will naturally occur at first view, that a discourse upon the passions should commence with explaining the qualities now mentioned. But upon trial, I found this could not be done distinctly, till the difference were ascertained betwixt an emotion and a passion, and till their causes were evolved.

Great obscurity may be observed among writers with regard to the present point. No care, for example, is taken to distinguish agreeable from pleasant, disagreeable from painful; or rather these terms are deemed synonymous. This is an error not at all venial in the science of ethics; as instances can and shall be given, of painful passions that are agreeable, and of pleasant passions that are disagreeable. These terms, it is true, are used indifferently in familiar conversations, and in composition for amusement, where accuracy is not required. But for those to use them so who profess to explain the passions, is a capital error. In writing upon the critical art, I would avoid every refinement that may seem more curious than useful. But the proper meaning of the terms under consideration must be ascertained, in order to understand the passions, and some of their effects that are intimately connected with criticism.

I shall endeavour to explain these terms by familiar examples. Viewing a fine garden, I perceive it to be beautiful or agreeable; and I consider the beauty or agreeableness as belonging to the object, or as one of its qualities. Again, when I turn my thoughts from the garden to what passes in my mind, I am conscious of a pleasant emotion of which the garden is the cause. The pleasure here is felt, not as a quality of the garden, but of the emotion produced by it. I give an opposite example. A rotten carcass is loathsome and disagreeable, and raises in the spectator a painful emotion. The disagreeableness is a quality of the object: the pain is a quality of the emotion produced by it. Agreeable and disagreeable, then, are qualities of the object we perceive: pleasant and painful are qualities of the emotions we feel. The former qualities are perceived as adhering to objects; the latter are felt as existing within us.

But a passion or emotion, beside being felt, is frequently made an object of thought or reflection: we examine it; we inquire into its nature, its cause, and its effects. In this view it partakes the nature of other objects: it is either agreeable or disagreeable. Hence clearly appear the different significations of the terms under consideration, as applied to passion. When a passion is termed *pleasant* or *painful*, we refer to the actual feeling: when termed *agreeable* or *disagreeable*, it is considered as an object of thought or reflection. A passion is pleasant or painful to the person in whom it exists: it is agreeable or disagreeable to the person who makes it a subject of contemplation.

When the terms thus defined are applied to particular emotions and passions, they do not always coincide. And in order to make this evident, we must endeavour to ascertain, first, what passions and emotions are pleasant what painful, and next, what are agreeable what disagreeable. With respect to both, there are general rules, which, so far as I gather from induction, admit not any exceptions. The nature of an emotion or passion as pleasant or painful, depends entirely on its cause. An agreeable object produceth always a pleasant emotion; and a disagreeable object produceth always a painful emotion[12]. Thus a lofty oak, a generous action, a valuable discovery in art or science, are agreeable objects that unerringly produce pleasant emotions. A stinking puddle, a treacherous action, an irregular ill-contrived edifice, being disagreeable objects, produce painful emotions. Selfish passions are pleasant; for they arise from self, an agreeable object or cause. A social passion directed upon an agreeable object is always pleasant: directed upon an object in distress, is painful[13]. Lastly, all dissocial passions, such as envy, resentment, malice, being caused by disagreeable objects, cannot fail to be painful.

It requires a greater compass to evolve the general rule that concerns the agreeableness or disagreeableness of emotions and passions. An action conformable to the common nature of our species, is perceived by us to be regular and good[14]; and consequently every such action appears agreeable to us. The same observation is applicable to passions and emotions. Every feeling that is conformable to the common nature of our species, is perceived by us to be regular and as it ought to be; and upon that account it must appear agreeable. By this general rule we can ascertain what emotions are agreeable what disagreeable.

---

12. See part 7. of this chapter.
13. Ibid.
14. See this doctrine fully explained, chap. 25. Standard of Taste.

Every emotion that is conformable to the common nature of man, ought to appear agreeable. And that this holds true with respect to pleasant emotions, will readily be admitted. But why should painful emotions be an exception, when they are not less natural than the other? The proportion holds true in both. Thus the painful emotion raised by a monstrous birth or brutal action, is not less agreeable upon reflection, than the pleasant emotion raised by a flowing river or a lofty dome. With respect to passions as opposed to emotions, it will be obvious from the foregoing proposition, that their agreeableness or disagreeableness, like the actions of which they are productive, must be regulated entirely by the moral sense. Every action vicious or improper is disagreeable to a spectator, and so is the passion that prompts it. Every action virtuous or proper is agreeable to a spectator, and so is the passion that prompts it.

This deduction may be carried a great way farther; but to avoid intricacy and obscurity, I make but one other step. A passion, which, as aforesaid, becomes an object of thought to a spectator, may have the effect to produce a passion or emotion in him; for it is natural that a social being should be affected with the passions of others. Passions or emotions thus generated, submit, in common with others, to the general law above mentioned, *viz.* that an agreeable object produces a pleasant emotion, and a disagreeable object a painful emotion. Thus the passion of gratitude, being to a spectator an agreeable object, produceth in him the pleasant passion of love to the grateful person. Thus malice, being to a spectator a disagreeable object, produceth in him the painful passion of hatred to the malicious person.

We are now prepared for examples of pleasant passions that are disagreeable, and of painful passions that agreeable. Self-love, so long as confined within just bounds, is a passion both pleasant and agreeable. In excess it is disagreeable, though it continues to be still pleasant. Our appetites are precisely in the same condition. Again, vanity, though pleasant, is disagreeable. Resentment, on the other hand, is, in every stage of the passion, painful; but is not disagreeable unless in excess. Pity is always painful, yet always agreeable. But however distinct these qualities are, they coincide, I acknowledge, in one class of passions. All vicious passions tending to the hurt of others, are equally painful and disagreeable.

The foregoing distinctions among passions and emotions, may serve the common affairs of life, but they are not sufficient for the critical art. The qualities of pleasant and painful are too familiar to carry us far into human nature, or to form an accurate judgement in the fine arts. It is further necessary, that we be made acquainted with the several modifications of these qualities, with the modifications at least that make the greatest figure. Even at first view everyone is sensible, that the pleasure or pain of one passion differs from that of another. How distant the pleasure of revenge from that of love? So distant, as that we cannot without reluctance admit them to be anyway related. That the same quality of pleasure should be so differently modified in different passions, will not be surprising, when we reflect on the boundless variety of pleasant sounds, tastes, and smells, daily felt. Our discernment reaches differences still more nice, in objects even of the same sense. We have no difficulty to distinguish different sweets, different sours, and different bitters. Honey is sweet, and so is sugar; and yet they never pass the one for the other. Our sense of smelling is sufficiently acute, to distinguish varieties in sweet-smelling flowers without end. With respect to passions and emotions, their different feelings have no limits; for when we attempt the more delicate modifications, they elude our search, and are scarce discernible. In this matter, however, there is an analogy betwixt our internal and external senses. The latter generally are sufficiently acute for all the useful purposes of life, and so are the former. Some persons indeed, Nature's favourites, have a wonderful acuteness of sense, which to them unfolds many a delightful scene totally hid from vulgar eyes. But if such refined pleasure be refused to the bulk of mankind, it is however wisely ordered that they are not sensible of the defect; and it detracts not from their happiness that others secretly are more happy. With relation to the fine arts only, this qualification seems essential; and there it is termed *delicacy of taste*.

Should an author of such a taste attempt to describe all those differences and shades of pleasant and painful emotions which he himself feels, he would soon meet an invincible obstacle in the poverty of language. No known tongue hitherto has reached such perfection, as to express clearly the more delicate feelings. A people must be thoroughly refined, before their language become so comprehensive. We must therefore rest satisfied with an explanation of the more obvious modifications.

In forming a comparison betwixt pleasant passions of different kinds, we conceive some of them to be *gross* some *refined*. Those pleasures of external sense that are felt as at the organ of sense, are conceived to be corporeal or gross[15]. The pleasures of the eye and ear are felt to be internal; and for that reason are conceived to be more pure and refined.

The social affections are conceived by all to be more refined than the selfish. Sympathy and humanity are reckoned the finest temper of mind; and for that reason, the prevalence of the social affections in the progress of society, is held to be a refinement in our nature. A savage is unqualified for any pleasure but what is thoroughly or nearly selfish: therefore a savage is incapable of comparing selfish and social pleasure. But a man after acquiring a high relish of the latter, loses not thereby a taste for the former. This man can judge, and he will give preference to social pleasures as more sweet and refined. In fact they maintain that character, not only in the direct feeling, but also when we make them the subject of reflection. The social passions are by far more agreeable than the selfish, and rise much higher in our esteem.

Refined manners and polite behaviour, must not be deemed altogether artificial. Men accustomed to the sweets of society, who cultivate humanity, find an elegant pleasure in preferring others and making them happy, of which the proud or selfish scarce have a conception.

Ridicule, which chiefly arises from pride, a selfish passion, is at best but a gross pleasure. A people, it is true, must have emerged out of barbarity before they can have a taste for ridicule. But it is too rough an entertainment for those who are highly polished and refined. Ridicule is banished France, and is losing ground daily in England.

Other modifications of pleasant passions will be occasionally mentioned hereafter. Particularly the modifications of *high* and *low* are handled in the chapter of grandeur and sublimity; and the modifications of *dignified* and *mean*, in the chapter of dignity and meanness.

Part III

*Interrupted existence of emotions and passions.—
Their growth and decay.*

Were emotions of the same nature with colour and figure, to continue in their present state till varied by some operating cause, the condition of man would be deplorable. It is ordered wisely, that emotions should more resemble another attribute of matter, *viz.* motion, which requires

---

15. See the Introduction.

the constant exertion of an operating cause, and ceases when the cause is withdrawn. An emotion may subsist while its cause is present; and when its cause is removed, may subsist by means of an idea, though in a fainter degree. But the moment another thought breaks in and occupies the mind, so as to exclude not only this cause, but also its idea, the emotion is gone: it is no longer felt. If it return with its cause or idea, it again vanisheth with them when other thoughts crowd in. This observation is applicable to emotions and passions of every kind. And these accordingly are connected with perceptions and ideas, so intimately as not to have any independent existence. A strong passion, it is true, hath a mighty influence to detain its object in the mind; but not so as to detain it forever. A succession of perceptions or ideas is unavoidable[16]: the object of the passion may be often recalled; but however interesting, it must by intervals yield to other objects. For this reason, a passion rarely continues long with an equal degree of vigour. It is felt strong and moderate, in a pretty quick succession. The same object makes not always the same impression; because the mind, being of a limited capacity, cannot, at the same instant, give great attention to a plurality of objects. The strength of a passion depends on the impression made by its cause; and a cause makes its strongest impression, when happening to be the single interesting object, it attracts our whole attention[17]. Its impression is slighter when our attention is divided betwixt it and other objects; and at that time the passion is slighter in proportion.

When emotions and passions are felt thus by intervals and have not a continued existence, it may be thought a nice problem, to ascertain their identity, and to determine when they are the same when different. In a strict philosophic view, every single impression made even by the same object, is distinguishable from what have gone before, and from what succeed. Neither is an emotion raised by an idea the same with what is raised by a sight of the object. But such accuracy is not found in common apprehension, nor is necessary in common language. The emotions raised by a fine landscape in its successive appearances, are not distinguished from each other, nor even from those raised by successive ideas of the object: all of them are held to be the same. A passion also is always reckoned the same, so long as it is fixed upon the same object. Thus love and hatred may continue the same for life. Nay, so loose are

---

16. See this point explained afterward, chap. 9.
17. See the Appendix, containing definitions, and explanation of terms, sect. 33.

we in this way of thinking, that many passions are reckoned the same even after a change of object. This is the case of all passions that proceed from some peculiar propensity. Envy, for example, is considered to be the same passion, not only while it is directed upon the same person, but even where it comprehends many persons at once. Pride and malice are in the same condition. So much was necessary to be said upon the identity of a passion and emotion, in order to prepare for examining their growth and decay.

The growth and decay of passions and emotions, is a subject too extensive to be exhausted in an undertaking like the present. I pretend only to give a cursory view of it, so far as necessary for the purposes of criticism. Some emotions are produced in their utmost perfection, and have a very short endurance. This is the case of surprise, of wonder, and sometimes of terror. Emotions raised by insensible objects, such as trees, rivers, buildings, pictures, arrive at perfection almost instantaneously, and have a long endurance: a second view produceth nearly the same pleasure with the first. Love, hatred, and someother passions, increase gradually to a certain pitch, and thereafter decay gradually. Envy, malice, pride, scarce ever decay. Again, some passions, such as gratitude and revenge, are often exhausted by a single act of gratification. Other passions, such as pride, malice, envy, love, hatred, are not so exhausted; but having a long continuance, demand frequent gratification.

In order to explain these differences, it would be an endless work to examine every emotion and passion in particular. We must be satisfied at present with some general views. And with respect to emotions, which are quiescent and not productive of desire, their growth and decay are easily explained. An emotion caused by an external object, cannot naturally take longer time to arrive at perfection, than is necessary for a leisurely survey. Such emotion also must continue long stationary, without any sensible decay; a second or third view of the object being nearly as agreeable as the first. This is the case of an emotion produced by a fine prospect, an impetuous river, or a towering hill. While a man remains the same, such objects ought to have the same effect upon him. Familiarity, however, hath an influence here, as it hath everywhere. Frequency of view, after short intervals especially, weans the mind gradually from the object, which at last loses all relish. The noblest object in the material world, a clear and serene sky, is quite disregarded, unless perhaps after a course of bad weather. An emotion raised by human virtues, qualities, or actions, may grow imperceptibly by reiterated views of the object, till it become so vigorous as to generate desire. In this condition it must be handled as a passion.

As to passion, I observe first, that when nature requires a passion to be sudden, it is commonly produced in perfection. This is frequently the case of fear and of anger. Wonder and surprise are always produced in perfection. Reiterated impressions made by their cause, exhaust these passions in place of inflaming them. This will be explained afterward[18].

In the next place, when a passion hath for its foundation an original propensity peculiar to some men, it generally comes soon to perfection. The propensity, upon representing a proper object, is immediately enlivened into a passion. This is the case of pride, of envy, and of malice.

In the third place, love and hatred have often a slow growth. The good qualities or kind offices of a person, raise in me pleasant emotions; which, by reiterated views, are swelled into a passion involving desire of that person's happiness. This desire being often put in exercise, works gradually a change internally; and at last produceth in me a settled habit of affection for that person, now my friend. Affection thus produced, operates precisely like an original propensity. To enliven it into a passion, no more is required but the real or ideal presence of the object. The habit of aversion or hatred is brought on in the same manner. And here I must observe by the way, that love and hatred signify commonly affection, not passion. The bulk indeed of our passions, are these affections inflamed into a passion by different circumstances. The affection of love I bear to my son, is inflamed into the passion of fear, when he is in danger; becomes hope, when he hath a prospect of good fortune; becomes admiration, when he performs a laudable action; and shame, when he commits any wrong. Aversion, again, becomes fear when there is a prospect of good fortune to my enemy; becomes hope when he is in danger; becomes joy when he is in distress; and sorrow when a laudable action is performed by him.

Fourthly, the growth of some passions depends often on occasional circumstances. Obstacles to gratification never fail to augment and inflame a passion. A constant endeavour to remove the obstacle, preserves the object of the passion ever in view, which swells the passion by impressions frequently reiterated. Thus the restraint of conscience, when an obstacle to love, agitates the mind and inflames the passion:

---

18. Chap. 6.

> *Quod licet, ingratum est: quod non licet, acrius urit.*
> *Si nunquam Danaën habuisset ahenea turris,*
> *Non esset Danaë de Jove facta parens.*
>
> —*Ovid. Amor. l. 2*

At the same time, the mind distressed with the obstacle, is disposed to indulge its distress by magnifying the pleasure of gratification; which naturally inflames desire. Shakespear expresses this observation finely:

> *All impediments in fancy's course,*
> *Are motives of more fancy.*

We need no better example than a lover who hath many rivals. Even the caprices of a mistress have the effect to inflame love. These occasioning uncertainty of success, tend naturally to make the anxious lover overvalue the happiness of fruition.

So much upon the growth of passions. Their continuance and decay come next under consideration. And first, it is a general law of nature, that things sudden in their growth, are equally sudden in their decay. This is commonly the case of anger; and with respect to wonder and surprise, another reason concurs, that their causes are of short duration. Novelty soon degenerates into familiarity; and the unexpectedness of an object, is soon sunk in the pleasure which the object affords us. Fear, which is a passion of greater importance as tending to self-preservation, is often instantaneous, and yet is of equal duration with its cause. Nay it frequently subsists after the cause is removed.

In the next place, a passion founded on a peculiar propensity, subsists generally forever. This is the case of pride, envy, and malice. Objects are never wanting, to inflame the propensity into a passion.

Thirdly, it may be laid down as a general law of nature, that every passion ceases upon attaining its ultimate end. To explain this law, we must distinguish betwixt a particular and a general end. I call a particular end what may be accomplished by a single act. A general end, on the contrary, admits acts without number; because it cannot be said that a general end is ever fully accomplished while the object of the passion subsists. Gratitude and revenge are examples of the first kind. The ends they aim at may be accomplished by a single act; and when this act is performed, the passions are necessarily at an end. Love and hatred are examples of the other kind. The desire of doing good or of doing mischief to an individual, is a general end, which admits acts without number, and which seldom is fully accomplished. Therefore these passions have frequently the same duration with their objects.

Lastly, it will afford us another general view, to consider the difference betwixt an original propensity and an affection produced by custom. The former adheres too close to the constitution ever to be eradicated; and for that reason the passions to which it gives birth, endure during life with no remarkable diminution of strength. The latter, which owes its birth and increment to time, owes its decay to the same cause. Affection decays gradually as it grew. Hence long absence extinguisheth hatred as well as love. Affection wears out more gradually betwixt persons, who, living together, are objects to each other of mutual good-will and kindness. But here habit comes in luckily, to supply decayed affection. It makes these persons necessary to the happiness of each other, by the pain of separation[19]. Affection to children hath a long endurance, longer perhaps than any other affection. Its growth keeps pace with that of its objects. They display new beauties and qualifications daily, to feed and augment the affection. But whenever the affection becomes stationary, it must begin to decay; with a slow pace indeed, in proportion to its increment. In short, man with respect to this life, is a temporary being. He grows, becomes stationary, decays; and so must all his powers and passions.

Part IV

Coexistent emotions and passions.

To have a thorough knowledge of the human passions and emotions, it is not sufficient that they be examined singly and separately. As a plurality of them are sometimes felt at the same instant, the manner of their coexistence, and the effects thereby produced, ought also to be examined. This subject is extensive, and it will be difficult to evolve all the laws that govern its endless variety of cases. Such an undertaking may be brought to perfection, but it must be by degrees. The following hints may suffice for a first attempt.

---

19. See chap. 14.

We begin with emotions raised by different sounds, as the simplest case. Two sounds that mix, and are, as it were, incorporated before they reach the ear, are said to be concordant. That each sound produceth an emotion of its own, must be admitted. But then these emotions, like the sounds that produce them, mix so intimately, as to be rather one complex emotion than two emotions in conjunction. Two sounds, again, that refuse incorporation or mixture, are said to be discordant. Being however heard at the same instant, the emotions produced by them are conjoined; and in that condition are unpleasant, even where separately they are each of them pleasant.

Similar to the emotion raised by mixed sounds, is the emotion that an object of sight raises by means of its several qualities. A tree, for example, with its qualities of colour, figure, size, &c. is perceived to be one object; and the emotion it raises is one, not different emotions combined. But though the emotion be one, it is however not simple. The perception of the tree is complex, and the emotion raised by it must also be complex.

With respect to coexistent emotions produced by different causes or objects, it must be observed, that there cannot be a concordance among objects of sight like what is perceived in sounds. Objects of sight are never mixed or incorporated in the act of vision. Each object is perceived as it exists, separately from others; and each raiseth its own emotion, which is felt distinctly however intimately connected the objects may be. This doctrine holds in all the causes of emotion or passion, sounds only excepted.

To explain the manner in which such emotions coexist, similar emotions must be distinguished from those that are dissimilar. Two emotions are said to be similar, when they tend each of them to produce the same tone of mind. Chearful emotions, however different their causes may be, are similar; and so are those which are melancholy. Dissimilar emotions are easily explained by their opposition to what are similar. Grandeur and littleness, gaiety and gloominess, are dissimilar emotions.

Emotions perfectly similar, readily combine and unite[20], so as in a manner to become one complex emotion; witness the emotions

---

20. It is easier to conceive the manner of co-existence of similar emotions than to describe it. They cannot be said to mix or incorporate, like concordant sounds; their union is rather of agreement or concord; and therefore I have chosen the words in the text, not

produced by a number of flowers in a parterre, or of trees in a wood. Emotions again that are opposite or extremely dissimilar, never combine nor unite. The mind cannot simultaneously take on opposite tones: it cannot at the same instant be both joyful and sad, angry and satisfied, proud and humble. Dissimilar emotions may succeed each other with rapidity, but they cannot exist simultaneously.

Betwixt these two extremes, emotions will unite more or less, in proportion to the degree of their resemblance and the greater or less connection of their causes. The beauty of a landscape and the singing of birds, produce emotions that are similar in a considerable degree; and these emotions therefore, though proceeding from very different causes, readily combine and unite. On the other hand, when the causes are intimately connected, the emotions, though but slightly resembling each other, are forced into a sort of union. I give for an example a mistress in distress. When I consider her beauty, I feel a pleasant emotion; and a painful emotion when I consider her distress. These two emotions, proceeding from different views of the object, have very little resemblance to each other: and yet their causes are so intimately connected, as to force them into a sort of complex emotion, partly pleasant partly painful. This clearly explains some expressions common in poetry, *a sweet distress, a pleasant pain*.

We proceed to the effects produced by means of the different manners of coexistence above described; first, the effects produced within the mind, and next, those that appear externally. I discover two mental effects clearly distinguishable from each other. The one may be represented by addition and subtraction in numbers, and the other by harmony in sounds. Two pleasant emotions that are similar, readily unite when they are coexistent; and the pleasure felt in the union, is the sum of the two pleasures. The combined emotions are like multiplied effects from the co-operation of different powers. The same emotions in succession, are far from making the same figure; because the mind at no instant of the succession is conscious of more than a single emotion. This doctrine may aptly be illustrated by a landscape comprehending hills, vallies, plains, rivers, trees, *&c*. The emotions produced by these several objects, being similar in a high degree as falling in easily and sweetly with the same tone of mind, are in conjunction extremely

---

as sufficient to express clearly the manner of their co-existence, but only as less liable to exception than any other I can find.

pleasant. And this multiplied effect is felt from objects even of different senses; as where a landscape is conjoined with the music of birds and odor of flowers. Such multiplied effect, as above hinted, depends partly on the resemblance of the emotions and partly on the connection of their causes; whence it follows, that the effect must be the greatest, where the causes are intimately connected and the emotions perfectly similar.

The other pleasure arising from coexistent emotions, which may be termed *the pleasure of concord or harmony*, is ascertained by a different rule. It is directly in proportion to the degree of resemblance betwixt the emotions, and inversely in proportion to the degree of connection betwixt the causes. To feel this pleasure in perfection, the resemblance cannot be too strong, nor the connection too slight. Where the causes are intimately connected, the similar emotions they produce are felt like one complex emotion. But the pleasure of harmony, is not felt from one emotion single or complex. It is felt from various similar emotions, distinct from each other, and yet sweetly combining in the mind; and the less connection the causes have, the more entire is the emotion of harmony. This matter cannot be better illustrated, than by the foregoing example of a landscape, where the sight, hearing, and smelling, are employed. The accumulated pleasure of so many different similar emotions, is not what delights us the most in this combination of objects. The sense of harmony from these emotions sweetly uniting in the mind, is still more delightful. We feel this harmony in the different emotions proceeding from the visible objects; but we feel it still more sensibly in the emotions proceeding from the objects of different senses. This emotion of concord or harmony, will be more fully illustrated, when the emotions produced by the sound of words and their meaning are taken under consideration[21].

This emotion of concord from conjoined emotions, is felt even where the emotions are not perfectly similar. Love is a pleasant passion; but then its sweetness and tenderness make it resemble in a considerable degree the painful passion of pity or grief; and for that reason, love accords better with these passions than with what are gay and sprightly. I give the following example from Catullus, where the concord betwixt love and grief, has a fine effect even in so slight a subject as the death of a sparrow.

---

21. Chap. 18, sect. 3.

> *Lugete, ô Veneres, Cupidinesque,*
> *Et quantum est hominum venustiorum!*
> *Passer mortuus est meæ puellæ,*
> *Quem plus illa oculis suis amabat.*
> *Nam mellitus erat, suamque norat*
> *Ipsam tam bene, quam puella matrem:*
> *Nec sese a gremio illius movebat;*
> *Sed circumsiliens modo huc, modo illuc,*
> *Ad solam dominam usque pipilabat.*
> *Qui nunc it per iter tenebricosum,*
> *Illuc, unde negant redire quemquam.*
> *At vobis male sit, malæ tenebræ*
> *Orci, quæ omnia bella devoratis;*
> *Tarn bellum mihi passerem abstulistis.*
> *O factum male, ô miselle passer,*
> *Tua nunc opera, meæ puellæ*
> *Flendo turgiduli rubent ocelli.*

To complete this branch of the subject, I proceed to consider the effects of dissimilar emotions. These effects obviously must be opposite to what are above described; and in order to explain them with accuracy, dissimilar emotions proceeding from connected causes, must be distinguished from what proceed from causes that are unconnected. Dissimilar emotions of the former kind, being forced into a sort of unnatural union, produce a feeling of discord instead of harmony. It holds also that in computing their force, subtraction must be used in place of addition, which will be evident from what follows. Dissimilar emotions forced into union, are felt obscurely and imperfectly; for each tends to vary the tone of mind that is suited to the other; and the mind thus distracted betwixt two objects, is at no instant in a condition to receive a full impression from either. Dissimilar emotions proceeding from unconnected causes, are in a very different condition. Dissimilar emotions in general are averse to union; and as there is nothing to force them into union when their causes are unconnected emotions of this kind are never felt but in succession. By that means, they are not felt to be discordant, and each hath an opportunity to make a full impression.

This curious theory must be illustrated by examples. In reading the description of the dismal waste, book 1. of *Paradise Lost*, we are sensible of a confused feeling, arising from dissimilar emotions forced into union, *viz.* the beauty of the description and the horror of the object described.

> *Seest thou yon dreary plain, forlorn and wild,*
> *The seat of desolation, void of light,*
> *Save what the glimmering of these livid flames*
> *Casts pale and dreadful?*

Many other passages in this justly celebrated poem produce the same effect; and we always observe, that if the disagreeableness of the subject be obscured by the beautiful description, this beauty is not less obscured by its discordant union with the disagreeableness of the subject. For the same reason, ascending smoke in a calm morning is improper in a picture full of violent action. The emotion of stillness and tranquillity inspired by the former, accords not with the lively and animated emotion inspired by the latter. A parterre, partly ornamented partly in disorder, produces a mixt feeling of the same sort. Two great armies in act to engage, mix the dissimilar emotions of grandeur and of terror.

> *Sembra d'alberi densi alta foresta*
> *L' un campo, e l' altro; di tant' aste abbonda.*
> *Son tesi gli archi, e son le lance in resta:*
> *Vibransi i dardi, e rotasi ogni fionda.*
> *Ogni cavallo in guerra anco s' appresta:*
> *Gli odii, e'l furor del suo signor seconda:*
> *Raspa, batte, nitrisce, e si raggira,*
> *Gonfia le nari; e fumo, e fuoco spira.*
>
> *Bello in sì bella vista anco è l'orrore:*
> *E di mezzo la tema esce il diletto.*
> *Ne men le trombe orribili, e canore*
> *Sono a gli orecchi lieto, e fero oggetto.*
> *Pur il campo fedel, benchè minore,*
> *Par di suon più mirabile, e d'aspetto.*
> *E canta in più guerriero, e chiaro carme*
> *Ogni sua tromba, e maggior luce han l'arme.*

—*Gerusalemme liberata, cant. 20. st. 29. & 30*

A virtuous man has drawn on himself a great misfortune, by a fault incident to human nature, and therefore venial. The remorse he feels aggravates his distress, and consequently raises our pity to a high pitch. We indeed blame the man; and the indignation raised by the fault he has committed, is dissimilar to pity. These two passions however proceeding from different views of the same object, are forced into a sort of union. But the indignation is so slight as scarce to be felt in the mixture with pity. Subjects of this kind, are of all the fittest for tragedy. But of this afterward[22].

Opposite emotions are so dissimilar as not to admit any sort of union, even where they proceed from causes the most intimately connected. Love to a mistress, and resentment for her infidelity, are of this nature. They cannot exist otherwise than in succession, which by the connection of their causes is commonly rapid. And these emotions will govern alternately, till one of them obtain the ascendent, or both be obliterated. A succession opens to me by the death of a worthy man, who was my friend as well as my kinsman. When I think of my friend I am grieved; but the succession gives me joy. These two causes are intimately connected, for the succession is the direct consequence of my friend's death. The emotions however being opposite, do not mix: they prevail alternately, perhaps for a course of time, till grief for my friend's death be banished by the pleasures of opulence. A virtuous man suffering unjustly, is an example of the same kind. I pity him, and I have great indignation at the author of the wrong. These emotions proceed from causes nearly connected; but being directed upon different objects, they are not forced into union. The opposition preserves them distinct; and accordingly they are found to govern alternately, the one sometimes prevailing and sometimes the other.

Next of dissimilar emotions arising from unconnected causes. Good and bad news of equal importance arriving at the same instant from different quarters, produce opposite emotions, the discordance of which is not felt because they are not forced into union. They govern alternately, commonly in a quick succession, till their force be spent. In the same manner, good news arriving to a man labouring under distress, occasions a vibration in his mind from the one to the other.

---

22. Chap. 22.

OSMYN: By heav'n thou'st rous'd me from my lethargy.
   The spirit which was deaf to my own wrongs,
   And the loud cries of my dead father's blood,
   Deaf to revenge—nay, which refus'd to hear
   The piercing sighs and murmurs of my love
   Yet unenjoy'd; what not Almeria could
   Revive, or raise, my people's voice has waken'd.
   O my Antonio, I am all on fire,
   My soul is up in arms, ready to charge
   And bear amidst the foe with conqu'ring troops.
   I hear 'em call to lead 'em on to liberty,
   To victory; their shouts and clamours rend
   My ears, and reach the heav'ns: where is the king?
   Where is Alphonso? ha! where! where indeed?
   O I could tear and burst the strings of life,
   To break these chains. Off, off, ye stains of royalty!
   Off, slavery! O curse, that I alone
   Can beat and flutter in my cage, when I
   Would soar and stoop at victory beneath!

—Mourning Bride, act 3. sc. 2

If the emotions be unequal in force, the stronger after a conflict will extinguish the weaker. Thus the loss of a house by fire or of a sum of money by bankruptcy, will make no figure in opposition to the birth of a long-expected son, who is to inherit an opulent fortune. After some slight vibrations, the mind settles in joy, and the loss is forgot.

The foregoing observations, will be found of great use in the fine arts. Many practical rules are derived from them, which I shall have occasion afterward to mention. For instant satisfaction in part, I propose to show the use of these observations in music, a theme I insist upon at present, not being certain of another opportunity more favourable. It will be admitted, that no combination of sounds but what is agreeable to the ear, is intitled to the name of music. Melody and harmony are separately agreeable and in union delightful. The agreeableness of vocal music differs from that of instrumental. The former being intended to accompany words, ought to be expressive of the sentiment that is conveyed by the words. But the latter having no connection with words, may be agreeable without expressing any sentiment. Harmony properly so called, though delightful when in perfection, is not expressive of sentiment; and we often find good melody without the least tincture of it.

These preliminaries being established, I proceed directly to the point. In vocal music, the intimate connection of sense and sound rejects dissimilar emotions, those especially that are opposite. Similar emotions produced by the sense and sound go naturally into union; and at the same time are felt to be concordant or harmonious. Dissimilar emotions, on the other hand, forced into union by causes intimately connected, not only obscure each other, but are also unpleasant by discordance. From these principles it is easy to say what sort of poetical compositions are fitted for music. It is evident that no poem expressing the sentiments of any disagreeable passion is proper. The pain a man feels who is actuated with malice or unjust revenge, disqualifies him for relishing music or anything that is entertaining. And supposing him disposed, against nature, to vent his sentiments in music, the mixture would be unpleasant; for these passions raise disgust and aversion in the audience, a tone of mind opposite to every emotion that music can inspire. A man seized with remorse cannot bear music, because every sort of it must be discordant with his tone of mind; and when these by an unskilful artist are forced into union, the mixture is unpleasant to the audience.

In general, music never can have a good effect in conjunction with any composition expressive of malice, envy, peevishness, or any other dissocial passion. The pleasure of music, on the other hand, is similar to all pleasant emotions; and music is finely qualified for every song where such emotions are expressed. Music particularly in a chearful tone, is concordant in the highest degree with every emotion in the same tone; and hence our taste for chearful airs expressive of mirth and jollity. Music is peculiarly well qualified for accompanying every sympathetic emotion. Sympathetic joy associates finely with chearful music, and sympathetic pain not less finely with music that is tender and melancholy. All the different emotions of love, *viz.* tenderness, concern, anxiety, pain of absence, hope, fear, *&c.* accord delightfully with music. A person in love, even when unkindly treated, is soothed by music. The tenderness of love still prevailing, accords with a melancholy strain. This is finely exemplified by Shakespear in the fourth act of *Othello*, where Desdemona calls for a song expressive of her distress. Wonderful is the delicacy of that writer's taste, which fails him not even in the most refined emotions of human nature. Melancholy music again is suitable to slight grief, which requires or admits consolation. But deep grief, which refuses all consolation, rejects for that reason even melancholy music. For a different reason, music is improper for accompanying pleasant emotions of the more important kind. These totally ingross the mind, and leave no place for music or any sort of amusement. In a perilous enterprise to dethrone a tyrant, music would be impertinent, even where hope prevails, and the prospect of success is great. Alexander attacking the Indian town and mounting the wall, had certainly no impulse to exert his prowess in a song. It is true, that not the least regard is paid to these rules either in the French or Italian opera; and the attachment we have to these compositions, may at first sight be considered as a proof that the foregoing doctrine cannot be founded on human nature. But the general taste for operas is at bottom no authority against me. In our operas the passions are so imperfectly expressed, as to leave the mind free for relishing music of any sort indifferently. It cannot be disguised, that the pleasure of an opera is derived chiefly from the music, and scarce at all from the sentiments. A happy coincidence of emotions raised by the song and by the music, is extremely rare; and I venture to affirm, that there is no example of it unless where the emotion raised by the former is pleasant as well as that raised by the latter.

The subject we have run through, appears not a little entertaining. It is extremely curious to observe, in many instances, a plurality of causes producing in conjunction a great pleasure: in other instances, not less frequent, no conjunction, but each cause acting in opposition. To enter bluntly upon a subject of such intricacy, might gravel an acute philosopher; and yet by taking matters in a train, the intricacy vanisheth.

Next in order, according to the method proposed, come external effects. And this leads to passions in particular, which involving desire are the causes of action. Two coexistent passions that have the same tendency, must be similar. They accordingly readily unite, and in conjunction have double force; which must hold whether the two passions have the same or different causes. This is verified by experience; from which we learn, that different passions having the same end in view, impel the mind to action with united force. The mind receives not impulses alternately from these passions, but one strong impulse from the whole in conjunction. And indeed it is not easy to conceive what should bar the union of passions that have all of them the same tendency.

Two passions having opposite tendencies, may proceed from the same object or cause considered in different lights. Thus a mistress may at once be the object both of love and resentment. Her beauty inflames the passion of love: her cruelty or inconstancy causes resentment. When two such passions coexist in the same breast, the opposition of their aim prevents any sort of union. They are not felt otherwise than in succession. And the consequence must be one of two things: the passions will balance each other, and prevent external action; or one of them will prevail, and accomplish its end. Guarini, in his *Pastor Fido*, describes beautifully the struggle betwixt love and resentment directed upon the same object.

> CORISCA: Chi vide mai, chi mai udi più strana
> E più folle, e più sera, e più importuna
> Passione amorosa? amore, ed odio
> Con sì mirabil tempre in un cor misti,
> Che l'un per l'altro (e non so ben dir come)
> E si strugge, e s'avanza, e nasce, e more.
> S' i' miro alle bellezze di Mirtillo
> Dal piè leggiadro al grazioso volto,
> Il vago portamento, il bel sembiante.
> Gli atti, i costumi, e le parole, e 'l guardo;
> M'assale Amore con sì possente foco
> Ch'i' ardo tutta, e par, ch' ogn' altro affetto
> Da questo sol sia superato, e vinto:
> Ma se poi penso all' ostinato amore,
> Ch' ei porta ad altra donna, e che per lei
> Di me non cura, e sprezza (il vo' pur dire)
> La mia famosa, e da mill' alme, e mille
> Inchinata beltà, bramata grazia;
> L'odio così, così l'aborro, e schivo,
> Che impossibil mi par, ch'unqua per lui
> Mi s'accendesse al cor siamma amorosa.
> Tallor meco ragiono: o s'io petessi
> Gioir del mio dolcissimo Mirtillo,
> Sicche fosse mio tutto, e ch'altra mai
> Posseder no 'l potesse, o più d' ogn' altra
> Beata, e felicissima Corisca!

> Ed in quel punto in me sorge un talento
> Verso di lui sì dolce, e sì gentile,
> Che di seguirlo, e di pregarlo ancora,
> E di scoprirgli il cor prendo consiglio.
> Che più? così mi stimola il desio,
> Che se potessi allor l'adorerei.
> Dall' altra parte i' mi risento, e dico,
> Un ritroso? uno schifo? un che non degna?
> Un, che può d'altra donna esser amante?
> Un, ch'ardisce mirarmi, e non m'adora?
> E dal mio volto si difende in guisa,
> Che per amor non more? ed io, che lui
> Dovrei veder, come molti altri i' veggio
> Supplice, e lagrimosa a' piedi miei,
> Supplice, e lagrimoso a' piedi suoi
> Sosterro di cadere? ah non fia mai.
> Ed in questo pensier tant' ira accoglio
> Contra di lui, contra di me, che volsi
> A seguirlo il pensier, gli occhi a mirarlo,
> Che 'l nome di Mirtillo, e l'amor mio
> Odio più che la morte; e lui vorrei
> Veder il più dolente, il più infelice
> Pastor, che viva; e se potessi allora,
> Con le mie proprie man l'anciderei.
> Così sdegno, desire, odio, ed amore
> Mi fanno guerra, ed io, che stata sono
> Sempre sin qui di mille cor la fiamma,
> Di mill' alme il tormento, ardo, e languisco:
> E provo nel mio mal le pene altrui.

—Act 1. sc. 3

Ovid paints in lively colours the vibration of mind betwixt two opposite passions directed upon the same object. Althea had two brothers much beloved, who were unjustly put to death by her son Meleager in a fit of passion. She was strongly impelled to revenge; but the criminal was her own son. This ought to have with-held her hand. But the story makes a better figure and is more interesting, by the violence of the struggle betwixt resentment and maternal love.

Dona Deum templis nato victore ferebat;
Cum videt extinctos fratres Althæa referri.
Quæ plangore dato, mæstis ululatibus urbem
Implet; et auratis mutavit vestibus atras.
At simul est auctor necis editus; excidit omnis
Luctus: et a lacrymis in pœnæ versus amorem est.
Stipes erat, quem, cum partus enixa jaceret
Thestias, in flammam triplices posuêre sorores;
Staminaque impresso fatalia pollice nentes,
Tempora, dixerunt, eadem lignoque, tibique,
O modo nate, damus. Quo postquam carmine dicto
Excessere deæ; flagrantem mater ab igne
Erripuit torrem: sparsitque liquentibus undis.
Ille diu fuerat penetralibus abditus imis;
Servatusque, tuos, juvenis, servaverat annos.
Protulit hunc genitrix, tædasque in fragmina poni
Imperat; et positis inimicos admovet ignes.
Tum conata quater flammis imponere ramum
Cœpta quater tenuit. Pugnat materque, sororque,
Et diversa trahunt unum duo nomina pectus.
Sæpe metu sceleris pallebant ora futuri:
Sæpe suum fervens oculis dabat ira ruborem,
Et modo nescio quid similis crudele minanti
Vultus erat; modo quem misereri credere posses:
Cumque ferus lacrymas animi siccaverat ardor;
Inveniebantur lacrymæ tamen. Utque carina,
Quam ventus, ventoque contrarius æstus,
Vim geminam sentit, paretque incerta duobus:
Thestias haud aliter dubiis affectibus errat,
Inque vices ponit, positamque resuscitat iram.
Incipit esse tamem melior germana parente;
Et, consanguineas ut sanguine leniat umbras,
Impietate pia est. Nam postqnam pestifer ignis
Convaluit: Rogus iste cremet mea viscera, dixit.
Utque manu dirâ lignum fatale tenebat;
Ante sepulchrales infelix adstitit aras.
Pœnarumque deæ triplices furialibus, inquit,
Eumenides, sacris vultus advertite vestros.
Ulciscor, facioque nefas. Mors morte pianda est;

> *In scelus addendum scelus est, in funera funus:*
> *Per coacervatos pereat domus impia luctus.*
> *An felix Oeneus nato victore fruetur;*
> *Thestius orbus erit? melius lugebitis ambo.*
> *Vos modo, fraterni manes, animæque recentes,*
> *Officium sentite meum; magnoque paratas*
> *Accipite inferias, uteri mala pignora nostri.*
> *Hei mihi! quo rapior? fratres ignoscite matri.*
> *Deficiunt ad cœpta manus. Meruisse fatemur*
> *Illum, cur pereat: mortis mihi displicet auctor.*
> *Ergo impune feret; vivusque, et victor, et ipso*
> *Successu tumidus regnum Calydonis habebit?*
> *Vos cinis exiguus, gelidæque jacebitis umbræ?*
> *Haud equidem patiar. Pereat sceleratus; et ille*
> *Spemque patris, regnique trahat, patriæque ruinam.*
> *Mens ubi materna est; ubi sunt pia jura parentum?*
> *Et, quos sustinui, bis mensûm quinque labores?*
> *O utinam primis arsisses ignibus infans;*
> *Idque ego passa forem! vixisti munere nostro:*
> *Nunc merito moriere tuo. Cape præmia facti;*
> *Bisque datam, primum partu, mox stipite rapto,*
> *Redde animam; vel me fraternis adde sepulchris.*
> *Et cupio, et nequeo. Quid agam? modo vulnera fratrum*
> *Ante oculos mihi sunt, et tantæ cædis imago;*
> *Nunc animum pietas, maternaque nomina frangunt.*
> *Me miseram! male vincetis, sed vincite, fratres:*
> *Dummodo, quæ dedero vobis solatia, vosque*
> *Ipsa sequar, dixit: dextraque aversa trementi*
> *Funereum torrem medios conjecit in ignes.*
> *Aut dedit, aut visus gemitus est ille dedisse,*
> *Stipes; et invitis correptus ab ignibus arsit.*
>
> —*Metamorph. lib. 8. l. 445*

In cases of this kind, one circumstance always augments the fluctuation. A resolution to prefer one action before another after balancing betwixt them, is an inchoated gratification of the prevailing passion, which softens it in some degree. This circumstance tends to give a superiority to the opposite passion. And another circumstance also concurs, that this opposite passion has by restraint acquired in the interim some additional force.

Love and jealousy connected by a common object, occupy the mind alternately. When the object is considered as beautiful, love prevails: when considered as possibly unfaithful, jealousy prevails. A situation of this kind, affords great scope for fluctuation of passion, which is painted to the life by several masterly hands in words as well as in colours. Shakespear handles the same subject, but in a manner uncommon and peculiar to himself. In Othello's soliloquy before putting his wife to death, love and jealousy are represented, each exerting its whole force, but without any struggle. Othello was naturally inflexible; and the tenderest love could not divert him from a purpose he approved as right, not even for a moment. But everything consistent with such a character is done to reconcile the two opposite passions. He is resolved to put her to death, but he will not shed her blood, nor so much as ruffle her skin.

> OTHELLO: It is the cause, it is the cause, my soul;—
>   Let me not name it to you, you chaste stars!
>   It is the cause.—Yet I'll not shed her blood,
>   Nor scar that whiter skin of hers than snow,
>   And smooth as monumental alabaster.
>   (*Lays down the sword*)
>   Yet she must die; else she'll betray more men.
>   Put out the light, and then—Put out the light?—
>   If I quench thee, thou flaming minister,
>   I can again thy former light restore,
>   Should I repent: but once put out *thy* light,
>   Thou cunning'st pattern of excelling nature,
>   I know not where is that Promethean heat
>   That can thy light relumine.—(*Sets down the taper*)
>   When I have pluck'd thy rose,
>   I cannot give it vital growth again;
>   It needs must wither.—I'll smell thee on the tree;
>   (*Kissing her*)
>   Oh balmy breath, that dost almost persuade
>   Justice to break her sword!—One more; one more;
>   Be thus when thou art dead, and I will kill thee,
>   And love thee after.—One more, that's the last;
>   So sweet was ne'er so fatal! I must weep,

> But they are cruel tears? this sorrow's heav'nly;
> It strikes where it doth love.—She wakes—
>
> *—Act 5. sc. 6*

In Otway's *Orphan*, we have an illustrious example of the address employed to gratify opposite passions directed upon the same object. Castalio and Polydore, brothers and rivals, had sworn mutual confidence. Castalio broke his faith by a private marriage. By this concealment, Polydore was unwarily betrayed into a dismal deed, that of polluting his brother's bed. Thus he had injured his brother, and was injured by him. Justice prompted him to make full atonement by his own death: resentment against his brother required a full atonement to be made to himself. In coexistent passions so contradictory, one of them commonly prevails after a struggle. But here happily an expedient occurred to gratify both; which was, that Polydore should provoke his brother to put him to death. Polydore's crime in his own opinion merited this punishment; and justice was satisfied when he fell by the hands of the man he had injured. He wanted at the same time to punish his brother for breach of faith; and he could not do this more effectually than by betraying his brother to be his executioner.

If difference of aim prevent the union of two passions though having the same object, much more will it prevent their union when their objects are also different. In both cases there is a fluctuation; but in the latter the fluctuation is slower than in the former. A beautiful situation of this kind is exhibited in the *Cid* of Corneille. Don Diegue, an old soldier worn out with age, having received a mortal affront from the Count father to Chimene, employs his son Don Rodrigue, Chimene's lover, to demand satisfaction. This situation occasions in the breast of Don Rodrigue a cruel struggle. It is a contest betwixt love and honour, one of which must be sacrificed. The scene is finely conducted, chiefly by making love in some degree take part with honour, Don Rodrigue reflecting, that if he lost his honour he could not deserve his mistress. Honour triumphs. The Count, provoked to a single combat, falls by the hand of Don Rodrigue.

This produceth another beautiful situation respecting Chimene, which for the sake of connection is placed here, though it properly belongs to the foregoing head. It became the duty of that lady to demand justice against her lover, for whose preservation, in other circumstances, she chearfully would have sacrificed her own life. The struggle betwixt these opposite passions directed upon the same object, is finely expressed in the third scene of the third act.

> ELVIRE: Il vous prive d'un pére, et vous l'aimez encore!
> CHIMENE: C'est peu de dire aimer, Elvire, je l'adore;
> Ma passion s'oppose à mon ressentiment,
> Dedans mon ennemi je trouve mon amant,
> Et je sens qu'en depit de toute ma colére,
> Rodrigue dans mon cœur combat encore mon pére.
> Il l'attaque, il le presse, il céde, il se défend,
> Tantôt fort, tantôt foible, et tantôt triomphant;
> Mais en ce dur combat de colére et de flame,
> Il déchire mon cœur sans partager mon ame,
> Et quoique mon amour ait sur moi de pouvoir,
> Je ne consulte point pour suivre mon devoir.
> Je cours sans balancer où mon honneur m'oblige;
> Rodrigue m'est bien cher, son interêt m'afflige,
> Mon cœur prend son parti; mais malgré son effort,
> Je sai ce que je suis, et que mon pére est mort.

Not less when the objects are different than when the same, are means sometimes afforded to gratify both passions; and such means are greedily embraced. In Tasso's *Gerusalem*, Edward and Gildippe, husband and wife, are introduced fighting gallantly against the Saracens. Gildippe receives a mortal wound by the hand of Soliman. Edward inflamed with revenge as well as concern for Gildippe, is agitated betwixt the two different objects. The poet[23] describes him endeavouring to gratify both at once, applying his right hand against Soliman the object of his resentment, and his left hand to support his wife the object of his love.

PART V

The power of passion to adjust our opinions and belief to its gratification.

There is such a connection among the perceptions passions and actions of the same person, that it would be wonderful if they should have no

---

23. Cante 20. st. 97.

mutual influence. That our actions are too much directed by passion, is a sad truth. It is not less certain, though not so commonly observed, that passion hath an irregular influence upon our opinions and belief. The opinions we form of men and things, are generally directed by affection. An advice given by a man of figure, hath great weight; the same advice from one in a low condition, is utterly neglected. A man of courage under-rates danger; and to the indolent, the slightest obstacle appears unsurmountable. Our opinions indeed, the result commonly of various and often opposite views, are so slight and wavering, as readily to be susceptible of a bias from passion and prejudice.

This subject is of great use in logic; and of still greater use in criticism, being intimately connected with many principles of the fine arts that will be unfolded in the course of this work. Being too extensive to be treated here at large, some cursory illustrations must suffice; leaving the subject to be prosecuted more particularly afterward when occasion shall offer.

Two principles that make an eminent figure in human nature, concur to give passion an undue influence upon our opinions and belief. The first and most extensive, is a strong tendency in the mind to fit objects for the gratification of its passions. We are prone to such opinions of men and things as correspond to our wishes. Where the object, in dignity or importance, corresponds to the passion bestowed on it, the gratification is complete and there is no occasion for artifice. But where the object is too mean for the passion so as not to afford a complete gratification, it is wonderful how apt the mind is to impose upon itself, and how disposed to proportion the object to its passion. The other principle is a strong tendency in our nature to justify our passions as well as our actions, not to others only, but even to ourselves. This tendency is extremely remarkable with respect to disagreeable passions. By its influence, objects are magnified or lessened, circumstances supplied or suppressed, everything coloured and disguised, to answer the end of justification. Hence the foundation of self-deceit, where a man imposes upon himself innocently, and even without suspicion of a bias.

Beside the influence of the foregoing principles to make us form opinions contrary to truth, the passions themselves, by subordinate means, contribute to the same effect. Of these means I shall mention two which seem to be capital. First, There was occasion formerly to observe[24], that though ideas seldom start up in the mind without

---

24. Chap. I.

connection, yet that ideas which correspond to the present tone of the mind are readily suggested by any slight connection. By this means, the arguments for a favourite opinion are always at hand, while we often search in vain for those that cross our inclination. Second, The mind taking delight in agreeable circumstances or arguments, is strongly impressed with them; while those that are disagreeable are hurried over so as scarce to make any impression. The self-same argument, accordingly as it is relished or not relished, weighs so differently, as in truth to make conviction depend more on passion than on reasoning. This observation is fully justified by experience. To confine myself to a single instance, the numberless absurd religious tenets that at different times have pestered the world, would be altogether unaccountable but for this irregular bias of passion.

We proceed to a more pleasant task, which is, to illustrate the foregoing observations by proper examples. Gratitude when warm, is often exerted upon the children of the benefactor; especially where he is removed out of reach by death or absence[25]. Gratitude in this case being exerted for the sake of the benefactor, requires no peculiar excellence in his children. To find however these children worthy of the benefits intended them, contributes undoubtedly to the more entire gratification of the passion. And accordingly, the mind, prone to gratify its passions, is apt to conceive a better opinion of these children than possibly they deserve. By this means, strong connections of affection are often formed among individuals, upon the slight foundation now mentioned.

Envy is a passion, which, being altogether unjustifiable, is always disguised under some more plausible name. But no passion is more eager than envy, to give its object such an appearance as to answer a complete gratification. It magnifies every bad quality, and fixes on the most humbling circumstances.

> Cassius: I cannot tell what you and other men
> Think of this life; but for my single self,
> I had as lief not be, as live to be
> In awe of such a thing as I myself.
> I was born free as Cæsar, so were you;
> We both have fed as well; and we can both

---

25. See part 1. sect. 1. of the present chapter.

> Endure the winter's cold as well as he.
> For once, upon a raw and gusty day,
> The troubled Tyber chasing with his shores,
> Cæsar says to me, Dar'st thou, Cassius, now
> Leap in with me into this angry flood,
> And swim to yonder point?—Upon the word,
> Accoutred as I was, I plunged in,
> And bid him follow; so indeed he did.
> The torrent roar'd, and we did buffet it
> With lusty sinews; throwing it aside,
> And stemming it with hearts of controversy.
> But ere we could arrive the point propos'd,
> Cæsar cry'd, Help me, Cassius, or I sink.
> I, as Æneas, our great ancestor,
> Did from the flames of Troy upon his shoulder
> The old Anchises bear; so from the waves of Tyber
> Did I the tired Cæsar: and this man
> Is now become a god, and Cassius is
> A wretched creature; and must bend his body,
> If Cæsar carelessly but nod on him.
> He had a fever when he was in Spain,
> And when the fit was on him, I did mark
> How he did shake. 'Tis true, this god did shake;
> His coward lips did from their colour fly,
> And that same eye whose bend doth awe the world,
> Did lose its lustre; I did hear him grone:
> Ay, and that tongue of his, that bade the Romans
> Mark him, and write his speeches in their books,
> Alas! it cry'd—Give me some drink, Titinius—
> As a sick girl. Ye gods, it doth amaze me,
> A man of such a feeble temper should
> So get the start of the majestic world,
> And bear the palm alone.
>
> —*Julius Cæsar, act I. sc. 3*

Glo'ster inflamed with resentment against his son Edgar, could even work himself into a momentary conviction that they were not related.

> *O strange fasten'd villain!*
> *Would he deny his letter?—I never got him.*
>
> *—King Lear, act 2. sc. 3*

When by a great sensibility of heart or other means, grief swells beyond what the cause can justify, the mind is prone to magnify the cause, in order to gratify the passion. And if the real cause admit not of being magnified, the mind seeks a cause for its grief in imagined future events.

> BUSHY: Madam, your Majesty is much too sad;
>   You promis'd, when you parted with the King,
>   To lay aside self-harming heaviness,
>   And entertain a chearful disposition.
> QUEEN: To please the King, I did; to please myself,
>   I cannot do it. Yet I know no cause
>   Why I should welcome such a guest as grief;
>   Save bidding farewell to so sweet a guest
>   As my sweet Richard: yet again, methinks,
>   Some unborn sorrow, ripe in Fortune's womb,
>   Is coming tow'rd me; and my inward soul
>   With something trembles, yet at nothing grieves,
>   More than with parting from my Lord the King.
>
> *—Richard II. act. 2. sc. 5*

The foregoing examples depend on the first principle. In the following, both principles concur. Resentment at first is wreaked on the relations of the offender, in order to punish him. But as resentment when so outrageous is contrary to conscience, the mind, to justify its passion as well as to gratify it, is disposed to paint these relations in the blackest colours; and it actually comes to be convinced, that they ought to be punished for their own demerits.

Anger raised by an accidental stroke upon a tender part, which gives great and sudden pain, is sometimes vented upon the undesigning cause. But as the passion in this case is absurd, and as there can be no solid gratification in punishing the innocent; the mind, prone to justify as well as to gratify its passion, deludes itself instantly into a conviction of the action's being voluntary. This conviction however is but momentary: the first reflection shows it to be erroneous; and the passion vanisheth almost instantaneously with the conviction. But anger, the most violent of all passions, has still greater influence. It sometimes forces the mind to personify a stock or a stone when it occasions bodily pain, in order to be a proper object of resentment. A conception is formed of it as a voluntary agent. And that we have really a momentary conviction of its being a voluntary agent, must be evident from considering, that without such conviction, the passion can neither be justified nor gratified. The imagination can give no aid. A stock or a stone may be imagined sensible; but a notion of this kind cannot be the foundation of punishment, so long as the mind is conscious that it is an imagination merely without any reality. Of such personification, involving a conviction of reality, there is one illustrious instance. When the first bridge of boats over the Hellespont was destroyed by a storm, Xerxes fell into a transport of rage, so excessive, that he commanded the sea to be punished with 300 stripes; and a pair of fetters to be thrown into it, enjoining the following words to be pronounced. "O thou salt and bitter water! thy master hath condemned thee to this punishment for offending him without cause; and is resolved to pass over thee in despite of thy insolence. With reason all men neglect to sacrifice to thee, because thou art both disagreeable and treacherous[26]."

Shakespear exhibits beautiful examples of the irregular influence of passion in making us conceive things to be otherwise than they are. King Lear, in his distress, personifies the rain, wind, and thunder; and in order to justify his resentment, conceives them to be taking part with his daughters.

> Lear: Rumble thy belly-full, spit fire, spout rain!
> Nor rain, wind, thunder, fire, are my daughters.
> I tax not you, you elements, with unkindness;
> I never gave you kingdom, call'd you children;
> You owe me no subscription. Then let fall
> Your horrible pleasure.—Here I stand, your brave;
> A poor, infirm, weak, and despis'd old man!
> But yet I call you servile ministers,
> That have with two pernicious daughters join'd

---

26. Herodotus, book 7.

> Your high engender'd battles, 'gainst a head
> So old and white as this. Oh! oh! 'tis foul.
>
> —*Act* 3. *sc.* 2

King Richard, full of indignation against his favourite horse for suffering Bolingbroke to ride him, conceives for a moment the horse to be rational.

> GROOM: O, how it yearn'd my heart, when I beheld,
> In London streets, that coronation-day;
> When Bolingbroke rode on Roan Barbary,
> That horse that thou so often hast bestrid,
> That horse that I so carefully have dress'd.
> K. RICH: Rode he on Barbary? tell me, gentle friend,
> How went he under him?
> GROOM: So proudly as he had disdain'd the ground.
> K. RICH: So proud that Bolingbroke was on his back!
> That jade had eat bread from my royal hand.
> This hand hath made him proud with clapping him.
> Would he not stumble? would he not fall down,
> (Since pride must have a fall), and break the neck
> Of that proud man that did usurp his back?
>
> —*Richard* II. *act* 5. *sc.* 11

Hamlet, swelled with indignation at his mother's second marriage, is strongly inclined to lessen the time of her widowhood; because this circumstance gratified his passion; and he deludes himself by degrees into the opinion of an interval shorter than the real one.

> HAMLET:—— That it should come to this!
> But two months dead! nay, not so much; not two;—
> So excellent a King, that was, to this,
> Hyperion to a satire: so loving to my mother,
> That he permitted not the wind of heav'n
> Visit her face too roughly. Heav'n and earth!
> Must I remember—why, she would hang on him,
> As if increase of appetite had grown
> By what it fed on; yet, within a month,—

> Let me not think—Frailty, thy name is *Woman*!
> A little month! or ere those shoes were old,
> With which she follow'd my poor father's body,
> Like Niobe, all tears—Why, she, ev'n she—
> (O heav'n! a beast that wants discourse of reason,
> Would have mourn'd longer—) married with mine uncle,
> My father's brother; but no more like my father,
> Than I to Hercules. Within a month!—
> Ere yet the salt of most unrighteous tears
> Had left the flushing in her gauled eyes,
> She married.—Oh, most wicked speed, to post
> With such dexterity to incestuous sheets!
> It is not, nor it cannot come to good.
> But break, my heart, for I must hold my tongue.
>
> *—Act 1. sc. 3*

The power of passion to falsify the computation of time, is the more remarkable, that time, which hath an accurate measure, is less obsequious to our desires and wishes, than objects which have no precise standard of less or more.

Even belief, though partly an act of the judgment, may be influenced by passion. Good news are greedily swallowed upon very slender evidence. Our wishes magnify the probability of the event as well as the veracity of the relater; and we believe as certain what at best is doubtful.

> *Quel, che l'huom vede, amor li fa invisibile*
> *E l'invisibil fa veder amore.*
> *Questo creduto fu, che'l miser suole*
> *Dar facile credenza a' quel, che vuole.*
>
> *—Orland. Furios. cant. 1. st. 56*

For the same reason, bad news gain also credit upon the slightest evidence. Fear, if once alarmed, has the same effect with hope to magnify every circumstance that tends to conviction. Shakespear, who shows more knowledge of human nature than any of our philosophers, hath in his *Cymbeline*[27] represented this bias of the mind: for he makes the

---

27. Act 2. sc. 6.

person who alone was affected with the bad news, yield to evidence that did not convince any of his companions. And Othello[28] is convinced of his wife's infidelity from circumstances too slight to move an indifferent person.

If the news interest us in so low a degree as to give place to reason, the effect will not be quite the same. Judging of the probability or improbability of the story, the mind settles in a rational conviction either that it is true or not. But even in this case, it is observable, that the mind is not allowed to rest in that degree of conviction which is produced by rational evidence. If the news be in any degree favourable, our belief is augmented by hope beyond its true pitch; and if unfavourable, by fear.

The observation holds equally with respect to future events. If a future event be either much wished or dreaded, the mind, to gratify its passion, never fails to augment the probability beyond truth.

The credit which in all ages has been given to wonders and prodigies, even the most absurd and ridiculous, is a strange phenomenon. Nothing can be more evident than the following proposition, That the more singular any event is, the more evidence is required. A familiar event daily occurring, being in itself extremely probable, finds ready credit, and therefore is vouched by the slightest evidence. But a strange and rare event, contrary to the course of nature, ought not to be easily believed. It starts up without connection, and without cause, so far as we can discover; and to overcome the improbability of such an event, the very strongest evidence is required. It is certain, however, that wonders and prodigies are swallowed by the vulgar, upon evidence that would not be sufficient to ascertain the most familiar occurrence. It has been reckoned difficult to explain this irregular bias of the mind. We are now no longer at a loss about its cause. The proneness we have to gratify our passions, which displays itself upon so many occasions, produces this irrational belief. A story of ghosts or fairies, told with an air of gravity and truth, raiseth an emotion of wonder, and perhaps of dread. These emotions tending strongly to their own gratification, impose upon a weak mind, and impress upon it a thorough conviction contrary to all sense and reason.

Opinion and belief are influenced by propensity as well as by passion; for the mind is disposed to gratify both. A natural propensity is all we have to convince us, that the operations of nature are uniform.

---

28. Act 3. sc. 8.

Influenced by this propensity, we often rashly conceive, that good or bad weather will never have an end; and in natural philosophy, writers, influenced by the same propensity, stretch commonly their analogical reasonings beyond just bounds.

Opinion and belief are influenced by affection as well as by propensity. The noted story of a fine lady and a curate viewing the moon through a telescope is a pleasant illustration. I perceive, says the lady, two shadows inclining to each other, they are certainly two happy lovers. Not at all, replies the curate, they are two steeples of a cathedral.

Appendix to Part V

Concerning the methods which nature hath afforded for computing time and space.

I introduce here the subject proposed, because it affords several curious examples of the power of passion to adjust objects to its gratification; a lesson that cannot be too much inculcated, as there is not perhaps another bias in human nature that hath an influence so universal, and that is so apt to make us wander from truth as well as from justice.

I begin with time; and the question shortly is, What was the measure of time before artificial measures were invented? and, What is the measure at present when these are not at hand? I speak not of months and days, which we compute by the moon and sun; but of hours, or in general of the time that runs betwixt any two occurrences when there is not access to the sun. The only natural measure we have, is the train of our thoughts; and we always judge the time to be long or short, in proportion to the number of perceptions that have passed through the mind during that interval. This is indeed a very imperfect measure; because in the different conditions of a quick or slow succession, the computation is different. But however imperfect, it is the only measure by which a person naturally calculates time; and this measure is applied on all occasions, without regard to any occasional variation in the rate of succession.

This natural measure of time, imperfect as it is, would however be tolerable, did it labour under no other imperfection than the ordinary variations that happen in the motion of our perceptions. But in many particular circumstances, it is much more fallacious; and in order to explain these distinctly, I must analize the subject. Time is generally computed at two different periods; one while time is passing, another after it is past. I shall consider these separately, with the errors to which each of them is liable. It will be found that these errors often produce very different computations of the same period of time. The computation of time while it is passing, comes first in order. It is a common and trite observation, That to lovers absence appears immeasurably long, every minute an hour, and every hour a day. The same computation is made in every case where we long for a distant event; as where one is in expectation of good news, or where a profligate heir watches for the death of an old man who keeps him from a great estate. Opposite to these are instances not fewer in number. To a criminal the interval betwixt sentence and execution appears miserably short; and the same holds in every case where one dreads an approaching event. Of this even a schoolboy can bear witness: the hour allowed him for play, moves, in his apprehension, with a very swift pace: before he is thoroughly engaged, the hour is gone. A reckoning founded on the number of ideas, will never produce computations so regularly opposite to each other; for a slow succession of ideas is not connected with our wishes, nor a quick succession with our fears. What is it then, that, in the cases mentioned, moves nature to desert her common measure for one very different? I know not that this question ever has been resolved. The false reckonings I have suggested are so common and familiar, that no writer has thought of inquiring for their cause. And indeed, to enter upon this matter at short hand, without preparation, might occasion some difficulty. But to encounter the difficulty, we luckily are prepared by what is said above about the power of passion to fit objects for its gratification. Among the other circumstances that terrify a condemned criminal, the short time he has to live is one. Terror, like our other passions, prone to its gratification, adjusts everyone of these circumstances to its own tone. It magnifies in particular the shortness of the interval betwixt the present time and that of the execution; and forces upon the criminal a conviction that the hour of his death approaches with a swift pace. In the same manner, among the other distresses of an absent lover, the time of separation is a capital circumstance, which for that reason is greatly magnified by his anxiety and impatience. He imagines that the time of meeting comes on very slow, or rather that it will never come. Every minute is thought of an intolerable length. Here is a fair and I hope satisfactory account, why we reckon time to be tedious when we long for a future event, and not less fleet when we dread the event. This account is confirmed by other instances. Bodily pain fixt to one part, produceth a slow train of perceptions, which, according to the common measure of time, ought to make it appear short. Yet we know, that in such a state time has the opposite appearance. Bodily pain is always attended with a degree of impatience and an anxiety to be rid of it, which make us judge every minute to be an hour. The same holds where the pain shifts from place to place; but not so remarkably, because such a pain is not attended with the same degree of impatience. The impatience a man hath in travelling through a barren country or in bad roads, makes him imagine, during the journey, that time goes on with a very slow pace. We shall show afterward that he makes a very different computation when his journey is at an end.

How ought it to stand with a man who apprehends bad news? It will probably be thought, that the case of this man resembles that of a criminal, who, in reckoning the short time he has to live, imagines every hour to be but a minute, and that time flies swift away. Yet the computation here is directly opposite. Reflecting upon this difficulty, there appears one capital circumstance in which the two cases differ. The fate of the criminal is determined: in the case under consideration, the man is still in suspense. Everyone knows how distressful suspense is to the bulk of mankind. Such distress we wish to get rid of at any rate, even at the expence of bad news. This case therefore, upon a more narrow inspection, resembles that of bodily pain. The present distress in both cases, makes the time appear extremely tedious.

The reader probably will not be displeased, to have this branch of the subject illustrated in a pleasant manner, by an author acquainted with every maze of the human heart, and who bestows ineffable grace and ornament upon every subject he handles.

> ROSALINDA: I pray you, what is't a clock?
>
> ORLANDO: You should ask me, what time o' day; there's no clock in the forest.
>
> Ros.: Then there is no true lover in the forest; else, sighing every minute, and groaning every hour, would detect the lazy foot of Time, as well as a clock.
>
> ORLA.: Why not the swift foot of Time? Had not that been as proper?
>
> Ros.: By no means, Sir. Time travels in diverse paces with diverse persons. I'll tell you who Time ambles withal, who Time

trots withal, who Time gallops withal, and who he stands still withal.

ORLA.: I pr'y thee whom doth he trot withal?

ROS.: Marry, he trots hard with a young maid, between the contract of her marriage, and the day it is solemnized: if the interim be but a se'ennight, Time's pace is so hard that it seems the length of seven years.

ORLA.: Who ambles Time withal?

ROS.: With a priest that lacks Latin, and a rich man that hath not the gout: for the one sleeps easily, because he cannot study; and the other lives merrily, because he feels no pain: the one lacking the burden of lean and wasteful learning; the other knowing no burthen of heavy tedious penury. These Time ambles withal.

ORLA.: Whom doth he gallop withal?

ROS.: With a thief to the gallows: for though he go as softly as foot can fall, he thinks himself too soon there.

ORLA.: Whom stays it still withall?

ROS.: With lawyers in the vacation; for they sleep between term and term, and then they perceive not how Time moves.

—*As you like it*, act 3. sc. 8

Reflecting upon the natural method of computing present time, it shows how far from truth we may be led by the irregular power of passion. Nor are our eyes immediately opened when the scene is past: the deception continues while there remain any traces of the passion. But looking back upon past time when the joy or distress is no longer remembered, the computation we make is very different. In this situation, passion being out of the question, we apply the ordinary measure, *viz.* the course of our perceptions; and I shall now proceed to the errors that this measure is subjected to. In order to have an accurate notion of this matter, we must distinguish betwixt a train of perceptions, and a train of ideas. Real objects make a strong impression, and are faithfully remembered. Ideas, on the contrary, however entertaining at the time, are apt to escape an after recollection. Hence it is, that in retrospection, the time that was employed upon real objects, appears longer than the time that was employed upon ideas. The former are more accurately recollected than the latter; and we measure the time by the number that is recollected. I proceed to particulars. After finishing a journey through a populous country, the frequency of agreeable objects distinctly recollected by the traveller, makes the time spent in the journey appear to him longer than it was in reality. This is chiefly remarkable in a first journey, where every object is new and makes a strong impression. On the other hand, after finishing a journey through a barren country thinly peopled, the time appears short, being measured by the number of objects, which were few and far from interesting. Here in both instances a reckoning is brought out, directly opposite to that made during the journey. And this, by the way, serves to account for a thing which may appear singular, that in a barren country the computed miles are always longer, than near the capital, where the country is rich and populous. The traveller has no natural measure of the space gone through, other than the time bestowed upon it; nor any natural measure of the time, other than the number of his perceptions. These being proportioned to the number of visible objects, he imagines that he hath consumed more time on his day's journey, and accomplished a greater number of miles, in a populous than in a waste country. By this method of calculation, every computed mile in the former must in reality be shorter than in the latter.

Again, the travelling with an agreeable companion produceth a short computation both of the road and of time; especially if there be few objects that demand attention, or if the objects be familiar. The case is the same of young people at a ball, or of a joyous company over a bottle. The ideas with which they have been entertained, being transitory, escape the memory. After all is over, they reflect that they have been much diverted, but scarce can say about what.

When one is totally occupied in any agreeable work that admits not many objects, time runs on without observation; and upon an after recollection must appear short, in proportion to the paucity of objects. This is still more remarkable in close contemplation and in deep thinking, where the train, composed wholly of ideas, proceeds with an extreme slow pace. Not only are the ideas few in number, but are apt to escape an after-reckoning. The like false reckoning of time may proceed from an opposite state of mind. In a reverie, where ideas float at random without making any impression, time goes on unheeded and the reckoning is lost. A reverie may be so profound as to prevent the recollection of anyone idea: that the mind was busied in a train of thinking, will in general be remembered; but what was the subject, has quite escaped the memory. In such a case, we are altogether at a loss about the time: we have no *data* for making a computation. No cause produceth so false a reckoning of time, as immoderate grief. The mind, in this state, is violently attached to a single object, and admits not a different thought. Any other object breaking in, is instantly banished, so as scarce to give an appearance of succession. In a reverie, we are uncertain of the time that is past: but in the example now given, there is an appearance of certainty, so far as the natural measure of time can be trusted, that the time must have been short, when the perceptions are so few in number.

The natural measure of space appears more obscure than that of time. I venture however to enter upon it, leaving it to be further prosecuted, if it be thought of any importance.

The space marked out for a house, appears considerably larger after it is divided into its proper parts. A piece of ground appears larger after it is surrounded with a fence; and still larger when it is made a garden and divided into different copartments.

On the contrary, a large plain looks less after it is divided into parts. The sea must be excepted, which looks less from that very circumstance of not being divided into parts.

A room of a moderate size appears larger when properly furnished. But when a very large room is furnished, I doubt whether it be not lessened in appearance.

A room of a moderate size, looks less by having a ceiling lower than in proportion. The same low ceiling makes a very large room look larger than it is in reality.

These experiments are by far too small a stock for a general theory. But they are all that occur at present; and without attempting any regular system, I shall satisfy myself with a few conjectures.

The largest angle of vision seems to me the natural measure of space. The eye is the only judge; and in examining with it the size of any plain, or the length of any line, the most accurate method that can be taken is, to run over the object in parts. The largest part that can be taken in at one stedfast look, determines the largest angle of vision; and when that angle is given, one may institute a calculation by trying with the eye how many of these parts are in the whole.

Whether this angle be the same in all men, I know not. The smallest angle of vision is ascertained; and to ascertain the largest angle, would not be less curious.

But supposing it known, it would be a very imperfect measure; perhaps more so than the natural measure of time. It requires great steadiness of eye to measure a line with any accuracy, by applying to it the largest angle of distinct vision. And suppose this steadiness to be acquired by practice, the measure will be imperfect from other circumstances. The space comprehended under this angle, will be different according to the distance, and also according to the situation of the object. Of a perpendicular this angle will comprehend the smallest space. The space will be larger in looking upon an inclined plain; and will be larger or less in proportion to the degree of inclination.

This measure of space, like the measure of time, is liable to some extraordinary errors from certain operations of the mind, which will account for some of the erroneous judgements above mentioned. The space marked out for a dwelling-house, where the eye is at any reasonable distance, is seldom greater than can be seen at once without moving the head. Divide this space into two or three equal parts, and none of these parts will appear much less than what can be comprehended at one distinct look; consequently each of them will appear equal, or nearly equal, to what the whole did before the division. If, on the other hand, the whole be very small, so as scarce to fill the eye at one look, its divisions into parts will, I conjecture, make it appear still less. The minuteness of the parts is, by an easy transition of ideas, transferred to the whole. Each part hath a diminutive appearance, and by the intimate connection of these parts with the whole, we pass the same judgement upon all.

The space marked out for a small garden, is surveyed almost at one view; and requires a motion of the eye so slight, as to pass for an object that can be comprehended under the largest angle of distinct vision. If not divided into too many parts, we are apt to form the same judgement of each part; and consequently to magnify the garden in proportion to the number of its parts.

A very large plain without protuberances, is an object not less rare than beautiful; and in those who see it for the first time, it must produce an emotion of wonder. This emotion, however slight, tending to its own gratification, imposes upon the mind, and makes it judge that the plain is larger than it is in reality. Divide this plain into parts, and our wonder ceases. It is no longer considered as one great plain, but as so many different fields or inclosures.

The first time one beholds the sea, it appears to be large beyond all bounds. When it becomes familiar, and raises our wonder in no degree, it appears less than it is in reality. In a storm it appears larger, being distinguishable by the rolling waves into a number of great parts. Islands scattered at considerable distances, add in appearance to its size. Each intercepted part looks extremely large, and we silently apply arithmetic to increase the appearance of the whole. Many islands scattered at hand, give a diminutive appearance to the sea, by its connection with its diminutive parts. The Lomond lake would undoubtedly look larger without its islands.

Furniture increaseth in appearance the size of a small room, for the same reason that divisions increase in appearance the size of a garden. The emotion of wonder which is raised by a very large room without furniture, makes it look larger than it is in reality. If completely furnished, we view it in parts, and our wonder is not raised.

A low ceiling hath a diminutive appearance, which, by an easy transition of ideas, is communicated to the length and breadth, provided they bear any sort of proportion to the height. If they be out of all proportion, the opposition seizes the mind, and raises some degree of wonder, which makes the difference appear greater than it really is.

Part VI

Of the resemblance emotions bear to their causes.

That many emotions bear a certain resemblance to their causes, is a truth that can be made clear by induction; though, so far as I know, the observation has not been made by any writer. Motion, in its different circumstances, is productive of feelings that resemble it. Sluggish motion, for example, causeth a languid unpleasant feeling; slow uniform motion, a feeling calm and pleasant; and brisk motion, a lively feeling that rouses the spirits and promotes activity. A fall of water through rocks, raises in the mind a tumultuous confused agitation, extremely similar to its cause. When force is exerted with any effort, the spectator feels a similar effort as of force exerted within his mind. A large object swells the heart. An elevated object makes the spectator stand erect.

Sounds also produce emotions that resemble them. A sound in a low key, brings down the mind. Such a sound in a full tone, hath a certain solemnity, which it communicates to the emotion produced by it. A sound in a high key, chears the mind by raising it. Such a sound in a full tone, both elevates and swells the mind.

Again, a wall or pillar that declines from the perpendicular, produceth a painful emotion, as of a tottering and falling within the mind. An emotion somewhat similar is produced by a tall pillar that stands so ticklish as to look like falling. For this reason, a column upon a base looks better than upon the naked ground. The base, which makes a part of the column, inspires a feeling of firmness and stability. The ground supporting a naked column, is too large to be considered as its base. And for the same reason, a cube as a base, is preferred before a cylinder, though the latter is a more beautiful figure. The angles of a cube, being extended to a greater distance from the centre than the circumference of a cylinder, give the column a greater appearance of stability. This excludes not a different reason, that the base, shaft, and capital, of a pillar, ought, for the sake of variety, to differ from each other. If the shaft be round, the base and capital ought to be square.

A constrained posture, uneasy to the man himself, is disagreeable to the spectator; which makes it a rule in painting, that the drapery ought not to adhere to the body, but hang loose, that the figures may appear easy and free in their movements. Hence the disagreeable figure of a French dancing-master is one of Hogarth's pieces. It is also ridiculous, because the constraint is assumed and not forced.

The foregoing observation is not confined to emotions raised by still life. It holds also in those which are raised by the qualities, actions, and passions, of a sensible being. Love inspired by a fine woman, assumes her qualities. It is sublime, soft, tender, severe, or gay, according to its cause. This is still more remarkable in emotions raised by human actions. It hath already been remarked[29], that any signal instance of gratitude, beside procuring esteem for the author, raiseth in the spectator a vague emotion of gratitude, which disposeth him to be grateful. I now further remark, that this vague emotion, being of the same kind with what produced the grateful action, hath a strong resemblance to its cause. Courage exerted inspires the reader as well as the spectator with a like emotion of courage. A just action fortifies our love to justice, and a generous action rouses our generosity. In short, with respect to all virtuous actions, it will be found by induction, that they lead us to imitation by inspiring emotions resembling the passions that produced these actions. And hence the benefit of dealing in choice books and in choice company.

Grief as well as joy are infectious: the emotions they raise in a spectator resemble them perfectly. Fear is equally infectious: and hence

---

29. Part 1. of this chapter, sect. 4.

in an army, fear, even from the slighted cause, making an impression on a few, spreads generally through all, and becomes an universal panic. Pity is similar to its cause. A parting scene betwixt lovers or friends, produceth in the spectator a sort of pity, which is tender like the distress. The anguish of remorse, produceth pity of a harsh kind; and if the remorse be extreme, the pity hath a mixture of horror. Anger I think is singular; for even where it is moderate and causeth no disgust, it disposes not the spectator to anger in any degree[30]. Covetousness, cruelty, treachery, and other vicious passions, are so far from raising any emotion similar to themselves, to incite a spectator to imitation, that they have an opposite effect. They raise abhorrence, and fortify the spectator in his aversion to such actions. When anger is immoderate, it cannot fail to produce the same effect.

Part VII

Final causes of the more frequent emotions and passions.

It is a law in our nature, that we never act but by the impulse of desire; which in other words is saying, that it is passion, by the desire included in it, which determines the will. Hence in the conduct of life, it is of the utmost importance, that our passions be directed upon proper objects, tend to just and rational ends, and with relation to each other be duly balanced. The beauty of contrivance, so conspicuous in the human frame, is not confined to the rational part of our nature, but is visible over the whole. Concerning the passions in particular, however irregular, headstrong, and perverse, in an overly view, they may appear, I propose to show, that they are by nature adjusted and tempered with admirable wisdom, for the good of society as well as for private good. This subject is extensive: but as the nature of the present undertaking will not admit a complete discussion, it shall suffice to give a few observations in general upon the sensitive part of our nature, without regarding that strange irregularity of passion discovered in some individuals. Such topical irregularities, if I may use the term, cannot fairly be held an objection to the present theory. We are frequently, it is true, misled

---

30. Aristotle, Poet. cap. 18. sect. 3. says, that anger raiseth in the spectator a similar emotion of anger.

by inordinate passion: but we are also, and perhaps not less frequently, misled by wrong judgement.

In order to a distinct apprehension of the present subject, it must be premised, that an agreeable object produceth always a pleasant emotion, and a disagreeable object one that is painful. This is a general law of nature, which admits not a single exception. Agreeableness in the object or cause is indeed so essentially connected with pleasure in the emotion its effect, that an agreeable object cannot be better defined, than by its power of producing a pleasant emotion. Disagreeableness in the object or cause, has the same necessary connection with pain in the emotion produced by it.

From this preliminary it appears, that to inquire for what end an emotion is made pleasant or painful, resolves into an inquiry for what end its cause is made agreeable or disagreeable. And from the most accurate induction it will be discovered, that no cause of an emotion is made agreeable or disagreeable arbitrarily; but that these qualities are so distributed as to answer wise and good purposes. It is an invincible proof of the benignity of the Deity, that we are surrounded with things generally agreeable, which contribute remarkably to our entertainment and to our happiness. Somethings are made disagreeable, such as a rotten carcass, because they are noxious. Others, a dirty marsh, for example, or a barren heath, are made disagreeable in order to excite our industry. And with respect to the few things that are neither agreeable nor disagreeable; it will be made evident, that their being left indifferent is not a work of chance but of wisdom. Of such I shall have occasion to give several instances.

Having attempted to assign the final causes of emotions and passions considered as pleasant or painful, we proceed to the final causes of the desires involved in them. This seems a work of some difficulty; for the desires that accompany different passions have very different aims, and seldom or never demand precisely the same gratification. One passion moves us to cling to its object, one to fly from it; one passion impels to action for our own good, and one for the good of others; one passion prompts us to do good to ourselves or others, and one to do mischief, frequently to others, and sometimes even to ourselves. Deliberating upon this intricate subject, and finding an intimate correspondence betwixt our desires and their objects, it is natural to think that the former must be regulated in some measure by the latter. In this view, I begin with desire directed upon an inanimate object.

Any pleasure we have in an agreeable object of this kind, is enjoyed by the continuance of the pleasant impression it makes upon us; and accordingly the desire involved in the pleasant emotion tends to that end, and is gratified by dwelling upon the agreeable object. Hence such an object may be properly termed *attractive*. Thus a flowing river, a towering hill, a fine garden, are attractive objects. They fix the attention of the spectator, by inspiring pleasant emotions, which are gratified by adhering to these objects and enjoying them. On the other hand, a disagreeable object of the same kind, raises in us a painful emotion including a desire to turn from the object, which relieves us of course from the pain; and hence such an object may be properly termed *repulsive*. A monstrous birth, for example, a rotten carcass, a confusion of jarring sounds, are repulsive. They repel the mind, by inspiring painful or unpleasant emotions, which are gratified by flying from such objects. Thus in general, with regard to inanimate objects, the desire included in every pleasant passion tends to prolong the pleasure, and the desire included in every painful passion tends to put an end to the pain. Here the final cause is evident. Our desires, so far, are modelled in such a manner as to correspond precisely to the sensitive part of our nature, prone to happiness and averse to misery. These operations of adhering to an agreeable inanimate object, and flying from one that is disagreeable, are performed in the beginning of life by means of desire impelling us, without the intervention of reason or reflection. Reason and reflection directing self-love, become afterward motives that unite their force with desire; because experience informs us, that the adhering to agreeable objects and the flying from those that are disagreeable, contribute to our happiness.

Sensible Beings considered as objects of passion, lead us into a more complex theory. A sensible being that is agreeable by its attributes, inspires us with a pleasant emotion; and the desire included in this emotion has evidently different means of gratification. A man regarding himself only, may be satisfied with viewing and contemplating this being, precisely as if it were inanimate; or he may desire the more generous gratification of making it happy. Were man altogether selfish, it would be conformable to his nature, that he should indulge the pleasant emotion without making any acknowledgement to the person who gives him pleasure, more than to a pure air or temperate clime when he enjoys these benefits. But as man is endued with a principle of benevolence as well as of selfishness, he is prompted by his nature to desire the good of every sensible being that gives him pleasure. And the final cause of desire so directed, is illustrious. It contributes to a man's own happiness, by affording him more means of gratification than he can have when his desire terminates upon himself alone; and at the same time it tends eminently to improve the happiness of those with whom he is connected. The directing our desires in this manner, occasions a beautiful coalition of self-love with benevolence; for both are equally promoted by the same internal impulse, and by the same external conduct. And this consideration, by the way, ought to silence those minute philosophers, who, ignorant of human nature, teach a most disgustful doctrine. That to serve others unless with a view to our own good, is weakness and folly; as if self-love only contributed to happiness and not benevolence. The hand of God is too visible in the human frame, to permit us to think seriously, that there ever can be any jarring or inconsistency among natural principles, those especially of self-love and benevolence, which regulate the bulk of our actions.

Next in order come sensible Beings that are in affliction or pain. It is disagreeable to behold a person in distress; and therefore this object must raise in the spectator an uneasy emotion. Were man purely a selfish being, he would be prompted by his nature to turn from every object, animate or inanimate, that gives him uneasiness. But the principle of benevolence gives an opposite direction to his desire. It impels him to afford relief; and by relieving the person from distress, his desire is fully gratified. Our benevolence to a person in distress is inflamed into an emotion of sympathy, signifying in Greek the painful emotion that is raised in us by that person. Thus sympathy, though a painful emotion, is in its nature attractive. And with respect to its final cause, we can be at no loss. It not only tends to relieve a fellow-creature from pain, but in its gratification is greatly more pleasant than if it were repulsive.

We in the last place bring under consideration persons hateful by vice or wickedness. Imagine a wretch who has lately perpetrated some horrid crime. He is disagreeable to every spectator; and consequently raises in every spectator a painful emotion. What is the natural gratification of the desire that accompanies this painful emotion? I must here again observe, that supposing man to be entirely a selfish being, he would be prompted by his nature to relieve himself from the pain by averting his eye, and banishing the criminal from his thoughts. But man is not so constituted. He is composed of many principles, which, though seemingly contradictory, are perfectly concordant. The principle of benevolence influences his conduct, not less remarkably than that of selfishness. And in order to answer the foregoing question, I must introduce a third principle, not less remarkable in its influence than either of those mentioned. It is that principle common to all, which prompts us to punish those who do wrong. An envious, malicious, or cruel action, is disagreeable to me even where I have no connection with the sufferer, and raises in me the painful emotion of resentment. The gratification of this emotion, when accompanied with desire, is directed by the principle now unfolded. Being prompted by my nature to punish guilt as well as to reward virtue, my desire is not gratified but by inflicting punishment. I must chastise the wretch by indignation at least and hatred, if not more severely. Here the final cause is self-evident.

An injury done to myself, touching me more than when done to others, raises my resentment in a higher degree. The desire accordingly included in this passion, is not satisfied with so slight a punishment as indignation or hatred. It is not fully gratified without retaliation; and the author must by my hand suffer mischief, as great at least as he has done me. Neither can we be at any loss about the final cause of this higher degree of resentment. The whole vigor of this passion is required to secure individuals from the injustice and oppression of others[31].

A wicked or disgraceful action, is disagreeable not only to others, but even to the delinquent himself. It raises in him as well as in others a painful emotion including a desire of punishment. The painful emotion which the delinquent feels, is distinguished by the name of *remorse*; and in this case the desire he has to punish is directed against himself. There cannot be imagined a better contrivance to deter us from vice; for remorse is the severest of all punishments. This passion and the desire of self-punishment derived from it, are touched delicately by Terence.

MENEDEMUS: Ubi comperi ex iis, qui ei fuere conscii,
    Domum revortor mœstus, atque animo fere
    Perturbato, atque incerto præ ægritudine:
    Adsido, adcurrunt servi, soccos detrahunt:
    Video alios festinare, lectos sternere,

---

31. See Historical Law Tracts, Tract 1.

> Cœnam adparare: pro se quisque sedulo
> Faciebat, quo illam mihi lenirent miseriam.
> Ubi video hæc, cœpi cogitare: Hem! tot mea
> Solius solliciti sint causa, ut me unum expleant?
> Ancillæ tot me vestiant? sumptus domi
> Tantos ego solus faciam? sed gnatum unicum,
> Quem pariter uti his decuit, aut etiam amplius,
> Quod illa ætas magis ad hæc utenda idonea 'st,
> Eum ego hinc ejeci miserum injustitia mea.
> Malo quidem me dignum quovis deputem,
> Si id faciam. nam usque dum ille vitam illam colet
> Inopem, carens patria ob meas injurias,
> Interea usque illi de me supplicium dabo:
> Laborans, quærens, parcens, illi serviens,
> Ita facio prorsus: nihil relinquo in ædibus,
> Nec vas, nec vestimentum: conrasi omnia,
> Ancillas, servos, nisi eos, qui opere rustico
> Faciundo facile sumptum exercerent suum:
> Omnes produxi ac vendidi: inscripsi ilico
> Ædeis mercede: quasi talenta ad quindecim
> Coëgi: agrum hunc mercatus sum: hic me exerceo.
> Decrevi tantisper me minus injuriæ,
> Chreme, meo gnato facere, dum fiam miser:
> Nec fas esse ulla me voluptate hic frui,
> Nisi ubi ille huc salvos redierit meus particeps.
>
> —*Heautontimerumenos, act 1. sc. 1*

Otway reaches the same sentiment:

> MONIMIA: Let mischiefs multiply! let ev'ry hour
> Of my loath'd life yield me increase of horror!
> Oh let the sun to these unhappy eyes
> Ne'er shine again, but be eclips'd forever!
> May everything I look on seem a prodigy,
> To fill my soul with terror, till I quite
> Forget I ever had humanity,
> And grow a curser of the works of nature!
>
> —*Orphan, act 4*

The cases mentioned are, where benevolence alone or where desire of punishment alone, governs without a rival. And it was necessary to handle these cases separately, in order to elucidate a subject which by writers is left in great obscurity. But neither of these principles operates always without rivalship. Cases may be figured, and cases actually exist, where the same person is an object both of sympathy and of desire to punish. Thus the sight of a profligate in the venereal disease, overrun with botches and sores, actuates both principles. While his distress fixes my attention, sympathy exerts itself; but so soon as I think of his profligacy, hatred prevails, and a desire to punish. This in general is the case of distress occasioned by immoral actions that are not highly criminal. And if the distress and the immoral action be in any proportion, sympathy and hatred counterbalancing each other will not suffer me either to afford relief or to inflict punishment. What then will be the result of the whole? The principle of self-love solves the question. Abhorring an object so loathsome, I naturally avert my eye, and walk off as fast as I can, in order to be relieved from the pain.

The present subject gives birth to several other observations, for which I could not find room above, without relaxing more from the strictness of order and connection, than with safety could be indulged in discoursing upon a matter that with difficulty is made perspicuous, even with all the advantages of order and connection. These observations I shall throw out loosely as they occur, without giving myself any further trouble about method.

No action good or bad is altogether indifferent even to a mere spectator. If good, it inspires esteem; and indignation, if wicked. But it is remarkable, that these emotions seldom are accompanied with desire. The abilities of man are limited, and he finds sufficient employment, in relieving the distressed, in requiting his benefactors, and in punishing those who wrong him, without moving out of his own sphere for the benefit or chastisement of those with whom he has no connection.

If the good qualities of others excite my benevolence, the same qualities in myself must produce a similar effect in a superior degree, upon account of the natural partiality every man hath for himself. This increases self-love. If these qualities be of a high rank, they produce a feeling of superiority, which naturally leads me to assume some sort of government over others. Mean qualities, on the other hand, produce in me a feeling of inferiority, which naturally leads me to submit to others.

Unless such feelings were distributed among individuals in society by measure and proportion, there could be no natural subordination of some to others, which is the principal foundation of government.

No other branch of the human constitution shows more visibly our destination for society, nor tends more to our improvement, than appetite for fame or esteem. The whole conveniencies of life being derived from mutual aid and support in society, it ought to be a capital aim, to form connections with others so strict and so extensive as to produce a firm reliance on many for succour in time of need. Reason dictates this lesson. But reason solely is not relied on in a matter of such consequence. We are moved by a natural appetite, to be solicitous about esteem and respect as we are about food when hungry. This appetite, at the same time, is finely adjusted to the moral branch of our constitution, by promoting all the moral virtues. For what infallible means are there to attract love and esteem, other than a virtuous course of life? If a man be just and beneficent, if he be temperate modest and prudent, he will infallibly gain the esteem and love of all who know him.

The communication of passion to related objects, is an illustrious instance of the care of Providence, to extend social connections as far as the limited nature of man can admit. This communication of passion is so far unhappy as to spread the malevolent passions beyond their natural bounds. But let it be remarked, that this unhappy effect regards savages only, who give way to malevolent passions. Under the discipline of society, these passions are subdued, and in a good measure eradicated. In their place succeed the kindly affections, which, meeting with all encouragement, take possession of the mind and govern our whole actions. In this condition, the progress of passion along related objects, by spreading the kindly affections through a multitude of individuals, hath a glorious effect.

Nothing can be more entertaining to a rational mind, than the œconomy of the human passions, of which I have attempted to give some faint notion. It must however be confessed, that our passions, when they happen to swell beyond their proper limits, take on a less regular appearance. Reason may proclaim our duty, but the will influenced by passion, makes gratification always welcome. Hence the power of passion, which, when in excess, cannot be resisted but by the utmost fortitude of mind. It is bent upon gratification; and where proper objects are wanting, it clings to any object at hand without distinction. Thus joy inspired by a fortunate event, is diffused upon every person around by acts of benevolence; and resentment for an atrocious injury done by one out of reach, seizes the first object that occurs to vent itself upon. Those who believe in prophecies, even wish the accomplishment; and a weak mind is disposed voluntarily to fulfil a prophecy, in order to gratify its wish. Shakespear, whom no particle of human nature hath escaped, however remote from common observation, describes this weakness:

> K. HENRY: Doth any name particular belong
> Unto that lodging where I first did swoon?
> WARWICK: 'Tis call'd *Jerusalem*, my Noble Lord.
> K. HENRY: Laud be to God! even there my life must end.
> It hath been prophesy'd to me many years,
> I should not die but in Jerusalem,
> Which vainly I suppos'd the holy land.
> But bear me to that chamber, there I'll lie:
> In that Jerusalem shall Henry die.
>
> *—Second part, Henry IV. act 4. sc. last*

I could not deny myself the amusement of the foregoing observation, though it doth not properly come under my plan. The irregularities of passion proceeding from peculiar weaknesses and biasses, I do not undertake to justify; and of these we have had many examples.[32] It is sufficient that passions common to all and as generally exerted, are made subservient to beneficial purposes. I shall only observe, that in a polished society instances of irregular passions are rare, and that their mischief doth not extend far.

---

32. Part 5. of the present chapter.

III

Beauty

Having discoursed in general of emotions and passions, I proceed to a more narrow inspection of some particulars that serve to unfold the principles of the fine arts. It is the province of a writer upon ethics, to give a full enumeration of all the passions; and of each separately to assign the nature, the cause, the gratification, and the effects. But a treatise of ethics is not my province. I carry my view no farther than to the elements of criticism, in order to show that the fine arts are a subject of reasoning as well as of taste. An extensive work would be ill suited to a design so limited; and to keep within moderate bounds, the following plan may contribute. It has already been observed, that things are the causes of emotions, by means of their properties and attributes[1]. This furnisheth a hint for distribution. Instead of a painful and tedious examination of the several passions and emotions, I propose to confine my inquiries to such attributes, relations, and circumstances, as in the fine arts are chiefly employed to raise agreeable emotions. Attributes of single objects, as the most simple, shall take the lead; to be followed with particulars that depend on the relations of objects, and are not found in anyone object singly considered. Dispatching next some coincident matters, I approach nearer to practice, by applying the principles unfolded in the foregoing parts of the work. This is a general view of the intended method; reserving however a privilege to vary it in particular instances, where a different method may be more commodious. I begin with beauty, the most noted of all the qualities that belong to single objects.

The term *beauty*, in its native signification, is appropriated to objects of sight. Objects of the other senses may be agreeable, such as the sounds of musical instruments, the smoothness and softness of some surfaces: but the agreeableness denominated *beauty* belongs to objects of sight.

Of all the objects of the external senses, an object of sight is the most complex. In the very simplest, colour is perceived, figure, and length

---

1. Chap. 2. part. 1. sect. 1. first note.

breadth and thickness. A tree is composed of a trunk, branches, and leaves. It has colour, figure, size, and sometimes motion. By means of each of these particulars, separately considered, it appears beautiful: how much more so, when they enter all into one complex perception? The beauty of the human figure is extraordinary, being a composition of numberless beauties arising from the parts and qualities of the object, various colours, various motions, figure, size, &c.; all uniting in one complex perception, and striking the eye with combined force. Hence it is, that beauty, a quality so remarkable in visible objects, lends its name to express everything that is eminently agreeable. Thus, by a figure of speech, we say a beautiful sound, a beautiful thought or expression, a beautiful theorem, a beautiful event, a beautiful discovery in art or science. But as figurative expression is not our present theme, this chapter is confined to beauty in its genuine signification.

It is natural to suppose, that a perception so various as that of beauty, comprehending sometimes many particulars, sometimes few, should occasion emotions equally various. And yet all the various emotions of beauty maintain one general character of sweetness and gaiety.

Considering attentively the beauty of visible objects, we discover two kinds. One may be termed *intrinsic* beauty, because it is discovered in a single object viewed apart without relation to any other object. The examples above given, are of that kind. The other may be termed *relative* beauty, being founded on the relation of objects. The former is a perception of sense merely; for to perceive the beauty of a spreading oak or of a flowing river, no more is required but singly an act of vision. The latter is accompanied with an act of understanding and reflection; for of a fine instrument or engine, we perceive not the relative beauty, until we be made acquainted with its use and destination. In a word, intrinsic beauty is ultimate: relative beauty is that of means relating to some good end or purpose. These different beauties agree in one capital circumstance, that both are equally perceived as spread upon the object. This will be readily admitted with respect to intrinsic beauty; but is not so obvious with respect to the other. The utility of the plough, for example, may make it an object of admiration or of desire; but why should utility make it appear beautiful? A principle mentioned above[2], will explain this doubt. The beauty of the effect, by an easy transition of ideas, is transferred to the cause, and is perceived as one of the qualities

---

2. Chap. 2. part. 1. sect. 5.

of the cause. Thus a subject void of intrinsic beauty, appears beautiful from its utility. An old Gothic tower that has no beauty in itself, appears beautiful, considered as proper to defend against an enemy. A dwelling-house void of all regularity, is however beautiful in the view of convenience; and the want of form or symmetry in a tree, will not prevent its appearing beautiful, if it be known to produce good fruit.

When these two beauties concur in any object, it appears delightful. Every member of the human body possesses both in a high degree. The slender make of a horse destined for running, pleases every taste; partly from symmetry, and partly from utility.

The beauty of utility, being proportioned accurately to the degree of utility, requires no illustration. But intrinsic beauty, so complex as I have said, cannot be handled distinctly without being analized into its constituent parts. If a tree be beautiful by means of its colour, its figure, its size, its motion, it is in reality possessed of so many different beauties, which ought to be examined separately, in order to have a clear notion of the whole. The beauty of colour is too familiar to need explanation. The beauty of figure requires an accurate discussion, for in it many circumstances are involved. When any portion of matter is viewed as a whole, the beauty of its figure arises from regularity and simplicity. Viewing the parts with relation to each other, uniformity, proportion, and order, contribute to its beauty. The beauty of motion deserves a chapter by itself; and another chapter is destined for grandeur, being distinguishable from beauty in a strict sense. For the definitions of regularity, uniformity, proportion, and order, if thought necessary, I remit my reader to the appendix at the end of the book. Upon simplicity I must make a few cursory observations, such as may be of use in examining the beauty of single objects.

A multitude of objects crowding into the mind at once, disturb the attention, and pass without making any impression, or any lasting impression. In a group, no single object makes the figure it would do apart, when it occupies the whole attention[3]. For the same reason, even a single object, when it divides the attention by the multiplicity of its parts, equals not, in strength of impression, a more simple object comprehended in a single view. Parts extremely complex must be considered in portions successively; and a number of impressions in succession, which cannot unite because not simultaneous, never touch

---

3. See the Appendix, containing definitions and explanation of terms, sect. 33.

the mind like one entire impression made as it were at one stroke. This justifies simplicity in works of art, as opposed to complicated circumstances and crowded ornaments. There is an additional reason for simplicity, in works that make an impression of dignity or elevation. The mind attached to beauties of a high rank, cannot descend to inferior beauties. And yet, notwithstanding these reasons, we find profuse decoration prevailing in works of art. But this is no argument against simplicity, For authors and architects who cannot reach the higher beauties, endeavour to supply their want of genius by dealing in those that are inferior. In all ages, the best writers and artists have been governed by a taste for simplicity.

These things premised, I proceed to examine the beauty of figure, as arising from the above-mentioned particulars, *viz.* regularity, uniformity, proportion, order, and simplicity. To exhaust this subject, would of itself require a large volume. I limit myself to a few cursory remarks, as matter for future disquisition. To inquire why an object, by means of the particulars mentioned, appears beautiful, would I am afraid be a vain attempt. It seems the most probable opinion, that the nature of man was originally framed with a relish for them, in order to answer wise and good purposes. The final causes have not hitherto been ascertained, though they are not probably beyond our reach. One thing is clear, that regularity, uniformity, order, and simplicity, contribute each of them to readiness of apprehension; and enable us to form more distinct images of objects, than can be done with the utmost attention where these particulars are not found. This final cause is, I acknowledge, too slight, to account satisfactorily for a taste that makes a figure so illustrious in the nature of man. That this branch of our constitution hath a purpose still more important, we have great reason to believe. With respect to proportion, I am still less successful. In several instances, accurate proportion is connected with utility. This in particular is the case of animals; for those that are the best proportioned, are the strongest and most active. But instances are still more numerous, where the proportions we relish the most, have no connection, so far as we see, with utility. Writers on architecture insist much upon the proportions of a column; and assign different proportions to the Doric, Ionic, and Corinthian. But no architect will maintain, that the most accurate proportions contribute more to use, than several that are less accurate and less agreeable. Neither will it be maintained, that the proportions assigned for the length breadth and height of rooms, tend to make them the more commodious. It appears then, so far as we can discover, that we have a taste for proportion independent altogether of utility. One thing indeed is certain, that any external object proportioned to our taste, is delightful. This furnishes a hint. May it not be thought a good final cause of proportion, that it contributes to our entertainment? The author of our nature has given many signal proofs, that this end is not below his care. And if so, why should we hesitate in assigning this as an additional final cause of regularity, and the other particulars above mentioned? We may be confirmed in this thought, by reflecting, that our taste, with respect to these, is not occasional or accidental, but uniform and universal, making an original branch of human nature.

One might fill a volume with the effects that are produced by the endless combinations of the principles of beauty. I have room only for a slight specimen, confined to the simplest figures. A circle and a square are each of them perfectly regular, being equally confined to a precise form, and admitting not the slightest variation. A square however is less beautiful than a circle, because it is less simple. A circle has parts as well as a square; but its parts not being distinct like those of a square, it makes one entire impression; whereas the attention is divided among the sides and angles of a square. The effect of simplicity may be illustrated by another example. A square, though not more regular than a hexagon or octagon, is more beautiful than either; for what other reason, than that a square is more simple, and the attention less divided? This reasoning will appear still more solid when we consider any regular polygon of very many sides; for of such figure the mind can never have any distinct perception. Simplicity thus contributes to beauty.

A square is more beautiful than a parallelogram. The former exceeds the latter in regularity and in uniformity of parts. But this holds with respect to intrinsic beauty only; for in many instances, utility comes in to cast the balance on the side of the parallelogram. This figure for the doors and windows of a dwelling-house, is preferred because of utility; and here we find the beauty of utility prevailing over that of regularity and uniformity.

A parallelogram again depends, for its beauty, on the proportion of its sides. The beauty is lost by a great inequality of sides. It is also lost, on the other hand, by the approximation toward equality. Proportion in this circumstance degenerates into imperfect uniformity; and the figure upon the whole appears an unsuccessful attempt toward a square.

An equilateral triangle yields not to a square in regularity nor in uniformity of parts, and it is more simple. But an equilateral triangle is less beautiful than a square, which must be owing to inferiority of order in the position of its parts. The sides of an equilateral triangle incline to each other in the same angle, which is the most perfect order they are susceptible of. But this order is obscure, and far from being so perfect as the parallelism of the sides of a square. Thus order contributes to the beauty of visible objects, not less than simplicity and regularity.

A parallelogram exceeds an equilateral triangle in the orderly disposition of its parts; but being inferior in uniformity and simplicity, it is less beautiful.

Uniformity is singular in one capital circumstance, that it is apt to disgust by excess. A number of things contrived for the same use, such as chairs spoons, &c. cannot be too uniform. But a scrupulous uniformity of parts in a large garden or field, is far from being agreeable. Uniformity among connected objects, belongs not to the present subject. It is handled in the chapter of uniformity and variety.

In all the works of nature, simplicity makes an illustrious figure. The works of the best artists are directed by it. Profuse ornament in painting, gardening, or architecture, as well as in dress and language, shows a mean or corrupted taste.

> *Poets, like painters, thus unskill'd to trace*
> *The naked nature and the living grace,*
> *With gold and jewels cover ev'ry part,*
> *And hide with ornaments their want of art.*
>
> —*Pope's Essay on criticism*

No one property recommends a machine more than its simplicity; not singly for better answering its purpose, but by appearing in itself more beautiful. Simplicity hath a capital effect in behaviour and manners; no other particular contributing more to gain esteem and love. The artificial and intricate manners of modern times, have little of dignity in them. General theorems, abstracting from their importance, are delightful by their simplicity, and by the easiness of their application to a variety of cases. We take equal delight in the laws of motion, which, with the greatest simplicity, are boundless in their influence.

A gradual progress from simplicity to complex forms and profuse ornament, seems to be the fate of all the fine arts; resembling behaviour, which from original candor and simplicity has degenerated into artificial refinements. At present, written productions are crowded with words, epithets, figures, &c. In music, sentiment is neglected, for the luxury of harmony, and for difficult movement which surprises in its execution. In *taste* properly so called, poignant sauces with complicated mixtures of different favours, prevail among people of condition. The French, accustomed to the artificial red on their women's cheeks, think the modest colouring of nature displayed on a fine face altogether insipid.

The same tendency appears in the progress of the arts among the ancients. Of this we have traces still remaining in architecture. Some vestiges of the oldest Grecian buildings prove them to be of the Doric order. The Ionic succeeded, and seems to have been the favourite order, while architecture was in its height of glory. The Corinthian came next in vogue: and in Greece, the buildings of that order appear mostly to have been erected after the Romans got footing there. At last came the Composite with all its extravagancies, where proportion is sacrificed to finery and crowded ornament.

But what taste is to prevail next? for fashion is in a continual flux, and taste must vary with it. After rich and profuse ornaments become familiar, simplicity appears by contrast lifeless and insipid. This would be an unsurmountable obstruction, should any man of genius and taste endeavour to restore ancient simplicity.

In reviewing what is said above, I am under some apprehension of an objection, which, as it may possibly occur to the reader, ought to be obviated. A mountain, it will be observed, is an agreeable object, without so much as the appearance of regularity; and a chain of mountains still more agreeable, without being arranged in any order. But these facts considered in a proper light, afford not an objection. Regularity, order, and uniformity, are intimately connected with beauty; and in this view only, have I treated them. Every regular object, for example, must in respect of its regularity be beautiful. But I have not said, that regularity, order, and uniformity, are essential to beauty, so as that it cannot exist without them. The contrary appears in the beauty of colour. Far less have I said, that an object cannot be agreeable in any respect independent of these qualities. Grandeur, as distinguished from beauty, requires very little regularity. This will appear more fully when that article is handled. In the mean time, to show the difference betwixt beauty and grandeur with respect to regularity, I shall give a few examples. Imagine a small body, let it be a globe, in a continual flux of figure, from the most perfect regularity till there remain no appearance of that quality. The beauty of this globe, depending on its regular figure, will gradually wear away with its regularity; and when it is no longer regular, it no longer will appear beautiful. The next example shall be of the same globe, gradually enlarging its size, but retaining its figure. In this body, we at first perceive the beauty of regularity only. But so soon as it begins to swell into a great size, it appears agreeable by its greatness, which joins with the beauty of regularity to make it a delightful object. In the last place, let it be imagined, that the figure as well as the quantity of matter are in a continual flux; and that the body, while it increases in size, becomes less and less regular, till it lose altogether the appearance of that quality. In this case, the beauty of regularity wearing off gradually, gives place to an agreeableness of a different sort, *viz.* that of greatness: and at last the emotion arising from greatness will be in perfection, when the beauty of regularity is gone. Hence it is, that in a large object the want of regularity is not much regarded by the spectator who is struck with its grandeur. A swelling eminence is agreeable, though not strictly regular. A towering hill is delightful, if it have but any distant resemblance of a cone. A small surface ought to be smooth; but in a wide-extended plain, considerable inequalities are overlooked. This observation holds equally in works of art. The slightest irregularity in a house of a moderate size hurts the eye; while the mind, struck with the grandeur of a superb edifice, which occupies it totally, cannot bear to descend to its irregularities unless extremely gross. In a large volume we pardon many defects that would make an epigram intolerable. In short, the observation holds in general, that beauty is connected with regularity in great objects as well as in small; but with a remarkable difference, that in passing from small to great, regularity is less and less required.

The distinction betwixt primary and secondary qualities in matter, seems now fully established. Heat and cold, though seeming to exist in bodies, are discovered to be effects caused by these bodies in a sensitive being. Colour, which the eye represents as spread upon a substance, has no existence but in the mind of the spectator. Perceptions of this kind, which, by a delusion of sense, are attributed to external subjects, are termed *secondary qualities*, in contradistinction to figure, extension, solidity, which are primary qualities, and which are not separable, even in imagination, from the subjects they belong to. This suggests a curious inquiry, Whether beauty be a primary or only a secondary quality of objects? The question is easily determined with respect to the beauty of colour; for if colour be a secondary quality existing no where but in the mind of the spectator, its beauty must be of the same kind. This conclusion must also hold with respect to the beauty of utility, which is plainly a conception of the mind, arising not merely from sight, but from reflecting that the thing is fitted for some good end or purpose. The question is more intricate with respect to the beauty of regularity. If regularity be a primary quality, why not also its beauty? That this is not a good consequence, will appear from considering, that beauty, in its very conception, refers to a percipient; for an object is said to be beautiful, for no other reason but that it appears so to a spectator. The same piece of matter which to man appears beautiful, may possibly to another being appear ugly. Beauty therefore, which for its existence depends upon the percipient as much as upon the object perceived, cannot be an inherent property of either. What else then can it be, but a perception in the mind occasioned by certain objects? The same reasoning is applicable to the beauty of order, of uniformity, of grandeur. Accordingly, it may be pronounced in general, that beauty in no case whatever is a real quality of matter. And hence it is wittily observed by the poet, that beauty is not in the countenance, but in the lover's eye. This reasoning is undoubtedly solid: and the only cause of doubt or hesitation is, that we are taught a different lesson by sense. By a singular determination of nature, we perceive both beauty and colour as belonging to the object; and, like figure or extension, as inherent properties. This mechanism is uncommon; and when nature, to fulfil her intention, chuseth any singular method of operation, we may be certain of some final cause that cannot be reached by ordinary means. It appears to me, that a perception of beauty in external objects, is requisite to attach us to them. Doth not this mechanism, in the first place, greatly promote industry, by prompting a desire to possess things that are beautiful? Doth it not further join with utility, in prompting us to embellish our houses and enrich our fields? These however are but slight effects, compared with the connections which are formed among individuals in society by means of this singular mechanism. The qualifications of the head and heart, are undoubtedly the most solid and most permanent foundations of such connections. But as external beauty lies more in view, and is more obvious to the bulk of mankind than the qualities now mentioned, the sense of beauty possesses the more universal influence in forming these connections. At any rate, it concurs in an eminent degree with mental qualifications, to produce social intercourse, mutual good-will, and consequently mutual aid and support, which are the life of society.

It must not however be overlooked, that this sense doth not tend to advance the interests of society, but when in a due mean with respect to strength. Love in particular arising from a sense of beauty, loses, when excessive, its sociable character. The appetite for gratification, prevailing over affection for the beloved object, is ungovernable; and tends violently to its end, regardless of the misery that must follow. Love in this state is no longer a sweet agreeable passion. It becomes painful like hunger or thirst; and produceth no happiness but in the instant of fruition. This discovery suggests a most important lesson, that moderation in our desires and appetites, which fits us for doing our duty, contributes at the same time the most to happiness. Even social passions, when moderate, are more pleasant than when they swell beyond proper bounds.

IV

Grandeur and Sublimity

Nature hath not more remarkably distinguished us from the other animals by an erect posture, than by a capacious and aspiring mind, inclining us to everything great and elevated. The ocean, the sky, or any large object, seizes the attention, and makes a strong impression[1]. Robes of state are made large and full to draw respect. We admire elephants and whales for their magnitude, notwithstanding their unwieldiness.

The elevation of an object affects us not less than its magnitude. A high place is chosen for the statue of a deity or hero. A tree growing upon the brink of a precipice viewed from the plain below, affords by that circumstance an additional pleasure. A throne is erected for the chief magistrate, and a chair with a high seat for the president of a court.

In some objects, greatness and elevation concur to make a complicated impression. The Alps and the pike of Teneriff are proper examples; with the following difference, that in the former greatness seems to prevail, elevation in the latter.

The emotions raised by great and by elevated objects, are clearly distinguishable, not only in the internal feeling, but even in their external expressions. A great object dilates the breast, and makes the spectator endeavour to enlarge his bulk. This is remarkable in persons, who, neglecting delicacy in behaviour, give way to nature without reserve. In describing a great object, they naturally expand themselves by drawing in air with all their force. An elevated object produces a different expression. It makes the spectator stretch upward and stand a tiptoe. Great and elevated objects considered with relation to the emotions produced by them, are termed *grand* and *sublime*. Grandeur and sublimity have a double signification. They generally signify the quality or circumstance in the objects by which the emotions are produced; sometimes the emotions themselves.

Whether magnitude singly in an object of sight, have the effect to

---

1. Longinus observes, that nature inclines us to admire, not a small rivulet, however clear and transparent, but the Nile, the Ister, the Rhine, or still more the ocean. The sight of a small fire produceth no emotion; but we are struck with the boiling furnaces of Ætna, pouring out whole rivers of liquid flame. *Treatise of the Sublime, chap.* 29.

produce an emotion distinguishable from the beauty or deformity of that object; or whether it be only a circumstance modifying the beauty or deformity, is an intricate question. If magnitude produce an emotion of its own distinguishable from others, this emotion must either be pleasant or painful. But this seems to be contradicted by experience; for magnitude, as it would appear, contributes in some instances to beauty, in some to deformity. A hill, for instance, is agreeable, and a great mountain still more so. But an ugly monster, the larger, the more horrid. Greatness in an enemy, great power, great courage, serve but to augment our terror. Hath not this an appearance as if grandeur were not an emotion distinct from all others, but only a circumstance that qualifies beauty and deformity?

I am notwithstanding satisfied, that grandeur is an emotion, not only distinct from all others, but in every circumstance pleasant. These propositions must be examined separately. I begin with the former, and shall endeavour to prove, that magnitude produceth a peculiar emotion distinguishable from all others. Magnitude is undoubtedly a real property of bodies, not less than figure, and more than colour. Figure and colour, even in the same body, produce separate emotions, which are never misapprehended one for the other. Why should not magnitude produce an emotion different from both? That it has this effect, will be evident from a plain experiment of two bodies, one great and one little, which produce different emotions, though they be precisely the same as to figure and colour. There is indeed an obscurity in this matter, occasioned by the following circumstance, that the grandeur and beauty of the same object mix so intimately as scarce to be distinguished. But the beauty of colour comes in happily to enable us to make the distinction. For the emotion of colour unites with that of figure, not less intimately than grandeur does with either. Yet the emotion of colour is distinguishable from that of figure; and so is grandeur, attentively considered: though when these three emotions are blended together, they are scarce felt as different emotions.

Next, that grandeur is an emotion in every circumstance pleasant, appears from the following considerations. Magnitude or greatness, abstracted from all other circumstances, swells the heart and dilates the mind. We feel this to be a pleasant effect; and we feel no such effect in contracting the mind upon little objects. This may be illustrated by considering grandeur in an enemy. Beauty is an agreeable quality, whether in a friend or enemy; and when the emotion it raiseth is mixed with resentment against an enemy, it must have the effect to moderate our resentment. In the same manner, grandeur in an enemy, undoubtedly softens and blunts our resentment. Grandeur indeed may indirectly and by reflection produce an unpleasant effect. Grandeur in an enemy, like courage, may increase our fear, when we consider the advantage he hath over us by this quality. But the same indirect effect may be produced by many other agreeable qualities, such as beauty or wisdom.

The magnitude of an ugly object, serves, it is true, to augment our horror or aversion. But this proceeds not from magnitude separately considered. It proceeds from the following circumstance, that in a large object a great quantity of ugly parts are presented to view.

The same chain of reasoning is so obviously applicable to sublimity, that it would be losing time to show the application. Grandeur therefore and sublimity shall hereafter be considered both of them as pleasant emotions.

The pleasant emotion raised by large objects, has not escaped the poets:

—— He doth bestride the narrow world
Like a Colossus; and we petty men
Walk under his huge legs.

—*Julius Cæsar, act I. sc. 3*

CLEOPATRA: I dreamt there was an Emp'ror Antony;
  Oh such another sleep, that I might see
  But such another man!
  His face was as the heav'ns: and therein stuck
  A sun and moon, which kept their course and lighted
  The little O o' th' earth.
  His legs bestrid the ocean, his rear'd arm
  Crested the world.

—*Antony and Cleopatra, act 5. sc. 3*

—— Majesty
Dies not alone, but, like a gulf, doth draw
What's near it with it. It's a massy wheel
Fixt on the summit of the highest mount;
To whose huge spokes, ten thousand lesser things

> *Are mortis'd and adjoin'd; which when it falls,*
> *Each small annexment, petty consequence,*
> *Attends the boist'rous ruin.*
>
> —*Hamlet, act 3. sc. 8*

The poets have also made good use of the emotion produced by the elevated situation of an object.

> *Quod si me lyricis varibus inferes,*
> *Sublimi feriam sidera vertice.*
>
> —*Horace, Carm. l. 1. ode 1*

> *Oh thou! the earthly author of my blood,*
> *Whose youthful spirit, in me regenerate,*
> *Doth with a twofold vigour lift me up,*
> *To reach at victory above my head.*
>
> —*Richard II. act 1. sc. 4*

> *Northumberland, thou ladder wherewithal*
> *The mounting Bolingbroke ascends my throne.*
>
> —*Richard II. act 5. sc. 2*

ANTHONY: Why was I rais'd the meteor of the world,
  Hung in the skies and blazing as I travell'd,
  Till all my fires were spent; and then cast downward
  To be trod out by Cæsar?

> —*Dryden, All for love, act 1*

Though the quality of magnitude produceth a pleasant emotion, we must not conclude that the opposite quality of littleness produceth a painful emotion. It would be unhappy for man, were an object disagreeable from its being of a small size merely, when he is surrounded with so many objects of that kind. The same observation is applicable to elevation of place. A body placed high is agreeable; but the same body placed low, is not by that circumstance rendered disagreeable. Littleness, and lowness of place, are precisely similar in the following particular, that they neither give pleasure nor pain. And in this may visibly be discovered peculiar attention in fitting the internal constitution of man to his external circumstances. Were littleness, and lowness of place agreeable, greatness and elevation could not be so. Were littleness, and lowness of place disagreeable, they would occasion uninterrupted uneasiness.

The difference betwixt great and little with respect to agreeableness, is remarkably felt in a series when we pass gradually from the one extreme to the other. A mental progress from the capital to the kingdom, from that to Europe—to the whole earth—to the planetary system—to the universe, is extremely pleasant: the heart swells and the mind is dilated, at every step. The returning in an opposite direction is not positively painful, though our pleasure lessens at every step, till it vanish into indifference. Such a progress may sometimes produce a pleasure of a different sort, which arises from taking a narrower and narrower inspection. The same observation is applicable to a progress upward and downward. Ascent is pleasant because it elevates us. But descent is never painful: it is for the most part pleasant from a different cause, that it is according to the order of nature. The fall of a stone from any height, is extremely agreeable by its accelerated motion. I feel it pleasant to descend from a mountain: the descent is natural and easy. Neither is looking downward painful. On the contrary, to look down upon objects, makes part of the pleasure of elevation. Looking down becomes then only painful when the object is so far below as to create dizziness: and even when that is the case, we feel a sort of pleasure mixt with the pain. Witness Shakespear's description of Dover cliffs:

> —— *How fearful*
> *And dizzy 'tis, to cast one's eyes so low!*
> *The crows and choughs, that wing the midway-air,*
> *Shew scarce so gross as beetles. Half-way down*
> *Hangs one, that gathers samphire; dreadful trade!*
> *Methinks he seems no bigger than his head.*
> *The fishermen that walk upon the beach,*
> *Appear like mice; and yon tall anchoring bark*
> *Diminish'd to her cock; her cock, a buoy*
> *Almost too small for sight. The murmuring surge,*
> *That on th' unnumber'd idle pebbles chafes,*
> *Cannot be heard so high. I'll look no more,*

> *Lest my brain turn, and the deficient sight*
> *Topple down headlong.*
>
> —*King Lear*, act 4. sc. 6

An observation is made above, that the emotions of grandeur and sublimity are nearly allied. Hence it is, that the one term is frequently put for the other. I give an example. An increasing series of numbers produceth an emotion similar to that of mounting upward, and for that reason is commonly termed *an ascending series*. A series of numbers gradually decreasing, produceth an emotion similar to that of going downward, and for that reason is commonly termed *a descending series*. We talk familiarly of going up to the capital, and of going down to the country. From a lesser kingdom we talk of going up to a greater, whence the *anabasis* in the Greek language when one travels from Greece to Persia. We discover the same way of speaking in the language even of Japan[2]; and its universality proves it the offspring of a natural feeling.

The foregoing observation leads us naturally to consider grandeur and sublimity in a figurative sense, and as applicable to the fine arts. Hitherto I have considered these terms in their proper meaning, as applicable to objects of sight only: and I thought it of importance, to bestow some pains upon that article; because, generally speaking, the figurative sense of a word is derived from its proper sense; which will be found to hold in the present subject. Beauty in its original signification, is confined to objects of sight. But as many other objects, intellectual as well as moral, raise emotions resembling that of beauty, the resemblance of the effects prompts us naturally to extend the term *beauty* to these objects. This equally accounts for the terms *grandeur* and *sublimity* taken in a figurative sense. Every emotion, from whatever cause proceeding, that resembles an emotion of grandeur or elevation, is called by the same name. Thus generosity is said to be an elevated emotion, as well as great courage; and that firmness of soul which is superior to misfortunes, obtains the peculiar name of *magnanimity*. On the other hand, every emotion that contracts the mind and fixeth it upon things trivial or of no importance, is termed *low*, by its resemblance to an emotion produced by a little or low object of sight. Thus an appetite for trifling amusements, is called *a low taste*. The same terms are applied

---

2. Kempfer's history of Japan, b. v. ch. 2.

to characters and actions. We talk familiarly of an elevated genius, of a great man, and equally so of littleness of mind. Some actions are great and elevated, others are low and groveling. Sentiments and even expressions are characterised in the same manner. An expression or sentiment that raises the mind, is denominated *great* or *elevated*; and hence the sublime[3] in poetry. In such figurative terms, the distinction is lost that is made betwixt *great* and *elevated* in their proper sense; for the resemblance is not so entire, as to preserve these terms distinct in their figurative application. We carry this figure still farther. Elevation in its proper sense, includes superiority of place; and lowness, inferiority of place. Hence a man of superior talents, of superior rank, of inferior parts, of inferior taste, and such like. The veneration we have for our ancestors and for the ancients in general, being similar to the emotion produced by an elevated object of sight, justifies the figurative expression, of the ancients being raised above us, or possessing a superior place. And we may remark by the way, that as words are intimately connected with ideas, many, by this form of expression, are led to conceive their ancestors as really above them in place, and their posterity below them:

> *A grandam's name is little less in love*
> *Than is the doting title of a mother:*
> *They are as children but one step below.*
>
> —*Richard III.* act 4. sc. 5

The notes of the gamut, proceeding regularly from the blunter or grosser sounds to those which are more acute and piercing, produce in the hearer a feeling somewhat similar to what is produced by mounting upward; and this gives occasion to the figurative expressions, *a high note, a low note*.

---

3. Longinus gives a description of the sublime that is not amiss, though far from being just in every circumstance, "That the mind is elevated by it, and so sensibly affected, as to swell in transport and inward pride, as if what is only heard or read, were its own invention." But he adheres not to this description; in his 6th chapter, he justly observes, that many passions have nothing of the grand, such as grief, fear, pity, which depress the mind instead of raising it; and yet in chap. 8. he mentions Sappho's ode upon love as sublime: beautiful it is undoubtedly, but it cannot be sublime, because it really depresses the mind instead of raising it. His translator Boileaux is not more successful in his instances: in his 10th reflection, he cites a passage from Demosthenes and another from Herodotus as sublime, which have not the least tincture of that quality.

Such is the resemblance in feeling betwixt real and figurative grandeur, that among the nations on the east coast of Afric, who are directed purely by nature, the different dignities of the officers of state are marked by the length of the batoon each carries in his hand. And in Japan, princes and great lords shew their rank by the length and size of their sedan-poles[4]. Again, it is a rule in painting, that figures of a small size are proper for grotesque pieces; but that in an historical subject, which is grand and important, the figures ought to be as great as the life. The resemblance of these feelings is in reality so strong, that elevation in a figurative sense is observed to have the same effect even externally, that real elevation has:

K. Henry: This day is call'd the feast of Crispian.
He that outlives this day, and comes safe home,
Will stand a tiptoe when this day is nam'd,
And rouse him at the name of Crispian.

—*Henry V. act 4. sc. 8*

The resemblance in feeling betwixt real and figurative grandeur, is humorously illustrated by Addison in criticising upon the English tragedy. "The ordinary method of making an hero, is to clap a huge plume of feathers upon his head, which rises so high, that there is often a greater length from his chin to the top of his head, than to the sole of his foot. One would believe, that we thought a great man and a tall man the same thing. As these superfluous ornaments upon the head make a great man, a princess generally receives her grandeur from those additional incumbrances that fall into her tail. I mean the broad sweeping train that follows her in all her motions, and finds constant employment for a boy who stands behind her to open and spread it to advantage[5]." The Scythians, impressed with the fame of Alexander, were astonished when they found him a little man.

A gradual progress from small to great, is not less remarkable in figurative than in real grandeur or elevation. Everyone must have observed the delightful effect of a number of thoughts or sentiments, artfully disposed like an ascending series, and making impressions

---

4. Kempfer's history of Japan.
5. Spectator, No. 42.

stronger and stronger. Such disposition of members in a period, is distinguished by a proper name, being termed a *climax*.

In order to have a just conception of grandeur and sublimity, it is necessary to be observed, that within certain limits they produce their strongest effects, which lessen by excess as well as by defect. This is remarkable in grandeur and sublimity taken in their proper sense. The strongest emotion of grandeur is raised by an object that can be taken in at one view. An object so immense as not to be comprehended but in parts, tends rather to distract than satisfy the mind[6]. In like manner, the strongest emotion produced by elevation is where the object is seen distinctly. A greater elevation lessens in appearance the object, till it vanish out of sight with its pleasant emotion. The same is equally remarkable in figurative grandeur and elevation, which shall be handled together, because, as observed above, they are scarce distinguishable. Sentiments may be so strained, as to become obscure, or to exceed the capacity of the human mind. Against such licence of imagination, every good writer will be upon his guard. And therefore it is of greater importance to observe, that even the true sublime may be carried beyond that pitch which produces the highest entertainment. We are undoubtedly susceptible of a greater elevation than can be inspired by human actions the most heroic and magnanimous; witness what we feel from Milton's description of superior beings. Yet every man must be sensible of a more constant and pleasant elevation, when the history of his own species is the subject. He enjoys an elevation equal to that of the greatest hero, of an Alexander or a Cæsar, of a Brutus or an Epaminondas. He accompanies these heroes in their sublimest sentiments and most hazardous exploits, with a magnanimity equal to theirs; and finds it no stretch to preserve the same tone of mind for hours together, without sinking. The case is by no means the same in describing the actions or qualities of superior beings. The reader's imagination cannot keep pace with that of the poet; and the mind, unable to support itself in a strained elevation, falls as from a height; and the fall is immoderate like the elevation. Where this effect is not

---

6. It is justly observed by Addison, that perhaps a man would have been more astonished with the majestic air that appeared in one of Lysippus's statues of Alexander, though no bigger than the life, than he might have been with Mount Athos, had it been cut into the figure of the hero, according to the proposal of Phidias, with a river in one hand, and a city in the other.—*Spectator*, No. 415.

felt, it must be prevented by some obscurity in the conception, which frequently attends the description of unknown objects.

On the other hand, objects of sight that are not remarkably great or high, scarce raise any emotion of grandeur or sublimity; and the same holds in other objects. The mind is often roused and animated without being carried to the height of grandeur or sublimity. This difference may be discerned in many sorts of music, as well as in some musical instruments. A kettledrum rouses, and a hautboy is animating; but neither of them inspire an emotion of sublimity. Revenge animates the mind in a considerable degree; but I think it never produceth an emotion that can be termed *grand* or *sublime*; and I shall have occasion afterward to observe, that no disagreeable passion ever has this effect. I am willing to put this to the test, by placing before my reader the most spirited picture of revenge ever drawn. It is a speech of Antony wailing over the body of Cæsar.

> *Wo to the hand that shed this costly blood!*
> *Over thy wounds now do I prophesy,*
> *(Which, like dumb mouths, do ope their ruby lips,*
> *To beg the voice and utterance of my tongue),*
> *A curse shall light upon the kind of men;*
> *Domestic fury, and fierce civil strife,*
> *Shall cumber all the parts of Italy;*
> *Blood and destruction shall be so in use,*
> *And dreadful objects so familiar,*
> *That mothers shall but smile, when they behold*
> *Their infants quarter'd by the hands of war,*
> *All pity choak'd with custom of fell deeds.*
> *And Cæsar's spirit, ranging for revenge,*
> *With* Atè *by his side come hot from hell,*
> *Shall in these confines, with a monarch's voice,*
> *Cry* Havock, *and let slip the dogs of war.*
>
> —*Julius Cæsar*, act 3. sc. 4

When the sublime is carried to its due height and circumscribed within proper bounds, it inchants the mind and raises the most delightful of all emotions. The reader, ingrossed by a sublime object, feels himself raised as it were to a higher rank. When such is the case, it is not wonderful that the history of conquerors and heroes should be universally the favourite entertainment. And this fairly accounts for what I once erroneously suspected to be a wrong bias originally in human nature. The grossest acts of oppression and injustice, scarce blemish the character of a great conqueror. We notwithstanding warmly espouse his interest, accompany him in his exploits, and are anxious for his success. The splendor and enthusiasm of the hero transfused into the readers, elevate their minds far above the rules of justice, and render them in a great measure insensible of the wrong that is done:

> *For in those days might only shall be admir'd*
> *And valour and heroic virtue call'd;*
> *To overcome in battle, and subdue*
> *Nations, and bring home spoils with infinite*
> *Manslaughter, shall be held the highest pitch*
> *Of human glory, and for glory done*
> *Of triumph, to be styl'd great conquerors,*
> *Patrons of mankind, gods, and sons of gods.*
> *Destroyers rightlier called, and plagues of men.*
> *Thus fame shall be atchiev'd, renown on earth,*
> *And what most merits fame in silence hid.*
>
> —*Milton, b. 11*

The attachment we have to things grand or lofty may be thought to proceed from an unwearied inclination we have to be exalted. No desire is more universal than to be respected and honoured. Upon that account chiefly, are we ambitious of power, riches, titles, fame, which would suddenly lose their relish, did they not raise us above others, and command submission and deference[7]. But the preference given to things grand and sublime must have a deeper root in human nature. Many bestow their time upon low and trifling amusements, without showing any desire to be exalted. Yet these very persons talk the same language with the rest of mankind; and at least in their judgement, if not in their taste, prefer the more elevated pleasures. They acknowledge

---

[7]. Honestum per se esse expetendum indicant pueri, in quibus, ut in speculis, natura cernitur. Quanta studia decertantium sunt! Quanta ipsa certamina! Ut illi efferuntur lætitia, cum vicerint! Ut pudet victos! Ut se accusari nolunt! Ut cupiunt laudari! Quos illi lahores non perferunt, ut æqualium principes sint! *Cicero de frugibus.*

a more refined taste, and are ashamed of their own as low and groveling. This sentiment, constant and universal, must be the work of nature; and it plainly indicates an original attachment in human nature to every object that elevates the mind. Some men may have a greater relish for an object not of the highest rank: but they are conscious of the common nature of man, and that it ought not to be subjected to their peculiar taste.

The irregular influence of grandeur, reaches also to other matters. However good, honest, or useful, a man may be, he is not so much respected, as one of a more elevated character is, though of less integrity; nor do the misfortunes of the former affect us so much as those of the latter. I add, because it cannot be disguised, that the remorse which attends breach of engagement, is in a great measure proportioned to the figure that the injured person makes. The vows and protestations of lovers are an illustrious example of this observation; for these commonly are little regarded when made to women of inferior rank.

What I have said suggests a capital rule for reaching the sublime in such works of art as are susceptible of it; and that is, to put in view those parts or circumstances only which make the greatest figure, keeping out of sight everything that is low or trivial. Such judicious selection of capital circumstances, is by an eminent critic styled *grandeur of manner*[8]. The mind, from an elevation inspired by important objects, cannot, without reluctance, be forced down to bestow any share of its attention upon trifles. In none of the fine arts is there so great scope for this rule as in poetry, which, by that means, enjoys a remarkable power of bestowing upon objects and events an air of grandeur. When we are spectators, every minute object presents itself in its order. But in describing at second hand, these are laid aside, and the capital objects are brought close together. A judicious taste in selecting, after this manner, the most interesting incidents to give them an united force, accounts for a fact which at first sight may appear surprising, that we are more moved by a poetical narrative at second hand, than when we are spectators of the event itself in all its circumstanccs.

Longinus exemplifies the foregoing rule by a comparison of two passages[9]. The first from Aristæus is thus translated.

---

8. Spectator, No. 415.
9. Chap. 8. of the Sublime.

> *Ye pow'rs, what madness! how on ships so frail*
> *(Tremendous thought!) can thoughtless mortals sail?*
> *For stormy seas they quit the pleasing plain,*
> *Plant woods in waves and dwell amidst the main.*
> *Far o'er the deep (a trackless path) they go,*
> *And wander oceans in pursuit of wo.*
> *No ease their hearts, no rest their eyes can find,*
> *On heaven their looks, and on the waves their mind.*
> *Sunk are their spirits, while their arms they rear,*
> *And gods are wearied with their fruitless prayer.*

The other from Homer I shall give in Pope's translation.

> *Bursts as a wave that from the cloud impends,*
> *And swell'd with tempests on the ship descends.*
> *White are the decks with foam: the winds aloud*
> *Howl o'er the masts, and sing through every shrowd.*
> *Pale, trembling, tir'd, the sailors freeze with fears,*
> *And instant death on every wave appears.*

In the latter passage, the most striking circumstances are selected to fill the mind with the grand and terrible. The former is a collection of minute and low circumstances, which scatter the thought and make no impression. The passage at the same time is full of verbal antitheses and low conceit, extremely improper in a scene of distress. But this last observation is made occasionally only, as it belongs not to the present subject.

The following passage from the twenty-first book of the Odyssey, deviates widely from the rule above laid down. It concerns that part of the history of Penelope and her suitors, in which she is made to declare in favour of him who should prove the most dexterous in shooting with the bow of Ulysses.

> *Now gently winding up the fair ascent,*
> *By many an easy step, the matron went:*
> *Then o'er the pavement glides with grace divine,*
> *(With polish'd oak the level pavements shine);*
> *The folding gates a dazling light display'd,*
> *With pomp of various architrave o'erlay'd.*

> *The bolt, obedient to the silken string,*
> *Forsakes the staple as she pulls the ring;*
> *The wards respondent to the key turn round;*
> *The bars fall back; the flying valves resound.*
> *Loud as a bull makes hill and valley ring;*
> *So roar'd the lock when it releas'd the spring.*
> *She moves majestic through the wealthy room*
> *Where treasur'd garments cast a rich perfume;*
> *There from the column where aloft it hung,*
> *Reach'd, in its splendid case, the bow unstrung.*

Virgil sometimes errs against this rule. In the following passages minute circumstances are brought into full view; and what is still worse, they are described in all the sublimity of poetical description. *Æneid, L. 1. l. 214. to 219. L. 6. l. 176. to 182. L. 6. l. 212. to 231.* And the last, which is a description of a funeral, is the less excuseable, as it relates to a man who makes no figure in the poem.

The speech of Clytemnestra, descending from her chariot in the Iphigenia of Euripides, beginning of act 3. is stuffed with a number of low, common, and trivial circumstances.

But of all writers Lucan in this article is the most injudicious. The sea-fight betwixt the Romans and Massilians[10], is described so much in detail without exhibiting any grand or general view, that the reader is quite fatigued with endless circumstances, and never feels any degree of elevation. And yet there are some fine incidents, those for example of the two brothers, and of the old man and his son, which, separated from the rest, would affect us greatly. But Lucan once engaged in a description, knows no bounds. See other passages of the same kind, *L. 4. l. 292. to 337. L. 4. l. 750. to 765.* The episode of the sorceress Erictho, end of book 6. is intolerably minute and prolix.

To these I venture to oppose a passage from an old historical ballad:

> *Go, little page, tell Hardiknute*
> *That lives on hill so high*[11],
> *To draw his sword, the dread of faes,*
> *And haste to follow me.*

---

10. Lib. 3. beginning at line 567.
11. *High*, in the old Scotch language, is pronounced *hee*.

> *The little page flew swift as dart*
> *Flung by his master's arm.*
> *Come down, come down, Lord Hardiknute,*
> *And rid your king from harm.*

This rule is also applicable to other fine arts. In painting it is established, that the principal figure must be put in the strongest light; that the beauty of attitude consists in placing the nobler parts most in view, and in suppressing the smaller parts as much as possible; that the folds of the drapery must be few and large; that foreshortenings are bad, because they make the parts appear little; and that the muscles ought to be kept as entire as possible, without being divided into small sections. Everyone at present is sensible of the importance of this rule when applied to gardening, in opposition to the antiquated taste of parterres split into a thousand small parts in the strictest regularity of figure. Those who have succeeded best in architecture, have governed themselves by this rule in all their models.

Another rule chiefly regards the sublime, though it may be applied to every literary performance intended for amusement; and that is, to avoid as much as possible abstract and general terms. Such terms, perfectly well fitted for reasoning and for conveying instruction, serve but imperfectly the ends of poetry. They stand upon the same footing with mathematical signs, contrived to express our thoughts in a concise manner. But images, which are the life of poetry, cannot be raised in any perfection, otherwise than by introducing particular objects. General terms, that comprehend a number of individuals, must be excepted from this rule. Our kindred, our clan, our country, and words of the like import, though they scarce raise any image, have notwithstanding a wonderful power over our passions. The greatness of the complex object over-balances the obscurity of the image.

What I have further to say upon this subject, shall be comprehended in a few observations. A man is capable of being raised so much above his ordinary pitch by an emotion of grandeur, that it is extremely difficult by a single thought or expression to produce that emotion in perfection. The rise must be gradual and the result of reiterated impressions. The effect of a single expression can be but momentary; and if one feel suddenly somewhat like a swelling or exaltation of mind, the emotion vanisheth as soon as felt. Single expressions, I know, are often justly cited as examples of the sublime. But then their effect is nothing compared with a grand subject displayed in its capital parts. I shall give a few examples, that the reader may judge for himself. In the famous action of Thermopylæ, where Leonidas the Spartan King with his chosen band fighting for their country, were cut off to the last man, a saying is reported of Dieneces one of the band, which, expressing chearful and undisturbed bravery, is well intitled to the first place in examples of this kind. Talking of the number of their enemies, it was observed, that the arrows shot by such a multitude would intercept the light of the sun. So much the better, says he; for we shall then fight in the shade[12].

SOMERSET: Ah! Warwick, Warwick, wert thou as we are,
    We might recover all our loss again.
    The Queen from France hath brought a puissant power,
    Ev'n now we heard the news. Ah! couldst thou fly!
WARWICK: Why, then I would not fly.

—*Third part, Henry VI. act 5. sc. 3*

Such a sentiment from a man expiring of his wounds, is truly heroic, and must elevate the mind to the greatest height that can be done by a single expression. It will not suffer in a comparison with the famous sentiment *Qu'il mourut* in Corneille's Horace. The latter is a sentiment of indignation merely, the former of invincible fortitude.

In opposition to these examples, to cite many a sublime passage, enriched with the finest images, and dressed in the most nervous expressions, would scarce be fair. I shall produce but one instance from Shakespear, which sets a few objects before the eye, without much pomp of language. It works its effect, by representing these objects in a climax, raising the mind higher and higher till it feel the emotion of grandeur in perfection.

> *The cloud-capt tow'rs, the gorgeous palaces,*
> *The solemn temples, the great globe itself,*
> *Yea all which it inherit, shall dissolve,* &c.

The cloud-capt tow'rs produce an elevating emotion, heightened by the *gorgeous palaces*. And the mind is carried still higher and higher

---

12. Herodotus, book 7.

by the images that follow. Successive images, making thus stronger and stronger impressions, must elevate more than any single image can do.

I proceed to another observation. In the chapter of beauty it is remarked, that regularity is required in small figures, and order in small groups; but that in advancing gradually from small to great, regularity and order are less and less required. This remark serves to explain the extreme delight we have in viewing the face of nature, when sufficiently enriched and diversified by objects. The bulk of the objects seen in a natural landscape are beautiful, and some of them grand. A flowing river, a spreading oak, a round hill, an extended plain, are delightful; and even a rugged rock or barren heath, though in themselves disagreeable, contribute by contrast to the beauty of the whole. Joining to these, the verdure of the fields, the mixture of light and shade, and the sublime canopy spread over all; it will not appear wonderful, that so extensive a group of glorious objects should swell the heart to its utmost bounds, and raise the strongest emotion of grandeur. The spectator is conscious of an enthusiasm, which cannot bear confinement nor the strictness of regularity and order. He loves to range at large; and is so inchanted with shining objects, as to neglect slight beauties or defects. Thus it is, that the delightful emotion of grandeur, depends little on order and regularity. And when the emotion is at its height by a survey of the greatest objects, order and regularity are almost totally disregarded.

The same observation is applicable in some measure to works of art. In a small building the slightest irregularity is disagreeable. In a magnificent palace or a large Gothic church, irregularities are less regarded. In an epic poem we pardon many negligences, which would be intolerable in a sonnet or epigram. Notwithstanding such exceptions, it may be justly laid down for a rule, That in all works of art, order and regularity ought to be governing principles. And hence the observation of Longinus, "In works of art we have regard to exact proportion; in those of nature, to grandeur and magnificence."

I shall add but one other observation, That no means can be more successfully employed to sink and depress the mind than grandeur or sublimity. By the artful introduction of an humbling object, the fall is great in proportion to the former elevation. Of this doctrine Shakespear affords us a beautiful illustration, in a passage part of which is cited above for another purpose:

> *The cloud-capt tow'rs, the gorgeous palaces,*
> *The solemn temples, the great globe itself,*
> *Yea all which it inherit, shall dissolve,*
> *And like the baseless fabric of a vision*
> *Leave not a rack behind—*
>
> *—Tempest, act 4. sc. 4*

The elevation of the mind in the former part of this beautiful passage, makes the fall great in proportion when the most humbling of all images is introduced, that of an utter dissolution of the earth and its inhabitants. A sentiment makes not the same impression in a cool state, that it does when the mind is warmed; and a depressing or melancholy sentiment makes the strongest impression, when it brings down the mind from its highest state of elevation or chearfulness.

This indirect effect of elevation to sink the mind, is sometimes produced without the intervention of any humbling image. There was occasion above to remark, that in describing superior beings, the reader's imagination, unable to support itself in a strained elevation, falls often as from a height, and sinks even below its ordinary tone. The following instance comes luckily in view; for a better illustration cannot be given: "God said, Let there be light, and there was light." Longinus cites this passage from Moses as a shining example of the sublime; and it is scarce possible in fewer words, to convey so clear an image of the infinite power of the Deity. But then it belongs to the present subject to remark, that the emotion of sublimity raised by this image is but momentary; and that the mind, unable to support itself in an elevation so much above nature, immediately sinks down into humility and veneration for a being so far exalted above us groveling mortals. Everyone is acquainted with a dispute about this passage betwixt two French critics[13], the one positively affirming, the other as positively denying, it to be sublime. What I have opened, shows that both of them have reached the truth, but neither of them the whole truth. Everyone of taste must be sensible, that the primary effect of this passage is an emotion of grandeur. This so far justifies Boileau. But then everyone of taste must be equally sensible, that the emotion is merely a flash, which vanisheth instantly, and gives way to

---

13. Boileau and Huet.

the deepest humility and veneration. This indirect effect of sublimity, justifies Huet on the other hand, who being a man of true piety, and perhaps of inferior imagination, felt the humbling passions more sensibly than his antagonist. And even laying aside any peculiarity of character, Huet's opinion may I think be defended as the more solid; upon the following account, that in such images, the depressing emotions are the more sensibly felt, and have the longer endurance.

The straining an elevated subject beyond due bounds and beyond the reach of an ordinary conception, is not a vice so frequent as to require the correction of criticism. But false sublime is a rock which writers of more fire than judgement generally split on. And therefore a collection of examples may be of use as a beacon to future adventurers. One species of false sublime, known by the name of *bon bast*, is common among writers of a mean genius. It is a serious endeavour, by strained description, to raise a low or familiar subject above its rank; which instead of being sublime, never fails to be ridiculous. I am extremely sensible how prone the mind is, in some animating passions, to magnify its objects beyond natural bounds. But such hyperbolical description has its limits. If carried beyond the impulse of the propensity, the colouring no longer pleases: it degenerates into the burlesque. Take the following examples.

> S<small>EJANUS</small>:—— Great and high
> The world knows only two, that's Rome and I.
> My roof receives me not; 'tis air I tread,
> And at each step I feel my advanc'd head
> Knock out a star in heav'n.
>
> —*Sejanus, Ben Johnson, act 5*

A writer who has no natural elevation of genius, is extremely apt to deviate into bombast. He strains above his genius; and the violent effort he makes carries him generally beyond the bounds of propriety. Boileau expresses this happily:

> *L'autre à peur de ramper, il se perd dans la nue*[14].

---

14. L'art poet, chant. 1. 1. 58.

The same author Ben Johnson abounds in the bombast:

―――― *The mother,*
Th'expulsed Apicata, finds them there;
Whom when she saw lie spread on the degrees,
After a world of fury on herself,
Tearing her hair, defacing of her face,
Beating her breasts and womb, kneeling amaz'd.
Crying to heav'n, then to them; at last
Her drowned voice got up above her woes:
And with such black and bitter execrations,
(As might affright the gods, and force the sun
Run backward to the east; nay, make the old
Deformed Chaos rise again t' o'erwhelm
Them, us, and all the world) she fills the air,
Upbraids the heavens with their partial dooms,
Defies their tyrannous powers, and demands
What she and those poor innocents have transgress'd,
That they must suffer such a share in vengeance.

—*Sejanus,* act 5. sc. last

―――― *Lentulus, the man,*
If all our fire were out, would fetch down new,
Out of the hand of Jove; and rivet him
To Caucasus, should he but frown; and let
His own gaunt eagle fly at him to tire.

—*Catiline,* act 3

Can these, or such, be any aids to us?
Look they as they were built to shake the world,
Or be a moment to our enterprise?
A thousand, such as they are, could not make
One atom of our souls. They should be men
Worth heaven's fear, that looking up, but thus,
Would make Jove stand upon his guard, and draw
Himself within his thunder; which, amaz'd,
He should discharge in vain, and they unhurt.
Or, if they were, like Capaneus at Thebes,

> *They should hang dead upon the highest spires,*
> *And ask the second bolt to be thrown down.*
> *Why Lentulus talk you so long? This time*
> *Had been enough t' have scatter'd all the stars,*
> *T' have quench'd the sun and moon, and made the world*
> *Despair of day, or any light but ours.*

> —*Catiline, act 4*

This is the language of a madman:

GUILFORD: Give way, and let the gushing torrent come,
  Behold the tears we bring to swell the deluge,
  Till the flood rise upon the guilty world
  And make the ruin common.

> —*Lady Jane Gray, act 4. near the end*

Another species of false sublime, is still more faulty than bombast; and that is, to force an elevation by introducing imaginary beings without preserving any propriety in their actions; as if it were lawful to ascribe every extravagance and inconsistence to beings of the poet's creation. No writers are more licentious in this article than Johnson and Dryden.

> *Methinks I see Death and the furies waiting*
> *What we will do, and all the heaven at leisure*
> *For the great spectacle. Draw then your swords:*
> *And if our destiny envy our virtue*
> *The honour of the day, yet let us care*
> *To sell ourselves at such a price, as may*
> *Undo the world to buy us, and make Fate,*
> *While she tempts ours, to fear her own estate.*

> —*Catiline, act 5*

> ———— *The furies stood on hills*
> *Circling the place, and trembled to see men*
> *Do more than they: whilst Piety left the field,*
> *Griev'd for that side, that in so bad a cause*
> *They knew not what a crime their valour was.*

> *The Sun stood still, and was, behind the cloud*
> *The battle made, seen sweating to drive up*
> *His frighted horse, whom still the noise drove backward.*

—*Ibid. act. 5*

Osmyn: While we indulge our common happiness,
 He is forgot by whom we all possess,
 The brave Almanzor, to whose arms we owe
 All that we did, and all that we shall do;
 Who like a tempest that outrides the wind,
 Made a just battle ere the bodies join'd.
Abdalla: His victories we scarce could keep in view,
 Or polish 'em so fast as he rough drew.
Abdemelech: Fate after him below with pain did move,
 And Victory could scarce keep pace above.
 Death did at length so many slain forget,
 And lost the tale, and took 'em by the great.

—*Conquest of Granada, act. 2. at beginning*

> *The gods of Rome fight for ye; loud Fame calls ye,*
> *Pitch'd on the topless Apenine, and blows*
> *To all the under world, all nations,*
> *The seas and unfrequented deserts, where the snow dwells,*
> *Wakens the ruin'd monuments, and there*
> *Where nothing but eternal death and sleep is,*
> *Informs again the dead bones.*

—*Beaumont and Fletcher, Bonduca, act. 3. sc. 3*

I close with the following observation, That an actor upon the stage may be guilty of bombast as well as an author in his closet. A certain manner of acting, which is grand when supported by dignity in the sentiment and force in the expression, is ridiculous where the sentiment is mean, and the expression flat.

V

Motion and Force

That motion is agreeable to the eye without relation to purpose or design, may appear from the amusement it gives to infants. Juvenile exercises are relished chiefly upon that account.

If to see a body in motion be agreeable, one will be apt to conclude, that to see it at rest is disagreeable. But we learn from experience, that this would be a rash conclusion. Rest is one of those circumstances that are neither agreeable nor disagreeable. It is viewed with perfect indifference. And happy it is for mankind that the matter is so ordered. If rest were agreeable, it would disincline us to motion, by which all things are performed. If it were disagreeable, it would be a source of perpetual uneasiness; for the bulk of the things we see appear to be at rest. A similar instance of designing wisdom I have had occasion to explain, in opposing grandeur to littleness, and elevation to lowness of place[1]. Even in the simplest matters, the finger of God is conspicuous. The happy adjustment of the internal nature of man to his external circumstances, displayed in the instances here given, is indeed admirable.

Motion is certainly agreeable in all its varieties of quickness and slowness. But motion long continued admits some exceptions. That degree of continued motion which corresponds to the natural course of our perceptions, is the most agreeable[2]. The quickest motion is for an instant delightful. But it soon appears to be too rapid. It becomes painful, by forcibly accelerating the course of our perceptions. Slow continued motion becomes disagreeable for an opposite reason, that it retards the natural course of our perceptions.

There are other varieties in motion, beside quickness and slowness, that make it more or less agreeable. Regular motion is preferred before what is irregular, witness the motion of the planets in orbits nearly circular. The motion of the comets in orbits less regular, is less agreeable.

Motion uniformly accelerated, resembling an ascending series of numbers, is more agreeable than when uniformly retarded. Motion

---

1. See Chap. 4.
2. This will be explained more fully afterward, chap. 9.

upward is agreeable by the elevation of the moving body. What then shall we say of downward motion regularly accelerated by the force of gravity, compared with upward motion regularly retarded by the same force? Which of these is the most agreeable? This question is not easily solved.

Motion in a straight line is no doubt agreeable. But we prefer undulating motion, as of waves, of a flame, of a ship under sail. Such motion is more free, and also more natural. Hence the beauty of a serpentine river.

The easy and sliding motion of fluids, from the lubricity and incoherence of their parts, is agreeable upon that account. But the agreeableness chiefly depends upon the following circumstance, that the motion is perceived, not as of one body, but as of an endless number moving together with order and regularity. Poets struck with this beauty, draw more images from fluids than from solids.

Force is of two kinds; one quiescent, and one exerted by motion. The former, dead weight for example, must be laid aside; for a body at rest is not by that circumstance either agreeable or disagreeable. Moving force only belongs to the present subject; and though it is not separable from motion, yet by the power of abstraction, either of them may be considered independent of the other. Both of them are agreeable, because both of them include activity. It is agreeable to see a thing move: to see it moved, as when it is dragged or pushed along, is neither agreeable nor disagreeable, more than when at rest. It is agreeable to see a thing exert force; but it makes not the thing either agreeable or disagreeable, to see force exerted upon it.

Though motion and force are each of them agreeable, the impressions they make are different. This difference, clearly felt, is not easily described. All we can say is, that the emotion raised by a moving body, resembles its cause: it feels as if the mind were carried along. The emotion raised by force exerted, resembles also its cause: it feels as if force were exerted within the mind.

To illustrate this difference, I give the following examples. It has been explained why smoke ascending in a calm day, suppose from a cottage in a wood, is an agreeable object[3]. Landscape-painters are fond of this object, and introduce it upon all occasions. As the ascent is natural and without effort, it is delightful in a calm state of mind. It

---

3. Chap. 1.

makes an impression of the same sort with that of a gently-flowing river, but more agreeable, because ascent is more to our taste than descent. A fire-work or a *jet d'eau* rouses the mind more; because the beauty of force visibly exerted, is superadded to that of upward motion. To a man reclining indolently upon a bank of flowers, ascending smoke in a still morning is delightful. But a fire-work or a *jet d'eau* rouses him from this supine posture, and puts him in motion.

A *jet d'eau* makes an impression distinguishable from that of a waterfall. Downward motion being natural and without effort, tends rather to quiet the mind than to rouse it. Upward motion, on the contrary, overcoming the resistance of gravity, makes an impression of a great effort, and thereby rouses and enlivens the mind.

The public games of the Greeks and Romans, which gave so much entertainment to the spectators, consisted chiefly in exerting force, wrestling, leaping, throwing great stones, and such like trials of strength. When great force is exerted, the effort felt within the mind produces great life and vivacity. The effort may be such, as in some measure to overpower the mind. Thus the explosion of gun-powder, the violence of a torrent, the weight of a mountain, and the crush of an earthquake, create astonishment rather than pleasure.

No quality nor circumstance contributes more to grandeur than force, especially as exerted by sensible beings. I cannot make this more evident than by the following citations.

> —— *Him the almighty power*
> *Hurl'd headlong flaming from th' ethereal sky,*
> *With hideous ruin and combustion, down*
> *To bottomless perdition, there to dwell*
> *In adamantine chains and penal fire,*
> *Who durst defy th' Omnipotent to arms.*
>
> —*Paradise Lost, book 1*

> —— *Now storming fury rose,*
> *And clamour such as heard in heaven till now*
> *Was never; arms on armour clashing bray'd*
> *Horrible discord, and the madding wheels*
> *Of brazen chariots rag'd; dire was the noise*
> *Of conflict; over head the dismal hiss*

> *Of fiery darts in flaming vollies flew,*
> *And flying vaulted either host with fire.*
> *So under fiery cope together rush'd*
> *Both battles main, with ruinous assault*
> *And inextinguishable rage: all heav'n*
> *Resounded; and had earth been then, all earth*
> *Had to her centre shook.*
>
> —*Ibid, book 6*

> *They ended parle, and both address'd for fight*
> *Unspeakable; for who, though with the tongue*
> *Of angels, can relate, or to what things*
> *Liken on earth conspicuous, that may lift*
> *Human imagination to such height*
> *Of godlike pow'r? for likest gods they seem'd,*
> *Stood they or mov'd, in stature, motion, arms,*
> *Fit to decide the empire of great Heav'n.*
> *Now wav'd their fiery swords, and in the air*
> *Made horrid circles: two broad suns their shields*
> *Blaz'd opposite, while Expectation stood*
> *In horror: from each hand with speed retir'd,*
> *Where erst was thickest fight, th' angelic throng,*
> *And left large field, unsafe within the wind*
> *Of such commotion; such as, to set forth*
> *Great things by small, if Nature's concord broke,*
> *Among the constellations war were sprung,*
> *Two planets, rushing from aspéct malign*
> *Of fiercest opposition, in mid sky,*
> *Should combat, and their jarring spheres confound.*
>
> —*Ibid, book 6*

We shall now consider the effect of motion and force in conjunction. In contemplating the planetary system, what strikes us the most, is the spherical figures of the planets and their regular motions. The conception we have of their activity and enormous bulk is more obscure. The beauty accordingly of this system, raises a more lively emotion than its grandeur. But if we could imagine ourselves spectators comprehending the whole system at one view, the activity and irresistible force of these immense bodies would fill us with amazement. Nature cannot furnish another scene so grand.

Motion and force, agreeable in themselves, are also agreeable by their utility when employed as means to accomplish some beneficial end. Hence the superior beauty of some machines, where force and motion concur to perform the work of numberless hands. Hence the beautiful motions, firm and regular, of a horse trained for war. Every single step is the fittest that can be for obtaining the end proposed. But the grace of motion is visible chiefly in man, not only for the reasons mentioned, but also because every gesture is significant. The power however of agreeable motion is not a common talent. Every limb of the human body has a good and a bad, an agreeable and disagreeable action. Some motions are extremely graceful, others are plain and vulgar: some express dignity, others meanness. But the pleasure here, arising not singly from the beauty of motion, but from indicating character and sentiment, belongs to a different chapter[4].

I should conclude with the final cause of the relish we have for motion and force, were it not so evident as to require no explanation. We are placed here in such circumstances as to make industry essential to our well-being; for without industry the plainest necessaries of life are not to be obtained. When our situation therefore in this world requires activity and a constant exertion of motion and force, Providence indulgently provides for our welfare in making these agreeable to us. It would be a blunder in our nature, to make things disagreeable that we depend on for existence; and even to make them indifferent, would tend to make us relax greatly from that degree of activity which is indispensable.

---

4. Chap. 11. and 15.

VI

Novelty, and the unexpected appearance of objects

Of all the particulars that contribute to raise emotions, not excepting beauty, or even greatness, novelty hath the most powerful influence. A new spectacle attracts multitudes. It produceth instantaneously an emotion which totally occupies the mind, and for a time excludes all other objects. The soul seems to meet the strange appearance with a certain elongation of itself; and all is hushed in close contemplation. In some instances, there is perceived a degree of agony, attended with external symptoms extremely expressive. Conversation among the vulgar never is more interesting, than when it runs upon strange objects and extraordinary events. Men tear themselves from their native country in search of things rare and new; and curiosity converts into a pleasure, the fatigues, and even perils of travelling. To what cause shall we ascribe these singular appearances? The plain account of the matter follows. Curiosity is implanted in human nature, for a purpose extremely beneficial, that of acquiring knowledge. New and strange objects, above all others, excite our curiosity; and its gratification is the emotion above described, known by the name of *wonder*. This emotion is distinguished from *admiration*. Novelty where-ever found, whether in a quality or action, is the cause of wonder: admiration is directed upon the operator who performs anything wonderful.

During infancy, every new object is probably the occasion of wonder, in some degree; because, during infancy, every object at first is strange as well as new. But as objects are rendered familiar by custom, we cease by degrees to wonder at new appearances that have any resemblance to what we are acquainted with. A thing must be singular as well as new, to excite our curiosity and to raise our wonder. To save multiplying words, I would be understood to comprehend both circumstances when I hereafter talk of novelty.

In an ordinary train of perceptions where one thing introduces another, not a single object makes its appearance unexpectedly[1]. The

---

1. See chap. 1.

mind thus prepared for the reception of its objects, admits them one after another without perturbation. But when a thing breaks in unexpectedly and without the preparation of any connection, it raises a singular emotion known by the name of *surprise*. This emotion may be produced by the most familiar object, as when one accidentally meets a friend who was reported to be dead; or a man in high life, lately a beggar. On the other hand, a new object, however strange, will not produce this emotion if the spectator be prepared for the fight. An elephant in India will not surprise a traveller who goes to see one; and yet its novelty will raise his wonder. An Indian in Britain would be much surprised to stumble upon an elephant feeding at large in the open fields; but the creature itself, to which he was accustomed, would not raise his wonder.

Surprise thus in several respects differs from wonder. Unexpedtedness is the cause of the former emotion: novelty is the cause of the latter. Nor differ they less in their nature and circumstances, as will be explained by and by. With relation to one circumstance they perfectly agree, which is the shortness of their duration. The instantaneous production of these emotions in perfection, may contribute to this effect, in conformity to a general law, That things soon decay which soon come to perfection. The violence of the emotions may also contribute; for an ardent emotion, which is not susceptible of increase, cannot have a long course. But their short duration is occasioned chiefly by that of their causes. We are soon reconciled to an object, however unexpected; and novelty soon degenerates into familiarity.

Whether these emotions be pleasant or painful, is not a clear point. It may appear strange, that our own feelings and their capital qualities should afford any matter for a doubt. But when we are ingrossed by any emotion, there is no place for speculation; and when sufficiently calm for speculation, it is not easy to recal the emotion with sufficient accuracy. New objects are sometimes terrible, sometimes delightful. The terror which a tyger inspires is greatest at first, and wears off gradually by familiarity. On the other hand, even women will acknowledge, that it is novelty which pleases the most in a new fashion. At this rate, it should be thought, that wonder is not in itself pleasant or painful, but that it assumes either quality according to circumstances. This doctrine, however plausible, must not pass without examination. And when we reflect upon the principle of curiosity and its operations, a glimpse of light gives some faint view of a different theory. Our curiosity is never more thoroughly gratified, than by new and singular objects. That very gratification is the emotion of wonder, which therefore, according to the analogy of nature, ought always to be pleasant. And indeed it would be a great defect in human nature, were the gratification of so useful a principle unpleasant. But upon a more strict scrutiny, we shall not have occasion to mark curiosity as an exception from the general rule. A new object, it is true, that hath a threatening appearance, adds to our terror by its novelty. But from this experiment it doth not follow, that novelty is in itself disagreeable. It is perfectly consistent, that we should be delighted with an object in one view, and terrified with it in another. A river in flood swelling over its banks, is a grand and delightful object; and yet it may produce no small degree of fear when we attempt to cross it. Courage and magnanimity are agreeable; and yet when we view these qualities in an enemy, they serve to increase our terror. In the same manner, novelty has two effects clearly distinguishable from each other. A new object, by gratifying curiosity, must always be agreeable. It may, at the same time, have an opposite effect indirectly, which is, to inspire terror. For when a new object appears in any degree dangerous, our ignorance of its powers and qualities affords ample scope for the imagination to dress it in the most frightful colours[2]. Thus the first sight of a lion at some distance, may at the same instant produce two opposite feelings, the pleasant emotion of wonder, and the painful passion of terror. The novelty of the object, produces the former directly, and contributes to the latter indirectly. Thus, when the subject is analized, we find, that the power which novelty hath indirectly to inflame terror, is perfectly consistent with its being in every case agreeable. The matter may be put in a still clearer light by varying the scene. If a lion be first seen from a place of safety, the spectacle is altogether agreeable without the least mixture of terror. If again the first sight put us within reach of this dangerous animal, our terror may be so great as quite to exclude any sense of novelty. But this fact proves not that wonder is painful: it proves only that wonder may be excluded by a more powerful passion. And yet it is this fact, which, in superficial thinking, has thrown the subject into obscurity. I presume we may now boldly affirm, that wonder is in every case a pleasant emotion. This is acknowledged as to all new objects that appear inoffensive. And even as to objects that appear offensive, I urge that the same must hold so long as the spectator can attend to the novelty.

---

2. Essays on the Principles of Morality and Natural Religion, part 2. ess. 6.

Whether surprise be in itself pleasant or painful, is a question not less intricate than the former. It is certain, that surprise inflames our joy when unexpectedly we meet with an old friend: and not less our terror, when we stumble upon anything noxious. To clear this point, we must trace it step by step. And the first thing to be remarked is, that in some instances an unexpected object overpowers the mind so as to produce a momentary stupefaction. An unexpected object, not less than one that is new, is apt to sound an alarm and to raise terror. Man, naturally a defenceless being, is happily so constituted as to apprehend danger in all doubtful cases. Accordingly, where the object is dangerous, or appears so, the sudden alarm it gives, without preparation, is apt totally to unhinge the mind, and for a moment to suspend all the faculties, even thought itself[3]. In this state a man is quite helpless; and if he move at all, is as likely to run upon the danger as from it. Surprise carried to this height, cannot be either pleasant or painful; because the mind, during such momentary stupefaction, is in a good measure, if not totally, insensible.

If we then inquire for the character of this emotion, it must be where the unexpected object or event produceth less violent effects. And while the mind remains sensible of pleasure and pain, is it not natural to suppose, that surprise, like wonder, should have an invariable character? I am inclined however to think, that surprise has no invariable character, but assumes that of the object which raises it. Wonder is the gratification of a natural principle, and upon that account must be pleasant. There, novelty is the capital circumstance, which, for a time, is intitled to possess the mind entirely in one unvaried tone. The unexpected appearance of an object, seems not equally intitled to produce an emotion distinguishable from the emotion, pleasant or painful, that is produced by the object in its ordinary appearance. It ought not naturally to have any effect, other than to swell that emotion, by making it more pleasant or more painful than it commonly is. And this conjecture is confirmed by experience, as well as by language, which is built upon experience. When a man meets a friend unexpectedly, he is said to be agreeably surprised; and when he meets an enemy unexpectedly, he is said to be disagreeably surprised. It appears then, that the sole effect of surprise is to swell the emotion raised by the object. And this effect can be clearly explained. A tide of

---

3. Hence the Latin names for surprise, *torpor, animi stupor.*

connected perceptions, glides gently into the mind, and produceth no perturbation. An object on the other hand breaking in unexpectedly, sounds an alarm, rouses the mind out of its calm state, and directs its whole attention upon the object, which, if agreeable, becomes doubly so. Several circumstances concur to produce this effect. On the one hand, the agitation of the mind and its keen attention, prepare it in the most effectual manner for receiving a deep impression. On the other hand, the object by its sudden and unforeseen appearance, makes an impression, not gradually as expected objects do, but as at one stroke with its whole force. The circumstances are precisely similar, where the object is in itself disagreeable.

The pleasure of novelty is easily distinguished from that of variety. To produce the latter, a plurality of objects is necessary. The former arises from a circumstance found in a single object. Again, where objects, whether coexistent or in succession, are sufficiently diversified, the pleasure of variety is complete, though every single object of the train be familiar. But the pleasure of novelty, directly opposite to familiarity, requires no diversification.

There are different degrees of novelty, and its effects are in proportion. The lowest degree is found in objects that are surveyed a second time after a long interval. That in this case an object takes on some appearance of novelty, is certain from experience. A large building of many parts variously adorned, or an extensive field embellished with trees, lakes, temples, statues, and other ornaments, will appear new oftener than once. The memory of an object so complex is soon lost; of its parts at least, or of their arrangement. But experience teaches, that even without any decay of remembrance, absence alone will give an air of novelty to a once familiar object; which is not surprising, because familiarity wears off gradually by absence. Thus a person with whom we have been intimate, returning after a long interval, appears like a new acquaintance. Distance of place contributes to this appearance, not less than distance of time. A friend after a short absence in a remote country, has the same air of novelty as if he had returned after a longer interval from a place nearer home. The mind forms a connection betwixt him and the remote country, and bestows upon him the singularity of the objects he has seen. When two things equally new and singular are presented, the spectator balances betwixt them. But when told that one of them is the product of a distant quarter of the world, he no longer hesitates, but clings to this as the more singular. Hence the preference given to foreign luxuries and to foreign curiosities, which appear rare in proportion to their original distance.

The next degree of novelty, mounting upward, is found in objects of which we have some information at second hand. For description, though it contribute to familiarity, cannot altogether remove the appearance of novelty when the object itself is presented. The first sight of a lion occasions some wonder, after a thorough acquaintance with the corrected pictures or statues of that animal.

A new object that bears some distant resemblance to a known species, is an instance of a third degree of novelty. A strong resemblance among individuals of the same species, prevents almost entirely the effect of novelty; unless distance of place or someother circumstance concur. But where the resemblance is faint, some degree of wonder is felt; and the emotion rises in proportion to the faintness of the resemblance.

The highest degree of wonder ariseth from unknown objects that have no analogy to any species we are acquainted with. Shakespear in a simile introduces this species of novelty.

> *As glorious to the sight*
> *As is a winged messenger from heaven*
> *Unto the white upturned wondring eye*
> *Of mortals, that fall back to gaze on him*
> *When he bestrides the lazy-pacing clouds,*
> *And sails upon the bosom of the air.*
>
> —*Romeo and Juliet*

One example of this species of novelty deserves peculiar attention; and that is, when an object altogether new is seen by one person only, and but once. These circumstances heighten remarkably the emotion. The singularity of the condition of the spectator concurs with the singularity of the object, to inflame wonder to its highest pitch.

In explaining the effects of novelty, the place a being occupies in the scale of existence, is a circumstance that must not be omitted. Novelty in the individuals of a low class, is perceived with indifference, or with a very slight emotion. Thus a pebble, however singular in its appearance, scarce moves our wonder. The emotion rises with the rank of the object; and, other circumstances being equal, is strongest in the highest order of existence. A strange animal affects us more than a strange vegetable;

and were we admitted to view superior beings, our wonder would rise proportionably; and accompanying Nature in her amazing works, be completed in the contemplation of the Deity.

However natural the love of novelty may be, it is a matter of experience, that those who relish novelty the most, are careful to conceal its influence. This relish, it is true, prevails in children, in idle people, and in men of a weak mind. And yet, after all, why should one be ashamed for indulging a natural propensity? A distinction will explain this difficulty. No man is ashamed to own, that he loves to contemplate new or strange objects. He neither condemns himself nor is censured by others, for this appetite. But every man studies to conceal, that he loves a thing or performs an action, merely for its novelty. The reason of the difference will set the matter in a clear light. Curiosity is a natural principle directed upon new and singular objects, in the contemplation of which its gratification consists, without leading to any end other than knowledge. The man therefore who prefers anything merely because it is new, hath not this principle for his justification; nor indeed any good principle. Vanity is at the bottom, which easily prevails upon those who have no taste, to prefer things odd, rare, or singular, in order to distinguish themselves from others. And in fact, the appetite for novelty, as above mentioned, reigns chiefly among persons of a mean taste, who are ignorant of refined and elegant pleasures.

The gratification of curiosity, as mentioned above, is distinguished by a proper name, *viz. wonder*; an honour denied to the gratification of any other principle, emotion, or passion, so far as I can recollect. This singularity indicates some important final cause, which I endeavour to unfold. An acquaintance with the various things that may affect us, and with their properties, is essential to our well-being. Nor will a slight or superficial acquaintance be sufficient. It ought to be so deeply ingraved on the mind, as to be ready for use upon every occasion. Now, in order to a deep impression, it is wisely contrived, that things should be introduced to our acquaintance, with a certain pomp and solemnity productive of a vivid emotion. When the impression is once fairly made, the emotion of novelty, being no longer necessary, vanisheth almost instantaneously; never to return, unless where the impression happens to be obliterated by length of time or other means; in which case the second introduction is nearly as solemn as the first.

Designing wisdom is no where more legible than in this part of the human frame. If new objects did not affect us in a very peculiar manner, their impressions would be so slight as scarce to be of any use in life. On the other hand, did objects continue to affect us as deeply as at first, the mind would be totally ingrossed with them, and have no room left either for action or reflection.

The final cause of surprise is still more evident than of novelty. Self-love makes us vigilantly attentive to self-preservation. But self-love, which operates by means of reason and reflection, and impells not the mind to any particular object or from it, is a principle too cool for a sudden emergency. An object breaking in unexpectedly, affords no time for deliberation; and, in this case, the agitation of surprise is artfully contrived to rouse self-love into action. Surprise gives the alarm, and if there be any appearance of danger, our whole force is instantly summoned up to shun or to prevent it.

VII

Risible Objects

Such is the nature of man, that his powers and faculties are soon blunted by exercise. The returns of sleep, suspending all activity, are not alone sufficient to preserve him in vigor. During his waking hours, amusement by intervals is requisite to unbend his mind from serious occupation. The imagination, of all our faculties the most active, and not always at rest even in sleep, contributes more than any other cause to recruit the mind and restore its vigor, by amusing us with gay and ludicrous images; and when relaxation is necessary, such amusement is much relished. But there are other sources of amusement beside the imagination. Many objects, natural as well as artificial, may be distinguished by the epithet of *risible*, because they raise in us a peculiar emotion expressed externally by *laughter*. This is a pleasant emotion; and being also mirthful, it most successfully unbends the mind and recruits the spirits.

Ludicrous is a general term, signifying, as we may conjecture from its derivation, what is playsome, sportive, or jocular. *Ludicrous* therefore seems the genus, of which *risible* is a species, limited as above to what makes us laugh.

However easy it may be, concerning any particular object, to say whether it be risible or not; it seems difficult, if at all practicable, to establish beforehand any general character by which objects of this kind may be distinguished from others. Nor is this a singular case. Upon a review, we find the same difficulty in most of the articles already handled. There is nothing more easy, viewing a particular object, than to pronounce that it is beautiful or ugly, grand or little: but were we to attempt general rules for ranging objects under different classes, according to these qualities, we should find ourselves utterly at a loss. There is a separate cause which increases the difficulty of distinguishing risible objects by a general character. All men are not equally affected by risible objects; and even the same person is more disposed to laugh at one time than another. In high spirits a thing will make us laugh outright, that will scarce provoke a smile when we are in a grave mood. We must therefore abandon the thought of attempting general rules for distinguishing risible objects from others. Risible objects however are circumscribed within certain limits, which I shall suggest, without pretending to any degree of accuracy. And, in the first place, I observe, that no object is risible but what appears slight, little, or trifling. For man is so constituted as to be seriously affected with everything that is of importance to his own interest or to that of others. Secondly, with respect to the works both of nature and of art, nothing is risible but what deviates from the common nature of the subject: it must be some particular out of rule, some remarkable defect or excess, a very long visage, for example, or a very short one. Hence nothing just, proper, decent, beautiful, proportioned, or grand, is risible. A real distress raises pity, and therefore cannot be risible. But a slight or imaginary distress, which moves not pity, is risible. The adventure of the fulling-mills in Don Quixote is extremely risible; so is the scene where Sancho, in a dark night, tumbles into a pit, and attaches himself to the side by hand and foot, there hanging in terrible dismay till the morning, when he discovers himself to be within a foot of the bottom. A nose remarkably long or short is risible; but to want the nose altogether, far from provoking laughter, raises horror in the spectator.

From what is said, it will readily be conjectured, that the emotion raised by a risible object is of a nature so singular as scarce to find place while the mind is occupied with any other passion or emotion. And this conjecture is verified by experience. We scarce ever find this emotion blended with any other. One emotion I must except, and that is contempt raised by some sort of improprieties. Every improper act inspires us with some degree of contempt for the author. And if an improper act be at the same time risible and provoke laughter, of which blunders and absurdities are noted instances, the two emotions of contempt and of laughter unite intimately in the mind, and produce externally what is termed *a laugh of derision* or *of scorn*. Hence objects that cause laughter, may be distinguished into two kinds. They are either *risible* or *ridiculous*. A risible object is mirthful only; a ridiculous object is both mirthful and contemptible. The first raises an emotion of laughter that is altogether pleasant: the emotion of laughter raised by the other, is qualified with that of contempt; and the mixed emotion, partly pleasant partly painful, is termed *the emotion of ridicule*. I avenge myself of the pain a ridiculous object gives me by a laugh of derision. A risible object, on the other hand, gives me no pain: it is altogether pleasant by a certain sort of titillation, which is expressed externally by mirthful laughter. Ridicule will be more fully explained afterward: the present chapter is appropriated to the other emotion.

Risible objects are so common and so well understood, that it is unnecessary to consume paper or time upon them. Take the few following examples.

> FALSTAFF: I do remember him at Clement's inn, like a man made after supper of a cheese-paring. When he was naked, he was for all the world like a forked radish, with a head fantastically carved upon it with a knife.
>
> —*Second part, Henry IV. act 3. sc. 5*

The foregoing is of disproportion. The following examples are of slight or imaginary misfortunes.

> FALSTAFF: Go fetch me a quart of sack, put a toast in't. Have I liv'd to be carried in a basket, like a barrow of butcher's offal, and to be thrown into the Thames? Well, if I be serv'd such another trick, I'll have my brains ta'en out and butter'd, and give them to a dog for a new-year's gift. The rogues slighted me into the river with as little remorse as they would have drown'd a bitch's blind puppies, fifteen i' th' litter; and you may know by my size, that I have a kind of alacrity in sinking: if the bottom were as deep as hell, I should down. I had been drown'd, but that the shore was shelvy and shallow; a death that I abhor; for the water swells a man: and what a thing should I have been, when I had been swell'd? I should have been a mountain of mummy.
>
> —*Merry wives of Windsor, act 3. sc. 15*

> FALSTAFF: Nay, you shall hear, Master Brook, what I have suffer'd to bring this woman to evil for your good. Being thus cramm'd in the basket, a couple of Ford's knaves, his hinds, were call'd forth by their mistress, to carry me in the name of foul cloaths to Datchet-lane. They took me on their shoulders, met the jealous knave their master in the door, who ask'd them once or twice what they had in their basket. I quak'd for fear, left the lunatic knave would have search'd it; but Fate,

ordaining he should be a cuckold, held his hand. Well, on went he for a search, and away went I for foul cloaths. But mark the sequel, Master Brook. I suffer'd the pangs of three egregious deaths: first, an intolerable fright, to be detected by a jealous rotten bell weather; next, to be compass'd like a good bilbo, in the circumference of a peck, hilt to point, heel to head; and then to be stopt in, like a strong distillation, with stinking cloaths that fretted in their own grease. Think of that, a man of my kidney; think of that, that am as subject to heat as butter; a man of continual dissolution and thaw; it was a miracle to 'scape suffocation. And in the height of this bath, when I was more than half-stew'd in grease, like a Dutch dish, to be thrown into the Thames, and cool'd glowing hot, in that surge, like a horse-shoe; think of that; hissing hot; think of that, Master Brook.

—*Merry wives of Windsor, act 3. sc. 17*

VIII

Resemblance and Contrast

Having discussed those qualities and circumstances of single objects that seem peculiarly connected with criticism, we proceed, according to the method proposed in the chapter of beauty, to the relations of objects, beginning with the relations of resemblance and contrast.

Man being unavoidably connected with the beings around him, some acquaintance with their nature, their powers, and their qualities, is requisite for regulating his conduct. As an incentive to acquire a branch of knowledge so essential to our well-being, motives alone of reason and interest are not sufficient. Nature hath providently superadded curiosity, a vigorous propensity which never is at rest. It is this propensity which attaches us to every new object[1]; and in particular incites us to consider objects in the way of comparison, in order to discover their differences and resemblances.

Resemblance among objects of the same kind, and dissimilitude among objects of different kinds, are too obvious and familiar to gratify our curiosity in any degree. The gratification lies in discovering differences among things where resemblance prevails, and in discovering resemblances where difference prevails. Thus a difference in individuals of the same kind of plants or animals is deemed a discovery, while the many particulars in which they agree are neglected: and in different kinds, any resemblance is greedily remarked, without attending to the many particulars in which they differ.

A comparison however may be too far stretched. When differences or resemblances are carried beyond certain bounds, they appear slight and trivial; and for that reason will not be relished by one of taste. Yet such propensity is there to gratify passion, curiosity in particular, that even among good writers, we find many comparisons too slight to afford satisfaction. Hence the frequent instances among logicians, of distinctions without any solid difference: and hence the frequent instances among poets and orators, of similes without any just resemblance. With regard to the latter, I shall confine myself to one

---

1. See chap. 6.

instance, which will probably amuse the reader, being a citation not from a poet nor orator, but from a grave author writing an institute of law. "Our student shall observe, that the knowledge of the law is like a deep well, out of which each man draweth according to the strength of his understanding. He that reacheth deepest, seeth the amiable and admirable secrets of the law, wherein I assure you the sages of the law in former times have had the deepest reach. And as the bucket in the depth is easily drawn to the uppermost part of the water, (for *nullum elementum in suo proprio loco est grave*), but take it from the water it cannot be drawn up but with a great difficulty; so, albeit beginnings of this study seem difficult, yet when the professor of the law can dive into the depth, it is delightful, easy, and without any heavy burden, so long as he keep himself in his own proper element[2]." Shakespear with much wit ridicules this disposition to simile-making, by putting in the mouth of a weak man a resemblance much of a piece with that now mentioned.

> FLUELLEN: I think it is in Macedon where Alexander is porn: I tell you, Captain, if you look in the maps of the orld, I warrant that you sall find, in the comparisons between Macedon and Monmouth, that the situations, look you, is both alike. There is a river in Macedon, there is also moreover a river in Monmouth: it is call'd *Wye* at Monmouth, but it is out of my prains what is the name of the other river; but it is all one, 'tis as like as my fingers to my fingers, and there is salmons in both. If you mark Alexander's life well, Harry of Monmouth's life is come after it indifferent well; for there is figures in all things. Alexander, God knows, and you know, in his rages, and his furies, and his wraths, and his cholers, and his moods, and his displeasures, and his indignations, and also being a little intoxicates in his prains, did, in his ales and his angers, look you, kill his pest friend Clytus.
>
> GOWER: Our King is not like him in that, he never kill'd any of his friends.
>
> FLUELLEN: It is not well done, mark you now, to take the tales out of my mouth, ere it is made and finished. I speak but in figures, and comparisons of it: As Alexander kill'd his friend Clytus, being in his ales and his cups; so also Harry

---

2. Coke upon Lyttleton. p. 71.

> Monmouth, being in his right wits and his good judgments, turn'd away the fat knight with the great belly-doublet; he was full of jests, and gypes, and knaveries, and mocks: I have forgot his name.
>
> GOWER: Sir John Falstaff.
>
> FLUELLEN: That is he: I tell you, there is good men porn at Monmouth.
>
> —*K. Henry* V. *act 4. sc. 13*

Instruction, no doubt, is the chief end of comparison, but not the only end. In works addressed to the imagination, comparison may be employed with great success to put a subject in a strong point of view. A lively idea is formed of a man's courage, by likening it to that of a lion; and eloquence is exalted in our imagination, by comparing it to a river overflowing its banks, and involving all in its impetuous course. The same effect is produced by contrast. A man in prosperity, becomes more sensible of his happiness, by opposing his condition to that of a person in want of bread. Thus comparison is subservient to poetry as well as to philosophy; and with respect to both, the foregoing observation holds equally, that resemblance among objects of the same kind, and contrast among objects of different kinds, have no effect. Such a comparison neither tends to gratify our curiosity, nor to set the objects compared in a stronger light. Two apartments in a palace, similar in shape, size, and furniture, make separately as good a figure as when compared; and the same observation applies to two similar copartments in a garden. On the other hand, oppose a regular building to a fall of water, or a good picture to a towering hill, or even a little dog to a large horse, and the contrast will produce no effect. But resemblance, where the objects compared are of different kinds, and contrast where the objects compared are of the same kind, have each of them remarkably an enlivening effect. The poets, such of them as have a just taste, draw all their similes from things that in the main differ widely from the principal subject; and they never attempt a contrast but where the things have a common genus and a resemblance in the capital circumstances. Place together a large and a small sized animal of the same species, the one will appear greater the other less, than when viewed separately. When we oppose beauty to deformity, each makes a greater figure by the comparison.

Upon a subject not only in itself curious, but of great importance in all the fine arts, I must be more particular. That resemblance and contrast have an enlivening effect upon objects of sight, is made sufficiently evident; and that they have the same effect upon objects of the other senses, will appear from induction. Nor is this law confined to the external senses. Characters contrasted, make a greater figure by the opposition. Iago, in the tragedy of *Othello*, says

> *He hath a daily beauty in his life,*
> *That makes me ugly.*

The character of a fop, and of a rough warrior, are no where more successfully contrasted than by Shakespear.

HOTSPUR: My liege, I did deny no prisoners;
　　But I remember, when the fight was done,
　　When I was dry with rage, and extreme toil,
　　Breathless and faint, leaning upon my sword;
　　Came there a certain Lord, neat, trimly dress'd,
　　Fresh as a bridegroom; and his chin, new-reap'd,
　　Shew'd like a stubble-land at harvest-home.
　　He was perfumed like a milliner;
　　And 'twixt his finger and his thumb he held
　　A pouncet-box, which ever and anon
　　He gave his nose;—and still he smil'd, and talk'd;
　　And as the soldiers bare dead bodies by,
　　He call'd them untaught knaves, unmannerly,
　　To bring a slovenly, unhandsome corse
　　Betwixt the wind and his nobility.
　　With many holiday and lady terms
　　He question'd me: amongst the rest, demanded
　　My pris'ners, in your Majesty's behalf.
　　I then all smarting with my wounds; being gal'd
　　To be so pester'd with a popinjay,
　　Out of my grief, and my impatience,
　　Answer'd, neglectingly, I know not what:
　　He should, or should not; for he made me mad,
　　To see him shine so brisk, and smell so sweet,
　　And talk so like a waiting-gentlewoman,

> Of guns, and drums, and wounds; (God save the mark!)
> And telling me, the sovereign'st thing on earth
> Was parmacity, for an inward bruise;
> And that it was great pity, so it was,
> This villanous saltpetre should be digg'd
> Out of the bowels of the harmless earth,
> Which many a good, tall fellow had destroy'd
> So cowardly: and but for these vile guns,
> He would himself have been a soldier.—
>
> —*First part, Henry IV. act 1. sc. 4*

Passions and emotions are also inflamed by comparison. A man of high rank humbles the bystanders so far as almost to annihilate them in their own opinion. Cæsar, beholding the statue of Alexander, felt a great depression of spirits, when he reflected, that now at the age of thirty-two, when Alexander died, he had not performed one memorable action.

Our opinions also are much influenced by comparison. A man whose opulence exceeds the ordinary standard, is reputed richer than he is in reality; and the character of wisdom or weakness, if at all remarkable is generally carried beyond the truth.

The opinion a man forms of his present condition as to happiness or misery, depends in a great measure on the comparison he makes betwixt it and his former condition:

> *Could I forget*
> *What I have been, I might the better bear*
> *What I am destin'd to. I'm not the first*
> *That have been wretched: but to think how much*
> *I have been happier.*
>
> —*Southern's Innocent adultery, act 2*

The distress of a long journey makes even an indifferent inn pass current. And in travelling, when the road is good and the horseman well covered, a bad day may be agreeable, by making him sensible how snug he is.

The same effect is equally remarkable, when a man sets his condition in opposition to that of others. A ship tossed about in a storm, makes the spectator reflect upon his own security and ease, and puts these in the strongest light:

> *Suave, mari magno turbantibus æquora ventis,*
> *E terra magnum alterius spectare laborem,*
> *Non quia vexari quemquam est jocunda voluptas,*
> *Sed quibus ipse malis careas, quia cernere suave est.*
>
> —*Lucret. l. 2. principio*

A man in grief cannot bear mirth. It gives him a more lively notion of his unhappiness, and of course makes him more unhappy. Satan contemplating the beauties of the terrestrial paradise, breaks out in the following exclamation.

> *With what delight could I have walk'd thee round,*
> *If I could joy in ought, sweet interchange*
> *Of hill and valley, rivers, woods, and plains,*
> *Now land, now sea, and shores with forest crown'd,*
> *Rocks, dens, and caves! but I in none of these*
> *Find place or refuge; and the more I see*
> *Pleasures about me, so much more I feel*
> *Torment within me, as from the hateful siege*
> *Of contraries: all good to me becomes*
> *Bane, and in heav'n much worse would be my state.*
>
> —*Paradise Lost, book 9. l. 114*

GAUNT: All places that the eye of heaven visits,
    Are to a wise man ports and happy havens.
    Teach thy necessity to reason thus:
    There is no virtue like necessity.
    Think not the King did banish thee;
    But thou the King. Wo doth the heavier sit,
    Where it perceives it is but faintly borne.
    Go say, I sent thee forth to purchase honour;
    And not, the King exil'd thee. Or suppose,
    Devouring pestilence hangs in our air,
    And thou art flying to a fresher clime,
    Look what thy soul holds dear, imagine it

> To lie that way thou go'st, not whence thou com'st.
> Suppose the singing birds, musicians;
> The grass whereon thou tread'st, the presence-floor;
> The flow'rs, fair ladies; and thy steps, no more
> Than a delightful measure, or a dance.
> For gnarling Sorrow hath less power to bite
> The man that mocks at it, and sets it light.
> BOLINGBROKE: Oh, who can hold a fire in his hand,
> By thinking on the frosty Caucasus?
> Or cloy the hungry edge of Appetite,
> By bare imagination of a feast?
> Or wallow naked in December snow,
> By thinking on fantastic summer's heat?
> Oh, no! the apprehension of the good
> Gives but the greater feeling to the worse.
>
> —*King Richard II. act 1. sc. 6*

The appearance of danger gives sometimes pleasure, sometimes pain. A timorous person upon the battlements of a high tower, is seized with terror, which even the consciousness of security cannot dissipate. But upon one of a firm head, this situation has a contrary effect. The appearance of danger heightens by opposition the consciousness of security, and of consequence the satisfaction that arises from security. The feeling here resembles that above mentioned occasioned by a ship labouring in a storm.

This effect of magnifying or lessening objects by means of comparison, is so familiar, that no philosopher has thought of searching for a cause[3]. The obscurity of the subject may possibly have contributed to their silence. But luckily in treating other subjects, a principle is unfolded which will clearly account for this phenomenon. It depends upon the power of passion to model our opinion of objects for its gratification[4]. We have had occasion to see many illustrious examples of this singular power of passion; and the present subject affords an additional instance.

---

3. Practical writers upon the fine arts will attempt anything, being blind both to the difficulty and danger. De Piles, accounting why contrast is agreeable, says, "That it is a sort of war, which puts the opposite parties in motion." Thus, to account for an effect of which there is no doubt, any cause, however foolish, is made welcome.
4. Chap. 2. part 5.

That this is the cause, will evidently appear, by reflecting in what manner a spectator is affected, when a very large animal is for the first time placed beside a very small one of the same species. The opposition is the first thing that strikes the mind: the unusual appearance gives surprise; and the spectator, prone to gratify this emotion, conceives the opposition to be the greatest that can be. He sees, or seems to see, the one animal extremely little, and the other extremely large. The emotion of surprise arising from any unusual resemblance, serves equally to explain why at first view we are apt to think such resemblance more entire than it is in reality. And it must be observed, that the circumstances of more and less, which are the proper subjects of comparison, raise a perception so indistinct and vague as to facilitate the effect described. We have no mental standard of great and little, nor of the several degrees of any attribute; and the mind thus unrestrained, is naturally disposed to indulge its surprise to the utmost extent.

In exploring the operations of the mind, some of which are extremely nice and slippery, it is necessary to proceed with the utmost circumspection. And after all, seldom it happens that speculations of this kind afford any strong conviction. Luckily, in the present case, we have at hand facts and experiments that support the foregoing theory in a satisfactory manner. In the first place, the opposing a small object of one species to a great object of another, produces not, in any degree, that effect of contrast, which is so remarkable when both objects are of the same species. There is no difference betwixt these two cases that promiseth to have any influence, but only that the former is common, the latter rare. May we not then fairly conclude, that surprise from the rarity of appearance is the cause of contrast, when we find no such effect where the appearance is common? In the next place, if surprise be the sole cause of the effects that appear in making a comparison, it follows necessarily that these effects will vanish so soon as a comparison becomes familiar. This holds so unerringly, as to leave no reasonable doubt that surprise is the prime mover in this operation. Our surprise is great the first time a small lapdog is seen with a large mastiff: but when two such animals are constantly together, there is no surprise; and it makes no difference whether they be viewed separately or in company. We put no bounds to the riches of a man who has recently made his fortune. The opposition betwixt his present and past situation, or betwixt his present situation and that of others, is carried to an extreme. With regard to a family that for many generations hath enjoyed great wealth, the same false reckoning is not made. It is equally remarkable, that a simile loses its effect by repetition. A lover compared to a moth scorching itself at the flame of a candle, is a sprightly simile, which by frequent use has lost all force. Love cannot now be compared to fire, without some degree of disgust. It has been justly objected against Homer, that the lion is too often introduced in his similes. All the variety he is able to throw into them, is not sufficient to keep alive the reader's surprise.

To explain the influence of comparison upon the mind, I have chosen the simplest case, that of two animals of the same kind, differing in size only, seen for the first time. To complete the theory, other circumstances must be taken in. And the next supposition I shall make, is where both animals, separately familiar to the spectator, are brought together for the first time. In this case, the effect of magnifying and diminishing, will be found remarkably greater than in that first mentioned. And the reason will appear upon analyzing the operation. The first thing we feel is surprise, occasioned by the uncommon difference of two creatures of the same species. We are next sensible, that the one appears less, the other larger, than they did formerly. This new circumstance is a second cause of surprise, and augments it so as to make us imagine a still greater opposition betwixt the animals, than if we had formed no notion of them beforehand.

I shall confine myself to one other supposition, That the spectator was acquainted beforehand with one of the animals only, the lapdog for example. This new circumstance will vary the effect. Instead of widening the natural difference by enlarging in appearance the one animal and diminishing the other in proportion, the whole apparent alteration will rest upon the lapdog. The surprise to find it less than judged to be formerly, will draw the whole attention of the mind upon it; and this surprise will be gratified, by conceiving it to be of the most diminutive size possible. The mastiff in the mean time is quite neglected. I am able to illustrate this effect by a very familiar example. Take a piece of paper or linen reckoned to be a good white, and compare it with something of the same kind that is a pure white. The judgement we formed of the first object is instantly varied; and the surprise occasioned by finding it not so white as was thought, produceth a hasty conviction that it is much less white than it is in reality. Withdrawing now the pure white, and putting in its place a deep black, the surprise occasioned by this new circumstance carries our thought to the other extreme, and we now conceive the original object to be a pure white. Thus experience forces us to acknowledge, that our emotions have an influence even upon our eye-sight. This experiment leads to a general observation, That whatever is found more strange or beautiful than was expected, is judged to be more strange or beautiful than it is in reality. Hence it is a common artifice, to depreciate beforehand what we wish to make a figure in the eyes of others.

The comparisons employed by poets and orators, coincide with the last-mentioned supposition. It is always a known object that is to be aggrandized or lessened. The former is effectuated by likening it to some grand object, or by contrasting it with one that has the opposite character. To effectuate the latter, the method must be reversed. The object must be contrasted with something superior to itself, or likened to something inferior. The whole effect is produced upon the principal subject, which by this means is elevated above its rank or depressed below it.

In accounting for the effect that any unusual resemblance or contrast has upon the mind, I have hitherto assigned no other cause but surprise; and to prevent confusion and obscurity, I thought it proper to discuss that principle first. But surprise is not the only cause of the effect described. Another cause concurs, which operates perhaps not less powerfully than surprise. This cause is a principle in human nature that lies still in obscurity, not having been evolved by any writer, though its effects are extensive. As it is not distinguished by a proper name, the reader must be satisfied with the following description. No man who studies himself or others but must be sensible of a tendency or propensity in the mind to complete every work that is begun, and to carry things to their full perfection. This principle has little opportunity to display itself upon natural operations, which are seldom left imperfect. But in the operations of art it hath great scope; and displays itself remarkably, by making us persevere in our own work, and by making us wish for the completion of what is done by another. We feel a sensible pleasure when the work is brought to perfection; and our pain is not less sensible when we are disappointed. Hence our uneasiness, when an interesting story is broke off in the middle, when a piece of music ends without a close, or when a building or garden is left imperfect. The same principle operates in making collections, such as the whole works good and bad of any author. A certain person endeavoured to collect prints of all the capital paintings, and succeeded except as to a few. La Bruyere remarks, that an anxious search was made for these, not on account of their value, but to complete the set[5].

The final cause of this principle is an additional proof of its existence. Human works are of no significancy till they be completed. Reason is not always a sufficient counterbalance to indolence: and some principle over and above is necessary, to excite our industry, and to prevent our stopping short in the middle of the course.

We need not lose time in describing the co-operation of the foregoing principle with surprise in producing the effect that is felt upon the appearance of any unusual resemblance or contrast. Surprise first operates, and carries our opinion of the resemblance or contrast beyond the truth. The principle we have been describing carries us still farther; for being bent upon gratification, it forces upon the mind

---

5. The examples above given, are of things that can be carried to an end or conclusion. But the same uneasiness is perceptible with respect to things that admit not any conclusion; witness a series that has no end, commonly called *an infinite series*. The mind moving along such a series, begins soon to feel an uneasiness, which becomes more and more sensible, in continuing its progress without hope of an end.

An unbounded prospect doth not long continue agreeable; we soon feel a slight uneasiness, which increases with the time we bestow upon the prospect. An avenue without a terminating object, is one instance of an unbounded prospect; and we might hope to find the cause of its disagreeableness, if it resembled an infinite series. The eye indeed promises no resemblance: for the sharpest eye commands but a certain length of space, and there it is bounded, however obscurely. But the mind perceives things as they exist, and the line is carried on in idea without end; in which respect an unbounded prospect is similar to an infinite series. In fact, the uneasiness of an unbounded prospect differs very little in its feeling from that of an infinite series; and therefore we may reasonably presume, that both proceed from the same cause.

We next consider a prospect unbounded every way, as, for example, a great plain or the ocean viewed from an eminence. We feel here an uneasiness occasioned by the want of an end or termination precisely as in the other cases. A prospect, unbounded every way, is indeed so far singular, as at first to be more pleasant than a prospect that is unbounded in one direction only, and afterward to be more painful. But these circumstances are easily explained, without wounding the general theory: the pleasure we feel at first is a vivid emotion of grandeur, arising from the immense extent of the object; and to increase the pain we feel afterward for the want of a termination, there occurs a pain of a different kind, occasioned by stretching the eye to comprehend so wide a prospect; a pain that gradually increases with the repeated efforts we make to grasp the whole.

It is the same principle, if I mistake not, which operates imperceptibly with respect to quantity and number. Another's property indented into my field, gives me uneasiness, and I am eager to make the purchase, not for profit, but in order to square my field. Xerxes and his army, in their passage to Greece, were sumptuously entertained by Pythius the Lydian: Xerxes recompensed him with 7000 darics, which he wanted to complete the sum of four millions.

a conviction that the resemblance or contrast is complete. We need no better illustration than the resemblance that is fancied in some pebbles to a tree or an insect. The resemblance, however faint in reality, is conceived to be wonderfully perfect. This tendency to complete a resemblance acting jointly with surprise, carries the mind sometimes so far as even to presume upon future events. In the Greek tragedy, intitled, *Phineides*, those unhappy women, seeing the place where it was intended they should be slain, cried out with anguish, "They now saw their cruel destiny had condemned them to die in that place, being the same where they had been exposed in their infancy[6]."

This remarkable principle which inclines us to advance everything to its perfection, not only co-operates with surprise to deceive the mind, but of itself is able to produce that effect. Of this we see many instances where there is no place for surprise. The first instance I shall give is of resemblance. *Unumquodque eodem modo dissolvitur quo colligatum est*, is a maxim in the Roman law that has no foundation in truth. For tying and loosing, building and demolishing, are acts opposite to each other, and are performed by opposite means. But when these acts are connected by their relation to the same subject, their connection leads us to imagine a sort of resemblance betwixt them, which the foregoing principle makes us conceive to be as complete as possible. The next instance shall be of contrast. Addison observes[7], "That the palest features look the most agreeable in white; that a face which is overflushed appears to advantage in the deepest scarlet; and that a dark complexion is not a little alleviated by a black hood." The foregoing principle serves to account for these appearances. To make this evident, one of the cases shall suffice. A complexion, however dark, never approaches to black. When these colours appear together, their opposition strikes us; and the propensity we have to complete the opposition, makes the darkness of complexion vanish out of sight.

The operation of this principle, even where there is no ground for surprise, is not confined to opinion or conviction. So powerful is it, as to make us sometimes proceed to action in order to complete a resemblance or contrast. If this appear obscure, it will be made clear by the following instances. Upon what principle is the *lex talionis* founded other than to make the punishment resemble the mischief? Reason

---

6. Aristotle, poet. cap. 17.
7. Spectator. No, 265.

dictates, that there ought to be a conformity or resemblance betwixt a crime and its punishment; and the foregoing principle impells us to make the resemblance as complete as possible. Titus Livius, influenced by this principle, accounts for a certain punishment by a resemblance betwixt it and the crime, far too subtle for common apprehension. Speaking of Mettus Fuffetius, the Alban general, who, for treachery to the Romans, his allies, was sentenced to be torn to pieces by horses, he puts the following speech in the mouth of Tullus Hostilius, who decreed the punishment. "Mette Fuffeti, inquit, si ipse discere posses fidem ac fœdera servare, vivo tibi ea disciplina a me adhibita esset. Nunc, quoniam tuum insanabile ingenium est, at tu tuo supplicio doce humanum genus, ea sancta credere, quæ a te violata sunt. Ut igitur paulo ante animum inter Fidenatem Romanamque rem ancipitem gessisti, ita jam corpus passim distrahendum dabis[8]." By the same influence, the sentence is often executed upon the very spot where the crime was committed. In the *Electra* of Sophocles, Egistheus is dragged from the theatre into an inner room of the supposed palace, to suffer death where he murdered Agamemnon. Shakespear, whose knowledge of nature is not less profound than extensive, has not overlooked this propensity:

OTHELLO: Get me some poison, Iago, this night; I'll not expostulate with her, lest her body and her beauty unprovide my mind again; this night, Iago.
IAGO: Do it not with poison; strangle her in her bed, even in the bed she hath contaminated.
OTHELLO: Good, good: The justice of it pleases; very good.

—Othello, act 4. sc. 5

WARWICK: From off the gates of York fetch down the head,
Your father's head which Clifford placed there.
Instead whereof let his supply the room.
Measure for measure must be answered.

—Third Part of Henry VI. act 2. sc. 9

Persons in their last moments are generally seized with an anxiety to be buried with their relations. In the *Amynta* of Tasso, the lover, hearing

---

8. Lib. 1. sect. 28.

that his mistress was torn to pieces by a wolf, expresses a desire to die the same death[9].

Upon the subject in general, I have two remarks to add. The first concerns resemblance, which when too entire hath no effect, however different in kind the things compared may be. This remark is applicable to works of art only; for natural objects of different kinds, have scarce ever an entire resemblance. Marble is a sort of matter, very different from what composes an animal; and marble cut into a human figure, produces great pleasure by the resemblance. But let a marble statue be coloured like a picture, the resemblance is so entire as to produce no effect. At a distance, it appears a real person. We discover the mistake when we approach; and no other emotion is raised but surprise occasioned by the deception. The idea of resemblance is sunk into that of identity. The figure still appears to our eyes rather to be a real person than a resemblance of it; and we must make use of our reflection to correct the mistake. This cannot happen in a picture; for the resemblance can never be so entire as to disguise the imitation.

The other remark regards contrast. Emotions make the greatest figure when contrasted in succession. But then the succession ought neither to be precipitate nor immoderately slow. If too slow, the effect of contrast becomes faint by the distance of the emotions; and if precipitate, no single emotion has room to expand itself to its full size; but is stifled as it were in the birth by a succeeding emotion. The funeral oration of the Bishop of Meaux upon the Duchess of Orleans, is a perfect hotchpotch of chearful and melancholy representations following each other in the quickest succession. Opposite emotions are best felt in succession: but each emotion separately should be raised to its due pitch, before another be introduced.

What is above laid down, will enable us to determine a very important question concerning emotions raised by the fine arts, *viz.* What ought to be the rule of succession; whether ought resemblance to be studied or contrast? The emotions raised by the fine arts, are generally too nearly related to make a figure by resemblance; and for that reason, their succession ought to be regulated as much as possible by contrast. This holds confessedly in epic and dramatic compositions: and the best writers, led perhaps by a good taste more than by reasoning, have generally aimed at this beauty. In the same cantata, all the variety

---

9. Act iv. sc. 2.

of emotions that are within the power of music, may not only be indulged, but, to make the greatest figure, ought to be contrasted. In gardening there is an additional reason for the rule. The emotions raised by that art, are at best so faint, that every artifice should be used to give them their utmost strength. A field may be laid out in grand, sweet, gay, neat, wild, melancholy scenes. When these are viewed in succession, grandeur ought to be contrasted with neatness, regularity with wildness, and gaiety with melancholy; so as that each emotion may succeed its opposite. Nay it is an improvement to intermix in the succession, rude uncultivated spots as well as unbounded views, which in themselves are disagreeable, but in succession heighten the feeling of the agreeable objects. And we have nature for our guide, who in her most beautiful landscapes often intermixes rugged rocks, dirty marshes, and barren stony heaths. The greatest matters of music, have the same view in their compositions: the second part of an Italian song seldom conveys any sentiment; and, by its harshness, seems purposely contrived to give a greater relish for the interesting parts of the composition.

A small garden comprehended under a single view, affords little opportunity for this embellishment. Dissimilar emotions require different tones of mind; and therefore in conjunction can never make a good figure[10]. Gaiety and sweetness may be combined, or wildness and gloominess; but a composition of gaiety and gloominess is distasteful. The rude uncultivated copartment of furze and broom in Richmond garden, hath a good effect in the succession of objects; but a spot of this nature would be insufferable in the midst of a polished parterre or flower-plot. A garden therefore, if not of great extent, will not admit of dissimilar emotions. And in ornamenting a small garden, the safest course is to confine it to a single expression. For the same reason, a landscape ought also to be confined to a single expression. It is accordingly a rule in painting, That if the subject be gay, every figure ought to contribute to that emotion.

It follows from the foregoing train of reasoning, that a garden near a great city, ought to have an air of solitude. The solitariness again of a waste country ought to be contrasted in forming a garden; no temples, no obscure walks; but *jets d'eau*, cascades, objects active, gay, and splendid. Nay such a garden should in some measure avoid imitating

---

10. See chap. 2. part 4.

nature, by taking on an extraordinary appearance of regularity and art, to show the busy hand of man, which in a waste country has a fine effect by contrast.

It may be gathered from what is said above[11], that wit and ridicule make not an agreeable mixture with grandeur. Dissimilar emotions have a fine effect in a slow succession; but in a rapid succession, which approaches to co-existence, they will not be relished. In the midst of a laboured and elevated description of a battle, Virgil introduces a ludicrous image, which is certainly out of its place:

> *Obvius ambustum torrem Chorinæus ab ara*
> *Corripit, et venienti Ebuso plagamque ferenti*
> *Occupat os flammis: illi ingens barba reluxit,*
> *Nidoremque ambusta dedit.*
>
> —*Æn.* xii. 298

The following image is not less ludicrous, nor less improperly placed.

> *Mentre fan questi i bellici stromenti*
> *Perche debbiano tosto in uso porse,*
> *Il gran nemico de l'humane genti,*
> *Contra i Christiani i lividi occhi torse:*
> *E lor veggendo a le bell' opre intenti,*
> *Ambo le labra per furor si morse:*
> *E qual tauro ferito, il suo dolore*
> *Verso mugghiando e sospirando fuore.*
>
> —*Gierusal. cant. 4. st. 1*

It would however be too austere, to banish altogether ludicrous images from an epic poem. This poem doth not always soar above the clouds. It admits great variety; and upon occasions can descend even to the ground without sinking. In its more familiar tones, a ludicrous scene may be introduced without impropriety. This is done by Virgil[12] in describing a foot-race; the circumstances of which, not excepting

---

11. Ibid.
12. Æs. lib.5.

the ludicrous part, are copied from Homer[13]. After a fit of merryment, we are, it is true, the less disposed to the serious and sublime: but then, a ludicrous scene, by unbending the mind from severe application to more interesting subjects, may prevent fatigue, and preserve our relish entire.

---

13. Iliad, book 23. 1. 789.

IX

Of Uniformity and Variety

When I apply myself to explain uniformity and variety, and to show how we are affected by these circumstances, it appears doubtful what method ought to be followed. I foresee several difficulties in keeping close to my text; and yet by indulging a range, such as may be necessary for a clear view, I shall certainly incur the censure of wandering.—Be it so. One ought not to abandon the right track for fear of censure. The collateral matters, beside, that will be introduced, are curious, and not of slight importance in the science of human nature.

The necessary succession of perceptions, is a subject formerly handled, so far as it depends on the relations of objects and their mutual connections. But that subject is not exhausted; and I take the liberty to introduce it a second time, in order to explain in what manner we are affected by uniformity and variety. The world we inhabit is replete with things not less remarkable for their variety than their number. These, unfolded by the wonderful mechanism of external sense, furnish the mind with many perceptions, which, joined with ideas of memory, of imagination, and of reflection, form a complete train that has not a gap or interval. This tide of objects, in a continual flux, is in a good measure independent of will. The mind, as has been observed[1], is so constituted, "That it can by no effort break off the succession of its ideas, nor keep its attention long fixt upon the same object." We can arrest a perception in its course; we can shorten its natural duration, to make room for another; we can vary the succession by change of place or amusement; and we can in some measure prevent variety, by frequently recalling the same object after short intervals: but still there must be a succession, and a change from one thing to another. By artificial means, the succession may be retarded or accelerated, may be rendered more various or more uniform, but in one shape or other is unavoidable.

The rate of succession, even when left to its ordinary course, is not always the same. There are natural causes that accelerate or retard it considerably. The first I shall mention depends on a peculiar constitution

---

1. Locke, book 2. chap. 14.

of mind. One man is distinguished from another, by no circumstance more remarkably than the movement of his train of perceptions. A cold languid temper is accompanied with a slow course of perceptions, which occasions dulness of apprehension and sluggishness in action. To a warm temper, on the contrary, belongs a quick course of perceptions, which occasions quickness of apprehension and activity in business. The Asiatic nations, the Chinese especially, are observed to be more cool and deliberate than the Europeans: may not the reason be, that heat enervates by exhausting the spirits? A certain degree of cold, such as is felt in the middle regions of Europe, by bracing the fibres, rouses the mind, and produces a brisk circulation of thought, accompanied with vigour in action. In youth there is observable a quicker succession of perceptions, than in old age. Hence in youth a remarkable avidity for variety of amusements, which in riper years give place to more uniform and more sedate occupation. This qualifies men of middle age for business, where activity is required, but with a greater proportion of uniformity than variety. In old age, a slow and languid succession makes variety unnecessary; and for that reason, the aged, in all their motions, are generally governed by an habitual uniformity. Whatever be the cause, we may venture to pronounce, that heat in the imagination and temper, is always connected with a brisk flow of perceptions.

The natural rate of succession, depends also in some degree upon the particular perceptions that compose the train. An agreeable object, taking a strong hold of the mind, occasions a slower succession than when the objects are indifferent. Grandeur and novelty fix the attention for a considerable time, excluding all other ideas; and the mind thus occupied feels no vacuity. Some emotions, by hurrying the mind from object to object, accelerate the succession. Where the train is composed of connected objects, the succession is quick. For it is so ordered by nature, that the mind goes easily and sweetly along connected objects[2]. On the other hand, the succession must be slow where the train is composed of unconnected objects. An unconnected object, finding no ready access to the mind, requires time to make an impression. And that it is not admitted without a struggle, appears from the unsettled state of the mind for some moments after it is presented, wavering betwixt it and the former train. During this short period, one or other of the former objects will intrude, perhaps oftener than once, till the

---

2. See chap. 1.

attention be fixt entirely upon the new object. The same observations are applicable to ideas suggested by language. The mind can bear a quick succession of related ideas. But an unrelated idea, for which the mind is not prepared, takes time to make a distinct impression; and therefore a train composed of such ideas, ought to proceed with a slow pace. Hence an epic poem, a play, or any story connected in all its parts, may be perused in a shorter time, than a book of maxims or apothegms, of which a quick succession creates both confusion and fatigue.

Such latitude hath nature indulged in the rate of succession. What latitude it indulges with respect to uniformity we proceed to examine. The uniformity or variety of a train, so far as composed of external objects, depends on the particular objects that surround the percipient at the time. The present occupation must also have an influence; one is sometimes engaged in a multiplicity of affairs, sometimes altogether vacant. A natural train of ideas of memory is more circumscribed, each object being linked, by some connection, to what precedes and to what follows it. These connections, which are many and of different kinds, afford scope for a sufficient degree of variety; and at the same time prevent any excess that is unpleasant. Temper and constitution also have an influence here, as well as upon the rate of succession. A man of a calm and sedate temper, admits not willingly any idea but what is regularly introduced by a proper connection. One of a roving disposition embraces with avidity every new idea, however slender its relation be to those that go before it. Neither must we overlook the nature of the perceptions that compose the train; for their influence is not less with respect to uniformity and variety, than with respect to the rate of succession. The mind ingrossed by any passion, love or hatred, hope or fear, broods over its object, and can bear no interruption. In such a state, the train of perceptions must not only be slow, but extremely uniform. Anger newly inflamed eagerly grasps its object, and leaves not a cranny in the mind for another thought than of revenge. In the character of Hotspur, this state of mind is represented to the life; a picture remarkable for high colouring as well as for strictness of imitation:

> WORCESTER: Peace, cousin, say no more.
>   And now I will unclasp a secret book,
>   And to your quick-conceiving discontents
>   I'll read you matter, deep and dangerous;

> As full of peril and advent'rous spirit
> As to o'erwalk a current, roaring loud,
> On the unsteadfast footing of a spear.
>
> HOTSPUR: If he fall in, goodnight. Or sink or swim,
> Send danger from the east into the west,
> So honour cross it from the north to south;
> And let them grapple. O! the blood more stirs
> To rouse a lion than to start a hare.
>
> WORCESTER: Those same Noble Scots,
> That are your prisoners—
>
> HOTSPUR: I'll keep them all.
> By Heav'n, he shall not have a Scot of them:
> No, if a Scot would save his soul, he shall not;
> I'll keep them, by this hand.
>
> WORCESTER: You start away,
> And lend no ear unto my purposes;
> Those pris'ners you shall keep.
>
> HOTSPUR: I will; that's flat:
> He said, he would not ransom Mortimer:
> Forbad my tongue to speak of Mortimer:
> But I will find him when he lies asleep,
> And in his ear I'll holla *Mortimer*!
> Nay, I will have a starling taught to speak
> Nothing but *Mortimer*, and give it him,
> To keep his anger still in motion.
>
> WORCESTER: Hear you, cousin, a word.
>
> HOTSPUR: All studies here I solemnly defy,
> Save how to gall and pinch this Bolingbroke:
> And that same sword-and-buckler Prince of Wales,
> (But that I think his father loves him not,
> And would be glad he met with some mischance),
> I'd have him poison'd with a pot of ale.
>
> WORCESTER: Farewel, my kinsman, I will talk to you,
> When you are better temper'd to attend.
>
> *—First part, Henry* IV. *act 1. sc. 4*

Having viewed a train of perceptions as directed by nature, and the variations it is susceptible of from different necessary causes, we proceed to examine how far it is subjected to will; for that will hath some influence, more or less, is observed above. And first, the rate of succession may be retarded by insisting upon one object, and propelled by dismissing another before its time. But such voluntary mutations in the natural course of succession, have limits that cannot be extended by the most painful efforts. The mind circumscribed in its capacity, cannot, at the same instant, admit many perceptions; and when replete, it has no place for new perceptions till others be removed. For this reason, a voluntary change of perceptions cannot be instantaneous; and the time it requires sets bounds to the velocity of succession. On the other hand, the power we have to arrest a flying perception, is equally limited. The longer we detain any perception, the more difficulty we find in the operation; till, the difficulty becoming unsurmountable, we are forced to quit our hold, and to permit the train to take its usual course.

The power we have over this train as to uniformity and variety, is in some cases very great, in others very little. A train so far as composed of external objects, depends entirely on the place we occupy, and admits not more or less variety but by change of place. A train composed of ideas of memmory, is still less under our power. Objects which are connected, afford the mind an easy passage from one to another. They suggest each other in idea by the same means; and we cannot at will call up any idea that is not connected with the train[3]. But a train of ideas suggested by reading, may be varied at will, provided we have books in store.

This power which nature hath given us over our train of perceptions, may be greatly strengthened by proper discipline, and by an early application to business. Its improved strength is remarkable in those who have a strong genius for the mathematics: nor less remarkable in persons devoted to religious exercises, who pass whole days in contemplation, and impose upon themselves long and severe penances. It is not to be conceived, what length a habit of activity in affairs will carry some men. Let a stranger, or let any person to whom the sight is not familiar, attend the Chancellor of Great Britain through the labours but of one day, during a session of parliament: how great will be his astonishment! what multiplicity of law-business, what deep thinking, and what elaborate application to matters of government! The train of perceptions must in this great man be accelerated far beyond

---

3. See chap. I.

the common course of nature. Yet no confusion nor hurry; but in every article the greatest order and accuracy. Such is the force of habit! How happy is man, to have the command of a principle of action, that can elevate him so far above the ordinary condition of humanity[4]!

We are now ripe for considering a train of perceptions with respect to pleasure and pain: and to this speculation we must give peculiar attention, because it serves to explain the effects that uniformity and variety have upon the mind. A man is always in a pleasant state of mind, when his perceptions flow in their natural course. He feels himself free, light, and easy, especially after any forcible acceleration or retardation. On the other hand, the resistance felt in retarding or accelerating the natural course, excites a pain, which, though scarcely felt in small removes, becomes considerable toward the extremes. An aversion to fix on any single object for a long time, or to take in a multiplicity of objects in a short time, is remarkable in children; and equally so in men unaccustomed to business. A man languishes when the succession is very slow; and, if he grow not impatient, is apt to fall asleep. During a rapid succession, he hath a feeling as if his head were turning round. He is fatigued, and his pain resembles that of weariness after bodily labour. External objects, when they occasion a very slow or a very quick succession, produce a pain of the same sort with what it felt in a voluntary retardation or acceleration: which shows that the pain proceeds not from the violence of the action, but from the retardation or acceleration itself, disturbing that free and easy course of succession which is naturally pleasant.

But the mind is not satisfied with a moderate course alone: its perceptions must also be sufficiently diversified. Number without variety constitutes not an agreeable train. In comparing a few objects, uniformity is agreeable: but the frequent reiteration of uniform objects becomes unpleasant. One tires of a scene that is not diversified; and soon feels a sort of unnatural restraint when confined within a narrow range, whether occasioned by a retarded succession or by too great uniformity. An excess in variety is, on the other hand, fatiguing. This is even perceptible in a train composed of related objects: much more where the objects are unrelated; for an object, unconnected with the former train, gains not admittance without effort; and this effort, though scarce perceptible in a single instance, becomes by frequent

---

4. This chapter was composed in the year 1753.

reiteration exceeding painful. Whatever be the cause, the fact is certain, that a man never finds himself more at ease, than when his perceptions succeed each other with a certain degree, not only of velocity, but also of variety. Hence it proceeds, that a train consisting entirely of ideas of memory, is never painful by too great variety; because such ideas are not introduced otherwise than according to their natural connections. The pleasure of a train of ideas, is the most remarkable in a reverie; especially where the imagination interposes, and is active in coining new ideas, which is done with wonderful facility. One must be sensible, that the serenity and ease of the mind in this state, makes a great part of the enjoyment. The case is different where external objects enter into the train; for these, making their appearance without any order, and without any connection save that of contiguity, form a train of perceptions that may be extremely uniform or extremely diversified; which, for opposite reasons, are both of them painful.

Any acceleration or retardation of the natural run of perceptions, is painful even where it is voluntary. And it is equally painful to alter that degree of variety which nature requires. Contemplation, when the mind is long attached to one thing, soon becomes painful by restraining the free range of perception. Curiosity and the prospect of advantage from useful discoveries, may engage a man to prosecute his studies, notwithstanding the pain they give him; and a habit of close attention, formed by frequent exercise, may soften the pain. But it is deeply felt by the bulk of mankind, and produceth in them an aversion to all abstract sciences. In any profession or calling, a train of operation that is simple and reiterated without intermission, makes the operator languish, and lose his vigor. He complains neither of too great labour nor of too little action; but regrets the want of variety, and his being obliged to do the same thing over and over. Where the operation is sufficiently varied, the mind retains its vigor, and is pleased with its condition. Actions again create an uneasiness when excessive in number or variety, though in every other respect agreeable. This uneasiness is extremely remarkable, where strict attention must be given, at the same time, to a number of different things. Thus a throng of business in law, in physic, or in traffick, distresseth and distracts the mind, unless where a habit of application is acquired by long and constant exercise. The excessive variety is the distressing circumstance; and the mind suffers grievously by being kept constantly upon the stretch.

With relation to involuntary causes disturbing that degree of variety which nature requires, a slight pain affecting one part of the body without variation, becomes, by its constancy and long duration, almost insupportable. The patient, sensible that the pain is not increased in degree, complains of its constancy more than of its severity, that it ingrosses his whole thoughts, and gives admission to no other object. Pain, of all feelings, seizes the attention with the greatest force; and the mind, after fruitless efforts to turn its view to objects more agreeable, must abandon itself to its tormentor. A shifting pain gives less uneasiness, because change of place contributes to variety. An intermitting pain, suffering other objects to intervene, is not increased by reiteration. Again, any single colour or sound often returning, becomes disagreeable; as may be observed in viewing a train of similar apartments painted with the same colour, and in hearing the prolonged tollings of a bell. Colour and sound varied within certain limits, though without any order, are agreeable; witness a field variegated with many colours of plants and flowers, and the various notes of birds in a thicket. Increase the number or variety, and the feeling becomes unpleasant. Thus a great variety of colours, crowded upon a small canvas or in quick succession, create an uneasy feeling, which is prevented by putting the colours at a greater distance either of place or time. A number of voices in a crowded assembly, a number of animals collected in a market, produce an unpleasant emotion; though a few of them together, or all of them in a moderate succession, would be agreeable. And because of the same excess in variety, a number of pains felt in different parts of the body, at the same instant or in a rapid succession, make an exquisite torture.

The foregoing doctrine concerning the train of perceptions, and the pleasure or pain resulting from that train in different circumstances, will be confirmed by attending to the final cause of these effects. And as I am sensible that the mind, inflamed with speculations of this kind so highly interesting, is beyond measure disposed to conviction, I shall be watchful to admit no argument nor remark but what appears solidly founded. With this caution I proceed to the inquiry. It is occasionally observed above, that persons of a phlegmatic temperament, having a sluggish train of perceptions, are indisposed to action; and that activity constantly accompanies a brisk motion of perceptions. To ascertain this fact, a man need not go abroad for experiments. Reflecting upon things passing in his own mind, he will find, that a brisk circulation of thought constantly prompts him to action; and that he is averse to action when his perceptions languish in their course. But man by nature is formed for action, and he must be active in order to be happy. Nature therefore hath kindly provided against indolence, by annexing pleasure to a moderate course of perceptions, and by making every remarkable retardation painful. A slow course of perceptions is attended with another bad effect. Man in a few capital cases is governed by propensity or instinct; but in matters that admit deliberation and choice, reason is assigned him for a guide. Now, as reasoning requires often a great compass of ideas, their succession ought to be so quick, as readily to furnish every motive that may be necessary for mature deliberation. In a languid succession, motives will often occur after action is commenced, when it is too late to retreat.

Nature hath guarded man, her favourite, against a succession too rapid, not less carefully than against one too slow. Both are equally painful, though the pain is not the same in both. Many are the good effects of this contrivance. In the first place, as the bodily faculties are by certain painful sensations confined within proper limits, beyond which it would be dangerous to strain the tender organs, Nature, in like manner, is equally provident with respect to the nobler faculties of the mind. Thus the pain of an accelerated course of perceptions, is Nature's admonition to relax our pace, and to admit a more gentle exertion of thought. Another valuable purpose may be gathered, from considering in what manner objects are imprinted upon the mind. To make such an impression as to give the memory fast hold of the object, time is required, even where attention is the greatest; and a moderate degree of attention, which is the common case, must be continued still longer to produce the same effect. A rapid succession then must prevent objects from making impressions so deep as to be of real service in life; and Nature accordingly for the sake of memory, has by a painful feeling guarded against a rapid succession. But a still more valuable purpose is answered by this contrivance. As, on the one hand, a sluggish course of perceptions indisposeth to action; so, on the other, a course too rapid impels to rash and precipitant action. Prudent conduct is the child of deliberation and clear conception, for which there is no place in a rapid course of thought. Nature therefore, taking measures for prudent conduct, has guarded us effectually from precipitancy of thought, by making it painful.

Nature not only provides against a succession too slow or too quick, but makes the middle course extremely pleasant. Nor is this middle course confined within narrow bounds. Every man can naturally without pain accelerate or retard in some degree the rate of his perceptions; and he can do this in a still greater degree by the force of habit. Thus a habit of contemplation annihilates the pain of a retarded course of perceptions; and a busy life, after long practice, makes acceleration pleasant.

Concerning the final cause of our taste for variety, it will be considered, that human affairs, complex by variety as well as number, require the distributing our attention and activity, in measure and proportion. Nature therefore, to secure a just distribution corresponding to the variety of human affairs, has made too great uniformity or too great variety in the course of our perceptions equally unpleasant. And indeed, were we addicted to either extreme, our internal constitution would be ill suited to our external circumstances. At the same time, where a frequent reiteration of the same operation is required, as in several manufactures, or a quick circulation, as in law or physic, Nature, attentive to all our wants, hath also provided for these cases. She hath implanted in the breast of every person, an efficacious principle, which leads to habit. By an obstinate perseverance in the same occupation, the pain of excessive uniformity vanisheth; and by the like perseverance in a quick circulation of different occupations, the pain of excessive variety vanisheth. And thus we come to take delight in several occupations, that by nature, without habit, are not a little disgustful.

A middle rate also in our train of perceptions betwixt uniformity and variety, is not less pleasant, than betwixt quickness and slowness. The mind of man thus constituted, is wonderfully adapted to the course of human affairs, which are continually changing, but not without connection. It is equally adapted to the acquisition of knowledge, which results chiefly from discovering resemblances among differing objects, and differences among resembling objects. Such occupation, even abstracting from the knowledge we acquire, is in itself delightful, by preserving a middle rate betwixt too great uniformity and too great variety.

We are now arrived at the chief purpose of the present chapter; and that is to examine how far uniformity or variety ought to be studied in the fine arts. And the knowledge we have obtained, will even at first view suggest a general observation, That in every work of art, it must be agreeable to find that degree of variety which corresponds to the natural course of our perceptions; and that an excess in variety or in uniformity, must be disagreeable by varying that natural course. For this reason, works of art admit more or less variety according to the nature of the subject. In a picture that strongly attaches the spectator to a single object, the mind relisheth not a multiplicity of figures or of ornaments. A picture again representing a gay subject, admits great variety of figures and ornaments; because these are agreeable to the mind in a chearful tone. The same observation is applicable to poetry and to music.

It must at the same time be remarked, that one can bear a greater variety of natural objects than of objects in a picture; and a greater variety in a picture than in a description. A real object presented to the view, makes an impression more readily than when represented in colours, and much more readily than when represented in words. Hence it is, that the profuse variety of objects in some natural landscapes, neither breed confusion nor fatigue. And for the same reason, there is place for greater variety of ornament in a picture, than in a poem.

From these general observations I proceed to particulars. In works exposed continually to public view, variety ought to be studied. It is a rule accordingly in sculpture, to contrast the different limbs of a statue, in order to give it all the variety possible. Though the cone in a single view be more beautiful than the pyramid; yet a pyramidal steeple, because of its variety, is justly preferred. For the same reason, the oval in compositions is preferred before the circle; and painters, in copying buildings or any regular work, endeavour to give an air of variety by representing the subject in an angular view: we are pleased with the variety without losing sight of the regularity. In a landscape representing animals, those especially of the same kind, contrast ought to prevail. To draw one sleeping another awake, one sitting another in motion, one moving toward the spectator another from him, is the life of such a performance.

In every sort of writing intended for amusement, variety is necessary in proportion to the length of the work. Want of variety is sensibly felt in Davila's history of the civil wars of France. The events are indeed important and various: but the reader languisheth by a tiresome uniformity of character; every person engaged being figured a consummate politician, governed by interest only. It is hard to say, whether Ovid disgusts more by too great variety or too great uniformity. His stories are all of the same kind, concluding invariably with the transformation of one being into another. So far he is tiresome with excess in uniformity. He also fatigues with excess in variety, by hurrying his reader incessantly from story to story. Ariosto is still more fatiguing than Ovid, by exceeding the just bounds of variety. Not satisfied, like Ovid, with a succession in his stories, he distracts the reader by jumbling together a multitude of unconnected events. Nor is the Orlando Furioso less tiresome by its uniformity than the Metamorphoses, though in a different manner. After a story is brought to a crisis, the reader, intent upon the catastrophe, is suddenly snatched away to a new story, which is little regarded so long as the mind is occupied with the former. This tantalizing method, from which the author never once swerves during the course of a long work, beside its uniformity, hath another bad effect: it prevents that sympathy which is raised by an interesting event when the reader meets with no interruption.

The emotions produced by our perceptions in a train, have been little considered, and less understood. The subject therefore required an elaborate discussion. It may surprise some readers, to find variety treated as only contributing to make a train of perceptions pleasant, when it is commonly held to be a necessary ingredient in beauty of whatever kind; according to the definition, "That beauty consists in uniformity amidst variety." But after the subject is explained and illustrated as above, I presume it will be evident, that this definition, however applicable to one or other species, is far from being just with respect to beauty in general. Variety contributes no share to the beauty of a moral action, nor of a mathematical theorem; and numberless are the beautiful objects of sight that have little or no variety in them. A globe, the most uniform of all figures, is of all the most beautiful; and a square, though more beautiful than a trapezium, hath less variety in its constituent parts. The foregoing definition, which at best is but obscurely expressed, is only applicable to a number of objects in a group or in succession, among which indeed a due mixture of uniformity and variety is always agreeable, provided the particular objects, separately considered, be in any degree beautiful. Uniformity amidst variety among ugly objects, affords no pleasure. This circumstance is totally omitted in the definition; and indeed to have mentioned it, would at first glance show the definition to be imperfect. To define beauty as arising from beautiful objects blended together in a due proportion of uniformity and variety, would be too gross to pass current; as nothing can be more gross, than to employ in a definition the very term that is proposed to be explained.

Appendix to Chap. IX

Concerning the works of nature.

In natural objects, whether we regard their internal or external structure, beauty and design are equally conspicuous. We shall begin with the outside of nature, as what first presents itself.

The figure of an organic body, is generally regular. The trunk of a tree, its branches, and their ramifications, are nearly round, and form a series regularly decreasing from the trunk to the smallest fibre. Uniformity is no where more remarkable than in the leaves, which, in the same species, have all the same colour, size, and shape. The seeds and fruits are all regular figures, approaching for the most part to the globular form. Hence a plant, especially of the larger kind, with its trunk, branches, foliage, and fruit, is a delightful object.

In an animal, the trunk, which is much larger than the other parts, occupies a chief place. Its shape, like that of the stem of plants, is nearly round; a figure which of all is the most agreeable. Its two sides are precisely similar. Several of the under parts go off in pairs; and the two individuals of each pair are accurately uniform. The single parts are placed in the middle. The limbs, bearing a certain proportion to the trunk, serve to support it, and to give it a proper elevation. Upon one extremity are disposed the neck and head, in the direction of the trunk. The head being the chief part, possesses with great propriety the chief place. Hence, the beauty of the whole figure, is the result of many equal and proportional parts orderly disposed; and the smallest variation in number, equality, proportion, or order, never fails to produce a perception of ugliness and deformity.

Nature in no particular seems more profuse of ornament, than in the beautiful colouring of her works. The flowers of plants, the furs of beasts, and the feathers of birds, vie with each other in the beauty of their colours, which in lustre as well as in harmony are beyond the power of imitation. Of all natural appearances, the colouring of the human face is the most exquisite. It is the strongest instance of the ineffable art of nature, in adapting and proportioning its colours to the magnitude, figure, and position, of the parts. In a word, colour seems to live in nature only, and to languish under the finest touches of art.

When we examine the internal structure of a plant or animal, a wonderful subtilty of mechanism is displayed. Man, in his mechanical operations, is confined to the surface of bodies. But the operations of nature are exerted through the whole substance, so as to reach even the elementary parts. Thus the body of an animal, and of a plant, are composed of certain great vessels; these of smaller; and these again of still smaller, without end so far we can discover. This power of diffusing mechanism through the most intimate parts, is peculiar to nature; and distinguishes her operations, most remarkably, from every work of art. Such texture, continued from the grosser parts to the most minute, preserves all along the strictest regularity. The fibres of plants are a bundle of cylindric canals, lying in the same direction, and parallel or nearly parallel to each other. In some instances, a most accurate arrangement of parts is discovered, as in onions, formed of concentric coats one within another to the very centre. An animal body is still more admirable, in the disposition of its internal parts, and in their order and symmetry. There is not a bone, a muscle, a blood-vessel, a nerve, that hath not one corresponding to it on the opposite side of the animal; and the same order is carried through the most minute parts. The lungs are composed of two parts, which are disposed upon the sides of the thorax; and the kidneys, in a lower situation, have a position not less orderly. As to the parts that are single, the heart is advantageously situated nigh the middle. The liver, stomach, and spleen, are disposed in the upper region of the abdomen, about the same height: the bladder is placed in the middle of the body; as well as the intestinal canal, which fills the whole cavity by its convolutions.

The mechanical power of nature, not confined to small bodies, reacheth equally those of the greatest size; witness the bodies that compose the solar system, which, however large, are weighed, measured, and subjected to certain laws, with the utmost accuracy. Their places around the sun, with their distances, are determined by a precise rule, corresponding to their quantities of matter. The superior dignity of the central body, in respect of its bulk and lucid appearance, is suited to the place it occupies. The globular figure of these bodies, is not only in itself beautiful, but is above all others fitted for regular motion. Each planet revolves about its own axis in a given time; and each moves round the sun, in an orbit nearly circular, and in a time proportioned to its distance. Their velocities, directed by an established law, are perpetually changing by regular accelerations and retardations. In fine, the great variety of regular appearances, joined with the beauty of the system itself, cannot fail to produce the highest delight in every person who can taste design, power, or beauty.

Nature hath a wonderful power of connecting systems with each other, and of propagating that connection through all her works. Thus the constituent parts of a plant, the roots, the stem, the branches, the leaves, the fruit, are really different systems, united by a mutual dependence on each other. Thus in an animal, the lymphatic and lacteal ducts, the blood-vessels and nerves, the muscles and glands, the bones and cartilages, the membranes and viscera, with the other organs, form distinct systems, which are united into one whole. There are, at the same time, other connections less intimate. Thus every plant is joined to the earth by its roots; it requires rain and dews to furnish it with juices; and it requires heat to preserve these juices in fluidity and motion. Thus every animal, by its gravity, is connected with the earth, with the element in which it breathes, and with the sun, by deriving from it cherishing and enlivening heat. The earth furnisheth aliment to plants, these to animals, and these again to other animals, in a long train of dependence. That the earth is part of a greater system, comprehending many bodies mutually attracting each other, and gravitating all toward one common centre, is now thoroughly explored. Such a regular and uniform series of connections, propagated through so great a number of beings and through such wide spaces, is wonderful: and our wonder must increase, when we observe this connection propagated from the minutest atoms to bodies of the most enormous size, and widely diffused, so as that we can neither perceive its beginning nor its end. That it doth not terminate within our own planetary system, is certain. The connection is diffused over spaces still more remote, where new bodies and systems rise to our view, without end. All space is filled with the works of God, which, being the operation of one hand, are formed by one plan, to answer one great end.

But the most wonderful connection of all, though not the most conspicuous, is that of our internal frame with the works of nature. Man is obviously fitted for contemplating these works, because in this contemplation he has great delight. The works of nature are remarkable in their uniformity not less than in their variety; and the mind of man is fitted to receive pleasure equally from both. Uniformity and variety are interwoven in the works of nature with surprising art. Variety, however great, is never without some degree of uniformity; nor the greatest uniformity, without some degree of variety. There is great variety in the same plant, by the different appearances of its stem, branches, leaves, blossoms, fruit, size, and colour; and yet when we trace this variety through different plants, especially of the same kind, there is discovered a surprising uniformity. Again, where nature seems to have intended the most exact uniformity, as among individuals of the same kind, there still appears a diversity, which serves readily to distinguish one individual from another. It is indeed admirable, that the human visage, in which uniformity is so prevalent, should yet be so marked as to leave no room for mistaking one person for another. The difference, though clearly perceived, is often so minute as to go beyond the reach of description. A correspondence so perfect betwixt the human mind and the works of nature, is extremely remarkable. The opposition betwixt variety and uniformity is so great, that one would not readily imagine they could both be relished by the same palate; at least not in the same object, nor at the same time. It is however true, that the pleasures they afford, being happily adjusted to each other, and readily mixing in intimate union, are frequently produced in perfection by the same individual object. Nay further, in the objects that touch us the most, uniformity and variety are constantly combined; witness natural objects, where this combination is always found in perfection. It is for that reason, that natural objects readily form themselves into groups, and are agreeable in whatever manner combined: a wood with its trees, shrubs, and herbs, is agreeable: the music of birds, the lowing of cattle, and the murmuring of a brook, are in conjunction delightful; though they strike the ear without modulation or harmony. In short, nothing can be more happily accommodated to the inward constitution of man, than that mixture of uniformity with variety which the eye discovers in natural objects. And accordingly, the mind is never more highly gratified than in contemplating a natural landscape.

End of the FIRST VOLUME

VOLUME II

X

Congruity and Propriety

Man is distinguished from the brute creation, not more remarkably by the superiority of his rational faculties, than by the greater delicacy of his perceptions and feelings. With respect to the gross pleasures of sense, man probably has little superiority over other animals. Some obscure perception of beauty may also fall to their share. But they are probably not acquainted with the more delicate conceptions of regularity, order, uniformity, or congruity. Such refined conceptions, being connected with morality and religion, are reserved to dignify the chief of the terrestrial creation. Upon this account, no discipline is more suitable to man, or more *congruous* to the dignity of his nature, than that by which his taste is refined, to distinguish in every subject, what is regular, what is orderly, what is suitable, and what is fit and proper[1].

No discerning person can be at a loss about the meaning of the terms *congruity* and *propriety*, when applied to dress, behaviour, or language; that a decent garb, for example, is proper for a judge, modest behaviour for a young woman, and a lofty style for an epic poem. In the following examples everyone is sensible of an unsuitableness or incongruity: a little woman sunk in an overgrown farthingale, a coat richly embroidered covering coarse and dirty linen, a mean subject in an elevated style, or an elevated subject in a mean style, a first minister darning his wife's stocking, or a reverend prelate in lawn sleeves dancing a hornpipe.

But it is not sufficient that these terms be understood in practice; the critical art requires, that their meaning be traced to its foundation in human nature. The relations that connect objects together, have

---

[1]. Nec vero illa parva vis naturæ est rationisque, quod unum hoc animal sentit quid sit ordo, quid sit quod deceat in factis dictisque, qui modus. Itaqne eorum ipsorum, quæ aspectu sentiuntur, nullum aliud animal, pulcritudinem, venustatem, convenientiam partium sentit. Quam similitudinem natura ratioque ab oculis ad animum transferens, multo etiam magis pulcritudinem, constantiam, ordinem in consiliis factisque conservandum putat, cavetque ne quid indecore effeminateve faciat; tum in omnibus et opinionibus et factis ne quid libidinose aut faciat aut cogitet. Quibus ex rebus conflatur et efficitur id quod quærimus, honestum.—*Cicero de officiis, l.* 1.

been examined in more than one view. Their influence in directing the train of our perceptions, is handled in the first chapter; and in the second, their influence in generating passion. Here they must be handled in a new view; for they are clearly the occasion of congruity and propriety. We are so framed by nature, as to require a certain suitableness or correspondence among things connected by any relation. This suitableness or correspondence is termed *congruity* or *propriety*; and the want of it, *incongruity* or *impropriety*. Among the many principles that compose the nature of man, a sense of congruity or propriety is one. Destitute of this sense, we could have no notion of congruity or propriety: the terms to us would be unintelligible[2].

As this sense is displayed upon relations, it is reasonable beforehand to expect, that we should be so formed, as to require among connected objects a degree of congruity proportioned to the degree of the relation. And upon examination we find this to hold in fact. Where the relation is strong and intimate as betwixt a cause and its effect, a body and its members, we require that the things be suited to each other in the strictest manner. On the other hand, where the relation is slight, or accidental, as among things jumbled together in the same place, we demand little or no congruity. The strictest propriety is required in behaviour and manner of living; because a man is connected with these by the relation of cause and effect. The situation of a great house ought to be lofty; for the relation betwixt an edifice and the ground it stands upon, is of the most intimate kind. Its relation to neighbouring hills, rivers, plains, being that of propinquity only, demands but a small share of congruity. Among members of the same club, the congruity ought to be considerable, as well as among things placed for show in the

---

2. From many things that pass current in the world without being generally condemned, one, at first view; would imagine, that the sense of congruity or propriety had scarce any foundation in nature; and that it is rather an artificial refinement of those who affect to distinguish themselves from others. The fulsome panegyrics bestowed upon the great and opulent, in epistles dedicatory, and other such compositions, would incline us to think so. Did there prevail in the world, it will be said, or did nature suggest, a taste of what is suitable, decent, or proper, would any good writer deal in such compositions, or any man of sense receive them without disgust. Can it be supposed that Lewis XIV of France was endued by nature with any sense of propriety, when in a dramatic performance purposely composed for his entertainment, he suffered himself, publicly and in his presence, to be styled the greatest king ever the earth produced? These, it is true, are strong facts: but luckily they do not prove the sense of propriety to be artificial: they only prove, that the sense of propriety is at times overpowered by pride and vanity; which is no singular case, for that sometimes is the fate even of the sense of justice.

same niche. Among passengers in a stage-coach, we require very little congruity; and less still at a public spectacle.

Congruity is so nearly allied to beauty, as commonly to be held a species of it. And yet they differ so essentially, as never to coincide. Beauty, like colour, is placed upon a single subject; congruity upon a plurality. Further, a thing beautiful in itself, may, with relation to other things, produce the strongest sense of incongruity.

Congruity and propriety are commonly reckoned synonymous terms; and hitherto in opening the subject they are used indifferently. But they are distinguishable; and the precise meaning of each must be ascertained. Congruity is the genus, of which propriety is a species. For we call nothing propriety, but that congruity or suitableness which ought to subsist betwixt sensible beings and their thoughts, words, and actions.

In order to give a full view of this subject, I shall trace it through some of the most considerable relations. The relation of a part to the whole, being extremely intimate, demands the utmost degree of congruity. For that reason, the slightest deviation is disgustful. Everyone must be sensible of a gross incongruity in the *Lutrin*, a burlesque poem, being closed with a serious and warm panegyric on Lamoignon, one of the King's judges:

—— Amphora cœpit
Institui; currente rota, cur urceus exit?

No relation affords more examples of congruity and incongruity, than that betwixt a subject and its ornaments. A literary performance intended merely for amusement, is susceptible of much ornament, as well as a music-room or a play-house. In gaiety, the mind hath a peculiar relish for show and decoration. The most gorgeous apparel, however unsuitable to an actor in a regular tragedy, disgusts not at an opera. The truth is, an opera, in its present form, is a mighty fine thing; but as it deviates from nature in its capital circumstances, we look not for anything natural in those which are accessory. On the other hand, a serious and important subject, admits not much ornament[3]: nor a

---

3. Contrary to this rule, the introduction to the third volume of the *Characteristics*, is a continued chain of metaphors: these in such profusion are too florid for the subject; and have beside the bad effect of removing our attention from the principal subject, to fix it upon splendid trifles.

subject that of itself is extremely beautiful. And a subject that fills the mind with its loftiness and grandeur, appears best in a dress altogether plain.

To a person of a mean appearance, gorgeous apparel is unsuitable: which, beside the incongruity, has a bad effect; for by contrast it shows the meanness of appearance in the strongest light. Sweetness of look and manner, requires simplicity of dress joined with the greatest elegance. A stately and majestic air requires sumptuous apparel, which ought not to be gaudy, or crowded with little ornaments. A woman of consummate beauty can bear to be highly adorned, and yet shows best in a plain dress:

> ——*For loveliness*
> *Needs not the foreign aid of ornament,*
> *But is when unadorn'd, adorn'd the most.*
>
> —*Thomson's Autumn*, 208

In judging of the propriety of ornament, we must attend, not only to the nature of the subject that is to be adorned, but also to the circumstances in which it is placed. The ornaments that are proper for a ball, will appear not altogether so decent at public worship; and the same person ought to dress differently for a marriage-feast and for a burial.

Nothing is more intimately related to a man, than his sentiments, words, and actions; and therefore we require here the strictest conformity. When we find what we thus require, we have a lively sense of propriety: when we find the contrary, our sense of impropriety is not less lively. Hence the universal distaste of affectation, which consists in making a shew of greater delicacy and refinement than is suited either to the character or circumstances of the person. Nothing hath a worse effect in a story than impropriety of manners. In Corneille's tragedy of *Cinna*, Æmilia, a favourite of Augustus, receives daily marks of his affection, and is loaded with benefits; yet all the while is laying plots to assassinate her benefactor, directed by no other motive but to avenge her father's death[4]. Revenge against a benefactor founded solely upon filial piety, will never suggest unlawful means; because it can never

---

4. See act 1. sc. 2.

exceed the bounds of justice. And yet the crime here attempted, murder under trust reposed, is what even a miscreant will scarce attempt against his bitterest enemy.

What is said may be thought sufficient to explain the qualities of congruity and propriety. But the subject is not exhausted. On the contrary, the prospect enlarges upon us, when we take under view the effects these qualities produce in the mind. Congruity and propriety, where-ever perceived, appear agreeable; and every agreeable object produceth in the mind a pleasant emotion. Incongruity and impropriety, on the other hand, are disagreeable; and consequently produce painful emotions. An emotion of this kind sometimes vanisheth without any consequence; but more frequently is the occasion of other emotions. When any slight incongruity is perceived in an accidental combination of persons or things, as of passengers in a stage-coach or of individuals dining at an ordinary, the emotion of incongruity, after a momentary existence, vanisheth without producing any effect. But this is not the case of propriety and impropriety. Voluntary acts, whether words or deeds, are imputed to the author: when proper, we reward him with our esteem: when improper, we punish him with our contempt. Let us suppose, for example, an heroic action suitable to the character of the author, which raises in him and in every spectator the pleasant emotion of propriety. This emotion generates in the author both self-esteem and joy; the former when he considers his relation to the action, and the latter when he considers the good opinion that others will entertain of him. The same emotion of propriety, produceth in the spectators, esteem for the author of the action: and when they think of themselves, it also produceth, by means of contrast, an emotion of humility. To discover the effects of an unsuitable action, we must invert each of these circumstances. The painful emotion of impropriety, generates in the author of the action both humility and shame; the former when he considers his relation to the action, and the latter when he considers what others will think of him. The same emotion of impropriety, produceth in the spectators, contempt for the author of the action; and it also produceth, by means of contrast when they think of themselves, an emotion of self-esteem. Here then are many different emotions, derived from the same action considered in different views by different persons; a machine provided with many springs, and not a little complicated. Propriety of action, it would seem, is a chief favourite of nature, or of the author of nature, when such care and solicitude is bestowed upon it. It is not left to our own choice; but, like justice, is required at our hands; and, like justice, inforced by natural rewards and punishments. A man cannot, with impunity, do anything unbecoming or improper. He suffers the chastisement of contempt inflicted by others, and of shame inflicted by himself. An apparatus so complicated and so singular, ought to rouse our attention. Nature doth nothing in vain; and we may conclude with great certainty, that this curious branch of the human constitution is intended for some valuable purpose. To the discovery of this purpose I shall with ardor apply my thoughts, after discoursing a little more at large upon the punishment, for I may now call it so, that Nature hath provided for indecent or unbecoming behaviour. This, at any rate, is necessary, in order to give a full view of the subject; and who knows whether it may not, over and above, open some track that will lead us to what we are in quest of?

A gross impropriety is punished with contempt and indignation, which are vented against the offender by every external expression that can gratify these passions. And even the slightest impropriety raises some degree of contempt. But there are improprieties, generally of the slighter kind, that provoke laughter; of which we have examples without end in the blunders and absurdities of our own species. Such improprieties receive a different punishment, as will appear by what follows. The emotions of contempt and of laughter occasioned by an impropriety of this kind, uniting intimately in the mind of the spectator, are expressed externally by a peculiar sort of laugh, termed *a laugh of derision* or *scorn*[5]. An impropriety that thus moves not only contempt but laughter, is distinguished by the epithet of *ridiculous*; and a laugh of derision or scorn is the punishment provided for it by nature. Nor ought it to escape observation, that we are so fond of inflicting this punishment, as sometimes to exert it even against creatures of an inferior species; witness a Turkycock swelling with pride, and strutting with displayed feathers. This object appears ridiculous, and in a gay mood is apt to provoke a laugh of derision.

We must not expect that the improprieties to which these different punishments are adapted, can be separated by any precise boundaries. Of improprieties, from the slightest to the most gross, from the most risible to the most serious, a scale may be formed ascending by degrees almost imperceptible. Hence it is, that in viewing some unbecoming

---

5. See chap. 7.

actions, too risible for anger and too serious for derision, the spectator feels a sort of mixt emotion partaking both of derision and of anger. This accounts for an expression, common with respect to the impropriety of some actions, That we know not whether to laugh or be angry.

It cannot fail to be observed, that in the case of a risible impropriety, which is always slight, the contempt we have for the offender is extremely faint, though derision, its gratification, is extremely pleasant. This disproportion betwixt a passion and its gratification, seems not conformable to the analogy of nature. In looking about for a solution, I reflect upon what is laid down above, that an improper action, not only moves our contempt for the author, but also, by means of contrast, swells the good opinion we have of ourselves. This contributes, more than any other article, to the pleasure we feel in ridiculing the follies and absurdities of others. And accordingly, it is well known, that they who put the greatest value upon themselves, are the most prone to laugh at others. Pride is a vivid passion, as all are which have self for their object. It is extremely pleasant in itself, and not less so in its gratification. This passion singly would be sufficient to account for the pleasure of ridicule, without borrowing any aid from contempt. Hence appears the reason of a noted observation, That we are the most disposed to ridicule the blunders and absurdities of others, when we are in high spirits; for in high spirits, self-conceit displays itself with more than ordinary vigor.

Having with wary steps traced an intricate road, not without danger of wandering; what remains to complete our journey, is to account for the final cause of congruity and propriety, which make so great a figure in the human constitution. One final cause, regarding congruity, is pretty obvious. The sense of congruity, as one of the principles of the fine arts, contributes in a remarkable degree to our entertainment. This is the final cause assigned above for our sense of proportion[6], and need not be enlarged upon here. Congruity indeed with respect to quantity, coincides with proportion. When the parts of a building are nicely adjusted to each other, it may be said indifferently, that it is agreeable by the congruity of its parts, or by the proportion of its parts. But propriety, which regards voluntary agents only, can never in any instance be the same with proportion. A very long nose is disproportioned, but cannot be termed *improper*. In some instances, it is true, impropriety coincides with disproportion in the same subject, but never in the same

---

6. See chap. 3.

respect. I give for an example a very little man buckled to a long toledo. Considering the man and the sword with respect to size, we perceive a disproportion. Considering the sword as the choice of the man, we perceive an impropriety.

The sense of impropriety with respect to mistakes, blunders, and absurdities, is happily contrived for the good of mankind. In the spectators it is productive of mirth and laughter, excellent recreation in an interval from business. The benefit is still more extensive. It is not agreeable to be the subject of ridicule; and to punish with ridicule the man who is guilty of an absurdity, tends to put him more upon his guard in time coming. Thus even the most innocent blunder is not committed with impunity; because, were errors licensed where they do no hurt, inattention would grow into a habit, and be the occasion of much hurt.

The final cause of propriety as to moral duties, is of all the most illustrious. To have a just notion of it, the two sorts of moral duties must be kept in view, *viz.* those that respect others, and those that respect ourselves. Fidelity, gratitude, and the forbearing injury, are examples of the first sort; temperance, modesty, firmness of mind, are examples of the other. The former are made duties by means of the moral sense; the latter, by means of the sense of propriety. Here is a final cause of the sense of propriety, that must rouse our attention. It is undoubtedly the interest of every man, to regulate his behaviour suitably to the dignity of his nature, and to the station allotted him by Providence. Such rational conduct contributes in every respect to happiness: it contributes to health and plenty: it gains the esteem of others: and, which is of all the greatest blessing, it gains a justly-founded self-esteem. But in a matter so essential to our well-being, even self-interest is not relied on. The sense of propriety superadds the powerful authority of duty to the motive of interest. The God of nature, in all things essential to our happiness, hath observed one uniform method. To keep us steady in our conduct, he hath fortified us with natural principles and feelings. These prevent many aberrations, which would daily happen were we totally surrendered to so fallible a guide as is human reason. The sense of propriety cannot justly be considered in another light, than as the natural law that regulates our conduct with respect to ourselves; as the sense of justice is the natural law that regulates our conduct with respect to others. I call the sense of propriety a law, because it really is so, not less than the sense of justice. If by law be meant a rule of conduct that we are conscious ought to be obeyed, this definition, which I conceive to be strictly accurate, is applicable undoubtedly to both. The sense of propriety includes this consciousness; for to say an action is proper, is, in other words, to say, that it *ought* to be performed; and to say it is improper, is, in other words, to say, that it *ought* to be forborn. It is this very consciousness of *ought* and *should* included in the moral sense, that makes justice a law to us. This consciousness of duty, when applied to propriety, is perhaps not so vigorous or strong as when applied to justice: but the difference is in degree only, not in kind: and we ought, without hesitation or reluctance, to submit equally to the government of both.

But I have more to urge upon this head. It must, in the next place, be observed, that to the sense of propriety as well as of justice are annexed the sanctions of rewards and punishments; which evidently prove the one to be a law as well as the other. The satisfaction a man hath in doing his duty, joined with the esteem and good-will of others, is the reward that belongs to both equally. The punishments also, though not the same, are nearly allied; and differ in degree more than in quality. Disobedience to the law of justice, is punished with remorse; disobedience to the law of propriety, with shame, which is remorse in a lower degree. Every transgression of the law of justice raises indignation in the beholder; and so doth every flagrant transgression of the law of propriety. Slighter improprieties receive a milder punishment: they are always rebuked with some degree of contempt, and frequently with derision. In general, it is true, that the rewards and punishments annexed to the sense of propriety are slighter in degree than those annexed to the sense of justice. And that this is wisely ordered, will appear from considering, that to the well-being of society, duty to others is still more essential than duty to ourselves; for society could not subsist a moment, were individuals not protected from the headstrong and turbulent passions of their neighbours.

Reflecting coolly and carefully upon the subject under consideration, the constitution of man, admirable in all its parts, appears here in a fine light. The final cause now unfolded of the sense of propriety, must, to every discerning eye, appear delightful; and yet hitherto we have given but a partial view of it. The sense of propriety reaches another illustrious end; which is, to co-operate with the sense of justice in inforcing the performance of social duties. In fact, the sanctions visibly contrived to compel a man to be just to himself, are equally serviceable to compel him to be just to others. This will be evident from a single reflection, That an action, by being unjust, ceases not to be improper. An action never appears more eminently improper, than when it is unjust. It is obviously becoming and suitable to human nature, that each man do his duty to others; and accordingly every transgression of duty with respect to others, is at the same time a transgression of duty with respect to self. This is an undisguised truth without exaggeration; and it opens a new and delightful view in the moral landscape. The prospect is greatly enriched, by the multiplication of agreeable objects. It appears now, that nothing is overlooked, nothing left undone, that can possibly contribute to the enforcing social duty. For to all the sanctions that belong to it singly, are superadded the sanctions of self-duty. A familiar example shall suffice for illustration. An act of ingratitude considered in itself, is to the author disagreeable as well as to every spectator: considered by the author with relation to himself, it raises self-contempt: considered by him with relation to the world, it makes him ashamed. Again, considered by others, it raises their contempt and indignation against the author. These feelings are all of them occasioned by the impropriety of the action. When the action is considered as unjust, it occasions another set of feelings. In the author it produces remorse, and a dread of merited punishment; and in others, the benefactor chiefly, indignation and hatred directed upon the ungrateful person. Thus shame and remorse united in the ungrateful person, and indignation united with hatred in the hearts of others, are the punishments provided by nature for injustice. Stupid and insensible must he be in extreme, who, in a contrivance so exquisite, perceives not the hand of the Sovereign Architect.

XI

Of Dignity and Meanness

These terms are applied to man in point of character, sentiment, and behaviour. We say, for example, of one man, that he hath a natural dignity in his air and manner; of another, that he makes a mean figure. There is a dignity in every action and sentiment of some persons: the actions and sentiments of others are mean and vulgar. With respect to the fine arts, some performances are said to be manly and suitable to the dignity of human nature: others are termed low, mean, trivial. Such expressions are common, though they have not always a precise meaning. With respect to the art of criticism, it must be a real acquisition to ascertain what these terms truly import; which possibly may enable us to rank every performance in the fine arts according to its dignity.

Inquiring first to what subjects the terms *dignity* and *meanness* are appropriated, we soon discover, that they are not applicable to anything inanimate. The most magnificent palace ever built, may be lofty, may be grand, but it has no relation to dignity. The most diminutive shrub may be little, but it is not mean. These terms must belong to sensitive beings, probably to man only; which will be evident when we advance in the inquiry.

Of all objects, human actions produce in a spectator the greatest variety of feelings. They are in themselves grand or little: with respect to the author, they are proper or improper: with respect to those affected by them, just or unjust. And I must now add, that they are also distinguished by dignity and meanness. It may possibly be thought, that with respect to human actions, dignity coincides with grandeur, and meanness with littleness. But the difference will be evident upon reflecting, that we never attribute dignity to any action but what is virtuous, nor meanness to any but what in some degree is faulty. But an action may be grand without being virtuous, or little without being faulty. Every action of dignity creates respect and esteem for the author; and a mean action draws upon him contempt. A man is always admired for a grand action, but frequently is neither loved nor esteemed for it: neither is a man always contemned for a low or little action.

As it appears to me, dignity and meanness are founded on a natural principle not hitherto mentioned. Man is endued with a sense of the worth and excellence of his nature. He deems it to be more perfect than that of the other beings around him; and he feels that the perfection of his nature consists in virtue, particularly in virtue of the highest rank. To express this sense, the term *dignity* is appropriated. Further, to behave with dignity, and to refrain from all mean actions, is felt to be, not a virtue only, but a duty: it is a duty every man owes to himself. By acting in this manner, he attracts love and esteem. By acting meanly or below himself, he is disapproved and contemned.

According to the description here given of dignity and meanness, they will be found to be a species of propriety and impropriety. Many actions may be proper or improper, to which dignity or meanness cannot be applied. To eat when one is hungry is proper, but there is no dignity in this action. Revenge fairly taken, if against law, is improper, but it is not mean. But every action of dignity is also proper, and every mean action is also improper.

This sense of the dignity of human nature, reaches even our pleasures and amusements. If they enlarge the mind by raising grand or elevated emotions, or if they humanize the mind by exercising our sympathy, they are approved as suited to our nature: if they contract the mind by fixing it on trivial objects, they are contemned as low and mean. Hence in general, every occupation, whether of use or amusement, that corresponds to the dignity of man, obtains the epithet of *manly*; and every occupation below his nature, obtains the epithet of *childish*.

To those who study human nature, there is a point which has always appeared intricate. How comes it that generosity and courage are more valued and bestow more dignity, than good-nature, or even justice, though the latter contribute more than the former, to private as well as to public happiness? This question bluntly proposed, might puzzle a cunning philosopher; but by means of the foregoing observations will easily be solved. Human virtues, like other objects, obtain a rank in our estimation, not from their utility, which is a subject of reflection, but from the direct impression they make on us. Justice and good-nature are a sort of negative virtues, that make no figure unless when they are transgressed. Courage and generosity producing elevated emotions, enliven greatly the sense of a man's dignity, both in himself and in others; and for that reason, courage and generosity are in higher regard than the other virtues mentioned. We describe them as grand and elevated, as of greater dignity, and more praise-worthy.

This leads us to examine more directly emotions and passions with respect to the present subject. And it will not be difficult to form a scale of them, beginning at the meanest, and ascending gradually to those of the highest rank and dignity. Pleasure felt as at the organ of sense, named *corporeal pleasure*, is perceived to be low; and when indulged to excess, beyond what nature demands, is perceived also to be mean. Persons therefore of any delicacy, dissemble the pleasure they have in eating and drinking. The pleasures of the eye and ear, which have no organic feeling[1], are free from any sense of meanness; and for that reason are indulged without any shame. They even arise to a certain degree of dignity, when their objects are grand or elevated. The same is the case of the sympathetic passions. They raise the character considerably, when their objects are of importance. A virtuous person behaving with fortitude and dignity under the most cruel misfortunes, makes a capital figure; and the sympathising spectator feels in himself the same dignity. Sympathetic distress at the same time never is mean: on the contrary, it is agreeable to the nature of a social being, and has the general approbation. The rank that love possesses in this scale, depends in a great measure on its object. It possesses a low place when founded on external properties merely; and is mean when bestowed upon a person of a rank much inferior without any extraordinary qualification. But when founded on the more elevated internal properties, it assumes a considerable degree of dignity. The same is the case of friendship. When gratitude is warm, it animates the mind; but it scarce rises to dignity. Joy bestows dignity when it proceeds from an elevated cause.

So far as I can gather from induction, dignity is not a property of any disagreeable passion. One is slight another severe, one depresses the mind another rouses and animates it; but there is no elevation, far less dignity, in any of them. Revenge, in particular, though it inflame and swell the mind, is not accompanied with dignity, not even with elevation. It is not however felt as mean or groveling, unless when it takes indirect measures for its gratification. Shame and remorse, though they sink the spirits, are not mean. Pride, a disagreeable passion, bestows no dignity

---

1. See the Introduction.

in the eye of a spectator. Vanity always appears mean; and extremely so where founded, as commonly happens, on trivial qualifications.

I proceed to the pleasures of the understanding, which possess a high rank in point of dignity. Of this everyone will be sensible, when he considers the important truths that have been laid open by science; such as general theorems, and the general laws that govern the material and moral worlds. The pleasures of the understanding are suited to man as a rational and contemplative being; and they tend not a little to ennoble his nature. Even to the Deity he stretches his contemplations, which, in the discovery of infinite power wisdom and benevolence, afford delight of the most exalted kind. Hence it appears, that the fine arts studied as a rational science, afford entertainment of great dignity; superior far to what they afford as a subject of taste merely.

But contemplation, though in itself valuable, is chiefly respected as subservient to action; for man is intended to be more an active than a contemplative being. He accordingly shows more dignity in action than in contemplation. Generosity, magnanimity, heroism, raise his character to the highest pitch. These best express the dignity of his nature, and advance him nearer to divinity than any other of his attributes.

By every production that shows art and contrivance, our curiosity is excited upon two points; first how it was made, and next to what end. Of the two, the latter is the more important inquiry, because the means are ever subordinate to the end; and in fact our curiosity is always more inflamed by the final than by the efficient cause. This preference is no where more visible, than in contemplating the works of nature. If in the efficient cause, wisdom and power be displayed, wisdom is not less conspicuous in the final cause; and from it only can we infer benevolence, which of all the divine attributes is to man the most important. Having endeavoured to assign the efficient cause of dignity and meanness, and to unfold the principle on which they are founded, we proceed to explain the final cause of the dignity or meanness bestowed upon the several particulars above mentioned, beginning with corporeal pleasures. These, so far as useful, are like justice fenced with sufficient sanctions to prevent their being neglected. Hunger and thirst are painful sensations; and we are incited to animal love by a vigorous propensity. Were they dignified over and above with a place in a high class, they would infallibly overturn the balance of the mind, by outweighing the social affections. This is a satisfactory final cause for refusing to corporeal pleasures any degree of dignity. And the final cause is not less evident of their meanness, when they are indulged to excess. The more refined pleasures of external sense, conveyed by the eye and the ear from natural objects and from the fine arts, deserve a high place in our esteem, because of their singular and extensive utility. In some cases they arise to a considerable dignity. The very lowest pleasures of the kind, are never esteemed mean or groveling. The pleasure arising from wit, humour, ridicule, or from what is simply ludicrous, is useful, by relaxing the mind after the fatigue of more manly occupation. But the mind, when it surrenders itself to pleasure of this kind, loses its vigor, and sinks gradually into sloth. The place this pleasure occupies in point of dignity, is adjusted to these views. To make it useful as a relaxation, it is not branded with meanness. To prevent its usurpation, it is removed from this place but a single degree. No man values himself upon this pleasure, even during the gratification; and if more time have been given to it than is requisite for relaxation, a man looks back with some degree of shame.

In point of dignity, the social passions rise above the selfish, and much above the pleasures of the eye and ear. Man is by his nature a social being; and to qualify him for society, it is wisely contrived, that he should value himself more for being social than selfish.

The excellency of man is chiefly discernible in the great improvements he is susceptible of in society. These, by perseverance, may be carried on progressively to higher and higher degrees of perfection, above any assignable limits; and, even abstracting from revelation, there is great probability, that the progress begun in this life will be completed in some future state. Now, as all valuable improvements proceed from the exercise of our rational faculties, the author of our nature, in order to excite us to a due use of these faculties, hath assigned a high rank to the pleasures of the understanding. Their utility, with respect to this life as well as a future, intitles them to this rank.

But as action is the end of all our improvements, virtuous actions justly possess the highest of all the ranks. These, I find, are by nature distributed into different classes, and the first in point of dignity assigned to actions which appear not the first in point of use. Generosity, for example, in the sense of mankind, is more respected than justice, though the latter is undoubtedly more essential to society. And magnanimity, heroism, undaunted courage, rise still higher in our esteem. One would readily think, that the moral virtues should be esteemed according to their importance. Nature has here deviated from her ordinary path, and great wisdom is shown in the deviation. The efficient cause is explained above; and the final cause is explained in the Essays of morality and natural religion[2].

---

2. Part 1. essay 2. chap. 4.

XII

Ridicule

This subject has puzzled and vexed all the critics. Aristotle gives a definition of ridicule, obscure and imperfect[1]. Cicero handles it at great length[2]; but without giving any satisfaction. He wanders in the dark, and misses the distinction betwixt risible and ridiculous. Quintilian is sensible of this distinction[3]; but has not attempted to explain it. Luckily this subject lies no longer in obscurity. A risible object produceth an emotion of laughter merely[4]. A ridiculous object is improper as well as risible; and produceth a mixt emotion, which is vented by a laugh of derision or scorn[5].

Having therefore happily unravelled the abstruse and knotty part, I proceed to what may be thought further necessary upon this subject.

Burlesque is one great engine of ridicule. But it is not confined to that subject; for it is clearly distinguishable into burlesque that excites laughter merely, and burlesque that provokes derision or ridicule. A grave subject in which there is no impropriety, may be brought down by a certain colouring so as to be risible. This is the case of *Virgil Travestie*[6]. And it is the case of the *Secchia Rapita*[7]. The authors laugh first at every turn, in order to make their readers laugh. The *Lutrin* is a burlesque poem of the other sort. The author Boileau, lays hold of a low and trifling incident to expose the luxury, indolence, and contentious spirit of a set of monks. He turns the subject into ridicule by dressing it in the heroic style, and affecting to consider it as of the utmost dignity and importance; and though ridicule is the poet's aim, he himself carries all along a grave face, and never once bewrays a smile. The opposition betwixt the subject and the manner of handling it, is what produces the

---

1. Poet cap. 5.
2. L. 2. De Oratore.
3. Ideoque anceps ejus rei ratio est, quod a derisu non procul abest risus, lib. 6. cap. 3. sect. 1.
4. See chap. 7.
5. See chap. 10.
6. Scarron.
7. Tassoni.

ridicule. In a composition of this kind, no image professedly ludicrous ought to have quarter; because such images destroy the contrast.

Though the burlesque that aims at ridicule, produces its effect by elevating the style far above the subject, yet it has limits beyond which the elevation ought not to be carried. The poet, consulting the imagination of his readers, ought to confine himself to such images as are lively and readily apprehended. A strained elevation, soaring above an ordinary reach of fancy, makes not a pleasant impression. The mind fatigued with being always upon the stretch, is soon disgusted; and if it perseveres, becomes thoughtless and indifferent. Further, a fiction gives no pleasure, unless where painted in so lively colours as to produce some perception of reality; which never can be done effectually where the images are formed with labour or difficulty. For these reasons, I cannot avoid condemning the *Batrachomuomachia* said to be the composition of Homer. It is beyond the power of imagination, to form a clear and lively image of frogs and mice acting with the dignity of the highest of our species: nor can we form a conception of the reality of such an action, in any manner so distinct as to interest our affections even in the slightest degree.

The *Rape of the Lock* is of a character clearly distinguishable from those now mentioned. It is not properly a burlesque performance, but what may rather be termed *an heroi-comical poem*. It treats a gay and familiar subject, with pleasantry and with a moderate degree of dignity. The author puts not on a mask like Boileau, nor professes to make us laugh like Tassoni. The *Rape of the Lock* is a genteel and gay species of writing, less strained than the others mentioned; and is pleasant or ludicrous without having ridicule for its chief aim; giving way however to ridicule where it arises naturally from a particular character, such as that of Sir Plume. Addison's *Spectator* upon the exercise of the fan[8] is extremely gay and ludicrous, resembling in its subject the *Rape of the Lock*.

Humour belongs to the present chapter, because it is undoubtedly connected with ridicule. Congreve defines humour to be "a singular and unavoidable manner of doing or saying anything, peculiar and natural to one man only, by which his speech and actions are distinguished from those of other men." Were this definition just, a majestic and commanding air, which is a singular property, is humour; as also that natural flow of eloquence and correct elocution which is a rare talent.

---

8. No. 102.

Nothing just or proper is denominated humour; nor any singularity of character, words, or actions, that is valued or respected. When we attend to the character of an humorist, we find that the peculiarity of this character lessens the man in our esteem: we find that this character arises from circumstances both risible and improper, and therefore in some measure ridiculous.

Humour in writing is very different from humour in character. When an author insists upon ludicrous subjects with a professed purpose to make his readers laugh, he may be styled *a ludicrous writer*; but is scarce intitled to be styled *a writer of humour*. This quality belongs to an author, who, affecting to be grave and serious, paints his objects in such colours as to provoke mirth and laughter. A writer that is really an humorist in character, does this without design. If not, he must affect the character in order to succeed. Swift and Fontaine were humorists in character, and their writings are full of humour. Addison was not an humorist in character; and yet in his prose writings a most delicate and refined humour prevails. Arbuthnot exceeds them all in drollery and humorous painting; which shows a great genius, because, if I am not misinformed, he had nothing of this peculiarity in his character.

There remains to show, by examples, the manner of treating subjects so as to give them a ridiculous appearance.

Il ne dit jamais, je vous donne, mais, je vous prete le bon jour.

—Moliere

ORLEANS: I know him to be valiant.
CONSTABLE: I was told that by one that knows him better than you.
ORLEANS: What's he?
CONSTABLE: Marry, he told me so himself; and he said, he car'd not who knew it.

—Henry V. Shakespear

He never broke any man's head but his own, and that was against a post when he was drunk.

—Ibid

MILLAMENT: Sententious Mirabell! pr'ythee don't look with that violent and inflexible wise face, like Solomon at the dividing of the child in an old tapestry hanging.

—*Way of the world*

A true critic in the perusal of a book, is like a dog at a feast, whose thoughts and stomach are wholly set upon what the guests fling away, and consequently is apt to snarl most when there are the fewest bones.

Tale of a Tub

In the following instances the ridicule is made to appear from the behaviour of the persons introduced.

MASCARILLE: Te souvient-il, vicomte, de cette demi-lune, que nous emportâmes sur les ennemis au siege d'Arras?
JEDELET: Que veux tu dire avec ta demi-lune? c'etoit bien une lune toute entiere.

—*Moliere les Precieuses Ridicules, sc. 11*

SLENDER: I came yonder at Eaton to marry Mrs. Anne Page; and she's a great lubberly boy.
PAGE: Upon my life then you took the wrong.
SLENDER: What need you tell me that? I think so, when I took a boy for a girl: if I had been marry'd to him, for all he was in woman's apparel, I would not have had him.

—*Merry Wives of Windsor*

VALENTINE: Your blessing, Sir.
SIR SAMPSON: You've had it already, Sir: I think I sent it you today in a bill for four thousand pound; a great deal of money, Brother Foresight.
FORESIGHT: Ay indeed, Sir Sampson, a great deal of money for a young man; I wonder what can he do with it.

—*Love for Love, act 2. sc. 7*

MILLAMANT: I nauseate walking; 'tis a country-diversion; I lothe the country, and everything that relates to it.

SIR WILFUL: Indeed! hah! look ye, look ye, you do? nay, 'tis like you may—here are choice of pastimes here in town, as plays and the like; that must be confess'd indeed.

MILLAMANT: Ah l'etourdie! I hate the town too.

SIR WILFUL: Dear heart, that's much—hah! that you should hate 'em both! hah! 'tis like you may; there are some can't relish the town, and others can't away with the country—'tis like you may be one of those, Cousine.

—Way of the world, act 4. sc. 4

LORD FROTH: I assure you, Sir Paul, I laugh at no body's jest but my own, or a lady's: I assure you, Sir Paul.

BRISK: How? how, my Lord? what, affront my wit! Let me perish, do I never say anything worthy to be laugh'd at?

LORD FROTH: O foy, don't misapprehend me, I don't say so, for I often smile at your conceptions. But there is nothing more unbecoming a man of quality, than to laugh; 'tis such a vulgar expression of the passion! everybody can laugh. Then especially to laugh at the jest of an inferior person, or when anybody else of the same quality does not laugh with one; ridiculous! To be pleas'd with what pleases the crowd! Now, when I laugh I always laugh alone.

—Double Dealer, act 1. sc. 4

So sharp-sighted is pride in blemishes, and so willing to be gratified, that it will take up with the very slightest improprieties; such as a blunder by a foreigner in speaking our language, especially if the blunder can bear a sense that reflects upon the speaker:

QUICKLY: The young man is an honest man.

CAIUS: What shall de honest man do in my closet? dere is no honest man dat shall come in my closet.

—Merry Wives of Windsor

Love-speeches are finely ridiculed in the following passage.

Quoth he, My faith as adamantine,
As chains of destiny, I'll maintain;
True as Apollo ever spoke,
Or oracle from heart of oak;
And if you'll give my flame but vent,
Now in close hugger-mugger pent,
And shine upon me but benignly,
With that one, and that other pigsneye,
The sun and day shall sooner part,
Than love, or you, shake off my heart;
The sun that shall no more dispense
His own, but your bright influence:
I'll carve your name on barks of trees,
With true love knots, and flourishes;
That shall infuse eternal spring,
And everlasting flourishing:
Drink ev'ry letter on't in stum,
And make it brisk champaign become.
Where-e'er you tread, your foot shall set
The primrose and the violet;
All spices, perfumes, and sweet powders,
Shall borrow from your breath their odours;
Nature her charter shall renew
And take all lives of things from you;
The world depend upon your eye,
And when you frown upon it, die.
Only our loves shall still survive,
New worlds and natures to outlive;
And, like to herald's moons, remain
All crescents, without change or wane.

—Hudibras, part 2. canto 1

Irony turns things into ridicule in a peculiar manner. It consists in laughing at a man under disguise, by appearing to praise or speak well of him. Swift affords us many illustrious examples of this species of ridicule. Take the following example. "By these methods, in a few weeks, there starts up many a writer, capable of managing the profoundest and most universal subjects. For what though his head be empty, provided his commonplace book be full? And if you will bate him but the circumstances of method, and style, and grammar, and invention; allow him but the common privileges of transcribing from others, and digressing from himself, as often as he shall see occasion; he will desire no more ingredients towards fitting up a treatise that shall make a very comely figure on a bookseller's shelf, there to be preserved neat and clean, for a long eternity, adorned with the heraldry of its title, fairly inscribed on a label; never to be thumbed or greased by students, nor bound to everlasting chains of darkness in a library; but when the fullness of time is come, shall happily undergo the trial of purgatory, in order to ascend the sky[9]." The following passage from Arbuthnot is not less ironical. "If the Reverend clergy showed more concern than others, I charitably impute it to their great charge of souls; and what confirmed me in this opinion was, that the degrees of apprehension and terror could be distinguished to be greater or less, according to their ranks and degrees in the church[10]."

A parody must be distinguished from every species of ridicule. It enlivens a gay subject by imitating some important incident that is serious. It is ludicrous, and may be risible. But ridicule is not a necessary ingredient. Take the following examples, the first of which refers to an expression of Moses.

> *The skilful nymph reviews her force with care:*
> *Let spades be trumps! she said, and trumps they were.*
>
> —*Rape of the Lock*, canto iii. 45

The next is an imitation of Achilles's oath in Homer.

> *But by this lock, this sacred lock, I swear,*
> *(Which never more shall join its parted hair,*
> *Which never more its honours shall renew,*
> *Clip'd from the lovely head where late it grew),*
> *That while my nostrils draw the vital air,*

---

9. Tale of a Tub, sect. 7.
10. A true and faithful narrative of what passed in London during the general consternation of all ranks and degrees of mankind.

> *This hand, which won it, shall forever wear.*
> *He spoke, and speaking, in proud triumph spread*
> *The long contended honours of her head.*

> —*Ibid. canto* iv. 133

The following imitates the history of Agamemnon's sceptre in Homer.

> *Now meet thy fate, incens'd Belinda cry'd,*
> *And drew a deadly bodkin from her side,*
> *(The same, his ancient personage to deck,*
> *Her great-great-grandsire wore about his neck,*
> *In three seal rings; which after, melted down,*
> *Form'd a vast buckle for his widow's gown:*
> *Her infant grandame's whistle next it grew,*
> *The bells she jingled, and the whistle blew;*
> *Then in a bodkin grac'd her mother's hairs,*
> *Which long she wore, and now Belinda wears.)*

> —*Ibid. canto* v. 87

Ridicule, as observed above, is no necessary ingredient in a parody. But I did not intend to say, that there is any opposition betwixt them. A parody, no doubt, may be successfully employed to promote ridicule; witness the following example, in which the goddess of Dullness is addressed upon the subject of modern education.

> *Thou gav'st that ripeness, which so soon began,*
> *And ceas'd so soon, he ne'er was boy nor man;*
> *Through school and college, thy kind cloud o'ercast,*
> *Safe and unseen the young Æneas past*[11];
> *Thence bursting glorious, all at once let down,*
> *Stunn'd with his giddy larum half the town.*

> —*Dunciad, b.* iv. 287

The interposition of the gods in the manner of Homer and Virgil, ought to be confined to ludicrous subjects, which are much enlivened by

---

11. Æn. I. 1. *At Venus obscuro,* &c.

such interposition handled in the form of a parody; witness the cave of Spleen, *Rape of the Lock, canto* 4.; the goddess of Discord; *Lutrin, canto* 1.; and the goddess of Indolence, *canto* 2.

Those who have a talent for ridicule, which is seldom united with a taste for delicate and refined beauties, are quick-sighted in improprieties; and these they eagerly lay hold of, in order to gratify their favourite propensity. The persons galled have no other refuge but to maintain, that ridicule ought not to be applied to grave subjects. It is yielded, on the other hand, that subjects really grave and important, are by no means fit for ridicule: but then it is urged, that ridicule is the only proper test for discovering whether a subject be really grave, or be made so artificially by custom and fashion. This dispute has produced a celebrated question, Whether ridicule be or be not a test of truth? I give this question a place here, because it tends to illustrate the nature of ridicule.

The question stated in accurate terms is, Whether the sense of ridicule be the proper test for distinguishing ridiculous objects from those that are not so? To answer this question with precision, I must premise, that ridicule is not a subject of reasoning, but of sense or taste[12]. This being taken for granted, I proceed thus. No person doubts that our sense of beauty is the true test of what is beautiful, and our sense of grandeur, of what is great or sublime. Is it more doubtful whether our sense of ridicule be the true test of what is ridiculous? It is not only the true test, but indeed the only test. For this is a subject that comes not, more than beauty or grandeur, under the province of reason. If any subject, by the influence of fashion or custom, have acquired a degree of veneration or esteem to which naturally it is not intitled, what are the proper means for wiping off the artificial colouring, and displaying the subject in its true light? Reasoning, as observed, cannot be applied. And therefore the only means is to judge by taste. The test of ridicule which separates it from its artificial connections, exposes it naked with all its native improprieties.

But it is urged, that the gravest and most serious matters may be set in a ridiculous light. Hardly so; for where an object is neither risible nor improper, it lies not open in any quarter to an attack from ridicule. But supposing the fact, I foresee not any harmful consequence. By the same sort of reasoning, a talent for wit ought to be condemned,

---

12. See chap. 10. compared with chap. 7.

because it may be employed to burlesque a great or lofty subject. Such irregular use made of a talent for wit or ridicule, cannot long impose upon mankind. It cannot stand the test of correct and delicate taste; and truth will at last prevail even with the vulgar. To condemn a talent for ridicule because it may be perverted to wrong purposes, is not a little ridiculous. Could one forbear to smile, if a talent for reasoning were condemned because it also may be perverted? And yet the conclusion in the latter case, would be not less just than in the former; perhaps more just, for no talent is so often perverted as that of reason.

We had best leave Nature to her own operations. The most valuable talents may be abused, and so may that of ridicule. Let us bring it under proper culture if we can, without endeavouring to pull it up by the root. Were we destitute of this test of truth, I know not what might be the consequences: I see not what rule would be left us to prevent splendid trifles passing for matters of importance, show and form for substance, and superstition or enthusiasm for pure religion.

XIII

Wit

Wit is a quality of certain thoughts and expressions. The term is never applied to an action or a passion, and as little to an external object.

However difficult it may be in every particular instance to distinguish a witty thought or expression from one that is not so, yet in general it may be laid down, that the term *wit* is appropriated to such thoughts and expressions as are ludicrous, and also occasion some degree of surprise by their singularity. Wit also in a figurative sense expresses that talent which some men have of inventing ludicrous thoughts or expressions. We say commonly, *a witty man*, or *a man of wit*.

Wit in its proper sense, as suggested above, is distinguishable into two kinds; wit in the thought, and wit in the words or expression. Again, wit in the thought is of two kinds; ludicrous images, and ludicrous combinations of things that have little or no natural relation.

Ludicrous images that occasion surprise by their singularity, as having little or no foundation in nature, are fabricated by the imagination. And the imagination is well qualified for the office; being of all our faculties the most active, and the least under restraint. Take the following example.

> SHYLOCK: You knew (none so well, none so well as you) of my daughter's flight.
> SALINO: That's certain; I, for my part, knew the tailor that made the wings she flew withal.
>
> —*Merchant of Venice, act 3. sc. 1*

The image here is undoubtedly witty. It is ludicrous: and it must occasion surprise; for having no natural foundation, it is altogether unexpected.

The other branch of wit in the thought, is that only which is taken notice of by Addison, following Locke, who defines it "to lie in the assemblage of ideas; and putting those together with quickness and variety, wherein can be found any resemblance or congruity, thereby to make up pleasant pictures and agreeable visions in the fancy[1]." It may be defined more curtly, and perhaps more accurately, "A junction of things by distant and fanciful relations, which surprise because they are unexpected[2]." The following is a proper example.

> *We grant although he had much wit,*
> *H' was very shie of using it,*
> *As being loth to wear it out;*
> *And therefore bore it not about,*
> *Unless on holidays, or so,*
> *As men their best apparel do.*
>
> —*Hudibras, canto 1*

Wit is of all the most elegant recreation. The image enters the mind with gaiety, and gives a sudden flash which is extremely pleasant. Wit thereby gently elevates without straining, raises mirth without dissoluteness, and relaxes while it entertains.

Wit in the expression, commonly called *a play of words*, being a bastard sort of wit, is reserved for the last place. I proceed to examples of wit in the thought. And first of ludicrous images.

Falstaff, speaking of his taking Sir John Colevile of the Dale:

> Here he is, and here I yield him; and I beseech your Grace, let it be book'd with the rest of this day's deeds; or, by the Lord, I will have it in a particular ballad else, with mine own picture on the top of it, Colevile kissing my foot: to the which course if I be inforc'd, if you do not all shew like gilt twopences to me; and I, in the clear sky of fame, o'er-shine you as much as the full moon doth the cinders of the element, which shew like pins' heads to her; believe not the word of the Noble. Therefore let me have right, and let desert mount.
>
> *Second part, Henry IV. act 4. sc. 6*

---

1. B. 2. ch. 11. § 2.
2. See chap. 1.

I knew, when seven justices could not take up a quarrel, but when the parties were met themselves, one of them thought but of an *if*; as, if you said so, then I said so; and they shook hands, and swore brothers. Your *if* is the only peacemaker; much virtue is in *if*.

Shakespear

For there is not through all nature, another so callous and insensible a member as the world's posteriors, whether you apply to it the toe or the birch.

Preface to a Tale of a tub

The war hath introduced abundance of polysyllables, which will never be able to live many more campaigns. Speculations, operations, preliminaries, ambassadors, palisadoes, communication, circumvallation, battalions, as numerous as they are, if they attack us too frequently in our coffeehouses, we shall certainly put them to flight, and cut off the rear.

Tatler, No 230

Speaking of Discord, "She never went abroad, but she brought home such a bundle of monstrous lies, as would have amazed any mortal, but such as knew her; of a whale that had swallowed a fleet of ships; of the lions being let out of the tower to destroy the Protestant religion; of the Pope's being seen in a brandy-shop at Wapping," *&c.*

History of John Bull, part. 1. ch. 16

The other branch of wit in the thought, *viz.* ludicrous combinations and oppositions, may be traced through various ramifications. And, first, fanciful causes assigned that have no natural relation to the effects produced.

LANCASTER: Fare you well, Falstaff; I, in my condition, Shall better speak of you than you deserve. (*Exit*)
FALSTAFF: I would you had but the wit; 'twere better than your dukedom. Good faith, this same young sober-blooded boy doth not love me; nor a man cannot make him laugh; but that's no marvel, he drinks no wine. There's never any of

these demure boys come to any proof; for thin drink doth so over-cool their blood, and making many fish-meals, that they fall into a kind of male green-sickness; and then, when they marry, they get wenches. They are generally fools and cowards; which some of us should be too, but for inflammation. A good sherris-sack hath a twofold operation in it; it ascends me into the brain; dries me there all the foolish, dull, and crudy vapours which environ it; makes it apprehensive, quick, forgetive, full of nimble, fiery, and delectable shapes; which deliver'd o'er to the voice, the tongue, which is the birth, becomes excellent wit. The second property of your excellent sherris, is, the warming of the blood; which before cold and settled left the liver white and pale; which is the badge of pusillanimity and cowardice: but the sherris warms it, and makes it course from the inwards, to the parts extreme; it illuminateth the face, which, as a beacon, gives warning to all the rest of this little kingdom, man, to arm; and then the vital commoners and inland petty spirits muster me all to their captain, the heart; who, great, and puff'd up with this retinue, doth any deed of courage: and this valour comes of sherris. So that skill in the weapon is nothing without sack, for that sets it a-work; and learning a mere hoard of gold kept by a devil, till sack commences it, and sets it in act and use. Hereof comes it, that Prince Harry is valiant; for the cold blood he did naturally inherit of his father, he hath, like lean, steril, and bare land, manured, husbanded, and till'd, with excellent endeavour of drinking good and good store of fertil sherris, that he is become very hot and valiant. If I had a thousand sons, the first human principle I would teach them, should be to forswear thin potations, and to addict themselves to sack.

—*Second part of Henry* IV. *act. 4. sc. 7*

The trenchant blade, toledo trusty,
For want of fighting was grown rusty,
And ate into itself, for lack
Of somebody to hew and hack.

> *The peaceful scabbard where it dwelt,*
> *The rancor of its edge had felt:*
> *For of the lower end two handful,*
> *It had devoured, 'twas so manful;*
> *And so much scorn'd to lurk in case,*
> *As if it durst not shew its face.*
>
> —*Hudibras, canto 1*

Speaking of physicians,

Le bon de cette profession est, qu'il y a parmi les morts une honnêteté, une discretion la plus grande du monde; jamais on n'en voit se plaindre du médicin qui l'a tué.

Le medicin malgré lui

> *Admirez les bontez, admirez les tendresses,*
> *De ces vieux esclaves du sort.*
> *Ils ne sont jamais las d'aquérir des richesses,*
> *Pour ceux qui souhaitent leur mort.*

BELINDA: Lard, he has so pester'd me with flames and stuff—I think I shan't endure the sight of a fire this twelvemonth.

—*Old Bachelor, act 2. sc. 8*

To account for effects by such fantastical causes, being highly ludicrous, is quite improper in any serious composition. Therefore the following passage from Cowley, in his poem on the death of Sir Henry Wooton, is in a bad taste.

> *He did the utmost bounds of Knowledge find,*
> *He found them not so large as was his mind.*
> *But, like the brave Pellæan youth, did moan,*
> *Because that Art had no more worlds than one.*
> *And when he saw that he through all had past,*
> *He dy'd, lest he should idle grow at last.*

Fanciful reasoning,

FALSTAFF: Imbowell'd!—if thou imbowel me today, I'll give you leave to powder me, and eat me tomorrow! 'Sblood, 'twas time to counterfeit, or that hot termagant Scot had paid me scot and lot too. Counterfeit? I lie, I am no counterfeit; to die is to be a counterfeit; for he is but the counterfeit of a man, who hath not the life of a man: but to counterfeit dying, when a man thereby liveth, is to be no counterfeit, but the true and perfect image of life, indeed.

—First Part Henry IV. act 1. sc. 10

CLOWN: And the more pity that great folk should have countenance in this world to drown or hang themselves, more than their even Christian.

—Hamlet, Act 5. sc. 1

PEDRO: Will you have me, Lady?
BEATRICE: No, my Lord, unless I might have another for working days. Your Grace is too costly to wear everyday.

—Much ado about nothing, act 2. sc. 5

JESSICA: I shall be saved by my husband; he hath made me a Christian.
LAUNCELOT: Truly the more to blame he; we were Christians enough before, e'en as many as could well live by one another: this making of Christians will raise the price of hogs; if we grow all to be pork-eaters, we shall not have a rasher on the coals for money.

—Merchant of Venice, act 3. sc. 6

In western clime there is a town,
To those that dwell therein well known;
Therefore there needs no more be said here,
We unto them refer our reader:
For brevity is very good,
When w' are, or are not understood.

—Hudibras, canto 1

> *But Hudibras gave him a twitch,*
> *As quick as lightning, in the breech,*
> *Just in the place where honour's lodg'd,*
> *As wise philosophers have judg'd;*
> *Because a kick in that part, more*
> *Hurts honour, than deep wounds before.*

—*Ibid. canto 3*

Ludicrous junction of small things with great, as of equal importance.

> *This day black omens threat the brightest fair*
> *That e'er deserv'd a watchful spirit's care;*
> *Some dire disaster, or by force, or flight;*
> *But what, or where, the fates have wrapt in night:*
> *Whether the nymph shall break Diana's law;*
> *Or some frail china jar receive a flaw;*
> *Or stain her honour, or her new brocade;*
> *Forget her pray'rs, or miss a masquerade;*
> *Or lose her heart, or necklace, at a ball;*
> *Or whether Heav'n has doom'd that Shock must fall.*

—*Rape of the Lock, canto* ii. 101

> *One speaks the glory of the British Queen,*
> *And one describes a charming Indian screen.*

—*Ibid. canto* iii. 13

> *Then flash'd the living lightning from her eyes,*
> *And screams of horror rend th' affrighted skies.*
> *Not louder shrieks to pitying heav'n are cast,*
> *When husbands, or when lapdogs breathe their last;*
> *Or when rich china vessels fall'n from high,*
> *In glitt'ring dust, and painted fragments lie!*

—*Ibid. canto* iii. 155

> *Not youthful kings in battle seiz'd alive,*
> *Not scornful virgins who their charms survive,*
> *Not ardent lovers robb'd of all their bliss,*
> *Not ancient ladies when refus'd a kiss,*

> *Not tyrants fierce that unrepenting die,*
> *Not Cynthia when her manteau's pinn'd awry,*
> *E'er felt such rage, resentment, and despair,*
> *As thou, sad virgin! for thy ravish'd hair.*
>
> —*Ibid. canto* iv. 3

Joining things that in appearance are opposite. As for example, where Sir Roger de Coverley, in the Spectator, speaking of his widow, "That he would have given her a coal-pit to have kept her in clean linen; and that her finger should have sparkled with one hundred of his richest acres."

Premisses that promise much and perform nothing. Cicero upon this article says, "Sed scitis esse notissimum ridiculi genus, cum aliud expectamus, aliud dicitur: hic nobismetipsis noster error risum movet[3]."

> BEATRICE:—— With a good leg and a good foot, uncle, and money enough in his purse, such a man would win any woman in the world, if he could get her good-will.
>
> —*Much ado about nothing, act 2. sc. 1*

> BEATRICE: I have a good eye, uncle, I can see a church by day-light.
>
> —*ibid*

> *Le medecin que l'on m'indique*
> *Sait le Latin, le Grec, l'Hebreu,*
> *Les belles lettres, la physique,*
> *La chimie et la botanique.*
> *Chacun lui donne son aveu:*
> *Il auroit aussi ma pratique;*
> *Mais je veux vivre encore un peu.*

---

[3]. De oratore, I. 2. cap. 63.

Again,

> *Vingt fois le jour le bon Grégoire*
> *A soin de fermer son armoire.*
> *De quoi pensez vous qu'il a peur?*
> *Belle demande! Qu'un voleur*
> *Trouvant une facile proie,*
> *Ne lui ravisse tout son bien.*
> *Non; Gregoire a peur qu'on ne voie*
> *Que dan son armoire il n'a rien.*

Again,

> *L'athsmatique Damon a cru que l'air des champs*
> *Repareroit en lui le ravage des ans,*
> *Il s'est fait, a grands fraix, transporter en Bretagne.*
> *Or voiez ce qu'a fait l'air natal qu'il a pris!*
> *Damon seroit mort à Paris:*
> *Damon est mort à la campagne.*

Having discussed wit in the thought, we proceed to what is verbal only, commonly called *a play of words*. This sort of wit depends for the most part upon chusing words that have different significations. By this artifice, hocus-pocus tricks are played in language; and thoughts plain and simple take on a very different appearance. Play is necessary for man, in order to refresh him after labour; and accordingly man loves play. He even relisheth a play of words; and it is happy for us, that words can be employed, not only for useful purposes, but also for our amusement. This amusement accordingly, though humble and low, is relished by some at all times, and by all at sometimes, in order to unbend the mind.

It is remarkable, that this low species of wit, has, at one time or other, made a figure in most civilized nations, and has gradually gone into disrepute. So soon as a language is formed into a system, and the meaning of words are ascertained with tolerable accuracy, opportunity is afforded for expressions, which, by the double meaning of some words, give a familiar thought the appearance of being new. And the penetration of the reader or hearer, is gratified in detecting the true sense disguised under the double meaning. That this sort of wit was in England deemed a reputable amusement, during the reigns of

Elisabeth and James I is vouched by the works of Shakespear, and even by the writings of grave divines. But it cannot have any long endurance: for as language ripens, and the meaning of words is more and more ascertained, words held to be synonymous diminish daily; and when those that remain have been more than once employed, the pleasure vanisheth with the novelty.

I proceed to examples, which, as in the former case, shall be distributed into different classes.

A seeming resemblance from the double meaning of a word.

> *Beneath this stone my wife doth lie:*
> *She's now at rest, and so am I.*

A seeming contrast from the same cause, termed *a verbal antithesis*, which hath no despicable effect in ludicrous subjects.

> *Whilst Iris his cosmetic wash would try*
> *To make her bloom revive, and lovers die.*
> *Some ask for charms, and others philters chuse,*
> *To gain Corinna, and their quartans lose,*
>
> —*Dispensary, canto 2*
>
> *And how frail nymphs, oft by abortion, aim*
> *To lose a substance, to preserve a name.*
>
> —*Ibid. canto 3*

Other seeming connections from the same cause.

> *Will you employ your conqu'ring sword,*
> *To break a fiddle and your word.*
>
> —*Hudibras, canto 2*
>
> *To whom the knight with comely grace*
> *Put off his hat to put his case.*
>
> —*Hudibras, Part 3. canto 3*

> *Here Britain's statesmen oft the fall foredoom*
> *Of foreign tyrants, and of nymphs at home;*
> *Here thou, great Anna! whom three realms obey,*
> *Does sometimes counsel take—and sometimes tea.*
>
> —*Rape of the Lock, canto 3. l. 5*

> *O'er their quietus where fat judges dose,*
> *And lull their cough and conscience to repose.*
>
> —*Dispensary, canto 1*

Speaking of Prince Eugene. "This General is a great taker of snuff as well as of towns."

> *Pope, Key to the Lock*

> *Exul mentisque domusque.*
> —*Metamorphoses, lib.* ix. 409

A seeming inconsistency from the same cause.

> *Hic quiescit qui nunquam quievit.*

Again,

> *Quel âge a cette Iris, dont on fait tant de bruit?*
> *Me demandoit Cliton n'aguere.*
> *Il faut, dis-je, vous satisfaire,*
> *Elle a vingt ans le jour, et cinquante ans la nuit.*

Again,

> *So like the chances are of love and war,*
> *That they alone in this distinguish'd are;*
> *In love the victors from the vanguish'd fly,*
> *They fly that wound, and they pursue that die.*
>
> —*Waller*

> *What new-found witchcraft was in thee,*
> *With thine own cold to kindle me?*
> *Strange art; like him that should devise*
> *To make a burning-glass of ice.*

> —*Cowley*

Wit of this kind is unsuitable in a serious poem; witness the following line in Pope's Elegy to the memory of an unfortunate lady:

> *Cold is that breast which warm'd the world before.*

This sort of writing is finely burlesqued by Swift:

> *Her hands, the softest ever felt,*
> *Though cold would burn, though dry would melt.*

> —*Strephon and Chloe*

Taking a word in a different sense from what is meant, comes under wit, because it occasions some slight degree of surprise.

BEATRICE: I may sit in a corner, and cry *Heigh ho!* for a husband.
PEDRO: Lady Beatrice, I will get you one.
BEATRICE: I would rather have one of your father's getting: hath your Grace ne'er a brother like you? Your father got excellent husbands, if a maid could come by them.

> —*Much ado about nothing, act 2. sc. 5*

FALSTAFF: My honest lads, I will tell you what I am about.
PISTOL: Two yards and more.
FALSTAFF: No quips now, Pistol: indeed, I am in the waste two yards about; but I am now about no waste; I am about thrift.

> —*Merry wives of Windsor, act 1. sc. 7*

LO. SANDS:—— By your leave, sweet ladies, If I chance to talk a little wild, forgive me: I had it from my father.
ANNE BULLEN: Was he mad, Sir?

SANDS: O, very mad, exceeding mad, in love too; But he would bite none——

—K. Henry VIII

An assertion that bears a double meaning, one right, one wrong; but so connected with other matters as to direct us to the wrong meaning. This species of bastard wit is distinguished from all others by the name *pun*. For example,

PARIS:—— Sweet Helen, I must woo you,
To help unarm our Hector: his stubborn buckles,
With these your white inchanting fingers touch'd,
Shall more obey, than to the edge of steel,
Or force of Greekish sinews: you shall do more
Than all the island kings, disarm great Hector.

—Troilus and Cressida, act 3. sc. 2

The pun is in the close. The word *disarm* has a double meaning. It signifies to take off a man's armour, and also to subdue him in fight. We are directed to the latter sense by the context. But with regard to Helen the word holds only true in the former sense. I go on with other examples.

Esse nihil dicis quicquid petis, improbe Cinna:
Si nil, Cinna, petis, nil tibi, Cinna, nego.

—Martial, l. 3. epigr. 61

Jocondus geminum imposuit tibi, Sequana, pontem;
Hunc tu jure potes dicere pontificem.

—Sanazarius

N. B. *Jocondus was a monk.*

CHIEF JUSTICE: Well! the truth is, Sir John, you live in great infamy.
FALSTAFF: He that buckles him in my belt, cannot live in less.
CHIEF JUSTICE: Your means are very slender, and your waste is great.

FALSTAFF: I would it were otherwise: I would my means were greater, and my waste slenderer.

—Second part, Henry IV. act. 1 sc. 5

CELIA: I pray you bear with me, I can go no further.
CLOWN: For my part, I had rather bear with you than bear you: yet I should bear no cross if I did bear you; for I think you have no money in your purse.

—As you like it, act 2. sc. 4

He that imposes an oath makes it,
Not he that for convenience takes it;
Then how can any man be said,
To break an oath he never made?

—Hudibras, part 2. canto 2

The seventh satire of the first book of Horace, is purposely contrived to introduce at the close a most execrable pun. Talking of some infamous wretch whose name was *Rex Rupilius*.

Persius exclamat, Per magnos, Brute, deos te
Oro, qui reges consueris tollere, cur non
Hunc regem jugulas? Operum hoc, mihi crede, tuorum est.

Though playing with words is a mark of a mind at ease, and disposed for any sort of amusement, we must not thence conclude that playing with words is always ludicrous. Words are so intimately connected with thought, that if the subject be really grave, it will not appear ludicrous even in this fantastic dress. I am, however, far from recommending it in any serious performance. On the contrary, the discordance betwixt the thought and expression must be disagreeable; witness the following specimen.

He hath abandoned his physicians, Madam, under whose practices he hath persecuted time with hope: and finds no other advantage in the process, but only the losing of hope by time.

All's well that ends well, act 1. sc. 1

K. Henry: O my poor kingdom, sick with civil blows!
When that my care could not with-hold thy riots,
What wilt thou do when riot is thy care?

—Second part, K. Henry IV

A smart repartee may be considered as a species of wit. A certain petulant Greek, objecting to Anacharsis that he was a Scythian: True, says Anacharsis, my country disgraces me, but you disgrace your country.

XIV

Custom and Habit

Inquiring into the nature of man as a sensitive being, and finding him affected in a high degree with novelty, would anyone conjecture that he is equally affected with custom? Yet these frequently take place, not only in the same person, but even with relation to the same subject: when new, it is inchanting; familiarity renders it indifferent; and custom, after a longer familiarity, makes it again desirable. Human nature, diversified with many and various springs of action, is wonderfully, and, indulging the expression, intricately constructed.

Custom hath such influence upon many of our feelings, by warping and varying them, that we must attend to its operations if we would be acquainted with human nature. This subject, in itself obscure, has been much neglected; and to give a complete analysis of it will be no easy task. I pretend only to touch it cursorily; hoping, however, that what is here laid down, will dispose more diligent inquirers to attempt further discoveries.

Custom respects the action, *habit* the actor. By custom we mean, a frequent reiteration of the same act; and by habit, the effect that custom has on the mind or body. This effect may be either active, witness the dexterity produced by custom in performing certain exercises; or passive, as when, by custom, a peculiar connection is formed betwixt a man and some agreeable object, which acquires thereby a greater power to raise emotions in him than it hath naturally. Active habits come not under the present undertaking; and therefore I confine myself to those that are passive.

This subject is thorny and intricate. Some pleasures are fortified by custom; and yet custom begets familiarity, and consequently indifference[1]. In many instances, satiety and disgust are the consequences of reiteration.

1.
If all the year were playing holidays,
To sport would be as tedious as to work:
But when they seldom come, they wish'd for come,
And nothing pleaseth but rare accidents.

—First part, Henry IV. act 1. sc. 3

Again, though custom blunts the edge of distress and of pain; yet the want of anything to which we have long been accustomed, is a sort of torture. A clue to guide us through all the intricacies of this labyrinth, would be an acceptable present.

Whatever be the cause, it is an established fact, that we are much influenced by custom. It hath an effect upon our pleasures, upon our actions, and even upon our thoughts and sentiments. Habit makes no figure during the vivacity of youth; in middle age it gains ground; and in old age it governs without control. In that period of life, generally speaking, we eat at a certain hour, take exercise at a certain hour, go to rest at a certain hour, all by the direction of habit. Nay a particular seat, table, bed, comes to be essential. And a habit in any of these, cannot be contradicted without uneasiness.

Any slight or moderate pleasure frequently reiterated for a long time, forms a connection betwixt us and the thing that causes the pleasure. This connection, termed *habit*, has the effect to raise our desire or appetite for that thing when it returns not as usual. During the course of enjoyment, the pleasure grows insensibly stronger till a habit be established; at which time the pleasure is at its height. It continues not however stationary. The same customary reiteration which carried it to its height, brings it down again by insensible degrees, even lower than it was at first. But of this circumstance afterward. What at present we have in view, is to prove by experiments, that those things which at first are but moderately agreeable, are the aptest to become habitual. Spirituous liquors, at first scarce agreeable, readily produce an habitual appetite; and custom prevails so far, as even to make us fond of things originally disagreeable, such as coffee, assa-sœtida, and tobacco. This is pleasantly illustrated by Congreve:

> FAINALL: For a passionate lover, methinks you are a man somewhat too discerning in the failings of your mistress.
> MIRABELL: And for a discerning man, somewhat too passionate a lover; for I like her with all her faults; nay like her for her faults. Her follies are so natural, or so artful, that they become her; and those affectations which in another woman would be odious, serve but to make her more agreeable. I'll tell thee, Fainall, she once us'd me with that insolence, that in revenge I took her to pieces, sifted her, and separated her failings; I study'd 'em, and got 'em by rote. The catalogue was

so large, that I was not without hopes, one day or other, to hate her heartily: to which end I so us'd myself to think of 'em, that at length, contrary to my design and expectation, they gave me every hour less and less disturbance; till in a few days it became habitual to me, to remember 'em without being displeased. They are now grown as familiar to me as my own frailties; and in all probability, in a little time longer, I shall like 'em as well.

—*The way of the world, act 1. sc. 3*

A walk upon the quarterdeck, though intolerably confined, becomes however so agreeable by custom, that a sailor in his walk on shore, confines himself commonly within the same bounds. I knew a man who had relinquished the sea for a country-life. In the corner of his garden he reared an artificial mount with a level summit, resembling most accurately a quarterdeck, not only in shape but in size; and this was his choice walk. Play or gaming, at first barely amusing by the occupation it affords, becomes in time extremely agreeable; and is frequently prosecuted with avidity, as if it were the chief business of life. The same observation is applicable to the pleasures of the internal senses, those of knowledge and virtue in particular. Children have scarce any sense of these pleasures; and men very little, who are in the state of nature without culture. Our taste for virtue and knowledge improves slowly; but is capable of growing stronger than any other appetite in human nature.

To introduce a habit, frequency of acts is not alone sufficient: length of time is also necessary. The quickest succession of acts in a short time, is not sufficient; nor a slow succession in the longest time. The effect must be produced by a moderate soft action, and a long series of easy touches removed from each other by short intervals. Nor are these sufficient, without regularity in the time, place, and other circumstances of the action. The more uniform any operation is, the sooner it becomes habitual; and this holds equally in a passive habit. Variety in any remarkable degree, prevents the effect. Thus any particular food will scarce ever become habitual, where the manner of dressing is varied. The circumstances then requisite to augment any pleasure and at the long run to form a habit, are weak uniform acts, reiterated during a long course of time without any considerable interruption. Every agreeable cause which operates in this manner, will grow habitual.

Affection and *aversion*, as distinguished from passion on the one hand, and on the other from original disposition, are in reality habits respecting particular objects, acquired in the manner above set forth. The pleasure of social intercourse with any person, must originally be faint, and frequently reiterated, in order to establish the habit of affection. Affection thus generated, whether it be friendship or love, seldom swells into any tumultuous or vigorous passion; but is however the strongest cement that can bind together two individuals of the human species. In like manner, a slight degree of disgust often reiterated with any degree of regularity, grows into the habit of aversion, which generally subsists for life.

Those objects of taste that are the most agreeable, are so far from having a tendency to become habitual, that too great indulgence fails not to produce satiety and disgust. No man contracts a habit of taking sugar, honey, or sweet-meats, as he doth of tobacco:

> *Dulcia non ferimus: succo renovamur amaro.*
>
> —*Ovid. art. Amand. l. 3*

> *Insipido è quel dolce, che condito*
> *Non è di qualche amaro, e tosto satia.*
>
> —*Aminta di Tasso*

> *These violent delights have violent ends,*
> *And in their triumph die. The sweetest honey*
> *Is loathsome in its own deliciousness,*
> *And in the taste confounds the appetite;*
> *Therefore love mod'rately, long love doth so:*
> *Too swift arrives as tardy as too slow.*
>
> —*Romeo and Juliet, act 2. sc. 6*

The same holds in the causes of all violent pleasures: these causes are not naturally susceptible of habit. Great passions suddenly raised are incompatible with a habit of any sort. In particular they never produce affection or aversion. A man who at first sight falls violently in love, has a strong desire of enjoyment, but no affection for the woman[2]. A man who is surprised with an unexpected savour, burns for an opportunity to exert his gratitude, without having any affection for his benefactor. Neither does desire of vengeance for an atrocious injury involve aversion.

It is perhaps not easy to say why moderate pleasures gather strength by custom. But two causes concur to prevent this effect in the more intense pleasures. These, by an original law in our nature, increase quickly to their full growth, and decay with no less precipitation[3]; and custom is too slow in its operation to overcome this law. Another cause is not less powerful. The mind is exhausted with pleasure as well as with pain. Exquisite pleasure is extremely fatiguing; occasioning, as a naturalist would say, great expence of animal spirits[4]. And therefore, of such the mind cannot bear so frequent gratification as to superinduce a habit. If the thing which raises the pleasure return before the mind have recovered its tone and relish, disgust ensues instead of pleasure.

---

2. Violent love without affection is finely exemplified in the following story. When Constantinople was taken by the Turks, Irene, a young Greek of an illustrious family, fell into the hands of Mahomet II, who was at that time in the prime of youth and glory. His savage heart being subdued by her charms, he shut himself up with her, denying access even to his ministers. Love obtained such ascendant as to make him frequently abandon the army, and fly to his Irene. War relaxed, for victory was no longer the monarch's favourite passion. The soldiers, accustomed to booty, began to murmur; and the infection spread even among the commanders. The basha Mustapha, consulting the fidelity he owed his master, was the first who durst acquaint him of the discourses held publicly to the prejudice of his glory.

The sultan, after a gloomy silence, formed his resolution. He ordered Mustapha to assemble the troops next morning; and then with precipitation retired to Irene's apartment. Never before did that princess appear so charming; never before did the prince bestow so many warm caresses. To give a new lustre to her beauty, be exhorted her women next morning, to bestow their utmost art and care on her dress. He took her by the hand, led her into the middle of the army, and, pulling off her veil, demanded of the bashas with a fierce look, whether they ever had beheld such a beauty? After an awful pause, Mahomet, with one hand laying hold of the young Greek by her beautiful locks, and with the other pulling out his scimitar, severed the head from the body at one stroke. Then turning to his grandees, with eyes wild and furious, "This sword," said he, "when it is my will, knows to cut the bands of love." However strange it may appear, we learn from experience, that desire of enjoyment may consist with the most brutal aversion, directed both to the same woman. Of this we have a noted example in the first book of Sully's Memoirs; to which I choose to refer the reader, for it is too gross to be transcribed.

3. See chap. 2. part 3.

4. Lady Easy, upon her husband's reformation, expresses to her friend the following sentiment: "Be satisfied; Sir Charles has made me happy, even to a "pain of joy."

A habit never fails to admonish us of the wonted time of gratification, by raising a pain for want of the object, and a desire to have it. The pain of want is always first felt; the desire naturally follows; and upon presenting the object, both vanish instantaneously. Thus a man accustomed to tobacco, feels, at the end of the usual interval, a confused pain of want, which in its first appearance points at nothing in particular, though it soon settles upon its accustomed object. The same may be observed in persons addicted to drinking, who are often in an uneasy restless state before they think of their bottle. In pleasures indulged regularly and at equal intervals, the appetite, remarkably obsequious to custom, returns regularly with the usual time of gratification; and a sight of the object in the interim, has scarce any power to move it. This pain of want arising from habit, seems directly opposite to that of satiety. Singular it must appear, that frequency of gratification should produce effects so opposite as are the pains of excess and of want.

The appetites that respect the preservation and propagation of our species, are attended with a pain of want similar to that occasioned by habit. Hunger and thirst are uneasy sensations of want, which always precede the desire of eating or drinking: and a pain for want of carnal enjoyment precedes the desire of a proper object. The pain being thus felt independent of an object, cannot be cured but by gratification. An ordinary passion, in which desire precedes the pain of want, is in a different condition. It is never felt but while the object is in view; and therefore by removing the object out of thought, it vanisheth with its desire and pain of want[5].

These natural appetites above mentioned, differ from habit in the following particular, They have an undetermined direction toward all objects of gratification in general; whereas an habitual appetite is directed upon a particular object. The attachment we have by habit to a particular woman, differs widely from the natural passion which comprehends the whole sex; and the habitual relish for a particular dish, is far from being the same with a vague appetite for food. Notwithstanding this difference, it is still remarkable, that nature hath inforced the gratification of certain natural appetites essential to the species, by a pain of the same sort with that which habit produceth.

The pain of habit is less under our power, than any other pain for want of gratification. Hunger and thirst are more easily endured,

---

5. See chap. 2. part 3.

especially at first, than an unusual intermission of any habitual pleasure. We often hear persons declaring, they would forego sleep or food, rather than snuff or any other habitual trifle. We must not however conclude, that the gratification of an habitual appetite affords the same delight with the gratification of one that is natural. Far from it: the pain of want only is greater.

The slow and reiterated acts that produce a habit, strengthen the mind to enjoy the habitual pleasure in greater quantity and more frequency than originally; and by this means a habit of intemperate gratification is often formed. After unbounded acts of intemperance, the habitual relish is soon restored, and the pain for want of enjoyment returns with fresh vigor.

The causes of the pleasant emotions hitherto in view, are either an individual, such as a companion, a certain dwelling-place, certain amusements, &c.; or a particular species, such as coffee, mutton, or any particular food. But habit is not confined to these. A constant train of trifling diversions, may form such a habit in the mind, as that it cannot be easy a moment without amusement. Variety in the objects prevents a habit as to anyone in particular; but as the train is uniform with respect to amusement in general, the habit is formed accordingly; and this sort of habit may be denominated *a generic habit*, in opposition to the former, which may be called *a specific habit*. A habit of a town-life, of country-sports, of solitude, of reading, or of business, where sufficiently varied, are instances of generic habits. It ought to be remarked, that every specific habit hath a mixture of the generic. The habit of one particular sort of food, makes the taste agreeable; and we are fond of this taste where-ever found. A man deprived of an habitual object, takes up with what most resembles it: deprived of tobacco, any bitter herb will do, rather than want. The habit of drinking punch, makes wine a good resource. A man accustomed to the sweet society and comforts of matrimony, being unhappily deprived of his beloved object, inclines the sooner to a second choice. In general, the quality which the most affects us in an habitual object, produceth, when we are deprived of it, a strong appetite for that quality in any other object.

The reasons are assigned above, why the causes of intense pleasure become not readily habitual. But now I must observe, that these reasons conclude only against specific habits. With regard to any particular object that is the cause of a weak pleasure, a habit is formed by frequency and uniformity of reiteration, which in the case of an intense pleasure cannot obtain without satiety and disgust. But it is remarkable, that satiety and disgust have no effect, except as to that thing which occasions them. A surfeit of honey produceth not a loathing of sugar; and intemperance with one woman, produceth no disrelish of the same pleasure with others. Hence it is easy to account for a generic habit in any strong pleasure. The disgust of intemperance, is confined to the object by which it is produced. The delight we had in the gratification of the appetite, inflames the imagination, and makes us, with avidity, search for the same gratification in whatever other object it can be found. And thus frequency and uniformity in gratifying the same passion upon different objects, produceth at the longrun a habit. In this manner, a man acquires an habitual delight in high and poignant sauces, rich dress, fine equipage, crowds of company, and in whatever is commonly termed *pleasure*. There concurs at the same time to introduce this habit, a peculiarity observed above, that reiteration of acts enlarges the capacity of the mind, to admit a more plentiful gratification than originally, with regard to frequency as well as quantity.

Hence it appears, that though a specific habit can only take place in the case of a moderate pleasure, yet that a generic habit may be formed with respect to every sort of pleasure, moderate or immoderate, that can be gratified by a variety of objects indifferently. The only difference is, that any particular object which causes a weak pleasure, runs naturally into a specific habit; whereas a particular object that causes an intense pleasure, is altogether incapable of such a habit. In a word, it is but in singular cases that a moderate pleasure produces a generic habit: an intense pleasure, on the other hand, cannot produce any other habit.

The appetites that respect the preservation and propagation of the species, are formed into habit in a peculiar manner. The time as well as measure of their gratification, are much under the power of custom; which, by introducing a change upon the body, occasions a proportional change in the appetites. Thus, if the body be gradually formed to a certain quantity of food at regular times, the appetite is regulated accordingly; and the appetite is again changed when a different habit of body is introduced by a different practice. Here it would seem, that the change is not made upon the mind, which is commonly the case in passive habits, but only upon the body.

When rich food is brought down by ingredients of a plainer taste, the composition is susceptible of a specific habit. Thus the sweet taste of sugar, rendered less poignant in a mixture, may, in course of time, produce a specific habit for such mixture. As moderate pleasures, by becoming more intense, tend to generic habits; so intense pleasures, by becoming more moderate, tend to specific habits.

The beauty of the human figure, by a special recommendation of nature, appears to us supreme, amid the great variety of beauteous forms bestowed upon animals. The various degrees in which individuals enjoy this property, render it an object sometimes of a moderate sometimes of an intense passion. The moderate passion, admitting frequent reiteration without diminution, and occupying the mind without exhausting it, becomes gradually stronger till it settle in a habit. So true this is, that instances are not wanting, of an ugly face, at first disagreeable, afterward rendered indifferent by familiarity, and at the longrun agreeable. On the other hand, consummate beauty, at the very first view, fills the mind so as to admit no increase. Enjoyment in this case lessens the pleasure[6]; and if often repeated, ends commonly in satiety and disgust. Constant experience shows, that the emotions created by great beauty become weaker by familiarity. The impressions made successively by such an object, strong at first and lessening by degrees, constitute a series opposite to that of the weak and increasing emotions, which grow into a specific habit. But the mind, when accustomed to beauty, contracts a relish for it in general, though often repelled from particular objects by the pain of satiety. Thus a generic habit is formed, of which inconstancy in love is the necessary consequence. For a generic habit, comprehending every beautiful object, is an invincible obstruction to a specific habit, which is confined to one.

But a matter which is of great importance to the youth of both sexes, deserves more than a cursory view. Though the pleasant emotion of beauty differs widely from the corporeal appetite, yet both may concur upon the same object. When this is the case, they inflame the imagination; and produce a very strong complex passion[7], which is incapable of increase, because the mind as to pleasure is limited rather more than as to pain. Enjoyment in this case must be exquisite, and therefore more apt to produce satiety than in any other case whatever. This is a never-failing effect, where consummate beauty on the one side, meets with a warm imagination and great sensibility on the other. What I am here explaining, is the naked truth without exaggeration. They

---

6. See chap, 2. part 3.
7. See chap. 2. part 4.

must be insensible upon whom this doctrine makes no impression; and it deserves well to be pondered by the young and the amorous, who in forming a society which is not dissolvable, are too often blindly impelled by the animal pleasure merely, inflamed by beauty. It may indeed happen after this pleasure is gone, and go it must with a swift pace, that a new connection is formed upon more dignified and more lasting principles. But this is a dangerous experiment. For even supposing good sense, good temper, and internal merit of every sort, which is a very favourable supposition, yet a new connection upon these qualifications is rarely formed. It generally or rather always happens, that such qualifications, the only solid foundation of an indissoluble connection, are rendered altogether invisible by satiety of enjoyment creating disgust.

One effect of custom, different from any that have been explained, must not be omitted, because it makes a great figure in human nature. Custom augments moderate pleasures, and diminishes those that are intense. It has a different effect with respect to pain; for it blunts the edge of every sort of pain and distress great and small. Uninterrupted misery therefore is attended with one good effect. If its torments be incessant, custom hardens us to bear them.

It is extremely curious, to remark the gradual changes that are made in forming habits. Moderate pleasures are augmented gradually by reiteration till they become habitual; and then are at their height. But they are not long stationary; for from that point they gradually decay till they vanish altogether. The pain occasioned by the want of gratification, runs a very different course. This pain increases uniformly; and at last becomes extreme, when the pleasure of gratification is reduced to nothing.

—— *It so falls out*
That what we have we prize not to the worth,
Whiles we enjoy it; but being lack'd and lost,
Why then we rack the value; then we find
The virtue that possession would not shew us
Whilst it was ours.

—*Much ado about nothing, act 4. sc. 2*

The effect of custom with relation to a specific habit, is displayed through all its varieties in the use of tobacco. The taste of this plant is at first extremely unpleasant. Our disgust lessens gradually till it vanish altogether; at which period the plant is neither agreeable nor disagreeable. Continuing the use, we begin to relish it; and our relish increases by use till it come to its utmost extent. From this state it gradually decays, while the habit becomes stronger and stronger, and consequently the pain of want. The result is, that when the habit has acquired its greatest vigor, the pleasure of gratification is gone. And hence it is, that we often smoke and take snuff habitually, without so much as being conscious of the operation. We must except gratification after the pain of want; because gratification in that case is at the height when the habit is strongest. It is of the same kind with the joy one feels upon being delivered from the rack, the cause of which is explained above[8]. This pleasure however is but occasionally the effect of habit; and however exquisite, is guarded against as much as possible, by preventing want.

With regard to the pain of want, I can discover no difference betwixt a generic and specific habit: the pain is the same in both. But these habits differ widely with respect to the positive pleasure. I have had occasion to observe, that the pleasure of a specific habit decays gradually till it become imperceptible. Not so the pleasure of a generic habit. So far as I can discover, this pleasure suffers little or no decay after it comes to its height. The variety of gratification preserves it entire. However it may be with other generic habits, the observation I am certain holds with respect to the pleasures of virtue and of knowledge. The pleasure of doing good has such an unbounded scope, and may be so variously gratified, that it can never decay. Science is equally unbounded; and our appetite for knowledge has an ample range of gratification, where discoveries are recommended by novelty, by variety, by utility, or by all of them.

Here is a large field of facts and experiments, and several phenomena unfolded, the causes of which have been occasionally suggested. The efficient cause of the power of custom over man, a fundamental point in the present chapter, has unhappily evaded my keenest search; and now I am reduced to hold it an original branch of the human constitution, though I have no better reason for my opinion, than that I cannot resolve it into any other principle. But with respect to the final cause, a point of still greater importance, I promise myself more success. It cannot indeed have escaped any thinking person, that the power of custom

---

8. Chap, 2. part 1. sect. 3.

is a happy contrivance for our good. Exquisite pleasure produceth satiety: moderate pleasure becomes stronger by custom. Business is our province, and pleasure our relaxation only. Hence, satiety is necessary to check exquisite pleasures, which otherwise would ingross the mind, and unqualify us for business. On the other hand, habitual increase of moderate pleasure, and even conversion of pain into pleasure, are admirably contrived for disappointing the malice of Fortune, and for reconciling us to whatever course of life may be our lot:

> *How use doth breed a habit in a man!*
> *This shadowy desert, unfrequented woods,*
> *I better brook than flourishing peopled towns.*
> *Here I can sit alone, unseen of any,*
> *And to the nightingale's complaining notes*
> *Tune my distresses, and record my woes.*
>
> —*Two Gentlemen of Verona*, act 5. sc. 4

The foregoing distinction betwixt intense and moderate, holds in pleasure only, not in pain, every degree of which is softened by time and custom. Custom is a catholicon for pain and distress of every sort; and of this regulation the final cause is so evident as to require no illustration.

Another final cause of custom will be highly relished by every person of humanity; and yet has in a great measure been overlooked. Custom hath a greater influence than any other known principle, to put the rich and poor upon a level. Weak pleasures, which fall to the share of the latter, become fortunately stronger by custom; while voluptuous pleasures, the lot of the former, are continually losing ground by satiety. Men of fortune, who possess palaces, sumptuous gardens, rich fields, enjoy them less than passengers do. The goods of Fortune are not unequally distributed: the opulent possess what others enjoy.

And indeed, if it be the effect of habit to produce the pain of want in a high degree while there is little pleasure in enjoyment, a voluptuous life is of all the least to be envied. Those who are accustomed to high feeding, easy vehicles, rich furniture, a crowd of valets, much deference and flattery, enjoy but a small share of happiness, while they are exposed to manifold distresses. To such a man, inslaved by ease and luxury, even the petty inconveniencies of a rough road, bad weather, or homely fare on a journey, are serious evils. He loses his tone of mind, becomes peevish, and would wreak his resentment even upon the common accidents of life. Better far to use the goods of Fortune with moderation. A man who by temperance and activity has acquired a hardy constitution, is, on the one hand, guarded against external accidents, and is, on the other, provided with great variety of enjoyment ever at command.

I shall close this chapter with the discussion of a question more delicate than abstruse, *viz.* What authority custom ought to have over our taste in the fine arts? It is proper to be premised, that we chearfully abandon to its authority everything that nature leaves to our choice, and where the preference we bestow has no foundation other than whim or fancy. There appears no original difference betwixt the right and the left hand: custom however has established a difference, so as to make it aukward and disagreeable to use the left where the right is commonly used. The various colours, though they affect us differently, are all of them agreeable in their purity. But custom has regulated this matter in another manner: a black skin upon a human creature, is to us disagreeable; and a white skin probably not less so to a negro. Thus things originally indifferent, become agreeable or disagreeable by the force of custom. Nor ought this to be surprising after the discovery made above, that the original agreeableness or disagreeableness of an object, is, by the influence of custom, often converted into the opposite quality.

Concerning now those matters of taste where there is naturally a preference of one thing before another; it is certain, in the first place, that our faint and more delicate feelings are readily susceptible of a bias from custom; and therefore that it is no proof of a defective taste, to find these in some measure under the government of custom. Dress, and the modes of external behaviour, are justly regulated by custom in every country. The deep red or vermilion with which the ladies in France cover their cheeks, appears to them beautiful in spite of nature; and strangers cannot altogether be justified in condemning this practice, considering the lawful authority of custom, or of the *fashion*, as it is called. It is told of the people who inhabit the skirts of the Alps facing the north, that the swelling they universally have in the neck is to them agreeable. So far has custom power to change the nature of things, and to make an object originally disagreeable take on an opposite appearance.

But as to the emotions of propriety and impropriety, and in general as to all emotions involving the sense of right or wrong, custom has little authority, and ought to have none at all. Emotions of this kind, being qualified with the consciousness of duty, take naturally place of every other feeling; and it argues a shameful weakness or degeneracy of mind, to find them in any case so far subdued as to submit to custom.

These few hints may enable us to judge in some measure of foreign manners, whether exhibited by foreign writers or our own. A comparison betwixt the ancients and the moderns, was sometime ago a favourite subject. Those who declared for the former, thought it a sufficient justification of ancient manners, that they were supported by the authority of custom. Their antagonists, on the other hand, refusing submission to custom as a standard of taste, condemned ancient manners in several instances as irrational. In this controversy, an appeal being made to different principles, without the slightest attempt on either side to establish a common standard, the dispute could have no end. The hints above given tend to establish a standard, for judging how far the lawful authority of custom may be extended, and within what limits it ought to be confined. For the sake of illustration, we shall apply this standard in a few instances.

Human sacrifices, the cruellest effect of blind and groveling superstition, wore gradually out of use by the prevalence of reason and humanity. In the days of Sophocles and Euripides, the traces of this savage practice were still recent; and the Athenians, through the prevalence of custom, could without disgust suffer human sacrifices to be represented in their theatre. The Iphigenia of Euripides is a proof of this fact. But a human sacrifice, being altogether inconsistent with modern manners, as producing horror instead of pity, cannot with any propriety be introduced upon a modern stage. I must therefore condemn the Iphigenia of Racine, which, instead of the tender and sympathetic passions, substitutes disgust and horror. But this is not all. Another objection occurs against every fable that deviates so remarkably from improved notions and sentiments. If it should even command our belief, by the authority of genuine history, its fictitious and unnatural appearance, however, would prevent its taking such hold of the mind as to produce a perception of reality[9]. A human sacrifice is so unnatural, and to us so improbable, that few will be affected with the representation of it more than with a fairy tale. The objection first mentioned strikes also against the *Phedra* of this author. The queen's passion for her stepson, being unnatural and beyond all bounds, creates

---

9. See chap. 2. part 1. sect. 7.

aversion and horror rather than compassion. The author in his preface observes, that the queen's passion, however unnatural, was the effect of destiny and the wrath of the gods; and he puts the same excuse in her own mouth. But what is the wrath of a heathen god to us Christians? We acknowledge no destiny in passion; and if love be unnatural, it never can be relished. A supposition, like what our author lays hold of, may possibly cover slight improprieties; but it will never engage our sympathy for what appears to us frantic or extravagant.

Neither can I relish the catastrophe of this tragedy. A man of taste may peruse, without disgust, a Grecian performance describing a sea-monster sent by Neptune to destroy Hippolytus. He considers, that such a story might agree with the religious creed of Greece; and, entering into ancient opinions, may be pleased with the story, as what probably had a strong effect upon a Grecian audience. But he cannot have the same indulgence for such a representation upon a modern stage; for no story which carries a violent air of fiction, can ever move us in any considerable degree.

In the *Coëphores* of Eschylus[10], Orestes is made to say, that he was commanded by Apollo to avenge his father's murder; and yet if he obeyed, that he was to be delivered to the furies, or be struck with some horrible malady. The tragedy accordingly concludes with a chorus, deploring the fate of Orestes, obliged to take vengeance against a mother, and involved thereby in a crime against his will. It is impossible for any man at present to accommodate his mind to opinions so irrational and absurd, which must disgust him in perusing even a Grecian story. Among the Greeks again, grossly superstitious, it was a common opinion, that the report of a man's death was a presage of his death; and Orestes, in the first act of *Electra*, spreading a report of his own death in order to blind his mother and her adulterer, is even in this case affected with the presage. Such imbecility can never find grace with a modern audience. It may indeed produce some degree of compassion for a people afflicted to such a degree with absurd terrors, similar to what is felt in perusing a description of the Hottentotes: but manners of this kind will not interest our affections, nor excite any degree of social concern.

---

10. Act 2.

XV

External Signs of Emotions and Passions

So intimately connected are the soul and body, that there is not a single agitation in the former, but what produceth a visible effect upon the latter. There is, at the same time, a wonderful uniformity in this operation; each class of emotions being invariably attended with an external appearance peculiar to itself[1]. These external appearances or signs, may not improperly be considered as a natural language, expressing to all beholders the several emotions and passions as they arise in the heart. We perceive display'd externally, hope, fear, joy, grief: we can read the character of a man in his face; and beauty, which makes so strong an impression, is known to result, not so much from regular features and a fine complexion, as from good nature, good sense, sprightliness, sweetness, or other mental quality, expressed some way upon the countenance. Though perfect skill in this language be rare, yet so much knowledge of it is diffused through mankind, as to be sufficient for the ordinary events of life. But by what means we come to understand this language, is a point of some intricacy. It cannot be by sight merely; for upon the most attentive inspection of the human visage, all that can be discerned are figure, colour, and motion; and yet these, singly or combined, never can represent a passion or a sentiment. The external sign is indeed visible. But to understand its meaning, we must be able to connect it with the passion that causes it; an operation far beyond the reach of eye-sight. Where then is the instructor to be found, that can unvail this secret connection? If we apply to experience, it is yielded, that from long and diligent observation, we may gather in some measure in what manner those we are acquainted with express their passions externally. But with respect to strangers, of whom we have no experience, we are left in the dark. And yet we are not puzzled about the meaning of these external expressions in a stranger, more than in a bosom-companion. Further, had we no other means but experience for understanding the external signs of passion, we could not expect any uniformity or any degree of skill in the bulk of individuals. But

---

1. Omnis enim motus animi suum quemdam a natura habet vultum et sonum et gestam. *Cicero, l. 3. De Oratore.*

matters are ordered so differently, that the external expressions of passion form a language understood by all, by the young as well as the old, by the ignorant as well as the learned. I talk of the plain and legible characters of this language; for undoubtedly we are much indebted to experience in deciphering the dark and more delicate expressions. Where then shall we apply for a solution of this intricate problem, which seems to penetrate deep into human nature? In my mind it will be convenient to suspend the inquiry, till we be better acquainted with the nature of external signs and with their operations. These articles therefore shall be premised.

The external signs of passion are of two kinds, voluntary and involuntary. The voluntary signs are also of two kinds: some are arbitrary and some natural. Words are arbitrary signs, excepting a few simple sounds expressive of certain internal emotions; and these sounds, being the same in all languages, must be the work of nature. But though words are arbitrary, the manner of employing them is not altogether so; for each passion has by nature peculiar expressions and tones suited to it. Thus the unpremeditated tones of admiration, are the same in all men; as also of compassion, resentment, and despair. Dramatic writers ought to be well acquainted with this natural manner of expressing passion. The chief talent of a fine writer, is a ready command of the expressions that nature dictates to every man when any vivid emotion struggles for utterance; and the chief talent of a fine reader, is a ready command of the tones suited to these expressions.

The other kind of voluntary signs, comprehends certain attitudes and gestures that naturally accompany certain emotions with a surprising uniformity. Thus excessive joy is expressed by leaping, dancing, or some elevation of the body; and excessive grief by sinking or depressing it. Thus prostration and kneeling have been employ'd by all nations and in all ages to signify profound veneration. Another circumstance, still more than uniformity, demonstrates these gestures to be natural, *viz.* their remarkable conformity or resemblance to the passions that produce them[2]. Joy, which produceth a chearful elevation of mind, is expressed by an elevation of body. Pride, magnanimity, courage, and the whole tribe of elevating passions, are expressed by external gestures that are the same as to the circumstance of elevation, however distinguishable in other respects. Hence it comes, that an erect posture is a sign or expression of dignity:

---

2. See chap. 2, part 6.

> *Two of far nobler shape, erect and tall,*
> *Godlike erect, with native honour clad,*
> *In naked majesty, seem'd lords of all.*
>
> —*Paradise Lost*, book 4

Grief, on the other hand, as well as respect, which depress the mind, cannot for that reason be expressed more significantly than by a similar depression of the body. Hence, *to be cast down*, is a common phrase, signifying to be grieved or dispirited.

One would not imagine, who has not given peculiar attention, that the body is susceptible of such a variety of attitude and motion, as readily to accompany every different emotion with a corresponding gesture. Humility, for example, is expressed naturally by hanging the head; arrogance, by its elevation; and langour or despondence, by reclining it to one side. The expressions of the hands are manifold. By different attitudes and motions, the hands express desire, hope, fear: they assist us in promising, in inviting, in keeping one at a distance: they are made instruments of threatening, of supplication, of praise, and of horror: they are employ'd in approving, in refusing, in questioning; in showing our joy, our sorrow, our doubts, our regret, our admiration. These gestures, so obedient to passion, are extremely difficult to be imitated in a calm state. The ancients, sensible of the advantage as well as difficulty of having these expressions at command, bestowed much time and care, in collecting them from observation, and in digesting them into a practical art, which was taught in their schools as an important branch of education.

The foregoing signs, though in a strict sense voluntary, cannot however be restrained but with the utmost difficulty when they are prompted by passion. Of this we scarce need a stronger proof, than the gestures of a keen player at bowls. Observe only how he wreaths his body, in order to restore a stray bowl to the right track. It is one article of good breeding, to suppress, as much as possible, these external signs of passion, that we may not in company appear too warm or too interested. The same observation holds in speech. A passion, it is true, when in extreme, is silent[3]; but when less violent, it must be vented in words, which have a peculiar force, not to be equalled in a sedate

---

3. See chap. 17.

composition. The ease and trust we have in a confident, encourages us no doubt to talk of ourselves and of our feelings. But the cause is more general; for it operates when we are alone as well as in company. Passion is the cause; for in many instances it is no slight gratification to vent a passion externally by words as well as by gestures. Some passions, when at a certain height, impel us so strongly to vent them in words, that we speak with an audible voice even where there is none to listen. It is this circumstance in passion, that justifies soliloquies; and it is this circumstance that proves them to be natural[4]. The mind sometimes favours this impulse of passion, by bestowing a temporary sensibility upon any object at hand, in order to make it a confident. Thus in the *Winter's Tale*[5], Antigonus addresses himself to an infant whom he was ordered to expose:

> *Come, poor babe,*
> *I have heard, but not believ'd, the spirits of the dead*
> *May walk again: if such thing be, thy mother*
> *Appear'd to me last night; for ne'er was dream*
> *So like a waking.*

The involuntary signs, which are all of them natural, are either peculiar to one passion or common to many. Every violent passion hath an external expression peculiar to itself, not excepting pleasant passions: witness admiration and mirth. The pleasant emotions that are less vivid, have one common expression; from which we may gather the strength of the emotion, but scarce the kind: we perceive a chearful or contented look; and we can make no more of it. Painful passions, being

---

[4]. Though a soliloquy in the perturbation of passion is undoubtedly natural, and, indeed, not unfrequent in real life, yet Congreve, who himself has penned several good soliloquies, yields, with more candour than knowledge, that they are unnatural, and he only pretends to justify them from necessity. This he does in his dedication of the *Double Dealer* in the following words: "When a man in a soliloquy reasons with himself, and *pro's* and *con's*, and weighs all his designs, we ought not to imagine that this man either talks to us or to himself; he is only thinking, and thinking (frequently) such matter as it were inexcusable folly in him to speak. But because we are concealed spectators of the plot in agitation, and the poet finds it necessary to let us know the whole mystery of his contrivance, he is willing to inform us of this person's thoughts, and to that end is forced to make use of the expedient of speech, no other better way being yet invented for the communication of thought."

[5]. Act 3. sc. 6.

all of them violent, are distinguishable from each other by their external expressions. Thus fear, shame, anger, anxiety, dejection, despair, have each of them peculiar expressions; which are apprehended without the least confusion. Some of these passions produce violent effects upon the body, such as trembling, starting, and swooning. But these effects, depending in a good measure upon singularity of constitution, are not uniform in all men.

The involuntary signs, such of them as are display'd upon the countenance, are of two kinds. Some make their appearance occasionally with the emotions that produce them, and vanish with the emotions: others are formed gradually by some violent passion often recurring; and, becoming permanent signs of this prevailing passion, serve to denote the disposition or temper. The face of an infant indicates no particular disposition, because it cannot be marked with any character to which time is necessary. And even the temporary signs are extremely aukward, being the first rude essays of Nature to discover internal feelings. Thus the shrieking of a new-born infant, without tears or sobbings, is plainly an attempt to weep. Some of the temporary signs, as smiling and frowning, cannot be observed for some months after birth. The permanent signs, formed in youth while the body is soft and flexible, are preserved entire by the firmness and solidity which the body acquires; and are never obliterated even by a change of temper. Permanent signs are not produced after a certain age when the fibres become rigid; some violent cases excepted, such as reiterated fits of the gout or stone through a course of time. But these signs are not so obstinate as what are produced in youth; for when the cause is removed, they gradually wear away, and at last vanish.

The natural signs of emotions, voluntary and involuntary, being nearly the same in all men, form an universal language, which no distance of place, no difference of tribe, no diversity of tongue, can darken or render doubtful. Education, though of mighty influence, hath not power to vary or sophisticate, far less to destroy, their signification. This is a wise appointment of Providence. For if these signs were, like words, arbitrary and variable, it would be an intricate science to decipher the actions and motives of our own species, which would prove a great or rather invincible obstruction to the formation of societies. But as matters are ordered, the external appearances of joy, grief, anger, fear, shame, and of the other passions, forming an universal language, open a direct avenue to the heart. As the arbitrary signs vary in every country, there could be no communication of thoughts among different nations, were it not for the natural signs in which all agree. Words are sufficient for the communication of science, and of all mental conceptions: but the discovering passions instantly as they arise, being essential to our well-being and often necessary for self-preservation, the author of our nature, attentive to our wants, hath provided a passage to the heart, which never can be obstructed while our external senses remain entire.

In an inquiry concerning the external signs of passion, actions ought not altogether to be overlooked: for though singly they afford no clear light, they are upon the whole the best interpreters of the heart[6]. By observing a man's conduct for a course of time, we discover unerringly the various passions that move him to action, what he loves and what he hates. In our younger years, every single action is a mark not at all ambiguous of the temper; for in childhood there is little or no disguise. The subject becomes more intricate in advanced age; but even there, dissimulation is seldom carried on for any length of time. And thus the conduct of life is the most perfect expression of the internal disposition. It merits not indeed the title of an universal language; because it is not thoroughly understood but by those who either have a penetrating genius or extensive observation. It is a language, however, which everyone can decipher in some measure; and which, joined with the other external signs, affords sufficient means for the direction of our conduct with regard to others. If we commit any mistake when such light is afforded, it never can be the effect of unavoidable ignorance, but of rashness or inadvertence.

In reflecting upon the various expressions of our emotions, voluntary and involuntary, we must recognise the anxious care of Nature to discover men to each other. Strong emotions, as above hinted, beget an impatience

---

6. The actions here chiefly in view are what a passion suggests in order to its gratification. Beside these, actions are occasionally exerted to give some vent to a passion, without any view to an ultimate gratification. Such occasional action is characteristical of the passion in a high degree; and for that reason, when happily invented, has a wonderful good effect:

HAMLET: Oh most pernicious woman!
  Oh villain! villain! smiling damned villain!
  My tables—meet it as I set it down,
  That one may smile, and smile, and be a villain!
  At least I'm sure it may be so in Denmark.   (Writing)
  So, uncle, there you are.

—Hamlet, act 1. sc. 8

to express them externally by speech and other voluntary signs, which cannot be suppressed without a painful effort. Thus a sudden fit of passion is a common excuse for indecent behaviour or harsh words. As to the involuntary signs, these are altogether unavoidable. No volition or effort can prevent the shaking of the limbs or a pale visage, when one is agitated with a violent fit of terror. The blood flies to the face upon a sudden emotion of shame, in spite of all opposition:

> *Vergogna, che'n altrui stampo natura,*
> *Non si puo' rinegar: che se tu' tenti*
> *Di cacciarla dal cor, fugge nel volto.*
>
> —*Pastor Fido*, act 2. sc. 5

Emotions indeed properly so called, which are quiescent, produce no remarkable signs externally; nor is it necessary that the more deliberate passions should, because the operation of such passions is neither sudden nor violent. These however remain not altogether in the dark. Being more frequent than violent passion, the bulk of our actions are directed by them. Actions therefore display, with sufficient evidence, the more deliberate passions, and complete the admirable system of external signs, by which we become skilful in human nature.

Next in order comes an article of great importance, which is, to examine the effects produced upon a spectator by external signs of passion. None of these signs are beheld with indifference: they are productive of various emotions tending all of them to ends wise and good. This curious article makes a capital branch of human nature. It is peculiarly useful to writers who deal in the pathetic; and with respect to history-painters, it is altogether indispensable.

When we enter upon this article, we gather from experience, that each passion, or class of passions, hath its peculiar signs; and that these invariably make certain impressions on a spectator. The external signs of joy, for example, produce a chearful emotion, the external signs of grief produce pity, and the external signs of rage produce a sort of terror even in those who are not aimed at.

Secondly, it is natural to think, that pleasant passions should express themselves externally by signs that appear agreeable, and painful passions by signs that appear disagreeable. This conjecture, which Nature suggests, is confirmed by experience. Pride seems to be an exception; its external signs being disagreeable, though it be commonly reckoned a pleasant passion. But pride is not an exception; for in reality it is a mixed passion, partly pleasant partly painful. When a proud man confines his thoughts to himself, and to his own dignity or importance, the passion is pleasant, and its external signs agreeable: but as pride chiefly consists in undervaluing or contemning others, it is so far painful, and its external signs disagreeable.

Thirdly, it is laid down above, that an agreeable object produceth always a pleasant emotion, and a disagreeable object one that is painful[7]. According to this law, the external signs of a pleasant passion, being agreeable, must produce in the spectator a pleasant emotion; and the external signs of a painful passion, being disagreeable, must produce in him a painful emotion.

Fourthly, in the present chapter it is observed, that pleasant passions are, for the most part, expressed externally in one uniform manner; and that only the painful passions are distinguishable from each other by their external expressions. In the emotions accordingly raised by external signs of pleasant passions, there is little variety. They are pleasant or chearful, and we have not words to reach a more particular description. But the external signs of painful passions produce in the spectator emotions of different kinds: the emotions, for example, raised by external signs of grief, of remorse, of anger, of envy, of malice, are clearly distinguishable from each other.

Fifthly, emotions raised by the external signs of painful passions, are some of them *attractive*, some *repulsive*. Every painful passion that is also disagreeable[8], raises by its external signs a repulsive emotion, repelling the spectator from the object. Thus the emotions raised by external signs of envy and rage, are repulsive. But this is not the case of painful passions that are agreeable. Their external signs, it is true, are disagreeable, and raise in the spectator a painful emotion. But this painful emotion is not repulsive. On the contrary, it is attractive; and produceth in the spectator good-will to the man who is moved by the passion, and a desire to relieve or comfort him. This cannot be better exemplified than by distress painted on the countenance, which instantaneously inspires the spectator with pity, and impels him to afford relief. The cause of this difference among the painful emotions

---

7. See chap. 2. part 7.
8. See passions explained as agreeable or disagreeable, chap. 2. part 2.

raised by external signs of passion, may be readily gathered from what is laid down chapter Emotions and passions, part 7.

It is now time to look back to the question proposed in the beginning, How we come to understand external signs, so as readily to ascribe each sign to its proper passion? We have seen that this branch of knowledge, cannot be derived originally from sight, nor from experience. Is it then implanted in us by nature? The following considerations will help us to answer this question in the affirmative. In the first place, the external signs of passion must be natural; for they are invariably the same in every country, and among the different tribes of men. Pride, for example, is always expressed by an erect posture, reverence by prostration, and sorrow by a dejected look. Secondly, we are not even indebted to experience for the knowledge that these expressions are natural and universal. We are so framed as to have an innate conviction of the fact. Let a man change his habitation to the other side of the globe; he will, from the accustomed signs, infer the passion of fear among his new neighbours, with as little hesitation as he did at home. And upon second thoughts, the question may be answered without any preliminaries. If the branch of knowledge we have been inquiring about be not derived from sight nor from experience, there is no remaining source from whence it can be derived but from nature.

We may then venture to pronounce, with some degree of confidence, that man is provided by nature with a sense or faculty which lays open to him every passion by means of its external expressions. And I imagine that we cannot entertain any reasonable doubt of this fact, when we reflect, that even infants are not ignorant of the meaning of external signs. An infant is remarkably affected with the passions of its nurse expressed on her countenance: a smile chears it, and a frown makes it afraid. Fear thus generated in the infant, must, like every other passion, have an object. What is the object of this passion? Surely not the frown considered abstractly, for a child never abstracts. The nurse who frowns is evidently the object. Fear, at the same time, cannot arise but from apprehending danger. But what danger can a child apprehend, if it be not sensible that the person who frowns is angry? We must therefore admit, that a child can read anger in its nurse's face; and it must be sensible of this intuitively, for it has no other means of knowledge. I have no occasion to affirm, that these particulars are clearly apprehended by the child. To produce clear and distinct perceptions, reflection and experience are requisite. But that even an infant, when afraid, must have some notion of its being in danger, is extremely evident.

That we should be conscious intuitively of a passion from its external expressions, is conformable to the analogy of nature. The knowledge of this language is of too great importance to be left upon experience. To rest it upon a foundation so uncertain and precarious, would prove a great obstacle to the formation of societies. Wisely therefore is it ordered, and agreeably to the system of Providence, that we should have Nature for our instructor.

Manifold and admirable are the purposes to which the external signs of passion are made subservient by the author of our nature. What are occasionally mentioned above, make but a part. Several final causes remain to be unfolded; and to this task I apply myself with alacrity. In the first place, the signs of internal agitation that are displayed externally to every spectator, tend to fix the signification of many terms. The only effectual means to ascertain the meaning of any doubtful word, is an appeal to the thing it represents. Hence the ambiguity of words expressive of things that are not objects of external sense; for in that case an appeal is denied. Passion, strictly speaking, is not an object of external sense: but its external signs are; and by means of these signs, passions may be appealed to, with tolerable accuracy. Thus the words that denote our passions, next to those that denote external objects, have the most distinct meaning. Words signifying internal action and the more delicate feelings, are less distinct. This defect with respect to internal action, is what chiefly occasions the intricacy of logic. The terms of that science are far from being sufficiently ascertained, even after the care and labour bestowed by an eminent writer[9]: to whom however the world is greatly indebted, for removing a mountain of rubbish, and moulding the subject into a rational and correct form. The same defect is remarkable in criticism, which has for its object the more delicate feelings. The terms that denote these feelings, are not more distinct than those of logic. To reduce this science of criticism to any regular form, has never once been attempted. However rich the ore may be, no critical chymist has been found to give us a regular analysis of its constituent parts, and to distinguish each by its own name.

In the second place, society among individuals is greatly promoted by this universal language. The distance and reserve that strangers naturally discover, show its utility. Looks and gestures give direct access to the heart; and lead us to select with tolerable accuracy the persons

---

9. Locke.

who may be trusted. It is surprising how quickly, and for the most part how correctly, we judge of character from external appearances.

Thirdly, after social intercourse is commenced, these external signs contribute above all other means to the strictest union, by diffusing through a whole assembly the feelings of each individual. Language no doubt is the most comprehensive vehicle for communicating emotions: but in expedition, as well as in the power of conviction, it falls short of the signs under consideration; the involuntary signs especially, which are incapable of deceit. Where the countenance, the tones, the gestures, the actions, join with the words, in communicating emotions, these united have a force irresistible. Thus all the agreeable emotions of the human heart, with all the social and virtuous affections, are, by means of these external signs, not only perceived but felt. By this admirable contrivance, social intercourse becomes that lively and animating amusement, without which life would at best be insipid. One joyful countenance spreads chearfulness instantaneously through a multitude of spectators.

Fourthly, dissocial passions being hurtful by prompting violence and mischief, are noted by the most conspicuous external signs, in order to put us upon our guard. Thus anger and revenge, especially when suddenly provoked, display themselves on the countenance in legible characters[10]. The external signs again of every passion that threatens danger, raise in us the passion of fear. Nor is this passion occasioned by consciousness of danger, though it may be inflamed by such consciousness. It is an instinctive passion, which operating without reason or reflection, moves us by a sudden impulse to avoid the impending danger[11].

---

10. Rough and blunt manners are allied to anger by an internal feeling, as well as by external expressions resembling in a faint degree those of anger; therefore such manners are easily heightened into anger; and savages for that reason are prone to anger. Thus rough and blunt manners are unhappy in two respects: first, they are readily converted into anger; and next, the change being imperceptible because of the similitude of their external signs, the person against whom the anger is directed is not put upon his guard. It is for these reasons a great object in society to correct such manners, and to bring on a habit of sweetness and calmness. This temper has two opposite good effects. First, it is not easily provoked to wrath. Next, the interval being great between it and real anger, a person of that temper who receives an affront, has many changes to go through before his anger be inflamed; these changes have each of them their external sign; and the offending party is put upon his guard to retire, or to endeavour a reconciliation.
11. See chap. 2. part 1. sect. 6.

In the fifth place, these external signs are made subservient in a curious manner to the cause of virtue. The external signs of a painful passion that is virtuous or innocent, and consequently agreeable, produce indeed a painful emotion. But this emotion is attractive, and connects the spectator with the person who suffers. Disagreeable passions only, are productive of repulsive emotions involving the spectator's aversion, and frequently his indignation. This artful contrivance makes us cling to the virtuous and abhor the wicked.

Sixthly, of all the external signs of passion, those of affliction or distress are the most illustrious with respect to a final cause; and deservedly merit a place of distinction. They are illustrious by the singularity of their contrivance; and they are still more illustrious by the sympathy they inspire, a passion to which human society is indebted for its greatest blessing, that of securing relief in all cases of distress. A subject so interesting, ought to be examined with leisure and attention. The conformity of the nature of man to his external circumstances, is in every particular wonderful. His nature makes him prone to society; and his situation makes it necessary for him. In a solitary state he is the most helpless of beings; destitute of support, and in his manifold distresses destitute of relief. Mutual support, the shining attribute of society, being essential to the well-being of man, is not left upon reason, but is inforced even instinctively by the passion of sympathy. Here sympathy makes a capital figure; and contributes, more than any other means, to make life easy and comfortable. But however essential sympathy be to comfortable existence, one thinking of it beforehand, would find difficulty in conjecturing how it could be raised by external signs of distress. For considering the analogy of nature, if these signs be agreeable, they must give birth to a pleasant emotion leading every beholder to be pleased with human misfortunes. If they be disagreeable, as they undoubtedly are, ought not the painful emotion they produce to repel the spectator from them, in order to be relieved from pain? Such would be the conjecture, in thinking of this matter beforehand; and such would be the effect, were man purely a selfish being. But the benevolence of our nature gives a very different direction to the painful passion of sympathy, and to the desire involved in it. Far from flying from distress, we fly to it in order to afford relief; and our sympathy cannot be otherwise gratified than by giving all the succour in our power[12].

---

12. See chap. 2. part 7.

Thus external signs of distress, though disagreeable, are attractive; and the sympathy they inspire us with is a powerful cause, impelling us to afford relief even to a stranger as if he were our friend or blood-relation.

This branch of human nature concerning the external signs of passion, is so finely adjusted to answer its end, that those who understand it the best will admire it the most. These external signs, being all of them resolvable into colour, figure, and motion, should not naturally make any deep impression on a spectator. And supposing them qualified for making deep impressions, we have seen above, that the effects they produce are not what would be expected. We cannot therefore account otherwise for the operation of these external signs, than by ascribing it to the original constitution of human nature. To improve the social state, by making us instinctively rejoice with the glad of heart, weep with the mourner, and shun those who threaten danger, is a contrivance illustrious for its wisdom as well as benevolence. With respect to the external signs of distress in particular, to judge of the excellency of their contrivance, we need only reflect upon several other means seemingly more natural, that would not have answered the end proposed. I am attracted by this amusing speculation, and will not ask pardon for indulging in it. We shall in the first place reverse the truth, by putting the case that the external signs of joy were disagreeable, and the external signs of distress agreeable. This is no whimsical supposition; for these external signs, so far as can be gathered from their nature, seem indifferent to the production of pleasure or pain. Admitting then the supposition, the question is, How would our sympathy operate? There is no occasion to deliberate for an answer. Sympathy, upon that supposition, would be not less destructive, than according to the real case it is beneficial. We should be incited, to cross the happiness of others if its external signs were disagreeable to us, and to augment their distress if its external signs were agreeable. I make a second supposition, That the external signs of distress were indifferent to us, and productive neither of pleasure nor pain. This would annihilate the strongest branch of sympathy, that which is raised by means of sight. And it is evident, that reflective sympathy, felt by those only who have more than an ordinary share of sensibility, would be far from being sufficient to fulfil the ends of the social state. I shall approach nearer truth in a third supposition, That the external signs of distress being disagreeable, were productive of a painful repulsive emotion. Sympathy upon this supposition would not be annihilated; but it would be rendered useless. For it would be gratified by flying from or avoiding the object, instead of clinging to it, and affording relief. The condition of man would in reality be worse than if sympathy were totally eradicated; because sympathy would only serve to plague those who feel it, without producing any good to the afflicted.

Loath to quit so interesting a subject, I add a reflection, with which I shall conclude. The external signs of passion are a strong indication, that man, by his very constitution, is framed to be open and sincere. A child, in all things obedient to the impulses of nature, hides none of its emotions: the savage and clown, who have no guide other than pure nature, expose their hearts to view by giving way to all the natural signs: and even when men learn to dissemble their sentiments, and when behaviour degenerates into art, there still remain checks, which keep dissimulation within bounds, and prevent a great part of its mischievous effects. The total suppression of the voluntary signs during any vivid passion, begets the utmost uneasiness, which cannot be endured for any considerable time. This operation becomes indeed less painful by habit: but luckily the involuntary signs, cannot by any effort be suppressed or even dissembled. An absolute hypocrisy, by which the character is concealed and a fictitious one assumed, is made impracticable; and nature has thereby prevented much harm to society. We may pronounce therefore, that nature, herself sincere and candid, intends that mankind should preserve the same character, by cultivating simplicity and truth, and banishing every sort of dissimulation that tends to mischief.

XVI

Sentiments

Every thought suggested by a passion or emotion, is termed *a sentiment*[1].

The knowledge of the sentiments peculiar to each passion considered abstractly, will not alone enable an artist to make a just representation of nature. He ought, over and above, to be acquainted with the various appearances of the same passion in different persons. Passions, it is certain, receive a tincture from every peculiarity of character; and for that reason, it rarely happens that any two persons vent their passions precisely in the same manner. Hence the following rule concerning dramatic and epic compositions, That a passion be adjusted to the character, the sentiments to the passion, and the language to the sentiments. If nature be not faithfully copied in each of these, a defect in execution is perceived. There may appear some resemblance; but the picture upon the whole will be insipid, through want of grace and delicacy. A painter, in order to represent the various attitudes of the body, ought to be intimately acquainted with muscular motion: not less intimately acquainted with emotions and characters ought a writer to be, in order to represent the various attitudes of the mind. A general notion of the passions, in their grosser differences of strong and weak, elevated and humble, severe and gay, is far from being sufficient. Pictures formed so superficially, have little resemblance, and no expression. And yet it will appear by and by, that in many instances our reputed masters are deficient even in this superficial knowledge.

In handling the present subject, it would be endless to trace even the ordinary passions through their nicer and more minute differences. Mine shall be an humbler task; which is, to select from the best writers instances of faulty sentiments, after paving the way by some general observations.

To talk in the language of music, each passion hath a certain tone, to which every sentiment proceeding from it ought to be tuned with the

---

1. See Appendix, § 32.

greatest accuracy. This is no easy work, especially where such harmony is to be supported during the course of a long theatrical representation. In order to reach such delicacy of execution, it is necessary that a writer assume the precise character and passion of the personage represented. This requires an uncommon genius. But it is the only difficulty; for the writer, who, forgetting himself, can thus personate another, so as to feel truly and distinctly the various agitations of the passion, need be in no pain about the sentiments: these will flow without the least study, or even preconception; and will frequently be as delightfully new to himself as afterward to his reader. But if a lively picture even of a single emotion require an effort of genius; how much greater must the effort be, to compose a passionate dialogue, in which there are as many different tones of passion as there are speakers? With what ductility of feeling ought a writer to be endued who aims at perfection in such a work; when, to execute it correctly, it is necessary to assume different and even opposite characters and passions, in the quickest succession? And yet this work, difficult as it is, yields to that of composing a dialogue in genteel comedy devoid of passion; where the sentiments must be tuned to the nicer and more delicate tones of different characters. That the latter is the more difficult task, appears from considering, that a character is greatly more complex than a passion, and that passions are more distinguishable from each other than characters are. Many writers accordingly who have no genius for characters, make a shift to represent, tolerably well, an ordinary passion in its plain movements. But of all works of this kind, what is truly the most difficult, is a characteristical dialogue upon any philosophical subject. To interweave characters with reasoning, by adapting to the peculiar character of each speaker a peculiarity not only of thought but of expression, requires the perfection of genius, taste, and judgement.

How hard dialogue-writing is, will be evident, even without reasoning, from the imperfect compositions of this kind found without number in all languages. The art of mimicking any singularity in voice or gesture, is a rare talent, though directed by sight and hearing, the acutest and most lively of our external senses: how much more rare must the talent be of imitating characters and internal emotions, tracing all their different tints, and representing them in a lively manner by natural sentiments properly expressed? The truth is, such execution is too delicate for an ordinary genius; and for that reason, the bulk of writers, instead of expressing a passion like one who is under its power, content themselves with describing it like a spectator. To awake passion by an internal effort merely, without any external cause, requires great sensibility; and yet this operation is necessary not less to the writer than to the actor; because none but they who actually feel a passion, can represent it to the life. The writer's part is much more complicated: he must join composition with action; and, in the quickest succession, be able to adopt every different character introduced in his work. But a very humble flight of imagination, may serve to convert a writer into a spectator, so as to figure, in some obscure manner, an action as passing in his sight and hearing. In this figured situation, he is led naturally to describe as a spectator, and at second hand to entertain his readers with his own observations, with cool description and florid declamation; instead of making them eye-witnesses, as it were, to a real event, and to every movement of genuine passion[2]. Thus, in the bulk of plays, a tiresome monotony prevails, a pompous declamatory style, without entering into different characters or passions.

This descriptive manner of expressing passion, has a very unhappy effect. Our sympathy is not raised by description: we must be lulled first into a dream of reality; and everything must appear as actually present and passing in our sight[3]. Unhappy is the player of genius who acts a capital part in what may be termed a *descriptive tragedy*. After he has assumed the very passion that is to be represented, how must he be cramped in his action, when he is forced to utter, not the sentiments of the passion he feels, but a cold description in the language of a by-stander? It is this imperfection, I am persuaded, in the bulk of our plays, that confines our stage almost entirely to Shakespear, his many irregularities notwithstanding. In our latest English tragedies, we sometimes find sentiments tolerably well

---

2. In the *Æneid*, the hero is made to describe himself in the following words: *Sum pius Æneas, fama super a thera notus.* Virgil could never have been guilty of an impropriety so gross, had he assumed the personage of his hero, instead of uttering the sentiments of a spectator. Nor would Xenophon have made the following speech for Cyrus, the younger, to his Grecian auxiliaries, whom he was leading against his brother Artaxerxes: "I have chosen you, O Greeks! my auxiliaries, not to enlarge my army, for I have *Barbarians* without number; but because you surpass all the *Barbarians* in valour and military discipline." This sentiment is Xenophon's; for surely Cyrus did not reckon his countrymen barbarians.
3. See chap. 2. part 1. sect. 7.

adapted to a plain passion. But it would be fruitless labour, to search in any of them for a sentiment expressive of character; and, upon that very account, all our modern performances of the dramatic kind, are intolerably insipid.

Looking back upon the foregoing observation, I am uncertain whether it will be sufficiently apprehended; for, upon this complicated subject, I find some difficulty to express myself with perspicuity. I despair not however to place this matter in the clearest light, by adding example to precept. In the front shall be set one or two examples of sentiments that appear the legitimate offspring of passion; and to them shall be opposed a few others that are descriptive only, and illegitimate. In making this comparison, I shall borrow my instances from Shakespear and Corneille, who for genius in dramatic composition stand uppermost in the rolls of fame.

SHAKESPEAR SHALL FURNISH THE FIRST instance, being of sentiments dictated by a violent and perturbed passion.

> LEAR:———Filial ingratitude!
>   Is it not, as if this mouth should tear this hand
>   For lifting food to't?—But I'll punish home;
>   No, I will weep no more.—In such a night,
>   To shut me out!—Pour on, I will endure.
>   In such a night as this! O Regan, Gonerill,
>   Your old kind father, whose frank heart gave all—
>   O, that way madness lies; let me shun that;
>   No more of that.—
> KENT: Good, my Lord, enter here.
> LEAR: Pr'ythee, go in thy self, seek thine own ease,
>   This tempest will not give me leave to ponder
>   On things would hurt me more—but I'll go in;
>   In, boy, go first. You houseless poverty—
>   Nay, get thee in; I'll pray, and then I'll sleep—
>   Poor naked wretches, wheresoe'er you are,
>   That bide the pelting of this pitiless storm!
>   How shall your houseless heads and unfed sides,
>   Your loop'd and window'd raggedness, defend you
>   From seasons such as these?—O I have ta'en
>   Too little care of this! take physic, Pomp;

> Expose thyself to feel what wretches feel,
> That thou may'st shake the superflux to them,
> And show the heavens more just.
>
> *—King Lear. act 3. sc 5*

To illustrate the foregoing doctrine, one other instance of the same kind may suffice, expressing sentiments arising from remorse and despair.

> OTHELLO: Lo! I have a weapon:
> A better never did itself sustain
> Upon a soldier's thigh. I've seen the day,
> That with this little arm, and this good sword,
> I've made my way through more impediments
> Than twenty times your stop. But, oh vain boast!
> Who can controul his fate? 'tis not so now.
> Be not afraid, though you do see me weapon'd;
> Here is my journey's end, here is my butt,
> The very sea mark of my outmost sail.
> Do you go back dismay'd? 'tis a lost fear.
> Man but a rush against Othello's breast,
> And he retires. Where should Othello go?
> Now—how dost thou look now? Oh ill starr'd wench!
> Pale as thy smoke! when we shall meet at compt,
> This look of thine will hurl my soul from heav'n,
> And fiends will snatch at it. Cold, cold, my girl,
> Ev'n like thy chastity. O cursed slave!
> Whip me, ye devils,
> From the possession of this heav'nly sight;
> Blow me about in winds, roast me in sulphur,
> Wash me in steep-down gulfs of liquid fire—
> Oh, Desdemona! Desdemona! dead! dead! oh, oh!
>
> *—Othello, act 5. sc. 9*

The sentiments here display'd flow so naturally from the passions represented, and are such genuine expressions of these passions, that it is not possible to conceive any imitation more perfect.

With regard to the French author, truth obliges me to acknowledge, that he describes in the style of a spectator, instead of expressing passion like one who feels it; and also that he is thereby betray'd into the other faults above mentioned, a tiresome monotony, and a pompous declamatory style[4]. It is scarce necessary to produce particular instances; for he never varies from this tone. I shall however take two passages at a venture, in order to be confronted with those transcribed above. In the tragedy of *Cinna*, Æmilia, after the conspiracy was discovered, having nothing in view but racks and death to herself and her lover, receives a pardon from Augustus, attended with the brightest circumstances of magnanimity and tenderness. This is a

---

4. This criticism reaches the French dramatic writers in general, with very few exceptions: their tragedies, excepting those of Racine, are mostly, if not totally, descriptive. Corneille led the way, and later writers, imitating his manner, have accustomed the French ear to a style, formal, pompous, declamatory, which suits not with any passion. Hence, to burlesque a French tragedy, is not more difficult than to burlesque a stiff solemn fop. The facility of the operation has in Paris introduced a singular amusement, which is, to burlesque the more successful tragedies in a sort of farce, called *a parody* La Motte, who himself appears to have been sorely galled by some of these productions, acknowledges, that no more is necessary to give them currency but barely to vary the *dramatis personæ*, and, instead of kings and heroes, queens and princesses, to substitute tinkers and taylors, milkmaids and seamstresses. The declamatory style, so different from the genuine expression of passion, passes in some measure unobserved, when great personages are the speakers; but in the mouths of the vulgar, the impropriety with regard to the speaker as well as to the passion represented, is so remarkable as to become ridiculous. A tragedy, where every passion is made to speak in its natural tone, is not liable to be thus burlesqued: the same passion is by all men expressed nearly in the same manner; and therefore the genuine expressions of passion cannot be ridiculous in the mouth of any man who is susceptible of the passion.

It is a well known fact, that to an English ear, the French actors appear to pronounce with too great rapidity: a complaint much insisted on by Cibber in particular, who had frequently heard the famous Baron upon the French stage. This may in some measure be attributed to our want of facility in the French tongue; as foreigners generally imagine that every language is pronounced too quick by natives. But that it is not the sole cause, will be probable from a fact directly opposite, that the French are not a little disgusted with the languidness, as they term it, of the English pronunciation. May not this difference of taste be derived from what is observed above. The pronunciation of the genuine language of a passion is necessarily directed by the nature of the passion, particularly by the slowness or celerity of its progress: plaintive passions, which are the most frequent in tragedy, having a slow motion, dictate a slow pronunciation: in declamation, on the contrary, the speaker warms gradually; and, as he warms, he naturally accelerates his pronunciation. But, as the French have formed their tone of pronunciation upon Corneille's declamatory tragedies, and the English upon the more natural language of Shakspeare, it is not surprising that custom should produce such difference of taste in the two nations.

happy situation for representing the passions of surprise and gratitude in their different stages. These passions, raised at once to the utmost pitch, are at first too big for utterance; and Æmilia's feelings must, for some moments, have been expressed by violent gestures only. So soon as there is a vent for words, the first expressions are naturally broken and interrupted. At last we ought to expect a tide of intermingled sentiments, occasioned by the fluctuation of the mind betwixt the two passions. Æmilia is made to behave in a very different manner. With extreme coolness she describes her own situation, as if she were merely a spectator; or rather the poet takes the task off her hands.

> *Et je me rens, Seigneur, à ces hautes bontés,*
> *Je recouvre la vûe auprés de leurs clartés,*
> *Je connois mon forfait qui me sembloit justice,*
> *Et ce que n'avoit pû la terreur du supplice,*
> *Je sens naitre en mon ame un repentir puissant;*
> *Et mon cœur en secret me dit, qu'il y consent.*
> *Le ciel a résolu votre grandeur suprême,*
> *Et pour preuve, Seigneur, je n'en veux que moi-même;*
> *J'ose avec vanité me donner cet éclat,*
> *Puisqu'il change mon cœur, qu'il veut changer l'état.*
> *Ma haine va mourir que j'ai crue immortelle,*
> *Elle est morte, et ce cœur devient sujet fidéle,*
> *Et prenant désormais cette haine en horreur,*
> *L'ardeur de vous servir succede à sa fureur.*

—Act 5. sc. 3

In the tragedy of *Sertorius*, the Queen, surprised with the news that her lover was assassinated, instead of venting any passion, degenerates into a cool spectator, even so much as to instruct the by-standers how a queen ought to behave on such an occasion.

> VIRIATE: Il m'en fait voir ensemble, et l'auteur, et la cause.
> Par cet assassinat c'est de moi qu'on dispose,
> C'est mon trône, c'est moi qu'on pretend conquerir,
> Et c'est mon juste choix qui seul l'a fait perir.
> Madame, aprés sa perte, et parmi ces alarmes,
> N'attendez point de moi de soupirs, ni de larmes;

> Ce sont amusemens que dédaigne aisement
> Le prompt et noble orgueil d'un vif ressentiment.
> Qui pleure, l'affoiblit, qui soupire, l'exhale,
> Il faut plus de fierté dans une ame royale;
> Et ma douleur soumise aux soins de le venger, &c.
>
> —*Act 5. sc. 3*

So much in general upon the genuine sentiments of passion. I proceed now to particular observations. And, first, Passions are seldom uniform for any considerable time: they generally fluctuate, swelling and subsiding by turns, often in a quick succession[5]. This fluctuation, in the case of a real passion, will be expressed externally by proper sentiments; and ought to be imitated in writing and acting. Accordingly, a climax shows never better than in expressing a swelling passion. The following passages shall suffice for an illustration.

> OROONOKO:—— Can you raise the dead?
> Pursue and overtake the wings of time?
> And bring about again, the hours, the days,
> The years, that made me happy?
>
> —*Oroonoko, act 2. sc. 2*

> ALMERIA:—— How hast thou charm'd
> The wildness of the waves and rocks to this?
> That thus relenting they have giv'n thee back
> To earth, to light and life, to love and me?
>
> —*Mourning Bride, act 1. sc. 7*

> *I would not be the villain that thou think'st*
> *For the whole space that's in the tyrant's grasp,*
> *And the rich earth to boot.*
>
> —*Macbeth, act 4. sc. 4*

The following passage expresses finely the progress of conviction.

---

5. See chap. 2. part 3.

> *Let me not stir, nor breathe, lest I dissolve*
> *That tender, lovely form, of painted air,*
> *So like Almeria. Ha! it sinks, it falls;*
> *I'll catch it ere it goes, and grasp her shade.*
> *'Tis life! 'tis warm! 'tis she! 'tis she herself!*
> *It is Almeria! 'tis, it is my wife!*
>
> *—Mourning Bride, act 2. sc. 6*

In the progress of thought, our resolutions become more vigorous as well as our passions.

> *If ever I do yield or give consent,*
> *By any action, word, or thought, to wed*
> *Another Lord; may then just Heav'n show'r down,* &c.
>
> *—Mourning Bride, act 1. sc. 1*

And this leads to a second observation, That the different stages of a passion, and its different directions, from its birth to its extinction, ought to be carefully represented in the sentiments, which otherwise will often be misplaced. Resentment, for example, when provoked by an atrocious injury, discharges itself first upon the author. Sentiments therefore of revenge take place of all others, and must in some measure be exhausted before the person injured think of pitying himself, or of grieving for his present distress. In the *Cid* of Corneille, Don Diegue having been affronted in a cruel manner, expresses scarce any sentiment of revenge, but is totally occupied in contemplating the low situation to which he was reduced by the affront.

> *O rage! ô desespoir! ô vieillesse ennemie!*
> *N'ai je donc tant vecu que pour cette infamie?*
> *Et ne suis-je blanchi dans les travaux guerriers,*
> *Que pour voir en une jour fletrir tant de lauriers?*
> *Mon bras, qu'avec respect toute l'Espagne admire,*
> *Mon bras, qui tant de fois a sauvé cet empire,*
> *Tant de fois affermi le trône de son roi,*
> *Trahit donc ma querelle, et ne fait rien pour moi!*
> *O cruel souvenir de ma gloire passée!*

> *Oeuvre de tant de jours en un jour effacée!*
> *Nouvelle dignité fatale à mon bonheur!*
> *Precipice élevé d'ou tombe mon honneur!*
> *Faut-il de votre éclat voir triompher le Comte,*
> *Et mourir sans vengeance, ou vivre dans la honte?*
> *Comte, fois de mon Prince à present gouverneur,*
> *Ce haut rang n'admet point un homme sans honneur;*
> *Et ton jaloux orgueil par cet affront insigne,*
> *Malgré le choix du Roi, m'en a su rendre indigne.*
> *Et toi, de mes exploits glorieux instrument,*
> *Mais d'un corps tout de glace inutile ornement,*
> *Fer jadis tant a craindre, et qui dans cette offense*
> *M'as servi de parade, et non pas de defense,*
> *Va quitte desormais le dernier des humains,*
> *Passe pour me vanger en de meilleures mains.*
>
> —*Le Cid*, act 1. sc. 4

These sentiments are certainly not what occur to the mind in the first movements of the passion. In the same manner as in resentment, the first movements of grief are always directed upon its object. Yet with relation to the hidden and severe distemper that seized Alexander bathing in the river Cydnus, Quintus Curtius describes the first emotions of the army as directed upon themselves, lamenting that they were left without a leader far from home, and had scarce any hopes of returning in safety. Their King's distress, which must naturally have been their first concern, occupies them but in the second place according to that author. In the *Aminta* of Tasso, Sylvia, upon a report of her lover's death, which she believed certain, instead of bemoaning the loss of a beloved object, turns her thoughts upon herself, and wonders her heart does not break.

> *Ohime, ben son di sasso,*
> *Poi che questa novella non m'uccide.*
>
> —*Act 4. sc. 2*

In the tragedy of *Jane Shore*, Alicia, in the full purpose of destroying her rival, has the following reflection:

> *Oh Jealousy! thou bane of pleasing friendship,*
> *Thou worst invader of our tender bosoms;*
> *How does thy rancour poison all our softness,*
> *And turn our gentle natures into bitterness?*
> *See where she comes! Once my heart's dearest blessing,*
> *Now my chang'd eyes are blasted with her beauty,*
> *Loathe that known face, and sicken to behold her.*
>
> —*Act 3. sc. 1*

These are the reflections of a cool spectator. A passion while it has the ascendant, and is freely indulged, suggests not to the man who feels it any sentiment to its own prejudice. Reflections like the foregoing, occur not to him readily till the passion have spent its vigor.

A person sometimes is agitated at once by different passions. The mind in this case vibrating like a pendulum, vents itself in sentiments which partake of the same vibration. This I give as a third observation:

QUEEN: 'Would I had never trod this English earth,
  Or felt the flatteries that grow upon it!
  Ye've angels faces, but Heav'n knows your hearts.
  What shall become of me now! wretched lady!
  I am the most unhappy woman living.
  Alas! poor wenches, where are now your fortunes? (*To her women*)
  Shipwreck'd upon a kingdom, where no pity,
  No friends, no hope! no kindred weep for me!
  Almost, no grave allow'd me.

—*Henry VIII. act 3. sc. 1*

OTHELLO: Oh devil, devil! If that the earth could teem with woman's tears, Each drop she falls, would prove a crocodile. Out of my sight.
DESDEMONA: I will not stay t'offend you. (*going*)
LODOVICO: Truly, an obedient lady: I do beseech your Lordship, call her back.
OTH.: Mistress——
DES.: My Lord.
OTH.: What would you with her, Sir?

Lod.: Who, I, my Lord?

Oth.: Ay; you did wish that I would make her turn: Sir, she can turn and turn, and yet go on; And turn again. And she can weep, Sir, weep; And she's obedient: as you say, obedient; Very obedient—proceed you in your tears—Concerning this, Sir,—oh well-painted passion!—I am commanded home—get you away, I'll send for you anon—Sir, I obey the mandate, And will return to Venice.—Hence, avaunt! (*Exit Desdemona*)

—Othello, act 4. sc. 6

Æmilia: Oh! my good Lord, I would speak a word with you.

Othello: Yes, 'tis Æmilia—by and by—she's dead. 'Tis like, she comes to speak of Cassio's death; The noise was high.—Ha, no more moving? Still as the grave. Shall she come in? were't good? I think she stirs again—No—what's the best? If she come in, she'll, sure, speak to my wife; My wife! my wife! What wife? I have no wife. Oh insupportable! oh heavy hour!

—Othello, act 5. sc. 7

A fourth observation is, that nature, which gave us passions, and made them extremely beneficial when moderate, intended undoubtedly that they should be subjected to the government of reason and conscience[6]. It is therefore against the order of nature, that passion in any case should take the lead in contradiction to reason and conscience. Such a state of mind is a sort of anarchy, which everyone is ashamed of, and endeavours to hide or dissemble. Even love, however laudable, is attended with a conscious shame when it becomes immoderate: it is covered from the world, and disclosed only to the beloved object:

> *Et que l'amour souvent de remors combattu*
> *Paroisse une foiblesse, et non une vertu.*
>
> *—Boileau, L'art poet. chant. 3. l. 101*

> *O, they love least that let men know their love.*
>
> *—Two Gentlemen of Verona, act 1. sc. 3*

---

6. See chap. 2. part 7.

Hence a capital rule in the representation of strong passions, that their genuine sentiments ought to be hid or dissembled as much as possible. And this holds in an especial manner with respect to criminal passions. One never counsels the commission of a crime in plain terms. Guilt must not appear in its native colours, even in thought: the proposal must be made by hints, and by representing the action in some favourable light. Of the propriety of sentiment upon such an occasion, Shakespear, in the *Tempest*, has given us a beautiful example. The subject is a proposal made by the usurping Duke of Milan to Sebastian, to murder his brother the King of Naples.

> ANTONIO:—— What might
> Worthy Sebastian—O, what might—no more.
> And yet, methinks, I see it in thy face,
> What thou should'st be: th'occasion speaks thee, and
> My strong imagination sees a crown
> Dropping upon thy head.
>
> *—Act 2. sc. 1*

There cannot be a finer picture of this sort, than that of King John soliciting Hubert to murder the young Prince Arthur.

> K. JOHN: Come hither, Hubert. O my gentle Hubert,
> We owe thee much; within this wall of flesh
> There is a soul counts thee her creditor,
> And with advantage means to pay thy love.
> And, my good friend, thy voluntary oath
> Lives in this bosom, dearly cherished.
> Give me thy hand, I had a thing to say—
> But I will fit it with some better time.
> By Heaven, Hubert, I'm almost asham'd
> To say what good respect I have of thee.
> HUBERT: I am much bounden to your Majesty.
> K. JOHN: Good friend, thou hast no cause to say so yet—
> But thou shalt have—and creep time ne'er so slow,
> Yet it shall come for me to do thee good.
> I had a thing to say—but, let it go:
> The sun is in the heav'n, and the proud day,

>   Attended with the pleasures of the world,
>   Is all too wanton, and too full of gawds,
>   To give me audience. If the midnight-bell
>   Did with his iron tongue and brazen mouth
>   Sound one into the drowsy race of night;
>   If this same were a church-yard where we stand,
>   And thou possessed with a thousand wrongs;
>   Or if that surly spirit Melancholy
>   Had bak'd thy blood and made it heavy-thick,
>   Which else runs tickling up and down the veins,
>   Making that idiot Laughter keep men's eyes,
>   And strain their cheeks to idle merriment,
>   (A passion hateful to my purposes);
>   Or if that thou could'st see me without eyes,
>   Hear me without thine ears, and make reply
>   Without a tongue, using conceit alone,
>   Without eyes, ears, and harmful sounds of words;
>   Then, in despight of broad-ey'd watchful day,
>   I would into thy bosom pour my thoughts.
>   But ah, I will not—Yet I love thee well;
>   And, by my troth, I think thou lov'st me well.
> HUBERT: So well, that what you bid me undertake,
>   Though that my death were adjunct to my act,
>   By Heav'n, I'd do't.
> K. JOHN: Do not I know, thou would'st?
>   Good Hubert, Hubert, Hubert, throw thine eye
>   On yon young boy. I'll tell thee what, my friend;
>   He is a very serpent in my way.
>   And, wheresoe'er this foot of mine doth tread,
>   He lies before me. Dost thou understand me?
>   Thou art his keeper.
>
>   —*King John*, act 3. sc. 5

As things are best illustrated by their contraries, I proceed to collect from classical authors, sentiments that appear faulty. The first class shall consist of sentiments that accord not with the passion; or, in other words, sentiments that the passion represented does not naturally suggest. In the second class, shall be ranged sentiments that may belong to an ordinary passion, but unsuitable to it as tinctured by a singular character. Thoughts that properly are not sentiments, but rather descriptions, make a third. Sentiments that belong to the passion represented, but are faulty as being introduced too early or too late, make a fourth. Vicious sentiments exposed in their native dress, instead of being concealed or disguised, make a fifth. And in the last class, shall be collected sentiments suited to no character or passion, and therefore unnatural.

THE FIRST CLASS CONTAINS FAULTY sentiments of various kinds, which I shall endeavour to distinguish from each other. And first sentiments that are faulty by being above the tone of the passion.

> OTHELLO:—— O my soul's joy!
> If after every tempest come such calms,
> May the winds blow till they have waken'd death:
> And let the labouring bark climb hills of seas
> Olympus high, and duck again as low
> As hell's from heaven!
>
> —*Othello, act 2. sc. 6*

This sentiment is too strong to be suggested by so slight a joy as that of meeting after a storm at sea.

> PHILASTER: Place me, some god, upon a pyramid
> Higher than hills of earth, and lend a voice
> Loud as your thunder to me, that from thence
> I may discourse to all the under-world
> The worth that dwells in him.
>
> —*Philaster of Beaumont and Fletcher, act 4*

Secondly, Sentiments below the tone of the passion. Ptolemy, by putting Pompey to death, having incurred the displeasure of Cæsar, was in the utmost dread of being dethroned. In this agitating situation, Corneille makes him utter a speech full of cool reflection, that is in no degree expressive of the passion.

> *Ah! si je t'avois crû, je n'aurois pas de maître,*
> *Je serois dans le trône où le Ciel m'a fait naître;*
> *Mais c'est une imprudence assez commune aux rois,*
> *D'ecouter trop d'avis, et se tromper au choix.*
> *Le Destin les aveugle au bord du précipice,*
> *Ou si quelque lumiere en leur ame se glisse,*
> *Cette fausse clarté dont il les eblouit,*
> *Le plonge dans une gouffre, et puis s'evanouit.*
>
> —*La mort de Pompée, act 4. sc. 1*

In *Les Freres ennemies* of Racine, the second act is opened with a love-scene. Hemon talks to his mistress of the torments of absence, of the lustre of her eyes, that he ought to die no where but at her feet, and that one moment of absence was a thousand years. Antigone on her part acts the coquette, and pretends she must be gone to wait on her mother and brother, and cannot stay to listen to his courtship. This is odious French gallantry, below the dignity of the passion of love. It would scarce be excusable in painting modern French manners; and is insufferable where the ancients are brought upon the stage. The manners painted in the *Alexandre* of the same author are not more just. French gallantry prevails there throughout.

THIRD. SENTIMENTS THAT AGREE NOT with the tone of the passion; as where a pleasant sentiment is grafted upon a painful passion, or the contrary. In the following instances the sentiments are too gay for a serious passion.

> *No happier talk these faded eyes pursue;*
> *To read and weep is all they now can do.*
>
> —*Eloisa to Abelard, l. 47*

Again,

> *Heav'n first taught letters for some wretch's aid,*
> *Some banish'd lover, or some captive maid;*
> *They live, they speak, they breathe what love inspires,*
> *Warm from the soul, and faithful to its fires;*
> *The virgin's wish without her fears impart,*

> *Excuse the blush, and pour out all the heart;*
> *Speed the soft intercourse from soul to soul,*
> *And waft a sigh from Indus to the pole.*
>
> —*Eloisa to Abelard, l. 51*

These thoughts are pretty; they suit Pope extremely, but not Eloisa.

SATAN, ENRAGED BY A THREATENING of the angel Gabriel, answers thus:

> *Then when I am thy captive talk of chains,*
> *Proud limitary cherub; but ere then*
> *Far heavier load thyself expect to feel*
> *From my prevailing arm, though Heaven's King*
> *Ride on thy wings, and thou with thy compeers,*
> *Us'd to the yoke, draw'st his triumphant wheels*
> *In progress through the road of heav'n* star-pav'd.
>
> —*Paradise Lost, book 4*

The concluding epithet forms a grand and delightful image, which cannot be the genuine offspring of rage.

FOURTH. SENTIMENTS TOO ARTIFICIAL FOR a serious passion. I give for the first example a speech of Piercy expiring:

> *O, Harry, thou hast robb'd me of my growth:*
> *I better brook the loss of brittle life,*
> *Than those proud titles thou hast won of me;*
> *They wound my thoughts, worse than thy sword my flesh.*
> *But thought's the slave of life, and life time's fool;*
> *And time, that takes survey of all the world,*
> *Must have a stop.*
>
> —*First part, Henry IV. act 5. sc. 9*

Livy inserts the following passage in a plaintive oration of the Locrenses accusing Pleminius the Roman legate of oppression.

"In hoc legato vestro, nec hominis quicquam est, Patres Conscripti, præter figuram et speciem; neque Romani civis, præter habitum vestitumque, et sonum linguæ Latinæ. Pestis et bellua immanis, quales fretum, quondam, quo ab Sicilia dividimur, ad perniciem navigantium circumsedisse, fabulæ ferunt[7]."

Congreve shows a fine taste in the sentiments of the *Mourning Bride*. But in the following passage the picture is too artful to be suggested by severe grief:

ALMERIA: O no! Time gives increase to my afflictions.
    The circling hours, that gather all the woes
    Which are diffus'd through the revolving year,
    Come heavy-laden with th' oppressing weight
    To me; with me, successively, they leave
    The sighs, the tears, the groans, the restless cares,
    And all the damps of grief, that did retard their flight,
    They shake their downy wings, and scatter all
    The dire collected dews on my poor head;
    Then fly with joy and swiftness from me.

—Act 1. sc. 1

In the same play, Almeria seeing a dead body, which she took to be Alphonso's, expresses sentiments strained and artificial, which nature suggests not to any person upon such an occasion:

Had they, or hearts, or eyes, that did this deed?
Could eyes endure to guide such cruel hands?
Are not my eyes guilty alike with theirs,
That thus can gaze, and yet not turn to stone?
—I do not weep! The springs of tears are dry'd,
And of a sudden I am calm, as if
All things were well; and yet my husband's murder'd!
Yes, yes, I know to mourn! I'll sluice this heart,
The source of wo, and let the torrent loose.

—Act 5. sc. 11

---

7. Titus Livius, I. 29. § 17.

LADY TRUEMAN: How could you be so cruel to defer giving me that joy which you knew I must receive from your presence? You have robb'd my life of some hours of happiness that ought to have been in it.

—*Drummer, act 5*

Pope's Elegy to the memory of an unfortunate lady, expresses delicately the most tender concern and sorrow for the deplorable fate of a person of worth. A poem of this kind, deeply serious and pathetic, rejects all fiction with disdain. We therefore can give no quarter to the following passage, which is eminently discordant with the subject. It is not the language of the heart, but of the imagination indulging its flights at ease. It would be a still more severe censure, if it should be ascribed to imitation, copying indiscreetly what has been said by others.

> *What though no weeping loves thy ashes grace,*
> *Nor polish'd marble emulate thy face?*
> *What though no sacred earth allow thee room,*
> *Nor hallow'd dirge be muttered o'er thy tomb?*
> *Yet shall thy grave with rising flow'rs be drest,*
> *And the green turf lie lightly on thy breast:*
> *There shall the morn her earliest tears bestow,*
> *There the first roses of the year shall blow;*
> *While angels with their silver wings o'ershade*
> *The ground, now sacred by thy reliques made.*

Fifth. Fanciful or sinical sentiments, sentiments that degenerate into point or conceit, however they may amuse in an idle hour, can never be the offspring of any serious or important passion. In the *Ierusalem* of Tasso, Tancred, after a single combat, spent with fatigue and loss of blood, falls into a swoon. In this situation, understood to be dead, he is discovered by Erminia, who was in love with him to distraction. A more happy situation cannot be imagined, to raise grief in an instant to its highest pitch; and yet, in venting her sorrow, she descends most abominably to antithesis and conceit, even of the lowest kind.

> *E in lui versò d'inessicabil vena*
> *Lacrime, e voce di sospiri mista.*
> *In che misero punto hor qui me mena*
> *Fortuna? a che veduta amara e trista?*
> *Dopo gran tempo i' ti ritrovo à pena*
> *Tancredi, e ti riveggio, e non son vista,*
> *Vista non son da te, benche presente*
> *E trovando ti perdo eternamente.*
>
> —*Cant. 19. st. 105*

Armida's lamentation respecting her lover Rinaldo[8], is in the same vitious taste.

> QUEEN: Give me no help in lamentation,
>   I am not barren to bring forth complaints:
>   All springs reduce their currents to mine eyes,
>   That I, being govern'd by the wat'ry moon,
>   May send forth plenteous tears to drown the world.
>   Ah, for my husband, for my dear Lord Edward.
>
> —*King Richard III. act 2. sc. 2*

> JANE SHORE: Let me be branded for the public scorn,
>   Turn'd forth, and driven to wander like a vagabond,
>   Be friendless and forsaken, seek my bread
>   Upon the barren wild, and desolate waste,
>   *Feed on my sighs, and drink my falling tears*;
>   Ere I consent to teach my lips injustice,
>   Or wrong the orphan who has none to save him.
>
> —*Jane Shore, act 4*

> *Give me your drops, ye soft-descending rains,*
> *Give me your streams, ye never-ceasing springs,*
> *That my sad eyes may still supply my duty,*
> *And feed an everlasting flood of sorrow.*
>
> —*Jane Shore, act 5*

---

8. Canto 29, stan. 124, 125, and 126.

Jane Shore utters her last breath in a witty conceit.

> *Then all is well, and I shall sleep in peace—*
> *'Tis very dark, and I have lost you now—*
> *Was there not something I would have bequeath'd you?*
> *But I have nothing left me to bestow,*
> *Nothing but one sad sigh. Oh mercy, Heav'n!* (Dies)

—*Act 5*

Gilford to Lady Jane Gray, when both were condemned to die:

> *Thou stand'st unmov'd;*
> *Calm temper sits upon thy beauteous brow;*
> *Thy eyes that flow'd so fast for Edward's loss,*
> *Gaze unconcern'd upon the ruin round thee,*
> *As if thou hadst resolv'd to brave thy fate,*
> *And triumph in the midst of desolation.*
> *Ha! see, it swells, the liquid crystal rises,*
> *It starts in spight of thee—but I will catch it,*
> *Nor let the earth be wet with dew so rich.*

—*Lady Jane Gray, act 4. near the end*

The concluding sentiment is altogether sinical, unsuitable to the importance of the occasion, and even to the dignity of the passion of love.

CORNEILLE, IN HIS *EXAMEN OF the Cid*[9], answering an objection, that his sentiments are sometimes too much refined for persons in deep distress, observes, that if poets did not indulge sentiments more ingenious or refined than are prompted by passion, their performances would often be low; and extreme grief would never suggest but exclamations merely. This is in plain language to assert, That forced thoughts are more relished than such as are natural, and therefore ought to be preferred.

---

9. Page 316.

The second class is of sentiments that may belong to an ordinary passion, but are not perfectly concordant with it, as tinctured by a singular character. In the last act of that excellent comedy, *The Careless Husband*, Lady Easy, upon Sir Charles's reformation, is made to express more violent and turbulent sentiments of joy, than are consistent with the mildness of her character.

> Lady Easy: O the soft treasure! O the dear reward of long-desiring love—Thus! thus to have you mine, is something more than happiness, 'tis double life, and madness of abounding joy.

If the sentiments of a passion ought to be suited to a peculiar character, it is still more necessary that sentiments devoid of passion be suited to the character. In the 5th act of the *Drummer*, Addison makes his gardener act even below the character of an ignorant credulous rustic: he gives him the behaviour of a gaping idiot.

The following instances are descriptions rather than sentiments, which compose a third class.

Of this descriptive manner of painting the passions, there is in the *Hippolytus* of Euripides, act 5. an illustrious instance, *viz.* the speech of Theseus, upon hearing of his son's dismal exit. In Racine's tragedy of *Esther*, the Queen hearing of the decree issued against her people, instead of expressing sentiments suitable to the occasion, turns her attention upon herself, and describes with accuracy her own situation.

> *Juste Ciel? Tout mon sang dans mes veines se glace.*
>
> —*Act 1. sc. 3*

Again,

> Aman: C'en est fait. Mon orgueil est forcé de plier,
> L'inexorable Aman est reduit a prier.
>
> —*Esther, act 3. sc. 5*

> Athalie: Quel prodige nouveau me trouble et m'embarrasse?
> La douceur de sa voix, son enfance, sa grace,

> Font insensiblement à mon inimitié
> Succéder—Je serois sensible a la pitié?
>
> *—Athalie, act 2. sc. 7*

> TITUS: O de ma passion fureur desesperée!
>
> *—Brutus of Voltaire, act 3. sc. 6*

What other are the foregoing instances than describing the passion another feels?

AN EXAMPLE IS GIVEN ABOVE of remorse and despair expressed by genuine and natural sentiments. In the fourth book of *Paradise Lost*, Satan is made to express his remorse and despair in sentiments, which though beautiful, are not altogether natural. They are rather the sentiments of a spectator, than of a person who actually is tormented with these passions.

The fourth class is of sentiments introduced too early or too late.

Some examples mentioned above belong to this class. Add the following from *Venice preserv'd*, act 5. at the close of the scene betwixt Belvidera and her father Priuli. The account given by Belvidera of the danger she was in, and of her husband's threatening to murder her, ought naturally to have alarmed her relenting father, and to have made him express the most perturbed sentiments. Instead of which he dissolves into tenderness and love for his daughter, as if he had already delivered her from danger, and as if there were a perfect tranquillity.

> *Canst thou forgive me all my follies past?*
> *I'll henceforth be indeed a father; never,*
> *Never more thus expose, but cherish thee,*
> *Dear as the vital warmth that feeds my life,*
> *Dear as these eyes that weep in fondness o'er thee:*
> *Peace to thy heart.*

Immoral sentiments exposed in their native colours, instead of being concealed or disguised, compose the fifth class.

THE LADY MACBETH PROJECTING THE death of the King, has the following soliloquy:

> *—— The raven himself's not hoarse*
> *That croaks the fatal entrance of Duncan*
> *Under my battlements. Come all you spirits*
> *That tend on mortal thoughts, unsex me here,*
> *And fill me from the crown to th' toe, top-full*
> *Of direct cruelty; make thick my blood,*
> *Stop up th' access and passage to remorse*
> *That no compunctious visitings of nature*
> *Shake my fell purpose.*
>
> —*Macbeth*, act 1. sc. 7

This speech is not natural. Murder under trust was never perpetrated even by the most hardened miscreant without compunction. And that the lady here must have been in horrible agitation appears, from her invoking the infernal spirits to fill her with cruelty, and to stop up all avenues to remorse. But in this state of mind, it is a never-failing device of self-deceit, to draw the thickest veil over the wicked action, and to extenuate it by all circumstances that imagination can suggest. And if the crime cannot bear disguise, the next attempt is, to thrust it out of mind altogether, and to rush on to action without thought. This last was the husband's method.

> *Strange things I have in head, that will to hand;*
> *Which must be acted, ere they must be scann'd.*
>
> —*Act 3. sc. 5*

The lady follows neither of these courses, but in a deliberate manner endeavours to fortify her heart in the commission of an execrable crime, without even attempting a disguise. This I think is not natural. I hope there is no such wretch to be found, as is here represented. In the *Pompey* of Corneille[10], Photine counsels a wicked action in the plainest terms without disguise.

> *Seigneur, n'attirez point le tonnerre en ces lieux,*
> *Rangez-vous du parti des destins et des dieux,*
> *Et sans les accuser d'injustice, ou d'outrage,*

---

10. Act 1. sc. 1.

Puis qu'ils font les heureux, adorez leur ouvrage;
Quels que soient leurs decrets, déclarez-vouz pour eux,
Et pour leur obéir, perdez le malheureux.
Pressé de toutes parts des coléres celestes,
Il en vient dessus vous faire fondre les restes;
Et sa tête qu'à peine il a pû dérober,
Tout prête de choir, cherche avec qui tomber.
Sa retraite chez vous en effet n'est qu'un crime;
Elle marque sa haine, et non pas son estime;
Il ne vient que vous perdre en venant prendre port,
Et vous pouvez douter s'il est digne de mort!
Il devoit mieux remplir nos vœux et notre attente,
Faire voir sur ses nefs la victoire flotante;
Il n'eût ici trouvé que joye et que festins,
Mais puisqu'il est vaincu, qu'il s'en prenne aux destins
J'en veux à sa disgrace et non à sa personne,
J'exécute à regret ce que le ciel ordonne,
Et du même poignard, pour César destiné,
Je perce en soupirant son cœur infortuné.
Vouz ne pouvez enfin qu'aux dépens de sa tête
Mettre à l'abri la vôtre et parer la tempête.
Laissez nommer sa mort un injuste attentat,
La justice n'est pas une vertu d'etat.
Le choix des actions, ou mauvaises, ou bonnes,
Ne fait qu'anéantir la force des couronnes;
Le droit des rois consiste à ne rien épargner;
La timide équité détruit l'art de regner,
Quand on craint d'être injuste on a toûjours à craindre,
Et qui veut tout pouvoir doit oser tout enfraindre,
Fuir comme un deshonneur la vertu qui le pert,
Et voler sans scrupule au crime qui lui fert.

In the tragedy of *Esther*[11], Haman acknowledges, without disguise, his cruelty, insolence, and pride. And there is another example of the same kind in the *Agamemnon* of Seneca[12]. In the tragedy of *Athalie*[13],

---

11. Act 2. sc. 1.
12. Beginning of act 2.
13. Act 3. sc. 3. at the close.

Mathan, in cool blood, relates to his friend many black crimes he had been guilty of to satisfy his ambition.

In Congreve's *Double-dealer*, Maskwell, instead of disguising or colouring his crimes, values himself upon them in a soliloquy:

> Cynthia, let thy beauty gild my crimes; and whatsoever I commit of treachery or deceit, shall be imputed to me as a merit.—Treachery! what treachery? Love cancels all the bonds of friendship, and sets men right upon their first foundations.
>
> *Act 2. sc. 8*

In French plays, love, instead of being hid or disguised, is treated as a serious concern, and of greater importance than fortune, family, or dignity. I suspect the reason to be, that in the capital of France, love, by the easiness of intercourse, has dwindled down from a real passion to be a connection that is regulated entirely by the mode or fashion[14]. This may in some measure excuse their writers, but will never make their plays be relished among foreigners.

> Maxime: Quoi, trahir, mon ami!
> Euphorbe:—— L'amour rend tout permis, Un véritable amant
>   ne connoît point d'amis.
>
> *—Cinna, act 3. sc. 1*

> Cesar: Reine, tout est paisible, et la ville calmée,
>   Qu'un trouble assez leger avoit trop alarmée,
>   N'a plus à redouter le divorce intestin
>   Du soldat insolent, et du peuple mutin.
>   Mais, ô Dieux! ce moment que je vous ai quittée,
>   D'un trouble bien plus grand à mon ame agitée,
>   Et ces soins importuns qui m'arrachoient de vous
>   Contre ma grandeur même allumoient mon courroux.

---

[14]. A certain author says, humorously, "Les mots mêmes d'amour et d'amant sont bannis de l'intime société des deux sexes, et relegués avec ceux de *chaine* et de *flamme* dans les Romans qu'on ne lit plus." And where nature is once banished, a fair field is open to every fantastic imitation, even the most extravagant.

> Je lui voulois du mal de m'être si contraire,
> De rendre ma presence ailleurs si necessaire.
> Mais je lui pardonnois au simple souvenir
> Du bonheur qu'a ma flâme elle fait obtenir.
> C'est elle dont je tiens cette haute espérance,
> Qui flate mes desirs d'une illustre apparence,
> Et fait croire à Cesar qu'il peut former de vœux,
> Qu'il n'est pas tout-à-fait indigne de vos feux,
> Et qu'il peut en pretendre une juste conquête,
> N'ayant plus que les Dieux au dessus de sa tête.
> Oui, Reine, si quelqu'un dans ce vaste univers
> Pouvoit porter plus haut la gloire de vos fers;
> S'il étoit quelque trône où vous puissiez paroître
> Plus dignement assise en captivant son maître,
> J'irois, j'irois à lui, moins pour le lui ravir,
> Que pour lui disputer le droit de vous servir;
> Et je n'aspirerois au bonheur de vous plaire,
> Qu'aprés avoir mis bas un si grand adversaire.
> C'etoit pour acquerir un droit si précieux,
> Que combatoit par tout mon bras ambitieux,
> Et dans Pharsale même il a tiré l'epée
> Plus pour le conserver, que pour vaincre Pompée.
> Je l'ai vaincu, Princesse, et le Dieu de combats
> M'y favorisoit moins que vos divins appas.
> Ils conduisoient ma main, ils enfloient mon courage,
> Cette pleine victoire est leur dernier ouvrage,
> C'est l'effet des ardeurs qu'ils daignoient m'inspirer;
> Et vos beaux yeux enfin m'ayant fait soûpirer,
> Pour faire que votre ame avec gloire y réponde,
> M'ont rendu le premier, et de Rome, et du monde;
> C'est ce glorieux titre, à présent effectif,
> Que je viens ennoblir par celui de captif;
> Heureux, si mon ésprit gagne tant sur le vôtre,
> Qu'il en estime l'un, et me permette l'autre.
>
> —*Pompée*, act 4. sc. 3

The last class comprehends sentiments that are unnatural, as being suited to no character nor passion. These may be subdivided into three branches: first, sentiments unsuitable to the constitution of man and the laws of his nature; second, inconsistent sentiments; third, sentiments that are pure rant and extravagance.

WHEN THE FABLE IS OF human affairs, every event, every incident, and every circumstance, ought to be natural, otherwise the imitation is imperfect. But an imperfect imitation is a venial fault, compared with that of running cross to nature. In the *Hippolytus* of Euripides[15], Hippolytus, wishing for another self in his own situation, How much (says he) should I be touched with his misfortune! as if it were natural to grieve more for the misfortunes of another than for one's own.

> OSMYN: Yet I behold her—yet—and now no more.
> Turn your lights inward, Eyes, and view my thought,
> So shall you still behold her—'twill not be.
> O impotence of sight! mechanic sense
> Which to exterior objects ow'st thy faculty,
> Not seeing of election, but necessity.
> Thus do our eyes, as do all common mirrors,
> Successively reflect succeeding images.
> Nor what they would, but must; a star or toad;
> Just as the hand of Chance administers!
>
> —*Mourning Bride, act 2. sc. 8*

No man, in his senses, ever thought of applying his eyes to discover what passes in his mind; far less of blaming his eyes for not seeing a thought or idea. In Moliere's *L'Avare*[16], Harpagon being robbed of his money, seizes himself by the arm, mistaking it for that of the robber. And again he expresses himself as follows:

> Je veux aller querir la justice, et faire donner la question à toute ma maison; à servantes, à valets, à fils, à fille, et à moi aussi.

This is so absurd as scarce to provoke a smile if it be not at the author.

---

15. Act 4. sc. 5.
16. Act 4. sc. 7.

OF THE SECOND BRANCH THE following are examples.

—— Now bid me run
And I will strive with things impossible,
Yea get the better of them.

—Julius Cæsar, act 2. sc. 3

Vos mains seules ont droit de vaincre un invincible.

—Le Cid, act 5. sc. last

Que son nom soit beni. Que son nom soit chanté.
Que l'on celebre ses ouvrages
Au de la de l'eternité.

—Esther, act 5. sc. last

Me miserable! which way shall I fly
Infinite wrath and infinite despair?
Which way I fly is hell: myself am hell:
And in the lowest *deep, a* lower *deep*
Still threat'ning to devour me, opens wide;
To which, the hell I suffer seems a heav'n.

—Paradise Lost, book 4

Of the third branch, take the following samples.

LUCAN, TALKING OF POMPEY'S SEPULCHRE,

—— Romanum nomen, et omne
Imperium Magno est tumuli modus. Obrue saxa
Crimine plena deûm. Si tota est Herculis Oete,
Et juga tota vacant Bromio Nyseia; quare
Unus in Egypto Magno lapis? Omnia Lagi
Rura tenere potest, si nullo cespite nomen
Hæserit. Erremus populi, cinerumque tuorum,
Magne, metu nullas Nili calcemus arenas.

—L. 8. l. 798

Thus in Rowe's translation:

> *Where there are seas, or air, or earth, or skies,*
> *Where-e'er Rome's empire stretches, Pompey lies.*
> *Far be the vile memorial then convey'd!*
> *Nor let this stone the partial gods upbraid.*
> *Shall Hercules all Oeta's heights demand,*
> *And Nysa's hill for Bacchus only stand;*
> *While one poor pebble is the warrior's doom*
> *That fought the cause of liberty and Rome?*
> *If fate decrees he must in Egypt lie,*
> *Let the whole fertile realm his grave supply,*
> *Yield the wide country to his awful shade,*
> *Nor let us dare on any part to tread,*
> *Fearful we violate the mighty dead.*

The following passages are pure rant. Coriolanus speaking to his mother,

> *What is this?*
> *Your knees to me? to your corrected son?*
> *Then let the pebbles on the hungry beach*
> *Fillop the stars: then let the mutinous winds*
> *Strike the proud cedars 'gainst the fiery sun:*
> *Murd'ring impossibility, to make*
> *What cannot be, slight work.*
>
> —*Coriolanus, act 5. sc. 3*

Cæsar:—— Danger knows full well,
 That Cæsar is more dangerous than he.
 We were two lions litter'd in one day,
 And I the elder and more terrible.

> —*Julius Cæsar, act 2. sc. 4*

Almahide: This day—
 I gave my faith to him, he his to me.
Almanzor: Good Heav'n, thy book of fate before me lay
 But to tear out the journal of this day.
 Or if the order of the world below,

> Will not the gap of one whole day allow,
> Give me that minute when she made that vow.
> That minute ev'n the happy from their bliss might give,
> And those who live in grief a shorter time would live.
> So small a link if broke, th' eternal chain
> Would like divided waters join again.
>
> —*Conquest of Granada, act 3*

> ALMANZOR:—— I'll hold it fast
> As life; and when life's gone, I'll hold this last.
> And if thou tak'st it after I am slain,
> I'll send my ghost to fetch it back again.
>
> —*Conquest of Granada, part 2. act 3*

> LYNAIRAXA: A crown is come, and will not fate allow.
> And yet I feel something like death is near.
> My guards, my guards—
> Let not that ugly skeleton appear.
> Sure Destiny mistakes; this death's not mine;
> She doats, and meant to cut another line.
> Tell her I am a queen—but 'tis too late;
> Dying, I charge rebellion on my fate;
> Bow down, ye slaves—
> Bow quickly down and your submission show;
> I'm pleas'd to taste an empire ere I go. (*Dies*)
>
> —*Conquest of Granada, part 2. act. 5*

> VENTIDIUS: But you, ere love misled your wand'ring eyes,
> Were, sure, the chief and best of human race,
> Fram'd in the very pride and boast of nature,
> So perfect, that the gods who form'd you wonder'd
> At their own skill, and cry'd, A lucky hit
> Has mended our design.
>
> —*Dryden, All for Love, act 1*

Not to talk of the impiety of this sentiment, it is ludicrous instead of being lofty.

The famous Epitaph on Raphael is not less absurd than any of the foregoing passages:

> *Raphael, timuit, quo sospite, vinci*
> *Rerum magna parens, et moriente mori.*

Imitated by Pope in his Epitaph on Sir Godfrey Kneller:

> *Living, great Nature fear'd he might outvie*
> *Her works; and dying, fears herself may die.*

Such is the force of imitation; for Pope of himself would never have been guilty of a thought so extravagant.

XVII

Language of Passion

Among the particulars that compose the social part of our nature, a propensity to communicate our opinions, our emotions, and everything that affects us, is remarkable. Bad fortune and injustice affect everyone greatly; and of these we are so prone to complain, that if we have no friend or acquaintance to take part in our sufferings, we sometimes utter our complaints aloud even where there are none to listen.

But this propensity, though natural, operates not in every state of mind. A man immoderately grieved, seeks to afflict himself; and self-affliction is the gratification of the passion. Immoderate grief is therefore mute; because complaining is struggling for relief:

> *It is the wretch's comfort still to have*
> *Some small reserve of near and inward wo,*
> *Some unsuspected hoard of inward grief,*
> *Which they unseen may wail, and weep, and mourn,*
> *And glutton-like alone devour.*
>
> —Mourning Bride, act 1. sc. 1

When grief subsides, it then and no sooner finds a tongue. We complain, because complaining is an effort to disburden the mind of its distress[1].

---

1. This observation is finely illustrated by a story which Herodotus records, b. 3. Cambyses, when he conquered Egypt, made Psammenitus, the king, prisoner; and, for trying his constancy, ordered his daughter to be dressed in the habit of a slave, and to be employed in bringing water from the river: his son also was led to execution with a halter about his neck. The Egyptians vented their sorrow in tears and lamentations; Psammenitus only, with a downcast eye, remained silent. Afterward meeting one of his companions, a man advanced in years, who, being plundered of all, was begging alms, he wept bitterly, calling him by his name. Cambyses, struck with wonder demanded an answer to the following question; "Psammenitus, thy master, Cambyses, is desirous to know, why after thou hadst seen thy daughter so ignominiously treated, and thy son led to execution, without exclaiming or weeping, thou shouldst be so highly concerned for a poor man, no way related to thee?" Psammenitus returned the following answer; "Son of Cyrus, the calamities of my family are too great to leave me the power of weeping; but the misfortunes of a companion, reduced in his old age to want of bread, is a fit subject for lamentation."

Surprise and terror are silent passions for a different reason: they agitate the mind so violently, as for a time to suspend the exercise of its faculties, and in particular that of speech.

Love and revenge, when immoderate, are not more loquacious than immoderate grief. But when these passions become moderate, they set the tongue free, and, like moderate grief, become loquacious. Moderate love, when unsuccessful, is vented in complaints; when successful, is full of joy expressed both in words and gestures.

As no passion hath any long uninterrupted existence[2] nor beats always with an equal pulse, the language suggested by passion is also unequal and interrupted. And even during an uninterrupted fit of passion, we only express in words the more capital sentiments. In familiar conversation, one who vents every single thought is justly branded with the character of *loquacity*. Sensible persons express no thoughts but what make some figure. In the same manner, we are only disposed to express the strongest impulses of passion, especially when it returns with impetuosity after some interruption.

I already have had occasion to observe[3], that the sentiments ought to be tuned to the passion, and the language to both. Elevated sentiments require elevated language: tender sentiments ought to be clothed in words that are soft and flowing: when the mind is depressed with any passion, the sentiments must be expressed in words that are humble, not low. Words have an intimate connection with the ideas they represent; and the representation must be imperfect, if the words correspond not precisely to the ideas. An elevated tone of language to express a plain or humble sentiment, has a bad effect by a discordant mixture of feeling. There is not less discord when elevated sentiments are dressed in low words:

> *Versibus exponi tragicis res comica non vult.*
> *Indignatur item privatis ac prope Socco*
> *Dignis carminibus narrari cœna Thyestæ.*
>
> —Horace, Ars poet. l. 89

This however excludes not figurative expression, which, within moderate bounds, communicates to the sentiment an agreeable elevation. We are sensible of an effect directly opposite, where figurative

---

2. See chap. 2 part 3.
3. Chap. 16.

expression is indulged beyond a just measure. The opposition betwixt the expression and the sentiment, makes the discord appear greater than it is in reality[4].

At the same time, all passions admit not equally of figures. Pleasant emotions, which elevate or swell the mind, vent themselves in strong epithets and figurative expression. Humbling and dispiriting passions, on the contrary, affect to speak plain:

> *Et tragicus plerumque dolet sermone pedestri*
> *Telephus et Peleus: cum pauper et exul uterque;*
> *Projicit ampullas et sesquipedalia verba,*
> *Si curat cor spectantis tetigisse querela.*
>
> —Horace, Ars poet. 95

Figurative expression is the work of an enlivened imagination, and for that reason cannot be the language of anguish or distress. A scene of this kind is painted by Otway in colours finely adapted to the subject. There is scarce a figure in it, except a short and natural simile with which the speech is introduced.

Belvidera talking to her father of her husband:

> *Think you saw what pass'd at our last parting;*
> *Think you beheld him like a raging lion,*
> *Pacing the earth, and tearing up his steps,*
> *Fate in his eyes, and roaring with the pain*
> *Of burning fury; think you saw his one hand*
> *Fix'd on my throat, while the extended other*
> *Grasp'd a keen threat'ning dagger; oh, 'twas thus*
> *We last embrac'd, when, trembling with revenge,*
> *He dragg'd me to the ground, and at my bosom*
> *Presented horrid death; cry'd out, My friends,*
> *Where are my friends? swore, wept, rag'd, threaten'd, lov'd;*
> *For he yet lov'd, and that dear love preserv'd me*
> *To this last trial of a father's pity.*
> *I fear not death, but cannot bear a thought*
> *That that dear hand should do th' unfriendly office;*

---

4. See this explained more particularly in chap. 8.

> *If I was ever then your care, now hear me;*
> *Fly to the senate, save the promis'd lives*
> *Of his dear friends, ere mine be made the sacrifice.*
>
> —*Venice preserv'd, act 5*

To preserve this resemblance betwixt words and their meaning, the sentiments of active and hurrying passions ought to be dressed in words where syllables prevail that are pronounced short or fast; for these make an impression of hurry and precipitation. Emotions, on the other hand, that rest upon their objects, are best expressed by words where syllables prevail that are pronounced long or slow. A person affected with melancholy has a languid and slow train of perceptions. The expression best suited to this state of mind, is where words not only of long but of many syllables abound in the composition. For that reason, nothing can be finer than the following passage:

> *In those deep solitudes, and awful cells,*
> *Where heav'nly-pensive Contemplation dwells,*
> *And ever-musing Melancholy reigns.*
>
> —*Pope, Eloisa to Abelard*

To preserve the same resemblance, another circumstance is requisite, that the language conformable to the emotion, be rough or smooth, broken or uniform. Calm and sweet emotions are best expressed by words that glide softly; surprise, fear, and other turbulent passions, require an expression both rough and broken.

It cannot have escaped any diligent inquirer into nature, that in the hurry of passion, one generally expresses that thing first which is most at heart. This is beautifully done in the following passage.

> *Me, me; adsum qui feci: in me convertite ferrum,*
> *O Rutuli, mea fraus omnis.*
>
> —*Æneid ix. 427*

Passion has often the effect of redoubling words, the better to make them express the strong conception of the mind. This is finely represented in the following examples:

> —— *Thou sun, said I, fair light!*
> *And thou enlighten'd earth, so fresh and gay!*
> *Ye hills and dales, ye rivers, woods, and plains!*
> *And ye that live, and move, fair creatures! tell*
> *Tell, if ye saw, how came I thus, how here.——*
>
> —*Paradise Lost, b. viii. 273*

> —— *Both have sinn'd! but thou*
> *Against God only; I, 'gainst God and thee:*
> *And to the place of judgement will return.*
> *There with my cries importune Heav'n; that all*
> *The sentence, from thy head remov'd, may light*
> *On me, sole cause to thee of all this woe;*
> *Me! Me! only just object of his ire.*
>
> —*Paradise Lost, book x. 930*

Shakespear is superior to all other writers in delineating passion. It is difficult to say in what part he most excels, whether in moulding every passion to peculiarity of character, in discovering the sentiments that proceed from various tones of passion, or in expressing properly every different sentiment. He imposes not upon his reader, general declamation and the false coin of unmeaning words, which the bulk of writers deal in. His sentiments are adjusted, with the greatest propriety, to the peculiar character and circumstances of the speaker; and the propriety is not less perfect betwixt his sentiments and his diction. That this is no exaggeration, will be evident to everyone of taste, upon comparing Shakespear with other writers, in similar passages. If upon any occasion he fall below himself, it is in those scenes where passion enters not. By endeavouring in this case to raise his dialogue above the style of ordinary conversation, he sometimes deviates into intricate thought and obscure expression[5]. Sometimes, to throw his

---

5. Of this take the following specimen.

> *They clepe us drunkards, and with swinish phrase*
> *Soil our ambition: and indeed it takes*
> *From our achievements, though perform'd at height.*
> *The pith and marrow of our attribute.*
> *So, oft it chances in particular men,*

language out of the familiar, he employs rhyme. But may it not in some measure excuse Shakespear, I shall not say his works, that he had no pattern, in his own or in any living language, of dialogue fitted for the theatre? At the same time, it ought not to escape observation, that the stream clears in its progress, and that in his later plays he has attained the purity and perfection of dialogue; an observation that, with greater certainty than tradition, will direct us to arrange his plays in the order of time. This ought to be considered by those who magnify every blemish that is discovered in the finest genius for the drama ever the world enjoy'd. They ought also for their own sake to consider, that it is easier to discover his blemishes, which lie generally at the surface, than his beauties, of which none can have a thorough relish but those who dive deep into human nature. One thing must be evident to the meanest capacity, that where-ever passion is to be display'd, Nature shows itself strong in him, and is conspicuous by the most delicate propriety of sentiment and expression[6].

I return to my subject from a digression I cannot repent of. That perfect harmony which ought to subsist among all the constituent parts of a dialogue, is a beauty, not less rare than conspicuous. As to

> *That for their vicious mole of nature in them,*
> *As, in their birth (wherein they are not guilty,*
> *Since Nature cannot choose his origin),*
> *By the o'ergrowth of some complexion*
> *Oft breaking down the pales and forts of reason;*
> *Or by some habit that too much o'er-leavens*
> *The form of plausive manners; that these men;*
> *Carrying, I say, the stamp of one defect,*
> *(Being Nature's livery, or Fortune's scar,)*
> *Their virtues else, be they as pure as grace,*
> *As infinite as man may undergo,*
> *Shall in the general censure take corruption*
> *From that particular fault.*

—Hamlet, act *1*. sc. 7

6. The critics seem not perfectly to comprehend the genius of Shakspeare. His plays are defective in the mechanical part; which is less the work of genius than of experience, and is not otherwise brought to perfection but by diligently observing the errors of former compositions. Shakspeare excels all the ancients and moderns in knowledge of human nature, and in unfolding even the most obscure and refined emotions. This is a rare faculty, and of the greatest importance in a dramatic author; and it is that faculty which makes him surpass all other writers in the comic as well as tragic vein.

expression in particular, were I to give instances, where, in one or other of the respects above mentioned, it corresponds not precisely to the characters, passions, and sentiments, I might from different authors collect volumes. Following therefore the method laid down in the chapter of sentiments, I shall confine my citations to the grosser errors, which every writer ought to avoid.

And, first, of passion expressed in words flowing in an equal course without interruption.

In the chapter above cited, Corneille is censured for the impropriety of his sentiments; and here, for the sake of truth, I am obliged to attack him a second time. Were I to give instances from that author of the fault under consideration, I might copy whole tragedies; for he is not less faulty in this particular, than in passing upon us his own thoughts as a spectator, instead of the genuine sentiments of passion. Nor would a comparison betwixt him and Shakespear upon the present point, redound more to his honour, than the former upon the sentiments. Racine here is less incorrect than Corneille, though many degrees inferior to the English author. From Racine I shall gather a few instances. The first shall be the description of the sea-monster in his *Phædra*, given by Theramene the companion of Hippolytus, and an eye-witness to the disaster. Theramene is represented in terrible agitation, which appears from the following passage, so boldly figurative as not to be excused but by violent perturbation of mind.

> *Le ciel avec horreur voit ce monstre sauvage,*
> *La terre s'en émeut, l'air en est infecté,*
> *Le flot, qui l'apporta, recule epouvanté.*

Yet Theramene gives a long pompous connected description of this event, dwelling upon every minute circumstance, as if he had been only a cool spectator.

> *A peine nous sortions des portes de Trézene,* &c.
>
> —*Act 5. sc. 6*

The last speech of Atalide, in the tragedy of *Bajazet*, of the same author, is a continued discourse, and but a faint representation of the violent passion which forc'd her to put an end to her own life.

> *Enfin, c'en est donc fait,* &c.
>
> —*Act 5. sc. last*

Though works, not authors, are the professed subject of this critical undertaking, I am tempted by the present speculation, to transgress once again the limits prescribed, and to venture a cursory reflection upon this justly-celebrated author, That he is always sensible, generally correct, never falls low, maintains a moderate degree of dignity without reaching the sublime, paints delicately the tender passions, but is a stranger to the true language of enthusiastic or fervid passion.

If in general the language of violent passion ought to be broken and interrupted, soliloquies ought to be so in a peculiar manner. Language is intended by nature for society; and a man when alone, though he always clothes his thoughts in words, seldom gives his words utterance unless when prompted by some strong emotion; and even then by starts and intervals only[7]. Shakespear's soliloquies may be justly established as a model; for it is not easy to conceive any model more perfect. Of his many incomparable soliloquies, I confine myself to the two following, being different in their manner.

> HAMLET: Oh, that this too too solid flesh would melt,
>   Thaw, and resolve itself into a dew!
>   Or that the Everlasting had not fix'd
>   His cannon 'gainst self slaughter? O God! O God!
>   How weary, stale, flat, and unprofitable
>   Seem to me all the uses of this world!
>   Fie on't! O fie! 'tis an unweeded garden,
>   That grows to seed: things rank and gross in nature
>   Possess it merely. That it should come to this!
>   But two months dead, nay not so much; not two—
>   So excellent a king, that was, to this,
>   Hyperion to a satyr: so loving to my mother,
>   That he permitted not the winds of heav'n
>   Visit her face too roughly. Heav'n and earth!
>   Must I remember,—why, she would hang on him,

---

7. Soliloquies accounted for chap. 15.

> As if increase of appetite had grown
> By what it fed on; yet, within a month—
> Let me not think—Frailty, thy name is *Woman*!
> A little month, or ere those shoes were old,
> With which she follow'd my poor father's body,
> Like Niobe, all tears—why she, ev'n she—
> (O Heav'n! a beast that wants discourse of reason
> Would have mourn'd longer—) married with mine uncle,
> My father's brother; but no more like my father
> Than I to Hercules—Within a month—
> Ere yet the salt of most unrighteous tears
> Had left the flushing in her gauled eyes,
> She married—Oh, most wicked speed, to post
> With such dexterity to incestuous sheets!
> It is not, nor it cannot come to good.
> But break, my heart, for I must hold my tongue.
>
> —*Hamlet*, act 1. sc. 3

> FORD: Hum! ha! is this a vision? is this a dream? do I sleep? Mr. Ford, awake; awake Mr. Ford; there's a hole made in your best coat, Mr. Ford! this 'tis to be married! this 'tis to have linen and buck baskets! Well, I will proclaim myself what I am; I will now take the leacher; he is at my house, he cannot 'scape me; 'tis impossible he should; he cannot creep into a halfpenny-purse, nor into a pepper-box. But lest the devil that guides him should aid him, I will search impossible places; though what I am I cannot avoid, yet to be what I would not, shall not make me tame.
>
> —*Merry Wives of Windsor*, act 3. sc. last

These soliloquies are accurate copies of nature. In a passionate soliloquy one begins with thinking aloud; and the strongest feelings only, are expressed. As the speaker warms, he begins to imagine one listening, and gradually slides into a connected discourse.

How far distant are soliloquies generally from these models? They are indeed for the most part so unhappily executed, as to give disgust instead of pleasure. The first scene of *Iphigenia* in Tauris discovers that princess, in a soliloquy, gravely reporting to herself her own history.

There is the same impropriety in the first scene of *Alcestes*, and in the other introductions of Euripides, almost without exception. Nothing can be more ridiculous. It puts one in mind of that ingenious device in Gothic paintings, of making every figure explain itself by a written label issuing from its mouth. The description a parasite, in the *Eunuch* of Terence[8], gives of himself in the form of a soliloquy, is lively; but against all the rules of propriety; for no man, in his ordinary state of mind, and upon a familiar subject, ever thinks of talking aloud to himself. The same objection lies against a soliloquy in the *Adelphi* of the same author[9]. The soliloquy which makes the third scene, act third, of his *Heicyra*, is insufferable; for there Pamphilus, soberly and circumstantially, relates to himself an adventure which had happened to him a moment before.

Corneille is not more happy in his soliloquies than in his dialogue. Take for a specimen the first scene of *Cinna*.

Racine also is extremely faulty in the same respect. His soliloquies, almost without exception, are regular harangues, a chain completed in every link, without interruption or interval. That of Antiochus in *Berenice*[10] resembles a regular pleading, where the parties *pro* and *con* display their arguments at full length. The following soliloquies are equally destitute of propriety: *Bajazet*, act 3. sc. 7. *Mithridate*, act 3. sc. 4. & act 4. sc. 5. *Iphigenia*, act 4. sc. 8.

Soliloquies upon lively or interesting subjects, but without any turbulence of passion, may be carried on in a continued chain of thought. If, for example, the nature and sprightliness of the subject prompt a man to speak his thoughts in the form of a dialogue, the expression must be carried on without break or interruption, as in a dialogue betwixt two persons. This justifies Falstaff's soliloquy upon honour:

> What need I be so forward with Death, that calls not on me? Well, 'tis no matter, Honour pricks me on. But how if Honour prick me off, when I come on? how then? Can Honour set a leg? No: or an arm? No: or take away the grief of a wound? No: Honour hath no skill in surgery then? No. What is Honour? A word.—What is that word *honour*? Air; a trim reckoning.—

---

8. Act 2. sc. 2.
9. Act 1. sc. 1.
10. Act 1. sc. 2.

Who hath it? He that dy'd a Wednesday. Doth he feel it? No. Doth he hear it? No. Is it insensible then? Yea, to the dead. But will it not live with the living? No: Why? Detraction will not suffer it. Therefore, I'll none of it; honour is a mere scutcheon, and so ends my catechism.

First part Henry IV. act 5. sc. 2

And even without dialogue, a continued discourse may be justified, where the soliloquy is upon an important subject that makes a strong impression, but without much agitation. For if it be at all excusable to think aloud, it is necessary that the language with the reasoning be carried on in a chain without a broken link. In this view that admirable soliloquy in *Hamlet* upon life and immortality, being a serene meditation upon the most interesting of all subjects, ought to escape censure. And the same consideration will justify the soliloquy that introduces the 5th act of Addison's *Cato*.

THE NEXT CLASS OF THE grosser errors which all writers ought to avoid, shall be of language elevated above the tone of the sentiment; of which take the following instances.

> ZARA: Swift as occasion, I
>   Myself will fly; and earlier than the morn
>   Wake thee to freedom. Now 'tis late; and yet
>   Some news few minutes past arriv'd, which seem'd
>   To shake the temper of the King—Who knows
>   What racking cares disease a monarch's bed?
>   Or love, that late at night still lights his lamp,
>   And strikes his rays through dusk, and folded lids,
>   Forbidding rest, may stretch his eyes awake,
>   And force their balls abroad at this dead hour.
>   I'll try.
>
> —*Mourning Bride, act 3. sc. 4*

The language here is undoubtedly too pompous and laboured for describing so simple a circumstance as absence of sleep. In the following passage, the tone of the language, warm and plaintive, is well suited to the passion, which is recent grief. But everyone will be sensible, that in the last couplet save one, the tone is changed, and the mind suddenly elevated to be let fall as suddenly in the last couplet.

> *Il déteste à jamais sa coupable victoire,*
> *Il renonce à la cour, aux humains, à la gloire;*
> *Et se fuïant lui-même, au milieu des deserts,*
> *Il va cacher sa peine au bout de l'univers;*
> *La, soit que le soleil rendit le jour au monde,*
> *Soit qu'il finit sa course au vaste sein de l'onde,*
> *Sa voix faisoit redire aux echos attendris,*
> *Le nom, le triste nom, de son malheureux fils.*

—*Henriade, chant. viii. 229*

Language too artificial or too figurative for the gravity, dignity, or importance, of the occasion, may be put in a third class.

CHIMENE DEMANDING JUSTICE AGAINST RODRIGUE who killed her father, instead of a plain and pathetic expostulation, makes a speech stuffed with the most artificial flowers of rhetoric:

> *Sire, mon pere est mort, mes yeux ont vû son sang*
> *Couler à gros bouillons de son généreux flanc;*
> *Ce sang qui tant de fois garantit vos murailles,*
> *Ce sang qui tant de fois vous gagna des batailles,*
> *Ce sang qui, tout sorti fume encore de courroux*
> *De se voir répandu pour d'autres que pour vous,*
> *Qu'au milieu des hazards n'osoit verser la guerre,*
> *Rodrigue en votre cour vient d'en couvrir la terre.*
> *J'ai couru sur le lieu sans force, et sans couleur;*
> *Je l'ai trouvé sans vie. Excusez ma douleur,*
> *Sire; la voix me manque à ce récit funeste,*
> *Mes pleurs et mes soupirs vous diront mieux le reste.*

And again:

> *Son flanc etoit ouvert, et, pour mieux m'emouvoir,*
> *Son sang sur la poussiére écrivoit mon devoire;*
> *Ou plutôt sa valeur en cet état réduite*

> *Me parloit par sa plaie, et hâtoit ma pursuite,*
> *Et pour se faire entendre au plus juste des Rois,*
> *Par cette triste bouche elle empruntoit ma voix.*
>
> —*Act 2. sc. 9*

Nothing can be contrived in language more averse to the tone of the passion than this florid speech. I should imagine it more apt to provoke laughter than to inspire concern or pity.

IN A FOURTH CLASS SHALL be given specimens of language too light or airy for a severe passion.

THE AGONY A MOTHER MUST feel upon the savage murder of two hopeful sons, rejects all imagery and figurative expression, as discordant in the highest degree. Therefore the following passage is undoubtedly in a bad taste:

> QUEEN: Ah, my poor princes! ah, my tender babes,
> My unblown flow'rs, new-appearing sweets!
> If yet your gentle souls fly in the air,
> And be not fixt in doom perpetual,
> Hover about me with your airy wings,
> And hear your mother's lamentation.
>
> —*Richard III. act 4. sc. 4*

Again,

> K. PHILIP: You are as fond of grief as of your child.
> CONSTANCE: Grief fills the room up of my absent child,
> Lies in his bed, walks up and down with me,
> Puts on his pretty looks, repeats his words,
> Remembers me of all his gracious parts,
> Stuffs out his vacant garment with his form;
> Then have I reason to be fond of grief.
>
> —*King John, act 3. sc. 6*

A thought that turns upon the expression instead of the subject, commonly called *a play of words*, being low and childish, is unworthy of any composition, whether gay or serious, that pretends to the smallest share of dignity. Thoughts of this kind make a fifth class.

IN THE *AMINTA* OF TASSO[11] the lover falls into a mere play of words, demanding how he who had lost himself, could find a mistress. And for the same reason, the following passage in Corneille has been generally condemned:

> CHIMENE: Mon pere est mort, Elvire, et la premiére épée
>   Dont s'est armé Rodrigue à sa trame coupée.
>   Pleurez, pleurez, mes yeux, et fondez-vous en eau,
>   La moitié de ma vie a mis l'autre au tombeau,
>   Et m'oblige à venger, aprés ce coup funeste,
>   Celle que je n'ai plus, sur celle qui me reste.
>
> —*Cid, act 3. sc. 3*

> *To die is to be banish'd from myself:*
> *And Sylvia is myself; banish'd from her,*
> *Is self from self; a deadly banishment!*
>
> —*Two Gentlemen of Verona, act 3. sc. 3*

> COUNTESS: I pray thee, Lady, have a better cheer:
>   If thou ingrossest all the griefs as thine,
>   Thou robb'st me of a moiety.
>
> —*All's well that ends well, act 3. sc. 3*

> K. HENRY: O my poor kingdom, sick with civil blows!
>   When that my care could not with-hold thy riots,
>   What wilt thou do when riot is thy care?
>   O, thou wilt be a wilderness again,
>   Peopled with wolves, thy old inhabitants.
>
> —*Second part, Henry IV. act 4. sc. 11*

> *Cruda Amarilli, che col nome ancora*
> *D'amar, ahi lasso, amaramente insegni.*
>
> —*Pastor Fido, act 1. sc. 2*

---

11. Act 1. sc. 2.

Antony, speaking of Julius Cæsar:

> *O world! thou wast the forest of this hart;*
> *And this, indeed, O world, the heart of thee.*
> *How like a deer, stricken by many princes,*
> *Dost thou here lie!*

> —*Julius Cæsar, act 3. sc. 3*

Playing thus with the sound of words, which is still worse than a pun, is the meanest of all conceits. But Shakespear, when he descends to a play of words, is not always in the wrong; for it is done sometimes to denote a peculiar character; as is the following passage.

KING PHILIP: What say'st thou, boy? look in the lady's face.
LEWIS: I do, my Lord, and in her eye I find
  A wonder, or a wond'rous miracle;
  The shadow of myself form'd in her eye;
  Which being but the shadow of your son,
  Becomes a sun, and makes your son a shadow.
  I do protest, I never lov'd myself,
  Till now infixed I beheld myself
  Drawn in the flatt'ring table of her eye.
FAULCONBRIDGE: Drawn in the flatt'ring table of her eye!
  Hang'd in the frowning wrinkle of her brow!
  And quarter'd in her heart! he doth espy
  Himself Love's traitor: this is pity now,
  That hang'd, and drawn, and quarter'd, there should be,
  In such a love so vile a lout as he.

> —*King John, act. 2. sc. 5*

A jingle of words is the lowest species of this low wit; which is scarce sufferable in any case, and least of all in an heroic poem. And yet Milton in some instances has descended to this puerility:

> *And brought into the world a world of wo.*
> —— *Begirt th' almighty throne*
> *Beseeching or besieging*——
> *Which tempted our attempt*——

> *At one slight bound high overleap'd all bound,*
> *—— With a shout*
> *Loud as from numbers without number.*

One should think it unnecessary to enter a caveat against an expression that has no meaning, or no distinct meaning; and yet somewhat of this kind may be found even among good writers. These make a sixth class.

> SEBASTIAN: I beg no pity for this mould'ring clay.
> For if you give it burial, there it takes
> Possession of your earth:
> If burnt and scatter'd in the air; the winds
> That strow my dust, diffuse my royalty,
> And spread me o'er your clime; for where one atom
> Of mine shall light, know there Sebastian reigns.
>
> —Dryden, *Don Sebastian King of Portugal*, act 1

> CLEOPATRA: Now, what news my Charmion?
> Will he be kind? and will he not forsake me?
> Am I to live or die? nay, do I live?
> Or am I dead? for when he gave his answer,
> Fate took the word, and then I liv'd or dy'd.
>
> —Dryden, *All for Love*, act 2

> *If she be coy, and scorn my noble fire,*
> *If her chill heart I cannot move;*
> *Why, I'll enjoy the very love,*
> *And make a mistress of my own desire.*
>
> —Cowley, *poem inscribed*, The Request

His whole poem, inscribed, *My Picture*, is a jargon of the same kind:

> —— 'Tis he, they cry, by whom
> Not men, but war itself is overcome.
>
> —Indian Queen

Such empty expressions are finely ridiculed in the *Rehearsal*:

> *Was't not unjust to ravish hence her breath,*
> *And in life's stead to leave us nought but death?*
>
> *—Act 4. sc 1*

XVIII

Beauty of Language

Of all the fine arts, painting only and sculpture are in their nature imitative. A field laid out with taste, is not, properly speaking, a copy or imitation of nature, but nature itself embellished. Architecture deals in originals, and copies not from nature. Sound and motion may in some measure be imitated by music; but for the most part music, like architecture, deals in originals. Language has no archetype in nature, more than music or architecture; unless where, like music, it is imitative of sound or motion. In the description of particular sounds, language sometimes happily furnisheth words, which, beside their customary power of exciting ideas, resemble by their softness or harshness the sound described: and there are words, which, by the celerity or slowness of pronunciation, have some resemblance to the motion they signify. This imitative power of words goes one step farther. The loftiness of some words, makes them proper symbols of lofty ideas: a rough subject is imitated by harsh-sounding words; and words of many syllables pronounced slow and smooth, are naturally expressive of grief and melancholy. Words have a separate effect on the mind, abstracting from their signification and from their imitative power. They are more or less agreeable to the ear, by the roundness, sweetness, faintness, or roughness, of their tones.

These are beauties, but not of the first rank: They are relished by those only, who have more delicacy of sensation than belongs to the bulk of mankind. Language possesseth a beauty superior greatly in degree, of which we are eminently conscious when a thought is communicated in a strong and lively manner. This beauty of language, arising from its power of expressing thought, is apt to be confounded with the beauty of the thought expressed; which beauty, by a natural transition of feeling among things intimately connected, is convey'd to the expression, and makes it appear more beautiful[1]. But these

---

1. Chap. 2. part 1. § 5. Demetrius Phalereus (of Elocution, § 75.) makes the same observation. We are apt, says that author, to confound the language with the subject, and if the latter be nervous, we judge the same of the former. But they are clearly distinguishable; and it is not uncommon to find subjects of great dignity dressed in mean

beauties, if we wish to think accurately, must be carefully distinguished from each other. They are indeed so distinct, that we sometimes are conscious of the highest pleasure language can afford, when the subject expressed is disagreeable. A thing that is loathsome, or a scene of horror to make one's hair stand on end, may be described in the liveliest manner. In this case, the disagreeableness of the subject, doth not even obscure the agreeableness of the description. The causes of the original beauty of language considered as significant, which is a branch of the present subject, will be explained in their order. I shall only at present observe, that this beauty is the beauty of means fitted to an end, *viz.* the communication of thought. And hence it evidently appears, that of several expressions all conveying the same thought, the most beautiful, in the sense now mentioned, is that which in the most perfect manner answers its end.

The several beauties of language above mentioned, being of different kinds and distinguishable from each other, ought to be handled separately. I shall begin with those beauties of language which arise from sound; after which will follow the beauties of language considered as significant. This order appears natural; for the sound of a word is attended to, before we consider its signification. In a third section come those singular beauties of language that are derived from a resemblance betwixt sound and signification. The beauties of verse I propose to handle in the last section. For though the foregoing beauties are found in verse as well as in prose; yet verse has many peculiar beauties, which for the sake of perspicuity must be brought under one view. And versification, at any rate, is a subject of so great importance, as to deserve a place by itself.

Section. I

Beauty of language with respect to sound.

I propose to handle this subject in the following order, which appears the most natural. The sounds of the different letters come first. Next, these sounds as united in syllables. Third, syllables united in words. Fourth, words united in a period. And in the last place, periods united in a discourse.

---

language. Theopompus is celebrated for the force of his diction, but erroneously; his subject indeed has great force, but his style very little.

With respect to the first article, every vowel is sounded by a single expiration of air from the wind-pipe through the cavity of the mouth; and by varying this cavity, the different vowels are sounded. The air in passing through cavities differing in size, produceth various sounds, some high or sharp, some low or flat. A small cavity occasions a high sound, a large cavity a low sound. The five vowels accordingly, pronounced with the same extension of the wind-pipe, but with different openings of the mouth, form a regular series of sounds, descending from high to low, in the following order, i, e, a^2, o, u. Each of these sounds is agreeable to the ear. And if it be inquired which of them is the most agreeable, it is perhaps the safest side to hold, that there is no universal preference of anyone before the rest. Probably those vowels which are farthest removed from the extremes, will generally be the most relished. This is all I have to remark upon the first article. For consonants being letters which of themselves have no sound, have no other power but to form articulate sounds in conjunction with vowels; and every such articulate sound being a syllable, consonants come naturally under the second article. To which therefore we proceed.

All consonants are pronounced with a less cavity than any of the vowels; and consequently they contribute to form a sound still more sharp than the sharpest vowel pronounced single. Hence it follows, that every articulate sound into which a consonant enters, must necessarily be double, though pronounced with one expiration of air, or with one breath as commonly expressed. The reason is, that though two sounds readily unite; yet where they differ in tone, both of them must be heard if neither of them be suppressed. For the same reason, every syllable must be composed of as many sounds as there are letters, supposing every letter to be distinctly pronounced.

We next inquire, how far articulate sounds into which consonants enter, are agreeable to the ear. With respect to this point, there is a noted observation, that all sounds of difficult pronunciation are to the ear harsh in proportion. Few tongues are so polished as entirely to have rejected sounds that are pronounced with difficulty; and such sounds must in some measure be disagreeable. But with respect to agreeable sounds, it appears, that a double sound is always more agreeable

---

2. In this scale of sounds the letter *i* must be pronounced as in the word *interest*, and as in other words beginning with the syllable *in;* the letter *e* as in *persuasion*; the letter *a* as in *bat;* and the letter *u* as in *number*.

than a single sound. Everyone who has an ear must be sensible, that the diphthongs *oi* or *ai* are more agreeable than any of these vowels pronounced singly. And the same holds where a consonant enters into the double sound. The syllable *le* has a more agreeable sound than the vowel *e* or than any vowel. And in support of experience, a satisfactory argument may be drawn from the wisdom of Providence. Speech is bestowed upon man, to qualify him for society. The provision he hath of articulate sounds, is proportioned to the use he hath for them. But if sounds that are agreeable singly were not also agreeable in conjunction, the necessity of a painful selection would render language intricate and difficult to be attained in any perfection. And this selection, at the same time, would tend to abridge the number of useful sounds, so as perhaps not to leave sufficient for answering the different ends of language.

In this view, the harmony of pronunciation differs widely from that of music properly so called. In the latter are discovered many sounds singly agreeable, that in conjunction are extremely disagreeable; none but what are called *concordant sounds* having a good effect in conjunction. In the former, all sounds singly agreeable are in conjunction concordant; and ought to be, in order to fulfil the purposes of language.

Having discussed syllables, we proceed to words; which make a third article. Monosyllables belong to the former head. Polysyllables open a different scene. In a cursory view, one will readily imagine, that the effect a word hath upon the ear, must depend entirely upon the agreeableness or disagreeableness of its component syllables. In part it doth; but not entirely; for we must also take under consideration the effect that a number of syllables composing a word have in succession. In the first place, syllables in immediate succession, pronounced, each of them, with the same or nearly the same aperture of the mouth, produce a weak and imperfect sound; witness the French words *détêté* (detested), *dit-il* (says he), *patetique* (pathetic). On the other hand, a syllable of the greatest aperture succeeding one of the smallest, or the opposite, makes a succession, which, because of its remarkable disagreeableness, is distinguished by a proper name, *viz. hiatus*. The most agreeable succession, is, where the cavity is increased and diminished alternately by moderate intervals. Secondly, words consisting wholly of syllables pronounced slow or of syllables pronounced quick, commonly called *long* and *short syllables*, have little melody in them. Witness the words *petitioner*, *fruiterer*, *dizziness*. On the other hand, the intermixture of long and short syllables is remarkably agreeable; for example, *degree*, *repent*, *wonderful*, *altitude*, *rapidity*, *independent*, *impetuosity*. The cause will be explained afterward, in treating of versification.

Distinguishable from the beauties above mentioned, there is a beauty of some words which arises from their signification. When the emotion raised by the length or shortness, the roughness or smoothness, of the sound, resembles in any degree what is raised by the sense, we feel a very remarkable pleasure. But this subject belongs to the third section.

The foregoing observations afford a standard to every nation, for estimating, pretty accurately, the comparative merit of the words that enter into their own language. And though at first view they may be thought equally useful for estimating the comparative merit of different languages; yet this holds not in fact, because no person can readily be found who is sufficiently qualified to apply the standard. What I mean is, that different nations judge differently of the harshness or smoothness of articulate sounds: a sound, harsh and disagreeable to an Italian, may be abundantly smooth to a northern ear. Where are we to find a judge to determine this controversy? and supposing a judge, upon what principle is his decision to be founded? The case here is precisely the same as in behaviour and manners. Plain-dealing and sincerity, liberty in words and actions, form the character of one people. Politeness, reserve, and a total disguise of every sentiment that can give offence, form the character of another people. To each the manners of the other are disagreeable. An effeminate mind cannot bear the least of that roughness and severity, which is generally esteemed manly when exerted upon proper occasions. Neither can an effeminate ear bear the least harshness in words that are deemed nervous and sounding by those accustomed to a rougher tone of language. Must we then relinquish all thoughts of comparing languages in the point of roughness and smoothness, as a fruitless inquiry? Not altogether so; for we may proceed a certain length, though without hope of an ultimate decision. A language with difficulty pronounced even by natives, must yield the preference to a smoother language. Again, supposing two languages pronounced with equal facility by natives, the preference, in my judgement, ought to be in favour of the rougher language; provided it be also stored with a competent share of more mellow sounds. This will be evident from attending to the different effects that articulate sound hath upon the mind. A smooth gliding sound is agreeable, by smoothing the mind and lulling it to rest. A rough bold sound, on the contrary, animates the mind. The effort perceived in pronouncing, is communicated to the hearers: they feel in their own minds a similar effort, which rouses their attention and disposes them to action. I must add another consideration. The agreeableness of contrast in the rougher language, for which the great variety of sounds gives ample opportunity, must, even in an effeminate ear, prevail over the more uniform sounds of the smoother language[3]. This appears to me all that can be safely determined upon the present point. With respect to the other circumstances that constitute the beauty of words, the standard above mentioned is infallible when apply'd to foreign languages as well as to our own. For every man, whatever be his mother-tongue, is equally capable to judge of the length or shortness of words, of the alternate opening and closing of the mouth in speaking, and of the relation which the sound bears to the sense. In these particulars, the judgement is susceptible of no prejudice from custom, at least of no invincible prejudice.

That the English tongue, originally harsh, is at present much softened by dropping in the pronunciation many redundant consonants, is undoubtedly true. That it is not capable of being farther mellowed, without suffering in its force and energy, will scarce be thought by anyone who possesses an ear. And yet such in Britain is the propensity for dispatch, that overlooking the majesty of words composed of many syllables aptly connected, the prevailing taste is, to shorten words, even at the expence of making them disagreeable to the ear and harsh in the pronunciation. But I have no occasion to insist upon this article, being prevented by an excellent writer, who possessed, if any man ever did, the true genius of the English tongue[4]. I cannot however forbear urging one observation borrowed from that author. Several tenses of our verbs are formed by adding the final syllable *ed*, which, being a weak sound, has remarkably the worse effect by possessing the most conspicuous place in the word. Upon that account, the vowel is in common speech generally suppressed, and the consonant is added to the foregoing syllable. Hence the following rugged sounds, *drudg'd*, *disturb'd*, *rebuk'd*, *fledg'd*. It is still less excuseable to follow this practice in writing; for the hurry of speaking may excuse what is altogether improper in a composition of

---

3. That the Italian tongue is too smooth, seems probable, from considering that in versification, vowels are frequently suppressed, in order to produce a rougher and bolder tone.

4. See Swift's proposal for correcting the English tongue, in a letter to the Earl of Oxford.

any value. The syllable *ed*, it is true, makes but a poor figure at the end of a word: but we ought to submit to that defect, rather than multiply the number of harsh words, which, after all that has been done, bear an overproportion in our tongue. The author above mentioned, by showing a good example, did all in his power to restore that syllable; and he well deserves to be imitated. Some exceptions however I would make. A word which signifies labour, or anything harsh or rugged, ought not to be smooth. Therefore *forc'd*, with an apostrophe, is better than *forced*, without it. Another exception is, where the penult syllable ends with a vowel. In that case the final syllable *ed* may be apostrophized without making the word harsh. Examples, *betray'd*, *carry'd*, *destroy'd*, *employ'd*.

The article next in order, is to consider the music of words as united in a period. And as the arrangement of words in succession so as to afford the greatest pleasure to the ear, depends on principles pretty remote from common view, it will be necessary to premise some general observations upon the effect that a number of objects have upon the mind when they are placed in an increasing or decreasing series. The effect of such a series will be very different, according as resemblance or contrast prevails. Where the members of a series vary by small differences, resemblance prevails; which, in ascending, makes us conceive the second object of no greater size than the first, the third of no greater size than the second, and so of the rest. This diminisheth in appearance the size of the whole. Again, when beginning at the largest object, we proceed gradually to the least, resemblance makes us imagine the second as large as the first, and the third as large as the second; which in appearance magnifies every object of the series except the first. On the other hand, in a series varying by great differences, where contrast prevails, the effects are directly opposite. A large object succeeding a small one of the same kind, appears by the opposition larger than usual: and a small object, for the same reason, succeeding one that is large, appears less than usual[5]. Hence a remarkable pleasure in viewing a series ascending by large intervals; directly opposite to what we feel when the intervals are small. Beginning at the smallest object of a series where contrast prevails, this object has the same effect upon the mind as if it stood single without making a part of the series. But this is not the case of the second object, which by means of contrast makes a much greater figure than when viewed singly and apart; and the same

---

5. See the reason, chap. 8.

effect is perceived in ascending progressively, till we arrive at the last object. The direct contrary effect is produced in descending; for in this direction, every object, except the first, makes a less figure than when viewed separately and independent of the series. We may then lay down as a maxim, which will hold in the composition of language as well as of other subjects, That a strong impulse succeeding a weak, makes a double impression on the mind; and that a weak impulse succeeding a strong, makes scarce any impression.

After establishing this maxim, we can be at no loss about its application to the subject in hand. The following rule is laid down by Diomedes[6]. "In verbis observandum est, ne a majoribus ad minora descendat oratio; melius enim dicitur, *Vir est optimus*, quam, *Vir optimus est.*" This rule is applicable not only to single words, but equally to entire members of a period, which, according to our author's expression, ought not more than single words to proceed from the greater to the less, but from the less to the greater. In arranging the members of a period, no writer equals Cicero. The beauty of the following examples out of many, will not suffer me to slur them over by a reference.

Quicum quæstor fueram,
Quicum me sors consuetudoque majorum,
Quicum me Deorum hominumque judicium conjunxerat.

Again:

Habet honorem quem petimus,
Habet spem quam præpositam nobis habemus,
Habet existimationem, multo sudore, labore, vigiliisque, collectam.

Again:

Eripite nos ex miseriis,
Eripite nos ex faucibus eorum,
Quorum crudelitas, nostro sanguine non potest expleri.

—*De oratore, l. 1. § 52*

---

6. De structura perfectæ orationis, 1. 2.

This order of words or members gradually increasing in length, may, so far as concerns the pleasure of sound singly, be denominated *a climax in sound*.

The last article is the music of periods as united in a discourse; which shall be dispatched in a very few words. By no other human means is it possible to present to the mind, such a number of objects and in so swift a succession, as by speaking or writing. And for that reason, variety ought more to be studied in these, than in any other sort of composition. Hence a rule regarding the arrangement of the members of different periods with relation to each other, That to avoid a tedious uniformity of sound and cadence, the arrangement, the cadence, and the length of these members, ought to be diversified as much as possible. And if the members of different periods be sufficiently diversified, the periods themselves will be equally so.

Section. II

Beauty of language with respect to signification.

It is well said by a noted writer[7], "That by means of speech we can divert our sorrows, mingle our mirth, impart our secrets, communicate our counsels, and make mutual compacts and agreements to supply and assist each other." Considering speech as contributing thus to so many good purposes, it follows, that the chusing words which have an accurate meaning, and tend to convey clear and distinct ideas, must be one of its capital beauties. This cause of beauty, is too extensive to be handled as a branch of any other subject. To ascertain with accuracy even the proper meaning of words, not to talk of their figurative power, would require a large volume; an useful work indeed; but not to be attempted without a large stock of time, study, and reflection. This branch therefore of the subject I must humbly decline. Nor do I propose to exhaust all the other beauties of language with respect to signification. The reader, in a work like the present, cannot fairly expect more than a slight sketch of those that make the greatest figure. This is a task which I attempt the more willingly, as it appears to be connected with some principles in human nature; and the rules I shall have occasion to lay down, will, if I judge aright, be agreeable illustrations of these principles. Every subject must

---

7. Scot's Christian life.

be of importance that tends in any measure to unfold the human heart; for what other science is more worthy of human beings?

The present subject is so extensive, that, to prevent confusion, it must be divided into parts; and what follows suggests a division into two parts. In every period, two things are to be regarded, equally capital; first, the words of which the period is composed; next, the arrangement of these words. The former resemble the stones that compose a building; and the latter resembles the order in which these stones are placed. Hence the beauty of language with respect to its meaning, may not improperly be distinguished into two kinds. The first consists in a right choice of words or materials for constructing the period; and the other consists in a due arrangement of these words or materials. I shall begin with rules that direct us to a right choice of words, and then proceed to rules that concern their arrangement.

And with respect to the former, communication of thought being the principal end of language, it is a rule, That perspicuity ought not to be sacrificed to any other beauty whatever. If it should be doubted whether perspicuity be a positive beauty, it cannot be doubted, that the want of it is the greatest defect. Nothing therefore in the structure of language ought more to be studied, than to prevent all obscurity in the expression; for to have no meaning, is but one degree worse than to express it so as not to be understood. Want of perspicuity from a wrong arrangement, belongs to the next branch. I shall give a few examples where the obscurity arises from a wrong choice of words; and as this defect is so common in ordinary writers as to make examples from them unnecessary, I confine myself to the most celebrated authors.

Livy, speaking of a rout after a battle,

> *Multique in ruina majore quam fuga oppressi obtruncatique.*
>
> —*L. 4. § 46*

> *Unde tibi reditum* certo subtemine *Parcæ Rupere.*
>
> —*Horace, epod. xiii. 22.*

> *Qui persæpe cava testudine flevit amorem,*
> Non elaboratum ad pedem.
>
> —*Horace, epod. xiv. 11*

Me fabulosæ Vulture in Appulo,
Altricis extra limen Apuliæ,
Ludo, fatigatumque somno,
Fronde nova puerum palumbes
Texere.

—Horace, Carm. l. 3. ode 4

Puræ rivus aquæ, silvaque jugerum
Paucorum, et segetis certa fides meæ,
Fulgentem imperio fertilis Africæ
Fallit sorte beatior.

—Horace, Carm. l. 3. ode 16

Cum fas atque nefas exiguo fine *libidinum*
Discernunt avidi.

—Horace, Carm. l. 1. ode 18

Ac spem fronte serenat.

—Æneid iv. 477

There is want of neatness even in an ambiguity so slight as that is which arises from the construction merely; as where the period commences with a member which is conceived to be in the nominative case, and which afterward is found to be in the accusative. Example: "Some emotions more peculiarly connected with the fine arts, I propose to handle in separate chapters[8]." Better thus: "Some emotions more peculiarly connected with the fine arts, are proposed to be handled in separate chapters."

THE RULE NEXT IN ORDER, because next in importance, is, That the language ought to correspond to the subject. Grand or heroic actions or sentiments require elevated language: tender sentiments ought to be expressed in words soft and flowing; and plain language devoid of ornament, is adapted to subjects grave and didactic. Language may be considered as the dress of thought; and where the one is not suited to the other, we are sensible of incongruity, in the same manner as where

---

8. Elements of Criticism, vol. i. p. 43. edit. 1.

a judge is dressed like a fop, or a peasant like a man of quality. The intimate connection that words have with their meaning, requires that both be in the same tone. Or, to express the thing more plainly, the impression made by the words ought as nearly as possible to resemble the impression made by the thought. The similar emotions mix sweetly in the mind, and augment the pleasure[9]. On the other hand, where the impressions made by the thought and the words are dissimilar, they are forc'd into a sort of unnatural union, which is disagreeable[10].

In the preceding chapter, concerning the language of passion, I had occasion to give many examples of deviations from this rule with regard to the manner of expressing passions and their sentiments. But as the rule concerns the manner of expressing thoughts and ideas of all kinds, it has an extensive influence in directing us to the choice of proper materials. In that view it must be branched out into several particulars. And I must observe, in the first place, that to write with elegance, it is not sufficient to express barely the conjunction or disjunction of the members of the thought. It is a beauty to find a similar conjunction or disjunction in the words. This may be illustrated by a familiar example. When we have occasion to mention the intimate connection that the soul has with the body, the expression ought to be *the soul and body*; because the particle *the*, relative to both, makes a connection in the expression, which resembles in some degree the connection in the thought. But when the soul is distinguished from the body, it is better to say *the soul and the body*, because the disjunction in the words resembles the disjunction in the thought. In the following examples the connection in the thought is happily imitated in the expression.

Constituit agmen; et expedire tela animosque, equitibus jussis, &c.

—*Livy, l. 38. § 25*

Again:

Quum ex paucis quotidie aliqui corum caderent aut vulnerarentur, et qui superarent, fessi et corporibus et animis essent, &c.

—*Livy, l. 38. § 29*

---

9. Chap. 2. part 4.
10. Ibid.

> *Post acer Mnestheus adducto constitit arcu,*
> *Alta petens, pariterque oculos telumque tetendit.*
>
> —*Æneid, l. v. 507*

The following passage of Tacitus appears to me not so happy. It approaches to wit by connecting in the foregoing manner things but slightly related, which is not altogether suitable to the dignity or gravity of history.

> *Germania omnis a Galliis, Rhætiisque, et Pannoniis,*
> *Rheno et Danubio fluminibus; a Sarmatis Dacisque,*
> *mutuo metu aut montibus separatur.*
>
> —*De moribus Germanorum*

I am more doubtful about this other instance:

> —— *The fiend look'd up, and knew*
> *His mounted scale aloft; nor more, but fled*
> *Murm'ring, and with him fled the shades of night.*
>
> —*Paradise Lost, B. 4. at the end*

I shall add someother examples where the opposition in the thought is imitated in the words; an imitation that is distinguished by the name of *antithesis*.

SPEAKING OF CORIOLANUS SOLICITING THE people to be made consul:

With a proud heart he wore his humble weeds.

Coriolanus

Had you rather Cæsar were living, and die all slaves; than that Cæsar were dead, to live all free men?

Julius Cæsar

He hath cool'd my friends and heated mine enemies.

Shakespear

> *Why, if two gods should play some* heav'nly *match,*
> *And on the wager lay two* earthly *women,*
> *And Portia one, there must be something else*
> *Pawn'd with the other; for the poor rude world*
> *Hath not her fellow.*
>
> —*Merchant of Venice, act 3. sc. 6*

This rule may be extended to govern the construction of sentences or periods. A sentence or period in language ought to express one entire thought or mental proposition; and different thoughts ought to be separated in the expression by placing them in different sentences or periods. It is therefore offending against neatness, to crowd into one period entire thoughts which require more than one; for this is conjoining in language things that are separated in reality; and consequently rejecting that uniformity which ought to be preserved betwixt thought and expression. Of errors against this rule take the following examples.

CÆSAR, DESCRIBING THE SUEVI:

> Atque in eam se consuetudinem adduxerunt, ut locis frigidissimis, neque vestitus, præter pelles, habeant quidquam, quarum, propter exiguitatem, magna est corporis pars operta, et laventur in fluminibus.
> *Commentaria, l. 4. prin*

Burnet, in the history of his own times, giving Lord Sunderland's character, says,

> His own notions were always good; but he was a man of great expence.
>   I have seen a woman's face break out in heats, as she has been talking against a great lord, whom she had never seen in her life; and indeed never knew a party-woman that kept her beauty for a twelvemonth.
> *Spectator*, No 57

Lord Bolingbroke, speaking of Strada:

> I single him out among the moderns, because he had the foolish presumption to censure Tacitus, and to write history himself:

and your Lordship will forgive this short excursion in honour of a favourite author.

Letters on history, vol. 1. let. 5

It seems to me, that in order to maintain the moral system of the world at a certain point, far below that of ideal perfection, (for we are made capable of conceiving what we are incapable of attaining), but however sufficient upon the whole to constitute a state easy and happy, or at the worst tolerable: I say, it seems to me, that the author of nature has thought fit to mingle from time to time, among the societies of men, a few, and but a few, of those on whom he is graciously pleased to bestow a larger proportion of the ethereal spirit than is given in the ordinary course of his providence to the sons of men.

Bolingbroke, on the spirit of patriotism, let. 1

To crowd into a single member of a period, different subjects, is still worse than to crowd them into one period.

——— Trojam, genitore Adamasto
Paupere (mansissetque utinam fortuna) profectus.

—Æneid. iii. 614

Where two things are so connected as to require but a copulative, it is pleasant to find a resemblance in the members of the period, were it even so slight as where both begin with the same letter:

The peacock, in all his pride, does not display half the colour that appears in the garments of a British lady, when she is either dressed for a ball or a birth-day.

Spectator, No 265

Had not my dog of a steward run away as he did, without making up his accounts, I had still been immersed in sin and sea-coal.

Ibid. No. 530

My life's companion, and my bosom-friend,
One faith, one fame, one fate shall both attend.

—Dryden, Translation of Æneid

There is obviously a sensible defect in neatness when uniformity is in this case totally neglected[11]; witness the following example, where the construction of two members connected by a copulative is unnecessarily varied.

> For it is confidently reported, that two young gentlemen of real hopes, bright wit, and profound judgment, who upon a thorough examination of causes and effects, and by the mere force of natural abilities, without the least tincture of learning, have made a discovery that there was no God, and *generously communicating* their thoughts for the good of the public, were sometime ago, by an unparallelled severity, and upon I know not what obsolete law, broke for blasphemy[12]. (Better thus): Having made a discovery that there was no God, and having generously communicated their thoughts for the good of the public, were sometime ago, &c.
>
> He had been guilty of a fault, for which his master would have put him to death, had he not found an opportunity to escape out of his hands, and *fled* into the deserts of Numidia.
>
> *Guardian*, No 139

> If all the ends of the revolution are already obtained, it is not only impertinent to argue for obtaining any of them, but *factious designs might be imputed*, and the name of incendiary be applied with some colour, perhaps, to anyone who should persist in pressing this point.
>
> *Dissertation upon parties, Dedication*

It is even unpleasant to find a negative and affirmative proposition connected by a copulative.

> *Nec excitatur classico miles truci,*
> *Nec horret iratum mare;*
> *Forumque vitat, et superba civium*
> *Potentiorum limina.*
>
> —*Horace, Epod. 2. l. 5*

---

11. See Girard's French Grammar, discourse 12.
12. An Argument against abolishing Christianity.—*Swift*.

> *If it appear not plain, and prove untrue,*
> *Deadly divorce step between me and you.*
>
> —*Shakespear*

An artificial connection among the words, is undoubtedly a beauty when it represents any peculiar connection among the constituent parts of the thought; but where there is no such connection, it is a positive deformity, because it makes a discordance betwixt the thought and expression. For the same reason, we ought also to avoid every artificial opposition of words where there is none in the thought. This last, termed *verbal antithesis*, is studied by writers of no taste; and is relished by readers of the same stamp, because of a certain degree of liveliness in it. They do not consider how incongruous it is, in a grave composition, to cheat the reader, and to make him expect a contrast in the thought, which upon examination is not found there.

> *A light wife doth make a heavy husband.*
>
> —*Merchant of Venice*

Here is a studied opposition in the words, not only without any opposition in the sense, but even where there is a very intimate connection, that of cause and effect; for it is the levity of the wife that vexes the husband.

> ——— *Will maintain*
> *Upon his bad life to make all this good.*
>
> —*King Richard II. act. 1. sc. 2*

Lucetta: What, shall these papers lie like tell-tales here?
Julia: If thou respect them, best to take them up.
Lucetta: Nay, I was taken up for laying them down.

> —*Two Gentlemen of Verona, act 1. sc. 3*

To conjoin by a copulative, members that signify things opposed in the thought, is an error too gross to be commonly practised. And yet writers are guilty of this fault in some degree, when they conjoin by a copulative things transacted at different periods of time. Hence a want of neatness in the following expression.

> The nobility too, whom the King had no means of retaining by suitable offices and preferments, had been seized with the general discontent, and unwarily threw themselves into the scale, which began already too much to preponderate.
> *History of G. Britain, vol. 1. p. 250*

In periods of this kind, it appears more neat to express the past time by the participle passive, thus:

> The nobility having been seized with the general discontent, unwarily threw themselves, *&c.* (or), The nobility who had been seized, *&c.* unwarily threw themselves, *&c.*

So much upon conjunction and disjunction in general. I proceed to apply the rule to comparisons in particular. Where a resemblance betwixt two objects is described, the writer ought to study a resemblance betwixt the two members that express these objects. For it makes the resemblance the more entire to find it extended even to the words. To illustrate this rule, I shall give various examples of deviations from it. I begin with the words that express the resemblance.

> I have observed of late, the style of some great *ministers* very much to exceed that of any other *productions*.
> *Letter to the Lord High Treasurer. Swift*

This, instead of studying the resemblance of words in a period that expresses a comparison, is going out of one's road to avoid it. Instead of *productions* which resemble not ministers great or small, the proper word is *writers* or *authors*.

> If men of eminence are exposed to censure on the one hand, they are as much liable to flattery on the other. If they receive reproaches which are not due to them, they likewise receive praises which they do not deserve.
> *Spectator*

Here the subject plainly demands uniformity in expression instead of variety; and therefore it is submitted whether the period would not do better in the following manner:

If men of eminence be exposed to censure on the one hand, they are as much exposed to flattery on the other. If they receive reproaches which are not due, they likewise receive praises which are not due.

I cannot but fancy, however, that this imitation, which passes so currently with *other judgements*, must at sometime or other have stuck a little with your *Lordship*[13]. (Better thus:) I cannot but fancy, however, that this imitation, which passes so currently with others, must at sometime or other have stuck a little with your Lordship.

*   *   *   *   *

A glutton or mere sensualist is as ridiculous as the other two characters.

Shaftesbury, vol. 1. p. 129

They wisely prefer *the generous efforts of good-will and affection*, to the reluctant compliances *of such as* obey by force.
Remarks on the history of England. Letter 5. Bolingbroke

Titus Livius, concerning the people of Enna demanding the keys from the Roman garrison, makes the governor say,

Quas simul tradiderimus, Carthaginiensium extemplo Enna erit, fœdiusque hic trucidabimir, quam Murgantiæ præsidium interfectum est.

L. 24. § 38

Quintus Curtius, speaking of Porus mounted on an elephant, and leading his army to battle:

Magnitudini Pori adjicere videbatur bellua qua vehebatur, tantum inter cæteras eminens, quanto aliis ipse præstabat.

L. 8. cap. 14

---

13. Letters concerning enthusiasm.—Shafteebary.

It is a still greater deviation from congruity, to affect not only variety in the words, but also in the construction. Describing Thermopylæ, Titus Livius says,

> Id jugum, sicut Apennini dorso Italia dividitur, ita mediam Græciam deremit.
>
> *L. 36. § 15*

Speaking of Shakespear:

> There may remain a suspicion that we over-rate the greatness of his genius; in the same manner as bodies appear more gigantic on account of their being disproportioned and mishapen.
> *History of G. Britain, vol. 1. p. 138*

This is studying variety in a period where the beauty lies in uniformity. Better thus:

> There may remain a suspicion that we over-rate the greatness of his genius, in the same manner as we over-rate the greatness of bodies which are disproportioned and mishapen.

Next as to the length of the members that signify the resembling objects. To produce a resemblance betwixt such members, they ought not only to be constructed in the same manner, but as nearly as possible be equal in length. By neglecting this circumstance, the following example is defective in neatness.

> As the performance of all other religious duties will not avail in the sight of God, *without charity*, so neither will the discharge of all other ministerial duties avail in the sight of men *without a faithful discharge of this principal duty*.
> *Dissertation upon parties, dedication*

In the following passage all the errors are accumulated that a period expressing a resemblance can well admit:

> Ministers are answerable for everything done to the prejudice of the constitution, in the same proportion as the preservation of

the constitution in its purity and vigour, or the perverting and weakening it, are of greater consequence to the nation, than any other instances of good or bad government.

Dissertation upon parties, dedication

The same rule obtains in a comparison where things are opposed to each other. Objects contrasted, not less than what are similar, require a resemblance in the members of the period that express them. The reason is, that contrast has no effect upon the mind, except where the things compared have a resemblance in their capital parts. Therefore, in opposing two circumstances to each other, it remarkably heightens the contrast, to make as entire as possible the resemblance betwixt the other parts, and in particular betwixt the members expressing the two circumstances contrasted. As things are often best illustrated by their contraries, I shall also give examples of deviations from the rule in this case.

ADDISON SAYS,

> A friend exaggerates a man's virtues, an enemy inflames his crimes.
>
> *Spectator*, No 399

Would it not be neater to study uniformity instead of variety? as thus:

> A friend exaggerates a man's virtues, an enemy his crimes.

For here the contrast is only betwixt a friend and an enemy; and betwixt all the other circumstances, including the members of the period, the resemblance ought to be preserved as entire as possible.

SPEAKING OF A LADY'S HEAD-DRESS:

> About ten years ago it shot up to a very great height, insomuch that the female part of our species were much taller than the men.
>
> *Spectator*, No 98

It should be,

than the male part.

The wise man is happy when he gains his own approbation; the fool when he recommends himself to the applause of those about him.

Ibid. No 73

Better:

The wise man is happy when he gains his own approbation; the fool when he gains that of others.

Sicut in frugibus pecudibusque, non tantum semina ad servandum indolem valent, quantum terræ proprietas cœlique, sub quo aluntur, mutat.

Livy, l. 38. § 17

Sallust, in his history of Catiline's conspiracy:

Per illa tempora quicumque rempublicam agitavere, honestis nominibus, alii, sicuti populi jura defenderent, pars, quo senati auctoritas maxuma foret, bonum publicum simulantes, pro sua quisque potentia certabant.

Cap. 38

We proceed to a rule of a different kind. During the course of a period, the same scene ought to be continued without variation. The changing from person to person, from subject to subject, or from person to subject, within the bounds of a single period, distracts the mind, and affords no time for a solid impression. I illustrate this rule by giving examples of deviations from it.

Honos alit artes, *omnesque* incenduntur ad studia gloriâ; jacentque *ea* semper quæ apud quosque improbantur.

Cicero, Tuscul. quæst. l. 1

Speaking of the distemper contracted by Alexander bathing in the river Cydnus and of the cure offered by Philip the physician:

Inter hæc à Parmenione fidissimo purpuratorum, literas *accipit*, quibus ei *denunciabat*, ne salutem suam Philippo committeret.

Quintus Curtius, l. 3. cap. 6

Hook, in his Roman history, speaking of Eumenes, who had been beat down to the ground with a stone, says,

> After a short time *he* came to himself; and the next day, *they* put him on board his ship, *which* conveyed him first to Corinth, and thence to the island of Ægina.

I give another example of a period which is unpleasant, even by a very slight deviation from the rule.

> That sort of instruction which is acquired by inculcating an important moral truth, *&c.*

This expression includes two persons, one acquiring, and one inculcating; and the scene is changed without necessity. To avoid this blemish, the thought may be expressed thus:

> That sort of instruction which is afforded by inculcating, *&c.*

The bad effect of this change of person is remarkable in the following passage.

> The *Britains*, daily harassed by cruel inroads from the Picts, were forced to call in the Saxons for their defence, *who* consequently reduced the greatest part of the island to their own power, drove the Britains into the most remote and mountainous parts, and *the rest of the country*, in customs, religion, and language, became wholly Saxons.
> *Letter to the Lord High Treasurer. Swift*

The following example is a change from subject to persons.

> *This prostitution of praise* is not only a deceit upon the gross of mankind, who take their notion of characters from the learned; but also *the better sort* must by this means lose some part at least of that desire of fame which is the incentive to generous actions, when they find it promiscuously bestowed on the meritorious and undeserving.
> *Guardian*, No 4

Even so slight a change as to vary the construction in the same period, is unpleasant:

Annibal luce prima, Balearibus levique alia armatura præmissa, transgressus flumen, ut quosque traduxerat, ita in acie locabat; Gallos Hispanosque equites prope ripam lævo in cornu adversus Romanum equitatum; dextrum cornu Numidis equitibus datum.
Tit. Liv. l. 22. § 46

Speaking of Hannibal's elephants drove back by the enemy upon his own army:

Eo magis ruere in suos belluæ, tantoque majorem stragem edere quam inter hostes ediderant, quanto acrius pavor consternatam agit, quam insidentis magistri imperio regitur.
Liv. l. 27. § 14

This passage is also faulty in a different respect, that there is no resemblance betwixt the members of the expression, though they import a comparison.

The present head, which relates to the choice of materials, shall be closed with a rule concerning the use of copulatives. Longinus observes, that it animates a period to drop the copulatives; and he gives the following example from Xenophon.

Closing their shields together, they were push'd, they fought, they slew, they were slain.
Treatise of the Sublime, cap. 16

The reason I take to be what follows. A continued sound, if not strong, tends to lay us asleep. An interrupted sound rouses and animates by its repeated impulses. Hence it is, that syllables collected into feet, being pronounced with a sensible interval betwixt each, make more lively impressions than can be made by a continued sound. A period, the members of which are connected by copulatives, produceth an effect upon the mind approaching to that of a continued sound: and therefore to suppress the copulatives must animate a description. To suppress the copulatives hath another good effect. The members of a period connected by the proper copulatives, glide smoothly and gently along;

and are a proof of sedateness and leisure in the speaker. On the other hand, a man in the hurry of passion, neglecting copulatives and other particles, expresses the principal image only. Hence it is, that hurry or quick action is best expressed without copulatives:

Veni, vidi, vici.

―― *Ite:*
Ferte cite flammas, date vela, impellite remos.

—*Æneid.* iv. 593

Quis globus, O Cives, caligine volvitur atra?
Ferte cite ferrum, date tela, scandite muros.
Hostis adest, eja.

—*Æneid.* ix. 36

In this view Longinus[14] justly compares copulatives in a period to strait tying, which in a race obstructs the freedom of motion.

It follows from the same premisses, that to multiply copulatives in the same period ought to be avoided. For if the laying aside copulatives give force and liveliness, a redundancy of them must render the period languid. I appeal to the following instance, though there are not more than two copulatives.

> Upon looking over the letters of my female correspondents, I find several from women complaining of jealous husbands; and at the same time protesting their own innocence, and desiring my advice upon this occasion.
>
> *Spectator*, No 170

I except the case where the words are intended to express the coldness of the speaker; for there the redundancy of copulatives is a beauty.

> Dining one day at an alderman's in the city, Peter observed him expatiating after the manner of his brethren, in the praises of

---

14. Treatise of the Sublime, cap. 16.

his sirloin of beef. "Beef," said the sage magistrate, "is the king of meat: Beef comprehends in it the quintessence of partridge, and quail, and venison, and pheasant, and plum-pudding, and custard."

Tale of Tub, § 4

And the author shows great taste in varying the expression in the mouth of Peter, who is represented more animated.

"Bread," says he, "dear brothers, is the staff of life, in which bread is contained, *inclusivè*, the quintessence of beef, mutton, veal, venison, partridge, plum-pudding, and custard."

We proceed to the second kind of beauty, which consists in a due arrangement of the words or materials. This branch of the subject is not less nice than extensive; and I despair to put it in a clear light, until a sketch be given of the general principles that govern the structure or composition of language.

Every thought, generally speaking, contains one capital object considered as acting or as suffering. This object is expressed by a substantive noun. Its action is expressed by an active verb; and the thing affected by the action is expressed by another substantive noun. Its suffering or passive state is expressed by a passive verb, and the thing which acts upon it, by a substantive noun. Beside these, which are the capital parts of a sentence or period, there are generally under-parts. Each of the substantives as well as the verb, may be qualified. Time, place, purpose, motive, means, instrument, and a thousand other circumstances, may be necessary to complete the thought. And in what manner these several parts are connected together in the expression, will appear from what follows.

In a complete thought or mental proposition, all the members and parts are mutually related, some slightly, some more intimately. In communicating such a thought, it is not sufficient that the component ideas be clearly expressed: it is also necessary, that all the relations contained in the thought be expressed according to their different degrees of intimacy. To annex a certain meaning to a certain sound or word, requires no art. The great nicety in all languages is, to express the various relations that connect together the parts of the thought. Could we suppose this branch of language to be still a secret, it would puzzle,

I am apt to think, the greatest grammarian ever existed, to invent an expeditious method. And yet, by the guidance merely of nature, the rude and illiterate have been led to a method so perfect, that it appears not susceptible of any improvement. Without a clear conception of the manner of expressing relations, one at every turn must be at a loss about the beauties of language; and upon that subject therefore I find it necessary to say a few words.

Words that import a relation, must be distinguished from those that do not. Substantives commonly imply no relation, such as *animal*, *man*, *tree*, *river*. Adjectives, verbs, and adverbs, imply a relation. The adjective *good* must be connected with some substantive, some being possessed of that quality. The verb *write* must be applied to some person who writes; and the adverbs *moderately*, *diligently*, have plainly a reference to some action which they modify. When in language a relative term is introduced, all that is necessary to complete the expression, is, to ascertain that thing to which the term relates. For answering this purpose, I observe in Greek and Latin two different methods. Adjectives are declined as well as substantives; and declension serves to ascertain the connection that is betwixt them. If the word that expresses the subject be, for example, in the nominative case, so also must the word be that expresses its quality. Example, *vir bonus*. Again, verbs are related, on the one hand, to the agent; and, on the other, to the subject upon which the action is exerted. A contrivance similar to that now mentioned, serves to express this double relation. The nominative case is appropriated to the agent, the accusative to the passive subject; and the verb is put in the first second or third person, to correspond the more intimately with both. Examples: *Ego amo Tulliam*; *tu amas Semproniam*; *Brutus amat Portiam*. The other method is by juxtaposition, which is necessary with respect to words only that are not declined, adverbs for example, articles, prepositions, and conjunctions. In the English language there are few declensions; and therefore juxtaposition is our chief resource. Adjectives accompany their substantives[15]; an adverb accompanies the word it qualifies;

---

15. "Taking advantage of a declension to separate an adjective from its substantive, as is commonly practised in Latin, though it detract not from perspicuity, is certainly less neat than the English method of juxtaposition. Contiguity is more expressive of an intimate relation, than resemblance merely of the final syllables. Latin, indeed, has evidently the advantage when the adjective and substantive happen to be connected by contiguity, as well as by resemblance of the final syllables.

and the verb occupies the middle place betwixt the active and passive subjects to which it relates.

It must be obvious, that those terms which have nothing relative in their signification, cannot be connected in so easy a manner. When two substantives happen to be connected, as cause and effect, as principal and accessory, or in any other manner, such connection cannot be expressed by contiguity solely; for words must often in a period be placed together which are not thus related. The relation betwixt substantives, therefore, cannot otherwise be expressed than by particles denoting the relation. Latin indeed and Greek, by their declensions, go a certain length to express such relations, without the aid of particles. The relation of property, for example, betwixt Cæsar and his horse is, expressed by putting the latter in the nominative case, the former in the genitive; *equus Cæsaris*. The like in English, *Cæsar's horse*. But in other instances, declensions not being used in the English language, relations of this kind are commonly expressed by prepositions.

This form of connecting by prepositions, is not confined to substantives. Qualities, attributes, manner of existing or acting, and all other circumstances, may in the same manner be connected with the substantives to which they relate. This is done artificially by converting the circumstance into a substantive, in which condition it is qualified to be connected with the principal subject by a preposition, in the manner above described. For example, the adjective *wise* being converted into the substantive *wisdom*, gives opportunity for the expression "a man *of* wisdom," instead of the more simple expression, *a wise man*. This variety in the expression, enriches language. I observe beside, that the using a preposition in this case, is not always a matter of choice. It is indispensable with respect to every circumstance that cannot be expressed by a single adjective or adverb.

To pave the way for the rules of arrangement, one other preliminary must be discussed, which is, to explain the difference betwixt a natural style, and that where transposition or inversion prevails. There are, it is true, no precise boundaries betwixt these two; for they run into each other, like the shades of different colours. No person however is at a loss to distinguish them in their extremes: and it is necessary to make the distinction; because though some of the rules I shall have occasion to mention are common to both, yet each has rules peculiar to itself. In a natural style, relative words are by juxtaposition connected with those to which they relate, going before or after, according to the peculiar genius of the language. Again, a circumstance connected by a preposition, follows naturally the word with which it is connected. But this arrangement may be varied, when a different order is more beautiful. A circumstance may be placed before the word with which it is connected by a preposition; and may be interjected even betwixt a relative word and that to which it relates. When such liberties are frequently taken, the style becomes inverted or transposed.

But as the liberty of inversion is a capital point in handling the present subject, it will be necessary to examine it more narrowly, and in particular to trace the several degrees in which an inverted style recedes more and more from that which is natural. And first, as to the placing a circumstance before the word with which it is connected, I observe, that it is the easiest of all inversion, even so easy as to be consistent with a style that is properly termed natural. Witness the following examples.

> In the sincerity of my heart, I profess, &c.
> By our own ill management, we are brought to so low an ebb of wealth and credit, that, &c.
> On Thursday morning there was little or nothing transacted in Change-alley.
> At St. Bride's church in Fleetstreet, Mr. Woolston, (who writ against the miracles of our Saviour), in the utmost terrors of conscience made a public recantation.

The interjecting a circumstance betwixt a relative word and that to which it relates, is more properly termed inversion; because, by a violent disjunction of words intimately connected, it recedes farther from a natural style. But this liberty has also degrees; for the disjunction is more violent in some cases than in others. This I must also explain: and to give a just notion of the difference, I must crave liberty of my reader to enter a little more into an abstract subject, than would otherwise be my choice.

In nature, though a substance cannot exist without its qualities, nor a quality without a substance; yet in our conception of these, a material difference may be remarked. I cannot conceive a quality but as belonging to some subject: it makes indeed a part of the idea which is formed of the subject. But the opposite holds not. Though I cannot form a conception of a subject devoid of all qualities, a partial conception may however be formed of it, laying aside or abstracting from any particular quality. I can, for example, form the idea of a fine Arabian horse without regard to his colour, or of a white horse without regard to his size. Such partial conception of a subject, is still more easy with respect to action or motion; which is an occasional attribute only, and has not the same permanency with colour or figure. I cannot form an idea of motion independent of a body; but there is nothing more easy than to form an idea of a body at rest. Hence it appears, that the degree of inversion depends greatly on the order in which the related words are placed. When a substantive occupies the first place, we cannot foresee what is to be said of it. The idea therefore which this word suggests, must subsist in the mind at least for a moment, independent of the relative words afterward introduced; and if it can so subsist, that moment may without difficulty be prolonged by interjecting a circumstance betwixt the substantive and its connections. Examples therefore of this kind, will scarce alone be sufficient to denominate a style inverted. The case is very different, where the word that occupies the first place, denotes a quality or an action; for as these cannot be conceived without a subject, they cannot without greater violence be separated from the subject that follows. And for that reason, every such separation by means of an interjected circumstance belongs to an inverted style.

To illustrate this doctrine examples being necessary, I shall begin with those where the word first introduced does not imply a relation.

—— Nor Eve to iterate
Her former trespass fear'd.

—— Hunger and thirst at once,
Powerful persuaders, quicken'd at the scent
Of that alluring fruit, urg'd me so keen.

Moon, that now meet'st the orient sun, now fli'st
With the fix'd stars, fix'd in their orb that flies,
And ye five other wand'ring fires that move
In mystic dance not without song, resound
His praise.

In the following examples, where the word first introduced imports a relation, the disjunction will be found more violent.

> *Of man's first disobedience, and the fruit*
> *Of that forbidden tree, whose mortal taste*
> *Brought death into the world, and all our wo,*
> *With loss of Eden, till one greater man*
> *Restore us, and regain the blessful seat,*
> *Sing heav'nly muse.*

> *—— Upon the firm opacous globe*
> *Of this round world, whose first convex divides*
> *The luminous inferior orbs, inclos'd*
> *From chaos and th' inroad of darkness old*
> *Satan alighted walks.*

> *—— On a sudden open fly,*
> *With impetuous recoil and jarring sound,*
> *Th' infernal doors.*

> *—— Wherein remain'd,*
> *For what could else? to our almighty foe*
> *Clear victory, to our part loss and rout.*

> *——Forth rush'd with whirlwind sound*
> *The chariot of paternal Deity.*

Language would have no great power, were it confined to the natural order of ideas. A thousand beauties may be compassed by inversion, that must be relinquished in a natural arrangement. I shall soon have an opportunity to make this evident. In the mean time, it ought not to escape observation, that the mind of man is happily so constituted as to relish inversion, though in one respect unnatural; and to relish it so much, as in many cases to admit a violent disjunction of words that by the sense are intimately connected. I scarce can say that inversion has any limits; though I may venture to pronounce, that the disjunction of articles, conjunctions, or prepositions, from the words to which they belong, never has a good effect. The following example with relation to a preposition, is perhaps as tolerable as any of the kind.

> He would neither separate *from*, nor act against them.

I give notice to the reader, that I am now ready to enter upon the rules of arrangement; beginning with a natural style, and proceeding gradually to what is the most inverted. And in the arrangement of a period, as well as in a right choice of words, the first and great object being perspicuity, it is above laid down as a rule, That perspicuity ought not to be sacrificed to any other beauty whatever. Ambiguities occasioned by a wrong arrangement are of two sorts; one where the arrangement leads to a wrong sense, and one where the sense is left doubtful. The first being the more culpable, shall take the lead, beginning with examples of words put in a wrong place.

How much the imagination of such a presence must exalt a genius, we may observe *merely* from the influence which an ordinary presence has over men.
Characteristics, vol. 1. p. 7

This arrangement leads to a wrong sense: The adverb *merely* seems by its position to affect the preceding word; whereas it is intended to affect the following words *an ordinary presence*; and therefore the arrangement ought to be thus.

How much the imagination of such a presence must exalt a genius, we may observe from the influence which an ordinary presence merely has over men.

The time of the election of a poet-laureat being now at hand, it may be proper to give some account of the rites and ceremonies anciently used at that solemnity, and only discontinued through the neglect and degeneracy of later times.
Guardian

The term *only* is intended to qualify the noun *degeneracy*, and not the participle *discontinued*; and therefore the arrangement ought to be as follows.

——— *and discontinued through the neglect and degeneracy only, of later times.*

Sixtus the Fourth was, if I mistake not, a great collector of books at least.
Letters on history, vol. 1. let. 6. Bolingbroke

The expression here leads evidently to a wrong sense. The adverb *at least*, ought not to be connected with the substantive *books*, but with *collector*, thus:

Sixtus the Fourth was a great collector at least, of books.

Speaking of Lewis XIV.

If he was not the greatest king, he was the best actor of majesty at least, that ever filled a throne.

Ibid. letter 7

Better thus:

If he was not the greatest king, he was at least the best actor of majesty, &c.

This arrangement removes the wrong sense occasioned by the juxtaposition of *majesty* and *at least*.

The following examples are of the wrong arrangement of members.

I have confined myself to those methods for the advancement of piety, which are in the power of a prince limited like ours by a strict execution of the laws.

A project for the advancement of religion. Swift

The structure of this period leads to a meaning which is not the author's, *viz.* power limited by a strict execution of the laws. This wrong sense is removed by the following arrangement.

I have confined myself to those methods for the advancement of piety, which, by a strict execution of the laws, are in the power of a prince limited like ours.

This morning when one of Lady Lizard's daughters was looking over some hoods and ribands brought by her tirewoman, with great care and diligence, I employed no less in examining the box which contained them.

Guardian, No 4

The wrong sense occasioned by this arrangement, may be easily prevented by varying it thus:

> This morning when, with great care and diligence, one of Lady Lizard's daughters was looking over some hoods and ribands, &c.
> A great stone that I happened to find after a long search by the sea-shore, served me for an anchor.
> Gulliver's Travels, part 1. chap. 8

One would think that the search was confined to the sea-shore; but as the meaning is, that the great stone was found by the sea-shore, the period ought to be arranged thus:

> A great stone, that, after a long search, I happened to find by the sea-shore, served me for anchor.

Next of a wrong arrangement where the sense is left doubtful; beginning, as in the former sort, with examples of the wrong arrangement of words in a member.

> These forms of conversation *by degrees* multiplied and grew troublesome.
> Spectator, No 119

Here it is left doubtful whether the modification *by degrees* relate to the preceding member or to what follows. It should be,

> These forms of conversation multiplied by degrees.
> Nor does this false modesty expose us *only* to such actions as are indiscreet, but very often to such as are highly criminal.
> Spectator, No 458

The ambiguity is removed by the following arrangement.

> Nor does this false modesty expose us to such actions only as are indiscreet, &c.
> The empire of Blefuscu is an island situated to the north-east side of Lilliput, from whence it is parted *only* by a channel of 800 yards wide.
> Gulliver's Travels, part 1. chap. 5

The ambiguity may be removed thus:

—— from whence it is parted by a channel of 800 yards wide only.

In the following examples the sense is left doubtful by a wrong arrangement of members.

The minister who grows less by his elevation, *like a little statue placed on a mighty pedestal*, will always have his jealousy strong about him.

Dissertation upon parties, dedication. Bolingbroke

Here, so far as can be gathered from the arrangement, it is doubtful, whether the object introduced by way of simile, relate to what goes before or to what follows. The ambiguity is removed by the following arrangement.

The minister who, like a little statue placed on a mighty pedestal, grows less by his elevation, will always, *&c.*

Since this is too much to ask of freemen, nay of slaves, *if his expectation be not answered*, shall he form a lasting division upon such transient motives?

Ibid

Better thus:

Since this is too much to ask of freemen, nay of slaves, shall he, if his expectation be not answered, form, *&c.*

Speaking of the superstitious practice of locking up the room where a person of distinction dies:

The knight, seeing his habitation reduced to so small a compass, and himself in a manner shut out of his own house, *upon the death of his mother* ordered all the apartments to be flung open, and exorcised by his chaplain.

Spectator, No 110

Better thus:

The knight, seeing his habitation reduced to so small a compass, and himself in a manner shut out of his own house, ordered, upon the death of his mother, all the apartments to be flung open.

Speaking of some indecencies in conversation:

As it is impossible for such an irrational way of conversation to last long among a people that make any profession of religion, or show of modesty, *if the country-gentlemen get into it*, they will certainly be left in the lurch.

Spectator, No. 119

The ambiguity vanishes in the following arrangement.

—— the country-gentlemen, if they get into it, will certainly be left in the lurch.

Speaking of a discovery in natural philosophy, that colour is not a quality of matter:

As this is a truth which has been proved incontestably by many modern philosophers, and is indeed one of the finest speculations in that science, *if the English reader would see the notion explained at large*, he may find it in the eighth chapter of the second book of Mr. Locke's essay on human understanding.

Spectator, No 413

Better thus:

As this is a truth, *&c.* the English reader, if he would see the notion explained at large, may find it, *&c.*

A woman seldom asks advice before she has bought her wedding-cloaths. When she has made her own choice, *for form's sake* she sends a *conge d'elire* to her friends.

Ibid. No 475

Better thus:

—— she sends for form's sake a *conge d'elire* to her friends.

And since it is necessary that there should be a perpetual intercourse of buying and selling, and dealing upon credit, *where fraud is permitted or connived at, or hath no law to punish it*, the honest dealer is always undone, and the knave gets the advantage.

Gulliver's Travels, part 1. chap. 6

Better thus:

And since it is necessary that there should be a perpetual intercourse of buying and selling, and dealing upon credit, the honest dealer, where fraud is permitted or connived at, or hath no law to punish it, is always undone, and the knave gets the advantage.

From these examples, the following observation will readily occur, that a circumstance ought never to be placed betwixt two capital members of a period; for by such situation it must always be doubtful, so far as we gather from the arrangement, to which of the two members it belongs. Where it is interjected, as it ought to be, betwixt parts of the member to which it belongs, the ambiguity is removed, and the capital members are kept distinct, which is a great beauty in composition. In general, to preserve members distinct which signify things distinguished in the thought, the sure method is, to place first in the consequent member some word that cannot connect with what precedes it.

If by anyone it shall be thought, that the objections here are too scrupulous, and that the defect of perspicuity is easily supplied by accurate punctuation; the answer is, That punctuation may remove an ambiguity, but will never produce that peculiar beauty which is felt when the sense comes out clearly and distinctly by means of a happy arrangement. Such influence has this beauty, that by a natural transition of feeling, it is communicated to the very sound of the words, so as in appearance to improve the music of the period. But as this curious subject comes in more properly afterward, it is sufficient at present to appeal to experience, that a period so arranged as to bring out the sense clear, seems always more musical than where the sense is left in any degree doubtful.

A rule deservedly occupying the second place, is, That words expressing things connected in the thought, ought to be placed as near together as possible. This rule is derived immediately from human nature, in which there is discovered a remarkable propensity to place together things that are in any manner connected[16]. Where things are arranged according to their connections, we have a sense of order: otherwise we have a sense of disorder, as of things placed by chance. And we naturally place words in the same order in which we would place the things they signify. The bad effect of a violent separation of words or members thus intimately connected, will appear from the following examples.

> For the English are naturally fanciful, and very often disposed, by that gloominess and melancholy of temper which is so frequent in our nation, to many wild notions and visions, to which others are not so liable.
>
> *Spectator*, No 419

Here the verb or assertion is, by a pretty long circumstance, violently separated from the subject to which it refers. This makes a harsh arrangement; the less excusable that the fault is easily prevented by placing the circumstance before the verb or assertion, after the following manner:

> For the English are naturally fanciful, and, by that gloominess and melancholy of temper which is so frequent in our nation, are often disposed to many wild notions, *&c.*

> For as no mortal author, in the ordinary fate and vicissitude of things, knows to what use his works may, sometime or other, be applied, *&c.*
>
> *Spectator*, No 85

---

[16]. See chap. 1.

Better thus:

For as, in the ordinary fate and vicissitude of things, no mortal author knows to what use, sometime or other, his works may be apply'd.

From whence we may date likewise the rivalship of the house of France, for we may reckon that of the Valois and that of Bourbon as one upon this occasion, and the house of Austria, that continues at this day, and has oft cost so much blood and so much treasure in the course of it.

Letters on history, vol. 1. letter 6. Bolingbroke

It cannot be impertinent or ridiculous therefore in such a country, whatever it might be in the Abbot of St. Real's, which was Savoy I think; or in Peru, under the Incas, where Garcilasso de la Vega says it was lawful for none but the nobility to study—for men of all degrees to instruct themselves in those affairs wherein they may be actors, or judges of those that act, or controllers of those that judge.

Letters on history, vol. 1. letter 5. Bolingbroke

If Scipio, who was naturally given to women, for which anecdote we have, if I mistake not, the authority of Polybius, as well as some verses of Nevius preserved by Aulus Gellius, had been educated by Olympias at the court of Philip, it is improbable that he would have restored the beautiful Spaniard.

Ibid. letter 3

If anyone have a curiosity for more specimens of this kind, they will be found without number in the works of the same author.

A pronoun, which saves the naming a person or thing a second time, ought to be placed as near as possible to the name of that person or thing. This is a branch of the foregoing rule; and with the reason there given, another concurs, *viz.* That if other ideas intervene, it is difficult to recal the person or thing by reference.

If I had leave to print the Latin letters transmitted to me from foreign parts, they would fill a volume, and be a full defence against all that Mr. Partridge, or his accomplices of the Portugal inquisition, will be ever able to object; *who*, by the way, are the only enemies my predictions have ever met with at home or abroad.

Better thus:

—— and be a full defence against all that can be objected by Mr. Partridge, or his accomplices of the Portugal inquisition; who, by the way, are, *&c.*

There being a round million of creatures in human figure, throughout this kingdom, *whose* whole subsistence, *&c.*

A modest proposal, &c. *Swift*

Better:

There being, throughout this kingdom, a round million of creatures in human figure, whose whole subsistence, *&c.*

Tom is a lively impudent clown, and has wit enough to have made him a pleasant companion, had *it* been polished and rectified by good manners.

Guardian, No 162

It is the custom of the Mahometans, if they see any printed or written paper upon the ground, to take it up, and lay it aside carefully, as not knowing but it may contain some piece of their Alcoran.

Spectator, No 85

The arrangement here leads to a wrong sense, as if the ground were taken up, not the paper. Better thus:

It is the custom of the Mahometans, if they see upon the ground any printed or written paper, to take it up, *&c.*

The following rule depends on the communication of emotions or feelings to related objects, a principle in human nature we have had more than one occasion to mention. We find this operation, even where the objects are not otherwise related than by the juxtaposition of the words that express them. Hence to elevate or depress an object, one method is, to join it in the arrangement to another that is naturally high or low. Witness the following speech of Eumenes to the Roman senate.

> Causam veniendi sibi Romam fuisse, præter cupiditatem visendi *deos hominesque*, quorum beneficio in ea fortuna esset, supra quam ne optare quidem auderet, etiam ut coram moneret senatum ut Persei conatus obviam iret.
>
> *Livy, l. 42. cap. 11*

To join the Romans with the gods in the same enunciation, is an artful stroke of flattery, because it tacitly puts them on a level. On the other hand, when the purpose is to degrade or vilify an object, this is done successfully by ranking it with one that is really low:

> I hope to have this entertainment in a readiness for the next winter; and doubt not but it will please more than the opera or puppet-show.
>
> *Spectator*, No 28

> Manifold have been the judgments which Heaven from time to time, for the chastisement of a sinful people, has inflicted upon whole nations. For when the degeneracy becomes common, 'tis but just the punishment should be general. Of this kind, in our own unfortunate country, was that destructive pestilence, whose mortality was so fatal as to sweep away, if Sir William Petty may be believed, five millions of Christian souls, besides women and Jews.
>
> *God's revenge against punning. Arbuthnot*

> Such also was that dreadful conflagration ensuing in this famous metropolis of London, which consumed, according to the computation of Sir Samuel Morland, 100,000 houses, not to mention churches and stables.
>
> *Ibid*

> But on condition it might pass into a law, I would gladly exempt both lawyers of all ages, subaltern and field officers, young heirs, dancing-masters, pickpockets, and players.
>
> *An infallible scheme to pay the public debts. Swift*

Circumstances in a period resemble small stones in a building employ'd to fill up vacancies among those of a larger size. In the arrangement of a period, such under-parts crowded together make a poor figure; and never are graceful but when interspersed among the capital parts. I shall illustrate this rule by the following example.

> It is likewise urged, that there are, by computation, in this kingdom, above 10,000 parsons, whose revenues, added to those of my Lords the bishops, would suffice to maintain, &c.
> *Argument against abolishing Christianity. Swift*

Here two circumstances, *viz. by computation* and *in this kingdom*, are crowded together unnecessarily. They make a better appearance separated in the following manner.

> It is likewise urged, that in this kingdom there are, by computation, above 10,000 parsons, &c.

If there be room for a choice, the sooner a circumstance be introduced, the better. Circumstances are proper for that coolness of mind, with which a period as well as a work is commenced. In the progress, the mind warms, and has a greater relish for matters of importance. When a circumstance is placed at the beginning or near the beginning of the period, the transition from it to the principal subject is agreeable: it is like ascending or mounting upward. On the other hand, to place it late in the period has a bad effect; for after being engaged in the principal subject, one is with reluctance brought down to give attention to a circumstance. Hence evidently the preference of the following arrangement,

> Whether in any country a choice altogether unexceptionable has been made, seems doubtful,

before this other,

> Whether a choice altogether unexceptionable has in any country been made, &c.

For this reason the following period is exceptionable in point of arrangement:

> I have considered formerly, with a good deal of attention, the subject upon which you command me to communicate my thoughts to you.
>
> *Bolingbroke of the study of history, letter 1*

which, with a slight alteration, may be improved thus:

> I have formerly, with a good deal of attention, considered the subject, *&c.*

The bad effect of placing a circumstance last or late in a period, will appear from the following examples.

> Let us endeavour to establish to ourselves an interest in him who holds the reins of the whole creation in his hand.
>
> *Spectator*, No 12

Better thus:

> Let us endeavour to establish to ourselves an interest in him, who, in his hand, holds the reins of the whole creation.
>
> Virgil, who has cast the whole system of Platonic philosophy, so far as it relates to the soul of man, into beautiful allegories, *in the sixth book of his Æneid*, gives us the punishment, *&c.*
>
> *Spectator*, No 90

Better thus:

> Virgil, who in the sixth book of his Æneid has cast, *&c.*
>
> And Philip the Fourth was obliged at last to conclude a peace, on terms repugnant to his inclination, to that of his people, to the interest of Spain, and to that of all Europe, in the Pyrenean treaty.
>
> *Letters on history, vol. 1. letter 6. Bolingbroke*

Better thus:

And at last, in the Pyrenean treaty, Philip the Fourth was obliged to conclude a peace, *&c.*

In arranging a period, it is of importance to determine in what part of it a word makes the greatest figure, whether in the beginning, during the currency, or at the close. The breaking silence rouses the attention to what is said; and therefore deeper impression is made at the beginning than during the currency. The beginning, however, must yield to the close; which being succeeded by a pause, affords time for a word to make its deepest impression. Hence the following rule, That to give the utmost force to a period, it ought if possible to be closed with that word which makes the greatest figure. The opportunity of a pause should not be thrown away upon accessories, but reserved for the principal object, in order that it may make a full impression. This is an additional reason against closing a period with a circumstance. There are however periods that admit not this structure; and in that case, the capital word ought if possible to be placed in the front, which next to the close is the most advantageous for making an impression. Hence, in directing our discourse to any man, we ought to begin with his name; and one will be sensible of a degradation, when this rule is neglected, as it frequently is for the sake of verse. I give the following examples.

> *Integer vitæ, scelerisque purus,*
> *Non eget Mauris jaculi, neque arcu,*
> *Nec venenatis gravidâ sagittis,*
> *Fusce, pharetrâ.*
>
> —Horat. Carm. l. 1. ode 22

Je crains Dieu, cher Abner, et n'ai point d'autre crainte.

In these examples the name of the person addressed to makes a mean figure, being like a circumstance slipt into a corner. That this criticism is well founded, we need no other proof than Addison's translation of the last example.

> *O Abner! I fear my God, and I fear none but him.*
>
> —*Guardian*, No 117

> *O father, what intends thy hand, she cry'd,*
> *Against thy only son? What fury, O son,*
> *Possesses thee to bend that mortal dart*
> *Against thy father's head?*
>
> —*Paradise Lost*, book 2. l. 727

Everyone must be sensible of a dignity in the invocation at the beginning, which that in the middle is far from reaching. I mean not however to censure this expression. On the contrary it appears beautiful, by distinguishing the respect due to a father and to a son.

THE SUBSTANCE OF WHAT IS said in this and the foregoing section, upon the method of arranging the words of a period so as to make the strongest impression with respect to sound as well as signification, is comprehended in the following observation. That order of the words in a period will always be the most agreeable, where, without obscuring the sense, the most important images, the most sonorous words, and the longest members, bring up the rear.

HITHERTO OF ARRANGING SINGLE WORDS, single members, and single circumstances. But the enumeration of many particulars in the same period is often necessary; and the question is, In what order they should be placed. It does not seem easy at first view to bring a subject apparently so loose under any general rules. But luckily reflecting upon what is said in the first chapter about order, we find rules laid down to our hand, so as to leave us no harder task than their application to the present question. And, first, with respect to the enumerating a number of particulars of equal rank, it is laid down in the place cited, that as there is no foundation for preferring anyone before the rest, it is indifferent to the mind in what order they be viewed. And it is only necessary to be added here, that for the same reason, it is indifferent in what order they be named. 2dly, If a number of objects of the same kind, differing only in size, are to be ranged along a straight line, the most agreeable order to the eye is that of an increasing series. In surveying a number of such objects, beginning at the least and proceeding to greater and greater, the mind swells gradually with the successive objects, and in its progress has a very sensible pleasure. Precisely for the same reason, the words expressive of such objects ought to be placed in the same order. The beauty of this figure, which may be termed *a climax in sense*, has escaped Lord Bolingbroke in the first member of the following period.

> Let but one great, brave, disinterested, active man arise, and he will be received, followed, and almost adored.

The following arrangement has sensibly a better effect.

> Let but one brave, great, active, disinterested man arise, *&c.*

Whether the same rule ought to be followed in enumerating men of different ranks, seems doubtful. On the one hand, a procession of a number of persons, presenting the lowest class first, and rising upon the eye in succession till it terminate upon the highest, is undoubtedly the most agreeable order. On the other hand, in every list of names, it is customary to set the person of the greatest dignity at the top, and to descend gradually through his inferiors. Where the purpose is to honour the persons named according to their rank, the latter order ought to be followed; but everyone who regards himself only, or his reader, will chuse the former order. 3dly, As the sense of order directs the eye to descend from the principal to its greatest accessory, and from the whole to its greatest part, and in the same order through all the parts and accessories till we arrive at the minutest; the same order ought to be followed in the enumeration of such particulars. I shall give one familiar example. Talking of the parts of a column, *viz.* the base, the shaft, the capital, these are capable of six different arrangements, and the question is, Which is the best? When one has in view the erection of a column, he will naturally be led to express the parts in the order above mentioned; which at the same time is agreeable by mounting upward. But considering the column as it stands without reference to its erection, the sense of order, as observed above, requires the chief part to be named first. For that reason we begin with the shaft; and the base comes next in order, that we may ascend from it to the capital. Lastly, In tracing the particulars of any natural operation, order requires that we follow the course of nature. Historical facts are related in the order of time. We begin at the founder of a family, and proceed from him to his descendents. But in describing a lofty oak, we begin with the trunk, and ascend to the branches.

When force and liveliness of expression are aimed at, the rule is, to suspend the thought as much as possible, and to bring it out full and entire at the close. This cannot be done but by inverting the natural arrangement, and by introducing a word or member before its time. By such inversion our curiosity is raised about what is to follow; and it is agreeable to have our curiosity gratified at the close of the period. Such arrangement produceth on the mind an effect similar to a stroke exerted upon the body by the whole collected force of the agent. On the other hand, where a period is so constructed as to admit more than one complete close in the sense, the curiosity of the reader is exhausted at the first close, and what follows appears languid or superfluous. His disappointment contributes also to this appearance, when he finds, that, contrary to his expectation, the period is not yet finished. Cicero, and after him Quintilian, recommend the verb to the last place. This method evidently tends to suspend the sense till the close of the period; for without the verb the sense cannot be complete. And when the verb happens to be the capital word, which is frequently the case, it ought at any rate to be put last, according to another rule, above laid down. I proceed as usual to illustrate this rule by examples. The following period is placed in its natural order.

> Were instruction an essential circumstance in epic poetry, I doubt whether a single instance could be given of this species of composition, in any language.

The period thus arranged admits a full close upon the word *composition*; after which it goes on languidly, and closes without force. This blemish will be avoided by the following arrangement.

> Were instruction an essential circumstance in epic poetry, I doubt whether, in any language, a single instance could be given of this species of composition.
>
> Some of our most eminent divines have made use of this Platonic notion, as far as it regards the subsistence of our passions after death, with great beauty and strength of reason.
>
> *Spectator*, No 90

Better thus:

Some of our most eminent divines have, with great beauty and strength of reason, made use of this Platonic notion, &c.

Men of the best sense have been touched, more or less, with these groundless horrors and presages of futurity, upon surveying the most indifferent works of nature.

Spectator, No 505

Better:

Upon surveying the most indifferent works of nature, men of the best sense, &c.

She soon informed him of the place he was in, which, notwithstanding all its horrors, appeared to him more sweet than the bower of Mahomet, in the company of his Balsora.

Guardian, No 167

Better:

She soon, &c. appeared to him, in the company of his Balsora, more sweet, &c.

The Emperor was so intent on the establishment of his absolute power in Hungary, that he exposed the Empire doubly to desolation and ruin for the sake of it.

Letters on history, vol. 1. let. 7. Bolingbroke

Better:

—— that for the sake of it he exposed the Empire doubly to desolation and ruin.

None of the rules for the composition of periods are more liable to be abused, than those last mentioned: witness many Latin writers, among the moderns especially, whose style, by inversions too violent, is rendered harsh and obscure. Suspension of the thought till the close of the period, ought never to be preferred before perspicuity. Neither ought such suspension to be attempted in a long period; because in that case the mind is bewildered among a profusion of words. A traveller, while he is puzzled about the road, relishes not the finest prospects.

> All the rich presents which Astyages had given him at parting, keeping only some Median horses, in order to propagate the breed of them in Persia, he distributed among his friends whom he left at the court of Ecbatana.
>
> *Travels of Cyrus, book 1*

The foregoing rules concern the arrangement of a single period. I shall add one rule more concerning the distribution of a discourse into different periods. A short period is lively and familiar. A long period, requiring more attention, makes an impression grave and solemn. In general, a writer ought to study a mixture of long and short periods, which prevents an irksome uniformity, and entertains the mind with variety of impressions. In particular, long periods ought to be avoided till the reader's attention be thoroughly engaged; and therefore a discourse, especially of the familiar kind, ought never to be introduced with a long period. For that reason, the commencement of a letter to a very young lady on her marriage is faulty.

> Madam, The hurry and impertinence of receiving and paying visits on account of your marriage, being now over, you are beginning to enter into a course of life, where you will want much advice to divert you from falling into many errors, fopperies, and follies, to which your sex is subject.
>
> *Swift*

See a stronger example in the commencement of Cicero's oration, *Pro Archia poeta*.

BEFORE WE PROCEED FARTHER, IT may be proper to take a review of the rules laid down in this and the preceding section, in order to make some general observations. The natural order of the words and members of a period, is undoubtedly the same with the natural order of the ideas that compose the thought. The tendency of many of the foregoing rules, is to substitute an artificial arrangement, in order to reach some beauty either of sound or meaning that cannot be reached in the natural order. But seldom it happens, that in the same period there is place for a plurality of these rules. If one beauty can be catched, another must be relinquished. The only question is, Which ought to be preferred? This is a question that cannot be resolved by any general rule. But practice, supported by a good taste, will in most instances make the choice easy. The component words and members of a period, are ascertained by the subject. If the natural order be not relished, a few trials will discover that artificial order which has the best effect. All that can be said in general is, that in making a choice, sound ought to yield to signification.

The transposing words and members out of their natural order, so remarkable in the learned languages, has been the subject of much speculation. It is agreed on all hands, that such transposition or inversion bestows upon a period a very sensible degree of force and elevation; and yet writers seem to be at a loss in what manner to account for this effect. Cerçeau[17] ascribes so much power to inversion, as to make it the characteristic of French verse, and the single circumstance which in that language distinguishes verse from prose. And yet he pretends not to say, that it hath any other power but to raise surprise; he must mean curiosity; which is done by suspending the thought during the period, and bringing it out entire at the close. This indeed is one power of inversion; but neither its sole power, nor even that which is the most remarkable, as is made plain above. But waving censure, which is not an agreeable task, I enter into the matter. And I begin with observing, that if a conformity betwixt words and their meaning be agreeable, it must of course be agreeable to find the same order or arrangement in both. Hence the beauty of a plain or natural style, where the order of the words corresponds precisely to the order of the ideas. Nor is this the single beauty of a natural style: it is also agreeable upon account of its simplicity and perspicuity. This observation throws light upon the subject. For if a natural style be in itself agreeable, a transposed style cannot be so. And therefore, it cannot otherwise be agreeable, but as contributing to some positive beauty which is excluded in a natural style. To be confirmed in this opinion, we need but reflect upon some of the foregoing rules, which make it evident, that language, by means of inversion, is susceptible of many beauties that are totally excluded in a natural arrangement of words. From these premisses it clearly follows, that inversion ought

---

17. Reflections sur la poësie François.

not to be indulged, unless in order to reach some beauty superior to that of a natural style. It may with great certainty be pronounced, that every inversion which is not governed by this rule, will appear harsh and strained, and be disrelished by everyone of taste. Hence the beauty of inversion when happily conducted; the beauty, not of an end, but of means, as furnishing opportunity for numberless ornaments that find no place in a natural style. Hence the force, the elevation, the harmony, the cadence, of some compositions. Hence the manifold beauties of the Greek and Roman tongues, of which living languages afford but faint imitations.

Section. III

Beauty of language from a resemblance betwixt sound and signification.

The resemblance betwixt the sound and signification of certain words, is a beauty, which has escaped no critical writer, and yet is not handled with accuracy by any of them. They have probably been erroneously of opinion, that a beauty so obvious in the feeling, requires no explanation in the understanding. In order to supply this defect, I shall give examples of the various resemblances betwixt sound and signification; and at the same time shall endeavour to explain why such resemblances are beautiful. I begin with examples where the resemblance betwixt the sound and signification is the most entire; proceeding to others, where the resemblance is less and less so.

There being frequently a strong resemblance betwixt different sounds, it will not be surprising to find a natural sound imitated by one that is articulate. Thus the sound of a bow-string is imitated by the words that express it.

> —— *The string let fly,*
> Twang'd short and sharp, *like the shrill swallow's cry.*
>
> —*Odyssey* xxi. 449

The sound of felling trees in a wood:

> *Loud sounds the ax, redoubling strokes on strokes;*
> *On all sides round the forest hurls her oaks*

> *Headlong. Deep-echoing groan the thickets brown,*
> *Then* rustling, crackling, crashing, *thunder down.*
>
> —*Iliad*, xxiii. 144
>
> *But when loud surges lash the sounding shore*
> *The hoarse rough verse should like the torrent roar!*
>
> —*Pope's Essay on Criticism*, 369

No person can be at a loss about the cause of this beauty. It is obviously that of imitation.

That there is any other natural resemblance betwixt sound and signification, must not be taken for granted. There is evidently no resemblance betwixt sound and motion, nor betwixt sound and sentiment. In this matter, we are apt to be deceived by artful reading or pronouncing. The same passage may be pronounced in many different tones, elevated or humble, sweet or harsh, brisk or melancholy, so as to accord with the thought or sentiment. Such concord, depending on artful pronunciation, must be distinguished from that concord betwixt sound and sense, which is perceived in some expressions independent of artful pronunciation. The latter is the poet's work: the former must be attributed to the reader. Another thing contributes still more to the deceit. In language, sound and sense are so intimately connected, as that the properties of the one are readily communicated to the other. An emotion of grandeur, of sweetness, of melancholy, or of compassion, though occasioned by the thought solely, is transferred upon the words, which by that means resemble in appearance the thought that is expressed by them[18]. I have great reason to recommend these observations to my reader, considering how inaccurately the present subject is handled by critics. Not one of them distinguishes the natural resemblance of sound and signification, from the artificial resemblance now described. Witness Vida in particular, who in a very long passage has given very few examples, but what are of the latter kind[19].

That there may be a resemblance betwixt natural and artificial sounds, is self-evident; and that in fact there exist such resemblances

---

18. See chap. 2. part 1. sect. 5.
19. Poet. L. 3. 365–454.

successfully employ'd by writers of genius, is clear from the foregoing examples, and many others that might be given. But we may safely pronounce, that this natural resemblance can be carried no farther. The objects of the several senses, differ so widely from each other as to exclude any resemblance. Sound in particular, whether articulate or inarticulate, resembles not in any degree taste, smell, or motion; and as little can it resemble any internal sentiment, feeling, or emotion. But must we then agree, that nothing but natural sound can be imitated by that which is articulate? Taking imitation in its proper sense, as involving a resemblance betwixt two objects, the proposition must be admitted. And yet in many passages that are not descriptive of natural sound, everyone must be sensible of a peculiar concord betwixt the sound of the words and their meaning. As there can be no doubt of the fact, what remains is, to inquire into its cause.

Resembling causes may produce effects that have no resemblance; and causes that have no resemblance may produce resembling effects. A magnificent building, for example, resembles not in any degree an heroic action; and yet the emotions they produce, being concordant, bear a resemblance to each other. We are still more sensible of this resemblance, in a song where the music is properly adjusted to the sentiment. There is no resemblance betwixt thought and sound; but there is the strongest resemblance betwixt the emotion raised by music tender and pathetic, and that raised by the complaint of an unsuccessful lover. To apply these examples to the present subject, I observe, that the sound even of a single word makes, in some instances, an impression resembling that which is made by the thing it signifies; witness the word *running*, composed of two short syllables; and more remarkably the words *rapidity*, *impetuosity*, *precipitation*. Brutal manners produce in the spectator, an emotion not unlike what is produced by a harsh and rough sound. Hence the figurative expression, *rugged* manners; an expression peculiarly agreeable by the relation of the sound to the sense. Again, the word *little*, being pronounced with a very small aperture of the mouth, has a weak and faint sound, which makes an impression resembling that made by any diminutive object. This resemblance of effects, is still more remarkable where a number of words are connected together in a period. Words pronounced in succession make often a strong impression; and when this impression happens to accord with that made by the sense, a peculiar pleasure arises. The thought or sentiment produces one pleasant emotion: the melody or tone of the words produces another. But the chief pleasure proceeds from having these two concordant emotions combined in perfect harmony, and carried on in the mind to a full close[20]. Except in the single case where sound is described, all the examples given by critics of sense being imitated in sound, resolve into a resemblance of effects. Emotions raised by sound and signification may have a resemblance; but sound itself cannot have a resemblance to anything but sound.

Proceeding now to particulars, and beginning with those cases where the emotions have the strongest resemblance, I observe, first, That in pronouncing a number of syllables in succession, an emotion is sometimes raised extremely similar to that raised by successive motion. This may be made evident even to those who are defective in taste, by the following fact, that the term *movement* in all languages is equally apply'd to both. In this manner, successive motion, such as walking, running, galloping, can be imitated by a succession of long or short syllables, or by a due mixture of both. For example, slow motion may be aptly imitated in a verse where long syllables prevail; especially when aided by a slow pronunciation:

Illi inter sese magnâ vi brachia tollunt.

—*Georg.* iv. 174

On the other hand, swift motion is imitated by a succession of short syllables:

Quadrupedante putrem sonitu quatit ungula campum.

Again:

Radit iter liquidum, celeres neque commovet alas.

Thirdly, a line composed of monosyllables, makes an impression, by the frequency of its pauses, similar to what is made by laborious interrupted motion:

---

20. See chap. 2. part 4.

> *With many a weary step, and many a groan,*
> *Up the high hill he heaves a huge round stone.*

—*Odyssey*, xi. 736

> *First march the heavy mules, securely slow;*
> *O'er hills, o'er dales, o'er craggs, o'er rocks, they go.*

—*Iliad*, xxiii. 138

Fourthly, the impression made by rough sounds in succession, resembles that made by rough or tumultuous motion. On the other hand, the impression of smooth sounds resembles that of gentle motion. The following is an example of both.

> *Two craggy rocks projecting to the main,*
> *The roaring wind's tempestuous rage restrain;*
> *Within, the waves in softer murmurs glide,*
> *And ships secure without their haulsers ride.*

—*Odyssey*, iii. 118

Another example of the latter:

> *Soft is the strain when Zephyr gently blows,*
> *And the smooth stream in smoother numbers flows.*

—*Essay on Crit.* 366

Fifthly, prolonged motion is expressed in an Alexandrine line. The first example shall be of slow motion prolonged:

> *A needless Alexandrine ends the song;*
> *That, like a wounded snake, drags its slow length along.*

—*Essay on Crit.* 356

The next example is of forcible motion prolonged:

> *The waves behind impel the waves before,*
> *Wide-rolling, foaming high, and tumbling to the shore.*

—*Iliad*, xiii. 1004

The last shall be of rapid motion prolonged:

> *Not so when swift Camilla scours the plain,*
> *Flies o'er th' unbending corn, and skims along the main.*
>
> —*Essay on Crit.* 373

Again, speaking of a rock torn from the brow of a mountain,

> *Still gath'ring force, it smokes, and, urg'd amain,*
> *Whirls, leaps, and thunders down, impetuous to the plain.*
>
> —*Iliad*, xiii. 197

Sixthly, a period consisting mostly of long syllables, that is, of syllables pronounced slow, produceth an emotion resembling faintly that which is produced by gravity and solemnity. Hence the beauty of the following verse.

> *Olli sedato respondit corde Latinus.*

Seventhly, a slow succession of ideas is a circumstance that belongs equally to settled melancholy, and to a period composed of polysyllables pronounced slow. Hence, by similarity of emotions, the latter is imitative of the former:

> *In those deep solitudes and awful cells,*
> *Where heav'nly-pensive Contemplation dwells,*
> *And ever-musing Melancholy reigns.*
>
> —*Pope. Eloisa to Abelard*

Eighthly, a long syllable made short, or a short syllable made long, raises, by the difficulty of pronouncing contrary to custom, a feeling similar to that of hard labour:

> *When Ajax strives some rock's* vast *weight to throw,*
> *The line too labours, and the words move slow.*
>
> —*Essay on Crit.* 370

Ninthly, harsh or rough words pronounced with difficulty, excite a feeling resembling that which proceeds from the labour of thought to a dull writer:

> *Just writes to make his barrenness appear,*
> *And strains from hard-bound brains eight lines a-year.*
>
> —Pope's epistle to Dr. Arbuthnot, l. 181

I shall close with one other example, which of all makes the finest figure. In the first section mention is made of a climax in sound, and in the second of a climax in sense. It belongs to the present subject to observe, that when these coincide in the same passage, the concordance of sound and sense is delightful. The reader is conscious not only of pleasure from the two climaxes separately, but of an additional pleasure from their concordance, and from finding the sense so justly imitated by the sound. In this respect, no periods are more perfect than those borrowed from Cicero in the first section.

The concord betwixt sense and sound is not less agreeable in what may be termed an *anticlimax*, where the progress is from great to little; for this has the effect to make diminutive objects appear still more diminutive. Horace affords a striking example:

> *Parturiunt montes, nascetur ridiculus mus.*

The arrangement here is singularly artful. The first place is occupied by the verb, which is the capital word by its sense as well as sound. The close is reserved for the word that is the meanest in sense as well as in sound. And it must not be overlooked, that the resembling sounds of the two last syllables give a ludicrous air to the whole.

Reviewing the foregoing examples, it appears to me, contrary to expectation, that in passing from the strongest resemblances to those that are fainter, the pleasure rises gradually in proportion. Can this be accounted for? or shall I renounce my taste as capricious? When I renew the experiment again and again, I feel no wavering, but the greatest pleasure constantly from the faintest resemblances. And yet how can this be? for if the pleasure lie in imitation, must not the strongest resemblance afford the greatest pleasure? From this vexing dilemma, I am happily relieved, by reflecting on a doctrine established in the chapter of resemblance and contrast, that the pleasure of resemblance is the greatest, where it is least expected, and where the objects compared are in their capital circumstances widely different. Nor will this appear surprising, when we descend to familiar examples. It raiseth not wonder in the smallest degree, to find the most perfect resemblance betwixt two eggs of the same animal. It is more rare to find such resemblance betwixt two human faces; and upon that account such an appearance raises some degree of wonder. But this emotion rises to a still greater height, when we find in a pebble, an aggat, or any natural production, a perfect resemblance to a tree or other organised body. We cannot hesitate a moment, in applying these observations to the present subject. What occasion of wonder can it be to find one sound resembling another, where both are of the same kind? It is not so common to find a resemblance betwixt an articulate sound and one not articulate; and accordingly the imitation here affords some slight pleasure. But the pleasure swells greatly, when we employ sound to imitate things it resembles not otherwise than by the effects produced in the mind.

I have had occasion to observe, that to complete the resemblance betwixt sound and sense, artful pronunciation contributes not a little. Pronunciation therefore may be considered as a branch of the present subject; and with some observations upon it I shall conclude the section.

In order to give a just idea of pronunciation, it must be distinguished from singing. The latter is carried on by notes, requiring each of them a different aperture of the windpipe. The notes properly belonging to the former, are expressed by different apertures of the mouth, without varying the aperture of the windpipe. This however doth not hinder pronunciation to borrow from singing, as a man sometimes is naturally led to do, in expressing a vehement passion.

In reading, as in singing, there is a key-note. Above this note the voice is frequently elevated, to make the sound correspond to the elevation of the subject. But the mind in an elevated state, is disposed to action. Therefore in order to a rest, it must be brought down to the key-note. Hence the term *cadence*.

The only general rule that can be given for directing the pronunciation, is, To sound the words in such a manner as to imitate the things they represent, or of which they are the symbols. The ideas which make the greatest figure, ought to be expressed with a peculiar emphasis. In expressing an elevated subject, the voice ought to be raised above its ordinary pitch; and words signifying dejection of mind, ought to be pronounced in a low note. A succession of sounds gradually ascending from low to high notes, represents an ascending series of objects. An opposite succession of sounds, is fitted for objects or sentiments that descend gradually. In Dryden's ode of *Alexander's feast*, the line, *Faln, faln, faln, faln*, ought to be pronounced with a falling voice; and is pronounced in that manner, by everyone of taste, without instruction. Another circumstance contributes to the resemblance betwixt sense and sound, which is slow or quick pronunciation. For though the length or shortness of the syllables with relation to each other, be in prose ascertained in some measure, and in verse always; yet taking a whole line or period together, it is arbitrary to pronounce it slow or fast. Hence it is, that a period expressing what is solemn or deliberate, ought to be pronounced slow; and ought to be pronounced quick, when it expresses anything brisk, lively, or impetuous.

The art of pronouncing with propriety and grace, being calculated to make the sound an echo to the sense, scarce admits of any other general rule than that above mentioned. This rule may indeed be branched out into many particular rules and observations: but these belong not properly to the present undertaking, because they cannot be explained in words. We have not words to signify the different degrees of high and low, loud and soft, fast and slow; and before these differences can be made the subject of regular instruction, notes must be invented resembling those employ'd in music. We have reason to believe, that in Greece every tragedy was accompanied with such notes, in order to ascertain the pronunciation. But the moderns hitherto have not thought of this refinement. Cicero indeed[21], without the help of notes, pretends to give rules for ascertaining the several tones of voice that are proper in expressing the several passions; and it must be acknowledged, that in this attempt he has exhausted the whole power of language. At the same time, every person of judgement must see, that these rules avail little in point of instruction. The very words he employs, are scarce intelligible, except to those who beforehand are acquainted with the subject.

---

21. De oratore, l. 3. cap. 58.

To vary the scene a little, I propose to close with a slight comparison betwixt singing and pronouncing. In this comparison the five following circumstances relative to articulate sound, must be kept in view. 1st, It is harsh or smooth. 2d, A sound or syllable, is long or short. 3d, It is pronounced high or low. 4th, It is pronounced loud or soft. And, lastly, a number of words in succession constituting a period or member of a period, are pronounced slow or quick. Of these five, the first depending on the component letters, and the second being ascertained by custom, admit not any variety in pronouncing. The three last are arbitrary, depending on the will of the person who pronounces; and it is chiefly in the artful management of these, that just pronunciation consists. With respect to the first circumstance, music has evidently the advantage; for all its notes are agreeable to the ear, which is not always the case of articulate sound. With respect to the second, long and short syllables variously combined, produce a great variety of feet; yet far inferior to the variety which is found in the multiplied combinations of musical notes. With respect to high and low notes, pronunciation is still more inferior to singing. For it is observed by Dionysius of Halicarnassus[22], that in pronouncing, *i.e.* without altering the aperture of the windpipe, the voice is confined within three notes and a half. Singing has a much greater compass. With respect to the two last circumstances, pronunciation equals singing.

IN THIS DISCOURSE, I HAVE mentioned none of the beauties of language, but what arise from words taken in their proper sense. Those beauties that depend on the metaphorical and figurative power of words, are reserved to be treated in chap. 20.

Section. IV

Versification.

The music of verse, though handled by every grammarian, merits more attention than has been given it. The subject is intimately connected with human nature; and to explain it thoroughly, several nice and delicate feelings must be employ'd. Entering upon this subject, it occurs as a preliminary point, By what mark is verse distinguished

---

22. De structura orationis, sect. 2.

from prose? The discussion of this point is necessary, were it for no other purpose but to ascertain the nature and limits of our subject. To produce this distinguishing mark, is a task not perhaps so easy as may at first be apprehended. Verse of every sort, has, it is true, rules for its construction. It is composed of feet, the number and variety of which are ascertained. Prose, though also composed of feet, is more loose and scarce subjected to any rules. But many are ignorant of these rules: Are such left without means to make the distinction? And even with respect to the learned, must they apply the rule before they can with certainty pronounce whether the composition be prose or verse? This will hardly be maintained; and therefore, instead of rules, the ear must be appealed to as the proper judge. But what gain we by being thus referred to another standard? It still recurs, by what mark does the ear distinguish verse from prose? The proper and satisfactory answer is, That these make different impressions, which are readily distinguishable by everyone who hath an ear. This advances us one step in our inquiry.

Taking it then for granted, that verse makes upon the ear a different impression from that of prose; nothing remains but to explain this difference, and to assign its cause. To these ends, I must call to my aid an observation made above in treating of the sound of words, that they are more agreeable to the ear when composed of long and short syllables than when all the syllables are of the same sort. A continued sound in the same tone, makes an impression that comes not up to any idea we have of music. The same note successively renewed by intervals, is more agreeable; but still makes not a musical impression. To produce this impression, variety is necessary as well as number. The successive sounds or syllables, must be some of them long, some of them short; and if also high and low, the music is the more perfect. Now if this impression can be made by single words, much more by a plurality in an orderly succession. The musical impression made by a period consisting of long and short syllables arranged in a certain order, is what the Greeks call *rhythmus*, the Latins, *numerus*, and we *modulation* or *measure*. Cicero justly observes, that in one continued sound there is no modulation: "Numerus in continuatione nullus est." But in what follows he is wide of the truth, if by *numerus* he means modulation or musical measure. "Distinctio, et æqualium et sæpe variorum intervallorum percussio, numerum conficit; quem in cadentibus guttis, quod intervallis distinguuntur, notare possumus." Falling drops, whether with equal or unequal intervals, are certainly not musical. We begin then only to be sensible of a musical expression, when the notes are varied. And this also was probably the opinion of the author cited, though his expression be a little unguarded[23].

It will probably occur, that modulation, so far as connected with long and short syllables combined in a sentence, may be found in prose as well as in verse; considering especially, that in both, particular words are accented or pronounced in a higher tone than ordinary; and therefore that the difference betwixt them cannot consist in modulation merely. The observation is just; and it follows, that the distinction betwixt prose and verse, since it depends not on modulation merely, must arise from the difference of the modulation. This is precisely the case, though the difference cannot with any accuracy be explained in words. Verse is more musical than prose; and of the former, the modulation is more perfect than of the latter. The difference betwixt verse and prose, resembles the difference in music properly so called betwixt the song and the recitative. And the resemblance is not the less complete, that these differences, like the shades of colours, approximate sometimes so nearly as scarce to be discernible. A recitative in its movement approaches sometimes to the liveliness of a song; which on the other hand degenerates sometimes toward a plain recitative. Nothing is more distinguishable from prose, than the bulk of Virgil's hexameters. Many of those composed by Horace, are very little removed from prose. Sapphic verse has a very sensible modulation. That on the other hand of an Iambic, is extremely faint[24].

This more perfect modulation of articulate sounds, is what distinguisheth verse from prose. Verse is subjected to certain inflexible laws. The number and variety of the component syllables are ascertained, and in some measure the order of succession. Such restraint makes it a matter of difficulty to compose in verse; a difficulty that is not to be surmounted but by a singular genius. Useful lessons of every sort

---

23. From this passage, however, we discover the etymology of the Latin term for musical impression. Everyone being sensible that there is no music in a continued sound; the first inquiries were probably carried no farther than to discover, that, to produce a musical impression, a number of sounds is necessary; and musical impression obtained the name of *numerus*, before it was clearly certained that variety is necessary as well as number.

24. Music, properly so called, is analyzed into melody and harmony. A succession of sounds so as to be agreeable to the ear, constitutes melody: harmony arises from co-existing sounds. Verse therefore can only reach melody, and not harmony.

convey'd to us in verse, are agreeable by the union of music with instruction. But are we for that reason to reject knowledge offered in a plainer dress? This would be ridiculous; for knowledge may be acquired without music, and music is entertaining independent of knowledge. Many there are, not less willing than capable to instruct us, who have no genius for verse. Hence the use of prose, which, for the reason now given, is not confined to precise rules. There belongs to it, a certain modulation of an inferior kind, which, being extremely ornamental, ought to be the aim of every writer. But to succeed in it, practice is necessary more than genius. Nor are we rigid on this article. Provided the work answer its chief end of instruction, we are the less solicitous about its dress.

Having ascertained the nature and limits of our subject, I proceed to the laws by which it is regulated. These would be endless, were verse of all different kinds to be taken under consideration. I propose therefore to confine the inquiry, to Latin or Greek hexameter, and to French and English heroic verse; which perhaps will carry me farther than the reader may chuse to follow. The observations I shall have occasion to make, will at any rate be sufficient for a specimen; and these with proper variations may easily be transferred to the composition of other sorts of verse.

Before I enter upon particulars, it must be premised in general, that to verse of every kind, five things are of importance. 1st, The number of syllables that compose a verse. 2d, The different lengths of syllables, *i.e.* the difference of time taken in pronouncing. 3d, The arrangement of these syllables combined in words. 4th, The pauses or stops in pronouncing. 5th, Pronouncing syllables in a high or low tone. The three first mentioned are obviously essential to verse. If any of them be wanting, there cannot be that higher degree of modulation which distinguisheth verse from prose. To give a just notion of the fourth, it must be observed, that pauses are necessary for three different purposes. One is, to separate periods and members of the same period according to the sense: another is, to improve the modulation of verse: and the last is, to afford opportunity for drawing breath in reading. A pause of the first kind is variable, being long or short, frequent or less frequent, as the sense requires. A pause of the second kind, is in no degree arbitrary; its place being determined by the modulation. The last sort again is in a measure arbitrary, depending on the reader's command of breath. This sort ought always to coincide with the first or second; for one cannot read with grace, unless, for drawing breath, opportunity be taken of a pause in the sense or in the melody; and for that reason this pause may be neglected. With respect then to the pauses of sense and of melody, it may be affirmed without hesitation, that their coincidence in verse is a capital beauty. But as it cannot be expected, in a long work especially, that every line should be so perfect; we shall afterward have occasion to see, that the pause necessary for sense must often, in some degree, be sacrificed to the verse-pause; and the latter sometimes to the former.

The pronouncing syllables in a high or low tone, contributes also to melody. In reading, whether verse or prose, a certain tone is assumed, which may be called *the key-note*; and in this tone the bulk of the words are sounded. Sometimes to humour the sense and sometimes the melody, a particular syllable is sounded in a higher tone; and this is termed *accenting a syllable*, or gracing it with an accent. Opposed to the accent, is the cadence, which I have not mentioned as one of the requisites of verse, because it is entirely regulated by the sense, and hath no peculiar relation to verse. The cadence is a falling of the voice below the key-note at the close of every period; and so little is it essential to verse, that in correct reading the final syllable of every line is accented, that syllable only excepted which closes the period, where the sense requires a cadence. The reader may be satisfied of this by experiments; and for that purpose I recommend to him the *Rape of the Lock*, which, in point of versification, is the most complete performance in the English language. Let him consult in particular a period canto 2. beginning at line 47. and closed line 52. with the word *gay*, which only of the whole final syllables is pronounced with a cadence. He may also examine another period in the 5th canto, which runs from line 45. to line 52.

Though the five requisites above mentioned, enter the composition of every species of verse, they are however governed by different rules, peculiar to each species. Upon quantity only, one general observation may be premised, because it is applicable to every species of verse. Syllables, with respect to the time taken in pronouncing, are distinguished into long and short; two short syllables, with respect to time, being precisely equal to one long. These two lengths are essential to verse of all kinds; and to no verse, so far as I know, is a greater variety of time necessary in pronouncing syllables. The voice indeed is frequently made to rest longer than commonly, upon a word that bears an important signification. But this is done to humour the sense, and is not necessary for the modulation. A thing not more necessary occurs with respect to accenting, similar to that now mentioned. A word signifying anything humble, low, or dejected, is naturally, in prose as well as in verse, pronounced in a tone below the key-note.

We are now sufficiently prepared for entering upon particulars; and Latin or Greek Hexameter, which are the same, coming first in order, I shall exhaust what I have to say upon this species of verse, under the four following heads; of number, arrangement, pause, and accent; for as to quantity, so far as concerns the present point, what is observed above may suffice.

Hexameter lines are, with respect to time, all of the same length. A line may consist of seventeen syllables; and when regular and not Spondaic, it never has fewer than thirteen. Hence it is plain, that where the syllables are many, the plurality must be short; where few, the plurality must be long. And upon the whole, the number of syllables in every line with respect to the time taken in pronouncing, are equivalent to twelve long syllables, or twenty-four short.

With regard to arrangement, this line is susceptible of much variety. The succession of long and short syllables, may be greatly varied without injuring the melody. It is subjected however to laws, that confine its variety within certain limits. For trying the arrangement, and for determining whether it be perfect or faulty, grammarians have invented a rule by Dactyles and Spondees, which they denominate *feet*. One at first view is led to think, that these feet are also intended to regulate the pronunciation. But this is far from being the case. It will appear by and by, that the rules of pronunciation are very different. And indeed were one to pronounce according to these feet, the melody of a Hexameter line would be destroy'd, or at best be much inferior to what it is when properly pronounced[25]. These feet then must be

---

25. After giving some attention to this subject, and weighing deliberately every circumstance, I was necessarily led to the foregoing conclusion, That the Dactyle and Spondee are no other than artificial measures, invented for trying the accuracy of composition. Repeated experiments have convinced me, that though the sense should he neglected, an Hexameter line read by Dactyles and Spondees will not be melodious. And the composition of an Hexameter line demonstrates this to be true, without necessity of an experiment; for, as will appear afterward, there must always, in this line, be a capital pause at the end of the fifth long syllable, reckoning, as above, two short for one long; and when we measure this line by Dactyles and Spondees, the pause now mentioned divides always a Dactyle or a Spondee, without once falling in after either of

confined to their sole province of regulating the arrangement, for they serve no other purpose. They are withal so artificial and complex, that, neglecting them altogether, I am tempted to substitute in their room, other rules, more simple and of more easy application; for example, the following. 1st, The line must always commence with a long syllable, and close with two long preceded by two short. 2d, More than two short can never be found in any part of the line, nor fewer than two if any. And, 3d, Two long syllables which have been preceded by two short, cannot also be followed by two short. These few rules fulfil all the conditions of a Hexameter line, with relation to order or arrangement. To these again a single rule may be substituted, for which I have a still greater relish, as it regulates more affirmatively the construction of every part. That I may put this rule into words with the greater facility, I take a hint from the twelve long syllables that compose an Hexameter line, to divide it into twelve equal parts or portions, being each of them one long syllable or two short. This preliminary being

---

these feet. Hence it is evident, that if a line be pronounced as it is scanned by Dactyles and Spondees, the pause must utterly be neglected; which destroys the melody, because this pause is essential to the melody of an Hexameter verse. If, on the other hand, the melody be preserved by making that pause, the pronouncing by Dactyles or Spondees must be abandoned.

What has led grammarians into the use of Dactyles and Spondees, seems not beyond the reach of conjecture. To produce melody, the Dactyle and the Spondee, which close every Hexameter line, must be distinctly expressed in the pronunciation. This discovery, joined with another, that the foregoing part of the verse could be measured by the same feet, probably led grammarians to adopt these artificial measures, and perhaps rashly to conclude, that the pronunciation is directed by these feet as the composition is: the Dactyle and the Spondee at the close serve indeed to regulate the pronunciation as well as the composition: but in the foregoing part of the line, they regulate the composition only, not the pronunciation.

If we must have feet in verse to regulate the pronunciation, and consequently the melody, these feet must be determined by the pauses. All the syllables interjected between two pauses ought to be deemed one musical foot; because, to preserve the melody, they must all be pronounced together without any stop. And therefore, whatever number there are of pauses in an Hexameter line, the parts into which it is divided by these pauses, make just so many musical feet.

Connexion obliges me here to anticipate, and to observe, that the same doctrine is applicable to English heroic verse. Considering its composition merely, it is of two kinds; one composed of five Iambi, and one of a Trochæus followed by four Iambi; but these feet afford no rule for pronouncing; the musical feet being obviously those parts of the line that are interjected between two pauses. To bring out the melody, these feet must be expressed in the pronunciation; or, which comes to the same, the pronunciation must be directed by the pauses without regard to the Iambus or Trochæus.

established, the rule is shortly what follows. The 1st, 3d, 5th, 7th, 9th, 11th, and 12th portions, must each of them be one long syllable; the 10th must always be two short syllables; the 2d, 4th, 6th, and 8th, may indifferently be one long or two short. Or to express the thing still more curtly, The 2d, 4th, 6th, and 8th portions may be one long syllable or two short; the 10th must be two short syllables; all the rest must consist of one long syllable. This fulfils all the conditions of an Hexameter line, and comprehends all the combinations of Dactyles and Spondees that this line admits.

NEXT IN ORDER COMES THE pause. At the end of every Hexameter line, no ear but must be sensible of a complete close or full pause. This effect is produced by the following means. Every line invariably is finished with two long syllables preceded by two short; a fine preparation for a full close. Syllables pronounced slow, resemble a slow and languid motion tending to rest. The mind put in the same tone by the pronunciation, is naturally disposed to a pause. And to this disposition the two preceding short syllables contribute; for these, by contrast, make the slow pronunciation of the final syllables the more conspicuous. Beside this complete close or full pause at the end, others are also requisite for the sake of melody. I discover two clearly, and perhaps there may be more. The longest and most remarkable, succeeds the 5th portion, according to the foregoing measure. The other, which being more faint, may be called *the semipause*, succeeds the 8th portion. So striking is the pause first mentioned, as to be distinguished even by the rudest ear. The monkish rhymes are evidently built upon it. In these, it is an invariable rule, to make the final word chime with that which immediately precedes the pause:

De planctu endo || mitrum cum carmine nudo
Mingere cum bumbis || res est soluberrima lumbis.

The difference of time in the pause and semipause, occasions another difference not less remarkable. The pause ought regularly to be at the end of a word; but it is lawful to divide a word by a semipause. The bad effect of dividing a word by the pause, is sensibly felt in the following examples.

Effusus labor, at||que inmitis rupta Tyranni

Again,

> *Observans nido im‖plumes detraxit; at illa*

Again,

> *Loricam quam De‖moleo detraxerat ipse*

The dividing a word by a semipause has not the same bad effect:

> *Jamque pedem referens ‖ casus e|vaserat omnes.*

Again,

> *Qualis populea ‖ mærens Philo|mela sub umbra*

Again,

> *Ludere quæ vellem ‖ calamo per|misit agresti.*

Lines, however, where words are left entire to be pronounced as they ought to be, without being divided even by a semipause, run by that means much the more sweetly.

> *Nec gemere aërea ‖ cessabit | turtur ab ulmo.*

Again,

> *Quadrupedante putrem ‖ sonitu quatit | ungula campum.*

Again,

> *Eurydicen toto ‖ referebant |flumine ripæ.*

The reason of these observations, will be evident upon the slightest reflection. Betwixt things so intimately connected as sense and sound in pronunciation, to find discordance is unpleasant to the ear; and for that reason, it is a matter of importance, to make the musical pauses coincide as much as possible with those of the sense. This is requisite, more especially, with respect to the pause. A deviation from the rule is less remarkable in a semipause, which makes but a slight impression. Considering the matter as to modulation solely, it is indifferent whether the pauses be at the end of words or in the middle. But when we carry the sense along, nothing is more disagreeable than to find a word split into two parts, neither of which separately have any meaning. This bad effect, though it regard the sense only, is by an easy transition of ideas transferred to the sound, with which the sense is intimately connected; and by this means, we conceive a line to be harsh and grating to the ear, which in reality is only so to the understanding[26].

To the rule which places the pause after the 5th portion, there is one exception, and no more. If the syllable succeeding the 5th portion be short, the pause is sometimes postponed to it:

Pupillis quos dura || *premit custodia matrum*

Again,

In terris oppressa || *gravi sub religione*

Again,

Et quorum pars magna || *fui; quis talia fando*

This contributes to diversify the melody; and where the words are smooth and liquid, is not ungraceful; as in the following examples.

Formosam resonare || *doces Amaryllida sylvas*

Again,

Agricolas, quibus ipsa || *procul discordibus armis*

If this pause, postponed as aforesaid to the short syllable, happen also to divide a word, the melody by these circumstances is totally

---

26. See chap. 2. part 1. sect. 5.

annihilated: witness the following line of Ennius, which is plain prose.

Romæ mœnia terru||*it impiger* | *Hannibal armis*

Hitherto the arrangement of the long and short syllables of an Hexameter line and its different pauses, have been considered with respect to melody. But to have a just notion of Hexameter verse, these particulars must also be considered with respect to sense. There is not perhaps in any other sort of verse, such a latitude in the long and short syllables. This circumstance contributes greatly to that richness of modulation which is remarkable in Hexameter verse; and which makes Aristotle pronounce, that an epic poem in any other sort would not succeed[27]. One defect however must not be dissembled. The same means that contribute to the richness of the melody, render it less fit than several other sorts for a narrative poem. With regard to the melody, as above observed, there cannot be a more artful contrivance than to close an Hexameter line with two long syllables preceded by two short. But unhappily this construction proves a great imbarrassment to the sense; as will be evident from what follows. As in general there ought to be a strict concordance betwixt every thought and the words in which it is dressed, so in particular, every close in the sense, complete and incomplete, ought to be accompanied with a similar close in the sound. In the composition of prose, there is sufficient latitude for applying this rule in the strictest manner. But the same strictness in verse, would occasion insuperable difficulties. Some share of the concordance betwixt thought and expression, may be justly sacrificed to the melody of verse; and therefore during the course of a line, we freely excuse the want of coincidence of the musical pause with that of the sense. But the close of an Hexameter line is too conspicuous to admit a total neglect of this coincidence. And hence it follows, that there ought to be always some pause in the sense at the end of every Hexameter line, were it but such a pause as is marked with a comma. It follows also, for the same reason, that there ought never to be a full close in the sense but at the end of a line, because there the modulation is closed. An Hexameter line, to preserve its melody, cannot well permit any greater relaxation; and yet

---

27. Poet, cap. 25.

in a narrative poem, it is extremely difficult to keep up to the rule even with these indulgences. Virgil, the greatest poet for versification that ever existed, is forc'd often to end a line without any close in the sense, and as often to close the sense during the running of a line: though a close in the melody during the movement of the thought, or a close in the thought during the movement of the melody, cannot fail to be disagreeable.

THE ACCENT, TO WHICH WE proceed, is not less essential than the other circumstances above handled. By a good ear it will be discerned, that in every line there is one syllable distinguishable from the rest by a strong accent. This syllable making the 7th portion, is invariably long; and in point of time occupies a place nearly at an equal distance from the pause which succeeds the 5th portion, and the semipause, which succeeds the 8th:

Nec bene promeritis || *capitûr nec* | *tangitur ira*

Again,

Non sibi sed toto || *genitûm se* | *credere mundo*

Again,

Qualis spelunca || *subitô com*|*mota columba*

In these examples, the accent is laid upon the last syllable of a word. And that this is a favourable circumstance for the melody, will appear from the following consideration. In reading, there must be some pause after every word, to separate it from what follows; and this pause, however short, supports the accent. Hence it is, that a line thus accented, has a more spirited air, than where the accent is placed on any other syllable. Compare the foregoing lines with the following.

Alba neque Assyrio || *fucâtur* | *lana veneno*

Again,

Panditur interea || domus ômnipo|tentis Olympi

Again,

Olli sedato || respôndit | corde Latinus

In lines where the pause comes after the short syllable succeeding the 5th portion, the accent is displaced and rendered less sensible. It seems to be split into two, and to be laid partly on the 5th portion, and partly on the 7th, its usual place; as in

Nuda genu, nodôque || sinûs col|lecta fluentes

Again,

Formosam resonâre || docês Amar|yllida sylvas

Beside this capital accent, slighter accents are laid upon other portions; particularly upon the 4th, unless where it consists of two short syllables; upon the 9th, which is always a long syllable; and upon the 11th, where the line concludes with a monosyllable. Such conclusion, by the by, lessens the melody, and for that reason is not to be indulged unless where it is expressive of the sense. The following lines are marked with all the accents.

Ludere quæ vêllem calamô permisit agresti

Again,

Et duræ quêrcus sudâbunt rôscida mella

Again,

Parturiunt môntes, nascêtur rîdiculûs mus

Inquiring into the melody of Hexameter verse, we soon discover, that order or arrangement doth not constitute the whole of it. Comparing different lines, equally regular as to the succession of long and short syllables, the melody is found in very different degrees of perfection. Nor does the difference arise from any particular combination of

Dactyles and Spondees, or of long and short syllables. On the contrary, we find lines where Dactyles prevail and lines where Spondees prevail, equally melodious. Of the former take the following instance:

Æneadum genetrix hominum divumque voluptas.

Of the latter:

Molli paulatim flavescet campus arista.

What can be more different as to melody than the two following lines, which, however, as to the succession of long and short syllables, are constructed precisely in the same manner?

Spond. Dact. Spond. Spond. Dact. Spond.
Ad talos stola dimissa et circumdata palla.

—*Hor.*

Spond. Dact. Spond. Spond. Dact. Spond.
Placatumque nitet diffuso lumine cœlum.

—*Lucret*

In the former, the pause falls in the middle of a word, which is a great blemish, and the accent is disturbed by a harsh elision of the vowel *a* upon the particle *et*. In the latter the pauses and the accent are all of them distinct and full: there is no elision: and the words are more liquid and sounding. In these particulars consists the beauty of an Hexameter line with respect to melody; and by neglecting these, many lines in the Satires and Epistles of Horace are less agreeable than plain prose; for they are neither the one nor the other in perfection. To make these lines sound, they must be pronounced without relation to the sense. It must not be regarded, that words are divided by pauses, nor that harsh elisions are multiplied. To add to the account, prosaic low sounding words are introduced; and which is still worse, accents are laid on them. Of such faulty lines take the following instances.

Candida rectaque sit, munda hactenus sit neque longa.
Jupiter exclamat simul atque audirit; at in se

Custodes, lectica, ciniflones, parasitæ
Optimus est modulator, ut Alfenus Vafer omni
Nunc illud tantum quæram, meritone tibi sit.

Next in order comes English heroic verse, which shall be examined under the whole five heads, of number, quantity, arrangement, pause, and accent. This verse sometimes employs rhymes and sometimes not, which distinguishes it into two kinds; one named *metre*, and one *blank verse*. In the former, the lines are connected two and two by similarity of sound in the final syllables; and such connected lines are termed *couplets*. Similarity of sound being avoided in the latter, banishes couplets. These two sorts must be handled separately, because there are many peculiarities in each. The first article with respect to rhyme or metre, shall be discussed in a few words. Every line consists of ten syllables, five short and five long. There are but two exceptions, both of them rare. A couplet can bear to be drawn out, by adding a short syllable at the end of each of the two lines:

> *There hero's wits are kept in pond'rous vases,*
> *And beau's in snuff-boxes and tweezer-cases.*

> *The piece, you think, is incorrect? Why, take it;*
> *I'm all submission; what you'd have it, make it.*

This licence is sufferable in a single couplet; but if frequent would soon become disgustful.

The other exception concerns the second line of a couplet, which is sometimes stretched out to twelve syllables, termed an *Alexandrine line*.

> *A needless Alexandrine ends the song,*
> *That, like a wounded snake, drags its slow length along.*

It doth extremely well when employ'd to close a period with a certain pomp and solemnity suitable to the subject.

With regard to the second article, it is unnecessary to mention a second time, that the quantities employ'd in verse are but two, the one double of the other; that every syllable is reducible to one or other of these standards; and that a syllable of the larger quantity is termed *long*, and of the lesser quantity *short*. It belongs more to the present article, to examine what peculiarities there may be in the English language as to long and short syllables. In every language, there are syllables that may be pronounced long or short at pleasure; but the English above all abounds in syllables of that kind. In words of three or more syllables, the quantity for the most part is invariable. The exceptions are more frequent in dissyllables; but as to monosyllables, they may without many exceptions be pronounced either long or short. Nor is the ear hurt by this liberty; being accustomed to the variation of quantity in the same word. This shows that the melody of English verse must depend less upon quantity, than upon other circumstances. In that particular it differs widely from Latin verse. There, every syllable having but one sound, strikes the ear constantly with its accustomed impression; and a reader must be delighted to find a number of such syllables, disposed so artfully as to raise a lively sense of melody. Syllables variable in quantity cannot possess this power. Custom may render familiar, both a long and short pronunciation of the same word; but the mind constantly wavering betwixt the two sounds, cannot be so much affected with a syllable of this kind as with one which bears always the same sound. What I have further to say upon quantity, will come in more properly under the following head, of arrangement.

And with respect to arrangement, which may be brought within a narrow compass, the English heroic line is commonly Iambic, the first syllable short, the second long, and so on alternately through the whole line. One exception there is, pretty frequent. Many lines commence with a Trochæus, *viz.* a long and a short syllable. But this affects not the order of the following syllables. These go on alternately as usual, one short and one long. The following couplet affords an example of each kind:

Sōme ĭn thĕ fields ŏf pūrĕst æthĕr plāy,
Ănd bāsk ănd whītĕn ĭn thĕ blāze ŏf dāy.

It is unhappy in the construction of English verse, that it excludes the bulk of polysyllables, though the most sounding words in our language; for upon examination it will be found, that very few of them are composed of such alternation of long and short syllables as to correspond to either of the arrangements mentioned. English verse accordingly is almost totally reduced to dissyllables and monosyllables. *Magnanimity* is a sounding word totally excluded. *Impetuosity* is still a finer word by the resemblance of the sound and sense; and yet a negative is put upon it, as well as upon numberless words of the same kind. Polysyllables composed of syllables long and short alternately, make a good figure in verse; for example, *observance, opponent, ostensive, pindaric, productive, prolific*, and such others of three syllables. *Imitation, imperfection, misdemeanour, mitigation, moderation, observator, ornamental, regulator*, and others similar of four syllables, beginning with two short syllables, the third long, and the fourth short, may find a place in a line commencing with a Trochæus. I know not if there be any of five syllables. One I know of six, *viz. misinterpretation*. But words so composed are not frequent in our language.

One would not imagine without trial, how uncouth false quantity appears in verse; not less than a provincial tone or idiom. The article *the* is one of the few monosyllables that is invariably short. See how harsh it makes a line where it must be pronounced long:

Thĭs nȳmph, tŏ thē dĕstrūctiŏn ōf mănkīnd,

Again:

Th' ădvēnt'rŏus bārŏn thē brĭght lōcks ădmīr'd.

Let the article be pronounced short, and it reduces the melody almost to nothing. Better so however than a false quantity. In the following examples we perceive the same defect.

And old impertinence || *expel by new.*

With varying vanities || *from ev'ry part.*

Love in these labyrinths || *his slaves detains.*

New stratagems || *the radiant lock to gain.*

Her eyes half-languishing || *half-drown'd in tears.*

Roar'd for the handkerchief || *that caus'd his pain.*

Passions like elements || *though born to fight.*

The great variety of modulation conspicuous in English verse, will be found upon trial to arise chiefly from the pauses and accents;

and therefore these circumstances are of greater importance than is commonly thought. There is a degree of intricacy in this branch of our subject, and it will require some pains to give a distinct view of it. But we must not be discouraged by difficulties. The pause, which paves the way to the accent, offers itself first to our examination. From a very short trial, the following facts will be verified. 1st, A line admits but one capital pause. 2d, In different lines, we find this pause after the fourth syllable, after the fifth, after the sixth, and after the seventh. These particulars lay a solid foundation for dividing English heroic lines into four sorts, distinguished by the different places of the pause. Nor is this an idle distinction. On the contrary, unless it be kept in view, we cannot have any just notion of the richness and variety of English versification. Each sort or order hath a melody peculiar to itself, readily distinguishable by a good ear; and, in the sequel, I am not without hopes to make the cause of this peculiarity sufficiently evident. It must be observed, at the same time, that the pause cannot be made indifferently at any of the places mentioned. It is the sense that regulates the pause, as will be seen more fully afterward; and consequently, it is the sense that determines of what order every line must be. There can be but one capital musical pause in a line; and this pause ought to coincide, if possible, with a pause in the sense; in order that the sound may accord with the sense.

What is said must be illustrated by examples of each sort or order. And first of the pause after the fourth syllable:

> *Back through the paths || of pleasing sense I ran*

Again,

> *Profuse of bliss || and pregnant with delight*

After the 5th:

> *So when an angel || by divine command,*
> *With rising tempests || shakes a guilty land,*

After the 6th:

> *Speed the soft intercourse || from soul to soul*

Again,

> *Then from his closing eyes || thy form shall part*

After the 7th:

> *And taught the doubtful battle || where to rage*

Again,

> *And in the smooth description || murmur still*

Beside the capital pause now mentioned, other inferior or semipauses will be discovered by a nice ear. Of these there are commonly two in each line; one before the capital pause, and one after it. The former is invariably placed after the first long syllable, whether the line begin with a long syllable or a short. The other in its variety imitates the capital pause. In some lines it follows the 6th syllable, in some the 7th, and in some the 8th. Of these semipauses take the following examples.

1st and 8th:

> *Led | through a sad || variety | of wo.*

1st and 7th:

> *Still | on that breast || enamour'd | let me lie*

2d and 8th:

> *From storms | a shelter || and from heat | a shade*

2d and 6th:

> *Let wealth | let honour || wait | the wedded dame*

2d and 7th:

> *Above | all pain || all passion | and all pride*

Even from these few examples, it appears, that the place of the last semipause, like that of the full pause, is directed in a good measure by the sense. Its proper place with respect to the melody is after the eighth syllable, so as to finish the line with an Iambus distinctly pronounced, which, by a long syllable after a short, is a preparation for rest. If this hold, the placing this semipause after the 6th or after the 7th syllable, must be directed by the sense, in order to avoid a pause in the middle of a word, or betwixt two words intimately connected; and so far melody is justly sacrificed to sense.

In discoursing of the full pause in a Hexameter line, it is laid down as a rule, That it ought never to divide a word. Such licence deviates too far from the connection that ought to be betwixt the pauses of sense and of melody. And in an English line, it is for the same reason equally wrong to divide a word by a full pause. Let us justify this reason by experiments.

A noble super||fluity it craves

Abhor, a perpe||tuity should stand

Are these lines distinguishable from prose? Scarcely, I think.

The same rule is not applicable to a semipause, which being short and faint, is not sensibly disagreeable when it divides a word.

Relent|less walls || whose darksome round | contains

For her | white virgins || hyme|neals sing

In these | deep solitudes || and aw|ful cells

It must however be acknowledged, that the melody here suffers in some degree. A word ought to be pronounced without any rest betwixt its component syllables. The semipause must bend to this rule, and thereby vanisheth almost altogether.

With regard to the capital pause, it is so essential to the melody, that a poet cannot be too nice in the choice of its place, in order to have it full, clear, and distinct. It cannot be placed more happily than with a pause in the sense; and if the sense require but a comma after the fourth, fifth, sixth, or seventh syllable, there can be no difficulty about this musical pause. But to make such coincidence essential, would cramp versification too much; and we have experience for our authority, that there may be a pause in the melody where the sense requires none. We must not however imagine, that a musical pause may be placed at the end of any word indifferently. Some words, like syllables of the same word, are so intimately connected as not to bear a separation even by a pause. No good poet ever attempted to separate a substantive from its article: the dividing such intimate companions, would be harsh and unpleasant. The following line, for example, cannot be pronounced with a pause as marked.

If Delia smile, the || flow'rs begin to spring

But ought to be pronounced in the following manner.

If Delia smile, || the flow'rs begin to spring.

If then it be not a matter of indifferency where to make the pause, there ought to be rules for determining what words may be separated by a pause and what are incapable of such separation. I shall endeavour to unfold these rules; not chiefly for their utility, but in order to exemplify some latent principles that tend to regulate our taste even where we are scarce sensible of them. And to that end, it seems the eligible method to run over the verbal relations, beginning with the most intimate. The first that presents itself, is that of adjective and substantive, being the relation of substance and quality, the most intimate of all. A quality cannot exist independent of a substance, nor is it separable from it even in imagination, because they make parts of the same idea; and for that reason, it must, with regard to melody, be disagreeable, to bestow upon the adjective a sort of independent existence, by interjecting a pause betwixt it and its substantive. I cannot therefore approve the following lines, nor any of the sort; for to my taste they are harsh and unpleasant.

Of thousand bright || inhabitants of air

The sprites of fiery || termagants inflame

The rest, his many-colour'd || robe conceal'd

The same, his ancient || personage to deck

Ev'n here, where frozen || *Chastity retires*

I sit, with sad || *civility, I read*

Back to my native || *moderation slide*

Or shall we ev'ry || *decency confound*

Time was, a sober || *Englishman wou'd knock*

And place, on good || *security, his gold*

Taste, that eternal || *wanderer, which flies*

But ere the tenth || *revolving day was run*

First let the just || *equivalent be paid*

Go, threat thy earth-born || *Myrmidons; but here*

Haste to the fierce || *Achilles' tent (he cries)*

All but the ever-wakeful || *eyes of Jove*

Your own resistless || *eloquence employ*

I have upon this article multiplied examples, that in a case where I have the misfortune to dislike what passes current in practice, every man upon the spot may judge by his own taste. The foregoing reasoning, it is true, appears to me just: it is however too subtile, to afford conviction in opposition to taste.

Considering this matter in a superficial view, one might be apt to imagine, that it must be the same, whether the adjective go first, which is the natural order, or the substantive, which is indulged by the laws of inversion. But we soon discover this to be a mistake. Colour cannot be conceived independent of the surface coloured; but a tree may be conceived, as growing in a certain spot, as of a certain kind, and as spreading its extended branches all around, without ever thinking of the colour. In a word, qualities, though related all to one subject, may be considered separately, and the subject may be considered with some of its qualities independent of others; though we cannot form an image of any single quality independent of the subject. Thus then, though an adjective named first be inseparable from the substantive, the proposition does not reciprocate. An image can be formed of the substantive independent of the adjective; and for this reason, they may be separated by a pause, when the former is introduced before the latter:

For thee, the fates || severely kind ordain

And curs'd with hearts || unknowing how to yield.

The verb and adverb are precisely in the same condition with the substantive and adjective. An adverb, which expresses a certain modification of the action expressed by the verb, is not separable from it even in imagination. And therefore I must also give up the following lines.

And which it much || becomes you to forget

'Tis one thing madly || to disperse my store

But an action may be conceived leaving out a particular modification, precisely as a subject may be conceived leaving out a particular quality; and therefore when by inversion the verb is first introduced, it has no bad effect to interject a pause betwixt it and the adverb which follows. This may be done at the close of a line, where the pause is at least as full as that is which divides the line:

While yet he spoke, the Prince advancing drew
Nigh to the lodge, &c.

The agent and its action come next, expressed in grammar by the active substantive and its verb. Betwixt these, placed in their natural order, there is no difficulty of interjecting a pause. An active being is not always in motion, and therefore it is easily separable in idea from its action. When in a sentence the substantive takes the lead, we know not that action is to follow; and as rest must precede the commencement of motion, this interval is a proper opportunity for a pause.

On the other hand, when by inversion the verb is placed first, is it lawful to separate it by a pause from the active substantive? I answer not, because an action is not in idea separable from the agent, more than a quality from the substance to which it belongs. Two lines of the first rate for beauty have always appeared to me exceptionable, upon account of the pause thus interjected betwixt the verb and the consequent substantive; and I have now discovered a reason to support my taste:

In these deep solitudes and awful cells,
Where heav'nly-pensive || Contemplation dwells,
And ever-musing || Melancholy reigns.

The point of the greatest delicacy regards the active verb and the passive substantive placed in their natural order. On the one side it will be observed, that these words signify things which are not separable in idea. Killing cannot be conceived without some being that is put to death, nor painting without a surface upon which the colours are spread. On the other side, an action and the thing on which it is exerted, are not, like substance and quality, united in one individual subject. The active subject is perfectly distinct from that which is passive; and they are connected by one circumstance only, that the action exerted by the former, is exerted upon the latter. This makes it possible to take the action to pieces, and to consider it first with relation to the agent, and next with relation to the patient. But after all, so intimately connected are the parts of the thought, that it requires an effort to make a separation even for a moment. The subtilising to such a degree is not agreeable, especially in works of imagination. The best poets however, taking advantage of this subtilty, scruple not to separate by a pause an active verb from its passive subject. Such pauses in a long work may be indulged; but taken singly, they certainly are not agreeable. I appeal to the following examples.

The peer now spreads || the glitt'ring forfex wide

As ever sully'd || the fair face of light

Repair'd to search || the gloomy cave of Spleen

Nothing, to make || philosophy thy friend

> *Shou'd chance to make* || *the well-dress'd rabble stare*
>
> *Or cross, to plunder* || *provinces, the main*
>
> *These madmen never hurt* || *the church or state*
>
> *How shall we fill* || *a library with wit*
>
> *What better teach* || *a foreigner the tongue?*
>
> *Sure, if I spare* || *the minister, no rules*
> *Of honour bind me, not to maul his tools.*

On the other hand, when the passive subject by inversion is first named, there is no difficulty of interjecting a pause betwixt it and the verb, more than when the active subject is first named. The same reason holds in both, that though a verb cannot be separated in idea from the substantive which governs it, and scarcely from the substantive it governs; yet a substantive may always be conceived independent of the verb. When the passive subject is introduced before the verb, we know not that an action is to be exerted upon it; therefore we may rest till the action commences. For the sake of illustration take the following examples.

> *Shrines! where their vigils* || *pale-ey'd virgins keep*
>
> *Soon as thy letters* || *trembling I unclose*
>
> *No happier task* || *these faded eyes pursue*

What is said about placing the pause, leads to a general observation, which I shall have occasion for afterwards. The natural order of placing the active substantive and its verb, is more friendly to a pause than the inverted order. But in all the other connections, inversion affords by far a better opportunity for a pause. Upon this depends one of the great advantages that blank verse hath over rhyme. The privilege of inversion, in which it far excels rhyme, gives it a much greater choice of pauses, than can be had in the natural order of arrangement.

We now proceed to the slighter connections, which shall be discussed in one general article. Words connected by conjunctions and prepositions freely admit a pause betwixt them, which will be clear from the following instances.

Assume what sexes || and what shape they please

The light militia || of the lower sky

Connecting particles were invented to unite in a period two substantives signifying things occasionally united in the thought, but which have no natural union. And betwixt two things not only separable in idea, but really distinct, the mind, for the sake of melody, chearfully admits by a pause a momentary disjunction of their occasional union.

ONE CAPITAL BRANCH OF THE subject is still upon hand, to which I am directed by what is just now said. It concerns those parts of speech which singly represent no idea, and which become not significant till they be joined to other words. I mean conjunctions, prepositions, articles, and such like accessories, passing under the name of *particles*. Upon these the question occurs, Whether they can be separated by a pause from the words that make them significant? Whether, for example, in the following lines, the separation of the accessory preposition from the principal substantive, be according to rule?

The goddess with || a discontented air

And heighten'd by || the diamond's circling rays

When victims at || yon altar's foot we lay

So take it in || the very words of Creech

An ensign of || the delegates of Jove

Two ages o'er || his native realm he reign'd

While angels, with || their silver wings o'ershade

Or separating the conjunction from the word it connects with what goes before:

Talthybius and || Eurybates the good

It will be obvious at the first glance, that the foregoing reasoning upon objects naturally connected, are not applicable to words which of themselves are mere ciphers. We must therefore have recourse to someother principle for solving the present question. These particles out of their place are totally insignificant. To give them a meaning, they must be joined to certain words. The necessity of this junction, together with custom, forms an artificial connection, which has a strong influence upon the mind. It cannot bear even a momentary separation, which destroys the sense, and is at the same time contradictory to practice. Another circumstance tends still more to make this separation disagreeable. The long syllable immediately preceding the full pause, must be accented; for this is required by the melody, as will afterward appear. But it is ridiculous to accent or put an emphasis upon a low word that raises no idea, and is confined to the humble province of connecting words that raise ideas. And for that reason, a line must be disagreeable where a particle immediately precedes the full pause; for such construction of a line makes the melody discord with the sense.

Hitherto we have discoursed upon that pause only which divides the line. Are the same rules applicable to the concluding pause? This must be answered by making a distinction. In the first line of a couplet, the concluding pause differs little, if at all, from the pause which divides the line; and for that reason, the rules are applicable to both equally. The concluding pause of the couplet, is in a different condition: it resembles greatly the concluding pause in a Hexameter line. Both of them indeed are so remarkable, that they never can be graceful, unless when they accompany a pause in the sense. Hence it follows, that a couplet ought always to be finished with some close in the sense; if not a point, at least a comma. The truth is, that this rule is seldom transgressed. In Pope's works, upon a cursory search indeed, I found but the following deviations from the rule.

> *Nothing is foreign: parts relate to whole;*
> *One all extending, all-preserving soul*
> *Connects each being——*

Another:

> *To draw fresh colours from the vernal flow'rs,*
> *To steal from rainbows ere they drop in show'rs*
> *A brighter wash———*

But now, supposing the connection to be so slender as to admit a pause, it follows not that a pause may always be put. There is one rule to which every other ought to bend, That the sense must never be wounded or obscured by the music; and upon that account, I condemn the following lines:

> *Ulysses, first || in public cares, she found.*

And,

> *Who rising, high || th' imperial sceptre rais'd.*

With respect to inversion, it appears both from reason and experiments, that many words which cannot bear a separation in their natural order, admit a pause when inverted. And it may be added, that when two words, or two members of a sentence, in their natural order, can be separated by a pause, such separation can never be amiss in an inverted order. An inverted period, which runs cross to the natural train of ideas, requires to be marked in some measure even by pauses in the sense, that the parts may be distinctly known. Take the following examples.

> *As with cold lips || I kiss'd the sacred veil.*

> *With other beauties || charm my partial eyes.*

> *Full in my view || set all the bright abode.*

> *With words like these || the troops Ulysses rul'd.*

> *Back to th' assembly roll || the thronging train.*

> *Not for their grief || the Grecian host I blame.*

The same where the separation is made at the close of the first line of the couplet:

> *For spirits, freed from mortal laws, with ease*
> *Assume what sexes and what shapes they please.*

The pause is tolerable even at the close of the couplet, for the reason just now suggested, that inverted members require some slight pause in the sense:

> *'Twas where the plane-tree spread its shades around:*
> *The altars heav'd; and from the crumbling ground*
> *A mighty dragon shot.*

Thus a train of reasoning hath insensibly led us to conclusions with regard to the musical pause, very different from those in the first section, concerning the separating by an interjected circumstance words intimately connected. One would conjecture, that where-ever words are separable by interjecting a circumstance, they should be equally separable by interjecting a pause. But, upon a more narrow inspection, the appearance of analogy vanisheth. To make this evident, I need only premise, that a pause in the sense distinguishes the different members of a period from each other; that two words of the same member may be separated by a circumstance, all the three making still but one member; and therefore that a pause in the sense has no connection with the separation of words by interjected circumstances. This sets the matter in a clear light. It is observed above, that the musical pause is intimately connected with the pause in the sense; so intimately indeed, that regularly they ought to coincide. As this would be too great a restraint, a licence is indulged, to place pauses for the sake of the music where they are not necessary for the sense. But this licence must be kept within bounds. And a musical pause ought never to be placed where a pause is excluded by the sense; as, for example, betwixt the adjective and following substantive which make parts of the same idea, and still less betwixt a particle and the word which makes it significant.

Abstracting at present from the peculiarity of modulation arising from the different pauses, it cannot fail to be observed in general, that they introduce into our verse no slight degree of variety. Nothing more fatigues the ear, than a number of uniform lines having all the same pause, which is extremely remarkable in the French versification. This imperfection will be discerned by a fine ear even in the shortest succession, and becomes intolerable in a long poem. Pope excels all the world in the variety of his modulation, which indeed is not less perfect of its kind than that of Virgil.

From what is now said, there ought to be one exception. Uniformity in the members of a thought, demands equal uniformity in the members of the period which expresses that thought. When therefore resembling objects or things are expressed in a plurality of verse-lines, these lines in their structure ought to be as uniform as possible, and the pauses in particular ought all of them to have the same place. Take the following examples.

> *By foreign hands || thy dying eyes were clos'd,*
> *By foreign hands || thy decent limbs compos'd,*
> *By foreign hands || thy humble grave adorn'd.*

Again,

> *Bright as the sun, || her eyes the gazers strike,*
> *And, like the sun, || they shine on all alike.*

Speaking of Nature, or the God of Nature:

> *Warms in the sun || refreshes in the breeze,*
> *Glows in the stars || and blossoms in the trees,*
> *Lives through all life || extends through all extent,*
> *Spreads undivided || operates unspent.*

Pauses are like to dwell longer upon hand than I imagined; for the subject is not yet exhausted. It is laid down above, that English heroic verse, considering melody only, admits no more than four capital pauses; and that the capital pause of every line is determined by the sense to be after the fourth, the fifth, the sixth, or seventh syllable. And that this doctrine holds true so far as melody alone is concerned, every good ear will bear testimony. At the same time, examples are not unfrequent, in Milton especially, of the capital pause being after the first, the second, or the third syllable. And that this licence may be taken, even gracefully, when it adds vigour to the expression, I readily admit. So far the sound may be justly sacrificed to the sense or expression. That this licence may be successfully taken, will be clear from the following example. Pope, in his translation of Homer, describes a rock broke off from a mountain, and hurling to the plain, in the following words.

From steep to steep the rolling ruin bounds;
At every shock the crackling wood resounds;
Still gath'ring force, it smokes; and urg'd amain,
Whirls, leaps, and thunders down, impetuous to the plain:
There stops || *So Hector. Their whole force he prov'd,*
Resistless when he rag'd; and when he stopt, unmov'd.

In the penult line the proper place of the musical pause is at the end of the fifth syllable; but it enlivens the expression by its coincidence with that of the sense at the end of the second syllable. The stopping short before the usual pause in the melody, aids the impression that is made by the description of the stone's stopping short. And what is lost to the melody by this artifice, is more than compensated by the force that is added to the description. Milton makes a happy use of this licence; witness the following examples from his *Paradise Lost*.

—— Thus with the year
Seasons return, but not to me returns
Day || *or the sweet approach of even or morn.*

Celestial voices to the midnight-air
Sole || *or responsive each to others note.*

And over them triumphant Death his dart
Shook || *but delay'd to strike.*

—— And wild uproar
Stood rul'd || *stood vast infinitude confin'd.*

—— And hard'ning in his strength
Glories || *for never since created man*
Met such embodied force.

From his slack hand the garland wreath'd for Eve
Down drop'd || *and all the faded roses shed.*

> *Of unessential night, receives him next,*
> *Wide gaping* || *and with utter loss of being*
> *Threatens him,* &c.

> *——For now the thought*
> *Both of lost happiness and lasting pain*
> *Torments him* || *round he throws his baleful eyes,* &c.

If we consider the foregoing passages with respect to melody singly, the pauses are undoubtedly out of their proper place. But being united with those of the sense, they inforce the expression and enliven it greatly. And the beauty of expression is communicated to the sound, which, by a natural deception, makes even the melody appear more perfect than if the musical pauses were regular.

To explain the rules of accenting, two general observations must be premised. The first is, That accents have a double effect. They contribute to the melody, by giving it air and spirit: they contribute not less to the sense, by distinguishing important words from others. These two effects ought never to be separated. If a musical accent be put where the sense rejects it, we feel a discordance betwixt the thought and the melody. An accent, for example, placed on a word that makes no figure, has the effect to burlesk it, by giving it an unnatural elevation. The injury thus done to the sense, is communicated to the melody by the intimacy of connection, and both seem to be wounded. This rule is applicable in a peculiar manner to particles. It is indeed ridiculous to put an emphasis on a word which of itself has no meaning, and like cement serves only to unite words significant. The other general observation is, That a word of whatever number of syllables, is not accented upon more than one of them. Nor is this an arbitrary practice. The object represented by the word, is set in its best light by a single accent: reiterated accents on different syllables in succession, make not the emphasis stronger; but have an air, as if the sound only of the accented syllables were regarded, and not the sense of the word.

Keeping in view the foregoing observations, the doctrine of accenting English heroic verse, is extremely simple. In the first place, accenting is confined to the long syllables; for the melody admits not an accent upon any short syllable. In the next place, as the melody is inriched in proportion to the number of accents, every word that has a long syllable ought to be accented, unless where the accent is rejected by the sense: a word, as observed, that makes no figure by its signification, cannot bear an accent. According to this rule, a line may admit five accents; a case by no means rare.

But supposing every long syllable to be accented, there is constantly, in every line, one accent which makes a greater figure than the rest. This capital accent is that which precedes the capital pause. Hence it is distinguishable into two kinds; one that is immediately succeeded by the pause, and one that is divided from the pause by a short syllable. The former belongs to lines of the first and third order: the latter to those of the second and fourth. Examples of the first kind.

> *Smooth flow the wâves* || *the zephyrs gently play,*
> *Belinda smîl'd* || *and all the world was gay.*
>
> *He rais'd his azure wând* || *and thus begun*

Examples of the second.

> *There lay three gârters* || *half a pair of gloves;*
> *And all the trôphies* || *of his former loves.*
>
> *Our humble prôvince* || *is to tend the fair,*
> *Not a less plêasing* || *though less glorious care.*
>
> *And hew triumphal ârches* || *to the ground*

These accents make different impressions on the mind, which will be the subject of a following speculation. In the mean time, it may be safely pronounced a capital defect in the composition of verse, to put a low word, incapable of an accent, in the place where this accent should be. This bars the accent altogether; and I know no other fault more subversive of the melody, if it be not that of barring a pause altogether. I may add affirmatively, that it is a capital beauty in the composition of verse, to have the most important word of the sentence, so placed as that this capital accent may be laid upon it. No single circumstance contributes more to the energy of verse, than to have this accent on a word, that, by the importance of its meaning, is intitled to a peculiar emphasis. To show the bad effect of excluding the capital accent, I refer the reader to some instances given above, p. ooo, where particles are separated by a pause from the capital words that make them significant, and which particles ought, for the sake of the melody, to be accented, were they capable of an accent. Add to these the following instances from the Essay on Criticism.

Oft, leaving what || is natural and fit,
—*line 448*

Not yet purg'd off, || of spleen and sour disdain
—*l. 528*

No pardon vile || obscenity should find
—*l. 531*

When love was all || an easy monarch's care
—*l. 537*

For 'tis but half || a judge's talk, to know
—*l. 562*

'Tis not enough, || taste, judgement, learning, join
—*l. 563*

That only makes || superior sense belov'd
—*l. 578*

Whose right it is, || uncensur'd, to be dull
—*l. 590*

'Tis best sometimes || your censure to restrain
—*l. 597*

When this fault is at the end of the line that closes a couplet, it leaves not the least trace of melody:

> *But of this frame the bearings, and the ties,*
> *The strong connections, nice dependencies*

In a line expressive of what is humble or dejected, it improves the resemblance betwixt the sound and sense, to exclude the capital accent. This, to my taste, is a beauty in the following lines.

> *In thêse deep sôlitudes || and awful cells*

> *The pôor inhâbitant || behôlds in vain*

To conclude this article, the accents are not, like the syllables, confined to a certain number. Some lines have no fewer than five, and there are lines that admit not above one. This variety, as we have seen, depends entirely on the different powers of the component words. Particles, even where they are long by position, cannot be accented; and polysyllables, whatever space they occupy, admit but one accent. Polysyllables have another defect, that they generally exclude the full pause. I have shown above, that few polysyllables can find place in the construction of English verse. Here are reasons for excluding them, could they find place.

I AM NOW PREPARED TO fulfil a promise concerning the four sorts of lines that enter into English heroic verse. That these have, each of them, a peculiar melody distinguishable by a good ear, I ventured to suggest, and promised to account for: and though this subject is extremely delicate, I am not without hopes of making good my engagement. First, however, like a wary general, I take all advantages the ground will permit. I do not aver, that this peculiarity of modulation is in every instance perceptible. Far from it. The impression made by a period, whether it be verse or prose, is occasioned chiefly by the thought, and in an inferior degree by the words; and these articles are so intimately united with the melody, that they have each of them a strong influence upon the others. With respect to the melody in particular, instances are without number, of melody, in itself poor and weak, passing for rich and spirited where it is supported by the thought and expression. I am therefore intitled to insist, that this experiment be tried upon lines of equal rank. And to avoid the perplexity of various cases, I must also insist, that the lines chosen for a trial be regularly accented before the pause: for upon a matter abundantly refined in itself, I would not willingly be imbarrassed with faulty and irregular lines. These preliminaries being adjusted, I begin with some general observations, that will save repeating the same thing over and over upon each particular case. And, first, an accent succeeded by a pause, makes sensibly a deeper impression than where the voice goes on without a stop: to make an impression requires time; and there is no time where there is no pause. The fact is so certain, that in running over a few lines, there is scarce an ear so dull as not readily to distinguish from others, that particular accent which immediately precedes the full pause. In the next place, the elevation of an accenting tone, produceth in the mind a similar elevation, which is continued during the pause. Every circumstance is different where the pause is separated from the accent by a short syllable. The impression made by the accent is more slight when there is no stop; and the elevation of the accent is gone in a moment by the falling of the voice in pronouncing the short syllable that follows. The pause also is sensibly affected by the position of the accent. In lines of the first and third order, the close conjunction of the accent and pause, occasions a sudden stop without preparation, which rouses the mind, and bestows on the melody a spirited air. When, on the other hand, the pause is separated from the accent by a short syllable, which always happens in lines of the second and fourth order, the pause is soft and gentle. This short unaccented syllable succeeding one that is accented, must of course be pronounced with a falling voice, which naturally prepares for a pause. The mind falls gently from the accented syllable, and slides into rest as it were insensibly. Further, the lines themselves, derive different powers from the position of the pause. A pause after the fourth syllable divides the line into two unequal portions, of which the largest comes last. This circumstance resolving the line into an ascending series, makes an impression in pronouncing like that of mounting upward. And to this impression contributes the redoubled effort in pronouncing the largest portion, which is last in order. The mind has a different feeling when the pause succeeds the fifth syllable. The line being divided into two equal parts by this pause, these parts, pronounced with equal effort, are agreeable by their uniformity. A line divided by a pause after the sixth syllable, makes an impression opposite to that first mentioned. Being divided into two unequal portions, of which the shortest is last in order, it appears like a slow descending series; and the second portion being pronounced with less effort than the first, the diminished effort prepares the mind for rest. And this preparation for rest is still more sensibly felt where the pause is after the seventh syllable, as in lines of the fourth order.

No person can be at a loss in applying these observations. A line of the first order is of all the most spirited and lively. To produce this effect, several of the circumstances above mentioned concur. The accent, being followed instantly by a pause, makes an illustrious figure: the elevated tone of the accent elevates the mind: the mind is supported in its elevation by the sudden unprepared pause which rouses and animates: and the line itself, representing by its unequal division an ascending series, carries the mind still higher, making an impression similar to that of mounting upward. The second order has a modulation sensibly sweet, soft, and flowing. The accent is not so sprightly as in the former, because a short syllable intervenes betwixt it and the pause: its elevation, by the same means, vanisheth instantaneously: the mind, by a falling voice, is gently prepared for a stop: and the pleasure of uniformity from the division of the line into two equal parts, is calm and sweet. The third order has a modulation not so easily expressed in words. It in part resembles the first order, by the liveliness of an accent succeeded instantly by a full pause. But then the elevation occasioned by this circumstance, is balanced in some degree by the remitted effort in pronouncing the second portion, which remitted effort has a tendency to rest. Another circumstance distinguisheth it remarkably. Its capital accent comes late, being placed on the sixth syllable; and this circumstance bestows on it an air of gravity and solemnity. The last order resembles the second in the mildness of its accent and softness of its pause. It is still more solemn than the third, by the lateness of its capital accent. It also possesses in a higher degree than the third, the tendency to rest; and by that circumstance is of all the best qualified for closing a period in the completest manner.

But these are not all the distinguishing characters of the different orders. Each order also, by means of its final accent and pause, makes a peculiar impression; so peculiar as to produce a melody clearly distinguishable from that of the others. This peculiarity is occasioned by the division which the capital pause makes in a line. By an unequal division in the first order, the mind has an impression of ascending; and is left at the close in the highest elevation, which is display'd on the concluding syllable. By this means, a strong emphasis is naturally laid upon the concluding syllable, whether by raising the voice to a sharper tone, or by expressing the word in a fuller tone. This order accordingly is of all the least proper for concluding a period, where a cadence is proper, and not an accent. In the second order, the final accent makes not so capital a figure. There is nothing singular in its being marked by a pause, for this is common to all the orders; and this order, being destitute of the impression of ascent, cannot rival the first order in the elevation of its accent, nor consequently in the dignity of its pause; for these always have a mutual influence. This order, however, with respect to its close, maintains a superiority over the third and fourth orders. In these the close is more humble, being brought down by the impression of descent, and by the remitted effort in pronouncing; considerably in the third order, and still more considerably in the last. According to this description, the concluding accents and pauses of the four orders being reduced to a scale, will form a descending series probably in an arithmetical progression.

After what is said, will it be thought refining too much to suggest, that the different orders are qualified for different purposes, and that a poet of genius will be naturally led to make a choice accordingly? I cannot think this altogether chimerical. It appears to me, that the first order is proper for a sentiment that is bold, lively, or impetuous; that the third order is proper for subjects grave, solemn, or lofty; the second for what is tender, delicate, or melancholy, and in general for all the sympathetic emotions; and the last for subjects of the same kind, when tempered with any degree of solemnity. I do not contend, that anyone order is fitted for no other talk, than that assigned it. At that rate, no sort of modulation would be left for accompanying ordinary thoughts, that have nothing peculiar in them. I only venture to suggest, and I do it with diffidence, that one order is peculiarly adapted to certain subjects, and better qualified than the others for expressing such subjects. The best way to judge is by experiment; and to avoid the imputation of a partial search, I shall confine my instances to a single poem, beginning with the first order.

> *On her white breast, a sparkling cross she wore,*
> *Which Jews might kiss, and Infidels adore.*
> *Her lively looks, a sprightly mind disclose,*

> *Quick as her eyes, and as unfix'd as those:*
> *Favours to none, to all she smiles extends;*
> *Oft she rejects, but never once offends.*
> *Bright as the sun, her eyes the gazers strike,*
> *And, like the sun, they shine on all alike.*
> *Yet graceful ease, and sweetness void of pride,*
> *Might hide her faults, if belles had faults to hide:*
> *If to her share some female errors fall,*
> *Look on her face, and you'll forget 'em all.*
>
> —Rape of the Lock

In accounting for the remarkable liveliness of this passage, it will be acknowledged by everyone who has an ear, that the modulation must come in for a share. The lines, all of them, are of the first order; a very unusual circumstance in the author of this poem, so eminent for variety in his versification. Who can doubt, that, in this passage, he has been led by delicacy of taste to employ the first order preferably to the others?

Second order.

> *Our humbler province is to tend the fair,*
> *Not a less pleasing, though less glorious care;*
> *To save the powder from too rude a gale,*
> *Nor let th' imprison'd essences exhale;*
> *To draw fresh colours from the vernal flow'rs;*
> *To steal from rainbows ere they drop their show'rs,* &c.

Again,

> *Oh, thoughtless mortals! ever blind to fate,*
> *Too soon dejected, and too soon elate.*
> *Sudden, these honours shall be snatch'd away,*
> *And curs'd forever this victorious day.*

Third order.

> *To fifty chosen sylphs, of special note,*
> *We trust th'important charge, the petticoat.*

Again,

> *Oh say what stranger cause, yet unexplor'd,*
> *Could make a gentle belle reject a lord?*

A plurality of lines of the fourth order, would not have a good effect in succession; because, by a remarkable tendency to rest, its proper office is to close a period. The reader, therefore, must be satisfied with instances where this order is mixed with others.

> *Not louder shrieks to pitying Heav'n are cast,*
> *When husbands, or when lapdogs, breathe their last.*

Again,

> *Steel could the works of mortal pride confound,*
> *And hew triumphal arches to the ground.*

Again,

> *She sees, and trembles at th' approaching ill,*
> *Just in the jaws of ruin, and codille.*

Again,

> *With earnest eyes, and round unthinking face,*
> *He first the snuff-box open'd, then the case.*

And this suggests another experiment, which is, to set the different orders more directly in opposition, by giving examples where they are mixed in the same passage.

First and second orders.

> *Sol through white curtains shot a tim'rous ray,*
> *And ope'd those eyes that must eclipse the day.*

Again,

> *Not youthful kings in battle seiz'd alive,*
> *Not scornful virgins who their charms survive,*

> *Not ardent lovers robb'd of all their bliss,*
> *Not ancient ladies when refus'd a kiss,*
> *Not tyrants fierce that unrepenting die,*
> *Not Cynthia when her manteau's pinn'd awry,*
> *E'er felt such rage, resentment, and despair,*
> *As thou, sad virgin! for thy ravish'd hair.*

First and third.

> *Think what an equipage thou hast in air,*
> *And view with scorn two pages and a chair.*

Again,

> *What guards the purity of melting maids,*
> *In courtly balls, and midnight-masquerades,*
> *Safe from the treach'rous friend, the daring spark,*
> *The glance by day, the whisper in the dark?*

Again,

> *With tender billet-doux he lights the pyre,*
> *And breathes three am'rous sighs to raise the fire;*
> *Then prostrate falls, and begs, with ardent eyes,*
> *Soon to obtain, and long possess the prize.*

Again,

> *Jove's thunder roars, heav'n trembles all around,*
> *Blue Neptune storms, the bellowing deeps resound,*
> *Earth shakes her nodding tow'rs, the ground gives way,*
> *And the pale ghosts start at the flash of day!*

Second and third.

> *Sunk in Thalestris' arms, the nymph he found,*
> *Her eyes dejected, and her hair unbound.*

Again,

> *On her heav'd bosom hung her drooping head,*
> *Which with a sigh she rais'd; and thus she said.*

Musing on the foregoing subject, I begin to doubt whether I have not been all this while in a reverie. Here unexpectedly a sort of fairy-scene opens, where every object is new and singular. Is there any truth in the appearance, or is it merely a work of imagination? The scene seems to be a reality; and if it can bear examination, it must exalt greatly the melody of English heroic verse. If uniformity prevail, in the arrangement, in the equality of the lines, and in the resemblance of the final sounds; variety is still more conspicuous in the pauses and accents, which are diversified in a surprising manner. The beauty that results from combined objects, is justly observed to consist in a due mixture of uniformity and variety[28]. Of this beauty many instances have already occurred, but none more illustrious than English versification. However rude it may be by the simplicity of arrangement, it is highly melodious by its pauses and accents, so as already to rival the most perfect species known in Greece or Rome. And it is no disagreeable prospect to find it susceptible of still greater refinement.

W E   P R O C E E D   T O   B L A N K   V E R S E, which hath so many circumstances in common with rhyme, that what is necessary to be said upon it may be brought within a narrow compass. With respect to form, it differs not from rhyme farther than in rejecting the jingle of similar sounds. But let us not think this difference a trifle, or that we gain nothing by it but the purifying our verse from a pleasure so childish. In truth, our verse is extremely cramped by rhyme; and the great advantage of blank verse is, that, being free from the fetters of rhyme, it is at liberty to attend the imagination in its boldest flights. Rhyme necessarily divides verse into couplets: each couplet makes a complete musical period; the parts of which are divided by pauses, and the whole summed up by a full close at the end: the modulation begins anew with the next couplet: and in this manner a composition in rhyme proceeds couplet after couplet. I have more than once had occasion to observe the influence that sound and sense have upon each other by their intimate union. If a couplet be a complete period with regard to the melody, it ought

---

28. See chap. 9.

regularly to be so also with regard to the sense. This, it is true, proves too great a cramp upon composition; and licences are indulged, as explained above. These however must be used with discretion, so as to preserve some degree of uniformity betwixt the sense and the music. There ought never to be a full close in the sense but at the end of a couplet; and there ought always to be some pause in the sense at the end of every couplet. The same period as to sense may be extended through several couplets; but in this case each couplet ought to contain a distinct member, distinguished by a pause in the sense as well as in the sound; and the whole ought to be closed with a complete cadence. Rules such as these, must confine rhyme within very narrow bounds. A thought of any extent, cannot be reduced within its compass. The sense must be curtailed and broken into pieces, to make it square with the curtness of melody: and it is obvious, that short periods afford no latitude for inversion. I have examined this point with the greater accuracy, in order to give a just notion of blank verse; and to show that a slight difference in form may produce a very great difference in substance. Blank verse has the same pauses and accents with rhyme; and a pause at the end of every line, like what concludes the first line of a couplet. In a word, the rules of melody in blank verse, are the same that obtain with respect to the first line of a couplet. But luckily, being disengaged from rhyme, or, in other words, from couplets, there is access to make every line run into another, precisely as the first line of a couplet may run into the second. There must be a musical pause at the end of every line; but it is not necessary that it be accompanied with a pause in the sense. The sense may be carried on through different lines; till a period of the utmost extent be completed, by a full close both in the sense and the sound. There is no restraint, other than that this full close be at the end of a line. This restraint is necessary in order to preserve a coincidence betwixt sense and sound; which ought to be aimed at in general, and is indispensable in the case of a full close, because it has a striking effect. Hence the aptitude of blank verse for inversion; and consequently the lustre of its pauses and accents; for which, as observed above, there is greater scope in inversion, than when words run in their natural order.

In the second section of this chapter it is shown, that nothing contributes more than inversion to the force and elevation of language. The couplets of rhyme confine inversion within narrow limits. Nor would the elevation of inversion, were there access for it in rhyme, be extremely concordant with the humbler tone of that sort of verse.

It is universally agreed, that the loftiness of Milton's style supports admirably the sublimity of his subject; and it is not less certain, that the loftiness of his style arises chiefly from inversion. Shakespear deals little in inversion. But his blank verse, being a sort of measured prose, is perfectly well adapted to the stage. Laboured inversion is there extremely improper, because in dialogue it never can appear natural.

Hitherto I have considered the advantage of laying aside rhyme, with respect to that superior power of expression which verse acquires thereby. But this is not the only advantage of blank verse. It has another not less signal of its kind; and that is, of a more extensive and more complete melody. Its music is not, like that of rhyme, confined to a single couplet; but takes in a great compass, so as in some measure to rival music properly so called. The intervals betwixt its cadences may be long or short at pleasure; and, by this means, its modulation, with respect both to richness and variety, is superior far to that of rhyme; and superior even to that of the Greek and Latin Hexameter. Of this observation no person can doubt who is acquainted with the *Paradise Lost*. In that work there are indeed many careless lines; but at every turn it shines out in the richest melody as well as in the sublimest sentiments. Take the following specimen.

Now Morn her rosy steps in th' eastern clime
Advancing, sow'd the earth with orient pearl,
When Adam wak'd, so custom'd, for his sleep
Was aëry light from pure digestion bred,
And temp'rate vapours bland, which th' only sound
Of leaves and fuming rills, Aurora's fan,
Lightly dispers'd, and the shrill matin song
Of birds on every bough; so much the more
His wonder was to find unwaken'd Eve
With tresses discompos'd, and glowing cheek,
As through unquiet rest: he on his side
Leaning half-rais'd, with looks of cordial love
Hung over her enamour'd, and beheld
Beauty, which, whether waking or asleep,
Shot forth peculiar graces; then with voice
Mild, as when Zephyrus on Flora breathes,
Her hand soft touching, whisper'd thus. Awake
My fairest, my espous'd, my latest found,
Heav'n's last best gift, my ever new delight,

> *Awake; the morning shines, and the fresh field*
> *Calls us; we lose the prime, to mark how spring*
> *Our tended plants, how blows the citron grove,*
> *What drops the myrrh, and what the balmy reed,*
> *How Nature paints her colours, how the bee*
> *Sits on the bloom extracting liquid sweet.*

—*Book 1. l. 1*

Comparing the Latin Hexameter and English heroic rhyme, the former has obviously the advantage in the following particulars. It is greatly preferable as to arrangement, by the latitude it admits in placing the long and short syllables. Secondly, the length of an Hexameter line hath a majestic air: ours, by its shortness, is indeed more brisk and lively, but much less fitted for the sublime. And, thirdly, the long high-sounding words that Hexameter admits, add greatly to its majesty. To compensate these advantages, English rhyme possesses a greater number and greater variety both of pauses and of accents. These two sorts of verse stand indeed pretty much in opposition: in the Hexameter, great variety of arrangement, none in the pauses or accents: in the English rhyme, great variety in the pauses and accents, very little in the arrangement.

In blank verse are united, in a good measure, the several properties of Latin Hexameter and English rhyme; and it possesses beside many signal properties of its own. If is not confined, like a Hexameter, by a full close at the end of every line; nor, like rhyme, by a full close at the end of every couplet. This form of construction, which admits the lines to run into each other, gives it a still greater majesty than arises from the length of a Hexameter line. By the same means, it admits inversion even beyond the Latin or Greek Hexameter, which suffer some confinement by the regular closes at the end of every line. In its music it is illustrious above all. The melody of Hexameter verse, is circumscribed to a line; and of English rhyme, to a couplet. The melody of blank verse is under no confinement, but enjoys the utmost privilege of which the melody of verse is susceptible, and that is to run hand in hand with the sense. In a word, blank verse is superior to the Hexameter in many articles; and inferior to it in none, save in the latitude of arrangement, and in the use of long words.

IN THE FRENCH HEROIC VERSE, there are found, on the contrary, all the defects of the Latin Hexameter and English rhyme, without the beauties of either. Subjected to the bondage of rhyme, and to the full close at the end of each couplet, it is further peculiarly disgustful by the uniformity of its pauses and accents. The line invariably is divided by the pause into two equal parts, and the accent is invariably placed before the pause.

> *Jeune et vaillant herôs || dont la haute sagesse*
> *Ne'st point la fruit tardif || d'une lente vieillesse.*

Here every circumstance contributes to a most tedious uniformity. A constant return of the same pause and of the same accent, as well as an equal division of every line; by which the latter part always answers to the former, and fatigues the ear without intermission or change. I cannot set this matter in a better light, than by presenting to the reader a French translation of the following passage of Milton.

> *Two of far nobler shape, erect and tall,*
> *Godlike erect, with native honour clad*
> *In naked majesty seem'd lords of all;*
> *And worthy seem'd, for in their looks divine*
> *The image of their glorious Maker shon,*
> *Truth, wisdom, sanctitude severe and pure,*
> *Severe, but in true filial freedom plac'd;*
> *Whence true authority in men: though both*
> *Not equal, as their sex not equal seem'd;*
> *For contemplation he and valour form'd,*
> *For softness she and sweet attractive grace,*
> *He for God only, she for God in him.*

Were the pauses of the sense and sound in this passage, but a little better assorted, nothing in verse could be more melodious. In general, the great defect of Milton's versification, in other respects admirable, is the want of coincidence betwixt the pauses of the sense and sound.

The translation is in the following words.

> *Ce lieu délicieux, ce paradis charmant,*
> *Reçoit deux objets son plus bel ornement;*
> *Leur port majestueux, et leur démarche altiere,*

> *Semble leur meriter sur la nature entiere*
> *Ce droit de commander que Dieu leur a donné.*
> *Sur leur auguste front de gloire couronné,*
> *Du souverain du ciel drille la resemblance:*
> *Dans leur simples regards éclatte l'innocence,*
> *L'adorable candeur, l'aimable vérité,*
> *La raison, la sagesse, et la sévérité*
> *Qu'adoucit la prudence, et cet air de droiture*
> *Du visage des rois respectable parure.*
> *Ces deux objets divins n'ont pas les mêmes traits,*
> *Ils paroissent formés, quoique tous deux parfaits;*
> *L'un pour la majesté, la force, et la noblesse;*
> *L'autre pour la douceur, la grace, et la tendresse:*
> *Celui-ci pour Dieu seul, l'autre pour l'homme encor.*

Here the sense is fairly translated, the words are of equal power, and yet how inferior the melody!

I take the liberty to add here a speculation, which, though collateral only, arises naturally from the subject, and shall be discussed in a few words. Many attempts have been made to introduce Hexameter verse into the living languages, but without success. The English language, I am inclined to believe, is not susceptible of this melody; and my reasons are these. First, the polysyllables in Latin and Greek are finely diversified by long and short syllables, a circumstance that qualifies them for the melody of Hexameter verse. Ours are extremely ill qualified for this service, because they superabound in short syllables. Secondly, the bulk of our monosyllables are arbitrary with regard to length, which is an unlucky circumstance in Hexameter. Custom, as observed above, may render familiar a long or short pronunciation of the same word: but the mind wavering betwixt the two sounds, cannot be so much arrested with either, as with a word that hath always the same sound; and for that reason, arbitrary sounds are ill fitted for a melody which is chiefly supported by quantity. In Latin and Greek Hexameter, invariable sounds direct and ascertain the melody: English Hexameter would be destitute of melody, unless by artful pronunciation; because of necessity the bulk of its sounds must be arbitrary. The pronunciation is easy in a simple movement of alternate short and long syllables; but would be perplexing and unpleasant in the diversified movement of Hexameter verse.

Rhyme makes so great a figure in modern poetry, as to deserve a solemn trial. I have for that reason reserved it to be examined with some deliberation; in order to discover, if possible, its peculiar beauties, and the degree of merit it is intitled to. The first view of this subject leads naturally to the following reflection, "That rhyme having no relation to sentiment, nor any effect upon the ear other than a mere jingle, ought to be banished all compositions of any dignity, as affording but a trifling and childish pleasure." It will also be observed, "That a jingle of words hath in some measure a ludicrous effect; witness the celebrated poem of *Hudibras*, the double rhymes of which contribute no small share to its drollery; that this effect would be equally remarkable in a serious work, were it not obscured by the nature of the subject; that having however a constant tendency to give a ludicrous air to the composition, it requires more than ordinary fire to support the dignity of the sentiments against such an undermining antagonist[29]."

These arguments are specious, and have undoubtedly some weight. Yet, on the other hand, it ought to be considered, that rhyme, in later times, has become universal among men as well as children; and that to give it a currency, it must have some foundation in human nature. In fact, it has been successfully employ'd by poets of genius, in their serious and grave compositions, as well as in those which are more light and airy. Here, in weighing authority against argument, the balance seems to hang pretty even; and therefore, to come at anything decisive, we must pierce a little deeper.

Music has great power over the soul; and may be successfully employ'd to inflame or sooth our passions, if not actually to raise them. A single sound, however sweet, is not music; but a single sound repeated after proper intervals, may have an effect upon the mind, by rousing the attention and keeping the hearer awake. A variety of similar sounds, succeeding each other after regular intervals, must have a still stronger effect. This is applicable to rhyme, which consists in the connection that two verse-lines have by closing with two words similar in sound. And considering deliberately the effect that this may have; we find, that it rouses the attention, and produceth an emotion moderately gay without dignity or elevation. Like the murmurings of a brook gliding through pebbles, it calms the mind when perturbed, and gently raises

---

29. Vossius *De Poematum Cantu*, p. 26, says, "Nihil æque gravitatem orationis afficit, quam in sono ludere syllabarum."

it when sunk. These effects are scarce perceived when the whole poem is in rhyme; but are extremely remarkable by contrast, in the couplets which close the several acts of our later tragedies. The tone of the mind is sensibly varied by them, from anguish, distress, or melancholy, to some degree of ease and alacrity. For the truth of this observation, I appeal to the speech of Jane Shore in the fourth act, when her doom was pronounced by Glo'ster; to the speech of Lady Jane Gray at the end of the first act; and to that of Calista, in the *Fair Penitent*, when she leaves the stage, about the middle of the third act. The speech of Alicia, at the close of the fourth act of *Jane Shore*, puts the matter beyond doubt. In a scene of deep distress, the rhymes which finish the act, produce a certain gaiety and chearfulness, far from according with the tone of the passion.

> ALICIA: Forever? Oh! Forever!
> Oh! who can bear to be a wretch forever!
> My rival too! his last thoughts hung on her:
> And, as he parted, left a blessing for her.
> Shall she be bless'd, and I be curs'd, forever!
> No; since her fatal beauty was the cause
> Of all my suff'rings, let her share my pains;
> Let her, like me, of ev'ry joy forlorn,
> Devote the hour when such a wretch was born:
> Like me to deserts and to darkness run,
> Abhor the day and curse the golden sun;
> Cast ev'ry good and ev'ry hope behind;
> Detest the works of nature, loathe mankind:
> Like me with cries distracted fill the air,
> Tear her poor bosom, and her frantic hair,
> And prove the torments of the last despair.

Having described, the best way I can, the impression that rhyme makes on the mind; I proceed to examine whether rhyme be proper for any subject, and to what subjects in particular it is best suited. Great and elevated subjects, which have a powerful influence, claim justly the precedence in this inquiry. In the chapter of grandeur and sublimity, it is established, that a grand or sublime object, inspires a warm enthusiastic emotion disdaining strict regularity and order. This observation is applicable to the present point. The moderately-enlivening music of rhyme, gives a tone to the mind very different from that of grandeur and sublimity. Supposing then an elevated subject to be expressed in rhyme, what must be the effect? The intimate union of the music with the subject, produces an intimate union of their emotions; one inspired by the subject, which tends to elevate and expand the mind; and one inspired by the music, which, confining the mind within the narrow limits of regular cadency and similar sound, tends to prevent all elevation above its own pitch. Emotions so little concordant, cannot in union have a happy effect.

But it is scarce necessary to reason upon a case, that never did, and probably never will happen, *viz.* an important subject clothed in rhyme, and yet supported in its utmost elevation. A happy thought or warm expression, may at times give a sudden bound upward; but it requires a genius greater than has hitherto existed, to support a poem of any length in a tone much more elevated than that of the melody. Tasso and Ariosto ought not to be made exceptions, and still less Voltaire. And after all, where the poet has the dead weight of rhyme constantly to struggle with, how can we expect an uniform elevation in a high pitch; when such elevation, with all the support it can receive from language, requires the utmost effort of the human genius?

But now, admitting rhyme to be an unfit dress for grand and lofty images; it has one advantage however, which is, to raise a low subject to its own degree of elevation. Addison[30] observes, "That rhyme, without any other assistance, throws the language off from prose, and very often makes an indifferent phrase pass unregarded; but where the verse is not built upon rhymes, there, pomp of sound and energy of expression are indispensably necessary, to support the style and keep it from falling into the flatness of prose." This effect of rhyme is remarkable in the French verse, which, being simple and natural and in a good measure unqualified for inversion, readily sinks down to prose where it is not artificially supported. Rhyme, by rousing the mind, raises it somewhat above the tone of ordinary language: rhyme therefore is indispensable in the French tragedy; and may be proper even for their comedy. Voltaire[31] assigns this very reason for adhering to rhyme in these compositions.

---

30. Spectator, No. 285.

31. Preface to his *Œdipus,* and in his discourse upon tragedy, prefixed to his tragedy of *Brutus*.

He indeed candidly owns, that even with the support of rhyme, the tragedies of his country are little better than conversation-pieces. This shows, that the French language is weak, and an improper dress for any grand subject. Voltaire was sensible of this imperfection; and yet Voltaire attempted an epic poem in that language.

The chearing and enlivening power of rhyme, is still more remarkable in poems of short lines, where the rhymes return upon the ear in a quick succession. And for that reason, rhyme is perfectly well adapted to gay, light, and airy subjects. Witness the following.

> *O the pleasing, pleasing anguish.*
> *When we love, and when we languish!*
> *Wishes rising,*
> *Thoughts surprising,*
> *Pleasure courting,*
> *Charms transporting,*
> *Fancy viewing,*
> *Joys ensuing,*
> *O the pleasing, pleasing anguish.*
>
> —Rosamond, act 1. sc. 2

For this reason, such frequent rhymes are very improper for any severe or serious passion: the dissonance betwixt the subject and the modulation, is very sensibly felt. Witness the following.

> *Ardito ti renda,*
> *T'accenda*
> *Di sdegno*
> *D'un figlio*
> *Il periglio*
> *D'un regno*
> *L' amor*
> *E' dolce ad un' alma*
> *Che aspetta*
> *Vendetta*
> *Il perder la calma*
> *Fra l'ire del cor.*
>
> —Metastasio. Artaserse, act 3. sc 3

Rhyme is not less unfit for deep distress, than for subjects elevated and lofty; and for that reason has been long disused in the English and Italian tragedy. In a work, where the subject is serious though not elevated, it has not a good effect; because the airiness of the modulation agrees not with the gravity of the subject. The *Essay on Man*, which treats a subject great and important, would show much better in blank verse. Sportive love, mirth, gaiety, humour, and ridicule, are the province of rhyme. The boundaries assigned it by nature, were extended in barbarous and illiterate ages, and in its usurpations it has long been protected by custom. But taste in the fine arts, as well as in morals, improves daily; and makes a progress, slowly indeed, but uniformly, towards perfection: and there is no reason to doubt, that rhyme in Britain will in time be forc'd to abandon its unjust conquests, and to confine itself within its natural limits.

Having thrown out what occurred upon rhyme, I close the section with a general observation. The melody of articulate sound so powerfully inchants the mind, as to draw a vail over very gross faults and imperfections. Of this power a stronger example cannot be given, than the episode of Aristæus, which closes the fourth book of the *Georgics*. To renew a stock of bees when the former is lost, Virgil asserts, that they will be produced in the intrails of a bullock, slain and managed in a certain manner. This leads him to say, how this strange receipt was invented; which is as follows. Aristæus having lost his bees by disease and famine, never dreams of employing the ordinary means for obtaining a new stock; but, like a froward child, complains heavily of his misfortune to his mother Cyrene, a water-nymph. She advises him to consult Proteus, a sea-god, not how he was to obtain a new stock, but only by what fatality he had lost his former stock; adding, that violence was necessary, because Proteus would say nothing voluntarily. Aristæus, satisfied with this advice, though it gave him no prospect of repairing his loss, proceeds to execution. Proteus is catched sleeping, bound with cords, and compelled to speak. He declares, that Aristæus was punished with the loss of his bees, for attempting the chastity of Euridice, the wife of Orpheus; she having got her death by the sting of a serpent in flying his embraces. Proteus, whose sullenness ought to have been converted into wrath by the rough treatment he met with, becomes on a sudden courteous and communicative. He gives the whole history of Orpheus's expedition to hell in order to recover his spouse; a very entertaining story indeed, but without the least relation to the affair on hand. Aristæus returning to his mother, is advised to deprecate by sacrifices the wrath of Orpheus, who was now dead. A bullock is sacrificed, and out of the intrails spring miraculously a swarm of bees. How should this have led any mortal to think, that, without a miracle, the same might be obtained naturally, as is supposed in the receipt?

A list of the different FEET, and of their NAMES.

1. PYRRHICHIUS, consists of two short syllables. Examples: *Deus, given, cannot, hillock, running.*
2. SPONDEUS, consists of two long syllables. Ex. *omnes, possess, forewarn, mankind, sometime.*
3. IAMBUS, composed of a short and a long. Ex. *pios, intent, degree, appear, consent, repent, demand, report, suspect, affront, event.*
4. TROCHÆUS, or CHOREUS, a long and a short. Ex. *fervat, whereby, after, legal, measure, burden, holy, lofty.*
5. TRIBRACHYS, three short. Ex. *melius, property.*
6. MOLOSSUS, three long. Ex. *delectant.*
7. ANAPÆSTUS, two short and a long. Ex. *animos, condescend, apprehend, overheard, acquiesce, immature, overcharge, serenade, opportune.*
8. DACTYLUS, a long and two short. Ex. *carmina, evident, excellence, estimate, wonderful, altitude, burdened, minister, tenement.*
9. BACCHIUS, a short and two long. Ex. *dolores.*
10. HYPPOBACCHIUS, or ANTIBACCHIUS, two long and a short. Ex. *pelluntur.*
11. CRETICUS, or AMPHIMACER, a short syllable betwixt two long. Ex. *infito, afternoon.*
12. AMPHIBRACHYS, a long syllable betwixt two short. Ex. *honore, consider, imprudent, procedure, attended, proposed, respondent, concurrence, apprentice, respective, revenue.*
13. PROCELEUSMATICUS, four short syllables. Ex. *hominibus, necessary.*
14. DISPONDEUS, four long syllables. Ex. *infinitis.*
15. DIIAMBUS, composed of two Iambi. Ex. *severitas.*
16. DITROCHÆUS, of two Trochæi. Ex. *permanere, procurator.*
17. IONICUS, two short syllables and two long. Ex. *properabant.*

18. Another foot passes under the same name, composed of two long syllables and two short. Ex. *calcaribus, possessory*.
19. CHORIAMBUS, two short syllables betwixt two long. Ex. *Nobilitas*.
20. ANTISPASTUS, two long syllables betwixt two short. Ex. *Alexander*.
21. PÆON 1st, one long syllable and three short. Ex. *temporibus, ordinary, inventory, temperament*.
22. PÆON 2d, the second syllable long, and the other three short. Ex. *potentia, rapidity, solemnity, minority, considered, imprudently, extravagant, respectfully, accordingly*.
23. PÆON 3d, the third syllable long and the other three short. Ex. *animatus, independent, condescendence, sacerdotal, reimbursement, manufacture*.
24. PÆON 4th, the last syllable long and the other three short. Ex. *Celeritas*.
25. EPITRITUS 1st, the first syllable short and the other three long. Ex. *voluptates*.
26. EPITRITUS 2d, the second syllable short and the other three long. Ex. *pænitentes*.
27. EPITRITUS 3d, the third syllable short and the other three long. Ex. *discordias*.
28. EPITRITUS 4th, the last syllable short and the other three long. Ex. *fortunatus*.
29. A word of five syllables composed of a Pyrrhichius and Dactylus. Ex. *ministerial*.
30. A word of five syllables composed of a Trochæus and Dactylus. Ex. *singularity*.
31. A word of five syllables composed of a Dactylus and Trochæus. Ex. *precipitation, examination*.
32. A word of five syllables, the second only long. Ex. *necessitated, significancy*.
33. A word of six syllables composed of two Dactyles. Ex. *impetuosity*.
34. A word of six syllables composed of a Tribrachys and Dactyle. Ex. *pusillanimity*.

N. B. Every word may be considered as a prose foot, because every word is distinguished by a pause; and every foot in verse may be considered as a verse word, composed of syllables pronounced at once without a pause.

End of the Second Volume

VOLUME III

XIX

Comparisons

Comparisons, as observed above[1]; serve two different purposes: When addressed to the understanding, their purpose is to instruct; when to the heart, their purpose is to give pleasure. With respect to the latter, a comparison may be employ'd to produce various pleasures by different means. First, by suggesting some unusual resemblance or contrast: second, by setting an object in the strongest light: third, by associating an object with others that are agreeable: fourth, by elevating an object: and, fifth, by depressing it. And that comparisons may produce various pleasures by these different means, appears from what is said in the chapter above cited; and will be made still more evident by examples, which shall be given after premising some general observations.

An object of one sense cannot be compared to an object of another; for such objects are totally separated from each other, and have no circumstance in common to admit either resemblance or contrast. Objects of hearing may be compared, as also of taste, and of touch. But the chief fund of comparison are objects of sight; because, in writing or speaking, things can only be compared in idea, and the ideas of visible objects are by far more lively than those of any other sense.

It has no good effect to compare things by way of simile that are of the same kind, nor to contrast things of different kinds. The reason is given in the chapter cited above; and the reason shall be illustrated by examples. The first is a resemblance instituted betwixt two objects so nearly related as to make little or no impression.

> *This just rebuke inflam'd the Lycian crew,*
> *They join, they thicken, and th' assault renew;*
> *Unmov'd th' embody'd Greeks their fury dare,*
> *And fix'd support the weight of all the war;*
> *Nor could the Greeks repel the Lycian pow'rs,*
> *Nor the bold Lycians force the Grecian tow'rs.*

---

1. Chap. 8.

> *As on the confines of adjoining grounds,*
> *Two stubborn swains with blows dispute their bounds;*
> *They tugg, they sweat; but neither gain, nor yield,*
> *One foot, one inch, of the contended field:*
> *Thus obstinate to death, they fight, they fall;*
> *Nor these can keep, nor those can win the wall.*

—*Iliad*, xii. 505

Another from Milton labours under the same defect. Speaking of the fallen angels searching for mines of gold:

> *A numerous brigade hasten'd: as when bands*
> *Of pioneers with spade and pick-ax arm'd*
> *Forerun the royal camp to trench a field*
> *Or cast a rampart.*

The next shall be of things contrasted that are of different kinds.

QUEEN: What, is my Richard both in shape and mind
   Transform'd and weak? Hath Bolingbroke depos'd
   Thine intellect? Hath he been in thy heart?
   The lion, dying, thrusteth forth his paw,
   And wounds the earth, if nothing else, with rage
   To be o'erpower'd: and wilt thou, pupil-like,
   Take thy correction mildly, kiss the rod,
   And fawn on rage with base humility?

—*Richard II. act 5. sc. 1*

This comparison has scarce any force. A man and a lion are of different species; and there is no such resemblance betwixt them in general, as to produce any strong effect by contrasting particular attributes or circumstances.

A third general observation is, That abstract terms can never be the subject of comparison, otherwise than by being personified. Shakespear compares adversity to a toad, and slander to the bite of a crocodile; but in such comparisons these abstract terms must be imagined sensible beings.

I now proceed to illustrate by particular instances the different means by which comparison can afford pleasure; and, in the order above established, I shall begin with those instances that are agreeable by suggesting some unusual resemblance or contrast:

> *Sweet are the uses of Adversity,*
> *Which, like the toad, ugly and venomous,*
> *Wears yet a precious jewel in her head.*
>
> —*As you like it, act 2, sc. 1*

GARDINER: Bolingbroke hath seiz'd the wasteful King.
  What pity is't that he had not so trimm'd
  And dress'd his land, as we this garden dress,
  And wound the bark, the skin of our fruit-trees;
  Left, being over proud with sap and blood,
  With too much riches it confound itself.
  Had he done so to great and growing men,
  They might have liv'd to bear, and he to taste
  Their fruits of duty. All superfluous branches
  We lop away, that bearing boughs may live:
  Had he done so, himself had borne the crown,
  Which waste and idle hours have quite thrown down.

  —*Richard II. act 3. sc. 7*

> *See, how the Morning opes her golden gates,*
> *And takes her farewell of the glorious sun;*
> *How well resembles it the prime of youth,*
> *Trim'd like a yonker prancing to his love.*
>
> —*Second Part Henry VI. act 2. sc. 1*

BRUTUS: O Cassius, you are yoked with a lamb,
  That carries anger as the flint bears fire;
  Who, much inforced, shows a hasty spark,
  And straight is cold again.

  —*Julius Cæsar, act 4. sc. 3*

> *Thus they their doubtful consultations dark*
> *Ended, rejoicing in their matchless chief:*
> *As when from mountain-tops the dusky clouds,*
> *Ascending, while the North-wind sleeps, o'erspread*
> *Heav'n's chearful face, the lowring element*
> *Scowls o'er the darken'd landscape, snow, and shower;*
> *If chance the radiant sun with farewell sweet*
> *Extend his ev'ning-beam, the fields revive,*
> *The birds their notes renew, and bleating herds*
> *Attest their joy, that hill and valley rings.*
>
> —*Paradise Lost*, book 2

The last exertion of courage compared to the blaze of a lamp before extinguishing, *Tasso Gierusalem*, canto 19. st. 22.

> *As the bright stars, and milky way,*
> *Shew'd by the night, are hid by day:*
> *So we in that accomplish'd mind,*
> *Help'd by the night, new graces find,*
> *Which, by the splendor of her view*
> *Dazzled before, we never knew.*
>
> —*Waller*

None of the foregoing similes, as it appears to me, have the effect to add any lustre to the principal subject; and therefore the pleasure they afford, must arise from suggesting resemblances that are not obvious: I mean the chief pleasure; for undoubtedly a beautiful subject introduced to form the simile affords a separate pleasure, which is felt in the similes mentioned, particularly in that cited from Milton.

The next effect of a comparison in the order mentioned, is to place an object in a strong point of view; which I think is done sensibly in the following similes.

> *As when two scales are charg'd with doubtful loads,*
> *From side to side the trembling balance nods,*
> *(While some laborious matron, just and poor,*
> *With nice exactness weighs her woolly store),*

> *Till pois'd aloft, the resting beam suspends*
> *Each equal weight; nor this nor that descends:*
> *So stood the war, till Hector's matchless might,*
> *With fates prevailing, turn'd the scale of fight.*
> *Fierce as a whirlwind up the walls he flies,*
> *And fires his host with loud repeated cries.*
>
> —*Iliad*, b. xii. 52

> *Ut flos in septis secretis nascitur hortis,*
> *Ignotus pecori, nullo contusus aratro,*
> *Quem mulcent auræ, firmat sol, educat imber,*
> *Multi illum pueri, multæ cupiere puellæ.*
> *Idem, cum tenui carptus defloruit ungui,*
> *Nulli illum pueri, nullæ cupiere puellæ.*
> *Sic virgo, dum intacta manet, dum cara suis; sed*
> *Cum castum amisit, polluto corpore, florem,*
> *Nec pueris jucunda manet, nec cara puellis.*
>
> —*Catullus*

The imitation of this beautiful simile by *Ariosto, canto 1. st. 42*. falls short of the original. It is also in part imitated by Pope[2].

> LUCETTA: I do not seek to quench your love's hot fire, But qualify the fires extreme rage, Lest it should burn above the bounds of reason.
>
> JULIA: The more thou damm'st it up, the more it burns: The current, that with gentle murmur glides, Thou know'st, being stopp'd, impatiently doth rage; But when his fair course is not hindered, He makes sweet music with th' enamel'd stones Giving a gentle kiss to every sedge He overtaketh in his pilgrimage. And so by many winding nooks he strays With willing sport, to the wild ocean. Then let me go, and hinder not my course; I'll be as patient as a gentle stream, And make a pastime of each weary step Till the last step have

---

2. Dunciad, b. 4. 1. 405.

brought me to my love; And there I'll rest, as, after much turmoil, A blessed soul doth in Elysium.

—Two Gentlemen of Verona, act 2. sc. 10

——————— *She never told her love,*
But let concealment, like a worm i' th' bud,
Feed on her damask cheek: she pin'd in thought;
And with a green and yellow melancholy,
She sat like Patience on a monument,
Smiling at Grief.

—Twelfth-Night, act 2. sc. 6

YORK: Then, as I said, the Duke, great Bolingbroke, Mounted upon a hot and fiery steed, Which his aspiring rider seem'd to know, With slow but stately pace, kept on his course: While all tongues cry'd, God save thee, Bolingbroke.

DUCHESS: Alas! poor Richard, where rides he the while?

YORK: As in a theatre, the eyes of men, After a well-grac'd actor leaves the stage, Are idly bent on him that enters next, Thinking his prattle to be tedious: Even so, or with much more contempt, mens eyes Did scowl on Richard; no man cry'd, God save him! No joyful tongue gave him his welcome home; But dust was thrown upon his sacred head; Which with such gentle sorrow he shook off, His face still combating with tears and smiles, The badges of his grief and patience; That had not God, for some strong purpose, steel'd The hearts of men, they must perforce have melted; And barbarism itself have pitied him.

—Richard II. *act 5. sc. 3*

NORTHUMBERLAND: How doth my son and brother?
Thou tremblest, and the whiteness in thy cheek
Is apter than thy tongue to tell thy errand.
Even such a man, so faint, so spiritless,
So dull, so dead in look, so wo-be-gone,
Drew Priam's curtain in the dead of night,
And would have told him, half his Troy was burn'd;

> But Priam found the fire, ere he his tongue:
> And I my Percy's death, ere thou report'st it.
>
> —*Second Part Henry* IV. *act 1. sc. 3*

> *Why, then I do but dream on sov'reignty,*
> *Like one that stands upon a promontory,*
> *And spies a far-off shore where he would tread,*
> *Wishing his foot were equal with his eye,*
> *And chides the sea that sunders him from thence,*
> *Saying, he'll lave it dry to have his way:*
> *So do I wish, the crown being so far off,*
> *And so I chide the means that keep me from it,*
> *And so (I say) I'll cut the causes off,*
> *Flatt'ring my mind with things impossible.*
>
> —*Third Part Henry* VI. *act 3. sc. 3*

> —— *Out, out, brief candle!*
> *Life's but a walking shadow, a poor player,*
> *That struts and frets his hour upon the stage,*
> *And then is heard no more.*
>
> —*Macbeth, act 5. sc. 5*

> *O thou Goddess,*
> *Thou divine Nature! how thyself thou blazon'st*
> *In these two princely boys! they are as gentle*
> *As zephyrs blowing below the violet,*
> *Not wagging his sweet head; and yet as rough,*
> *(Their royal blood inchas'd) as the rud'st wind,*
> *That by the top doth take the mountain-pine,*
> *And make him stoop to th' vale.*
>
> —*Cymbeline, act 4. sc. 4*

The sight obtained of the city of Jerusalem by the Christian army, compared to that of land discovered after a long voyage, Tasso's *Gierusalem, canto 3. st. 4.* The fury of Rinaldo subsiding when not opposed, to that of wind or water when it has a free passage, *canto 20. st. 58.*

As words convey but a faint and obscure notion of great numbers, a poet, to give a high notion of the object he describes with regard to number, does well to compare it to what is familiar and commonly known. Thus Homer[3] compares the Grecian army in point of number to a swarm of bees. In another passage[4] he compares it to that profusion of leaves and flowers which appear in the spring, or of insects in a summer's evening. And Milton,

> —— *As when the potent rod*
> *Of Amram's son in Egypt's evil day*
> *Wav'd round the coast, up call'd a pitchy cloud*
> *Of locusts, warping on the eastern wind,*
> *That o'er the realm of impious Pharaoh hung*
> *Like night, and darken'd all the land of Nile:*
> *So numberless were those bad angels seen,*
> *Hovering on wing under the cope of hell,*
> *'Twixt upper, nether, and surrounding fires.*
>
> —*Paradise Lost, book 1*

Such comparisons have, by some writers[5], been condemned for the lowness of the images introduced: but surely without reason; for, with regard to numbers, they put the principal subject in a strong light.

THE FOREGOING COMPARISONS OPERATE BY resemblance; others have the same effect by contrast:

YORK: I am the last of Noble Edward's sons,
    Of whom thy father, Prince of Wales, was first:
    In war, was never lion rag'd more fierce;
    In peace, was never gentle lamb more mild;
    Than was that young and princely gentleman.
    His face thou hast; for even so look'd he,
    Accomplish'd with the number of thy hours.
    But when he frown'd, it was against the French,
    And not against his friends. His noble hand

---

3. Book 2. 1. 111.
4. Book 2, 1. 551.
5. See Vidæ Poetic, lib. 2. 1. 282.

Did win what he did spend; and spent not that
Which his triumphant father's hand had won.
His hands were guilty of no kindred's blood,
But bloody with the enemies of his kin.
Oh, Richard! York is too far gone with grief,
Or else he never would compare between.

—*Richard* II. *act 2. sc. 3*

Milton has a peculiar talent in embellishing the principal subject by associating it with others that are agreeable, which is the third end of a comparison. Similes of this kind have, beside, a separate effect: they diversify the narration by new images that are not strictly necessary to the comparison: they are short episodes, which, without distracting us from the principal subject, afford great delight by their beauty and variety:

He scarce had ceas'd, when the superior fiend
Was moving toward the shore; his pond'rous shield,
Ethereal temper, massy, large, and round,
Behind him cast; the broad circumference
Hung on his shoulders like the moon, whose orb
Through optic glass the Tuscan artist views
At ev'ning from the top of Fesole,
Or in Valdarno, to descry new lands,
Rivers, or mountains, in her spotty globe.

—*Milton, b. 1*

—— *Thus far these, beyond*
Compare of mortal prowess, yet observ'd
Their dread commander. He, above the rest
In shape and gesture proudly eminent,
Stood like a tow'r; his form had yet not lost
All her original brightness, nor appear'd
Less than arch-angel ruin'd, and th' excess
Of glory obscur'd: as when the sun new-risen
Looks through the horizontal misty air
Shorn of his beams; or from behind the moon
In dim eclipse, disastrous twilight sheds

On half the nations, and with fear of change
Perplexes monarchs.

—Milton, b. 1

As when a vulture on Imaus bred,
Whose snowy ridge the roving Tartar bounds,
Dislodging from a region scarce of prey
To gorge the flesh of lambs, or yeanling kids,
On hills where flocks are fed, flies toward the springs
Of Ganges or Hydaspes, Indian streams,
But in his way lights on the barren plains
Of Sericana, where Chineses drive
With sails and wind their cany waggons light:
So on this windy sea of land, the fiend
Walk'd up and down alone, bent on his prey.

—Milton, b. 3

—— Yet higher than their tops
The verdurous wall of Paradise up sprung:
Which to our general sire gave prospect large
Into this nether empire neighbouring round.
And higher than that wall, a circling row
Of goodliest trees loaden with fairest fruit,
Blossoms and fruits at once of golden hue,
Appear'd, with gay enamel'd colours mix'd,
On which the sun more glad impress'd his beams
Than in fair evening cloud, or humid bow,
When God hath show'r'd the earth; so lovely seem'd
That landscape: and of pure now purer air
Meets his approach, and to the heart inspires
Vernal delight and joy, able to drive
All sadness but despair: now gentle gales
Fanning their odoriferous wings dispense
Native perfumes, and whisper whence they stole
Those balmy spoils. As when to them who sail
Beyond the Cape of Hope, and now are past
Mozambic, off at sea North-east winds blow
Sabean odour from the spicy shore

> *Of Arabie the Blest; with such delay*
> *Well pleas'd they slack their course, and many a league,*
> *Chear'd with the grateful smell, old Ocean smiles.*

> —*Milton, b.* 4

With regard to similes of this kind, it will readily occur to the reader, that when the resembling subject or circumstance is once properly introduced in a simile, the mind passes easily to the new objects, and is transitorily amused with them, without feeling any disgust at the slight interruption. Thus, in fine weather, the momentary excursions of a traveller for agreeable prospects or sumptuous buildings, chear his mind, relieve him from the langour of uniformity, and without much lengthening his journey in reality, shorten it greatly in appearance.

NEXT OF COMPARISONS THAT AGGRANDIZE or elevate. These make stronger impressions than any other sort; the reason of which may be gathered from the chapter of grandeur and sublimity, and, without reasoning, will be evident from the following instances.

> *As when a flame the winding valley fills,*
> *And runs on crackling shrubs between the hills,*
> *Then o'er the stubble up the mountain flies,*
> *Fires the high woods, and blazes to the skies,*
> *This way and that, the spreading torrent roars;*
> *So sweeps the hero through the wasted shores.*
> *Around him wide, immense destruction pours,*
> *And earth is delug'd with the sanguine show'rs.*

> —*Iliad* xx. 569

> *Through blood, through death, Achilles still proceeds,*
> *O'er slaughter'd heroes, and o'er rolling steeds.*
> *As when avenging flames with fury driv'n*
> *On guilty towns exert the wrath of Heav'n,*
> *The pale inhabitants, some fall, some fly,*
> *And the red vapours purple all the sky.*
> *So rag'd Achilles: Death, and dire dismay,*
> *And toils, and terrors, fill'd the dreadful day.*

> —*Iliad* xxi. 605

> *Methinks, King Richard and myself should meet*
> *With no less terror than the elements*
> *Of fire and water, when their thund'ring shock,*
> *At meeting tears the cloudy cheeks of heaven.*

> —*Richard* II. act. 3. sc. 5

I beg peculiar attention to the following simile, for a reason that shall be mentioned.

> *Thus breathing death, in terrible array,*
> *The close-compacted legions urg'd their way:*
> *Fierce they drove on, impatient to destroy;*
> *Troy charg'd the first, and Hector first of Troy.*
> *As from some mountain's craggy forehead torn,*
> *A rock's round fragment flies with fury born,*
> *(Which from the stubborn stone a torrent rends)*
> *Precipitate the pond'rous mass descends:*
> *From steep to steep the rolling ruin bounds:*
> *At every shock the crackling wood resounds;*
> *Still gath'ring force, it smoaks; and urg'd amain,*
> *Whirls, leaps, and thunders down, impetuous to the plain:*
> *There stops—So Hector. Their whole force he prov'd,*
> *Resistless when he rag'd; and when he stopt, unmov'd.*

> —*Iliad* xiii. 187

The image of a falling rock is certainly not elevating[6]. Yet undoubtedly the foregoing image fires and swells the mind. It is grand therefore, if not sublime. And that there is a real, though delicate distinction, betwixt these two feelings, will be illustrated from the following simile.

> *So saying, a noble stroke he lifted high,*
> *Which hung not, but so swift with tempest fell*
> *On the proud crest of Satan, that no sight,*
> *Nor motion of swift thought, less could his shield*
> *Such ruin intercept. Ten paces huge*

---

6. See chap. 4.

> *He back recoil'd; the tenth on bended knee*
> *His massy spear upstaid; as if on earth*
> *Winds under ground or waters forcing way*
> *Sidelong had push'd a mountain from his seat*
> *Half sunk with all pines.*
>
> —*Milton, b. 6*

A comparison by contrast may contribute to grandeur or elevation, not less than by resemblance; of which the following comparison of Lucan is a remarkable instance.

> *Victrix causa diis placuit, sed victa Catoni.*

Considering that the Heathen deities possessed a rank but one degree above that of mankind, I think it scarce possible, by a single expression, to elevate or dignify more one of the human species, than is done by this comparison. I am sensible, at the same time, that such a comparison among Christians, who entertain juster notions of the Deity, would justly be reckoned extravagant and absurd.

THE LAST ARTICLE MENTIONED, IS that of lessening or depressing a hated or disagreeable object; which is effectually done by resembling it to anything that is low or despicable. Thus Milton, in his description of the rout of the rebel-angels, happily expresses their terror and dismay in the following simile.

> ——— *As a herd*
> *Of goats or timorous flock together throng'd*
> *Drove them before him thunder-struck, pursu'd*
> *With terrors and with furies to the bounds*
> *And crystal wall of heav'n, which op'ning wide,*
> *Rowl'd inward, and a spacious gap disclos'd*
> *Into the wasteful deep; the monstrous sight*
> *Strook them with horror backward, but far worse*
> *Urg'd them behind; headlong themselves they threw*
> *Down from the verge of heav'n.*
>
> —*Milton, b. 6*

In the same view, Homer, I think, may be defended, in comparing the shouts of the Trojans in battle, to the noise of cranes[7], and to the bleating of a flock of sheep[8]: and it is no objection, that these are low images; for by opposing the noisy march of the Trojans to the silent and manly march of the Greeks, he certainly intended to lessen the former. Addison[9], imagining the figure that men make in the sight of a superior being, takes opportunity to mortify their pride by comparing them to a swarm of pismires.

A comparison that has none of the good effects mentioned in this discourse, but is built upon common and trifling circumstances, makes a mighty silly figure: "Non sum nescius, grandia consilia a multis plerumque causis, ceu magna navigia a plurimis remis, impelli."

By this time I imagine the different purposes of comparison, and the various impressions it makes on the mind, are sufficiently illustrated by proper examples. This was an easy work. It is more difficult to lay down rules about the propriety or impropriety of comparisons; in what circumstances they may be introduced, and in what circumstances they are out of place. It is evident, that a comparison is not proper upon every occasion; a man in his cool and sedate moments, is not disposed to poetical flights, nor to sacrifice truth and reality to the delusive operations of the imagination; far less is he so disposed, when oppressed with cares, or interested in some important transaction that occupies him totally. The region of comparison and of all figurative expression, lies betwixt these two extremes. It is observable, that a man, when elevated or animated by any passion, is disposed to elevate or animate all his objects: he avoids familiar names, exalts objects by circumlocution and metaphor, and gives even life and voluntary action to inanimate beings. In this warmth of mind, the highest poetical flights are indulged, and the boldest similes and metaphors relished[10]. But without soaring so high, the mind is frequently in a tone to relish chaste and moderate ornament; such as comparisons that set the principal object in a strong point of view, or that embellish and diversify the narration. In general, when by any animating passion, whether pleasant or painful, an impulse is given to the imagination; we

---

7. Beginning of book 3.
8. Book 4. 1. 498.
9. Guardian. No. 153.
10. It is accordingly observed by Longinus, in his Treatise of the Sublime, that the proper time for metaphor, is when the passions are so swelled as to hurry on like a torrent.

are in that condition wonderfully disposed to every sort of figurative expression, and in particular to comparisons. This in a great measure is evident from the comparisons already mentioned; and shall be further illustrated by other examples. Love, for example, in its infancy, rousing the imagination, prompts the heart to display itself in figurative language, and in similes:

> TROILUS: Tell me, Apollo, for thy Daphne's love,
>   What Cressid is, what Pandar, and what we?
> Her bed is India, there she lies, a pearl:
> Between our Ilium, and where she resides,
> Let it be call'd the wild and wandering flood;
> Ourself the merchant, and this sailing Pandar
> Our doubtful hope, our convoy, and our bark.
>
> —*Troilus and Cressida, act 1. sc. 1*

Again,

> *Come, gentle Night; come, loving black-brow'd Night!*
> *Give me my Romeo; and, when he shall die,*
> *Take him, and cut him out in little stars,*
> *And he will make the face of heav'n so fine,*
> *That all the world shall be in love with Night*
> *And pay no worship to the garish sun.*
>
> —*Romeo and Juliet, act 3. sc. 4*

The dread of a misfortune, however imminent, involving always some doubt and uncertainty, agitates the mind, and excites the imagination:

> WOLSEY:—— Nay, then, farewell;
>   I've touch'd the highest point of all my greatness;
> And from that full meridian of my glory
> I haste now to my setting. I shall fall,
> Like a bright exhalation in the evening,
> And no man see me more.
>
> —*Henry VIII. act 3. sc. 4*

But it will be a better illustration of the present head, to give examples where comparisons are improperly introduced. I have had already occasion to observe, that similes are not the language of a man in his ordinary state of mind, going about the common affairs of life. For that reason, the following speech of a gardiner to his servants, is extremely improper.

> *Go bind thou up yon dangling apricocks*
> *Which, like unruly children, make their sire*
> *Stoop with oppression of their prodigal weight:*
> *Give some supportance to the bending twigs.*
> *Go thou, and like an executioner,*
> *Cut off the heads of too-fast-growing sprays,*
> *That look too lofty in our commonwealth:*
> *All must be even in our government.*
>
> *—Richard II. act 3. sc. 7*

The fertility of Shakespear's vein betrays him frequently into this error. There is the same impropriety in another simile of his:

HERO: Good Margaret, run thee into the parlour;
    There shalt thou find my cousin Beatrice;
    Whisper her ear, and tell her, I and Ursula
    Walk in the orchard, and our whole discourse
    Is all of her; say, that thou overheard'st us:
    And bid her steal into the pleached bower,
    Where honeysuckles, ripen'd by the sun,
    Forbid the sun to enter; like to favourites,
    Made proud by princes, that advance their pride
    Against that power that bred it.

—Much ado about nothing, act 3. sc. 1

Rooted grief, deep anguish, terror, remorse, despair, and all the severe dispiriting passions, are declared enemies, perhaps not to figurative language in general, but undoubtedly to the pomp and solemnity of comparison. Upon this account the simile pronounced by young Rutland under terror of death from an inveterate enemy, and praying mercy, is unnatural:

> *So looks the pent-up lion o'er the wretch*
> *That trembles under his devouring paws;*
> *And so he walks insulting o'er his prey,*
> *And so he comes to rend his limbs asunder.*
> *Ah, gentle Clifford, kill me with thy sword,*
> *And not with such a cruel threat'ning look.*
>
> —*Third part Henry VI. act 1. sc. 5*

Nothing appears more out of place, or more aukwardly introduced, than the following simile.

> Lucia:————Farewell, my Portius,
>   Farewell, though death is in the word, *forever*!
> Portius: Stay, Lucia, stay; what dost thou say, *forever*?
> Lucia: Have I not sworn? If, Portius, thy success
>   Must throw thy brother on his fate, farewell:
>   Oh, how shall I repeat the word *forever*!
> Portius: Thus, o'er the dying lamp th' unsteady flame
>   Hangs quivering on a point, leaps off by fits,
>   And falls again, as loath to quit its hold.
>   —Thou must not go, my soul still hovers o'er thee,
>   And can't get loose.
>
> —*Cato, act 3. sc. 2*

Nor doth the simile which closes the first act of the same tragedy, make its appearance with a much better grace; the situation there represented, being too dispiriting for a simile. A simile is improper for one who dreads the discovery of a secret machination.

> Zara: The mute not yet return'd! Ha! 'twas the King,
>   The King that parted hence! frowning he went;
>   His eyes like meteors roll'd, then darted down
>   Their red and angry beams; as if his sight
>   Would, like the raging Dog-star, scorch the earth,
>   And kindle ruin in its course.
>
> —*Mourning Bride, act 5. sc. 3*

A man spent and dispirited after losing a battle, is not disposed to heighten or illustrate his discourse by similes:

> YORK: With this we charg'd again; but out! alas,
> We bodg'd again; as I have seen a swan
> With bootless labour swim against the tide,
> And spend her strength with over-matching waves.
> Ah! hark, the fatal followers do pursue.
> And I am faint and cannot fly their fury.
> The sands are number'd that make up my life;
> Here must I stay, and here my life must end.
>
> —*Third part Henry VI. act 1. sc. 6*

Far less is a man disposed to similes who is not only defeated in a pitch'd battle, but lies at the point of death mortally wounded.

> WARWICK:———— My mangled body shews,
> My blood, my want of strength, my sick heart shews,
> That I must yield my body to the earth,
> And, by my fall, the conquest to my foe.
> Thus yields the cedar to the ax's edge,
> Whose arms gave shelter to the princely eagle;
> Under whose shade the ramping lion slept,
> Whose top-branch overpeer'd Jove's spreading tree,
> And kept low shrubs from winter's pow'rful wind.
>
> —*Third part Henry VI. act 5. sc. 3*

Queen Katharine, deserted by the King and in the deepest affliction upon her divorce, could not be disposed to any sallies of imagination: and for that reason, the following simile, however beautiful in the mouth of a spectator, is scarce proper in her own.

> *I am the most unhappy woman living,*
> *Shipwreck'd upon a kingdom, where no pity,*
> *No friends, no hope! no kindred weep for me!*
> *Almost no grave allowed me! like the lily,*
> *That once was mistress of the field, and flourish'd,*
> *I'll hang my head and perish.*
>
> —*King Henry VIII. act 3. sc. 1*

Similes thus unseasonably introduced, are finely ridiculed in the *Rehearsal*:

BAYES: Now here she must make a simile.
SMITH: Where's the necessity of that, Mr. Bayes?
BAYES: Because she's surpris'd; that's a general rule; you must ever make a simile when you are surprised; 'tis a new way of writing.

A comparison is not always faultless, even where it is properly introduced. I have endeavoured above to give a general view of the different ends to which a comparison may contribute. A comparison, like other human productions, may fall short of its end; and of this defect instances are not rare even among good writers. To complete the present subject, it will be necessary to make some observations upon such faulty comparisons. I begin with observing, that nothing can be more erroneous than to institute a comparison too faint: a distant resemblance or contrast, fatigues the mind with its obscurity instead of amusing it, and tends not to fulfil anyone end of a comparison. The following similes seem to labour under this defect:

Albus ut obscuro deterget nubila cœlo
Sæpe Notus, neque parturit imbres
Perpetuos: sic tu sapiens finire memento
Tristitiam vitæque labores
Molli, Plance, mero.

—*Horace, Carm. l. 1. ode 7*

—— *Medio dux agmine Turnus*
Vertitur arma tenens, et toto vertice supra est,
Ceu septem surgens sedatis amnibus altus
Per tacitum Ganges: aut pingui flumine Nilus
Cum refluit campis, et jam se condidit alveo.

—*Æneid ix. 28*

Talibus orabat, talesque miserrima fletus
Fertque refertque soror; sed nullus ille movetur
Fletibus, aut voces ullas tractabilis audit.
Fata obstant: placidasque viri Deus obstruit aures.

> *Ac veluti annoso validam cum robore quercum*
> *Alpini Boreæ, nunc hinc, nunc flatibus illinc*
> *Eruere inter se certant; it stridor; et alte*
> *Consternunt terram concusso stipite frondes:*
> *Ipsa hæret scopulis: et quantum vertice ad auras*
> *Æthereas, tantum radice in tartara tendit.*
> *Haud secus assiduis hinc atque hinc vocibus heros*
> *Tunditur, et magno persentit pectore curas:*
> *Mens immota manet, lacrymæ volvuntur inanes.*

—Æneid iv. 437

K. RICH: Give me the crown.—Here, cousin, seize the crown,
Here, on this side, my hand; on that side, thine.
Now is this golden crown like a deep well,
That owes two buckets, filling one another;
The emptier ever dancing in the air,
The other down, unseen and full of water;
That bucket down, and full of tears, am I;
Drinking my griefs, whilst you mount up on high.

—Richard II. act 4. sc. 3

KING JOHN: Oh! Cousin, thou art come to set mine eye;
The tackle of my heart is crack'd and burnt;
And all the shrowds wherewith my life should sail,
Are turned to one thread, one little hair:
My heart hath one poor string to stay it by,
Which holds but till thy news be uttered.

—King John, act 5. sc. 10

YORK: My uncles both are slain in rescuing me:
And all my followers, to the eager foe
Turn back, and fly like ships before the wind,
Or lambs pursu'd by hunger-starved wolves.

—Third Part Henry VI. act 1. sc. 6

The latter of the two similes is good. The former, because of the faintness of the resemblance, produces no good effect, and crowds the narration with an useless image.

The next error I shall mention is a capital one. In an epic poem, or in any elevated subject, a writer ought to avoid raising a simile upon a low image, which never fails to bring down the principal subject. In general, it is a rule, that a grand object ought never to be resembled to one that is diminutive, however delicate the resemblance may be. It is the peculiar character of a grand object to fix the attention, and swell the mind: in this state, it is disagreeable to contract the mind to a minute object, however elegant. The resembling an object to one that is greater, has, on the contrary, a good effect, by raising or swelling the mind. One passes with satisfaction from a small to a great object; but cannot be drawn down, without reluctance, from great to small. Hence the following similes are faulty.

> *Meanwhile the troops beneath Patroculus' care,*
> *Invade the Trojans, and commence the war.*
> *As wasps, provok'd by children in their play,*
> *Pour from their mansions by the broad high-way,*
> *In swarms the guiltless traveller engage,*
> *Whet all their stings, and call forth all their rage;*
> *All rise in arms, and with a general cry*
> *Assert their waxen domes, and buzzing progeny:*
> *Thus from the tents the fervent legion swarms,*
> *So loud their clamours, and so keen their arms.*

—*Iliad* xvi. 312

> *So burns the vengeful hornet (soul all o'er)*
> *Repuls'd in vain, and thirsty still of gore;*
> *(Bold son of air and heat) on angry wings*
> *Untam'd, untir'd, he turns, attacks and stings.*
> *Fir'd with like ardour fierce Atrides flew,*
> *And sent his soul with ev'ry lance he threw.*

—*Iliad* xvii. 642

> *Instant ardentes Tyrii: pars ducere muros,*
> *Molirique arcem, er manibus subvolvere saxa;*
> *Pars aptare locum tecto, et concludere sulco.*
> *Jura magistratusque legunt, sanctumque senatum.*
> *Hic portus alii effodiunt: hic alta theatris*

> *Fundamenta locant alii, immanesque columnas*
> *Rupibus excidunt, scenis decora alta futuris.*
> *Quails apes æstate nova per florea rura*
> *Exercet sub sole labor, cum gentis adultos*
> *Educunt fœtus, aut cum liquentia mella*
> *Stipant, et dulci distendunt nectare cellas,*
> *Aut onera accipiunt venientum, aut agmine facto*
> *Ignavum fucos pecus a præsepibus arcent.*
> *Fervet opus, redolentque thymo fragrantia mella.*
>
> —*Æneid* i. 427

To describe bees gathering honey as resembling the builders of Carthage, would have a much better effect.

> *Tum vero Teucri incumbunt, et littore celsas*
> *Deducunt toto naves: natat uncta carina;*
> *Frondentesque ferunt remos, et robora sylvis*
> *Infabricata, fugæ studio.*
> *Migrantes cernas, totaque ex urbe ruentes.*
> *Ac veluti ingentem formicæ farris acervum*
> *Cum populant, hyemis memores, tectoque reponunt:*
> *It nigrum campis agmen, prædamque per herbas*
> *Convectant calle angusto: pars grandia trudunt*
> *Obnixæ frumenta humeris: pars agmina cogunt,*
> *Castigantque moras: opere omnis semita fervet.*
>
> —*Æneid.* iv. 397

The following simile has not anyone beauty to recommend it. The subject is Amata the wife of King Latinus.

> *Tum vero infelix, ingentibus excita monstris,*
> *Immensam sine more furit lymphata per urbem:*
> *Ceu quondam torto volitans sub verbere turbo,*
> *Quem pueri magno in gyro vacua atria circum*
> *Intenti ludo exercent. Ille actus habena*
> *Curvatis fertur spatiis: stupet inscia turba,*
> *Impubesque manus, mirata volubile buxum:*

> *Dant animos plagæ. Non cursu segnior illo*
> *Per medias urbes agitur, populosque feroces.*
>
> —*Æneid.* vii. 376

This simile seems to border upon the burlesque.

An error opposite to the former, is the introducing a resembling image, so elevated or great as to bear no proportion to the principal subject. The remarkable disparity betwixt them, being the most striking circumstance, seizes the mind, and never fails to depress the principal subject by contrast, instead of raising it by resemblance: and if the disparity be exceeding great, the simile takes on an air of burlesque; nothing being more ridiculous than to force an object out of its proper rank in nature, by equalling it with one greatly superior or greatly inferior. This will be evident from the following comparisons.

> *Fervet opus, redolentque thymo fragrantia mella.*
> *Ac veluti lentis Cyclopes fulmina massis*
> *Cum properant: alii taurinis follibus auras*
> *Accipiunt, redduntque: alii stridentia tingunt*
> *Æra lacu: gemit impositis incudibus Ætna:*
> *Illi inter sese magna vi brachia tollunt*
> *In numerum; versantque tenaci forcipe ferrum.*
> *Non aliter (si parva licet componere magnis)*
> *Cecropias innatus apes amor urget habendi,*
> *Munere quamque suo. Grandævis oppida curæ,*
> *Et munire favos, et Dædala fingere tecta.*
> *At fessæ multâ referunt se necte minores,*
> *Crura thymo plenæ: pascuntur et arbuta passim,*
> *Et glaucas salices, casiamque crocumque rubentem,*
> *Et pinguem tiliam, et ferrugineos hyacinthos.*
> *Omnibus una quies operum, labor omnibus unus.*
>
> —*Georgic.* iv. 169

> *Tum Bitian ardentem oculis animisque frementem;*
> *Non jaculo, neque enim jaculo vitam ille dedisset;*
> *Sed magnum stridens contorta falarica venit*
> *Fulminis acta modo, quam nec duo taurea terga,*
> *Nec duplici squama lorica fidelis et auro*

> *Sustinuit: collapsa ruunt immania membra:*
> *Dat tellus gemitum, et clypeum super intonat ingens.*
> *Qualis in Euboico Baiarum littore quondam*
> *Saxea pila cadit, magnis quam molibus ante*
> *Constructam jaciunt ponto: sic illa ruinam*
> *Prona trahit, penitusque vadis illisa recumbit:*
> *Miscent se maria, et nigræ attolluntur arenæ:*
> *Tum sonitu Prochyta alta tremit, durumque cubile*
> *Inarime Jovis imperiis imposta Typhoëo.*
>
> —*Æneid.* ix. 703

> *Loud as a bull makes hill and valley ring,*
> *So roar'd the lock when it releas'd the spring.*
>
> —*Odyssey* xxi. 51

Such a simile upon the simplest of all actions, that of opening a lock, is pure burlesque.

A writer of delicacy will avoid drawing his comparisons from any image that is nauseous, ugly, or remarkably disagreeable: for however strong the resemblance may be, more will be lost than gained by such comparison. Therefore I cannot help condemning, though with some reluctance, the following simile, or rather metaphor.

> *O thou fond many! with what loud applause*
> *Did'st thou beat heav'n with blessing Bolingbroke*
> *Before he was what thou wou'dst have him be?*
> *And now being trimm'd up in thine own desires,*
> *Thou, beastly feeder, art so full of him,*
> *That thou provok'st thyself to cast him up.*
> *And so, thou common dog, didst thou disgorge*
> *Thy glutton bosom of the royal Richard,*
> *And now thou wou'dst eat thy dead vomit up,*
> *And howl'st to find it.*
>
> —*Second Part Henry IV.* act 1. sc. 6

The strongest objection that can lie against a comparison, is, that it consists in words only, not in sense. Such false coin, or bastard wit, does extremely well in burlesque; but is far below the dignity of the epic, or of any serious composition:

> *The noble sister of Poplicola,*
> *The moon of Rome; chaste as the isicle*
> *That's curdled by the frost from purest snow,*
> *And hangs on Dian's temple.*
>
> —*Coriolanus,* act 5. sc. 3

There is evidently no resemblance betwixt an isicle and a woman, chaste or unchaste. But chastity is cold in a metaphorical sense, and an isicle is cold in a proper sense; and this verbal resemblance, in the hurry and glow of composing, has been thought a sufficient foundation for the simile. Such phantom similes are mere witticisms, which ought to have no quarter, except where purposely introduced to provoke laughter. Lucian, in his dissertation upon history, talking of a certain author, makes the following comparison, which is verbal merely.

This author's descriptions are so cold, that they surpass the Caspian snow, and all the ice of the north.

Virgil has not escaped this puerility:

> —— *Galathæa thymo mihi dulcior Hyblæ.*
>
> —*Bucol.* vii. 37
>
> —— *Ego Sardois videar tibi amarior herbis.*
>
> —*Ibid.* 41
>
> *Gallo, cujus amor tantum mihi crescit in horas,*
> *Quantum vere novo viridis se subjicit alnus.*
>
> —*Buccol.* x. 73

Nor Tasso, in his Aminta:

> *Picciola e' l'ape, e fa col picciol morso*
> *Pur gravi, e pur moleste le ferite;*
> *Ma, qual cosa é più picciola d'amore,*
> *Se in ogni breve spatio entra, e s'asconde*

> *In ogni breve spatio? hor, sotto a l'ombra*
> *De le palpebre, hor trà minuti rivi*
> *D'un biondo crine, hor dentro le pozzette,*
> *Che forma un dolce riso in bella guancia;*
> *E pur fá tanto grandi, e si mortali,*
> *E cosi immedicabili le piaghe.*
>
> —*Act 2. sc. 1*

Nor Boileau, the chastest of all writers; and that even in his art of poetry:

> *Ainsi tel autrefois, qu'on vit avec Faret*
> *Charbonner de ses vers les murs d'un cabaret,*
> *S'en va mal a' propos, d'une voix insolente,*
> *Chanter du peuple He'breu la suite triomphante,*
> *Et poursuivant Moise au travers des déserts,*
> *Court avec Pharaon se noyer dans les mers.*
>
> —*Chant. 1. l. 21*

> —— *But for their spirits and souls*
> *This word* rebellion *had froze them up*
> *As fish are in a pond.*
>
> —*Second Part Henry IV. act 1. sc. 3*

QUEEN: The pretty vaulting sea refus'd to drown me;
    Knowing, that thou wou'dst have me drown'd on shore
    With tears as salt as sea, through thy unkindness.

—*Second Part Henry VI. act 3. sc. 6*

Here there is no manner of resemblance but in the word *drown*; for there is no real resemblance betwixt being drown'd at sea, and dying of grief at land. But perhaps this sort of tinsel wit, may have a propriety in it, when used to express an affected, not a real, passion, which was the Queen's case.

Pope has several similes of the same stamp. I shall transcribe one or two from the *Essay on Man*, the gravest and most instructive of all his performances.

> *And hence one master-passion in the breast,*
> *Like Aaron's serpent, swallows up the rest.*
>
> —*Epist. 2. l. 131*

And again, talking of this same ruling or master passion.

> *Nature its mother, Habit is its nurse;*
> *Wit, spirit, faculties, but make it worse;*
> *Reason itself but gives it edge and pow'r;*
> *As heav'n's blest beam turns vinegar more sowr.*
>
> —*Ibid. l. 145*

Lord Bolingbroke, speaking of historians:

Where their sincerity as to fact is doubtful, we strike out truth by the confrontation of different accounts; as we strike out sparks of fire by the collision of flints and steel.

Let us vary the phrase a very little, and there will not remain a shadow of resemblance. Thus, for example:

We discover truth by the confrontation of different accounts; as we strike out sparks of fire by the collision of flints and steel.

Racine makes Pyrrhus say to Andromaque,

> *Vaincu, chargé de fers, de regrets consumé,*
> *Brulé de plus de feux que je n'en allumai,*
> *Helas! fus-je jamais si cruel que vous l'etés?*

And Orestes, in the same strain:

> *Que les Scythes sont moins cruels qu' Hermione.*

Similes of this kind put one in mind of a ludicrous French song:

> *Je croyois Janneton*
> *Aussi douce que belle:*
> *Je croyois Janneton*
> *Plus douce qu'un mouton;*

> *Helas! helas!*
> *Elle est cent fois, mille fois, plus cruelle*
> *Que n'est le tigre aux bois.*

Again,

> *Helas! l'amour m'a pris,*
> *Comme le chat fait la souris.*

A vulgar Irish ballad begins thus:

> *I have as much love in store*
> *As there's apples in Portmore.*

Where the subject is burlesque or ludicrous, such similes are far from being improper. Horace says pleasantly,

> *Quanquam tu levior cortice.*
>
> —*L. 3. ode 9*

And Shakespear,

In breaking oaths he's stronger than Hercules.

And this leads me to observe, that beside the foregoing comparisons, which are all serious, there is a species, the end and purpose of which is to excite gaiety or mirth. Take the following examples.

Falstaff, speaking to his page:

I do here walk before thee, like a sow that hath overwhelmed all her litter but one.

Second Part Henry IV. act 1. sc. 4

I think he is not a pick-purse, nor a horse-stealer; but for his verity in love, I do think him as concave as a cover'd goblet, or a worm-eaten nut.

As you like it, act 3. sc. 10

> *This sword a dagger had his page,*
> *That was but little for his age;*
> *And therefore waited on him so*
> *As dwarfs upon knights-errant do.*
>
> —*Hudibras, canto 1*

Desciption of Hudibras's horse:

> *He was well stay'd, and in his gait*
> *Preserv'd a grave, majestic state.*
> *At spur or switch no more he skipt,*
> *Or mended pace, than Spaniard whipt:*
> *And yet so fiery he would bound,*
> *As if he griev'd to touch the ground:*
> *That Cæsar's horse, who, as fame goes,*
> *Had corns upon his feet and toes,*
> *Was not by half so tender hooft,*
> *Nor trod upon the ground so soft.*
> *And as that beast would kneel and stoop,*
> *(Some write) to take his rider up;*
> *So Hudibras his ('tis well known)*
> *Would often do, to set him down.*
>
> —*Canto 1*

> *Honour is, like a widow, won*
> *With brisk attempt and putting on,*
> *With entering manfully, and urging;*
> *Not slow approaches, like a virgin.*
>
> —*Canto 1*

> *The sun had long since in the lap*
> *Of Thetis taken out his nap;*
> *And, like a lobster boil'd, the morn*
> *From black to red began to turn.*
>
> —*Part 2. canto 2*

Books, like men, their authors, have but one way of coming into the world; but there are ten thousand to go out of it, and return no more.

Tale of a Tub

And in this the world may perceive the difference between the integrity of a generous author, and that of a common friend. The latter is observed to adhere close in prosperity, but on the decline of fortune, to drop suddenly off: whereas the generous author, just on the contrary, finds his hero on the dunghill, from thence by gradual steps raises him to a throne, and then immediately withdraws, expecting not so much as thanks for his pains.

Tale of a Tub

The most accomplish'd way of using books at present is, to serve them as some do lords, learn their *titles*, and then brag of their acquaintance.

Tale of a Tub

Box'd in a chair, the beau impatient sits,
While spouts run clatt'ring o'er the roof by fits;
And ever and anon with frightful din
The leather sounds; he trembles from within.
So when Troy chairmen bore the wooden steed,
Pregnant with Greeks, impatient to be freed,
(Those bully Greeks, who, as the moderns do,
Instead of paying chairmen, run them through),
Laocoon struck the outside with his spear,
And each imprison'd hero quak'd for fear.

—*Description of a city shower. Swift*

Clubs, diamonds, hearts, in wild disorder seen,
With throngs promiscuous strow the level green.
Thus when dispers'd a routed army runs,
Of Asia's troops, and Afric's sable sons,
With like confusion different nations fly,
Of various habit, and of various dye,

> *The pierc'd battalions disunited, fall*
> *In heaps on heaps; one fate o'erwhelms them all.*
>
> —*Rape of the Lock, canto 3*

He does not consider, that sincerity in love is as much out of fashion as sweet snuff; no body takes it now.

Careless Husband

LADY EASY: My dear, I am afraid you have provoked her a little too far.

SIR CHARLES: O! Not at all. You shall see, I'll sweeten her, and she'll cool like a dish of tea.

—Ibid

XX

Figures

The reader must not expect to find here a complete list of the different tropes and figures that have been carefully noted by ancient critics and grammarians. Tropes and figures have indeed been multiplied with so little reserve, as to make it no easy matter to distinguish them from plain language. A discovery almost accidental, made me think of giving them a place in this work: I found that the most important of them depend on principles formerly explained; and I was glad of an opportunity to show the extensive influence of these principles. Confining myself therefore to figures that answer this purpose, I am luckily freed from much trash; without dropping, so far as I remember, any figure that merits a proper name. And I begin with Prosopopœia or personification, which is justly intitled to the first place.

Section. I

Personification.

This figure, which gives life to things inanimate, is so bold a delusion as to require, one should imagine, very peculiar circumstances for operating the effect. And yet, in the language of poetry, we find variety of expressions, which, though commonly reduced to this figure, are used without ceremony or any sort of preparation. I give, for example, the following expressions. *Thirsty* ground, *hungry* church-yard, *furious* dart, *angry* ocean. The epithets here, in their proper meaning, are attributes of sensible beings. What is the effect of such epithets, when apply'd to things inanimate? Do they raise in the mind of the reader a perception of sensibility? Do they make him conceive the ground, the church-yard, the dart, the ocean, to be endued with animal functions? This is a curious inquiry; and whether so or not, it cannot be declined in handling the present subject.

One thing is certain, that the mind is prone to bestow sensibility upon things inanimate, where that violent effect is necessary to gratify passion. This is one instance, among many, of the power of passion to adjust our opinions and belief to its gratification. I give the following examples. Antony, mourning over the body of Cæsar, murdered in the senate-house, vents his passion in the following words.

> ANTONY: O pardon me, thou bleeding piece of earth,
>   That I am meek and gentle with these butchers.
>   Thou art the ruins of the noblest man
>   That ever lived in the tide of times.
>
> —*Julius Cæsar*, act 3. sc. 4

Here Antony must have been impressed with some sort of notion, that the body of Cæsar was listening to him, without which the speech would be foolish and absurd. Nor will it appear strange, after what is said in the chapter above cited, that passion should have such power over the mind of man. Another example of the same kind is, where the earth, as a common mother, is animated to give refuge against a father's unkindness.

> ALMERIA: O Earth, behold, I kneel upon thy bosom,
>   And bend my flowing eyes to stream upon
>   Thy face, imploring thee that thou wilt yield;
>   Open thy bowels of compassion, take
>   Into thy womb the last and most forlorn
>   Of all thy race. Hear me thou, common parent;
>   —I have no parent else.—Be thou a mother,
>   And step between me and the curse of him,
>   Who was—who was, but is no more a father;
>   But brands my innocence with horrid crimes;
>   And for the tender names of *child* and *daughter*,
>   Now calls me *murderer* and *parricide*.
>
> —*Mourning Bride*, act. 4. sc. 7

Plaintive passions are extremely solicitous for vent. A soliloquy commonly answers the purpose. But when a passion swells high, it is not satisfied with so slight a gratification: it must have a person to complain to; and if none be found, it will animate things devoid of sense. Thus Philoctetes complains to the rocks and promontories of the isle of Lemnos[1]; and Alcestes dying, invokes the sun, the light of day, the clouds, the earth, her husband's palace, &c.[2]. Plaintive passions carry the mind still farther. Among the many principles that connect individuals in society, one is remarkable: it is that principle which makes us earnestly wish, that others should enter into our concerns and think and feel as we do. This social principle, when inflamed by a plaintive passion, will, for want of a more complete gratification, prompt the mind to give life even to things inanimate. Moschus, lamenting the death of Bion, conceives that the birds, the fountains, the trees, lament with him. The shepherd, who in Virgil bewails the death of Daphnis, expresseth himself thus:

> *Daphni, tuum Pœnos etiam ingemuisse leones*
> *Interitum, montesque feri sylvæque loquuntur.*
>
> —*Eclogue* v. 27

Again,

> *Illum etiam lauri, illum etiam flevere myricæ.*
> *Pinifer illum etiam sola sub rupe jacentem*
> *Mænalus, et gelidi fleverunt saxa Lycæi.*
>
> —*Eclogue* x. 13

Again,

> *Ho visto al pianto mio*
> *Responder per pietate i sassi e l'onde;*
> *E sospirar le fronde*
> *Ho visto al pianto mio.*
> *Ma non ho visto mai,*
> *Ne spero di vedere*
> *Compassion ne la crudele, e bella.*
>
> —*Aminta di Tasso*, act 1. sc. 2

---

1. Philoctetes of Sophocles, act 4. sc. 2.
2. Alcestes of Euripides, act 2. Sc. 1.

Earl Rivers carried to execution, says,

> *O Pomfret, Pomfret! O thou bloody prison,*
> *Fatal and ominous to Noble peers!*
> *Within the guilty closure of thy walls*
> *Richard the Second, here, was hack'd to death;*
> *And, for more slander to thy dismal seat,*
> *We give to thee our guiltless blood to drink.*
>
> —*Richard III, act 3. sc. 4*

King Richard having got intelligence of Bolingbroke's invasion, says, upon his landing in England from his Irish expedition, in a mixture of joy and resentment,

> ——— *I weep for joy*
> *To stand upon my kingdom once again.*
> *Dear earth, I do salute thee with my hand,*
> *Though rebels wound thee with their horses hoofs.*
> *As a long parted mother with her child*
> *Plays fondly with her tears, and smiles in meeting;*
> *So weeping, smiling, greet I thee my earth,*
> *And do thee favour with my royal hands.*
> *Feed not thy sovereign's foe, my gentle earth,*
> *Nor with thy sweets comfort his rav'nous sense:*
> *But let thy spiders that suck up thy venom,*
> *And heavy-gaited toads, lie in their way;*
> *Doing annoyance to the treach'rous feet,*
> *Which with usurping steps do trample thee.*
> *Yield stinging nettles to mine enemies;*
> *And, when they from thy bosom pluck a flower,*
> *Guard it, I pr'ythee, with a lurking adder;*
> *Whose double tongue may with a mortal touch*
> *Throw death upon thy sovereign's enemies.*
> *Mock not my senseless conjuration, Lords:*
> *This earth shall have a feeling; and these stones*
> *Prove armed soldiers, ere her native king*
> *Shall faulter under foul rebellious arms.*
>
> —*Richard II. act 3. sc. 2*

Among the ancients, it was customary after a long voyage to salute the natal soil. A long voyage, was of old a greater enterprise than at present: the safe return to one's country after much fatigue and danger, was a circumstance extremely delightful; and it was natural to give the natal soil a temporary life, in order to sympathise with the traveller. See an example, *Agamemnon* of Æschilus, act 3. in the beginning. Regret for leaving a place one has been accustomed to has the same effect[3].

Terror produceth the same effect. A man, to gratify this passion, extends it to everything around, even to things inanimate:

Speaking of Polyphemus,

> *Clamorem immensum tollit, quo pontus et omnes*
> *Intremuere undæ penitusque exterrita tellus*
> *Italiæ.*

—*Æneid.* iii. 672

> —— *As when old Ocean roars,*
> *And heaves huge surges to the* trembling *shores.*

—*Iliad* ii. 249

> *And thund'ring footsteps* shake *the sounding shore.*

—*Iliad* ii. 549

> *Then with a voice that* shook *the vaulted skies.*

—*Iliad* v. 431

Racine, in the tragedy of *Phedra*, describing the sea-monster that destroy'd Hippolitus, conceives the sea itself to be inspired with terror as well as the spectators; or more accurately transfers from the spectators their terror to the sea, with which they were connected:

> *Le flot qui l'apporta recule epouvanté.*

---

3. Philoctetes of Sophocles, at the close.

A man also naturally communicates his joy to all objects around, animate or inanimate:

> ——— *As when to them who sail*
> *Beyond the Cape of Hope, and now are past*
> *Mozambic, off at sea north-east winds blow*
> *Sabean odour from the spicy shore*
> *Of Araby the Blest; with such delay*
> *Well pleas'd, they slack their course, and many a league*
> *Chear'd with the grateful smell old Ocean smiles.*
>
> —Paradise Lost, b. 4

I have been profuse of examples, to show what power many passions have to animate their objects. In all the foregoing examples, the personification, if I mistake not, is so complete as to be derived from an actual conviction, momentary indeed, of life and intelligence. But it is evident from numberless instances, that personification is not always so complete. Personification is a common figure in descriptive poetry, understood to be the language of the writer, and not of any of his personages in a fit of passion. In this case, it seldom or never comes up to a conviction, even momentary, of life and intelligence. I give the following examples.

> *First in* his *east the glorious lamp was seen,*
> *Regent of day, and all th' horizon round*
> *Invested with bright rays; jocund to run*
> His *longitude through heav'n's high road: the gray*
> *Dawn, and the Pleiades before* him *danc'd,*
> *Shedding sweet influence. Less bright the moon*
> *But opposite, in levell'd west was set*
> His *mirror, with full face borrowing* her *light*
> *From* him; *for other light* she *needed none.*
>
> —Paradise Lost, b. 7. l. 370.[4]

---

[4]. The chastity of the English language, which in common usage distinguishes by genders no words but what signify beings male and female, gives thus a fine opportunity for the prosopopœia; a beauty unknown in other languages, where every word is masculine or feminine.

> *Night's candles are burnt out, and jocund day*
> *Stands tiptoe on the misty mountain-tops.*
>
> —*Romeo and Juliet, act 3. sc. 7*
>
> *But look, the morn, in russet mantle clad,*
> *Walks o'er the dew of yon high eastward hill.*
>
> —*Hamlet, act 1. sc. 1*

It may, I presume, be taken for granted, that, in the foregoing instances, the personification, either with the poet or his reader, amounts not to a conviction of intelligence; nor that the sun, the moon, the day, the morn, are here understood to be sensible beings. What then is the nature of this personification? Upon considering the matter attentively, I discover that this species of personification must be referred to the imagination. The inanimate object is imagined to be a sensible being, but without any conviction, even for a moment, that it really is so. Ideas or fictions of imagination have power to raise emotions in the mind[5]; and when anything inanimate is, in imagination, supposed to be a sensible being, it makes by that means a greater figure than when an idea is formed of it according to truth. The elevation however in this case, is far from being so great as when the personification arises to an actual conviction; and therefore must be considered as of a lower or inferior sort. Thus personification is of two kinds. The first or nobler, may be termed *passionate personification*: the other, or more humble, *descriptive personification*; because seldom or never is personification in a description carried the length of conviction.

The imagination is so lively and active, that its images are raised with very little effort; and this justifies the frequent use of descriptive personification. This figure abounds in Milton's *Allegro* and *Penseroso*.

Abstract and general terms, as well as particular objects, are often necessary in poetry. Such terms however are not well adapted to poetry, because they suggest not any image to the mind: I can readily form an image of Alexander or Achilles in wrath; but I cannot form an image of wrath in the abstract, or of wrath independent of a person. Upon that account, in works addressed to the imagination, abstract terms are frequently personified. But this personification never goes farther than the imagination.

---

5. See Appendix, containing definitions and explanations of terms, § 28.

> *Sed mihi vel Tellus optem prius ima dehiscat;*
> *Vel pater omnipotens adigat me fulmine ad umbras,*
> *Pallentes umbras Erebi, noctemque profundam,*
> *Ante pudor quam te violo, aut tua jura resolvo.*
>
> —*Æneid. 4. l. 24*

Thus, to explain the effects of slander, it is imagined to be a voluntary agent:

> —— *No, 'tis Slander;*
> *Whose edge is sharper than the sword; whose tongue*
> *Out venoms all the worms of Nile; whose breath*
> *Rides on the posting winds, and doth belie*
> *All corners of the world, kings, queens, and states,*
> *Maids, matrons: nay, the secrets of the grave*
> *This viperous Slander enters.*
>
> —*Shakespear, Cymbeline, act. 3. sc. 4*

As also human passions. Take the following example.

> ——*For Pleasure and Revenge*
> *Have ears more deaf than adders, to the voice*
> *Of any true decision.*
>
> —*Troilus and Cressida, act 2. sc. 4*

Virgil explains fame and its effects by a still greater variety of action[6]. And Shakespear personifies death and its operations in a manner extremely fanciful:

> —— *Within the hollow crown*
> *That rounds the mortal temples of a king,*
> *Keeps Death his court; and there the antic sits,*
> *Scoffing his state, and grinning at his pomp;*
> *Allowing him a breath, a little scene*
> *To monarchize, be fear'd, and kill with looks;*

---

6. Æneid, iv. 173.

> *Infusing him with self and vain conceit,*
> *As if his flesh, which walls about our life,*
> *Were brass impregnable; and humour'd thus,*
> *Comes at the last, and with a little pin*
> *Bores through his castle-walls, and farewell king!*

—Richard II. act 3. sc. 4

Not less successfully is life and action given even to sleep:

K. Henry: How many thousands of my poorest subjects
   Are at this hour asleep! O gentle Sleep,
   Nature's soft nurse, how have I frighted thee,
   That thou no more wilt weigh my eye-lids down,
   And steep my senses in forgetfulness?
   Why rather, Sleep, ly'st thou in smoky cribs,
   Upon uneasy pallets stretching thee,
   And hush'd with buzzing night-flies to thy slumber;
   Than in the perfum'd chambers of the great,
   Under the canopies of costly state,
   And lull'd with sounds of sweetest melody?
   O thou dull god, why ly'st thou with the vile
   In loathsome beds, and leav'st the kingly couch,
   A watch-case to a common larum-bell?
   Wilt thou, upon the high and giddy mast,
   Seal up the ship-boy's eyes, and rock his brains
   In cradle of the rude imperious surge;
   And in the visitation of the winds,
   Who take the ruffian billows by the top,
   Curling their monstrous heads, and hanging them
   With deaf'ning clamours in the slipp'ry shrouds,
   That, with the hurly, Death itself awakes:
   Can'st thou, O partial Sleep, give thy repose
   To the wet sea-boy in an hour so rude;
   And, in the calmest and the stillest night,
   With all appliances and means to boot,
   Deny it to a king? Then, happy low! lie down;
   Uneasy lies the head that wears a crown.

—Second Part Henry IV. act 3. sc. 1

I shall add one example more, to show that descriptive personification may be used with propriety, even where the purpose of the discourse is instruction merely:

> *Oh! let the steps of youth be cautious,*
> *How they advance into a dangerous world;*
> *Our duty only can conduct us safe:*
> *Our passions are seducers: but of all,*
> *The strongest Love: he first approaches us,*
> *In childish play, wantoning in our walks:*
> *If heedlessly we wander after him,*
> *As he will pick out all the dancing way,*
> *We're lost, and hardly to return again.*
> *We should take warning: he is painted blind,*
> *To show us, if we fondly follow him,*
> *The precipices we may fall into.*
> *Therefore let Virtue take him by the hand:*
> *Directed so, he leads to certain joy.*
>
> —Southern

Hitherto our progress has been upon firm ground. Whether we shall be so lucky in the remaining part of the journey, seems doubtful. For after acquiring some knowledge of the subject, when we now look back to the expressions mentioned in the beginning, *thirsty* ground, *furious* dart, and such like, it seems as difficult as at first to say what sort of personification it is. Such expressions evidently raise not the slighted conviction of sensibility. Nor do I think they amount to descriptive personification: in the expressions mentioned, we do not so much as figure the ground or the dart to be animated; and if so, they cannot at all come under the present subject. And to show this more clearly, I shall endeavour to explain what effect such expressions have naturally upon the mind. In the expression *angry ocean*, for example, do we not tacitly compare the ocean in a storm, to a man in wrath? It is by this tacit comparison, that the expression acquires a force or elevation, beyond what is found when an epithet is used proper to the object: for I have had occasion to show, that a thing inanimate acquires a certain elevation by being compared to a sensible being. And this very comparison is itself a demonstration, that there is no personification in such expressions. For, by the very nature of a comparison, the things compared are kept distinct, and the native appearance of each is preserved. It will be shown afterward, that expressions of this kind belong to another figure, which I term *a figure of speech*, and which employs the seventh section of the present chapter.

Though thus in general we can precisely distinguish descriptive personification from what is merely a figure of speech, it is however often difficult to say, with respect to some expressions, whether they are of the one kind or of the other. Take the following instances.

> *The moon shines bright: in such a night as this,*
> *When the sweet wind did gently* kiss *the trees,*
> *And they did make no noise; in such a night,*
> *Troilus methinks mounted the Trojan wall,*
> *And sigh'd his soul towards the Grecian tents*
> *Where Cressid lay that night.*
>
> —*Merchant of Venice, act 5. sc. 1*

> —— *I have seen*
> *Th' ambitious* ocean swell, and rage, and foam,
> *To be exalted with the threat'ning clouds.*
>
> —*Julius Cæsar, act 1. sc. 6*

JANE SHORE: My form, alas! has long forgot to please;
    The scene of beauty and delight is chang'd,
    No roses bloom upon my fading cheek,
    No laughing graces wanton in my eyes;
    But haggard Grief, lean-looking sallow Care,
    And pining Discontent, a rueful train,
    Dwell on my brow, all hideous and forlorn.

—*Jane Shore, act 1. sc. 2*

With respect to these and numberless other instances of the same kind, whether they be examples of personification or of a figure of speech merely, seems to be an arbitrary question. They will be ranged under the former class by those only who are endued with a sprightly imagination. Nor will the judgement even of the same person be steady: it will vary with the present state of the spirits, lively or composed.

Having thus at large explained the present figure, its different kinds, and the principles from whence derived; what comes next in order is to ascertain its proper province, by showing in what cases it is suitable, in what unsuitable. I begin with observing, upon passionate personification, that this figure is not promoted by every passion indifferently. All dispiriting passions are averse to it. Remorse, in particular, is too serious and severe, to be gratified by a phantom of the mind. I cannot therefore approve the following speech of Enobarbus, who had deserted his master Antony.

> *Be witness to me, O thou blessed moon,*
> *When men revolted shall upon record*
> *Bear hateful memory, poor Enobarbus did*
> *Before thy face repent———*
> *Oh sovereign mistress of true melancholy,*
> *The poisonous damp of night dispunge upon me,*
> *That life, a very rebel to my will,*
> *May hang no longer on me.*
>
> —*Antony and Cleopatra, act 4. sc. 7*

If this can be justified, it must be upon the Heathen system of theology, which converted into deities the sun, moon, and stars.

Secondly, After a passionate personification is properly introduced, it ought to be confined strictly to its proper province, that of gratifying the passion; and no sentiment nor action ought to be exerted by the animated object, but what answers that purpose. Personification is at any rate a bold figure, and ought to be employed with great reserve. The passion of love, for example, in a plaintive tone, may give a momentary life to woods and rocks, that the lover may vent his distress to them: but no passion will support a conviction so far stretched, as that these woods and rocks should be living witnesses to report the distress to others:

> *Ch'i' t'ami piu de la mia vita,*
> *Se tu nol fai, crudele,*
> *Chiedilo a queste selve,*
> *Che te'l diranno, et te'l diran con esso*

> *Le fere loro e i duri sterpi, e i sassi*
> *Di questi alpestri monti,*
> *Ch'i' ho si spesse volte*
> *Intenetiti al suon de' miei lamenti.*
>
> —*Pastor fido,* act 3. sc. 3

No lover who is not crazed will utter such a sentiment: it is plainly the operation of the writer, indulging his imagination without regard to nature. The same observation is applicable to the following passage.

> *In winter's tedious nights sit by the fire*
> *With good old folks, and let them tell thee tales*
> *Of woful ages, long ago betid:*
> *And ere thou bid goodnight, to quiet their grief,*
> *Tell them the lamentable fall of me,*
> *And send the hearers weeping to their beds.*
> *For why! the senseless brands will sympathise*
> *The heavy accent of thy moving tongue,*
> *And in compassion weep the fire out.*
>
> —*Richard II.* act 5. sc. 1

One must read this passage very seriously to avoid laughing. The following passage is quite extravagant: the different parts of the human body are too intimately connected with self, to be personified by the power of any passion; and after converting such a part into a sensible being, it is still worse to make it be conceived as rising in rebellion against self.

> CLEOPATRA: Haste, bare my arm, and rouze the serpent's fury.
>   Coward flesh————
> Would'st thou conspire with Cæsar, to betray me,
> As thou wert none of mine? I'll force thee to't.
>
> —*Dryden, All for Love,* act 5

Next comes descriptive personification; upon which I must observe in general, that it ought to be cautiously used. A personage in a tragedy, agitated by a strong passion, deals in strong sentiments; and the reader, catching fire by sympathy, relishes the boldest personifications. But a writer, even in the most lively description, ought to take a lower flight, and content himself with such easy personifications as agree with the tone of mind inspired by the description. In plain narrative, again, the mind, serious and sedate, rejects personification altogether. Strada, in his history of the Belgic wars, has the following passage, which, by a strained elevation above the tone of the subject, deviates into burlesk. "Vix descenderat a prætoria navi Cæsar; cum fœda illico exorta in portu tempestas, classem impetu disjecit, prætoriam hausit: quasi non vecturam amplius Cæsarem, Cæsarisque fortunam." Neither do I approve, in Shakespear, the speech of King John, gravely exhorting the citizens of Angiers to a surrender; though a tragic writer has much greater latitude than a historian. Take the following specimen of this speech.

The cannons have their bowels full of wrath;
And ready mounted are they to spit forth
Their iron-indignation 'gainst your walls.

—*Act 2. sc. 3*

Secondly, If extraordinary marks of respect put upon a person of the lowest rank be ridiculous, not less so is the personification of a mean object. This rule chiefly regards descriptive personification: for an object can hardly be mean that is the cause of a violent passion; in that circumstance, at least, it must be an object of importance. With respect to this point, it would be in vain to set limits to personification: taste is the only rule. A poet of superior genius hath more than others the command of this figure; because he hath more than others the power of inflaming the mind. Homer appears not extravagant in animating his darts and arrows: nor Thomson in animating the seasons, the winds, the rains, the dews. He even ventures to animate the diamond, and doth it with propriety.

—— That polish'd bright
And all its native lustre let abroad,
Dares, as it sparkles on the fair-one's breast,
With vain ambition emulate her eyes.

But there are things familiar and base, to which personification cannot descend. In a composed state of mind, to animate a lump of matter even in the most rapid flight of fancy, degenerates into burlesk.

> *How now? What noise? that spirit's possess'd with haste,*
> *That wounds th' unresisting postern with these strokes.*
>
> —Shakespear, Measure for Measure, act 4. sc. 6

The following little better:

> —— *Or from the shore*
> *The plovers when to scatter o'er the heath,*
> *And sing their wild notes to the list'ning waste.*
>
> —Thomson, Spring, l. 23

Speaking of a man's hand cut off in battle:

> *Te decisa suum, Laride, dextera quærit:*
> *Semianimesque micant digiti; ferrumque retractant.*
>
> —Æneid. x. 395

The personification here of a hand is insufferable, especially in a plain narration; not to mention that such a trivial incident is too minutely described.

The same observation is applicable to abstract terms, which ought not to be animated unless they have some natural dignity. Thomson, in this article, is quite licentious. Witness the following instances out of many.

> *O vale of bliss! O softly swelling hills!*
> *On which* the power of cultivation *lies,*
> *And joys to see the wonders of his toil.*
>
> —Summer, l. 1423

> *Then sated* Hunger *bids his brother* Thirst
> *Produce the mighty bowl:*
> *Nor wanting is the brown October, drawn*
> *Mature and perfect, from* his *dark retreat*

> *Of thirty years; and now* his honest front
> *Flames in the light refulgent.*
>
> *—Autumn, l. 516*

Thirdly, it is not sufficient to avoid improper subjects. Some preparation is necessary, in order to rouze the mind. The imagination refuses its aid, till it be warmed at least, if not inflamed. Yet Thomson, without the least ceremony or preparation, introduceth each season as a sensible being:

> *From brightening fields of æther fair disclos'd,*
> *Child of the sun, refulgent Summer comes,*
> *In pride of youth, and felt through Nature's depth.*
> *He comes attended by the sultry hours,*
> *And ever-fanning breezes, on his way,*
> *While from his ardent look, the turning Spring*
> *Averts her blushful face, and earth and skies*
> *All-smiling, to his hot dominion leaves.*
>
> *—Summer, l. 1*

> *See* Winter *comes, to rule the vary'd year,*
> *Sullen and sad with all his rising train,*
> Vapours, *and* clouds, *and* storms.
>
> *—Winter, l. 1*

This has violently the air of writing mechanically without taste. It is not natural, that the imagination of a writer should be so much heated at the very commencement; and, at any rate, he cannot expect such ductility in his readers: but if this practice can be justified by authority, Thomson has one of no mean note: Vida begins his first eclogue in the following words.

> *Dicite, vos Musæ, et juvenum memorate querelas;*
> *Dicite; nam motas ipsas ad carmina cautes*
> *Et requiesse suos perhibent vaga flumina cursus.*

Even Shakespear is not always careful to prepare the mind for this bold figure. Take the following instance:

> ———*Upon these taxations,*
> *The clothiers all, not able to maintain*
> *The many to them 'longing, have put off*
> *The spinsters, carders, fullers, weavers; who,*
> *Unfit for other life, compell'd by hunger*
> *And lack of other means, in desp'rate manner*
> *Daring th' event to th' teeth, are all in uproar,*
> *And* Danger *serves among them.*
>
> —*Henry VIII. act 1. sc. 4*

Fourthly, Descriptive personification ought never to be carried farther than barely to animate the subject: and yet poets are not easily restrained from making this phantom of their own creating behave and act in every respect as if it were really a sensible being. By such licence we lose sight of the subject; and the description is rendered obscure or unintelligible, instead of being more lively and striking. In this view, the following passage, describing Cleopatra on shipboard, appears to me exceptionable.

> *The barge she sat in, like a burnish'd throne,*
> *Burnt on the water; the poop was beaten gold,*
> *Purple the sails, and so perfumed, that*
> *The winds were love sick with 'em.*
>
> —*Antony and Cleopatra, act 2. sc. 3*

Let the winds be personified; I make no objection. But to make them love-sick, is too far stretched; having no resemblance to any natural action of wind. In another passage, where Cleopatra is also the subject, the personification of the air is carried beyond all bounds:

> ———*The city cast*
> *Its people out upon her; and Antony*
> *Inthron'd i' th' market-place, did sit alone,*
> *Whistling to th' air, which but for vacancy,*
> *Had gone to gaze on Cleopatra too,*
> *And made a gap in nature.*
>
> —*Antony and Cleopatra, act 2. sc. 3*

The following personification of the earth or soil is not less wild.

> *She shall be dignify'd with this high honour*
> *To bear my Lady's train; lest the base earth*
> *Should from her vesture chance to steal a kiss;*
> *And of so great a favour growing proud,*
> *Disdain to root the summer swelling flower,*
> *And make rough winter everlastingly.*

—*The Two Gentlemen of Verona*, act 2. sc. 7

Shakespear, far from approving such intemperance of imagination, puts this speech in the mouth of a ranting lover. Neither can I relish what follows.

> *Omnia quæ, Phœbo quondam meditante, beatus*
> *Audiit Eurotas, jussitque ediscere lauros,*
> *Ille canit.*

—*Virgil, Buc. vi. 82*

The chearfulness singly of a pastoral song, will scarce support personification in the lowest degree. But admitting, that a river gently flowing may be imagined a sensible being listening to a song, I cannot enter into the conceit of the river's ordering his laurels to learn the song. Here all resemblance to anything real is quite lost. This however is copied literally by one of our greatest poets; early indeed, before maturity of taste or judgement.

> *Thames heard the numbers as he flow'd along,*
> *And bade his willows learn the moving song.*

—*Pope's Pastorals, past. 4. l. 13*

This author, in riper years, is guilty of a much greater deviation from the rule. Dullness may be imagined a deity or idol, to be worshipped by bad writers: but then some sort of disguise is requisite, some bastard virtue must be bestowed, to give this idol a plausible appearance. Yet in the *Dunciad*, dullness, without the least disguise, is made the object of worship. The mind rejects such a fiction as unnatural; for dullness is a defect, of which even the dullest mortal is ashamed:

> *Then he: great tamer of all human art, &c.*
>
> —*Book i. 163*

The following instance is stretched beyond all resemblance. It is bold to take a part or member of a living creature, and to bestow upon it life, volition, and action: after animating two such members, it is still bolder to make them envy each other; for this is wide of any resemblance to reality:

> ———*De nostri baci*
> *Meritamente sia giudice quella, &c.*
>
> —*Pastor Fido, act 2. sc. 1*

Fifthly, The enthusiasm of passion may have the effect to prolong passionate personification: but descriptive personification cannot be dispatched in too few words. A minute description dissolves the charm, and makes the attempt to personify appear ridiculous. Homer succeeds in animating his darts and arrows: but such personification spun out in a French translation, is mere burlesk:

> *Et la fléche en furie, avide de son sang,*
> *Part, vole à lui, l'atteint, et lui perce le flanc.*

Horace says happily, "Post equitem sedet atra Cura." See how this thought degenerates by being divided, like the former, into a number of minute parts:

> *Un fou rempli d'erreurs, que le trouble accompagne*
> *Et malade à la ville ainsi qu'à la campagne,*
> *En vain monte à cheval pour tromper son ennui,*
> *Le Chagrin monte en croupe et galope avec lui.*

The following passage is, if possible, still more faulty.

> *Her fate is whisper'd by the gentle breeze,*
> *And told in sighs to all the trembling trees;*

> *The trembling trees, in ev'ry plain and wood,*
> *Her fate remurmur to the silver flood;*
> *The silver flood, so lately calm, appears*
> *Swell'd with new passion, and o'erflows with tears;*
> *The winds, and trees, and floods, her death deplore,*
> *Daphne, our grief! our glory! now no more.*

> —*Pope's Pastorals, iv. 61*

Let grief or love have the power to animate the winds, the trees, the floods, provided the figure be dispatched in a single expression. Even in that case, the figure seldom has a good effect; because grief or love of the pastoral kind, are causes rather too faint for so violent an effect as imagining the winds, trees, or floods, to be sensible beings. But when this figure is deliberately spread out with great regularity and accuracy through many lines, the reader, instead of relishing it, is struck with its ridiculous appearance.

Section. II

Apostrophe.

This figure and the former are derived from the same principle. If, to gratify a plaintive passion, we can bestow a momentary sensibility upon an inanimate object, it is not more difficult to bestow a momentary presence upon a sensible being who is absent.

> *Hinc Drepani me portus et illætabilis ora*
> *Accipit. Hic, pelagi tot tempestatibus actus,*
> *Heu! genitorem, omnis curæ casusque levamen,*
> *Amitto Anchisen:* hic me pater optime fessum
> Deseris, *heu! tantis nequiequam erepte periclis.*
> *Nec vates Helenus, cum multa horrenda moneret,*
> *Hos mihi prædixit luctus; non dira Celæno.*

> —*Æneid. iii. 707*

This figure is sometimes joined with the former: things inanimate, to qualify them for listening to a passionate expostulation, are not only personified, but also conceived to be present.

> *Et, si fata Deûm, si mens non læva fuisset,*
> *Impulerat ferro Argolicas fœdare latebras:*
> Trojaque nunc stares, Priamique arx alta maneres.
>
> —*Æneid. ii. 54*

> HELENA:—— Poor Lord, is't I
> That chase thee from thy country, and expose
> Those tender limbs of thine to the event
> Of non-sparing war? And is it I
> That drive thee from the sportive court, where thou
> Wast shot at with fair eyes, to be the mark
> Of smoky muskets? O you leaden messengers,
> That ride upon the violent speed of fire,
> Fly with false aim; pierce the still moving air,
> That sings with piercing; do not touch my Lord.
>
> —*All's well that ends well, act 3. sc. 4*

This figure, like all others, requires an agitation of mind. In plain narrative, as, for example, in giving the genealogy of a family, it has no good effect:

> ——*Fauno Picus pater; isque parentem*
> *Te, Saturne, refert; tu sanguinis ultimus auctor.*
>
> —*Æneid. vii. 48*

Section. III

Hyperbole.

In this figure we have another effect of the foregoing principle. An object uncommon with respect to size, either very great of its kind or very little, strikes us with surprise; and this emotion, like all others, prone to gratification, forces upon the mind a momentary conviction that the object is greater or less than it is in reality. The same effect, precisely, attends figurative grandeur or littleness. Every object that produceth surprise by its singularity, is always seen in a false light while the emotion subsists: circumstances are exaggerated beyond truth;

and it is not till after the emotion subsides, that things appear as they are. A writer, taking advantage of this natural delusion, enriches his description greatly by the hyperbole. And the reader, even in his coolest moments, relishes this figure, being sensible that it is the operation of nature upon a warm fancy.

It will be observed, that a writer is generally more successful in magnifying by a hyperbole than in diminishing: a minute object contracts the mind, and fetters its power of conception; but the mind, dilated and inflamed with a grand object, moulds objects for its gratification with great facility. Longinus, with respect to the diminishing power of a hyperbole, cites the following ludicrous thought from a comic poet. "He was owner of a bit of ground not larger than a Lacedemonian letter." But, for the reason now given, the hyperbole has by far the greater force in magnifying objects; of which take the following specimen.

> For all the land which thou seest, to thee will I give it, and to thy seed forever. And I will make thy seed as the dust of the earth: so that if a man can number the dust of the earth, then shall thy seed also be numbered.
>
> *Genesis xiii. 15. 16*

> *Illa vel intactæ segetis per summa volaret*
> *Gramina: nec teneras cursu læsisset aristas.*
>
> *—Æneid. vii. 808*

> —— *Atque imo barathri ter gurgite vastos*
> *Sorbet in abruptum fluctus, rursusque sub auras*
> *Erigit alternos, et sidera verberat undà.*
>
> *—Æneid. iii. 421*

> —— *Horrificis juxta tonat Ætna ruinis,*
> *Interdumque atram prorumpit ad æthera nubem,*
> *Turbine fumantem piceo et candente favilla:*
> *Attollitque globos flammarum, et sidera lambit.*
>
> *—Æneid. iii. 571*

---

7. Chap. 31. of his Treatise on the Sublime.

Speaking of Polyphemus,

> —— *Ipse arduus, altaque pulsat Sidera.*
>
> —*Æneid. iii. 619*

> —— *When he speaks,*
> *The air, a charter'd libertine, is still.*
>
> —*Henry V. act 1. sc. 1*

> *Now shield with shield, with helmet helmet clos'd,*
> *To armour armour, lance to lance oppos'd,*
> *Host against host with shadowy squadrons drew,*
> *The sounding darts in iron tempests flew,*
> *Victors and vanquish'd join promiscuous cries,*
> *And shrilling shouts and dying groans arise;*
> *With streaming blood the slipp'ry fields are dy'd,*
> *And slaughter'd heroes swell the dreadful tide.*
>
> —*Iliad iv. 508*

The following may also pass, though stretched pretty far.

> *Econjungendo à temerario ardire*
> *Estrema forza, e infaticabil lena*
> *Vien che si' impetuoso il ferro gire,*
> *Che ne trema la terra, e'l ciel balena.*
>
> —*Gierusalem, cant. 6. st. 46*

Quintilian[8] is sensible that this figure is natural. "For," says he, "not contented with truth, we naturally incline to augment or diminish beyond it; and for that reason the hyperbole is familiar even among the vulgar and illiterate." And he adds, very justly, "That the hyperbole is then proper, when the subject of itself exceeds the common measure." From these premisses, one would not expect the following conclusion, the only reason he can find for justifying this figure of speech. "Conceditur enim amplius dicere, quia dici quantum est, non

---

8. L. 8. cap. 6. in fin.

potest: meliusque ultra quam citra stat oratio." (We are indulged to say more than enough, because we cannot say enough; and it is better to be over than under). In the name of wonder, why this slight and childish reason, when immediately before he had made it evident, that the hyperbole is founded on human nature? I could not resist this personal stroke of criticism, intended not against our author, for no human creature is exempt from error; but against the blind veneration that is paid to the ancient classic writers, without distinguishing their blemishes from their beauties.

Having examined the nature of this figure, and the principle on which it is erected; I proceed, as in the first section, to some rules by which it ought to be governed. And in the first place, it is a capital fault to introduce an hyperbole in the description of an ordinary object or event which creates no surprise. In such a case, the hyperbole is altogether unnatural, being destitute of surprise, the only foundation that can support it. Take the following instance, where the subject is extremely familiar, *viz.* swimming to gain the shore after a shipwreck.

> *I saw him beat the surges under him,*
> *And ride upon their backs; he trode the water;*
> *Whose enmity he flung aside, and breasted*
> *The surge most swoln that met him: his bold head*
> *'Bove the contentious waves he kept, and oar'd*
> *Himself with his good arms, in lusty strokes*
> *To th' shore, that o'er his wave-born basis bow'd,*
> *As stooping to relieve him.*
>
> *—Tempest, act 2. sc. 1*

In the next place, it may be gathered from what is said, that an hyperbole can never suit the tone of any dispiriting passion. Sorrow in particular will never prompt such a figure; and for that reason the following hyperboles must be condemned as unnatural.

> K. Rich: Aumerle, thou weep'st, my tender-hearted cousin!
> We'll make foul weather with despised tears;
> Our sighs, and they, shall lodge the summer-corn,
> And make a dearth in this revolting land.
>
> *—Richard II. Act 3. Sc. 6*

> *Draw them to Tyber's bank, and weep your tears*
> *Into the channel, till the lowest stream*
> *Do kiss the most exalted shores of all.*
>
> —*Julius Cæsar, act 1. sc. 1*

Thirdly, a writer, if he wish to succeed, ought always to have the reader in his eye. He ought in particular never to venture a bold thought or expression, till the reader be warmed and prepared for it. For this reason, an hyperbole in the beginning of any work can never be in its place. Example:

> *Jam pauca aratro jugera regiæ*
> *Moles relinquent.*
>
> —*Horat. Carm. lib. 2. ode. 15*

In the fourth place, the nicest point of all, is to ascertain the natural limits of an hyperbole, beyond which being overstrained it has a bad effect. Longinus, in the above-cited chapter, with great propriety of thought, enters a caveat against an hyperbole of this kind. He compares it to a bowstring, which relaxes by overstraining, and produceth an effect directly opposite to what is intended. I pretend not to ascertain any precise boundary: the attempt would be difficult, if not impracticable. I must therefore be satisfied with an humbler task, which is, to give a specimen of what I reckon overstrained hyperboles; and I shall be also extremely curt upon this subject, because examples are to be found everywhere. No fault is more common among writers of inferior rank; and instances are found even among those of the finest taste; witness the following hyperbole, too bold even for an Hotspur.

Hotspur talking of Mortimer:

> *In single opposition hand to hand,*
> *He did confound the best part of an hour*
> *In changing hardiment with great Glendower.*
> *Three times they breath'd, and three times did they drink,*
> *Upon agreement, of swift Severn's flood;*
> *Who then affrighted with their bloody looks,*
> *Ran fearfully among the trembling reeds,*
> *And hid his crisp'd head in the hollow bank*
> *Blood-stained with these valiant combatants.*
>
> —*First Part Henry IV. act 1. sc. 4*

Speaking of Henry V.

> *England ne'er had a King until his time:*
> *Virtue he had, deserving to command:*
> *His brandish'd sword did blind men with its beams:*
> *His arms spread wider than a dragon's wings:*
> *His sparkling eyes, replete with awful fire,*
> *More dazzled, and drove back his enemies,*
> *Than mid-day sun fierce bent against their faces.*
> *What should I say? his deeds exceed all speech:*
> *He never lifted up his hand, but conquer'd.*
>
> —*First Part Henry VI. act 1. sc. 1*

Lastly, an hyperbole after it is introduced with all advantages, ought to be comprehended within the fewest words possible. As it cannot be relished but in the hurry and swelling of the mind, a leisurely view dissolves the charm, and discovers the description to be extravagant at least, and perhaps also ridiculous. This fault is palpable in a sonnet which passeth for one of the most complete in the French language. Phillis is made as far to outshine the sun as he outshines the stars.

> *Le silence regnoit sur la terre et sur l'onde,*
> *L'air devenoit serain,* &c.
>
> —*Collection of French epigrams, vol. 1. p. 66*

There is in Chaucer a thought expressed in a single line, which sets a young beauty in a more advantageous light, than the whole of this much-laboured poem.

> *Up rose the sun, and up rose Emelie.*

Section. IV

The means or instrument conceived to be the agent.

In viewing a group of things, we have obviously a natural tendency to bestow all possible perfection upon that particular object which makes the greatest figure. The emotion raised by the object, is, by this means, thoroughly gratified; and if the emotion be lively, it prompts us even to exceed nature in the conception we form of the object. Take the following examples.

For Neleus' sons Alcides' rage *had slain.*

A broken rock the force *of Pirus threw.*

In these instances, the rage of Hercules and the force of Pirus, being the capital circumstances, are so far exalted as to be conceived the agents that produce the effects.

In the following instance, hunger being the chief circumstance in the description, is itself imagined to be the patient.

Whose hunger has not tasted food these three days.

—Jane Shore

――――*As when the* force
Of subterranean wind transports a hill.

—Paradise Lost

――――*As when the* potent rod
Of Amram's son in Egypt's evil day
Wav'd round the coast, upcall'd a pitchy cloud
Of locusts.

—Paradise Lost

Section. V

A figure, which, among related objects, extends properties of one to another.

This figure is not dignified with a proper name, because it has been overlooked by all writers. It merits, however, place in this work; and must be distinguished from those formerly handled, as depending on a different principle. *Giddy brink, jovial wine, daring wound,* are examples of this figure. Here are expressions that certainly import not the ordinary relation of an adjective to its substantive. A *brink*, for example, cannot be termed *giddy* in a proper sense: neither can it be termed *giddy* in any figurative sense that can import any of its qualities or attributes. When we attend to the expression, we discover that a *brink* is termed *giddy* from producing that effect in those who stand on it. In the same manner a wound is said to be daring, not with respect to itself, but with respect to the boldness of the person who inflicts it: and wine is said to be jovial, as inspiring mirth and jollity. Thus the attributes of one subject, are extended to another with which it is connected; and such expression must be considered as a figure, because it deviates from ordinary language.

How are we to account for this figure, for we see it lies in the thought, and to what principle shall we refer it? Have poets a privilege to alter the nature of things, and at pleasure to bestow attributes upon subjects to which these attributes do not belong? It is an evident truth, which we have had often occasion to inculcate, that the mind, in idea, passeth easily and sweetly along a train of connected objects; and, where the objects are intimately connected, that it is disposed to carry along the good or bad properties of one to another; especially where it is in any degree inflamed with these properties[9]. From this principle is derived the figure under consideration. Language, invented for the communication of thought, would be imperfect, if it were not expressive even of the slighter propensities and more delicate feelings. But language cannot remain so imperfect, among a people who have received any polish; because language is regulated by internal feeling, and is gradually so improved as to express whatever passes in the mind. Thus, for example, a sword in the hand of a coward, is, in poetical diction, termed *a coward sword*: the expression is significative of an internal operation; for the mind, in passing from the agent to its instrument, is disposed to extend to the latter the properties of the former. Governed by the same principle, we say *listening* fear, by extending the attribute *listening* of the man who listens, to the passion with which he is moved. In the expression, *bold deed*, or *audax facinus*, we extend to the effect, what properly belongs to the cause. But not to waste time by making a commentary upon every expression of this kind, the best way to give a complete view of the subject, is to exhibit a table of the different connections that may give occasion to this figure. And in viewing this table, it will be observed, that the figure can never have any grace but where the connections are of the most intimate kind.

---

9. See chap. 2. part 1. sect. 5.

1. An attribute of the cause expressed as an attribute of the effect.

> *Audax facinus.*
> *Of yonder fleet a* bold *discovery make.*
> *An impious mortal gave the* daring *wound.*

> ——*To my* adventrous *song,*
> *That with no middle flight intends to soar.*
>
> —*Paradise Lost*

2. An attribute of the effect expressed as an attribute of the cause.

> *Quos periisse ambos* misera *censebam in mari.*
>
> —*Plautus*

> *No wonder, fallen such a* pernicious *height.*
>
> —*Paradise Lost*

3. An effect expressed as an attribute of the cause.
   Jovial wine, Giddy brink, Drowsy night, Musing midnight, Panting height, Astonish'd thought, Mournful gloom.

> *Casting a dim* religious *light.*
>
> —*Milton, Comus*

> *And the* merry *bells ring round,*
> *And the* jocund *rebecks sound.*
>
> —*Milton, Allegro*

4. An attribute of a subject bestowed upon one of its parts or members.

> *Longing arms.*

> *It was the nightingale, and not the lark,*
> *That pierc'd the* fearful *hollow of thine ear.*
>
> —*Romeo and Juliet, act 3. sc. 7*

> ———*Oh, lay by*
> *Those most ungentle looks and angry weapons;*
> *Unless you mean my griefs and killing fears*
> *Should stretch me out at your* relentless *feet.*
>
> —*Fair Penitent, act 3*

> ———*And ready now*
> *To stoop with* wearied *wing, and* willing *feet,*
> *On the bare outside of this world.*
>
> —*Paradise Lost, b. 3*

5. A quality of the agent given to the instrument with which it operates.

> *Why peep your* coward *swords half out their shells?*

6. An attribute of the agent given to the subject upon which it operates.

> *High-climbing hill.*
>
> —*Milton*

7. A quality of one subject given to another.

> *Icci,* beatis *nunc Arabum invides*
> *Gazis.*
>
> —*Hora. Carm. l. 1. ode 29*

> *When sapless age, and weak unable limbs,*
> *Should bring thy father to his* drooping *chair.*
>
> —*Shakespear*

> *By art, the pilot through the boiling deep*
> *And howling tempest, steers the* fearless *ship.*
>
> —*Iliad xxiii. 385*

> *Then, nothing loath, th' enamour'd fair he led,*
> *And sunk transported on the* conscious *bed.*
>
> —*Odyss.* viii. 337

> *A* stupid *moment motionless she stood.*
>
> —*Summer, l. 1336*

8. A circumstance connected with a subject, expressed as a quality of the subject.

> *Breezy summit.*

> *'Tis ours the chance of fighting fields to try.*
>
> —*Iliad* i. 301

> *Oh! had I dy'd before that well-fought wall.*
>
> —*Odyss.* v. 395

From this table it appears, that the expressing an effect as an attribute of the cause, is not so agreeable as the opposite expression. The descent from cause to effect is natural and easy: the opposite direction resembles retrograde motion[10]. *Panting height*, for example, *astonish'd thought*, are strained and uncouth expressions, which a writer of taste will avoid. For the same reason, an epithet is unsuitable, which at present is not applicable to the subject, however applicable it may be afterward.

> Submersasque *obrue puppes.*
>
> —*Æneid. i. 73*

> *And mighty* ruins *fall.*
>
> —*Iliad* v. 411

> *Impious sons their* mangled *fathers wound.*

---

10. See chap. 1.

Another rule regards this figure, That the property of one object ought not to be bestowed upon another with which it is incongruous:

K. Rich:—— How dare thy joints forget
To pay their *awful* duty to our presence.

—Richard II. *act 3. sc. 6*

The connection betwixt an awful superior and his submissive dependent is so intimate, that an attribute may readily be transferred from the one to the other. But awfulness cannot be so transferred, because it is inconsistent with submission.

Section. VI

Metaphor and Allegory.

A Metaphor differs from a simile, in form only, not in substance. In a simile the two different subjects are kept distinct in the expression, as well as in the thought: in a metaphor, the two subjects are kept distinct in thought only, not in expression. A hero resembles a lion, and upon that resemblance many similes have been made by Homer and other poets. But instead of resembling a lion, let us take the aid of the imagination, and feign or figure the hero to be a lion. By this variation the simile is converted into a metaphor; which is carried on by describing all the qualities of a lion that resemble those of the hero. The fundamental pleasure here, that of resemblance, belongs to thought as distinguished from expression. There is an additional pleasure which arises from the expression. The poet, by figuring his hero to be a lion, goes on to describe the lion in appearance, but in reality the hero; and his description is peculiarly beautiful, by expressing the virtues and qualities of the hero in new terms, which, properly speaking, belong not to him, but to a different being. This will better be understood by examples. A family connected with a common parent, resembles a tree, the trunk and branches of which are connected with a common root. But let us suppose, that a family is figured not barely to be like a tree, but to be a tree; and then the simile will be converted into a metaphor, in the following manner.

> *Edward's sev'n sons, whereof thyself art one,*
> *Were sev'n fair branches, springing from one root:*
> *Some of these branches by the dest'nies cut:*
> *But Thomas, my dear Lord, my life, my Glo'ster,*
> *One flourishing branch of his most royal root,*
> *Is hack'd down, and his summer leaves all faded,*
> *By Envy's hand and Murder's bloody axe.*
>
> —*Richard II. act 1. sc. 3*

Figuring human life to be a voyage at sea:

> *There is a tide in the affairs of men,*
> *Which, taken at the flood, leads on to fortune;*
> *Omitted, all the voyage of their life*
> *Is bound in shallows and in miseries.*
> *On such a full sea are we now afloat;*
> *And we must take the current when it serves,*
> *Or lose our ventures.*
>
> —*Julius Cæsar, act 4. sc. 5*

Figuring glory and honour to be a garland of fresh flowers:

HOTSPUR:—— Would to heav'n,
  Thy name in arms were now as great as mine!
PR. HENRY: I'll make it greater, ere I part from thee;
  And all the budding honours on thy crest
  I'll crop, to make a garland for my head.

—*First Part Henry IV. act 5. sc. 9*

Figuring a man who hath acquired great reputation and honour to be a tree full of fruit:

> ———*Oh, boys, this story*
> *The world may read in me: my body's mark'd*
> *With Roman swords; and my report was once*
> *First with the best of note. Cymbeline lov'd me;*
> *And when a soldier was the theme, my name*

> *Was not far off: then was I as a tree,*
> *Whose boughs did bend with fruit. But in one night,*
> *A storm or robbery, call it what you will,*
> *Shook down my mellow hangings, nay my leaves;*
> *And left me bare to weather.*
>
> —*Cymbeline, act 3. sc. 3*

I am aware that the term *metaphor* has been used in a more extensive sense than I give it; but I thought it of consequence, in matters of some intricacy, to separate things that differ from each other, and to confine words within their most proper sense. An allegory differs from a metaphor; and what I would chuse to call *a figure of speech*, differs from both. I shall proceed to explain these differences. A metaphor is defined above to be an operation of the imagination, figuring one thing to be another. An allegory requires no operation of the imagination, nor is one thing figured to be another: it consists in chusing a subject having properties or circumstances resembling those of the principal subject; and the former is described in such a manner as to represent the latter. The subject thus represented is kept out of view; we are left to discover it by reflection; and we are pleased with the discovery, because it is our own work. Quintilian[11] gives the following instance of an allegory,

> *O navis, referent in mare te novi*
> *Fluctus. O quid agis? fortiter occupa portum.*
>
> —*Horat. lib. 1. ode 14*

and explains it elegantly in the following words: "Totusque ille Horatii locus, quo navim pro republica, fluctuum tempestates pro bellis civilibus, portum pro pace atque concordia, dicit."

There cannot be a finer or more correct allegory than the following, in which a vineyard is put for God's own people the Jews.

> Thou hast brought a vine out of Egypt: thou hast cast out the heathen, and planted it. Thou didst cause it to take deep root, and it filled the land. The hills were covered with its shadow, and the boughs thereof were like the goodly cedars. Why hast thou then

---

11. L. 8. cap. 6. sect. 2.

broken down her hedges, so that all which pass do pluck her? The boar out of the wood doth waste it, and the wild beast doth devour it. Return, we beseech thee, O God of hosts: look down from heaven, and behold and visit this vine, and the vineyard thy right hand hath planted, and the branch thou madest strong for thyself.
Psalm 80

In a word, an allegory is in every respect similar to an hieroglyphical painting, excepting only, that words are used instead of colours. Their effects are precisely the same. A hieroglyphic raises two images in the mind; one seen, which represents one not seen. An allegory does the same. The representative subject is described; and it is by resemblance that we are enabled to apply the description to the subject represented.

In a figure of speech, neither is there any fiction of the imagination employ'd, nor a representative subject introduced. A figure of speech, as imply'd from its name, regards the expression only, not the thought; and it may be defined, the employing a word in a sense different from what is proper to it. Thus youth or the beginning of life, is expressed figuratively by *morning of life*. Morning is the beginning of the day; and it is transferred sweetly and easily to signify the beginning of any other series, life especially, the progress of which is reckoned by days.

Figures of speech are reserved for a separate section; but a metaphor and allegory are so much connected, that it is necessary to handle them together: the rules for distinguishing the good from the bad, are common to both. We shall therefore proceed to these rules, after adding some examples to illustrate the nature of an allegory. Horace speaking of his love to Pyrrha, which was now extinguished, expresses himself thus.

> ————*Me tabulâ sacer*
> *Votivâ paries indicat uvida*
> *Suspendisse potenti*
> *Vestimenta maris Deo.*
>
> —*Carm. l. 1. ode 5*

Again,

> *Phœbus volentem prælia me loqui,*
> *Victas et urbes, increpuit lyrâ:*

Ne parva Tyrrhenum per æquor
Vela darem.

—*Carm. l. 4. ode 15*

QUEEN: Great Lords, wise men ne'er sit and wail their loss,
  But chearly seek how to redress their harms.
  What though the mast be now blown overboard,
  The cable broke, the holding anchor lost,
  And half our sailors swallow'd in the flood?
  Yet lives our pilot still. Is't meet, that he
  Should leave the helm, and, like a fearful lad,
  With tearful eyes add water to the sea;
  And give more strength to that which hath too much?
  While in his moan the ship splits on the rock,
  Which industry and courage might have sav'd?
  Ah, what a shame! ah, what a fault were this!

—*Third Part Henry VI. act 5. sc. 5*

OROONOKO: Ha! thou hast rous'd
  The lion in his den, he stalks abroad
  And the wide forest trembles at his roar.
  I find the danger now.

—*Oroonoko, act 3. sc. 2*

The rules that govern metaphors and allegories, are of two kinds: those of the first kind concern the construction of a metaphor or allegory, and ascertain what are perfect and what are faulty: those of the other kind concern the propriety or impropriety of introduction, in what circumstances these figures may be admitted, and in what circumstances they are out of place. I begin with rules of the first kind; some of which coincide with those already given with respect to similes; some are peculiar to metaphors and allegories.

And in the first place, it has been observed, that a simile cannot be agreeable where the resemblance is either too strong or too faint. This holds equally in a metaphor and allegory; and the reason is the same in all. In the following instances, the resemblance is too faint to be agreeable.

> MALCOLM:—— But there's no bottom, none,
> In my voluptuousness: your wives, your daughters,
> Your matrons, and your maids, could not fill up
> The cistern of my lust.
>
> *—Macbeth, act 4. sc. 4*

The best way to judge of this metaphor, is to convert it into a simile; which would be bad, because there is scarce any resemblance betwixt lust and a cistern, or betwixt enormous lust and a large cistern.

Again,

> *He cannot buckle his distemper'd cause*
> *Within the belt of rule.*
>
> *—Macbeth, act 5. sc. 2*

There is no resemblance betwixt a distempered cause and anybody that can be confined within a belt.

Again,

> *Steep me in poverty to the very lips.*
>
> *—Othello, act 4. sc. 9*

Poverty here must be conceived a fluid, which it resembles not in any manner.

Speaking to Bolingbroke banish'd for six years.

> *The sullen passage of thy weary steps*
> *Esteem a foil, wherein thou art to set*
> *The precious jewel of thy home-return.*
>
> *—Richard II. act 1. sc. 6*

Again,

> *Here is a letter, lady,*
> *And every word in it a gaping wound*
> *Issuing life-blood.*
>
> *—Merchant of Venice, act 3. sc. 3*

The following metaphor is strained beyond all endurance. Timurbec, known to us by the name of Tamarlane the Great, writes to Bajazet Emperor of the Ottomans in the following terms.

> Where is the monarch who dares resist us? where is the potentate who doth not glory in being numbered among our attendants? As for thee, descended from a Turcoman sailor, since the vessel of thy unbounded ambition hath been wreck'd in the gulf of thy self-love, it would be proper, that thou shouldst take in the sails of thy temerity, and cast the anchor of repentance in the port of sincerity and justice, which is the port of safety; lest the tempest of our vengeance make thee perish in the sea of the punishment thou deservest.

Such strained figures, it is observable, are not unfrequent in the first dawn of refinement. The mind in a new enjoyment knows no bounds, and is generally carried to excess, till experience discover the just medium.

Secondly, whatever resemblance subjects may have, it is wrong to put one for another if they bear no mutual proportion. Where a very high and a very low subject are compared, the simile takes on an air of burlesk; and the same will be the effect, where the one is imagined to be the other, as in a metaphor, or made to represent the other, as in an allegory.

Thirdly, these figures, a metaphor in particular, ought not to be extended to a great length, nor be crowded with many minute circumstances; for in that case it is scarcely possible to avoid obscurity. It is difficult, during any course of time, to support a lively image of one thing being another. A metaphor drawn out to any length, instead of illustrating or enlivening the principal subject, becomes disagreeable by overstraining the mind. Cowley is extremely licentious in this way. Take the following instance:

> *Great, and wise conqu'ror, who where-e'er*
> *Thou com'st, dost fortify, and settle there!*
> *Who canst defend as well as get;*
> *And never hadst one quarter beat up yet;*
> *Now thou art in, thou ne'er will part*
> *With one inch of my vanquish'd heart;*

> *For since thou took'st it by assault from me,*
> *'Tis garrison'd so strong with thoughts of thee*
> *It fears no beauteous enemy.*

For the same reason, however agreeable at first long allegories may be by their novelty, they never afford any lasting pleasure: witness the *Fairy Queen*, which with great power of expression, variety of images, and melody of versification, is scarce ever read a second time.

In the fourth place, the comparison carried on in a simile, being in a metaphor sunk, and the principal subject being imagined that very thing which it only resembles, an opportunity is furnished to describe it in terms taken strictly or literally with respect to its imagined nature. This suggests another rule, That in constructing a metaphor, the writer ought to confine himself to the simplest expressions, and make use of such words only as are applicable literally to the imagined nature of his subject. Figurative words ought carefully to be avoided; for such complicated images, instead of setting the principal subject in a strong light, involve it in a cloud; and it is well if the reader, without rejecting by the lump, endeavour patiently to gather the plain meaning, regardless of the figures:

> *A stubborn and unconquerable flame*
> *Creeps in his veins, and drinks the streams of life.*
>
> —*Lady Jane Gray, act 1. sc. 1*

Copied from Ovid,

> *Sorbent avidæ præcordia flammæ.*
>
> —*Metamorphoses, lib. ix. 172*

Let us analize this expression. That a fever may be imagined a flame, I admit; though more than one step is necessary to come at the resemblance. A fever, by heating the body, resembles fire; and it is no stretch to imagine a fever to be a fire.

Again, by a figure of speech, flame may be put for fire, because they are commonly conjoined; and therefore a fever may also be imagined a flame. But now admitting a fever to be a flame, its effects ought to be explained in words that agree literally to a flame. This rule is not observed here; for a flame *drinks* figuratively only, not properly.

King Henry to his son Prince Henry:

> *Thou hid'st a thousand daggers in thy thoughts,*
> *Which thou hast whetted on thy stony heart*
> *To stab at half an hour of my frail life.*

> —*Second Part Henry IV. act 4. sc. 11*

Such faulty metaphors are pleasantly ridiculed in the *Rehearsal*:

PHYSICIAN: Sir, to conclude, the place you fill has more than amply exacted the talents of a wary pilot; and all these threatening storms, which, like impregnate clouds, hover o'er our heads, will, when they once are grasp'd but by the eye of reason, melt into fruitful showers of blessings on the people.
BAYES: Pray mark that allegory. Is not that good?
JOHNSON: Yes, that grasping of a storm with the eye, is admirable.

> —*Act 2. sc. 1*

Fifthly, The jumbling different metaphors in the same sentence, or the beginning with one metaphor and ending with another, is commonly called a mixt metaphor. Quintilian bears testimony against it in the bitterest terms: "Nam id quoque in primis est custodiendum, ut quo ex genere cœperis translationis, hoc desinas. Multi enim, cum initium a tempestate sumpserunt, incendio aut ruina finiunt: quæ est inconsequentia rerum fœdissima." *L. 8. cap. 6. § 2.*

K. HENRY:—— Will you again unknit
This churlish knot of all-abhorred war,
And move in that obedient orb again,
Where you did give a fair and natural light?

> —*First Part Henry IV. act 5. sc. 1*

> *Whether 'tis nobler in the mind, to suffer*
> *The stings and arrows of outrag'ous fortune;*
> *Or to take arms against a sea of troubles,*
> *And by opposing end them.*

> —*Hamlet, act 3. sc. 2*

In the sixth place, It is unpleasant to join different metaphors in the same period, even where they are preserved distinct. It is difficult to imagine the subject to be first one thing and then another in the same period without interval: the mind is distracted by the rapid transition; and when the imagination is put on such hard duty, its images are too faint to produce any good effect:

> *At regina gravi jamdudum saucia cura,*
> *Vulnus alit venis, et cæco carpitur igni.*
>
> —*Æneid. iv. 1*

> ——— *Est mollis flamma medullas*
> *Interea, et taciturn vivit sub pectore vulnus.*
>
> —*Æneid. iv. 66*

> *Motum ex Metello consule civicum,*
> *Bellique causas, et vitia, et modos,*
> *Ludumque fortunæ, gravesque*
> *Principum amicitias, et arma*
> *Nondum expiatis uncta cruoribus,*
> *Periculosæ plenum opus aleæ,*
> *Tractas, et incedis per ignes*
> *Subpositos cineri doloso.*
>
> —*Horat. Carm. l. 2, ode 1*

In the last place, It is still worse to jumble together metaphorical and natural expression, or to construct a period so as that it must be understood partly metaphorically partly literally. The imagination cannot follow with sufficient ease changes so sudden and unprepared. A metaphor begun and not carried on, hath no beauty; and instead of light there is nothing but obscurity and confusion. Instances of such incorrect composition are without number. I shall, for a specimen, select a few from different authors:

Speaking of Britain,

> *This precious stone set in the sea*
> *Which serves it in the office of a wall,*

> *Or as a moat defensive to a house*
> *Against the envy of less happier lands.*
>
> —*Richard II. act 2. sc. 1*

In the first line Britain is figured to be a precious stone. In the following lines, Britain, divested of her metaphorical dress, is presented to the reader in her natural appearance.

> *These growing feathers pluck'd from Cæsar's wing,*
> *Will make him fly an ordinary pitch,*
> *Who else would soar above the view of men,*
> *And keep us all in servile fearfulness.*
>
> —*Julius Cæsar, act 1. sc. 1*

> *Rebus angustis animosus atque*
> *Fortis adpare: sapienter idem*
> *Contrahes vento nimium secundo*
>
> —Turgida vela

The following is a miserable jumble of expressions, arising from an unsteady view of the subject betwixt its figurative and natural appearance.

> *But now from gath'ring clouds destruction pours,*
> *Which ruins with mad rage our halcyon hours:*
> *Mists from black jealousies the tempest form,*
> *Whilst late divisions reinforce the storm.*
>
> —*Dispensary, canto 3*

> *To thee, the world its present homage pays,*
> *The harvest early, but mature the praise.*
>
> —*Pope's imitation of Horace, b. 2*

> *Oui, sa pudeur n'est que franche grimace,*
> *Qu'une ombre de vertu qui garde mal la place,*
> *Et qui s'evanouit, comme l'on peut savoir*
> *Aux rayons du soleil qu'une bourse fait voir.*
>
> —*Molliere, L'Etourdi, act 3. sc. 2*

> *Et son feu depourvû de sense et de lecture,*
> *S'éteint a chaque pas, faute de nourriture.*
>
> —Boileau, L'art poetique, chant. 3. l. 319

Dryden, in his dedication to the translation of *Juvenal*, says,

When thus, as I may say, before the use of the loadstone, or knowledge of the compass, I was sailing in a vast ocean, without other help than the pole-star of the ancients, and the rules of the French stage among the moderns, &c.

There is a time when factions, by the vehemence of their own fermentation, stun and disable one another.

Bolingbroke

This fault of jumbling the figure and plain expression into one confused mass, is not less common in allegory than in metaphor. Take the following example.

> ———— *Heu! quoties fidem,*
> *Mutatosque Deos flebit, et aspera*
> *Nigris æquora ventis*
> *Emirabitur insolens,*
> *Qui nunc te fruitur credulus aureâ:*
> *Qui semper vacuam, semper amabilem*
> *Sperat, nescius auræ*
> *Fallacis.*
>
> —Horat. Carm. l. 1. ode 5

Lord Halifax, speaking of the ancient fabulists: "They (says he) wrote in signs and spoke in parables: all their fables carry a double meaning: the story is one and entire; the characters the same throughout; not broken or changed, and always conformable to the nature of the creature they introduce. They never tell you, that the dog which snapp'd at a shadow, lost his troop of horse; that would be unintelligible. This is his (Dryden's) new way of telling a story, and confounding the moral and the fable together." After instancing from the hind and panther, he goes on thus: "What relation has the hind to our Saviour? or what notion have we of a panther's bible? If you say he means the church, how does the church feed on lawns, or range in the forest? Let it be always a church or always a cloven-footed beast, for we cannot bear his shifting the scene every line."

A few words more upon allegory. Nothing gives greater pleasure than this figure, when the representative subject bears a strong analogy, in all its circumstances, to that which is represented. But the choice is seldom so lucky; the resemblance of the representative subject to the principal, being generally so faint and obscure, as to puzzle and not please. An allegory is still more difficult in painting than in poetry. The former can show no resemblance but what appears to the eye: the latter hath many other resources for showing the resemblance. With respect to what the Abbé du Bos[12] terms mixt allegorical compositions, these may do in poetry, because in writing the allegory can easily be distinguished from the historical part: no person mistakes Virgil's Fame for a real being. But such a mixture in a picture is intolerable; because in a picture the objects must appear all of the same kind, wholly real or wholly emblematical. The history of Mary de Medicis, in the palace of Luxembourg, painted by Rubens, is in a vicious taste, by a perpetual jumble of real and allegorical personages, which produce a discordance of parts and an obscurity upon the whole: witness in particular, the tablature representing the arrival of Mary de Medicis at Marseilles: mixt with the real personages, the Nereids and Tritons appear sounding their shells. Such a mixture of fiction and reality in the same group, is strangely absurd. The picture of Alexander and Roxana, described by Lucian, is gay and fanciful: but it suffers by the allegorical figures. It is not in the wit of man to invent an allegorical representation deviating farther from any appearance of resemblance, than one exhibited by Lewis XIV *anno* 1664; in which an overgrown chariot, intended to represent that of the sun, is dragg'd along, surrounded with men and women, representing the four ages of the world, the celestial signs, the seasons, the hours, *&c.*: a monstrous composition; and yet scarce more absurd than Guido's tablature of Aurora.

In an allegory, as well as in a metaphor, terms ought to be chosen that properly and literally are applicable to the representative subject. Nor ought any circumstance to be added, that is not proper to the representative subject, however justly it may be applicable figuratively to the principal. Upon this account the following allegory is faulty.

---

12. Reflections sur la Poesie, vol. 1. sect. 24.

> *Ferus et Cupido,*
> *Semper ardentes acuens sagittas*
> *Cote cruentâ.*
>
> —*Horat. l. 2. ode 8*

For though blood may suggest the cruelty of love, it is an improper or immaterial circumstance in the representative subject: water, not blood, is proper for a whetstone.

We proceed to the next head, which is, to examine in what circumstances these figures are proper, in what improper. This inquiry is not altogether superseded by what is said upon the same subject in the chapter of comparisons; because, upon trial, it will be found, that a short metaphor or allegory may be proper, where a simile, drawn out to a greater length, and in its nature more solemn, would scarce be relished. The difference however is not considerable; and in most instances the same rules are applicable to both. And, in the first place, a metaphor, as well as a simile, are excluded from common conversation, and from the description of ordinary incidents.

In the next place, in any severe passion which totally occupies the mind, metaphor is unnatural. For that reason, we must condemn the following speech of Macbeth.

> *Methought, I heard a voice cry, Sleep no more!*
> *Macbeth doth murther sleep; the innocent sleep;*
> *Sleep that knits up the ravell'd sleeve of Care,*
> *The birth of each day's life, sore Labour's bath,*
> *Balm of hurt minds, great Nature's second course,*
> *Chief nourisher in life's feast.——*
>
> —*Act 2. sc. 3*

The next example, of deep despair, beside the highly figurative style, hath more the air of raving than of sense:

Calista: Is it the voice of thunder, or my father?
　　Madness! Confusion! let the storm come on,
　　Let the tumultuous roar drive all upon me,
　　Dash my devoted bark; ye surges, break it;

> 'Tis for my ruin that the tempest rises.
> When I am lost, sunk to the bottom low,
> Peace shall return, and all be calm again.
>
> *—Fair Penitent, act 4*

The metaphor I next introduce, is sweet and lively, but it suits not the fiery temper of Chamont, inflamed with passion. Parables are not the language of wrath venting itself without restraint:

> CHAMONT: You took her up a little tender flower,
>   Just sprouted on a bank, which the next frost
>   Had nip'd; and with a careful loving hand,
>   Transplanted her into your own fair garden,
>   Where the sun always shines: there long she flourish'd,
>   Grew sweet to sense and lovely to the eye,
>   Till at the last a cruel spoiler came,
>   Cropt this fair rose, and rifled all its sweetness,
>   Then cast it like a loathsome weed away.
>
> *—Orphan, act 4*

The following speech, full of imagery, is not natural in grief and dejection of mind.

> GONSALEZ: O my son! from the blind dotage
>   Of a father's fondness these ills arose.
>   For thee I've been ambitious, base and bloody:
>   For thee I've plung'd into this sea of sin;
>   Stemming the tide with only one weak hand,
>   While t'other bore the crown, (to wreathe thy brow),
>   Whose weight has sunk me ere I reach'd the shore.
>
> *—Mourning Bride, act 5. sc. 6*

The finest picture that ever was drawn of deep distress, is in Macbeth[13], where Macduff is represented lamenting his wife and children, inhumanly murdered by the tyrant. Struck with the news, he questions the messenger over and over; not that he doubted the fact, but that his heart revolted

---

13. Act 4. sc. 6.

against so cruel a misfortune. After struggling sometime with his grief, he turns from his wife and children to their savage butcher; and then gives vent to his resentment; but still with manliness and dignity:

> *O, I could play the woman with mine eyes,*
> *And braggart with my tongue. But, gentle Heav'n!*
> *Cut short all intermission: front to front*
> *Bring thou this fiend of Scotland and myself;*
> *Within my sword's length set him—If he 'scape,*
> *Then Heav'n forgive him too.*

This passage is a delicious picture of human nature. One expression only seems doubtful. In examining the messenger, Macduff expresses himself thus:

> *He hath no children—all my pretty ones!*
> *Did you say all? what all? Oh, hell-kite! all?*
> *What! all my pretty little chickens and their dam,*
> *At one fell swoop!*

Metaphorical expression, I am sensible, may sometimes be used with grace, where a regular simile would be intolerable: but there are situations so overwhelming, as not to admit even the slightest metaphor. It requires great delicacy of taste to determine with firmness, whether the present case be of that nature. I incline to think it is; and yet I would not willingly alter a single word of this admirable scene.

But metaphorical language is proper when a man struggles to bear with dignity or decency a misfortune however great. The struggle agitates and animates the mind:

WOLSEY: Farewell, a long farewell, to all my greatness!
   This is the state of man; today he puts forth
   The tender leaves of hopes; tomorrow blossoms,
   And bears his blushing honours thick upon him;
   The third day comes a frost, a killing frost,
   And when he thinks, good easy man, full surely
   His greatness is a ripening, nips his root,
   And then he falls as I do.

—Henry VIII. act 3. sc. 6

Section. VII

Figure of Speech.

In the section immediately foregoing, a figure of speech is defined, "The employing a word in a sense different from what is proper to it"; and the new or uncommon sense of the word is termed *the figurative sense*. The figurative sense must have a relation to that which is proper; and the more intimate the relation is, the figure is the more happy. How ornamental this figure is to language, will not be readily imagined by anyone who hath not given peculiar attention. I shall endeavour to display its capital beauties and advantages. In the first place, a word used figuratively, together with its new sense, suggests what it commonly bears: and thus it has the effect to present two objects; one signified by the figurative sense, which may be termed *the principal object*; and one signified by the proper sense, which may be termed *accessory*. The principal makes a part of the thought; the accessory is merely ornamental. In this respect, a figure of speech is precisely similar to concordant sounds in music, which, without contributing to the melody, make it harmonious. I explain myself by examples. *Youth*, by a figure of speech, is termed *the morning of life*. This expression signifies *youth*, the principal object, which enters into the thought: but it suggests, at the same time, the proper sense of *morning*; and this accessory object being in itself beautiful and connected by resemblance to the principal object, is not a little ornamental. I give another example, of a different kind, where an attribute is expressed figuratively, *Imperious ocean*. Together with the figurative meaning of the epithet *imperious*, there is suggested its proper meaning, *viz.* the stern authority of a despotic prince. Upon this figurative power of words, Vida descants with great elegance:

> *Nonne vides, verbis ut veris sæpe relictis*
> *Accersant simulata, aliundeque nomina porro*
> *Transportent, aptentque aliis ea rebus; ut ipsæ,*
> *Exuviasque novas, res, insolitosque colores*
> *Indutæ, sæpe externi mirentur amictus*
> *Unde illi, lætæque aliena luce fruantur,*
> *Mutatoque habitu, nec jam sua nomina mallent?*
> *Sæpe ideo, cum bella canunt, incendia credas*
> *Cernere, diluviumque ingens surgentibus undis.*

Contrà etiam Martis pugnas imitabitur ignis,
Cum surit accensis acies Vulcania campis.
Nec turbato oritur quondam minor æquore pugna:
Confligunt animosi Euri certamine vasto
Inter se, pugnantque adversis molibus undæ.
Usque adeo passim sua res insignia lætæ
Permutantque, juvantque vicissim; & mutua sese
Altera in alterius transformat protinus ora.
Tum specie capti gaudent spectare legentes:
Nam diversa simul datur è re cernere eadem
Multarum simulacra animo subeuntia rerum.

—*Poet. lib. 3. l. 44*

In the next place, this figure possesses a signal power of aggrandising an object, by the following means. Words, which have no original beauty but what arises from their sound, acquire an adventitious beauty from their meaning. A word signifying anything that is agreeable, becomes by that means agreeable; for the agreeableness of the object is communicated to its name[14]. This acquired beauty, by the force of custom, adheres to the word even when used figuratively; and the beauty received from the thing it properly signifies, is communicated to the thing which it is made to signify figuratively. Consider the foregoing expression *Imperious ocean*, how much more elevated it is than *Stormy ocean*.

Thirdly, this figure hath a happy effect in preventing the familiarity of proper names. The familiarity of a proper name, is communicated to the thing it signifies by means of their intimate connection; and the thing is thereby brought down in our feeling[15]. This bad effect is prevented by using a figurative word instead of one that is proper; as, for example, when we express the sky by terming it *the blue vault of heaven*. For though no work made with hands can compare with the sky in magnificence, the expression however is good, by preventing the object from being brought down by the familiarity of its proper name. With respect to the degrading familiarity of proper names, Vida has the following passage.

---

14. See chap 2. part. 1. sect. 5.
15. I have often regretted, that a factious spirit of opposition to the reigning family makes it necessary in public worship to distinguish the King by his proper name. One will scarce imagine, who has not made the trial, how much better it sounds to pray for our Sovereign Lord the King, without any addition.

> *Hinc si dura mihi passus dicendus Ulysses,*
> *Non illum vero memorabo nomine, sed qui*
> *Et mores hominum multorum vidit, & urbes,*
> *Naufragus eversæ post sæva incendia Trojæ.*
>
> —*Poet. lib. 2. l. 46*

Lastly, by this figure language is enriched and rendered more copious. In that respect, were there no other, a figure of speech is a happy invention. This property is finely touched by Vida:

> *Quinetiam agricolas ea fandi nota voluptas*
> *Exercet, dum læta seges, dum trudere gemmas*
> *Incipiunt vites, sitientiaque ætheris imbrem*
> *Prata bibunt, ridentque satis surgentibus agri.*
> *Hanc vulgo speciem propriæ penuria vocis*
> *Intulit, indictisque urgens in rebus egestas.*
> *Quippe ubi se vera ostendebant nomina nusquam,*
> *Fas erat hinc atque hinc transferre simillima veris.*
>
> —*Poet. lib. 3. l. 90*

The beauties I have mentioned belong to every figure of speech. Several other beauties peculiar to one or other sort, I shall have occasion to remark afterward.

NOT ONLY SUBJECTS, BUT QUALITIES, actions, effects, may be expressed figuratively. Thus as to subjects, *the gates of breath* for the lips, *the watery kingdom* for the ocean. As to qualities, *fierce* for stormy, in the expression *Fierce winter*: *altus* for profundus, *altus puteus, altum mare*: *Breathing* for perspiring, *Breathing plants*. Again, as to actions, the sea *rages*: Time will *melt* her frozen thoughts: Time *kills* grief. An effect is put for the cause, as *lux* for the sun; and a cause for the effect, as *boum labores* for corn. The relation of resemblance is one plentiful source of figures of speech; and nothing is more common than to apply to one object the name of another that resembles it in any respect. Height, size, and worldly greatness, though in themselves they have no resemblance, produce emotions in the mind that have a resemblance; and, led by this resemblance, we naturally express worldly greatness by height or size. One feels a certain uneasiness in looking down to a great depth:

and hence depth is made to express anything disagreeable by excess; as *depth* of grief, *depth* of despair. Again, height of place and time long past, produce similar feelings; and hence the expression, *Ut altius repetam*. Distance in past time, producing a strong feeling, is put for any strong feeling: *Nihil mihi antiquius nostra amicitia*. Shortness with relation to space, for shortness with relation to time: *Brevis esse laboro; obscurus fio*. Suffering a punishment resembles paying a debt: hence *pendere pœnas*. Upon the same account, light may be put for glory, sun-shine for prosperity, and weight for importance.

Many words, originally figurative, having, by long and constant use, lost their figurative power, are degraded to the inferior rank of proper terms. Thus the words that express the operations of the mind, have in all languages been originally figurative. The reason holds in all, that when these operations came first under consideration, there was no other way of describing them but by what they resembled. It was not practicable to give them proper names, as may be done to objects that can be ascertained by sight and touch. A *soft* nature, *jarring* tempers, *weight* of wo, *pompous* phrase, *beget* compassion, *assuage* grief, *break* a vow, *bend* the eye downward, *shower* down curses, *drown'd* in tears, *wrapt* in joy, *warm'd* with eloquence, *loaden* with spoils, and a thousand other expressions of the like nature, have lost their figurative sense. Some terms there are, that cannot be said to be either purely figurative or altogether proper: originally figurative, they are tending to simplicity, without having lost altogether their figurative power. Virgil's *Regina saucia cura*, is perhaps one of these expressions. With ordinary readers, *saucia* will be considered as expressing simply the effect of grief; but one of a lively imagination will exalt the phrase into a figure.

To epitomise this subject, and at the same time to give a clear view of it, I cannot think of a better method, than to present to the reader a list of the several relations upon which figures of speech are commonly founded. This list I divide into two tables; one of subjects expressed figuratively, and one of attributes.

First Table

Subjects expressed figuratively.

1. A word proper to one subject employed figuratively to express a resembling subject.

There is no figure of speech so frequent, as what is derived from the relation of resemblance. Youth, for example, is signified figuratively by the *morning* of life. The life of a man resembles a natural day in several particulars. The morning is the beginning of day, youth the beginning of life: the morning is chearful, so is youth; &c. By another resemblance, a bold warrior is termed the *thunderbolt* of war; a multitude of troubles, a *sea* of troubles.

No other figure of speech possesses so many different beauties, as that which is founded on resemblance. Beside the beauties above mentioned, common to all sorts, it possesses in particular the beauty of a metaphor or of a simile. A figure of speech built upon resemblance, suggests always a comparison betwixt the principal subject and the accessory; and by this means every good effect of a metaphor or simile, may, in a short and lively manner, be produced by this figure of speech.

2. A word proper to the effect employ'd figuratively to express the cause.

    Lux for the sun. *Shadow* for cloud. A helmet is signified by the expression *glittering terror*. A tree by *shadow* or *umbrage*. Hence the expression,

    Nec habet Pelion umbras.

    —*Ovid*

    Where the dun umbrage hangs.

    —*Spring, l. 1023*

    A wound is made to signify an arrow:

    Vulnere non pedibus te consequar.

    —*Ovid*

There is a peculiar force and beauty in this figure. The word which signifies figuratively the principal subject, denotes it to be a cause by suggesting the effect.

3. A word proper to the cause, employ'd figuratively to express the effect.

Boumque labores for corn. *Sorrow* or *grief* for tears.

> *Again Ulysses veil'd his pensive head,*
> *Again unmann'd, a show'r of* sorrow *shed.*

> *Streaming* Grief *his faded cheek bedew'd.*

Blindness for darkness:

> *Cæcis erramus in undis.*
>
> —*Æneid. iii. 200*

There is a peculiar energy in this figure similar to that in the former. The figurative name denotes the subject to be an effect by suggesting its cause.

4. Two things being intimately connected, the proper name of the one employ'd figuratively to signify the other.

Day for light. *Night* for darkness. Hence, A sudden night. *Winter* for a storm at sea.

> *Interea magno misceri murmure pontum,*
> *Emissamque Hyemem sensit Neptunus.*
>
> —*Æneid. i. 128*

This last figure would be too bold for a British writer, as a storm at sea is not inseparably connected with winter in this climate.

5. A word proper to an attribute employ'd figuratively to denote the subject.

Youth and *beauty* for those who are young and beautiful:

> *Youth and beauty shall be laid in dust.*

Majesty for the King:

> *What art thou, that usurp'st this time of night,*
> *Together with that fair and warlike form,*

> *In which the Majesty of buried Denmark*
> *Did sometime march?*
>
> —*Hamlet*, act 1. sc. 1

> ——— *Or have ye chosen this place,*
> *After the toils of battle, to repose*
> *Your weary'd* virtue*?*
>
> —*Paradise Lost*

Verdure *for a green field.* Summer. l. 301.

Speaking of cranes:

> *To pigmy nations wounds and death they bring,*
> *And all the* war *descends upon the wing.*
>
> —*Iliad* iii. 10

> *Cool* age *advances venerably wise.*
>
> —*Iliad* iii. 149

The peculiar beauty of this figure arises from suggesting an attribute that embellishes the subject, or puts it in a stronger light.

6. A complex term employ'd figuratively to denote one of the component parts.
    Funus for a dead body. *Burial* for a grave.

7. The name of one of the component parts instead of the complex term.
    Tœda for a marriage. The *East* for a country situated east from us. *Jovis vestigia servat*, for imitating Jupiter in general.

8. A word signifying time or place employ'd figuratively to denote a connected subject.
    Clime for a nation, or for a constitution of government: Hence the expression, *Merciful clime. Fleecy winter* for snow. *Seculum felix.*

9. A part for the whole.

The *pole* for the earth. The *head* for the person.

> *Triginta minas pro capite tuo dedi.*
>
> —*Plautus*

Tergum for the man:

> *Fugiens tergum.*
>
> —*Ovid*

Vultus for the man:

> *Jam fulgor armorum fugaces*
> *Terret equos, equitumque vultus.*
>
> —*Horat*

> *Quis desiderio sit pudor aut modus*
> *Tam chari* capitis?
>
> —*Horat*

> *Dumque virent* genua.
>
> —*Horat*

> *Thy growing virtues justify'd my cares,*
> *And promis'd comfort to my* silver hairs.
>
> —*Iliad* ix. 616

> ——*Forthwith from the pool he rears*
> *His mighty* stature.
>
> —*Paradise Lost*

> *The silent* heart *which grief assails.*
>
> —*Parnell*

The peculiar beauty of this figure consists in marking out that part which makes the greatest figure.

10. The name of the container employ'd figuratively to signify what is contained.

    Grove for the birds in it: Vocal *grove*. *Ships* for the seamen: Agonizing *ships*. *Mountains* for the sheep pasturing upon them: Bleating *mountains*. *Zacynthus, Ithaca, &c.* for the inhabitants. *Ex mæstis domibus.* Livy.

11. The name of the sustainer employ'd figuratively to signify what is sustained.

    Altar for the sacrifice. *Field* for the battle fought upon it: Well-fought *field*.

12. The name of the materials employ'd figuratively to signify the things made of them.

    Ferrum for *gladius*.

13. The names of the Heathen deities employ'd figuratively to signify what they patronise.

    Jove for the air. *Mars* for war. *Venus* for beauty. *Cupid* for love. *Ceres* for corn. *Neptune* for the sea. *Vulcan* for fire.

This figure bestows great elevation upon the subject; and therefore ought to be confined to the higher strains of poetry.

Second Table

Attributes expressed figuratively.

1. When two attributes are connected, the name of the one may be employ'd figuratively to express the other.

    Purity and virginity are attributes of the same person. Hence the expression, *Virgin* snow for pure snow.

2. A word signifying properly an attribute of one subject, employ'd figuratively to express a resembling attribute of another subject.

    Tottering state. *Imperious* ocean. *Angry* flood. *Raging* tempest. *Shallow* fears.

> *My sure divinity shall bear the shield,*
> *And edge thy sword to* reap *the glorious field.*

—*Odyssey* xx. 61

Black omen, for an omen that portends bad fortune:

> Ater *odor.*
>
> —*Virgil*

The peculiar beauty of this figure arises from suggesting a comparison.

3. A word proper to the subject, employ'd to express one of its attributes.

> Mens *for* intellectus. Mens *for a resolution.*
> *Istam, oro, exue mentem.*

4. When two subjects have a resemblance by a common quality, the name of the one subject may be employ'd figuratively to denote that quality in the other.

> Summer *life for agreeable life.*

5. The name of the instrument, made to signify the power of employing it.

> —— *Melpomene, cui liquidam pater*
> *Vocem cum* cithara *dedit.*

The ample field of figurative expression display'd in these tables, affords great scope for reasoning and reflection. Several of the observations relating to metaphor, are applicable to figures of speech. These I shall slightly retouch, with some additions peculiarly adapted to the present subject.

In the first place, as the figure under consideration is built upon relation, we find from experience, and it must be obvious from reason, that the beauty of the figure depends on the intimacy of the relation betwixt the figurative and proper sense of the word. A slight resemblance, in particular, will never make this figure agreeable. The expression, for example, *drink down a secret*, for listening to a secret with attention, is harsh and uncouth, because there is scarce any resemblance betwixt *listening* and *drinking*. The expression *weighty crack*, used by Ben Johnson for *loud crack*, is worse if possible: a loud sound has not the slightest resemblance to a piece of matter that is weighty. The following expression of Lucretius is not less faulty. "Et lepido quæ sunt *fucata* sonore." i. 645.

———— Sed magis
Pugnas et exactos tyrannos
Densum humeris bibit *aure vulgus.*

—*Horat. Carm. l. 2. ode 13*

Phemius! let acts of gods, and heroes old,
What ancient bards in hall and bow'r have told,
Attemper'd to the lyre, your voice employ,
Such the pleas'd ear will drink *with silent joy,*

—*Odyssey* i. 433

Strepitumque exterritus hausit.

—*Æneid.* vi. 559

———— Write, my Queen,
And with mine eyes I'll drink *the words you send.*

—*Cymbeline, act 1. sc. 2*

As thus th' effulgence tremulous I drink.

—*Summer, l. 1684*

Neque audit *currus habenas.*

—*Georg.* i. 514

O Prince! (Lycaon's valiant son reply'd)
As thine the steeds, be thine the task to guide.
The horses practis'd to their lord's command,
Shall hear *the rein, and answer to thy hand.*

—*Iliad.* v. 288

The following figures of speech seem altogether wild and extravagant, the figurative and proper meaning having no connection whatever. *Moving* softness, freshness *breathes*, *breathing* prospect, *flowing* spring, *dewy* light, *lucid* coolness, and many others of this false coin may be found in Thomson's *Seasons*.

Secondly, the proper sense of the word ought to bear some proportion to the figurative sense, and not soar much above it, nor sink much below it. This rule, as well as the foregoing, is finely illustrated by Vida:

> *Hæc adeo cum sint, cum fas audere poetis*
> *Multa modis multis; tamen observare memento,*
> *Si quando haud propriis rem mavis dicere verbis,*
> *Translatisque aliunde notis, longeque petitis,*
> *Ne nimiam ostendas, quærendo talia, curam.*
> *Namque aliqui exercent vim duram, et rebus iniqui*
> *Nativam eripiunt formam, indignantibus ipsis,*
> *Invitasque jubent alienos sumere vultus.*
> *Haud magis imprudens mihi erit, et luminis expers,*
> *Qui puero ingentes habitus det ferre gigantis,*
> *Quam siquis stabula alta lares appellet equinos,*
> *Aut crines magnæ genitricis gramina dicat.*
>
> —*Poet. l. iii. 148*

Thirdly, in a figure of speech, every circumstance ought to be avoided that agrees with the proper sense only, not the figurative sense; for it is the latter that expresses the thought, and the former serves for no other purpose but to make harmony:

> *Zacynthus green with ever-shady groves,*
> *And Ithaca, presumptuous boast their loves;*
> *Obtruding on my choice a second lord,*
> *They press the Hymenean rite abhorr'd.*
>
> —*Odyssey* xix. 152

Zacynthus here standing figuratively for the inhabitants, the description of the island is quite out of place. It puzzles the reader, by making him doubt whether the word ought to be taken in its proper or figurative sense.

> *———— Write, my Queen,*
> *And with mine eyes I'll drink the words you send,*
> *Though ink be made of gall.*
>
> —*Cymbeline, act 1. sc. 2*

The disgust one has to drink ink in reality, is nothing to the purpose where the subject is drinking ink figuratively.

In the fourth place, to draw consequences from a figure of speech, as if the word were to be understood literally, is a gross absurdity, for it is confounding truth with fiction:

> *Be Moubray's sins so heavy in his bosom,*
> *That they may break his foaming courser's back,*
> *And throw the rider headlong in the lists,*
> *A caitiff recreant to my cousin Hereford.*
>
> —*Richard II. act 1. sc. 3*

Sin may be imagined heavy in a figurative sense: but weight in a proper sense belongs to the accessory only; and therefore to describe the effects of weight, is to desert the principal subject, and to convert the accessory into a principal.

CROMWELL: How does your Grace?
WOLSEY: Why, well;
   Never so truly happy, my good Cromwell.
   I know myself now, and I feel within me
   A peace above all earthly dignities,
   A still and quiet conscience. The King has cur'd me,
   I humbly thank his Grace; and, from these shoulders,
   These ruin'd pillars, out of pity taken
   A load would sink a navy, too much honour.

—*Henry VIII. act 3. sc. 6*

Ulysses speaking of Hector:

> *I wonder now how yonder city stands*
> *When we have here the base and pillar by us.*
>
> —*Troilus and Cressida, act 4. sc. 9*

OTHELLO: No, my heart is turn'd to stone: I strike it and it hurts my hand.

—*Othello, act 4. sc. 5*

Not less, even in this despicable now,
Than when my name fill'd Afric with affrights,
And froze your hearts beneath your torrid zone.

—*Don Sebastian King of Portugal, act 1*

How long a space, since first I lov'd, it is!
To look into a glass I fear,
And am surpris'd with wonder, when I miss
Grey hairs and wrinkles there.

—*Cowley, vol. 1. p. 86*

I chose the flourishing'st tree in all the park
With freshest boughs, and fairest head;
I cut my love into his gentle bark,
And in three days behold 'tis dead;
My very written flames so violent be,
They've burnt and wither'd up the tree.

—*Cowley, vol. 1. p. 136*

Ah, mighty Love, that it were inward heat
Which made this precious Limbeck sweat!
But what, alas, ah what does it avail
That she weeps tears so wond'rous cold,
As scarce the asses hoof can hold,
So cold, that I admire they fall not hail.

—*Cowley, vol. 1. p. 132*

Je crains que cette saison
Ne nous amenne la peste;
La gueule du chien celeste
Vomit feu sur l'horison.

> *A fin que je m'en délivre,*
> *Je veux lire ton gros livre*
> *Jusques au dernier feüillet:*
> *Tout ce que ta plume trace,*
> *Robinet, a de la glace*
> *A faire trembler Juillet.*
>
> —*Maynard*

> *In me tota ruens Venus*
> *Cyprum deseruit.*
>
> —*Horat. Carm. lib. 1. ode. 19*

ALMERIA: O Alphonso, Alphonso!
   Devouring seas have wash'd thee from my sight,
   No time shall rase thee from my memory;
   No, I will live to be thy monument:
   The cruel ocean is no more thy tomb;
   But in my heart thou art interr'd.

> —*Mourning Bride, act 1. sc. 1*

This would be very right, if there were any inconsistence in being interred in one place really and in another place figuratively.

From considering that a word employ'd in a figurative sense suggests at the same time its proper meaning, a fifth rule occurs, That to raise a figure of speech, we ought to use no word, the proper sense of which is inconsistent or incongruous with the subject: for no incongruity, far less inconsistency, whether real or imagined, ought to enter into the expression of any subject:

> *Interea genitor Tyberini ad fluminis undam*
> *Vulnera* siccabat *lymphis*——
>
> —*Æneid. x. 833*

> *Tres adeo incertos cæca caligine* soles
> *Erramus pelago, totidem sine sidere noctes.*
>
> —*Æneid.* iii. 203

The foregoing rule may be extended to form a sixth, That no epithet ought to be given to the figurative sense of a word that agrees not also with its proper sense:

> ——— *Dicat Opuntiæ*
> *Frater Megillæ, quo* beatus
> *Vulnere.*

—*Horat. Carm. lib. 1. ode 27*

> *Parcus deorum cultor, et infrequens,*
> Insanientis *dum sapientiæ*
> *Consultus erro.*

—*Horat. Carm. lib. 1. ode 34*

Seventhly, The crowding into one period or thought different figures of speech, is not less faulty than crowding metaphors in that manner. The mind is distracted in the quick transition from one image to another, and is puzzled instead of being pleased:

> *I am of ladies most deject and wretched,*
> *That suck'd the honey of his music vows.*

—*Hamlet*

> *My bleeding bosom sickens at the sound.*

—*Odyss.* i. 439

> ——— *Ah miser,*
> *Quantâ laboras in* Charybdi*!*
> *Digne puer meliore* flammâ.
> *Quæ saga, quis te solvere Thessalis*
> *Magus* venenis, *quis poterit deus?*
> *Vix illigatum te triformi*
> *Pegasus expediet* Chimærâ.

—*Horat. Carm. lib. 1. ode 27*

Eighthly, If crowding figures be bad, it is still worse to graft one figure upon another. For instance,

> *While his keen falchion drinks the warriors lives.*
>
> —*Iliad* xi. 211

A falchion drinking the warriors blood is a figure built upon resemblance, which is passable. But then in the expression, *lives* is again put for blood; and by thus grafting one figure upon another the expression is rendered obscure and unpleasant.

Ninthly, Intricate and involved figures, that can scarce be analized or reduced to plain language, are least of all tolerable:

> *Votis incendimus aras.*
>
> —*Æneid.* iii. 279

> —— *Onerantque canistris*
> *Dona laboratæ Cereris.*
>
> —*Æneid.* viii. 180

Vulcan to the Cyclopes,

> *Arma acri facienda viro: nunc viribus usus,*
> *Nunc manibus rapidis, omni nunc arte magistra:*
> Præcipitate *moras.*
>
> —*Æneid.* viii. 441

> ——— *Huic gladio, perque ærea suta*
> *Per tunicam squalentem auro, latus* haurit *apertum.*
>
> —*Æneid.* x. 313

> *Semotique prius tarda necessitas*
> *Lethi, corripuit gradum.*
>
> —*Horat. Carm. lib. 1. ode 3*

> *Scribêris Vario fortis, et hostium*
> *Victor, Mæonii carminis* alite.
>
> —*Horat. Carm. lib. 1. ode 6*

> *Else shall our fates be number'd with the dead.*
>
> —Iliad v. 294

> *Commutual death the fate of war confounds.*
>
> —Iliad viii. 85. and xi. 117

Speaking of Proteus,

> *Instant he wears, elusive of the rape,*
> *The mimic force of every savage shape.*
>
> —Odyss. iv. 563

> *Rolling convulsive on the floor, is seen*
> *The piteous object of a prostrate Queen.*
>
> —Ibid. iv. 952

> *The mingling tempest waves its gloom.*
>
> —Autumn, 337

> *A various sweetness swells the gentle race.*
>
> —Ibid. 640

> *A sober calm fleeces unbounded ether.*
>
> —Ibid. 967

> *The distant water-fall swells in the breeze.*
>
> —Winter, 738

In the tenth place, When a subject is introduced by its proper name, it is absurd to attribute to it the properties of a different subject to which the word is sometimes apply'd in a figurative sense:

> *Hear me, oh Neptune! thou whose arms are hurl'd*
> *From shore to shore, and gird the solid world.*
>
> —Odyss. ix. 617

Neptune is here introduced personally, and not figuratively for the ocean: the description therefore, which is only applicable to the ocean, is altogether improper.

It is not sufficient, that a figure of speech be regularly constructed, and be free from blemish: it requires taste to discern when it is proper when improper; and taste, I suspect, is the only guide we can rely on. One however may gather from reflection and experience, that ornaments and graces suit not any of the dispiriting passions, nor are proper for expressing anything grave and important. In familiar conversation, they are in some measure ridiculous. Prospero in the *Tempest*, speaking to his daughter Miranda, says,

> *The fringed curtains of thine eyes advance,*
> *And say what thou seest yond.*

No exception can be taken to the justness of the figure; and circumstances may be imagined to make it proper: but it is certainly not proper in familiar conversation.

In the last place, though figures of speech have a charming effect when accurately constructed and properly introduced, they ought however to be scattered with a sparing hand: nothing is more luscious, and nothing consequently more satiating, than redundant ornament of any kind.

XXI

Narration and Description

Horace, and many writers after him, give instructions for chusing a subject adapted to the genius of the author. But rules of criticism would be endless, did one descend to peculiarities in talent or genius. The aim of the present work is, to consider human nature in general, and to explore what is common to the species. The choice of a subject comes not under such a plan: but the manner of execution comes under it; because the manner of execution is subjected to general rules. These rules respect the things expressed, as well as the language or expression; which suggests a division of the present chapter into two parts; first of thoughts, and next of words. I pretend not to justify this division as entirely accurate. In discoursing of the thoughts, it is difficult to abstract altogether from words; and still more difficult, in discoursing of the words, to abstract altogether from thought.

The first observation is, That the thoughts which embellish a narration ought to be chaste and solid. While the mind is intent upon facts, it is little disposed to the operarations of the imagination. Poetical images in a grave history are intolerable; and yet Strada's Belgic history is full of poetical images. These being discordant with the subject, are disgustful; and they have a still worse effect, by giving an air of fiction to a genuine history. Such flowers ought to be scattered with a sparing hand, even in epic poetry; and at no rate are they proper, till the reader be warmed, and by an enlivened imagination be prepared to relish them: in that state of mind, they are extremely agreeable. But while we are sedate and attentive to an historical chain of facts, we reject with disdain every fiction. This Belgic history is indeed wofully vicious both in matter and form: it is stuffed with frigid and unmeaning reflections, as well as with poetical flashes, which, even laying aside the impropriety, are mere tinsel.

Vida[1], following Horace, recommends a modest commencement of an epic poem; giving for a reason, that the writer ought to husband his

---

1. Poet. lib. 2. 1. 30.

fire. This reason has weight; but what is said above suggests a reason still more weighty: Bold thoughts and figures are never relished till the mind be heated and thoroughly engaged, which is not the reader's case at the commencement. Shakespear, in the first part of his history of Henry VI begins with a sentiment too bold for the most heated imagination:

> BEDFORD: Hung be the heav'ns with black, yield day tonight!
> Comets, importing change of times and states,
> Brandish your crystal tresses in the sky,
> And with them scourge the bad revolting stars,
> That have consented unto Henry's death!
>
> Henry the Fifth, too famous to live long!
> England ne'er lost a king of so much worth.

The passage with which Strada begins his history, is too poetical for a subject of that kind; and at any rate too high for the beginning of a grave performance. A third reason ought to have not less influence than either of the former: A man who, upon his first appearance, endeavours to exhibit all his talents, is never relished; the first periods of a work ought therefore to be short, natural, and simple. Cicero, in his oration *pro Archia poeta*, errs against this rule: his reader is out of breath at the very first period, which seems never to end. Burnet begins the history of his own times with a period long and intricate.

A third rule or observation is, That where the subject is intended for entertainment solely, not for instruction, a thing ought to be described as it appears, not as it is in reality. In running, for example, the impulse upon the ground is accurately proportioned to the celerity of motion: in appearance it is otherwise; for a person in swift motion seems to skim the ground, and scarcely to touch it. Virgil, with great taste, describes quick running according to its appearance; and thereby raises an image far more lively, than it could have been by adhering scrupulously to truth:

> *Hos super advenit Volsca de gente Camilla,*
> *Agmen agens equitum et florentes ære catervas,*
> *Bellatrix: non illa colo calathisve Minervæ*
> *Fœmineas assueta manus; sed prælia virgo*
> *Dura pati, cursuque pedum prævertere ventos.*
> *Illa vel intactæ segetis per summa volaret*

> *Gramina: nec teneras cursu læsisset aristas:*
> *Vel mare per medium, fluctu suspensa tumenti,*
> *Ferret iter; celeres nec tingeret æquore plantas.*

—*Æneid* vii. 803

This example is copied by the author of *Telemachus*:

> *Les Brutiens sont legeres à la course comme les cerfs, et comme les daims. On croiroit que l'herbe même la plus tendre n'est point foulée sous leurs pieds; à peine laissent ils dans le sable quelques traces de leurs pas.*

—*Liv.* 10

Again,

> *Déja il avoit abattu Eusilas si léger à la course, qu'à peine il imprimoit la trace de ses pas dans le sable, et qui devançoit dans son pays les plus rapides flots de l'Eurotas et de l'Alphée.*

—*Liv.* 20

Fourthly, In narration as well as in description, facts and objects ought to be painted so accurately as to form in the mind of the reader distinct and lively images. Every useless circumstance ought indeed to be suppressed, because every such circumstance loads the narration; but if a circumstance be necessary, however slight, it cannot be described too minutely. The force of language consists in raising complete images[2]; which cannot be done till the reader, forgetting himself, be transported as by magic into the very place and time of the important action, and be converted, as it were, into a real spectator, beholding everything that passes. In this view, the narrative in an epic poem ought to rival a picture in the liveliness and accuracy of its representations: no circumstance must be omitted that tends to make a complete image; because an imperfect image, as well as any other imperfect conception, is cold and uninteresting. I shall illustrate this rule by several examples, giving the first place to a beautiful passage from Virgil.

---

2. Chap. ii. part 1. sect. 7.

> *Qualis* populeâ *mœrens Philomela sub umbrâ*
> *Amissos queritur fœtus, quos durus* arator
> *Observans nido* implumes *detraxit.*
>
> —*Georg. lib. 4. l. 511*

The poplar, plowman, and unfledged, though not essential in the description, are circumstances that tend to make a complete image, and upon that account are an embellishment.

Again,

> *Hic viridem Æneas frondenti ex ilice metam*
> *Constituit, signum nautis.*
>
> —*Æneid.* v. 129

Horace, addressing to Fortune:

> *Te pauper ambit sollicita prece*
> *Ruris colonus: te dominam æquoris,*
> *Quicumque Bithynâ lacessit*
> *Carpathium pelagus carinâ.*
>
> —*Carm. lib. 1. ode 35*

> ——— *Illum ex mœnibus hosticis*
> *Matrona bellantis tyranni*
> *Prospiciens, et adulta virgo,*
> *Suspiret: Eheu, ne rudis agminum*
> *Sponsus lacessat regius asperum*
> *Tactu leonem, quem cruenta*
> *Per medias rapit ira cædes.*
>
> —*Carm. lib. 3. ode 2*

Shakespear says[3], "You may as well go about to turn the sun to ice by fanning in his face with *a peacock's* feather." The peacock's feather, not to mention the beauty of the object, completes the image. An accurate image cannot be formed of this fanciful operation, without conceiving

---

3. Henry V. act 4. sc. 4.

a particular feather; and the mind is at some loss, when this is not specified in the decription. Again, "The rogues slighted me into the river with as little remorse, as they would have drown'd a bitch's blind puppies, fifteen i' th' litter[4]."

> OLD LADY: You would not be a queen?
> ANNE: No not for all the riches under heaven.
> OLD LADY: 'Tis strange: a three-pence bow'd
>   would hire me, old as I am, to queen it.

—Henry VIII. act 2. sc. 5

In the following passage, the action, with all its material circumstances, is represented so much to the life, that it could not be better conceived by a real spectator; and it is this manner of description which contributes greatly to the sublimity of the passage.

> *He spake; and to confirm his words, out-flew*
> *Millions of flaming swords, drawn from the thighs*
> *Of mighty cherubim: the sudden blaze*
> *Far round illumin'd hell: highly they rag'd*
> *Against the Highest, and fierce with grasped arms,*
> *Clash'd on their sounding shields the din of war,*
> *Hurling defiance toward the vault of heav'n.*

—Milton, b. I

A passage I am to cite from Shakespear, falls not much short of that now mentioned in particularity of description:

> *O you hard hearts! you cruel men of Rome!*
> *Knew you not Pompey? Many a time and oft*
> *Have you climb'd up to walls and battlements,*
> *To towers and windows, yea, to chimney-tops,*
> *Your infants in your arms; and there have sat*
> *The live-long day with patient expectation*
> *To see great Pompey pass the streets of Rome.*
> *And when you saw his chariot but appear,*

---

4. Merry Wives of Windsor, act 3. sc. 5.

> *Have you not made an universal shout,*
> *That Tyber trembled underneath his banks,*
> *To hear the replication of your sounds,*
> *Made in his concave shores?*

> —*Julius Cæsar*, act 1, sc. 1

The *Henriade* of Voltaire errs greatly against the foregoing rule: everything is touched in a summary way, without ever descending to the circumstances of an event. This manner is good in a general history, the purpose of which is to record important transactions: but in a fable, which hath a very different aim, it is cold and uninteresting; because it is impracticable to form distinct images of persons or things represented in a manner so superficial.

It is observed above, that every useless circumstance ought to be suppressed. To deal in such circumstances, is a fault, on the one hand, not less to be avoided, than the conciseness for which Voltaire is blamed, on the other. In the *Æneid*, Barce, the nurse of Sichæus, whom we never hear of before or after, is introduced for a purpose not more important than to call Anna to her sister Dido. And that it might not be thought unjust in Dido, even in this trivial incident, to prefer her husband's nurse before her own, the poet takes care to inform his reader, that Dido's nurse was dead. To this I must oppose a beautiful passage in the same book, where, after Dido's last speech, the poet, supposing her dead, hastens to describe the lamentation of her attendants:

> *Dixerat: atque illam media inter talia ferro*
> *Collapsam aspiciunt comites, ensemque cruore*
> *Spumantem, sparsasque manus. It clamor ad alta*
> *Atria, concussam bacchatur fama per urbem;*
> *Lamentis gemituque et fœmineo ululatu*
> *Tecta fremunt, resonat magnis plangoribus æther.*

> —*Lib. 4. l. 663*

As an appendix to the foregoing rule, I add the following observation, That to raise a sudden and strong impression, some single circumstance happily selected, has more power than the most laboured description.

---

5. Lib. 4. l. 632.

Macbeth, mentioning to his lady some voices he heard while he was murdering the King, says,

> *There's one did laugh in's sleep, and one cry'd Murder!*
> *They wak'd each other; and I stood and heard them;*
> *But they did say their prayers, and address them*
> *Again to sleep.*

LADY: There are two lodg'd together.
MACBETH: One cry'd, God bless us! and, Amen! the other;
    As they had seen me with these hangman's hands.
    Listening their fear, I could not say, Amen,
    When they did say, God bless us.
LADY: Consider it not so deeply.
MACBETH: But wherefore could not I pronounce, Amen?
    I had most need of blessing, and Amen
    Stuck in my throat.
LADY: These deeds must not be thought
    After these ways; so, it will make us mad.
MACBETH: Methought, I heard a voice cry, Sleep no more!
    Macbeth doth murder sleep, *&c.*

—Act 2. sc. 3

Describing Prince Henry:

> *I saw young Harry, with his beaver on,*
> *His cuisses on his thighs, gallantly arm'd,*
> *Rise from the ground like feather'd Mercury;*
> *And vaulted with such ease into his seat,*
> *As if an angel dropt down from the clouds,*
> *To turn and wind a fiery Pegasus,*
> *And witch the world with noble horsemanship.*

—First Part Henry IV. act 4. sc. 2

KING HENRY: Lord Cardinal, if thou think'st on heaven's bliss,
    Hold up thy hand, make signal of thy hope.
    He dies, and makes no sign!

—Second Part Henry VI. act 3. sc. 10

The same author, speaking ludicrously of an army debilitated with diseases, says,

> Half of them dare not shake the snow from off their cassocks, lest they shake themselves to pieces.

To draw a character is the master-stroke of description. In this Tacitus excels: his figures are natural, distinct, and complete; not a feature wanting or misplaced. Shakespear however exceeds Tacitus in the sprightliness of his figures: some characteristical circumstance is generally invented or laid hold of, which paints more to the life than many words. The following instances will explain my meaning, and at the same time prove my observation to be just.

> *Why should a man, whose blood is warm within,*
> *Sit like his grandsire cut in alabaster?*
> *Sleep when he wakes, and creep into the jaundice,*
> *By being peevish? I tell that what, Anthonio,*
> *(I love thee, and it is my love that speaks):*
> *There are a sort of men, whose visages*
> *Do cream and mantle like a standing pond;*
> *And do a wilful stillness entertain,*
> *With purpose to be dress'd in an opinion*
> *Of wisdom, gravity, profound conceit;*
> *As who should say, I am Sir Oracle,*
> *And when I ope my lips, let no dog bark!*
> *O my Anthonio, I do know of those,*
> *That therefore only are reputed wise,*
> *For saying nothing.*
>
> —*Merchant of Venice, act 1. sc. 1*

Again,

Gratiano speaks an infinite deal of nothing, more than any man in all Venice: his reasons are two grains of wheat hid in two bushels of chaff; you shall seek all day ere you find them, and when you have them, they are not worth the search.

Ibid

In the following passage a character is completed by a single stroke.

> SHALLOW: O the mad days that I have spent; and to see how many of mine old acquaintance are dead.
> SILENCE: We shall all follow, Cousin.
> SHALLOW: Certain, 'tis certain, very sure, very sure; Death (as the Psalmist saith) is certain to all: all shall die. How a good yoke of bullocks at Stamford fair?
> SLENDER: Truly, Cousin, I was not there.
> SHALLOW: Death is certain. Is old *Double* of your town living yet.
> SILENCE: Dead, Sir.
> SHALLOW: Dead! see, see; he drew a good bow: and dead? He shot a fine shoot. How a score of ewes now?
> SILENCE: Thereafter as they be. A score of good ewes may be worth ten pounds.
> SHALLOW: And is old *Double* dead?
>
> —*Second Part Henry IV. act 3. sc. 3*

Describing a jealous husband:

Neither press, coffer, chest, trunk, well, vault, but he hath an abstract for the remembrance of such places, and goes to them by his note. There is no hiding you in the house.
Merry Wives of Windsor, act 4. sc. 3

Congreve has an inimitable stroke of this kind in his comedy of *Love for Love*:

> BEN LEGEND: Well, father, and how do all at home? how does brother Dick, and brother Val?
> SIR SAMPSON: Dick, body o' me, Dick has been dead these two years, I writ you word, when you were at Leghorn.
> BEN: Mess, that's true; marry, I had forgot. Dick's dead, as you say.
>
> —*Act 3. sc. 6*

Falstaff speaking of Ancient Pistol,

He's no swaggerer, hostess; a tame cheater i' faith; you may stroak him as gently as a puppey-greyhound; he will not swagger with a Barbary hen, if her feathers turn back in any shew of resistence.

Second Part Henry IV. *act 2. sc. 9*

Some writers, through heat of imagination, fall into contradictions; some are guilty of downright inconsistencies; and some even rave like madmen. Against such capital errors one cannot be warned to better purpose than by collecting instances. The first shall be of a contradiction, the most venial of all. Virgil speaking of Neptune:

> *Interea magno misceri murmure pontum*
> *Emissamque hyemem sensit Neptunus, et imis*
> *Stagna refusa vadis:* graviter commotus, *et alto*
> *Prospiciens, summâ* placidum *caput extulit undâ.*
>
> —*Æneid.* i. 128

Again,

> *When first young Maro, in his boundless mind,*
> *A work t'outlast immortal Rome design'd.*
>
> —*Essay on Criticism, l. 130*

The following examples are of downright inconsistencies.

Alii pulsis e tormento catenis discerpti sectique, dimidiato corpore pugnabant sibi superstites, ac peremptæ partis ultores.

Strada, Dec. 2. L. 2

> *Il povér huomo, che non sen' era accorto,*
> *Andava combattendo, ed era morto.*
>
> —*Berni*

> *He fled, but flying, left his life behind.*
>
> —*Iliad* xi. 443

> *Full through his neck the weighty falchion sped;*
> *Along the pavement roll'd the mutt'ring head.*

—*Odyssey* xxii. 365

The last article is of raving like one mad. Cleopatra speaking to the aspick:

> —— *Welcome, thou kind deceiver,*
> *Thou best of thieves; who, with an easy key,*
> *Do'st open life, and unperceiv'd by us*
> *Ev'n steal us from ourselves; discharging so*
> *Death's dreadful office, better than himself,*
> *Touching our limbs so gently into slumber,*
> *That Death stands by, deceiv'd by his own image,*
> *And thinks himself but Sleep.*

—Dryden, *All for Love*, act 5

Reasons that are common and known to every person, ought to be taken for granted: to express them is childish and interrupts the narration. Quintus Curtius, relating the battle of Issus:

Jam in conspectu, sed extra teli jactum, utraque acies erat; quum priores Persæ inconditum et trucem sustulere clamorem. Redditur et a Macedonibus major, exercitus impar numero, sed jugis montium vastisque saltibus repercussus: *quippe semper circumjecta nemora petræque, quantamcumque accepere vocem, multiplicato sono referunt.*

Having discussed what observations occurred upon the thoughts or things expressed, I proceed to what more peculiarly concern the language or verbal dress. The language proper for expressing passion is the subject of a former chapter. Several observations there made, are applicable to the present subject; particularly, That words are intimately connected with the ideas they represent, and that the representation cannot be perfect unless the emotions raised by the sound and the sense be concordant. It is not sufficient, that the sense be clearly expressed: the words must correspond to the subject in every particular. An elevated subject requires an elevated style: what is familiar, ought to be familiarly expressed: a subject that is serious and important, ought to be cloathed in plain nervous language: a description, on the other hand, addressed to the imagination, is susceptible of the highest ornaments that sounding words, metaphor, and figurative expression, can bestow upon it.

I shall give a few examples of the foregoing doctrine. A poet of any genius will not readily dress a high subject in low words; and yet blemishes of this kind are found even in some classical works. Horace observing that men, perfectly satisfied with themselves, are seldom so with their condition, introduces Jupiter indulging to each his own choice:

> *Jam faciam quod vultis: eris tu, qui modo miles,*
> *Mercator: tu, consultus modo, rusticus: hinc vos,*
> *Vos hinc mutatis discedite partibus: eia,*
> *Quid? statis? nolint: atqui licet esse beatis.*
> *Quid causæ est, merito quin illis Jupiter ambas*
> *Iratus buccas inflet? neque se fore posthac*
> *Tam facilem dicat, votis ut præbeat aurem?*
>
> —*Serm, lib. 1. sat. 1. l. 16*

Jupiter in wrath puffing up both cheeks, is a ludicrous expression, far from suitable to the gravity of the subject: everyone must feel the discordance. The following couplet, sinking far below the subject, is not less ludicrous.

> *Not one looks backward, onward still he goes,*
> *Yet ne'er looks forward farther than his nose.*
>
> —*Essay on Man*, *ep.* iv. 223

On the other hand, to raise the expression above the tone of the subject, is a fault than which none is more common. Take the following instances.

> *Orcan le plus fidéle à server ses desseins,*
> *Né sous le ciel brûlant des plus noirs Affricains.*
>
> —*Bajazet, act 3. sc. 8*

> *Les ombres par trois fois ont obscurci les cieux*
> *Depuis que le sommeil n'est entré dans vos yeux;*
> *Et le jour a trois fois chassé la nuit obscure*
> *Depuis que votre corps languit sans nourriture.*
>
> —*Phedra, act 1. sc. 3*

Assuerus: Ce mortel, qui montra tant de zéle pour moi,
   Vit-il encore?
Asaph:—— Il voit l'astre qui vous éclaire.

> —*Esther, act 2. sc. 3*

> *Oui, c'est Agamemnon, c'est ton Roi qui t'eveille;*
> *Viens, reconnois la voix qui frape ton oreille.*
>
> —*Iphigenie*

> —— *In the inner room*
> *I spy a winking lamp, that weakly strikes*
> *The ambient air, scarce kindling into light.*
>
> —*Southerne, Fate of Capua, act 3*

In the funeral orations of the Bishop of Meaux, the following passages are raised far above the tone of the subject.

L'Ocean etonné de se voir traversé tant de fois en des appareils si divers, et pour des causes si differentes, &c.

p. 6

Grande Reine, je satisfais à vos plus tendres desirs, quand je célébre ce monarque; et ce cœur qui n'a jamais vêcu que pour lui, se eveille, tout poudre qu'il est, et devient sensible, même sous ce drap mortuaire, au nom d'un epoux si cher.

p. 32

Montesquieu, in a didactic work, *L'esprit des Loix*, gives too great indulgence to imagination: the tone of his language swells frequently above his subject. I give an example:

Mr. le Comte de Boulainvilliers et Mr. l'Abbé Dubos ont fait chacun un systeme, dont l'un semble être une conjuration contre le tiers-etat, et l'autre une conjuration contre la noblesse. Lorsque le Soleil donna à Phaéton son char à conduire, il lui dit: Si vous montez trop haut, vous brulerez la demeure céleste; si vous descendez trop bas, vous réduirez en cendres la terre: n'allez point trop a droite, vous tomberiez dans la constellation du serpent; n'allez point trop à gauche, vous iriez dans celle de l'autel: tenez-vous entre les deux.

L. ch. 10

The following passage, intended, one would imagine, as a receipt to boil water, is altogether burlesque by the laboured elevation of the diction.

> *A massy caldron of stupendous frame*
> *They brought, and plac'd it o'er the rising flame:*
> *Then heap the lighted wood; the flame divides*
> *Beneath the vase, and climbs around the sides:*
> *In its wide womb they pour the rushing stream;*
> *The boiling water bubbles to the brim.*
>
> —*Pope's Homer, book* xviii. 405

In a passage near the beginning of the 4th book of Telamachus, one feels a sudden bound upward without preparation, which accords not with the subject:

Calypso, qui avoit été jusqu' à ce moment immobile et transportée de plaisir en écoutant les avantures de Télémaque, l'interrompit pour lui faire prendre quelque repos. Il est tems, lui dit-elle, que vous alliez goûter la douceur du sommeil aprés tant de travaux. Vous n'avez rien à craindre ici; tout vous est favorable. Abandonnez-vous donc à la joye. Goûtez la paix, et tous les autres dons des dieux dont vous allez être comblé. Demain, *quand l'Aurore avec ses doigts de roses entr'ouvrira les portes dorées de l'Orient, et que les chevaux du soleil sortans de l'onde amére répandront les flames du jour, pour chasser devant eux toutes les etoiles du ciel*, nous reprendrons, mon cher Télémaque, l'histoire de vos malheurs.

This obviously is copied from a similar passage in the Æneid, which ought not to have been copied, because it lies open to the same censure: but the force of authority is great.

> *At regina gravi jamdudum saucia cura,*
> *Vulnus alit venis, & cæco carpitur igni.*
> *Multa viri virtus animo, multusque recursat*
> *Gentis honos: hærent infixi pectore vultus,*
> *Verbaque: nec placidam membris dat cura quietem.*
> Postera Phœbea lustrabat lampade terras,
> Humentemque Aurora polo dimoverat umbram;
> *Cum sic unanimem alloquitur malesana sororem:*

—*Lib.* iv. 1

Take another example where the words rise above the subject:

Ainsi les peuples y accoururent bientôt en foule de toutes parts; le commerce de cette ville étoit semblable au flux et reflux de la mer. Les trésors y entroient comme les flots viennent l'un sur l'autre. Tout y etoit apporté et en sortoit librement: tout ce qui y entroit, étoit utile; toute ce qui en sortoit, laissoit en sortant d'autres richesses en sa place. La justice sevére presidoit dans le port au milieu de tant de nations. La franchise, la bonne foi, la candeur, sembloient du haut de ces superbs tours appeller les marchands des terres les plus éloignées: chacun des ces marchands, *soit qu'il vint des rives orientales où le soleil sort chaque jour du sein des ondes, soit qu'il fût parti de cette grande mer ou le soleil assé de son cours va eteindre ses feux,* vivoit plaisible et en sureté dans Salente comme dans sa patrie!

Telemaque, l. 12

The language of Homer is suited to his subject, not less accurately than the actions and sentiments of his heroes are to their characters. Virgil, in this particular, falls short of perfection: his language is stately throughout; and though he descends at times to the simplest branches of cookery, roasting and boiling for example, yet he never relaxes a moment from the high tone[6]. In adjusting his language to his subject, no writer

---

6. See Æneid, lib. i. 188–219.

equals Swift. I can recollect but one exception, which at the same time is far from being gross. The journal of a modern lady, is composed in a style where sprightliness is blended with familiarity, perfectly suited to the subject. In one passage, however, the poet assumes a higher tone, which corresponds neither to the subject nor to the tone of language employ'd in the rest of that piece. The passage I have in view begins *l.* 116. "But let me now a while survey," &c. and ends at *l.* 135.

It is proper to be observed upon this head, that writers of inferior rank are continually upon the stretch to enliven and enforce their subject by exaggeration and superlatives. This unluckily has an effect opposite to what is intended: the reader, disgusted with language that swells above the subject, is led by contrast to think more meanly of the subject than it may possibly deserve. A man of prudence, beside, will be not less careful to husband his strength in writing than in walking: a writer too liberal of superlatives, exhausts his whole stock upon ordinary incidents, and reserves no share to express, with greater energy, matters of importance[7].

The power that language possesses to imitate thought, goes farther than to the capital circumstances above mentioned: it reacheth even the slighter modifications. Slow action, for example, is imitated by words pronounced slow; labour or toil, by words harsh or rough in their sound. But this subject has been already handled[8].

In dialogue-writing, the condition of the speaker is chiefly to be regarded in framing the expression. The centinel in *Hamlet*, interrogated about the ghost, whether his watch had been quiet? answers with great propriety for a man in his station, "Not a mouse stirring[9]."

I proceed to a second remark, not less important than the former. No person of reflection but must be sensible, that an incident makes

---

7. Montaigne, reflecting upon the then present modes, observes, that there never was at anytime so abject and servile prostitution of words in the addresses made by people of fashion to one another; the humblest tenders of life and soul, no professions under that of devotion and adoration; the writer constantly declaring himself a vassal, nay a slave; so that when anymore serious occasion of friendship or gratitude requires more genuine professions, words are wanting to express them.

8. Chap. 18. sect. 3.

9. One can scarce avoid smiling at the blindness of a certain critic, who with an air of self-sufficiency, condemns this expression as low and vulgar. A French poet, says he, would express the same thoughts in a more sublime manner: "Mais tout dort, et l'armée, et les vents, et Neptune." And he adds, "The English poet may please at London, but the French everywhere else."

a stronger impression on an eye-witness, than when heard at second hand. Writers of genius, sensible that the eye is the best avenue to the heart, represent everything as passing in our sight; and from readers or hearers, transform us, as it were, into spectators. A skilful writer conceals himself, and presents his personages. In a word, everything becomes dramatic as much as possible. Plutarch, *de gloria Atheniensium*, observes, that Thucydides makes his reader a spectator, and inspires him with the same passions as if he were an eye-witness. I am intitled to make the same observation upon our countryman Swift. From this happy talent arises that energy of style which is peculiar to him: he cannot always avoid narration; but the pencil is his choice, by which he bestows life and colouring upon his objects. Pope is richer in ornament, but possesses not in the same degree the talent of drawing from the life. A translation of the sixth satire of Horace, begun by the former and finished by the latter, affords the fairest opportunity for a comparison. Pope obviously imitates the picturesque manner of his friend: yet everyone of taste must be sensible, that the imitation, though fine, falls short of the original. In other instances, where Pope writes in his own style, the difference of manner is still more conspicuous.

Abstract or general terms have no good effect in any competition for amusement; because it is only of particular objects that images can be formed[10]. Shakespear's style in that respect is excellent. Every article in his descriptions is particular, as in nature; and if accidentally a vague expression slip in, the blemish is extremely discernible by the bluntness of its impression. Take the following example. Falstaff, excusing himself for running away at a robbery, says,

> By the Lord, I knew ye, as well as he that made ye. Why, hear ye, my masters; was it for me to kill the heir-apparent? should I turn upon the true prince? Why, thou knowest, I am as valiant as Hercules; but beware instinct, the lion will not touch the true prince: instinct is a great matter. I was a coward on instinct: I shall think the better of myself, and thee, during my life; I, for a valiant lion, and thou for a true prince. But, by the Lord, lads, I am glad you have the money. Hostess, clap to the doors; watch tonight, pray tomorrow. Gallants, lads, boys, hearts of gold, all

---

10. See chap. 4.

the titles of good fellowship come to you! What, shall we be merry? shall we have a play *extempore?*

First Part Henry IV. act 2. sc. 9

The particular words I object to are, *instinct is a great matter*, which make but a poor figure, compared with the liveliness of the rest of the speech. It was one of Homer's advantages, that he wrote before general terms were multiplied: the superior genius of Shakespear displays itself in avoiding them after they were multiplied. Addison describes the family of Sir Roger de Coverley in the following words.

You would take his valet de chambre for his brother, his butler is gray-headed, his groom is one of the gravest men that I have ever seen, and his coachman has the looks of a privy counsellor.
Spectator, No 106

The description of the groom is less lively than of the others; plainly because the expression, being vague and general, tends not to form any image. "Dives opum variarum[11]," is an expression still more vague; and so are the following.

———— *Mæcenas, mearum*
Grande decus, columenque rerum.

—*Horat. Carm. l. 2. ode 17*

———— *et fide Teia*
Dices laborantes in uno
Penelopen, vitreamque Circen.

—*Horat. Carm. l. 1. ode 17*

In the fine arts, it is a rule, to put the capital objects in the strongest point of view; and even to present them oftener than once, where it can be done. In history-painting, the principal figure is placed in the front, and in the best light: an equestrian statue is placed in a centre of streets, that it may be seen from many places at once. In no composition is there a greater opportunity for this rule than in writing:

---

11. Georg. ii. 468.

> ——— *Sequitur pulcherrimus Astur,*
> *Astur equo fidens et versicoloribus armis.*
>
> —*Æneid.* x. 180

> ———*Full many a lady*
> *I've ey'd with best regard, and many a time*
> *Th' harmony of their tongues hath into bondage*
> *Brought my too diligent ear, for several virtues*
> *Have I lik'd several women, never any*
> *With so full soul, but some defect in her*
> *Did quarrel with the noblest grace she ow'd,*
> *And put it to the foil. But you, O you,*
> *So perfect, and so peerless, are created*
> *Of every creature's best.*
>
> —*The Tempest,* act 3. sc. 1

> *With thee conversing I forget all time;*
> *All seasons and their change, all please alike.*
> *Sweet is the breath of morn, her rising sweet,*
> *With charm of earliest birds; pleasant the sun*
> *When first on this delightful land he spreads*
> *His orient beams, on herb, tree, fruit, and flow'r,*
> *Glistering with dew; fragrant the fertil earth*
> *After soft showers; and sweet the coming on*
> *Of grateful evening mild, the silent night*
> *With this her solemn bird, and this fair moon,*
> *And these the gems of heav'n, her starry train:*
> *But neither breath of morn, when she ascends*
> *With charm of earliest birds, nor rising sun*
> *On this delightful land, nor herb, fruit, flower,*
> *Glistering with dew, nor fragrance after showers,*
> *Nor grateful evening mild, nor silent night,*
> *With this her solemn bird, nor walk by moon,*
> *Or glittering star-light, without thee is sweet.*
>
> —*Paradise Lost, book* 4. l. 634

What mean ye, that ye use this proverb, The fathers have eaten sour grapes, and the children's teeth are set on edge? As I live, saith the Lord God, ye shall not have occasion to use this proverb in Israel. If a man keep my judgements to deal truly, he is just, he shall surely live. But if he be a robber, a shedder of blood; if he have eaten upon the mountains, and defiled his neighbour's wife; if he have oppressed the poor and needy, have spoiled by violence, have not restored the pledge, have lift up his eyes to idols, have given forth upon usury, and have taken increase: shall he live? he shall not live: he shall surely die; and his blood shall be upon him. Now, lo, if he beget a son, that seeth all his father's sins, and considereth, and doth not such like; that hath not eaten upon the mountains, hath not lift up his eyes to idols, nor defiled his neighbour's wife, hath not oppressed any nor with held the pledge, neither hath spoiled by violence, but hath given his bread to the hungry, and covered the naked with a garment; that hath not received usury nor increase, that hath executed my judgments, and walked in my statutes; he shall not die for the iniquity of his father; he shall surely live. The soul that sinneth, it shall die: the son shall not bear the iniquity of the father; neither shall the father bear the iniquity of the son; the righteousness of the righteous shall be upon him, and the wickedness of the wicked shall be upon him. Have I any pleasure that the wicked should die? saith the Lord God; and not that he should return from his ways and live.

Ezekiel xviii

The repetitions in Homer, which are frequent, have been the occasion of much criticism. Suppose we were at a loss about the reason, might not taste be sufficient to justify them? At the same time, one must be devoid of understanding not to be sensible, that they make the narration dramatic; and give an air of truth, by making things appear as passing in our sight.

A concise comprehensive style is a great ornament in narration; and a superfluity of unnecessary words, not less than of circumstances, a great nuisance. A judicious selection of the striking circumstances, cloathed in a nervous style, is delightful. In this style, Tacitus excels all writers, ancient and modern. Instances are numberless: take the following specimen.

Crebra hinc prælia, et sæpius in modum latrocinii: per saltus, per paludes; ut cuique sors aut virtus: temere, proviso, ob iram, ob prædam, jussu, et aliquando ignaris ducibus.

Annal. lib. 12. § 39

If a concise or nervous style be a beauty, tautology must be a blemish. And yet writers, fettered by verse, are not sufficiently careful to avoid this slovenly practice: they may be pitied, but they cannot be justified. Take for a specimen the following instances, from the best poet, for versification at least, that England has to boast of:

> *High on his helm celestial lightnings play,*
> *His beamy shield emits a living ray,*
> *Th' unweary'd blaze incessant streams supplies,*
> *Like the red star that fires th' autumnal skies.*
>
> —*Iliad* v. 5

> *Strength and omnipotence invest thy throne.*
>
> —*Iliad* viii. 576

> *So silent fountains, from a rock's tall head,*
> *In sable streams soft-trickling waters shed.*
>
> —*Iliad* ix. 19

> *His clanging armour rung.*
>
> —*Iliad* xii. 94

> *Fear on their cheek, and horror in their eye.*
>
> —*Iliad* xv. 4

> *The blaze of armour flash'd against the day.*
>
> —*Iliad* xvii. 736

> *As when the piercing blasts of Boreas blow.*
>
> —*Iliad* xix. 380

> *And like the moon, the broad refulgent shield*
> *Blaz'd with long rays, and gleam'd athwart the field.*
>
> —*Iliad* xix. 402

> *No—could our swiftness o'er the winds prevail,*
> *Or beat the pinions of the western gale,*
> *All were in vain—*

—*Iliad* xix. 460

> *The humid sweat from ev'ry pore descends.*

—*Iliad* xxiii. 829

Redundant epithets, such as *humid*, in the last citation, are by Quintilian disallowed to orators, but indulged to poets[12]; because his favourite poets, in a few instances, are reduced to such epithets for the sake of versification. For instance, *Prata canis albicant pruinis*, of Horace, and *liquidos fontes*, of Virgil.

As an apology for such careless expressions, it may well suffice, that Pope, in submitting to be a translator, acts below his genius. In a translation, it is hard to require the same spirit or accuracy, that is chearfully bestowed on an original work. And to support the reputation of this author, I shall give some instances from Virgil and Horace, more faulty by redundancy than any of those above mentioned:

> *Sæpe etiam immensum cœlo venit agmen aquarum,*
> *Et fœdam glomerant tempestatem imbribus atris*
> *Collectæ ex alto nubes: ruit arduus æther,*
> *Et pluviâ ingenti sata læta, boumque labores*
> *Diluit.*

—*Georg. lib.* i. 322

> *Postquam altum tenuere rates, nec jam amplius ullæ*
> *Apparent terræ; cœlum undique et undique pontus:*
> *Tum mihi cœruleus supra caput astitit imber,*
> *Noctem hyememque ferens: et inhorruit unda tenebris.*

—*Æneid. lib.* iii. 191

---

12. L. 7. chap. 6. sect. 2.

> ——— *Hinc tibi copia*
> *Manabit ad plenum benigno*
> *Ruris honorum opulenta cornu.*
>
> —Horat. Carm. lib. 1. ode 17

> *Videre fessos vomerem inversum boves*
> *Collo trahentes languido.*
>
> —Horat. Epod. ii. 63

Here I can luckily apply Horace's rule against himself:

> *Est brevitate opus, ut currat sententia, neu se*
> *Impediat verbis lassas onerantibus aures.*
>
> —Serm. lib. 1. sat. x. 9

I close this chapter with a curious inquiry. An object, however ugly to the sight, is far from being so when represented by colours or by words. What is the cause of this difference? The cause with respect to painting is obvious. A good picture, whatever the subject be, is agreeable, because of the pleasure we take in imitation: the agreeableness of imitation overbalances the disagreeableness of the subject; and the picture upon the whole is agreeable. It requires a greater compass to explain the cause with respect to the description of an ugly object. To connect individuals in the social state, no one particular contributes more than language, by the power it possesses of an expeditious communication of thought and a lively representation of transactions. But nature hath not been satisfied to recommend language by its utility merely: it is made susceptible of many beauties that have no relation to utility, which are directly felt without the intervention of any reflection[13]. And this unfolds the mystery; for the pleasure of language is so great, as in a lively description to overbalance the disagreeableness of the image raised by it[14]. This however is no encouragement to deal in disagreeable subjects; for the pleasure is out of sight greater where the subject and the description are both of them agreeable.

---

13. See chap. 18.
14. See chap. 2. part 4.

The following description is upon the whole agreeable, though the subject described is in itself dismal.

> *Nine times the space that measures day and night*
> *To mortal men, he with his horrid crew*
> *Lay vanquish'd, rowling in the fiery gulf*
> *Confounded though immortal: but his doom*
> *Reserv'd him to more wrath; for now the thought*
> *Both of lost happiness and lasting pain*
> *Torments him; round he throws his baleful eyes*
> *That witness'd huge affliction and dismay,*
> *Mix'd with obdurate pride and stedfast hate:*
> *At once as far as angels ken he views*
> *The dismal situation waste and wild:*
> *A dungeon horrible, on all sides round*
> *As one great furnace flam'd; yet from those flames*
> *No light, but rather darkness visible*
> *Serv'd only to discover sights of wo,*
> *Regions of sorrow, doleful shades, where peace*
> *And rest can never dwell, hope never comes*
> *That comes to all; but torture without end*
> *Still urges, and a fiery deluge, fed*
> *With ever burning sulphur unconsum'd:*
> *Such place eternal justice had prepar'd*
> *For those rebellious.*

—*Paradise Lost, book 1. l. 50*

An unmanly depression of spirits in time of danger is not an agreeable sight; and yet a fine description or representation of it will be relished:

K. RICHARD: What must the King do now? must he submit?
  The King shall do it: must he be depos'd?
  The King shall be contented: must he lose
  The name of King? O' God's name, let it go:
  I'll give my jewels for a set of beads;
  My gorgeous palace, for a hermitage;
  My gay apparel, for an almsman's gown;

> My figur'd goblets, for a dish of wood;
> My sceptre, for a palmer's walking staff;
> My subjects, for a pair of carved saints;
> And my large kingdom, for a little grave;
> A little, little grave;—an obscure grave.
> Or I'll be bury'd in the King's highway;
> Some way of common tread, where subjects feet
> May hourly trample on their sovereign's head:
> For on my heart they tread now, whilst I live;
> And, bury'd once, why not upon my head?

—Richard II. act 3. sc. 6

Objects that strike terror in a spectator, have in poetry and painting a fine effect. The picture, by raising a slight emotion of terror, agitates the mind; and in that condition every beauty makes a deep impression. May not contrast heighten the pleasure, by opposing our present security to the danger we would be in by encountering the object represented?

> ——— *The other shape,*
> *If shape it might be call'd, that shape had none*
> *Distinguishable in member, joint, or limb;*
> *Or substance might be call'd that shadow seem'd,*
> *For each seem'd either; black it stood as night,*
> *Fierce as ten furies, terrible as hell,*
> *And shook a dreadful dart.*

—Paradise Lost, book 2. l. 666

> ——— *Now storming fury rose,*
> *And clamour such as heard in heav'n till now*
> *Was never, arms on armour clashing bray'd*
> *Horrible discord, and the madding wheels*
> *Of brazen chariots rag'd; dire was the noise*
> *Of conflict; over-head the dismal hiss*
> *Of fiery darts in flaming vollies flew,*
> *And flying vaulted either host with fire.*
> *So under fiery cope together rush'd*
> *Both battles main, with ruinous assault*

> *And inextinguishable rage; all heav'n*
> *Resounded, and had earth been then, all earth*
> *Had to her centre shook.*

> —*Paradise Lost*, book 6. l. 207

> Ghost:——— But that I am forbid
> To tell the secrets of my prison-house,
> I could a tale unfold, whose lightest word
> Would harrow up thy soul, freeze thy young blood,
> Make thy two eyes, like stars, start from their spheres,
> Thy knotty and combined locks to part,
> And each particular hair to stand on end
> Like quills upon the fretful porcupine:
> But this eternal blazon must not be
> To ears of flesh and blood.
>
> —*Hamlet, act 1. sc. 8*

> Gratiano: Poor Desdemona! I'm glad thy father's dead:
> Thy match was mortal to him; and pure grief
> Shore his old thread in twain. Did he live now,
> This sight would make him do a desp'rate turn:
> Yea, curse his better angel from his side,
> And fall to reprobation.
>
> —*Othello, act 5. sc. 8*

Objects of horror must be excepted from the foregoing theory; for no description, however masterly, is sufficient to overbalance the disgust raised even by the idea of such an object. Everything horrible ought therefore to be avoided in a description. Nor is this a severe law: the poet will avoid such scenes for his own sake, as well as for that of his reader; and to vary his descriptions, nature affords plenty of objects that disgust us in some degree without raising horror. I am obliged therefore to condemn the picture of sin in the second book of *Paradise Lost*, though drawn with a masterly hand. The original would be a horrible spectacle; and the horror is not much softened in the copy.

> ——— *Pensive here I sat*
> *Alone, but long I sat not, till my womb*
> *Pregnant by thee, and now excessive grown*
> *Prodigious motion felt and rueful throes.*
> *At last this odious offspring whom thou seest,*
> *Thine own begotten, breaking violent way,*
> *Tore through my intrails, that with fear and pain*
> *Distorted, all my nether shape thus grew*
> *Transform'd; but he my inbred enemy*
> *Forth issu'd, brandishing his fatal dart,*
> *Made to destroy: I fled, and cry'd out Death;*
> *Hell trembl'd at the hideous name, and sigh'd*
> *From all her caves, and back resounded Death.*
> *I fled, but he pursu'd, (though more, it seems,*
> *Inflam'd with lust than rage), and swifter far,*
> *Me overtook, his mother all dismay'd,*
> *And in embraces forcible and foul*
> *Ingendring with me, of that rape begot*
> *These yelling monsters that with ceaseless cry*
> *Surround me, as thou saw'st, hourly conceiv'd*
> *And hourly born, with sorrow infinite*
> *To me; for when they list, into the womb*
> *That bred them they return, and howl and gnaw*
> *My bowels, their repast; then bursting forth*
> *Afresh with conscious terrors vex me round,*
> *That rest or intermission none I find.*
> *Before mine eyes in opposition sits*
> *Grim Death, my son and foe, who sets them on,*
> *And me his parent would full soon devour*
> *For want of other prey, but that he knows*
> *His end with mine involv'd; and knows that I*
> *Should prove a bitter morsel, and his bane,*
> *Whenever that shall be.*
>
> —Book 2. l. 777

Iago's character in the tragedy of *Othello*, is so monstrous and satanical, as not to be sufferable in a representation: not even Shakespear's masterly hand can make the picture agreeable.

THOUGH THE OBJECTS INTRODUCED IN the following scenes, are not altogether so horrible as Sin is in Milton's picture; yet with every person of taste, disgust will be the prevailing emotion.

> —— *Strophades Graio stant nomine dictæ*
> *Insulæ Ionio in magno: quas dira Celæno,*
> *Harpyiæque colunt aliæ: Phineia postquam*
> *Clausa domus, mensasque metu liquere priores.*
> *Tristius haud illis monstrum, nec sævior ulla*
> *Pestis et ira Deûm Stygiis sese extulit undis.*
> *Virginei volucrum vultus, fœdissima ventris*
> *Proluvies, uncæque manus, et pallida semper.*
> *Ora fame.*
> *Huc ubi delati portus intravimus: ecce*
> *Læta boum passim campis armenta videmus,*
> *Caprigenumque pecus, nullo custode, per herbas.*
> *Irruimus ferro, et Divos ipsumque vocamus*
> *In prædam partemque Jovem: tunc littore curvo*
> *Extruimusque toros, dapibusque epulamur opimis.*
> *At subitæ horrifico lapsu de montibus adsunt*
> *Harpyiæ: et magnis quatiunt clangoribus alas:*
> *Diripiuntque dapes, contactuque omnia fœdant*
> *Immundo: tum vox tetrum dira inter odorem.*
>
> —*Æneid. lib*. iii. 210

> *Sum patria ex Ithaca, comes infelicis Ulyssei,*
> *Nomen Achemenides: Trojam, genitore Adamasto*
> *Paupere (mansissetque utinam fortuna!) profectus.*
> *Hic me, dum trepidi crudelia limina linquunt,*
> *Immemores socii vasto Cyclopis in antro*
> *Deseruere. Domus sanie dapibusque cruentis,*
> *Intus opaca, ingens: ipse arduus, altaque pulsat*
> *Sidera: (Dii, talem terris avertite pestem)*
> *Nec visu facilis, nec dictu affabilis ulli.*
> *Visceribus miserorum, et sanguine vescitur atro.*
> *Vidi egomet, duo de numero cum corpora nostro,*
> *Prensa manu magna, medio resupinus in antro,*
> *Frangeret ad saxum, sanieque aspersa natarent*

Limina: vidi, atro cum membra fluentia tabo
Manderet, et tepidi tremerent sub dentibus artus.
Haud impune quidem: nec talia passus Ulysses,
Oblitusve sui est Ithacus discrimine tanto.
Nam simul expletus dapibus, vinoque sepultus
Cervicem inflexam posuit, jacuitque per antrum
Immensus, saniem eructans, ac frusta cruento
Per somnum commixta mero; nos, magna precati
Numina, sortitique vices, unà undique circum
Fundimur, et telo lumen terebramus acuto
Ingens, quod torva solum sub fronte latebat.

—*Æneid. lib.* iii 613

XXII

Epic and Dramatic Compositions

Tragedy differs from the epic more in form than in substance. The ends proposed by each are instruction and amusement; and each of them copy human actions as means to bring about these ends. They differ in the manner only of copying. Epic poetry deals in narration: Tragedy represents its facts as transacted in our sight. In the former, the poet introduces himself as an historian: in the latter he presents his actors and never himself[1].

This difference, regarding form only, may be thought slight; but the effects it occasions, are by no means so. What we see, makes a stronger impression than what we learn from others. A narrative poem is a story told by another: facts and incidents passing upon the stage, come under our own observation; and are beside much enlivened by action and gesture, expressive of many sentiments beyond the reach of language.

A dramatic composition has another property, independent altogether of action. A dialogue makes a deeper impression than a narration: because in the former persons express their own sentiments; whereas in the latter sentiments are related at second hand. For that reason, Aristotle, the father of critics, lays it down as a rule, That in an

---

1. The dialogue in a dramatic composition distinguishes it so clearly from other compositions, that no writer has thought it necessary to search for any other distinguishing mark. But much useless labour has been bestowed, to distinguish an epic poem by some peculiar mark. Bossu defines it to be, "A composition in verse, intended to form the manners by instructions disguised under the allegories of an important action"; which excludes every epic poem founded upon real facts, and perhaps includes several of Æsop's fables. Voltaire reckons verse so essential, as for that single reason to exclude the adventures of Telemachus. See his *Essay upon Epic Poetry*. Others, affected with substance more than with form, hesitate not to pronounce that poem to be epic. It is not a little diverting to see so many profound critics hunting for what is not; they take for granted, without the least foundation, that there must be some precise criterion to distinguish epic poetry from every other species of writing. Literary compositions run into each other precisely like colours: in their strong tints they are easily distinguished; but are susceptible of so much variety, and of so many different forms, that we never can say where one species ends and another begins. As to the general taste, there is little reason to doubt, that a work where heroicactions are related in an elevated style, will, without further requisite, be deemed an epic poem.

epic poem the author ought to take every opportunity to introduce his actors, and to confine the narrative part within the narrowest bounds[2]. Homer understood perfectly the advantage of this method; and his poems are both of them in a great measure dramatic. Lucan runs to the opposite extreme; and is guilty of a still greater fault: the *Pharsalia* is stuffed with cold and languid reflections; the merit of which the author assumes to himself, and deigns not to share with his personages. Nothing can be more impertinent, than a chain of such reflections, which suspend the battle of Pharsalia after the leaders had made their speeches, and the two armies are ready to engage[3].

Aristotle, from the nature of the fable, divides tragedy into simple and complex. But it is of greater moment, with respect to dramatic as well as epic poetry, to found a distinction upon the different ends attained by such compositions. A poem, whether dramatic or epic, that hath no tendency beyond moving the passions and exhibiting pictures of virtue and vice, may be distinguished by the name of *pathetic*. But where a story is purposely contrived to illustrate some important lesson of morality, by showing the natural connection betwixt disorderly passions and external misfortunes, such composition may be denominated *moral*[4]. It indeed conveys moral instruction with a perspicuity that is not exceeded by the most accurate reasoning; and makes a deeper impression than any moral discourse can do. To be satisfied of this, we need but reflect, that a man whose affections are justly balanced, hath a better chance to escape misfortunes, than one who is a slave to every passion. Indeed, nothing is more evident, than the natural connection that vice hath with misery, and virtue with happiness; and such connection may be illustrated, by stating a fact as well as by urging an argument. Let us assume, for example, the following moral truths, That discord among the chiefs, renders ineffectual all common measures; and that the consequences of a slightly-founded quarrel, fostered by pride and arrogance, are not less fatal than those of the grossest injury.

---

2. Poet. cap. 25. sect 6.

3. Lib. 7. from line 385 to line 460.

4. The same distinction is applicable to that sort of fable which is said to be the invention of Æsop. A moral, it is true, is by all critics considered as essential to such a fable. But nothing is more common than to be led blindly by authority; for, of the numerous collections I have seen, the fables that clearly inculcate a moral make a very small part. In many fables, indeed, proper pictures of virtue and vice are exhibited: but the bulk of these collections convey no instruction, nor afford any amusement, beyond what a child receives in reading an ordinary story.

These truths may be inculcated, by the quarrel betwixt Agamemnon and Achilles at the siege of Troy. In this view, it ought to be the poet's chief aim, to invent proper circumstances, presenting to our view the natural consequences of such discord. These circumstances must seem to arise in the common course of human affairs: no accidental or unaccountable event ought to be indulged; for the necessary or probable connection betwixt vice and misery, is learned from no events but what are governed by the characters and passions of the persons represented. A real event of which we see no cause, may be a lesson to us; because what hath happened may again happen: but this cannot be inferred from a story that is known to be fictitious.

Many are the good effects of such compositions. A pathetic composition, whether epic or dramatic, tends to a habit of virtue, by exciting emotions that produce good actions, and avert us from those that are vicious or irregular. It likewise, by its frequent pictures of human woes, humanizes the mind, and fortifies us in bearing our own misfortunes. A moral composition must obviously produce the same good effects, because by being moral it doth not cease to be pathetic. It enjoys beside an excellence peculiar to itself: for it not only improves the heart, as above mentioned, but instructs the head by the moral it contains. For my part, I cannot imagine any entertainment more suited to a rational being, than a work thus happily illustrating some moral truth; where a number of persons of different characters are engaged in an important action, some retarding, others promoting, the great catastrophe; and where there is dignity of style as well as of matter. A work of this kind, has our sympathy at command, and can put in motion the whole train of the social affections. We have at the same time great mental enjoyment, in perceiving every event and every subordinate incident connected with its proper cause. Our curiosity is by turns excited and gratified; and our delight is consummated at the close, upon finding, from the characters and situations exhibited at the commencement, that every circumstance down to the final catastrophe is natural, and that the whole in conjunction make a regular chain of causes and effects.

Considering an epic and dramatic poem as the same in substance, and having the same aim or end, it might be thought that they are equally fitted for the same subjects. But considering their difference as to form, there will be found reason to correct that thought, at least in some degree. Many subjects may indeed be treated with equal advantage in either form; but the subjects are still more numerous for which one of the forms is better qualified than the other; and there are subjects proper for the one and not for the other. To give some slight notion of the difference, as there is no room here for enlarging upon every article, I observe, that dialogue is better qualified for expressing sentiments, and narrative for displaying facts. These peculiarities tend to confine each within certain limits. Heroism, magnanimity, undaunted courage, and the whole tribe of the elevated virtues, figure best in action: tender passions and the whole tribe of sympathetic affections, figure best in sentiment. What we feel is the most remarkable in the latter: what we perform is the most remarkable in the former. It clearly follows, that tender passions are more peculiarly the province of tragedy, grand and heroic actions of epic poetry[5].

I have no occasion to say more upon the epic, considered as peculiarly adapted to certain subjects. But as dramatic subjects are more complex, I must take a narrower view of them; which I do the more willingly, in order to clear a point thrown into great obscurity by critics.

In the chapter of emotions and passions[6], it is occasionally shown, that the subject best fitted for tragedy is the story of a man who has himself been the cause of his misfortune. But this man must neither be deeply guilty nor altogether innocent. The misfortune must be occasioned by a fault incident to human nature, and therefore venial. Misfortunes of this kind, call forth the whole force of the social affections, and interest the spectator in the warmest manner. An accidental misfortune, if not extremely singular, doth not greatly move our pity. The person who suffers, being innocent, is freed from the greatest of all torments, *viz.* the anguish of mind occasioned by remorse:

> *Poco é funesta*
> *Laltrui fortuna,*
> *Quando non resta*
> *Ragione alcuna*
> *Ne di pentirsi, né darrossir.*
>
> —*Metastasio*

---

5. In Racine tender sentiments prevail; in Corneille, grand and heroic manners. Hence clearly the preference of the former before the latter, as dramatic poets. Corneille would have figured better in an heroic poem.
6. Part 4.

A criminal, on the other hand, who brings misfortunes upon himself, excites little pity, for a different reason. His remorse, it is true, aggravates his distress, and swells the first emotions of pity: but then our hatred to the criminal blending with pity, blunts its edge considerably. Misfortunes that are not innocent nor highly criminal, partake the advantages of each extreme: they are attended with remorse to embitter the distress, which raises our pity to a great height; and the slight indignation we have at a venial fault, detracts not sensibly from our pity. For this reason, the happiest of all subjects for tragedy, if such a one could be invented, would be where a man of integrity falls into a great misfortune by doing an innocent action, but which by some singular means he conceives to be criminal. His remorse aggravates his distress; and our compassion, unrestrained by indignation, rises to its highest pitch. Pity comes thus to be the ruling passion of a pathetic tragedy; and by proper representation, may be raised to a height scarce exceeded by anything felt in real life. A moral tragedy takes in a larger field; for, beside exercising our pity, it raises another passion, selfish indeed, but which deserves to be cherished equally with the social affections. When a misfortune is the natural consequence of some wrong bias in the temper, every spectator who is conscious of some such defect in himself, takes the alarm, and considers that he is liable to the same misfortune. This consideration raises in him an emotion of fear or terror; and it is by this emotion, frequently reiterated in a variety of moral tragedies, that the spectators are put upon their guard against the disorders of passion.

The commentators upon Aristotle and other critics, have been much graveled about the account given of tragedy by this author, "That by means of pity and terror it refines in us all sorts of passion." But no one who has a clear conception of the end and effects of a good tragedy, can have any difficulty about Aristotle's meaning. Our pity is engaged for the persons represented, and our terror is upon our own account. Pity indeed is here made to stand for all the sympathetic emotions, because of these it is the capital. There can be no doubt, that our sympathetic emotions are refined or improved by daily exercise; and in what manner our other passions are refined by terror I have just now said. One thing is certain, that no other meaning can justly be given to the foregoing doctrine than that now mentioned; and that it was really Aristotle's meaning, appears from his 13th chapter, where he delivers several propositions agreeable to the doctrine as here explained. These, at the same time, I the rather chuse to mention; because, so far as authority can go, they confirm the foregoing reasoning about the proper subjects for tragedy. His first proposition is, That it being the province of tragedy to excite pity and terror, an innocent person falling into adversity ought never to be the subject. This proposition is a necessary consequence of his doctrine as explained: a subject of this nature may indeed excite pity and terror; but the former in an inferior degree, and the latter in no degree for moral instruction. The second proposition is, That we must not represent a wicked person emerging from misery to good fortune. This excites neither terror nor compassion, nor is agreeable in any respect. The third is, That the misfortunes of a wicked person ought not to be represented. Such representation may be agreeable in some measure upon a principle of justice: but it will not move our pity; or any degree of terror, except in those of the same vicious disposition with the person represented. His last proposition is, That the only character fit for representation lies in the middle, neither eminently good nor eminently bad; where the misfortune is not the effect of deliberate vice, but of some involuntary fault, as our author expresses it[7]. The only objection I find to Aristotle's account of tragedy, is, that he confines it within too narrow bounds, by refusing admittance to the pathetic kind. For if terror be essential to tragedy, no representation deserves that name, but where the misfortunes exhibited are caused by a wrong balance of mind, or some disorder in the internal constitution. Such misfortunes always suggest moral instruction; and by such misfortunes only can terror be excited for our improvement.

Thus Aristotle's four propositions above mentioned, relate solely to tragedies of the moral kind. Those of the pathetic kind, are not confined within so narrow limits. Subjects fitted for the theatre, are not in such plenty, as to make us reject innocent misfortunes which rouse our sympathy, though they inculcate no moral. With respect to subjects of this kind, it may indeed be a doubtful question, whether the conclusion ought not always to be happy. Where a person of integrity is represented as suffering to the end under misfortunes purely accidental, we depart discontented, and with some obscure sense of injustice; for seldom is man so submissive to the course of Providence, as not to revolt against the tyranny and vexations of blind chance: he will be

---

7. If anyone can be amused with a grave discourse which promised much and performs nothing, I refer to Brumoy, in his *Theater Gree*, Preliminary discourse on the origin of tragedy.

inclined to say, This ought not to be. I give for an example the *Romeo and Juliet* of Shakespear, where the fatal catastrophe is occasioned by Friar Laurence's coming to the monument a minute too late. Such a story we think of with regret: we are vexed at the unlucky chance, and go away dissatisfied. This is a temper of mind which ought not to be cherished; and for that reason, I vote for excluding stories of this kind from the theatre. The misfortunes of a virtuous person arising from necessary causes, or from a chain of unavoidable circumstances, will, I am apt to think, be considered in a different light. Chance affords always a gloomy prospect, and in every instance gives an impression of anarchy and misrule. A regular chain, on the other hand, of causes and effects, directed by the general laws of nature, never fails to suggest the hand of Providence; to which we submit without resentment, being conscious that submission is our duty[8]. For that reason, we are not dissatisfied with the distresses of Voltaire's *Mariamne*, though redoubled on her till the moment of her death, without the least fault or failing on her part. Her misfortunes are owing to a cause extremely natural, and not unfrequent, the jealousy of a barbarous husband. The fate of Desdemona in the *Moor of Venice*, affects us in the same manner. We are not so easily reconciled to the fate of Cordelia in *King Lear*: the causes of her misfortune, are by no means so evident, as to exclude the gloomy notion of chance. In short, it appears, that a perfect character suffering under misfortunes is qualified for being the subject of a pathetic tragedy, provided chance be excluded. Nor is it altogether inconsistent with a moral tragedy: it may successfully be introduced as an under-part, supposing the chief place to be filled with an imperfect character from which a moral can be drawn. This is the case of Desdemona and Mariamne just now mentioned; and it is the case of Monimia and Belvidera, in Otway's two tragedies, *The Orphan*, and *Venice preserv'd*.

I had an early opportunity to unfold a curious doctrine, That fable operates on our passions, by representing its events as passing in our sight, and by deluding us into a conviction of reality[9]. Hence, in epic and dramatic compositions, it is of importance to employ every means that may promote the delusion, such as the borrowing from history some noted event, with the addition of circumstances that may answer the author's purpose. The principal facts are known to be true; and we

---

8. See Essays on the Principles of Morality, edit. 2. p. 291.
9. Chap. 2. part 1. sect. 7.

are disposed to extend our belief to every circumstance. But in chusing a subject that makes a figure in history, greater precaution is necessary than where the whole is invented. In the first place, no circumstances must be added, but such as connect naturally with what are known to be true: history may be supplied, but it must not be contradicted. In the next place, a pure fable, entirely new with respect to the persons as well as the incidents, may be supposed an ancient or a modern story. But if the poet build upon truth, the subject he chuses must be distant in time, or at least in place; for he ought by all means to avoid the familiarity of persons and events nearly connected with us. Familiarity ought more especially to be avoided in an epic poem, the peculiar character of which is dignity and elevation. Modern manners make but a poor figure in such a poem[10].

After Voltaire, no writer, it is probable, will think of erecting an epic poem upon a recent event in the history of his own country. But an event of this kind is perhaps not altogether unqualified for tragedy. It was admitted in Greece, and Shakespear has employ'd it successfully in several of his pieces. One advantage it possesses above fiction, that of more readily engaging our belief, which tends above any other particular to raise our sympathy. The scene of comedy is generally laid at home: familiarity is no objection; and we are peculiarly sensible of the ridicule of our own manners.

After a proper subject is chosen, there appears to me some delicacy in dividing it into parts. The conclusion of a book in an epic poem, or of an act in a play, cannot be altogether arbitrary; nor be intended for so slight a purpose as to make the parts of equal length. The supposed pause at the end of every book, and the real pause at the end of every act, ought always to coincide with some pause in the action. In this respect, a dramatic or epic poem, ought to resemble a sentence or period in language, divided into members that are distinguished from each other by regular pauses: or it ought to resemble a piece of music, having a full close at the end, preceded by imperfect closes that contribute to the melody. Every act therefore ought to close with some incident that

---

10. I would not from this observation be thought to undervalue modern manners. The roughness and impetuosity of ancient manners may be better fitted for an epic poem, without being better fitted for society. But with regard to that circumstance, it is the familiarity of modern manners that unqualifies them for a lofty subject. The dignity of our present manners will be better understood in future ages, when they are no longer familiar.

makes a pause in the action; for otherwise there can be no pretext for interrupting the representation. It would be absurd to break off in the very heat of action: against this everyone would exclaim. The absurdity still remains, though the action relents, if it be not actually suspended for sometime. This rule is also applicable to an epic poem; though there a deviation from the rule is less remarkable, because it is in the reader's power to hide the absurdity, by proceeding instantly to another book. The first book of the *Paradise Lost*, ends without any regular close, perfect or imperfect: it breaks off abruptly, where Satan, seated on his throne, is prepared to make a speech to the convocated host of the fall'n angels; and the second book begins with the speech. Milton seems to have copied the *Æneid*, of which the two first books are divided much in the same manner. Neither is there any proper pause at the end of the fifth book of the *Æneid*. There is no proper pause at end of the seventh book of *Paradise Lost*, nor at the end of the eleventh.

HITHERTO I HAVE CARRIED ON together the epic and dramatic compositions. I proceed to handle them separately, and to mention circumstances peculiar to each, beginning with the epic kind. In a theatrical entertainment, which employs both the eye and the ear, it would be a monstrous absurdity to introduce upon the stage invisible beings in a visible shape. But it has been much disputed, whether such beings may not be properly introduced in an epic poem. If we rest upon the authority of practice, we must declare for the affirmative; and Boileau, among many other critics, is a stout champion for this sort of machinery. But waving authority, which is apt to impose upon the judgement, let us draw what light we can from reason. I begin with a preliminary remark, That this matter is but indistinctly handled by critics. It is laid down above, that several passions incite the mind to animate its objects: the moral virtues become so many goddesses, and even darts and arrows are inspired with life and action. But then it must not be overlooked, that such personification, being the work of imagination, is descriptive only, and assumes not even an appearance of truth. This is very different from what is termed *machinery*, where deities, angels, devils, or other supernatural powers, are introduced as real personages, mixing in the action, and contributing to the catastrophe; and yet these two things are constantly jumbled together in the reasoning. The poetical privilege of animating insensible objects for the sake of description, cannot be controverted, because it is founded on a natural principle. But has the privilege of machinery, if it be a privilege, the same good foundation? Far from it: nothing can be more unnatural. Its effects, at the same time, are deplorable. First, it gives an air of fiction to the whole; and prevents that impression of reality which is requisite to interest our affections, and to move our passions[11]. This of itself is sufficient to explode machinery, whatever entertainment it may give to readers of a fantastic taste or irregular imagination. And next, were it possible to disguise the fiction, and to delude us into a notion of reality, which I think can hardly be, an insuperable objection would still remain, which is, that the aim or end of an epic poem can never be accomplished in any perfection where machinery is introduced. Virtuous emotions cannot be raised successfully but by the actions of those who are endued with passions and affections like our own, that is, by human actions. And as for moral instruction, it is evident, that we can draw none from beings who act not upon the same principles with us. A fable in Æsop's manner is no objection to this reasoning. His lions, bulls, and goats, are truly men under disguise: they act and feel in every respect as human beings; and the moral we draw is founded on that supposition. Homer, it is true, introduces the gods into his fable; and he was authorised to take that liberty by the religion of his country; it being an article in the Grecian creed, that the gods often interpose visibly and bodily in human affairs. I must however observe, that Homer's deities do no honour to his poems. Fictions that transgress the bounds of nature, seldom have a good effect: they may inflame the imagination for a moment, but will not be relished by any person of a correct taste. Let me add, that of whatever use such fictions may be to a mean genius, an able writer has much finer materials of Nature's production for elevating his subject, and making it interesting.

Boileau, a strenuous advocate for the Heathen deities, as observed, declares against angels and devils, though supported by the religious creed of his country. One would be apt to imagine, that a critic famed for his good taste, could have no other meaning than to justify the employing Heathen deities for enlivening or elevating the description. But as the Heathen deities make not a better figure in poetical language than angels and devils, Boileau, in pleading for the former, certainly meant, if he had any distinct meaning, that these may be introduced as actors. And, in fact, he himself is guilty of this glaring absurdity, where

---

11. See chap. 2. part 1. sect. 7.

it is not so pardonable as in an epic poem. In his ode upon the taking of Namur, he demands with a most serious countenance, whether the walls were built by Apollo or Neptune; and in relating the passage of the Rhine, *anno* 1672, he describes the god of that river as fighting with all his might to oppose the French monarch. This is confounding fiction with reality at a strange rate. The French writers in general run into this error: wonderful! that they should not be sensible how ridiculous it is.

That this is a capital error in the *Gierusalleme liberata*, Tasso's greatest admirers must acknowledge. A situation can never be intricate, nor the reader ever in pain about the catastrophe, so long as there is an angel, devil, or magician, to lend a helping hand. Voltaire, in his essay upon epic poetry, talking of the *Pharsalia*, observes judiciously, "That the proximity of time, the notoriety of events, the character of the age, enlightened and political, joined with the solidity of Lucan's subject, deprived him of all liberty of poetical fiction." Is it not amazing, that a critic who reasons so justly with respect to others, can be so blind with respect to himself? Voltaire, not satisfied to enrich his language with images drawn from invisible and superior beings, introduces them into the action. In the sixth canto of the *Henriade*, St. Louis appears in person, and terrifies the soldiers; in the seventh canto, St. Louis sends the god of Sleep to Henry; and, in the tenth, the demons of Discord, Fanaticism, War, &*c.* assist Aumale in a single combat with Turenne, and are chased away by a good angel brandishing the sword of God. To blend such fictitious personages in the same action with mortals, makes a bad figure at any rate; and is intolerable in a history so recent as that of Henry IV. This singly is sufficient to make the *Henriade* a short-liv'd poem, were it otherwise possessed of every beauty. I have tried serious reasoning upon this subject; but ridicule, I suppose, will be found a more successful weapon, which Addison has applied in an elegant manner: "Whereas the time of a general peace is, in all appearance, drawing near; being informed that there are several ingenious persons who intend to shew their talents on so happy an occasion, and being willing, as much as in me lies, to prevent that effusion of nonsense which we have good cause to apprehend; I do hereby strictly require every person who shall write on this subject, to remember that he is a Christian, and not to sacrifice his catechism to his poetry. In order to it, I do expect of him in the first place, to make his own poem, without depending upon Phœbus for any part of it, or calling out for aid upon any of the muses by name. I do likewise positively forbid the sending of Mercury with any particular message or dispatch relating to the peace; and shall by no means suffer Minerva to take upon her the shape of any plenipotentiary concerned in this great work. I do further declare, that I shall not allow the destinies to have had an hand in the deaths of the several thousands who have been slain in the late war; being of opinion that all such deaths may be very well accounted for by the Christian system of powder and ball. I do therefore strictly forbid the fates to cut the thread of man's life upon any pretence whatsoever, unless it be for the sake of the rhyme. And whereas I have good reason to fear, that Neptune will have a great deal of business on his hands in several poems which we may now suppose are upon the anvil, I do also prohibit his appearance, unless it be done in metaphor, simile, or any very short allusion; and that even here he be not permitted to enter, but with great caution and circumspection. I desire that the same rule may be extended to his whole fraternity of Heathen gods; it being my design to condemn every poem to the flames in which Jupiter thunders, or exercises any other act of authority which does not belong to him. In short, I expect that no Pagan agent shall be introduced, or any fact related which a man cannot give credit to with a good conscience. Provided always, that nothing herein contained shall extend, or be construed to extend, to several of the female poets in this nation, who shall still be left in full possession of their gods and goddesses, in the same manner as if this paper had never been written." *Spectator*, No 523.

The marvellous is indeed so much promoted by machinery, that it is not wonderful to find it embraced by the bulk of writers, and perhaps of readers. If indulged at all, it is generally indulged to excess. Homer introduces his deities with no greater ceremony than his mortals; and Virgil has still less moderation: an over-watched pilot cannot fall asleep and drop into the sea by natural means: the two lovers, Æneas and Dido, cannot take the same bed, without the immediate interposition of superior powers. The ridiculous in such fictions, must appear even through the thickest vail of gravity and solemnity.

Angels and devils serve equally with the Heathen deities, as materials for figurative language, perhaps better among Christians, because we believe in them, and not in the Heathen deities. But everyone is sensible, as well as Boileau, that the invisible powers in our creed make a much worse figure as actors in a modern poem, than the invisible powers in the Heathen creed did in ancient poems. The reason I take to be what follows. The Heathen deities, in the opinion of their votaries, were beings elevated one step only above mankind, actuated by the same passions, and directed by the same motives; therefore not altogether improper to mix with mankind in an important action. In our creed, superior beings are placed at such a mighty distance from us, and are of a nature so different, that with no propriety can they appear with us upon the same stage. Man is a creature so much inferior, that he loses all dignity when set in opposition.

There seems to be no doubt, that an historical poem admits the embellishment of allegory, as well as of metaphor, simile, or other figure. Moral truth, in particular, is finely illustrated in the allegorical manner. It amuses the fancy to find abstract terms, by a sort of magic, converted into active beings; and it is delightful to trace a general proposition in a pictured event. But allegorical beings should be confined within their own sphere; and never be admitted to mix in the principal action, nor to co-operate in retarding or advancing the catastrophe. This would have a still worse effect, than the introduction of invisible powers; and I am ready to assign the reason. An historical fable affords entertainment chiefly by making us conceive its personages to be really existing and acting in our presence: in an allegory, this agreeable delusion is denied; for we must not imagine an allegorical personage to be a real being, but the figure only of some virtue or vice; otherwise the allegory is lost. The impression of real existence, essential to an epic poem, is inconsistent with that figurative existence which is essential to an allegory; and therefore no method can be more effectual to destroy the impression of reality, than to introduce allegorical beings co-operating with those whom we conceive to be really existing. The love-episode in the *Henriade*[12], is insufferable by the discordant mixture of allegory with real life. This episode is copied from that of Rinaldo and Armida in the *Gierusalemme liberata*, which hath no merit to intitle it to be copied. An allegorical object, such as fame in the *Æneid*, and the temple of love in the *Henriade*, may find place in a description: but to introduce Discord as a real personage, imploring the assistance of Love as another real personage, to enervate the courage of the hero, is making these figurative beings act beyond their sphere, and creating a strange jumble of discordant materials, *viz.* truth and fiction. The allegory of Sin and Death in the *Paradise Lost*, is, I presume, not generally relished, though it is not entirely of the same nature with what I have been condemning.

---

12. Canto 9.

The *Paradise Lost* is not confined to the history of our first parents; and in a work comprehending the achievements of superior beings, there is more room for fancy than where it is confined to human actions.

What is the true notion of an episode? or how is it to be distinguished from what is really a part of the principal action? Every incident that promotes or retards the catastrophe, must be a part of the principal action. This clears the nature of an episode; which may be defined, "An incident connected with the principal action, but which contributes not either to advance or retard it." The descent of Æneas into hell doth not advance or retard the catastrophe; and therefore is an episode. The story of Nisus and Euryalus, producing an alteration in the affairs of the contending parties, is a part of the principal action. The family-scene in the sixth book of the *Iliad* is of the same nature: by Hector's retiring from the field of battle to visit his wife, the Grecians got liberty to breathe, and even to press upon the Trojans. It being thus the nature of an episode to break the unity of action, it ought never to be indulged unless to refresh and unbend the mind after the fatigue of a long narration. This purpose of an episode demands the following properties. It ought to be well connected with the principal action: it ought to be short: and it ought to be lively and interesting.

NEXT, UPON THE PECULIARITIES OF a dramatic poem. And the first I shall mention is a double plot; being naturally led to it by what is said immediately above. One of these double plots must be of the nature of an episode in an epic poem; for it would distract the spectator, instead of entertaining him, if he were forc'd to attend, at the same time, to two capital plots equally interesting. An under-plot in a tragedy has seldom a good effect; because a passionate piece cannot be too simple. The sympathetic emotions once roused, cling to their objects, and cannot bear interruption: when a subject fills the mind, it leaves no room for any separate concern[13]. Variety is more tolerable

---

13. Racine, in his preface to the tragedy of *Berenice,* is sensible that simplicity is a great beauty in tragedy, but mistakes the cause. "Nothing (says he) but verisimilitude pleases in tragedy: but where is the verisimilitude, that, within the compass of a day, events should be crowded which commonly are extended through months?" This is mistaking the accuracy of imitation for the probability or improbability of future events. I explain myself. The verisimilitude required in tragedy is, that the actions correspond to the manners, and the manners to nature. When this resemblance is preserved, the imitation is just, because it is a true copy of nature. But I deny that the verisimilitude of future events, meaning the probability of future events, is any rule in tragedy. A number of extraordinary events are,

in comedy, which pretends only to amuse, without totally occupying the mind. But even here, to make a double plot agreeable, a good deal of art is requisite. The under-plot ought not to vary greatly in its tone from that which is principal: passions may be varied, but discordant passions are unpleasant when jumbled together. This is a solid objection to tragi-comedy. For this reason, I blame the *Provok'd Husband*: all the scenes that bring the family of the Wrongheads into action, being ludicrous and farcical, agree very ill with the sharpness and severity of the principal subject, exhibiting the discord betwixt Lord Townly and his lady. The same objection touches not the double plot of the *Careless Husband*: the different subjects are sweetly connected; and have only so much variety as to resemble shades of colours harmoniously mixed. But this is not all. The under plot ought to be connected with the principal action, so as to employ the same persons: the intervals or pauses of the principal action ought to be filled with the under-plot; and both ought to be concluded together. This is the case of the *Merry Wives of Windsor*.

Violent action ought to be excluded from the stage. While the dialogue runs on, a thousand particulars concur to delude us into an impression of reality; genuine sentiments, passionate language, and persuasive gesture. The spectator once engaged, is willing to be deceived, loses sight of himself, and without scruple enjoys the spectacle as a reality. From this absent state, he is roused by violent action: he wakes as from a pleasing dream, and gathering his senses about him, finds all to be a fiction. Horace delivers the same rule; and sounds it upon the reason given:

Ne pueros coram populo Medea trucidet;
Aut humana palam coquat exta nefarius Atreus;
Aut in avem Progne vertatur, Cadmus in anguem.
Quodcunque ostendis mihi sic, incredulus odi.

---

it is true, seldom crowded within the compass of a day; but what seldom happens may happen; and when such events fall out, they appear no less natural than the most ordinary accidents. To make verisimilitude in the sense of probability a governing rule in tragedy, would annihilate that sort of writing altogether; for it would exclude all extraordinary events, in which the life of tragedy consists. It is very improbable or unlikely, pitching upon any man at random, that he will sacrifice his life and fortune for his mistress or for his country: yet when that event happens, supposing it conformable to the character, we recognize the verisimilitude as to nature, whatever want of verisimilitude or of probability there was *a priori* that such would be the event.

The French critics, as it appears to me, misapprehend the reason of this rule. Shedding blood upon the stage, say they, is barbarous and shocking to a polite audience. This no doubt is an additional reason for excluding bloodshed from the French stage, supposing the French to be in reality so delicate. But this evidently is not the reason that weighed with the Greeks: that polite people had no notion of such delicacy; witness the murder of Clytemnestra by her son Orestes, passing behind the scene, as represented by Sophocles. Her voice is heard calling out for mercy, bitter expostulations on his part, loud shrieks upon her being stabb'd, and then a deep silence. I appeal to every person of feeling, whether this scene be not more horrible, than if the deed had been committed in sight of the spectators upon a sudden gust of passion. According to the foregoing reasoning of the French critics, there is nothing to exclude from the stage a duel occasioned by an affair of honour, because in it there is nothing barbarous or shocking to a polite audience: yet a scene of this nature is excluded from the French stage; which shows, without more argument, that these critics have misapprehended the rule laid down by Horace. If Corneille, in representing the affair betwixt Horatius and his sister, upon which murder ensues behind the scene, had no other view than to remove from the spectators a scene of horror, he certainly was in a capital mistake: for murder in cold blood, which in some measure was the case as represented, is more horrible even where the conclusive stab is not seen, than the same act performed on the stage by violent and unpremeditated passion, as suddenly repented of as committed. I heartily agree with Addison[14], that no part of this incident ought to have been represented, but reserved for a narrative, with all the alleviating circumstances possible in favour of the hero. This is the only method to avoid the difficulties that unqualify this incident for representation, a deliberate murder on the one hand, and on the other a violent action performed on the stage, which must rouse the spectator from his dream of reality.

I SHALL FINISH WITH A few words upon the dialogue; which ought to be so conducted as to be a true representation of nature. I talk not here of the sentiments, nor of the language; for these come under different heads. I talk of what properly belongs to dialogue-writing; where every single speech, short or long, ought to arise from what is

---

14. Spectator. No. 44.

said by the former speaker, and furnish matter for what comes after, till the end of the scene. In this view, the whole speeches, from first to last, represent so many links, all connected together in one regular chain. No author, ancient or modern, possesses the art of dialogue equal to Shakespear. Dryden, in this particular, may justly be placed as his opposite. He frequently introduces three or four persons speaking upon the same subject, each throwing out his own sentiments separately, without regarding what is said by the rest. I give for an example the first scene of *Aurenzebe*. Sometimes he makes a number club in relating an event, not to a stranger, supposed ignorant of it, but to one another, for the sake merely of speaking. Of this notable sort of dialogue, we have a specimen in the first scene of the first part of the *Conquest of Granada*. In the second part of the same tragedy, scene second, the King, Abenamar, and Zulema, make their separate observations, like so many soliloquies, upon the fluctuating temper of the mob. It puts one in mind of a pastoral, where two shepherds are introduced reciting couplets alternately, each in praise of his own mistress, as if they were contending for a prize.

The bandying sentiments in this manner, beside an unnatural air, has another bad effect. It stays the course of the action, because it is not productive of any consequence. In Congreve's comedies, the action is often suspended to make way for a play of wit. But of this more particularly in the chapter immediately following.

XXIII

The three Unities

The first chapter unfolds the pleasure we have in a chain of connected facts. In histories of the world, of a country, of a people, this pleasure is but faint; because the connections are slight or obscure. We find more entertainment in biography, where the incidents are connected by their relation to one person, who makes a figure and commands our attention. But the greatest entertainment of the kind, is afforded by the history of a single event, supposing it to be interesting. The history of one event produceth a more entire connection among the parts, than the history of one person. In the latter, the circumstances are not otherwise connected than by their relation to that person: in the former, the circumstances are connected by the strongest of all relations, that of cause and effect. Thus, the circumstances of a single event, having a mutual connection extremely intimate, form a delightful train: we survey with peculiar pleasure a number of facts that give birth to each other; and we pass with ease and satisfaction from the first to the last.

But this subject merits a more particular discussion. When we consider the chain of causes and effects in the material world, independent of purpose, design, or thought, we find a train of incidents in succession, without beginning, middle, or end. Everything that happens is both a cause and an effect: it is the effect of something that goes before, and the cause of one or many things that follow. One incident may affect us more, another less; but all of them, great and small, are so many links in the universal chain. The mind, in viewing these incidents, cannot rest or settle ultimately upon anyone; but is carried along in the train without any close.

But when the intellectual world is taken under view, in conjunction with the material, the scene is varied. Man acts with deliberation, will, and choice; he acts with a view to some end, glory, for example, or riches, or conquest, the procuring happiness to individuals, or to his country in general; and he proposes means and lays schemes to attain the end proposed. Here is recognised a capital end or event, connected with subordinate events or incidents by the relation of causation. In running over a series of subordinate events, we cannot rest upon anyone; because they are presented to us as means only, leading to some end. But we rest with satisfaction upon the ultimate event; because there, the purpose, the plan, the aim, of the chief person or persons, is completed and brought to a final conclusion. This indicates a beginning, a middle, and an end, of what Aristotle calls *an entire action*[1]. The story naturally begins with describing those circumstances which move the distinguished person to form a plan, in order to compass some desired event. The prosecution of that plan, and the obstructions, carry the reader into the heat of action. The middle is properly where the action is the most involved; and the end is where the event is brought about, and the design accomplished.

A design or plan thus happily perfected, after many obstructions, affords wonderful delight to the reader. And to produce this delight, a principle mentioned above[2] mainly contributes; a principle that disposes the mind to complete every work commenced, and in general to carry everything to its ultimate conclusion.

I have given the foregoing example of a plan laid down and completed, because it affords the clearest conception of a beginning, a middle, and an end, in which consists unity of action: and indeed stricter unity cannot be imagined than in this case. But an action may have unity, or a beginning, middle, and end, without so intimate a relation of parts. The catastrophe may be different from what is intended or desired; which is frequently the case in our best tragedies. The *Æneid* is an instance of means employ'd to produce a certain event, and these means crowned with success. The *Iliad* is formed upon a different model. It begins with the quarrel betwixt Achilles and Agamemnon: it goes on to describe the several effects produced by that cause; and ends in a reconciliation. Here is unity of action, no doubt, a beginning, a middle, and an end: it must however be acknowledged, that the *Æneid* is more happy in point of connection. The mind hath a propensity to go forward in the chain of history: it keeps always in view the expected event; and when the incidents or under-parts are connected together by their relation to the event, the mind runs sweetly and easily along them. This pleasure we have in the *Æneid*. But it is not altogether so pleasant, as in the *Iliad*, to connect effects by their common cause; for such connection forces

---

1. Poet. cap. 6. See also cap. 7.
2. Chap. 8.

the mind to a continual retrospect: looking backward is like walking backward.

But Homer's plan is still more imperfect, for another reason, That the events described are but imperfectly connected with the wrath of Achilles as their cause. His wrath did not exert itself in action; and the misfortunes of his countrymen were but negatively the effects of his wrath, by depriving them of his assistance.

If unity of action be a capital beauty in a fable imitative of human affairs, a double action must be a capital defect, by carrying on together two trains of unconnected objects. For the sake of variety, we indulge an under-plot that contributes to the principal event. But two unconnected events are a great deformity; and it lessens the deformity but a very little, to engage the same actors in both. Ariosto is quite licentious in this particular: he carries on at the same time a plurality of unconnected stories. His only excuse is, that his plan is perfectly well adjusted to his subject; for everything in the *Orlando Furioso* is wild and extravagant.

To state facts according to the order of time, is the most natural and the most simple method: a method however not so essential, in an historical fable especially, as not to yield to some conspicuous beauties[3]. If a noted story, cold and simple in its first movements, be made the subject of an epic poem, the reader may be hurried into the heat of action, reserving the preliminaries for a conversation-piece, if it shall be thought necessary. This method, at the same time, being dramatic, hath a peculiar beauty, which narration cannot reach. Romance-writers, who give little attention to nature, deviate in this particular, among many, from a just standard. They make no difficulty of presenting to the reader, without the least preparation, unknown persons engaged in some adventure equally unknown. In *Cassandra*, two personages, who afterward are discovered to be the heroes of the story, start up completely armed upon the banks of the Euphrates, and engage in a single combat[4].

---

3. See chap. 1.
4. I am sensible that a commencement of this sort is much relished by readers disposed to the marvellous. Their curiosity is raised, and they are much tickled in its gratification. But curiosity is at an end with the first reading, because the personages are no longer unknown; and, therefore, at the second reading, a commencement so artificial loses its power even over the vulgar. A writer of genius prefers lasting beauties.

A play analyzed, is a chain of connected facts, of which each scene makes a link. Each scene, accordingly, ought to produce some incident relative to the catastrophe or ultimate event, by advancing or retarding it. If no incident be produced, such a scene, which may be termed barren, ought not to be indulged, because it breaks the unity of action. A barren scene can never be intitled to a place, because the chain is complete without it. In the *Old Bachelor*, the 3d scene of act 2. and all that follow to the end of that act, are mere conversation-pieces, without any consequence. The 10th and 11th scenes, act 3. *Double Dealer*, the 10th, 11th, 12th, 13th, and 14th scenes, act 1. *Love for Love*, are of the same kind. Neither is *The Way of the World* entirely guiltless of such scenes. It will be no justification, that they help to display characters. It were better, like Dryden, in his *dramatis personæ*, to describe characters beforehand, which would not interrupt the chain of action. But a writer of genius has no occasion for such artifice: he can display the characters of his personages much more to the life in sentiment and action. How successfully is this done by Shakespear! in whose works there is not to be found a single barren scene.

Upon the whole, it appears, that all the facts in an historical fable, ought to have a mutual connection by their common relation to the grand event or catastrophe. And this relation, in which the *unity* of action consists, is equally essential to epic and dramatic compositions.

How far the unities of time and of place are essential, is a question of greater intricacy. These unities were strictly observed in the Grecian and Roman theatres; and they are inculcated by the French and English critics as essential to every dramatic composition. In theory, these unities are also acknowledged by our best poets, though their practice is seldom correspondent: they are often forc'd to take liberties, which they pretend not to justify, against the practice of the Greeks and Romans, and against the solemn decision of their own countrymen. But in the course of this inquiry it will be made evident, that the example of the ancients ought, upon this point, to have no weight with us, and that our critics are guilty of a mistake, in admitting no greater latitude of place and time than was admitted in Greece and Rome.

Suffer me only to premise, that the unities of place and time, are not, by the most rigid critics, required in a narrative poem. In such a composition, if it pretend to copy nature, these unities would be absurd; because real events are seldom confined within narrow limits either of place or of time. And yet we can follow history, or an historical fable, through all its changes, with the greatest facility. We never once think of measuring the real time by what is taken in reading; nor of forming any connection betwixt the place of action and that which we occupy.

I am sensible, that the drama differs so far from the epic, as to admit different rules. It will be observed, "That an historical fable, which affords entertainment by reading solely, is under no limitation of time or of place, more than a genuine history; but that a dramatic composition cannot be accurately represented, unless it be limited, as its representation is, to one place and to a few hours; and therefore that no fable can be admitted but what has these properties, because it would be absurd to compose a piece for representation that cannot be justly represented." This argument, I acknowledge, has at least a plausible appearance; and yet one is apt to suspect some fallacy, considering that no critic, however strict, has ventured to confine the unities of place and of time within so narrow bounds[5].

A view of the Grecian drama, and a comparison betwixt it and our own, may perhaps help to relieve us from this dilemma. If they be differently constructed, as shall by and by be made evident, it is possible that the foregoing reasoning may not be applicable with equal force to both. This is an article, that, with relation to the present subject, has not, so far as I know, been examined by any writer.

All authors agree, that the first notion of tragedy in Greece, was derived from the hymns in praise of Bacchus, which were sung in parts by a chorus. Thespis, to relieve the singers, and for the sake of variety, introduced one actor; who gave a narrative of the subject, and sometimes represented one or other personage. Eschylus, introducing a second actor, formed the dialogue; by which the performance became dramatic: and the actors were multiplied when the subject represented made it necessary. But still, the chorus, which gave a beginning to tragedy, was considered as an essential part of its constitution. In the first scene, generally, are unfolded the preliminary circumstances that lead to the grand event. This scene is by Aristotle termed the *prologue*. In the second scene, where the action properly begins, the chorus is

---

5. Bossu, after observing, with wondrous critical sagacity, that winter is an improper season for an epic poem, and night no less improper for tragedy, admits, however, that an epic poem may be spread through the whole summer months, and a tragedy through the whole sunshine hours of the longest summer day. *Du Poeme, Epique, l.* 3. *chap.* 12. At that rate an English tragedy may be longer than a French tragedy; and in Nova Zembla the time of tragedy and of an epic poem may be the same.

introduced, which, as originally, continues upon the stage during the whole performance. Sophocles adheres to this plan religiously. Euripides is not altogether so correct. In some of his pieces it becomes necessary to remove the chorus. But this is seldom done; and when done, matters are so ordered as that their absence is but momentary. The chorus often mix in the dialogue; and when the dialogue happens to be suspended, the chorus, during the interval, is employ'd in singing. Nor does the removal of the chorus, when that unusual step is risked, interrupt the representation. They never leave the stage of their own accord, but at the command of some principal personage who constantly waits their return.

Thus the Grecian drama is a continued representation without any interruption; a circumstance that merits attention. A continued representation without a pause, affords not opportunity to vary the place of action; and has withal a very short duration. To a representation so confined in place and time, the foregoing reasoning is strictly applicable. A real or feigned action that is brought to a conclusion after considerable intervals of time and frequent change of place, cannot accurately be copied in a representation that admits of no latitude in either. Hence it is, that the unities of place and of time, were, or ought to have been, strictly observed in the Grecian tragedies. This is made necessary by the very constitution of their drama; for it is absurd to compose a tragedy that cannot be justly represented.

Modern critics, who for our drama pretend to establish rules founded on the practice of the Greeks, are guilty of an egregious blunder. The unities of place and of time, so much vaunted, were in Greece, as we see, a matter of necessity, not of choice. I am now ready to show, that if we submit to these fetters, it must be from choice not necessity. This will be evident upon taking a view of the construction of our drama, which differs widely from that of Greece; whether more or less perfect, is a separate question, which shall be handled afterward. By dropping the chorus, an opportunity is afforded to split our drama into parts or acts, which in the representation are distinguished by intervals of time; and during these intervals, the stage is totally evacuated and the spectacle suspended. This construction qualifies our drama for subjects spread through a wide space both of time and of place. The time supposed to pass during the suspension of the representation, is not measured by the time of the suspension; nor is any connection formed, betwixt the box we sit in and the place where things are supposed to be transacted in our absence: and by that means, many subjects can be justly represented in our theatres, for which there was no place in those of ancient Greece. This doctrine may be illustrated, by comparing a modern play to a set of historical pictures: let us suppose them five in number, and the resemblance will be complete. Each of the pictures resembles an act in one of our plays. There must necessarily be the strictest unity of place and of time in each picture; and the same necessity requires these two unities during each act of a play, because during an act there is no interruption in the spectacle. Now, when we view in succession a number of such historical pictures, let it be, for example, the history of Alexander by Le Brun, we have no difficulty to conceive, that months or years have passed betwixt the subjects exhibited in two different pictures, though the interruption is imperceptible in passing our eye from the one to the other. We have as little difficulty to conceive a change of place, however great. In this matter, there is truly no difference betwixt five acts of a modern play and five such pictures. Where the representation is suspended, we can with the greatest facility suppose any length of time or any change of place. The spectator, it is true, may be conscious, that the real time and place are not the same with what are employ'd in the representation, even including the intervals. But this is a work of reflection; and by the same reflection he may also be conscious, that Garrick is not King Lear, that the playhouse is not Dover cliffs, nor the noise he hears thunder and lightning. In a word, during an interruption of the representation, it is not more difficult for a spectator to imagine himself carried from place to place, and from one period of time to another, than at once, when the scene first opens, to be carried from London to Rome, or from the present time two thousand years back. And indeed, it must appear ridiculous, that a critic, who makes no difficulty of supposing candle-light to be sun-shine, and some painted canvasses a palace or a prison, should affect so much difficulty in imagining a latitude of place or of time in the story, beyond what is necessary in the representation.

There are, I acknowledge, some effects of great latitude in time that ought never to be indulged in a composition for the theatre. Nothing can be more absurd, than at the close to exhibit a full grown person who appears a child at the beginning. The mind rejects as contrary to all probability, such latitude of time as is requisite for a change so remarkable. The greatest change from place to place hath not altogether the same bad effect. In the bulk of human affairs place is not material;

and the mind, when occupied with an interesting event, is little regardful of minute circumstances. These may be varied at will, because they scarce make any impression.

But though I have thus taken arms to rescue modern poets from the slavish fetters of modern critics, I would not be understood to justify liberty without any reserve. An unbounded licence with relation to place and time, is faulty for a reason that seems to have been overlooked: it never fails to break in upon the unity of action. In the ordinary course of human affairs, single events, such as are fit to be represented on the stage, are confined to a narrow spot, and generally employ no great extent of time. We accordingly seldom find strict unity of action in a dramatic composition, where any remarkable latitude is indulged in these particulars. I must say farther, that a composition which employs but one place, and requires not a greater length of time than is necessary for the representation, is so far the more perfect: because the confining an event within so narrow bounds, contributes to the unity of action; and also prevents that labour, however slight, which the mind must undergo in imagining frequent changes of place and many intervals of time. But still I must insist, that the limitation of place and time which was necessary in the Grecian drama, is no rule to us; and therefore that though such limitation adds one beauty more to the composition, it is at best but a refinement, which may justly give place to a thousand beauties more substantial. And I may add, that it is extremely difficult, I was about to say impracticable, to contract within the Grecian limits, any fable so fruitful of incidents in number and variety as to give full scope to the fluctuation of passion.

It may now appear, that critics who put the unities of place and of time upon the same footing with the unity of action, making them all equally essential, have not attended to the nature and construction of the modern drama. If they admit an interrupted representation, with which no writer finds fault, it is plainly absurd to condemn the greatest advantage it procures us, that of representing many interesting subjects excluded from the Grecian stage. If there needs must be a reformation, why not restore the ancient chorus and the ancient continuity of action? There is certainly no medium: for to admit an interruption without relaxing from the strict unities of place and of time, is in effect to load us with all the inconveniencies of the ancient drama, and at the same time to with-hold from us its advantages.

And therefore the only proper question is, whether our model be or be not a real improvement. This indeed may justly be called in question; and in order to a fair comparative trial, some particulars must be premised. When a play begins, we have no difficulty to enter into the scene of action, however distant it be in time or in place. We know that the play is a representation only: and the imagination, with facility, accommodates itself to every circumstance. Our situation is very different after we are engaged. It is the perfection of representation to hide itself, to impose upon the spectator, and to produce in him an impression of reality, as if he were spectator of a real event[6]. Any interruption annihilates this impression: he is roused out of his waking dream, and unhappily restored to his senses. So difficult it is to support this impression of reality, that much slighter interruptions than the interval betwixt two acts are sufficient to dissolve the charm. In the 5th act of the *Mourning Bride*, the three first scenes are in a room of state; the fourth in a prison. This change is operated by shifting the scene, which is done in a trice. But however quick the transition may be, it is impracticable to impose upon the spectators so far as to make them conceive that they are actually carried from the palace to the prison. They immediately reflect, that the palace and prison are imaginary, and that the whole is a fiction.

From these premisses one will be naturally led, at first view, to declare against the frequent interruptions in the modern drama. It will occur, "That every interruption must have the effect to banish the dream of reality, and with it to banish our concern, which cannot subsist while we are conscious that all is a fiction; and therefore that in the modern drama sufficient time is not afforded for the fluctuation and swelling of passion, like what is afforded in the Grecian drama, where there is no interruption." This reasoning, it must be owned, has a specious appearance: but we must not turn faint-hearted upon the first repulse; let us rally our troops for a second engagement.

Considering attentively the ancient drama, we find, that though the representation is never interrupted, the principal action is suspended not less frequently than in the modern drama. There are five acts in each; and the only difference is, that in the former, when the action is suspended, as it is at the end of every act, opportunity is taken of the interval to employ the chorus in singing. Hence it appears, that the Grecian continuity of representation cannot have the effect to prolong the impression of reality. To banish this impression, a suspension of the

---

6. Chap. 2. part 1. sect. 7.

action while the chorus is employ'd in singing, is not less operative than a total suspension both of the representation and action.

But to open a larger view, I am ready to show, that a continued representation, without a single pause even in the principal action, so far from an advantage, would be really an imperfection; and that a representation with proper pauses, is better calculated for moving the audience, and making the strongest impressions. Representation cannot very long support an impression of reality: when the spirits are exhausted by close attention and by the agitation of passion, an uneasiness ensues, which never fails to banish the waking dream. Now supposing an act to employ as much time as can easily be given with strict attention to any incident, a supposition that cannot be far from the truth; it follows, that the impression of reality would not be prolonged beyond the space of an act, even supposing a continued representation. Hence it appears, that a continued representation without any pause, would be a bad contrivance: it would break the attention by overstraining it, and produce a total absence of mind. In this respect, the four pauses have a fine effect. By affording to the audience a seasonable respite when the impression of reality is gone, and while nothing material is in agitation, they relieve the mind from its fatigue; and consequently prevent a wandering of thought at the very time possibly of the most interesting scenes.

In one article indeed, the Grecian model has greatly the advantage: its chorus, during an interval, not only preserves alive the impressions made upon the audience, but also prepares their hearts finely for new impressions. In our theatres, on the contrary, the audience, at the end of every act, are in a manner solicited to withdraw their thoughts from what has been passing, and to trifle away the time the best way they can. Thus in the intervals betwixt the acts, every warm impression is banished; and the spectators begin the next act cool and indifferent, as at the commencement of the play. Here is a gross malady in our theatrical representations; but a malady that luckily is not incurable. To revive the Grecian chorus, would be to revive the Grecian slavery of place and time. But I can figure a detached chorus coinciding with a pause in the representation, as the ancient chorus did with a pause in the principal action. What objection, for example, can there lie against music betwixt the acts, vocal and instrumental, adapted to the subject? Such detached chorus, beside admitting the same latitude that we enjoy at present as to time and place, would have more than one happy effect: it would recruit the spirits; and it would preserve entire, the tone, if not the tide, of passion. The music that comes first, ought to accord with the tone of the preceding passion, and be gradually varied till it accord with the tone of the passion that is to succeed in the next act. The music and the representation would both of them be gainers by their conjunction; which will thus appear. Music that accords with the present tone of mind, is, upon that account, doubly agreeable; and accordingly, though music singly hath not power to raise any passion, it tends greatly to support a passion already raised. Further, music, though it cannot of itself raise a passion, prepares us for the passion that follows: by making chearful, tender, melancholy, or animated impressions, music has power to dispose the heart to various passions. Of this power, the first scene of the *Mourning Bride* is a shining instance: without the preparation of soft music in a melancholy strain, it would be extremely difficult to enter all at once into Almeria's deep distress. In this manner, music and representation support each other delightfully: the impression made upon the audience by the representation, is a fine preparation for the music that succeeds; and the impression made by the music, is a fine preparation for the representation that succeeds. It appears to me clear, that, by some such contrivance, the modern drama may be improved, so as to enjoy the advantage of the ancient chorus without its slavish limitation of place and time. And as to music in particular, I cannot figure any plan that would tend more to its improvement. Composers, those for the stage at least, would be reduced to the happy necessity of studying and imitating nature; instead of indulging, according to the present fashion, in wild, fantastic, and unnatural conceits. But we must return to our subject, and finish the comparison betwixt the ancient and the modern drama.

The numberless improprieties forc'd upon the Grecian dramatic poets by the constitution of their drama, are, of themselves one should think, a sufficient reason for preferring that of the moderns, even abstracting from the improvement proposed. To prepare the reader for this article, it must be premised, that as in the ancient drama the place of action never varies, a place necessarily must be chosen to which every person may have access without any improbability. This confines the scene to some open place, generally the court or area before a palace; which excludes from the Grecian theatre transactions within doors, though these commonly are the most important. Such cruel restraint is of itself sufficient to cramp the most pregnant invention; and accordingly the Grecian writers, in order to preserve unity of place, are reduced to woful improprieties. In the *Hippolytus* of Euripides[7], Phedra, distressed in mind and body, is carried without any pretext from her palace to the place of action, is there laid upon a couch unable to support herself upon her limbs, and made to utter many things improper to be heard by a number of women who form the chorus. What is still worse, her female attendant uses the strongest intreaties to make her reveal the secret cause of her anguish; which at last Phedra, contrary to decency and probability, is prevailed upon to do in presence of this very chorus[8]. Alcestes, in *Euripides*, at the point of death, is brought from the palace to the place of action, groaning and lamenting her untimely fate[9]. In the *Trachiniens* of Sophocles[10], a secret is imparted to Dejanira, the wife of Hercules, in presence of the chorus. In the tragedy of *Iphigenia*, the messenger employ'd to carry Clitemnestra the news that Iphigenia was sacrificed, stops short at the place of action, and with a loud voice calls the Queen from her palace to hear the news. Again, in the *Iphigenia in Tauris*, the necessary presence of the chorus forces Euripides into a gross absurdity, which is to form a secret plot in their hearing[11]; and to disguise the absurdity, much courtship is bestowed on the chorus, not one woman but a number, to engage them to secrecy. In the *Medea* of Euripides, that princess makes no difficulty, in presence of the chorus, to plot the death of her husband, of his mistress, and of her father the King of Corinth, all by poison. It was necessary to bring Medea upon the stage, and there is but one place of action, which is always occupied by the chorus. This scene closes the second act; and in the end of the third, she frankly makes the chorus her confidents in ploting the murder of her own children. Terence, by identity of place, is often forc'd to make a conversation within doors be heard on the open street: the cries of a woman in labour are there heard distinctly.

The Grecian poets are not more happy with respect to time than with respect to place. In the *Hippolytus* of Euripides, that prince is banished at the end of the fourth act. In the first scene of the following act, a messenger relates to Theseus the whole particulars of the death of Hippolytus by the sea-monster. This remarkable event must have

---

7. Act 1. sc. 6.
8. Act 2. sc. 2.
9. Act 2. sc. 1.
10. Act 2.
11. Act 4. at the close.

employ'd many hours; and yet in the representation it is confined to the time employ'd by the chorus upon the song at the end of the 4th act. The inconsistency is still greater in the *Iphigenia in Tauris*[12]. The song could not exhaust half an hour; and yet the incidents supposed to have happened in that time, could not naturally be transacted in less than half a day.

The Grecian artists are not less frequently obliged to transgress another rule, derived also from a continued representation, which is, that the place of action must constantly be occupied; for the very least vacuity is an interruption of the representation. Sophocles, with regard to this rule as well as others, is generally correct. But Euripides cannot bear such restraint: he often evacuates the stage, and leaves it empty for others in succession. *Iphigenia in Tauris*, after pronouncing a soliloquy in the first scene, leaves the place of action, and is succeeded by Orestes and Pylades. They, after some conversation, walk off; and Iphigenia re-enters, accompanied with the chorus. In the *Alcestes*, which is of the same author, the place of action is void at the end of the third act. It is true, that to cover this irregularity, and to preserve the representation in motion, Euripides is extremely careful to fill the stage without loss of time. But this is still an interruption, and a link of the chain broken: for during the change of the actors, there must always be a space of time, when we cannot justly say, that the stage is occupied by either set. It makes indeed a more remarkable interruption, to change the place of action as well as the actors; but that was not practicable upon the Grecian stage.

It is hard to say upon what model Terence has formed his plays. Having no chorus, there is a cessation in the representation at the end of every act. But advantage is not taken of this cessation, even to vary the place of action. The street is always chosen, where everything passing may be seen by every person: and by this choice, the most sprightly and interesting parts of the action, which commonly pass within doors, are excluded; witness the last act of the *Eunuch*. He hath submitted to the same slavery with respect to time. In a word, a play with a regular chorus, is not more confined in place and time than his plays are. Thus a zealous sectary follows implicitly ancient forms and ceremonies, without once considering whether their introductive cause be still subsisting. Plautus, of a bolder genius than Terence, makes good use of the liberty afforded

---

12. Act 5. sc. 4.

by an interrupted representation: he varies the place of action upon all occasions, when the variation suits his purpose.

The intelligent reader will by this time understand, that I plead for no change of place in our plays but after an interval, nor for any latitude in point of time but what falls in with an interval. The unities of place and time ought to be strictly observed during each act; for during the representation, there is no opportunity for the smallest deviation from either. Hence it is an essential requisite, that during an act the stage be always occupied; for even a momentary vacuity makes an interval. Another rule is not less essential: it would be a gross breach of the unity of action, to exhibit upon the stage two separate actions at the same time; and therefore to preserve this unity, it is necessary that each personage introduced during an act, be linked to those in possession of the stage, so as to join all in one action. These things follow from the very conception of an act, which admits not the slightest interruption. The moment the representation is intermitted, there is an end of that act; and we have no other notion of a new act, but where after a pause or interval, the representation is again put in motion. French writers, generally speaking, are extremely correct in this particular: the English, on the contrary, are so irregular as scarce to deserve a criticism: actors not only succeed each other in the same place without connection; but, what is still worse, they frequently succeed each other in different places. This change of place in the same act, ought never to be indulged; for, beside breaking the unity of the act, it has a disagreeable effect. After an interval, the mind can readily accommodate itself to any place that is necessary, just as readily as at the commencement of the play; but during the representation, the mind rejects change of place. From the foregoing censure must be excepted the *Mourning Bride* of Congreve, where regularity concurs with the beauty of sentiment and of language, to make it one of the most complete pieces England has to boast of. I must acknowledge, however, that in point of regularity, this elegant performance is not altogether unexceptionable. In the four first acts, the unities of place and time are strictly observed; but in the last act, there is a capital error with respect to unity of place. In the three first scenes of that act, the place of action is a room of state, which is changed to a prison in the fourth scene: the chain of the actors withal is broken; for the persons introduced in the prison, are different from those who made their appearance in the room of state. This remarkable interruption of the representation, makes in effect two acts instead of one: and therefore, if it be a rule, that a play ought not to consist of more acts than five, this performance is so far defective in point of regularity. I may add, that even admitting six acts, the irregularity would not be altogether removed, without a longer pause in the representation than is allowed in the acting; for it requires more than a momentary interruption, to enable the imagination readily to accommodate itself to a new place, or to prorogation of time. In *The Way of the World*, of the same author, unity of place is preserved during every act, and a stricter unity of time during the whole play than is necessary.

XXIV

Gardening and Architecture

The books that have been composed upon architecture and upon embellishing ground, abound in practical instruction necessary for a mechanic: but in vain would we rummage them for rational principles to improve our taste. In a general system, it might be thought sufficient to have unfolded the principles that govern these and other fine arts, leaving the application to the reader: but as I would neglect no opportunity of illustrating these principles, I propose to give a specimen of their application to gardening and architecture, being favourite arts, though I profess no peculiar skill in either.

Gardening was at first an useful art: in the garden of Alcinoous, described by Homer, we find nothing done for pleasure merely. But gardening is now improved into a fine art; and when we talk of a garden without any epithet, a pleasure garden, by way of eminence, is understood. The garden of Alcinoous, in modern language, was but a kitchen-garden. Architecture has run the same course. It continued many ages an useful art merely, before it aspired to be classed with the fine arts. Architecture therefore and gardening must be handled in a twofold view, as being useful arts as well as fine arts. The reader however will not here expect rules for improving any work of art in point of utility. It is no part of my plan to treat of any useful art as such. But there is a beauty in utility; and in discoursing of beauty, that of utility ought not to be neglected. This leads us to consider gardens and buildings in different views: they may be destined for use solely, for beauty solely, or for both. Such variety in the destination, bestows upon gardening and architecture a great command of beauties complex not less than various, which makes it difficult to form an accurate taste in these arts. And hence that difference and wavering of taste which is more remarkable here than in any art that has but a single destination.

Architecture and gardening cannot otherwise entertain the mind, than by raising certain agreeable emotions or feelings; and before we descend to particulars, these arts shall be presented in a general view, by showing what are the emotions or feelings that can be raised by them. Poetry, as to its power of raising emotions, possesses justly the first place among the fine arts; for scarce one emotion of human nature is beyond its reach. Painting and sculpture are more circumscribed, having the command of no emotions but what are produced by sight. They are peculiarly successful in expressing painful passions, which are display'd by external signs extremely legible[1]. Gardening, beside the emotions of beauty by means of regularity, order, proportion, colour, and utility, can raise emotions of grandeur, of sweetness, of gaiety, melancholy, wildness, and even of surprise or wonder. In architecture, regularity, order, and proportion, and the beauties that result from them, are still more conspicuous than in gardening. But with respect to the beauty of colour, architecture is far inferior. Grandeur can be expressed in a building, perhaps more successfully than in a garden; but as to the other emotions above mentioned, architecture hitherto has not been brought to the perfection of expressing them distinctly. To balance this defect, architecture can display the beauty of utility in the highest perfection.

But gardening possesses one advantage, which never can be equalled in the other art. A garden may be so contrived, as in various scenes to raise successively all its different emotions. But to operate this delicious effect, the garden must be extensive, so as to admit a slow succession: for a small garden, comprehended at one view, ought to be confined to one expression[2]: it may be gay, it may be sweet, it may be gloomy; but an attempt to mix these, would create a jumble of emotions not a little unpleasant. For the same reason, a building, even the most magnificent, is necessarily confined to one expression.

Architecture, considered as a fine art, instead of rivaling gardening in its progress toward perfection, seems not far advanced beyond its infant-state. To bring it to maturity, two things mainly are wanted. First, A greater variety of parts and ornaments than it seems provided with. Gardening here has greatly the advantage: it is provided with such plenty and such variety of materials, that it must be the fault of the artists, if the spectator be not entertained with different scenes, and affected with various emotions. But materials in architecture are so scanty, that artists hitherto have not been successful in raising emotions, other than those of beauty and grandeur. With respect to the former, there are indeed plenty of means, regularity, order, symmetry, simplicity; and with respect to the latter, the addition of size is sufficient. But though

---

1. See chap. 15.
2. See chap. 8.

it be evident, that every building ought to have a certain character or expression suitable to its destination; yet this is a refinement which artists have scarce ventured upon. A death's head and bones employ'd in monumental buildings, will indeed produce an emotion of gloom and melancholy: but every ornament of this kind, if these can be termed so, ought to be rejected, because they are in themselves disagreeable. The other thing wanted to bring the art to perfection, is, to ascertain the precise impression made by every single part and ornament, cupolas, spires, columns, carvings, statues, vases, &c. For in vain will an artist attempt rules for employing these, either singly or in combination, until the different emotions or feelings they produce be distinctly explained. Gardening in this particular hath also the advantage. The several emotions raised by trees, rivers, cascades, plains, eminences, and other materials it employs, are understood; and the nature of each can be described with some degree of precision, which is done occasionally in the foregoing parts of this work.

In gardening as well as in architecture, simplicity ought to be the governing taste. Profuse ornament hath no better effect than to confound the eye, and to prevent the object from making an impression as one entire whole. An artist destitute of genius for capital beauties, is naturally prompted to supply the defect by crowding his plan with slight embellishments. Hence in gardens, triumphal arches, Chinese houses, temples, obelisks, cascades, fountains, without end; and hence in buildings, pillars, vases, statues, and a profusion of carved work. Thus a woman who has no just taste, is apt to overcharge every part of her dress with ornament. Superfluity of decoration hath another bad effect: it gives the object a diminutive look. An island in a wide extended lake, makes it appear larger; but an artificial lake, which must always be little, appears still less by making an island in it[3].

In forming plans for embellishing a field, an artist void of taste deals in straight lines, circles, squares; because these show best upon paper. He perceives not, that to humour and adorn nature is the perfection of his art; and that nature, neglecting regularity, reacheth superior beauties by distributing her objects in great variety with a bold hand. A large field laid out with strict regularity, is stiff and artificial. Nature indeed, in organized bodies comprehended under one view, studies regularity; which, for the same reason, ought to be studied in architecture: but in

---

3. See appendix to part 5. chap. 2.

large objects, which cannot otherwise be surveyed than in parts and by succession, regularity and uniformity would be useless properties, because they cannot be discovered by the eye[4]. Nature therefore, in her large works, neglects these properties; and in copying nature the artist ought to neglect them.

HAVING THUS FAR CARRIED ON a comparison betwixt gardening and architecture, I proceed to rules peculiar to each; and I begin with gardening. The simplest idea of a garden, is that of a spot embellished with a number of natural objects, trees, walks, polish'd parterres, flowers, streams, &c. One more complex comprehends statues and buildings, that nature and art may be mutually ornamental. A third approaching nearer perfection, is of objects assembled together, in order to produce, not only an emotion of beauty, essential to gardens of every kind, but also someother particular emotion, grandeur, for example, gaiety, or any other of those above mentioned. The most perfect idea of a garden is an improvement upon the third, requiring the adjustment of the several parts, in such a manner as to inspire all the different emotions that can be raised by gardening. In this idea of a garden, the arrangement is an important circumstance; for it has been shown, that some emotions figure best in conjunction, and that others ought always to appear in succession and never in conjunction. I have had occasion to observe above[5], that when the most opposite emotions, such as gloominess and gaiety, stillness and activity, follow each other in succession, the pleasure on the whole will be the greatest; but that opposite or dissimilar emotions ought not to be united, because they produce an unpleasant mixture[6]. For that reason, a ruin, affording a sort of melancholy pleasure, ought not to be seen from a flower-parterre, which is gay and chearful. But to pass immediately from an exhilerating object to a ruin, has a glorious effect; for each of the emotions is the more sensibly felt by being contrasted with the other. Similar emotions, on the other hand, such as gaiety and sweetness, stillness and gloominess, motion and grandeur, ought to be raised together; for their effects upon the mind are greatly heightened by their conjunction.

---

[4]. A square field appears not such to the eye when viewed from any part of it: and the centre is the only place where a circular field preserves in appearance its regular figure.
[5]. Chap. 8.
[6]. Chap. 2. part 4.

Kent's method of embellishing a field, is admirable. It is painting a field with beautiful objects, natural and artificial, disposed like colours upon a canvas. It requires indeed more genius to paint in the gardening way. In forming a landscape upon a canvas, no more is required but to adjust the figures to each other: an artist who lays out ground in Kent's manner, has an additional task, which is to adjust his figures to the several varieties of the field.

One garden must be distinguished from a plurality; and yet it is not obvious wherein the unity of a garden consists. A notion of unity is indeed suggested from viewing a garden surrounding a palace, with views from each window, and walks leading to every corner. But there may be a garden without a house. In this case, I must pronounce, that what makes it one garden, is the unity of design, every single spot appearing part of a whole. The gardens of Versailles, properly expressed in the plural number, being no fewer than sixteen, are indeed all of them connected with the palace, but have scarce any mutual connection: they appear not like parts of one whole, but rather like small gardens in contiguity. Were these gardens at some distance from each other, they would have a better effect. Their junction breeds confusion of ideas, and upon the whole gives less pleasure than would be felt in a slower succession.

Regularity is required in that part of a garden which joins the dwelling-house; for being considered as a more immediate accessory, it ought to partake the regularity of the principal object[7]. But in proportion to the distance from the house considered as the centre, regularity ought less and less to be studied. In an extensive plan, it hath a fine effect to lead the mind insensibly from regularity to a bold

---

7. The influence of this connexion, surpassing all bounds, is still visible in many gardens formed of horizontal plains forced with great labour and expense, perpendicular faces of earth, supported by massy stone-walls, terrace walks in stages one above another, regular ponds and canals without the least motion, and the whole surrounded, like a prison, with high walls excluding every external object. At first view it may puzzle one to account for a taste so opposite to nature in every particular. But nothing happens without a cause. Perfect regularity and uniformity are required in a house; and this idea is extended to its accessory the garden, especially if it be a small spot incapable of grandeur or of much variety: the house is regular, so must the garden be; the floors of the house are horizontal, and the garden must have the same position; in the house we are protected from every intruding eye, so must we be in the garden. This, it must be confessed, is carrying the notion of resemblance very far: but where reason and taste are laid asleep, nothing is more common than to carry resemblance beyond proper bounds.

variety giving an impression of grandeur. And grandeur ought to be studied as much as possible, even in a more confined plan, by avoiding a multiplicity of small parts[8]. Nothing contributes more to grandeur, than a right disposition of trees. Let them be scattered extremely thin near the dwelling-house, and thickened in proportion to their distance: distant eminences to be filled with trees, and laid open to view. A small garden, on the other hand, which admits not grandeur, ought to be strictly regular.

Milton, describing the garden of Eden, prefers justly the grand taste to that of regularity.

> *Flowers worthy of paradise, which not nice art*
> *In beds and curious knots; but Nature boon*
> *Pour'd forth profuse on hill, and dale, and plain;*
> *Both where the morning sun first warmly smote*
> *The open field, and where the unpierc'd shade*
> *Imbrown'd the noontide-bow'rs.*
>
> —*Paradise Lost, b. 4*

In the manner of planting a wood or thicket, much art may be display'd. A common centre of walks, termed *a star*, from whence are seen a number of remarkable objects, appears too artificial to be agreeable. The crowding withal so many objects together, lessens the pleasure that would be felt in a slower succession. Abandoning therefore the star, being stiff and formal, let us try to substitute some form more natural, that will lay open all the remarkable objects in the neighbourhood. This may be done by openings in the wood at various distances, which, in walking, bring successively under the eye every object as by accident. Some openings display single objects, some a plurality in a line, and some a rapid succession of them. In this plan, the mind at intervals is roused and cheared by agreeable objects; and the scene is greatly heightened by the surprise it occasions when we stumble, as it were, upon objects of which we had no expectation.

As gardening is not an inventive art, but an imitation of nature, or rather nature itself ornamented; it follows necessarily, that everything unnatural ought to be rejected with disdain. Statues of wild beasts

---

8. See chap. 4.

vomiting water, a common ornament in gardens, prevails in those of Versailles. Is this ornament in a good taste? A *jet d'eau*, being purely artificial, may, without disgust, be tortured into a thousand shapes: but a representation of what really exists in nature, admits not any unnatural circumstance. These statues therefore in the gardens of Versailles must be condemned: and yet so insensible has the artist been to just imitation, as to have display'd his vicious taste without the least colour or disguise. A lifeless statue of an animal pouring out water, may be endured without much disgust. But here the lions and wolves are put in violent action: each has seized its prey, a deer or a lamb, in act to devour. And yet, instead of extended claws and open mouth, the whole, as by a hocus-pocus trick, is converted into a different scene: the lion, forgetting his prey, pours out water plentifully; and the deer, forgetting its danger, performs the same operation; a representation not less absurd than that in the opera, where Alexander the Great, after mounting the wall of a town besieged, turns about and entertains his army with a song.

In gardening, every lively exhibition of what is beautiful in nature has a fine effect: on the other hand, distant and faint imitations are displeasing to everyone of taste. The cutting evergreens in the shape of animals, is a very ancient practice; as appears from the epistles of Pliny, who seems to be a great admirer of this puerile conceit. The propensity to imitation gave birth to this practice; and has supported it wonderfully long, considering how faint and insipid the imitation is. But the vulgar, great and small, devoid of taste, are entertained with the oddness and singularity of a resemblance, however distant, betwixt a tree and an animal. An attempt, in the gardens of Versailles, to imitate a grove of trees by a group of *jets d'eau*, appears, for the same reason, not less ridiculous.

In laying out a garden, everything trivial or whimsical ought to be avoided. Is a labyrinth then to be justified? It is a mere conceit, like that of composing verses in the shape of an axe or an egg. The walks and hedges may be agreeable; but in the form of a labyrinth, they serve to no end but to puzzle. A riddle is a conceit not so mean; because the solution is a proof of sagacity, which affords no aid in tracing a labyrinth.

The gardens of Versailles, executed with infinite expence by men at that time in high repute, are a lasting monument of a taste the most vicious and depraved. The faults above mentioned, instead of being avoided, are chosen as beauties, and multiplied without end. Nature, it would seem, was deemed too vulgar to be imitated in the works of a magnificent monarch; and for that reason preference was given to things unnatural, which probably were mistaken for supernatural. I have often amused myself with a fanciful resemblance betwixt these gardens and the Arabian tales. Each of them is a performance intended for the amusement of a great king: in the sixteen gardens of Versailles there is no unity of design, more than in the thousand and one Arabian tales: and, lastly, they are equally unnatural; groves of *jets d'eau*, statues of animals conversing in the manner of Æsop, water issuing out of the mouths of wild beasts, give an impression of fairy-land and witchcraft, not less than diamond-palaces, invisible rings, spells and incantations.

A straight road is the most agreeable, because it shortens the journey. But in an embellished field, a straight walk has an air of stiffness and confinement: and at any rate is less agreeable than a winding or waving walk; for in surveying the beauties of a fine field, we love to roam from place to place at freedom. Winding walks have another advantage: at every step they open new views. In short, the walks in a field intended for entertainment, ought not to have any appearance of a road. My intention is not to make a journey, but to feast my eye with the beauties of art and nature. This rule excludes not long straight openings terminating upon distant objects. These, beside variety, never fail to raise an emotion of grandeur, by extending in appearance the size of the field. An opening without a terminating object, soon closes upon the eye: but an object, at whatever distance, continues the opening; and deludes the spectator into a conviction, that the trees which confine the view are continued till they join the object. Straight walks also in recesses do extremely well: they vary the scenery, and are favourable to meditation.

An avenue ought not to be directed in a straight line upon a dwelling-house: better far an oblique approach in a waving line, with single trees and other scattered objects interposed. In a direct approach, the first appearance continues the same to the end: we see a house at a distance, and we see it all along in the same spot without any variety. In an oblique approach, the intervening objects put the house seemingly in motion: it moves with the passenger, and appears to direct its course so as hospitably to intercept him. An oblique approach contributes also to variety: the house being seen successively in different directions, takes on at every step a new figure.

A garden on a flat ought to be highly and variously ornamented, in order to occupy the mind and prevent its regretting the insipidity of an uniform plain. Artificial mounts in this view are common: but no person has thought of an artificial walk elevated high above the plain. Such a walk is airy, and tends to elevate the mind: it extends and varies the prospect: and it makes the plain, seen from a height, appear more agreeable.

Whether should a ruin be in the Gothic or Grecian form? In the former, I say; because it exhibits the triumph of time over strength, a melancholy but not unpleasant thought. A Grecian ruin suggests rather the triumph of barbarity over taste, a gloomy and discouraging thought.

Fountains are seldom in a good taste. Statues of animals vomiting water, which prevail everywhere, stand condemned. A statue of a whale spouting water upward from its head, would in one sense be natural, as whales of a certain species have that power. The design however would scarce be relished, because its singularity would give it the appearance of being unnatural. There is another reason against it, that the figure of a whale is in itself not agreeable. In the many fountains in and about Rome, statues of fishes are frequently employ'd to support a large basin of water. This unnatural conceit cannot be otherwise explained, than by the connection betwixt water and the fish that swim in it; which by the way is a proof of the influence that even the slighter connections have on the mind. The only good design for a fountain I have met with, is what follows. In an artificial rock, rugged and abrupt, there is a cavity out of sight at the top: the water, convey'd to it by a pipe, pours or trickles down the broken parts of the rock, and is collected into a basin at the foot: it is so contrived, as to make the water fall in sheets or in rills at pleasure.

Hitherto a garden has been treated as a work intended solely for pleasure, or, in other words, for giving impressions of intrinsic beauty. What comes next in order is the beauty of a garden destined for use, termed *relative beauty*[9]; and this branch shall be dispatched in a few words. In gardening, luckily, relative beauty need never stand in opposition to intrinsic beauty. All the ground that can be requisite for use, makes but a small proportion of an ornamented field; and may be put in any corner without obstructing the disposition of the capital parts. At the same time, a kitchen-garden or an orchard is susceptible of intrinsic beauty; and may be so artfully disposed among the other parts, as by variety and contrast to contribute to the beauty of the

---

9. See these terms defined, chap. 3.

whole. In this respect, architecture is far more intricate, as will be seen immediately: for there, it being often requisite to blend intrinsic and relative beauty in the same building, it becomes a difficult task to attain both in any perfection.

As gardening is brought to greater perfection in China than in any other known country, an account of the means practised by Chinese artists to inspire all the various emotions of gardening, will be a fine illustration of the foregoing doctrine. In general, it is an indispensable law with them, never to deviate from nature: but in order to produce that degree of variety which is pleasing, every method is used that is consistent with nature. Nature is strictly imitated in the banks of their artificial lakes and rivers; which sometimes are bare and gravelly, sometimes covered with wood quite to the brink of the water. To flat spots adorned with flowers and shrubs, are opposed others steep and rocky. We see meadows covered with cattle; rice-grounds that run into the lakes; groves into which enter navigable creeks and rivulets. These generally conduct to some interesting object, a magnificent building, terraces cut in a mountain, a cascade, a grotto, an artificial rock, and other such inventions. Their artificial rivers are generally serpentine; sometimes narrow, noisy, and rapid; sometimes deep, broad, and slow: and to make the scene still more active, mills and other moving machines are often erected. In the lakes are interspersed islands; some barren, surrounded with rocks and shoals; others inriched with everything that art and nature can furnish. Even in their cascades they avoid regularity, as forcing nature out of its course: the waters are seen bursting out from among the caverns and windings of the artificial rocks; here an impetuous cataract, there many lesser falls: and in its passage, the water is often impeded by trees and heaps of stones, that seem brought down by the violence of the current. Straight lines, generally avoided, are sometimes indulged, in order to take the advantage of any interesting object at a distance, by directing openings upon it.

Sensible of the influence of contrast, the Chinese artists deal in sudden transitions, and in opposing to each other, forms, colours, and shades. The eye is conducted, from limited to extensive views, and from lakes and rivers to plains, hills, and woods: to dark and gloomy colours, are opposed the more brilliant: the different masses of light and shade are disposed in such a manner, as to render the composition distinct in its parts, and striking on the whole. In plantations, the trees are artfully mixed according to their shape and colour; those of spreading branches with the pyramidal, and the light with the deep green. They even introduce decay'd trees, some erect, and some half out of the ground[10]. In order to heighten contrast, much bolder strokes are risked. They sometimes introduce rough rocks, dark caverns, trees ill formed and seemingly rent by tempests, or blasted by lightning, a building in ruins or half consumed by fire. But to relieve the mind from the harshness of such objects, they are always succeeded by the sweetest and most beautiful scenes.

The Chinese study to give play to the imagination. They hide the termination of their lakes: the view of a cascade is frequently interrupted by trees, through which are seen obscurely the waters as they fall. The imagination once roused, is disposed to magnify every object.

Nothing is more studied in Chinese gardens than to raise wonder or surprise. In scenes calculated for that end, everything appears like fairy-land; a torrent, for example, convey'd under ground, producing an uncommon sound that puzzles a stranger to guess what it may be; and, to increase our wonder by multiplying such uncommon sounds, the rocks and buildings are contrived with cavities and interstices. Sometimes one is led insensibly into dark caverns, terminating unexpectedly in a landscape inriched with all that nature affords the most delicious. At other times, beautiful walks insensibly conduct us to a rough uncultivated field, where bushes briers and stones interrupt the passage: when we look about for an outlet, some rich prospect unexpectedly opens to view. Another artifice is, to obscure some capital part by trees or other interposed objects: our curiosity is raised to know what lies beyond; and after a few steps, we are greatly surprised with some scene totally different from what was expected.

I close these cursory observations upon gardening, with a remark that must touch every reader. Rough uncultivated ground, dismal to the eye, inspires peevishness and discontent. May not this be one cause of the harsh manners of savages? In a field richly ornamented, are collected beautiful objects of various kinds. Such a field displays in full lustre, the goodness of the Deity and the ample provision he has made for our happiness; which must fill every spectator, with gratitude to his Maker and with benevolence to his fellow-creatures. Other fine arts

---

10. Taste has suggested to Kent the same artifice. A decayed tree, placed properly, contributes to contrast; and also in a pensive or sedate state of mind, produces a sort of pity grounded on an imaginary personification.

may be perverted to excite irregular, and even vicious, emotions: but gardening, which inspires the purest and most refined pleasures, cannot but promote every good affection. The gaiety and harmony of mind it produceth, must naturally incline the spectator to communicate his satisfaction to others by acts of humanity and kindness.

Having finished what occurred on gardening, I proceed to rules and observations that more peculiarly concern architecture. Architecture being an useful as well as a fine art, buildings and parts of buildings must be distinguished into three kinds, *viz.* what are intended for utility solely, what for ornament solely, and what for both. A building intended for utility solely, such as detached offices, ought in every part to correspond precisely to that intention. The least deviation from use, though contributing to ornament, will be disagreeable. For every work of use being considered as a means to an end, its perfection as a means is the capital circumstance; and every other beauty, in opposition, is neglected as improper and impertinent. In things again intended for ornament, such as pillars, obelisks, triumphal arches, beauty solely ought to be regarded. A Heathen temple must be considered as merely ornamental; for being dedicated to some deity, and not intended for habitation, it is susceptible of any figure and any embellishment that fancy can suggest and beauty require. The great difficulty of contrivance, respects buildings that are intended for pleasure as well as for use. These ends, employing different and often opposite means, are with difficulty reconciled. In palaces, and other buildings sufficiently extensive to admit a variety of useful contrivance, regularity justly takes the lead. But in dwelling-houses that are too small for variety of contrivance, utility ought to prevail; neglecting regularity so far as it stands in opposition to convenience.

Intrinsic and relative beauty being founded on different principles, must be handled separately; and I begin with relative beauty, as of the greater importance.

The proportions of a door, are determined by the use to which it is destined. The door of a dwelling-house, which ought to correspond to the human size, is confined to seven or eight feet in height, and three or four in breadth. The proportions proper for the door of a barn or coach-house, are widely different. Another consideration enters. To study intrinsic beauty in a coach-house or barn, intended merely for use, is obviously improper. But a dwelling-house may admit ornaments; and the principal door of a palace demands all the grandeur that is consistent with the foregoing proportions dictated by utility. It ought to be elevated and approached by steps; and it may be adorned with pillars supporting an architrave, or in any other beautiful manner. The door of a church ought to be wide, in order to afford an easy passage for a multitude. The wideness, at the same time, regulates the height, as will appear by and by. The size of windows ought to be proportioned to that of the room they serve with light; for if the apperture be not sufficiently large to convey light to every corner, the room is dark and gloomy. Steps of stairs ought to be accommodated to the human figure, without regarding any other proportion: these steps accordingly are the same in large and in small buildings, because both are inhabited by men of the same size.

I proceed to consider intrinsic beauty blended with that which is relative. A cube in itself is more agreeable than a parallelopipedon, which will constantly hold in small figures. But a large building in the form a cube, appears lumpish and heavy; while the other figure, set on its smaller base, is by its elevation more agreeable: and hence the beauty of a Gothic tower. But let us suppose this parallelopipedon destin'd for a dwelling house, to make way for relative beauty. Here utility prevails over elevation and a parallelopipedon, inconvenient by its height, is set upon its larger base. The loftiness is gone; but that loss is more than compensated by additional convenience; and for that reason the form of a building spread more upon the ground than raised in height, is always preferred for a dwelling-house, without excepting even the most sumptuous palace.

With respect to the divisions within, utility requires that the rooms be rectangular; for otherwise void spaces will be left of no use. A hexagonal figure leaves no void spaces; but then it determines the rooms to be all of one size, which is extremely inconvenient. A cube will at first be pronounced the most agreeable figure; and this may hold in a room of a moderate size. But in a very large room, utility requires a different figure. The chief convenience of a great room, is unconfined motion. This directs us to the greatest length that can be obtained. But a square room of a great size is inconvenient, by removing far from the hand, chairs and tables, which, when unemploy'd, must be ranged along the sides of the room. Utility therefore requires a large room to be a parallelogram. This figure, at the same time, is the best calculated for receiving light; because, to avoid cross-light, all the windows ought to be in one wall; and if the opposite wall be at such distance as not to be fully lighted, the room must be obscure. The height of a room exceeding nine or ten feet, has little or no relation to utility; and therefore proportion is the only rule for determining the height when above that number of feet.

As all artists who deal in the beautiful are naturally prone to entertain the eye, they have great opportunity to exert their taste upon palaces and sumptuous buildings, where, as above observed, intrinsic beauty ought to have the ascendant over that which is relative. But such propensity is unhappy with respect to private dwelling-houses; because in these, relative beauty cannot be display'd in any perfection, without abandoning intrinsic beauty. There is no opportunity for great variety of form in a small house; and in an edifice of this kind, internal convenience has not hitherto been happily adjusted to external regularity. I am apt to believe, that an accurate coincidence here, is beyond the reach of art. And yet architects always split upon this rock; for they never will give over attempting to reconcile these two incompatibles. How else should it be accounted for, that of the endless variety of private dwelling-houses, there is not one to be found, that is generally agreed upon as a good pattern? The unwearied propensity to make a house regular as well as convenient, forces the architect, in some articles, to sacrifice convenience to regularity, and in others, regularity to convenience. By this means, the house, which turns out neither regular nor convenient, never fails to displease. The faults are obvious, and the difficulty of doing better is known to the artist only[11].

Nothing can be more evident, than that the form of a dwelling-house ought to be suited to the climate; and yet no error is more common, than to copy in Britain the form of Italian houses; not forgetting even those parts that are purposely contrived for air, and for excluding the sun. I shall give one or two instances. A colonnade along the front of a building, hath a fine effect in Greece and Italy, by producing coolness and obscurity, agreeable properties in warm and luminous climates. The cold climate of Britain is altogether averse to this ornament. A colonnade therefore, can never be proper in this country, unless when employ'd to communicate with a detached building. Again, a logio opening the house to the north, contrived in Italy for gathering cool air, is, if possible, still more improper for this climate. Scarce endurable in

---

11. "Houses are built to live in, and not to look on; therefore let use be preferred before uniformity, except where both may be had.'—*Lord Verulam, Essay* 45.

summer, it, in winter, exposes the house to the bitter blasts of the north, and to every shower of snow and rain.

Having discussed what appeared necessary to be said upon relative beauty, singly considered, or in combination with intrinsic beauty, the next step is, to view architecture as one of the fine arts, and to examine those buildings and parts of buildings that are solely calculated to please the eye. In the works of nature, grand and magnificent, variety prevails. The timid hand of art, is guided by rule and compass. Hence it is, that in works which imitate nature, the great art is to hide every appearance of art; which is done by avoiding regularity and indulging variety. But in works of art that are original and not imitative, such as architecture, strict regularity and uniformity ought to be studied so far as consistent with utility.

In buildings intended to please the eye, proportion is not less essential than regularity and uniformity; for we are so framed by nature, as to be pleased equally with each of these. By many writers it is taken for granted, that in all the parts of a building there are certain strict proportions which please the eye; precisely as there are certain strict proportions of sound which please the ear; and that in both the slightest deviation is equally disagreeable. Others again seem to relish more a comparison betwixt proportion in numbers and proportion in quantity; and hold that the same proportions are agreeable in both. The proportions, for example, of the numbers 16, 24, and 36 are agreeable; and so, say they, are the proportions of a room, the height of which is 16 feet, the breadth 24, and the length 36. This point, with relation to the present subject, being of importance, the reader will examine it with attention and impartiality. To refute the notion of a resemblance betwixt musical proportions and those of architecture, it might be sufficient to observe in general, that the one is addressed to the ear, the other to the eye; and that objects of different senses have no resemblance, nor indeed any relation to each other. But more particularly, what pleases the ear in harmony, is not the proportion of the strings of the instrument, but of the sounds that these strings produce. In architecture, on the contrary, it is the proportion of different quantities that pleases the eye, without the least relation to sound. Beside, were quantity here to be the sole ground of comparison, we have no reason to presume, that there is any natural analogy betwixt the proportions that please in a building and the proportions of strings that produce concordant sounds. I instance in particular an octave, the most complete of all concords. An octave is produced by two strings of the same tension and diameter, and as to length in the proportion of one to two. I do not know, that this proportion will be agreeable in any two parts of a building. I add, that concordant notes are produced by wind instruments, which, as to proportion, appear not to have even the slightest resemblance to a building.

With respect to the other notion instituting a comparison betwixt proportion in numbers and proportion in quantity, I urge, that number and quantity are so distinct from each other, as to afford no probability of any natural relation betwixt them. Quantity is a real quality of every substance or body: number is not a real quality, but merely a conception that arises upon viewing a plurality of things in succession. Because an arithmetical proportion is agreeable in numbers, have we any reason to conclude that it must also be agreeable in quantity? At this rate, a geometrical proportion and many others, ought also to be agreeable in both. A certain proportion may coincide in both; and among an endless variety of proportions, it would be wonderful, if there never should be a coincidence. One example is given of this coincidence, in the numbers 16, 24, and 36; but to be convinced that it is merely accidental, we need but reflect, that the same proportions are not applicable to the external figure of a house, and far less to a column.

That we are framed by nature to relish proportion as well as regularity, is indisputable: but that agreeable proportion, like concord in sounds, is confined to certain precise measures, is not warranted by experience: on the contrary, we learn from experience, that various proportions are equally agreeable, that proportion is never tied down to precise measures but admits more and less, and that we are not sensible of disproportion till the difference betwixt the quantities compared become the most striking circumstance. Columns evidently admit different proportions, equally agreeable. The case is the same in houses, rooms, and other parts of a building. And this opens an interesting reflection. The foregoing difference betwixt concord and proportion, is an additional instance of that admirable harmony which subsists among the several branches of the human frame. The ear is an accurate judge of sounds and of their smallest differences; and that concord in sounds should be regulated by accurate measures, is perfectly well suited to this accuracy of perception. The eye is more uncertain about the size of a large object, than of one that is small; and in different situations the same object appears of different sizes. Delicacy of feeling therefore with respect to proportion in quantities, would be an useless quality. It is much better ordered, that there should be such a latitude with respect to agreeable proportions, as to correspond to the uncertainty of the eye with respect to quantity.

But this scene is too interesting to be passed over in a cursory view: all its beauties are not yet display'd. I proceed to observe, that to make the eye as delicate with respect to proportion as the ear is with respect to concord, would not only be an useless quality, but be the source of continual pain and uneasiness. I need go no farther for a proof than the very room I possess at present: every step I take, varies to me, in appearance, the proportion of the length and breadth. At that rate, I should not be happy but in one precise spot, where the proportion appears agreeable. Let me further observe, that it would be singular indeed, to find in the nature of man, any two principles in perpetual opposition to each other. This would precisely be the case, if proportion were circumscribed like concord; for it would exclude all but one of those proportions that utility requires in different buildings, and in different parts of the same building.

It is ludicrous to observe all writers acknowledging the necessity of accurate proportions, and yet differing widely about them. Laying aside reasoning and philosophy, one fact universally agreed on ought to have undeceived them, that the same proportions which please in a model are not agreeable in a large building. A room 48 feet in length and 24 in breadth and height, is well proportioned; but a room 12 feet wide and high and 24 long, looks like a gallery.

Perrault, in his comparison of the ancients and moderns[12], is the only author who runs to the opposite extreme; maintaining, that the different proportions assigned to each order of columns are arbitrary, and that the beauty of these proportions is entirely the effect of custom. This bewrays ignorance of human nature, which evidently delights in proportion, as well as in regularity, order, and propriety. But without any acquaintance with human nature, a single reflection might have convinced him of his error; that if these proportions had not originally been agreeable, they could not have been established by custom. If a thing be universal, it must be natural.

To illustrate the present point, I shall add a few examples of the agreeableness of different proportions. In a sumptuous edifice, the capital rooms ought to be large, for otherwise they will not be proportioned to

---

12. Page 94.

the size of the building. On the other hand, a very large room in a small house, is disproportioned. But in things thus related, the mind requires not a precise or single proportion, rejecting all others; on the contrary, many different proportions are made equally welcome. It is only when a proportion becomes loose and distant, that the agreeableness abates, and at last vanisheth. In all buildings accordingly, we find rooms of different proportions equally agreeable, even where the proportion is not influenced by utility. With respect to the height of a room, the proportion it ought to bear to the length and breadth, is extremely arbitrary; and it cannot be otherwise, considering the uncertainty of the eye as to the height of a room, when it exceeds 17 or 18 feet. In columns again, even architects must confess, that the proportion of height and thickness varies betwixt 8 diameters and 10, and that every proportion betwixt these two extremes is agreeable. But this is not all. There must certainly be a further variation of proportion, depending on the size of the column. A row of columns 10 feet high, and a row twice that height, require different proportions. The intercolumniations must also differ in proportion according to the height of the row.

Proportion of parts is not only itself a beauty, but is inseparably connected with a beauty of the first magnitude. Parts that in conjunction appear proportional, never fail separately to produce similar emotions; which existing together, are extremely pleasant, as I have had occasion to show. Thus a room of which the parts are all finely adjusted to each other, strikes us with the beauty of proportion. It produceth at the same time a pleasure far superior. The length, the breadth, the height, the windows, raise each of them separately an emotion. These emotions are similar; and though faint when felt separately, they produce in conjunction the emotion of concord or harmony, which is extremely pleasant. On the other hand, where the length of a room far exceeds the breadth, the mind comparing together parts so intimately connected, immediately perceives a disagreement or disproportion which disgusts. But this is not all. Viewing them separately, different emotions are produced, that of grandeur from the great length, and that of meanness or littleness from the small breadth, which in union are disagreeable by their discordance. Hence it is, that a long gallery, however convenient for exercise, is not an agreeable figure of a room. We consider it, like a stable, as destined for use, and expect not that in any other respect it should be agreeable.

Regularity and proportion are essential in buildings destined chiefly or solely to please the eye, because they are the means to produce intrinsic beauty. But a skilful artist will not confine his view to regularity and proportion. He will also study propriety, which is perceived when the form and ornaments of a structure are suited to the purpose for which it is appointed. The sense of propriety dictates the following rule, That every building ought to have an expression corresponding to its destination. A palace ought to be sumptuous and grand; a private dwelling, neat and modest; a playhouse, gay and splendid; and a monument, gloomy and melancholy. A Heathen temple has a double destination: it is considered chiefly as a house dedicated to some divinity; and in that respect it ought to be grand, elevated, and magnificent: it is considered also as a place of worship; and in that respect it ought to be somewhat dark or gloomy; because dimness produces that tone of mind which is suited to humility and devotion. A Christian church is not considered as a house for the Deity, but merely a place of worship: it ought therefore to be decent and plain, without much ornament: a situation ought to be chosen, humble and retired; because the congregation, during worship, ought to be humble and disengaged from the world. Columns, beside their chief destination of being supports, contribute to that peculiar expression which the destination of a building requires: columns of different proportions, serve to express loftiness, lightness, &c. as well as strength. Situation also may contribute to expression: conveniency regulates the situation of a private dwelling-house; but, as I have had occasion to observe[13], the situation of a palace ought to be lofty.

And this leads me to examine, whether the situation of a great house, where the artist is limited in his choice, ought in any measure to regulate its form. The connection betwixt a great house and the neighbouring grounds, though not extremely intimate, demands however some congruity. It would, for instance, displease us to find an elegant building thrown away upon a wild uncultivated country: congruity requires a polished field for such a building; and beside the pleasure of congruity, the spectator is sensible of the pleasure of concordance from the similarity of the emotions produced by the two objects. The old Gothic form of building seems well suited to the rough uncultivated regions where it was invented. The only mistake was, the transferring this form to the fine plains of France and Italy, better fitted for buildings in the Grecian taste. But by refining upon the Gothic form, everything in the power of invention has been done, to reconcile it to its new situation.

---

13. Chap. 10.

The profuse variety of wild and grand objects about Inverary, demanded a house in the Gothic form; and everyone must approve the taste of the proprietor, in adjusting so finely, as he has done, the appearance of his house to that of the country where it is placed.

The external structure of a great house, leads naturally to its internal structure. A large and spacious room, receives us commonly upon our entrance. This seems to me a bad contrivance in several respects. In the first place, when immediately from the open air we step into such a room, its size in appearance is diminished by contrast: it looks little compared with the great canopy the sky. In the next place, when it recovers its grandeur, as it soon doth, it gives a diminutive appearance to the rest of the house: passing from it, every apartment looks little. This room therefore may be aptly compared to the swoln commencement of an epic poem.

Bella per Emathios plusquam civilia campos.

In the third place, by its situation it serves only for a waiting-room, and a passage to the principal apartments. And yet undoubtedly, the room of the greatest size ought to be reserved for company. A great room, which enlarges the mind and gives a certain elevation to the spirits, is destined by nature for conversation. Rejecting therefore this form, I take a hint from the climax in writing for another form that appears more suitable. My plan is, first a handsome portico, proportioned to the size and fashion of the front: this portico leads into a waiting-room of a larger size; and this again to the great room, all by a progression from small to great. If the house be very large, there may be space for the following suit of rooms; first, a portico; second, a passage within the house bounded by rows of columns on each side connected by arcades; third, an octagon room, or of any other figure, about the centre of the building; and, lastly, the great room.

Of all the emotions that can be raised by architecture, grandeur is that which has the greatest influence on the mind. It ought therefore to be the chief study of the artist, to raise this emotion in great buildings. But it seems unhappy for architecture, that it is necessarily governed by certain principles opposite to grandeur: the direct effect of regularity and proportion, is to make a building appear less than it is in reality. Any invention to reconcile these with grandeur, would be a capital improvement in architecture.

Next of ornaments, which contribute greatly to give buildings a peculiar expression. It has been a doubt with me, whether a building can regularly admit any ornament but what is useful, or at least appears to be useful. But considering the double aim of architecture, a fine as well as an useful art, there is no good reason why ornaments may not be added to please the eye without any relation to use. This liberty is allowed in poetry, painting, and gardening, and why not in architecture considered as a fine art? A private dwelling-house, it is true, and other edifices where use is the chief aim, admit not regularly any ornament but what has the appearance, at least, of use: but temples, triumphal arches, and other buildings intended chiefly or solely for show, may be highly ornamented.

This suggests a division of ornaments into three kinds, *viz.* ornaments that are beautiful without relation to use, such as statues in niches, vases, basso or alto relievo: next, things in themselves not beautiful, but possessing the beauty of utility by imposing on the spectator, and appearing to be of use, blind windows for example: the third kind is, where the thing is in itself beautiful, and also takes on the appearance of use; the case of a pilaster. With respect to the second, it is an egregious blunder, to contrive the ornament so as to make it appear useless. If a blind window therefore be necessary for regularity, it ought to be so disguised, as not to be distinguished from the real windows. If it appear to be a blind window, it is disgustful, as a vain attempt to supply the want of invention. It shows the irregularity in a stronger light; by signifying that a window ought to be there in point of regularity, but that the architect had not skill sufficient to connect external regularity with internal convenience.

From ornaments in general, we descend to a pillar, the chief ornament in great buildings. The destination of a pillar is to support, really or in appearance, another part termed *the architrave*. With respect to the form of this ornament, I observe, that a circle is a more agreeable figure than a square, a globe than a cube, and a cylinder than a parallelopipedon. This last, in the language of architecture, is saying, that a column is a more agreeable figure than a pilaster. For that reason, it ought to be preferred, all other circumstances being equal. Another reason concurs, that a column annexed to a wall, which is a plain surface, makes a greater variety than a pilaster. There is an additional reason for rejecting pilasters in the external front of a building, arising from a principle unfolded above[14], *viz.* a remarkable tendency in the mind of man, to advance

---

14. Chap. 4.

everything to its perfection as well as to its final issue. If I see a thing obscurely in a dim light, and by disjointed parts, my curiosity is roused, and prompts me, out of the disjointed parts to compose an entire whole. I suppose it to be, for example, a horse. My eye-sight being obedient to this conjecture, I immediately perceive a horse, almost as distinctly as in day-light. This principle is applicable to the case in hand. The most superb front, at a great distance, appears a plain surface: approaching gradually, we begin to perceive inequalities: these inequalities, advancing a few steps more, take on the appearance of pillars; but whether round or square, we are uncertain: our curiosity anticipating our progress, cannot rest in suspense: we naturally suppose the most complete pillar, or that which is the most agreeable to the eye; and we immediately perceive, or seem to perceive, a number of columns: if upon a near approach we find pilasters only, the disappointment makes these pilasters appear disagreeable; when abstracted from that circumstance, they would only have appeared somewhat less agreeable. But as this deception cannot happen in the inner front inclosing a court, I see no reason for excluding pilasters there, when there is any reason for preferring them before columns.

With respect now to the parts of a column, a bare uniform cylinder without base or capital, appears naked and scarce agreeable: it ought therefore to have some finishing at the top and at the bottom. Hence the three chief parts of a column, the shaft, the base, and the capital. Nature undoubtedly requires a certain proportion among these parts, but not limited within precise bounds. I suspect that the proportions in use have been influenced in some degree by the human figure; the capital being conceived as the head, the base as the feet. With respect to the base indeed, the principle of utility interposes to vary it from the human figure: the base must be so proportioned to the whole, as to give the column the appearance of stability.

In architecture as well as in gardening, contradictory expressions ought to be avoided. Firmness and solidity are the proper expressions of a pedestal: carved work, on the contrary, ought to be light and delicate. A pedestal therefore, whether of a column or of a statue, ought to be sparingly ornamented: the ancients never ventured any bolder ornament than the basso-relievo.

To succeed in allegorical or emblematic ornaments, is no slight effort of genius; for it is extremely difficult to dispose them so in a building as to produce any good effect. The mixing them with realities, makes a miserable jumble of truth and fiction[15]. In a basso-relievo on Antonin's pillar, rain obtained by the prayers of a Christian legion, is expressed by joining to the group of soldiers a rainy Jupiter, with water in abundance running from his head and beard. De Piles, fond of the conceit, carefully informs his reader, that he must not take this for a real Jupiter, but for a symbol which among the Pagans signified rain: an emblem ought not to make a part of the group representing real objects or real events, but be detached from it, so as even at first view to appear an emblem. But this is not all, nor the chief point. Every emblem ought to be rejected that is not clearly expressive of its meaning: if it be in any degree obscure, it never can be relished. The temples of Ancient and Modern Virtue in the gardens of Stow, appear not at first view emblematical; and when we are informed that they are so, it is not easy to gather their meaning. The spectator sees one temple in full repair, another in ruins: but without an explanatory inscription, he may guess, but cannot be certain, that the former being dedicated to Ancient Virtue, the latter to Modern Virtue, are intended a satire upon the present times. On the other hand, a trite emblem, like a trite simile, is disgustful[16]. Nor ought an emblem more than a simile to be founded on low or familiar objects; for if the objects be not agreeable, as well as their meaning, the emblem upon the whole will not be relished. A room in a dwelling-house containing a monument to a deceased friend, is dedicated to Melancholy. Its furniture is a clock that strikes every minute to signify how swiftly time passes: upon the monument, weeping figures and other hackney'd ornaments commonly found upon tomb-stones, with a stuff'd raven in a corner: verses on death, and other serious subjects, inscribed all around. The objects are too familiar, and the artifice too apparent, to produce the intended effect.

The statue of Moses striking a rock from which water actually issues, is also in a false taste; for it is mixing reality with representation: Moses himself may bring water out of the rock, but this miracle is too much for his statue. The same objection lies against a cascade where we see the statue of a water-god pouring out of his urn real water.

It is observed above of gardening, that it contributes to rectitude of manners, by inspiring gaiety and benevolence. I add another observation, That both gardening and architecture contribute to the same end, by

---

15. See chap. 20. sect. 5.
16. See chap. 8.

inspiring neatness and elegance. It is observed in Scotland, that even a turnpike-road has some influence of this kind upon the low people in the neighbourhood. They acquire a taste for regularity and neatness; which is display'd first upon their yards and little inclosures, and next within doors. A taste for regularity and neatness thus gathering strength, comes insensibly to be extended to dress, and even to behaviour and manners.

XXV

Standard of Taste

"That there is no disputing about taste," meaning taste in its most extensive sense, is a saying so generally received as to have become a proverb. One thing indeed is evident, that if the proverb hold true with respect to anyone external sense, it must hold true with respect to all. If the pleasures of the palate disdain a comparative trial and reject all criticism, the pleasures of touch, of smell, of sound, and even of sight, must be equally privileged. At this rate, a man is not within the reach of censure, even where, insensible to beauty, grandeur, or elegance, he prefers the Saracen's head upon a sign-post before the best tablature of Raphael, or a rude Gothic tower before the finest Grecian building: nor where he prefers the smell of a rotten carcass before that of the most odoriferous flower: nor jarring discords before the most exquisite harmony.

But we must not stop here. If the pleasures of external sense be exempted from criticism, why not everyone of our pleasures, from whatever source derived? If taste in the proper sense of the word cannot be disputed, there is as little room for disputing it in its figurative sense. The proverb accordingly comprehends both; and in that large sense may be resolved into the following general proposition, That with respect to the sensitive part of our nature, by which some objects are agreeable, some disagreeable, there is not such a thing as *good* or *bad*, a *right* or *wrong*; that every man's taste is to himself an ultimate standard without appeal; and consequently that there is no ground of censure against anyone, if such a one there be, who prefers Blackmore before Homer, selfishness before benevolence, or cowardice before magnanimity.

The proverb in the foregoing instances, is indeed carried very far. It seems difficult, however, to sap its foundation, or with success to attack it from any quarter. For in comparing the various tastes of individuals, it is not obvious what standard must be appealed to. Is not every man equally a judge of what is agreeable or disagreeable to himself? Doth it not seem odd, and perhaps absurd, that a man *ought not* to be pleased when he is, or that he *ought* to be pleased when he is not?

This reasoning may perplex, but, in contradiction to sense and feeling, will never afford conviction. A man of taste must necessarily feel the reasoning to be false, however unqualified to detect the fallacy. At the same time, though no man of taste will subscribe to the proverb as holding true in every case, no man will venture to affirm that it holds true in no case. Subjects there are undoubtedly, that we may like or dislike indifferently, without any imputation upon our taste. Were a philosopher to make a scale for human pleasures with many divisions, in order that the value of each pleasure may be denoted by the place it occupies, he would not think of making divisions without end, but would rank together many pleasures arising perhaps from different objects, either as being equally valuable, or differing so imperceptibly as to make a separation unnecessary. Nature hath taken this course, so far as appears to the generality of mankind. There may be subdivisions without end; but we are only sensible of the grosser divisions, comprehending each of them many pleasures of various kinds. To these the proverb is applicable in the strictest sense; for with respect to pleasures of the same rank, what ground can there be for preferring one before another? If a preference in fact be given by any individual, it cannot be taste, but custom, imitation, or some peculiarity of mind.

Nature in her scale of pleasures, has been sparing of divisions: she hath wisely and benevolently filled every division with many pleasures; in order that individuals may be contented with their own lot, without envying the happiness of others: many hands must be employ'd to procure us the conveniencies of life; and it is necessary that the different branches of business, whether more or less agreeable, be filled with hands. A taste too nice and delicate, would obstruct this plan; for it would crowd some employments, leaving others, not less useful, totally neglected. In our present condition, happy it is, that the plurality are not delicate in their choice. They fall in readily with the occupations, pleasures, food, and company, that fortune throws in their way; and if at first there be any displeasing circumstance, custom soon makes it easy.

The proverb will be admitted so far as it regards the particulars now explained. But when apply'd in general to every subject of taste, the difficulties to be encountered are insuperable. What shall we say, in particular, as to the difficulty that arises from human nature itself? Do we not talk of a good and a bad taste? of a right and a wrong taste? and upon that supposition, do we not, with great confidence, censure writers, painters, architects, and everyone who deals in the fine arts? Are such criticisms absurd and void of foundation? Have the foregoing expressions, familiar in all languages and among all people, no sort of meaning? This can hardly be: what is universal must have a foundation in nature. If we can reach this foundation, the standard of taste will no longer be a secret.

All living creatures are by nature distributed into classes; the individuals of each, however diversified by slighter differences, having a wonderful uniformity in their capital parts internal and external. Each class is distinguishable from others by an external form; and not less distinguishable by an internal constitution, manifested by certain powers, feelings, desires, and actions, peculiar to the individuals of each class. Thus each class may be conceived to have a common nature, which, in framing the individuals belonging to the class, is taken for a model or standard.

Independent altogether of experience, men have a sense or conviction of a common nature or standard, not only in their own species, but in every species of animals. And hence it is a matter of wonder, to find any individual deviating from the common nature of the species, whether in its internal or external construction: a child born with an aversion to its mother's milk, is a matter of wonder, not less than if born without a mouth, or with more than one[1].

With respect to this common nature or standard, we are so constituted as to conceive it to be *perfect* or *right*; and consequently that individuals *ought* to be made conformable to it. Every remarkable deviation accordingly from the standard, makes an impression upon us of imperfection, irregularity, or disorder: it is disagreeable and raises in us a painful emotion: monstrous births, exciting the curiosity of a philosopher, fail not at the same time to excite aversion in a high degree.

Lastly, we have a conviction, that the common nature of man is invariable not less than universal: we conceive that it hath no relation to time nor to place; but that it will be the same hereafter as at present, and as it was in time past; the same among all nations and in all corners of the earth. Nor are we deceived: giving allowance for the difference of culture and gradual refinement of manners, the fact corresponds to our conviction.

This conviction of a common nature or standard, and of its perfection, is the foundation of morality; and accounts clearly for that remarkable conception we have, of a right and a wrong taste in morals. It accounts

---

1. See Essays on Morality and Natural Religion, part 1. essay 2. chap. 1.

not less clearly for the conception we have of a right and a wrong taste in the fine arts. A person who rejects objects generally agreeable, and delights in objects generally disagreeable, is condemned as a monster: we disapprove his taste as bad or wrong; and we have a clear conception that he deviates from the common standard. If man were so framed as not to have any notion of a common standard, the proverb mentioned in the beginning would hold universally, not only in the fine arts but in morals: upon that supposition, the taste of every man, with respect to both, would to himself be an ultimate standard. But the conviction of a common standard being made a part of our nature, we intuitively conceive a taste to be right or good if conformable to the common standard, and wrong or bad if disconformable.

No particular concerning human nature is more universal, than the uneasiness a man feels when in matters of importance his opinions are rejected by others. Why should difference in opinion create uneasiness, more than difference in stature, in countenance, or in dress? The sense of a common standard is the only principle that can explain this mystery. Every man, generally speaking, taking it for granted that his opinions agree with the common sense of mankind, is therefore disgusted with those of a contrary opinion, not as differing from him, but as differing from the common standard. Hence in all disputes, we find the parties, each of them equally, appealing constantly to the common sense of mankind as the ultimate rule or standard. Were it not for this standard, of which the conviction is universal, I cannot discover the slightest foundation for rancor or animosity when persons differ in essential points more than in points purely indifferent. With respect to the latter, which are not supposed to be regulated by any standard, individuals are permitted to think for themselves with impunity. The same liberty is not indulged with respect to the former: for what reason, other than that the standard by which these are regulated, ought, as we judge, to produce an uniformity of opinion in all men? In a word, to this sense of a common standard must be wholly attributed the pleasure we take in those who espouse the same principles and opinions with ourselves, as well as the aversion we have at those who differ from us. In matters left indifferent by the standard, we find nothing of the same pleasure or pain. A bookish man, unless sway'd by convenience, relisheth not the contemplative more than the active part of mankind: his friends and companions are chosen indifferently out of either class. A painter consorts with a poet or musician, as readily as with those of his own art;

and one is not the more agreeable to me for loving beef, as I do, nor the less agreeable for preferring mutton.

I have said, that my disgust is raised, not by differing from me, but by differing from what I judge to be the common standard. This point, being of importance, ought to be firmly established. Men, it is true, are prone to flatter themselves, by taking it for granted, that their opinions and their taste are in all respects agreeable to the common standard. But there may be exceptions, and experience shows there are some. There are instances without number, of persons who cling to the grosser amusements of gaming, eating, drinking, without having any relish for more elegant pleasures, such, for example, as are afforded by the fine arts. Yet these very persons, talking the same language with the rest of mankind, pronounce in favour of the more elegant pleasures: they invariably approve those who have a more refined taste, and are ashamed of their own as low and sensual. It is in vain to think of giving a reason for this singular impartiality against self, other than the authority of the common standard. Every individual of the human species, the most groveling not excepted, hath a natural sense of the dignity of human nature[2]. Hence every man is esteemed and respected in proportion to the dignity of his character, sentiments, and actions. And from the instances now given we discover, that the sense of the dignity of human nature is so vigorous, as even to prevail over self-partiality, and to make us despise our own taste compared with the more elevated taste of others.

In our sense of a common standard and in the pleasure individuals give us by their conformity to it, a curious final cause is discovered. An uniformity of taste and sentiment in matters of importance, forms an intimate connection among individuals, and is a great blessing in the social state. With respect to morals in particular, unhappy it would be for mankind did not this uniformity prevail: it is necessary that the actions of all men be uniform with respect to right and wrong; and in order to uniformity of action, it is necessary that all men think the same way in these particulars: if they differ through any irregular bias, the common sense of mankind is appealed to as the rule; and it is the province of judges, in matters especially of equity, to apply that rule. The same uniformity, it is yielded, is not so strictly necessary in other matters of taste: men, though connected in general as members of the same state, are, by birth, office, or occupation, separated and

---

2. See chap. 11.

distinguished into different classes; and are thereby qualified for different amusements: variety of taste, so far, is no obstruction to the general connection. But with respect to the more capital pleasures, such as are best enjoy'd in common, uniformity of taste is necessary for two great ends, first to connect individuals the more intimately in the social life, and next to advance these pleasures to their highest perfection. With respect to the first, if instead of a common taste, every man had a taste peculiar to himself, leading him to place his happiness upon things indifferent or perhaps disagreeable to others, these capital pleasures could not be enjoy'd in common: every man would pursue his own happiness by flying from others; and instead of a natural tendency to union, remarkable in the human species, union would be our aversion: man would not be a consistent being: his interest would lead him to society, and his taste would draw him from it. The other end will be best explained by entering upon particulars. Uniformity of taste gives opportunity for sumptuous and elegant buildings, for fine gardens, and extensive embellishments, which please universally. Works of this nature could never have reached any degree of perfection, had every man a taste peculiar to himself: there could not be any suitable reward, either of profit or honour, to encourage men of genius to labour in such works. The same uniformity of taste is equally necessary to perfect the arts of music, sculpture, and painting; and to support the expence they require after they are brought to perfection. Nature is in every particular consistent with herself. We are formed by nature to have a high relish for the fine arts, which are a great source of happiness, and extremely friendly to virtue. We are, at the same time, formed with an uniformity of taste, to furnish proper objects for this high relish: if uniformity of taste did not prevail, the fine arts could never have made any figure.

Thus, upon a sense common to the species, is erected a standard of taste, which without hesitation is apply'd to the taste of every individual. This standard, ascertaining what actions are right what wrong, what proper what improper, hath enabled moralists to establish rules for our conduct from which no person is allowed to swerve. We have the same standard for ascertaining in all the fine arts, what is beautiful or ugly, high or low, proper or improper, proportioned or disproportioned. And here, as in morals, we justly condemn every taste that swerves from what is thus ascertained by the common standard.

The discovery of a rule or standard for trying the taste of individuals in the fine arts as well as in morals, is a considerable advance, but completes not our journey. We have a great way yet to travel. It is made out that there is a standard: but it is not made out, by what means we shall prevent mistaking a false standard for that of nature. If from opinion and practice we endeavour to ascertain the standard of nature, we are betray'd into endless perplexities. Viewing this matter historically, nothing appears more various and more wavering than taste in the fine arts. If we judge by numbers, the Gothic taste of architecture will be preferred before that of Greece; and the Chinese taste probably before both. It would be endless, to recount the various tastes of gardening that have prevailed in different ages, and still prevail in different countries. Despising the modest colouring of nature, women of fashion in France daub their cheeks with a red powder. Nay, the unnatural swelling in the neck, a disease peculiar to the inhabitants of the Alps, is relished by that people. But we ought not to be discouraged by such untoward instances. For do we not find the like contradictions with respect to morals? was it not once held lawful, for a man to expose his infant children, and, when grown up, to sell them for slaves? was it not held equally lawful, to punish children for the crime of their parents? was not the murder of an enemy in cold blood an universal practice? what stronger instance can be given, than the abominable practice of human sacrifices, not less impious than immoral? Such aberrations from the rules of morality, prove only, that men, originally savage and brutish, acquire not rationality or any delicacy of taste, till they be long disciplined in society. To ascertain the rules of morality, we appeal not to the common sense of savages, but of men in their more perfect state: and we make the same appeal, in forming the rules that ought to govern the fine arts. In neither can we safely rely on a local or transitory taste; but on what is the most universal and the most lasting among polite nations.

In this very manner, a standard for morals has been established with a good deal of accuracy; and so well fitted for practice, that in the hand of able judges it is daily apply'd with general satisfaction. The standard of taste in the fine arts, is not yet brought to such perfection. And there is an obvious reason for its slower progress. The sense of a right and a wrong in action, is conspicuous in the breast of every individual, almost without exception. The sense of a right and a wrong in the fine arts, is more faint and wavering: it is by nature a tender plant, requiring much culture to bring it to maturity: in a barren soil it cannot live; and in any soil, without cultivation, it is weak and sickly. I talk chiefly with relation to its more refined objects: for some objects make such lively impressions of beauty, grandeur, and proportion, as without exception to command the general taste. There appears to me great contrivance, in distinguishing thus the moral sense from a taste in the fine arts. The former, as a rule of conduct and as a law we ought to obey, must be clear and authoritative. The latter is not intitled to the same authority, since it contributes to our pleasure and amusement only. Were it more strong and lively, it would usurp upon our duty, and call off the attention from matters of greater moment. Were it more clear and authoritative, it would banish all difference of taste: a refined taste would not form a character, nor be intitled to esteem. This would put an end to rivalship, and consequently to all improvement.

But to return to our subject. However languid and cloudy the common sense of mankind may be with respect to the fine arts, it is yet the only standard in these as well as in morals. And when the matter is attentively considered, this standard will be found less imperfect than it appears to be at first sight. In gathering the common sense of mankind upon morals, we may safely consult every individual. But with respect to the fine arts, our method must be different: a wary choice is necessary; for to collect votes indifferently, will certainly mislead us: those who depend for food on bodily labour, are totally void of taste; of such a taste at least as can be of use in the fine arts. This consideration bars the greater part of mankind; and of the remaining part, many have their taste corrupted to such a degree as to unqualify them altogether for voting. The common sense of mankind must then be confined to the few that fall not under these exceptions. But as such selection seems to throw matters again into uncertainty, we must be more explicit upon this branch of our subject.

Nothing tends more than voluptuousness to corrupt the whole internal frame, and to vitiate our taste, not only in the fine arts, but even in morals. It never fails, in course of time, to extinguish all the sympathetic affections, and to bring on a beastly selfishness which leaves nothing of man but the shape. About excluding persons of this stamp there will be no dispute. Let us next bring under trial, the opulent whose chief pleasure is expence. Riches, coveted by most men for the sake of superiority and to command respect, are generally bestow'd upon costly furniture, numerous attendants, a princely dwelling, everything superb and gorgeous, to amaze and humble all beholders. Simplicity, elegance, propriety, and everything natural, sweet, or amiable, are despised or neglected; for these are not at the command of riches, and make no figure in the public eye. In a word, nothing is relished, but what serves to gratify pride, by an imagined exaltation of the possessor above those he reckons the vulgar. Such a tenor of life contracts the heart and makes every principle give way to self-interest. Benevolence and public spirit, with all their refined emotions, are little felt and less regarded. And if these be excluded, there can be no place for the faint and delicate emotions of the fine arts.

The exclusion of classes so many and various, reduces within a narrow compass those who are qualified to be judges in the fine arts. Many circumstances are necessary to form a judge of this sort: there must be a good natural taste: this taste must be improved by education, reflection, and experience: it must be preserved alive, by a regular course of life, by using the goods of fortune with moderation, and by following the dictates of improved nature which gives welcome to every rational pleasure without deviating into excess. This is the tenor of life which of all contributes the most to refinement of taste; and the same tenor of life contributes the most to happiness in general.

If there appear much uncertainty in a standard that requires so painful and intricate a selection, we may possibly be reconciled to it by the following consideration, That, with respect to the fine arts, there is less difference of taste than is commonly imagined. Nature hath marked all her works with indelible characters of high or low, plain or elegant, strong or weak. These, if at all perceived, are seldom misapprehended by any taste; and the same marks are equally perceptible in works of art. A defective taste is incurable; and it hurts none but the possessor, because it carries no authority to impose upon others. I know not if there be such a thing as a taste naturally bad or wrong; a taste, for example, that prefers a groveling pleasure before one that is high and elegant. Groveling pleasures are never preferred: they are only made welcome by those who know no better. Differences about objects of taste, it is true, are endless: but they generally concern trifles, or possibly matters of equal rank where the preference may be given either way with impunity. If, on any occasion, the dispute go deeper and persons differ where they ought not, a depraved taste will readily be discovered on one or other side, occasioned by imitation, custom, or corrupted manners, such as are described above.

If, after all that is said, the standard of taste be thought not yet sufficiently ascertained, there is still one resource in which I put great confidence. What I have in view, are the principles that constitute the sensitive part of our nature. By means of these principles, common to all men, a wonderful uniformity is preserved among the emotions and feelings of different individuals; the same object making upon every person the same impression; the same in kind, at least, if not in degree. There have been aberrations, as above observed, from these principles; but soon or late they always prevail, by restoring the wanderers to the right track. The uniformity of taste here accounted for, is the very thing that in other words is termed the common sense of mankind. And this discovery leads us to means for ascertaining the common sense of mankind or the standard of taste, more unerringly than the selection above insisted on. Every doubt with relation to this standard, occasioned by the practice of different nations and different times, may be cleared by applying to the principles that ought to govern the taste of every individual. In a word, a thorough acquaintance with these principles will enable us to form the standard of taste; and to lay a foundation for this valuable branch of knowledge, is the declared purpose of the present undertaking.

Appendix

Terms defined or explained.

1. Considering the things I am conscious of, some are internal or within my mind, some external or without. Passion, thinking, volition, are internal objects. Objects of sight, of hearing, of smell, of touch, of taste, are external.

2. The faculty by which I discover an internal object, is termed an internal sense: the faculty by which I discover an external object, is termed an external sense. This distinction among the senses is made with reference to their objects merely; for the senses, external and internal, are equally powers or faculties of the mind.

3. But as self is an object, and the only one that cannot be termed either external or internal, the faculty by which I am conscious of myself, must be distinguished from both the internal and external senses.

4. By sight we perceive the qualities of figure, colour, motion, &c.: by the ear we perceive the qualities high, low, loud, soft: by touch we perceive rough, smooth, hot, cold, &c.: by taste we perceive sweet, sour, bitter, &c.: by smell we perceive fragrant, stinking, &c. Qualities, from our very conception of them, are not capable of an independent existence; but must belong to something of which they are the qualities. A thing with respect to its qualities is termed a subject, or *substratum*; because its qualities rest, as it were, upon it, or are founded upon it. The subject or *substratum* of visible qualities, is termed *substance*, of audible qualities, *sound*; of tangible qualities, *body*. In like manner, *taste* is the *substratum* of qualities perceived by our sense of tasting; and *smell* is the *substratum* of qualities perceived by our sense of smelling.

5. Substance and sound are perceived existing in a certain place; often at a considerable distance from the organ. But smell, touch, and taste, are perceived at the organs of sense.

6. Objects of internal sense are conceived to be attributes: deliberation, reasoning, resolution, willing, consenting, are internal actions: passions

and emotions are internal agitations. With regard to the former, I am conscious of being active; with regard to the latter, I am conscious of being passive.

7. Again, we are conscious of internal action as in the head; of passions and emotions as in the heart.

8. Many actions may be exerted internally and many effects produced, of which we are not conscious. When we investigate the ultimate cause of animal motions, it is the most probable opinion, that they proceed from some internal power: and if so, we are, in this particular, unconscious of our own operations. But consciousness being imply'd in the very conception of deliberating, reasoning, resolving, willing, consenting, these operations cannot go on without our knowledge. The same is the case of passions and emotions; for no internal agitation is denominated a passion or emotion, but what we are conscious of.

9. The mind is not always in the same state: it is at times chearful, melancholy, severe, peevish. These different states may not improperly be denominated *tones*. An object, by making an impression, produceth an emotion or passion, which again gives the mind a certain tone suited to it.

10. *Perception* and *sensation* are commonly reckoned synonymous terms, signifying the consciousness we have of objects; but, in accurate language, they are distinguished. The consciousness we have of external objects, is termed *perception*. Thus we are said to perceive a certain animal, a certain colour, sound, taste, smell, &c. The consciousness we have of pleasure or pain arising from external objects, is termed *sensation*. Thus we have a sensation of cold, of heat, of the pain of a wound, of the pleasure of a landscape, of music, of beauty, of propriety, of behaviour, &c. The consciousness we have of internal action, such as deliberation, resolution, choice, is never termed either a perception or a sensation.

11. *Conception* ought to be distinguished from perception. External things and their attributes are objects of perception: relations among things are objects of conception. I see two men, James and John: the consciousness I have of them is a perception: but the consciousness I

have of their relation as father and son, is termed a *conception*. Again, perception relates to objects really existing: conception to fictitious objects, or to those framed by the imagination.

12. *Feeling*, beside denoting one of the external senses, has two different significations. Of these the most common includes not only sensation, but also that branch of consciousness which relates to passions and emotions: it is proper to say, I have a feeling of cold, of heat, or of pain; and it is not less proper to say, I have a feeling of love, of hatred, of anger, or of any other passion. But it is not applied to internal action: for it is not proper to say, that a man feels himself deliberating or resolving. In a sense less common, feeling is put for the thing that is felt; and in this sense it is a general term for everyone of our passions and emotions.

13. That we cannot perceive an external object till an impression be made upon our body, is probable from reason, and is ascertained by experience. But it is not necessary that we be made sensible of the impression. It is true, that in touching, tasting, and smelling, we feel the impression made at the organ of sense: but in seeing and hearing, we feel no impression. We know indeed by experience, that before we perceive a visible object, its image is spread upon the *retina tunica*; and that before we perceive a sound, an impression is made upon the drum of the ear: and yet here, we are not conscious either of the organic image or the organic impression: nor are we conscious of any other operation preparatory to the act of perception. All we can say, is, that we see that river, or hear that trumpet[1].

14. Objects once perceived may be recalled to the mind by the power of memory. When I recall an object in this manner, it appears to me the same as in the original survey, only more faint and obscure. For example, I saw yesterday a spreading oak growing on the brink of a river.

---

1. Yet a singular opinion that impressions are only objects of perception, has been espoused by some philosophers of no mean rank; not attending to the foregoing peculiarity in the senses of seeing and hearing, that we perceive objects without being conscious of an organic impression, or of any impression. See the Treatise upon Human Nature: where we find the following passage, book 1. p. 4. sect. 2. "Properly speaking, it is not our body we perceive when we regard our limbs and members; so that the ascribing a real and corporeal existence to these impressions, or to their objects, is an act of the mind as difficult to explain," &c.

I endeavour to recall it to my mind. How is this operation performed? Do I endeavour to form in my mind a picture of it or representative image? Not so. I transport myself ideally to the place where I saw the tree yesterday; upon which I have a perception of the tree and river, similar in all respects to the perception I had of it when I viewed it with my eyes, only more obscure. And in this recollection, I am not conscious of a picture or representative image, more than in the original survey: the perception is of the tree itself, as at first. I confirm this by another experiment. After attentively surveying a fine statue, I close my eyes. What follows? The same object continues, without any difference but that it is less distinct than formerly. This indistinct secondary perception of an object, is termed *an idea*. And therefore the precise and accurate definition of an idea, in contradistinction to an original perception, is, "That perception or consciousness of a real object, which a person has by exercising the power of memory." Everything one is conscious of, whether internal or external, passions, emotions, thinking, resolving, willing, heat, cold, &c. as well as external objects, may be recalled as above by the power of memory[2].

15. The original perceptions of external objects, are either simple or complex. A sound may be so simple as not to be resolvable into parts: so may a taste and a smell. A perception of touch, is generally compounded of the more simple perceptions of hardness or softness, joined with smoothness or roughness, heat or cold, &c. But of all the perceptions of external sense, that of a visible object is the most complex; because the eye takes in more particulars than any other organ. A tree is composed of its trunk, branches, leaves: it has colour, figure, size: everyone of these separately produceth a perception in the mind of the spectator, which are all combined into the complex perception of the tree.

---

2. From this definition of an idea, the following proposition must be evident, That there can be no such thing as an innate idea. If the original perception of an object be not innate, which is obvious, it is not less obvious that the idea or secondary perception of that object cannot be innate. And yet, to prove this self-evident proposition, Locke has bestowed a whole book of his Treatise upon Human Understanding. So necessary it is to give accurate definitions, and so preventive of dispute are definitions when accurate. Dr. Berkeley has taken great pains to prove another proposition equally evident, That there can be no such thing as a general idea; all our original perceptions are of particular objects, and our secondary perceptions or ideas must be equally so.

16. The original perception of an object of sight, is more complete, lively, and distinct, than that of any other external sense: and for that reason, an idea or secondary perception of a visible object, is more distinct and lively than that of any other object. A fine passage in music, may, for a moment, be recalled to the mind with tolerable accuracy: but the idea of any other object, and also of sound after the shortest interval, is extremely obscure.

17. As the range of an individual is commonly within narrow bounds of space, opportunities seldom offer of an enlarged acquaintance with external objects. Original perceptions therefore, and their corresponding ideas, are a provision too scanty for the purposes of life. Language is an admirable contrivance for supplying this deficiency; for by language, the original perceptions of each individual may be communicated to all; and the same may be done by painting and other imitative arts. It is natural to suppose, that the most lively ideas are the most susceptible of being communicated to others. This holds more especially when language is the vehicle of communication; for language hitherto has not arrived at any greater perfection than to express clear and lively ideas. Hence it is, that poets and orators, who are extremely successful in describing objects of sight, find objects of the other senses too faint and obscure for language. An idea thus acquired of an object at second hand, ought to be distinguished from an idea of memory; though their resemblance has occasioned the same term to be apply'd to both. This is to be regretted; for when knowledge is to be communicated by language, ambiguity in the signification of words is a great obstruction to accuracy of conception. Thus nature hath furnished the means of multiplying ideas without end, and of providing every individual with a sufficient stock to answer, not only the necessities, but even the elegancies of life.

18. Further, man is endued with a sort of creative power: he can fabricate images of things that have no existence. The materials employ'd in this operation, are ideas of sight, which may be taken to pieces and combined into new forms at pleasure: their complexity and vivacity make them fit materials. But a man has no such power over any of his other ideas, whether of the external or internal senses: he cannot, after the utmost effort, combine these into new forms: his ideas of such objects are too obscure for this operation. An image thus fabricated cannot be called a secondary perception, not being derived from an

original perception: the poverty of language however, as in the case immediately above mentioned, has occasioned the same term *idea* to be apply'd to all. This singular power of fabricating images independent of real objects, is distinguished by the name *imagination*.

19. As ideas are the chief materials employ'd in thinking, reasoning, and reflecting, it is of consequence that their nature and differences be understood. It appears now, that ideas may be distinguished into three kinds; first, Ideas or secondary perceptions, properly termed *ideas of memory*; second, Ideas communicated by language or other signs; and, third, Ideas of imagination. These ideas differ from each other in many respects; but the chief foundation of the distinction is the difference of their causes. The first kind are derived from real existences that have been objects of our senses: language is the cause of the second, or any other sign that has the same power with language; and a man's imagination is to himself the cause of the third. It is scarce necessary to add, that an idea, originally of imagination, being convey'd to others by language or any other vehicle, becomes in the mind of those to whom it is convey'd an idea of the second kind; and again, that an idea of this kind, being afterward recalled to the mind, becomes in that circumstance an idea of memory.

20. Human nature is not so constituted, as that its objects are perceived with indifferency: these, with very few exceptions, raise in us either pleasant or painful emotions. External objects, at the same time, appear in themselves agreeable or disagreeable; but with some difference betwixt those which produce organic impressions, and those which affect us from a distance. When we touch a soft and smooth body, we have a pleasant feeling as at the place of contact; and this feeling we distinguish not, at least not accurately, from the agreeableness of the body itself. The same holds in general with regard to all the organic impressions. It is otherwise in hearing and seeing. A sound is perceived as in itself agreeable; and, at the same time, raises in the hearer a pleasant emotion: an object of sight appears in itself agreeable; and, at the same time, raises in the seer a pleasant emotion. These are accurately distinguished. The pleasant emotion is felt as within the mind: the agreeableness of the object is placed upon the object, and is perceived as one of its qualities or properties. The agreeable appearance of an object of sight, is termed *beauty*; and the disagreeable appearance of such an object is termed *ugliness*.

21. But though beauty and ugliness, in their proper and genuine signification, are confined to objects of sight; yet in a more lax and figurative signification, they are apply'd to objects of the other senses. They are sometimes apply'd even to abstract terms; for it is not unusual to say, *a beautiful theorem, a beautiful constitution of government*. But I am inclined to think, that we are led to use such expression by conceiving the thing as delineated upon paper, and as in some sort an object of sight.

22. A line composed by a precise rule, is perceived and said to be regular. A straight line, a parabola, a hyperbola, the circumference of a circle, and of an ellipse, are all of them regular lines. A figure composed by a precise rule, is perceived and said to be regular. Thus a circle, a square, a hexagon, an equilateral triangle, are regular figures, being composed by a rule that determines the form of each. When the form of a line or of a figure is ascertained by a rule that leaves nothing arbitrary, the line and the figure are said to be perfectly regular: this is the case of the figures now mentioned; and it is the case of a straight line and of the circumference of a circle. A figure and a line are not perfectly regular where any part or circumstance is left arbitrary. A parallelogram and a rhomb are less regular than a square: the parallelogram is subjected to no rule as to the length of sides, other than that the opposite sides be equal: the rhomb is subjected to no rule as to its angles, other than that the opposite angles be equal. For the same reason, the circumference of an ellipse, the form of which is susceptible of much variety, is less regular than that of a circle.

23. Regularity, properly speaking, belongs, like beauty, to objects of sight: like beauty, it is also apply'd figuratively to other objects. Thus we say, *a regular government, a regular composition of music*, and, *regular discipline*.

24. When two figures are composed of similar parts, they are said to be uniform. Perfect uniformity is where the constituent parts of two figures are precisely similar to each other. Thus two cubes of the same dimensions are perfectly uniform in all their parts. An imperfect uniformity is, where the parts mutually correspond, but without being precisely similar. The uniformity is imperfect betwixt two squares or cubes of unequal dimensions; and still more so betwixt a square and a parallelogram.

25. Uniformity is also applicable to the constituent parts of the same figure. The constituent parts of a square are perfectly uniform: its sides are equal and its angles are equal. Wherein then differs regularity from uniformity? for a figure composed of similar or uniform parts must undoubtedly be regular. Regularity is predicated of a figure considered as a whole composed of resembling or uniform parts: uniformity again is predicated of these parts as related to each other by resemblance. We say, a square is a regular, not an uniform figure: but with respect to the constituent parts of a square, we say not that they are regular, but that they are uniform.

26. In things destined for the same use, as legs, arms, eyes, windows, spoons, we expect uniformity. Proportion ought to govern parts intended for different uses. We require a certain proportion betwixt a leg and an arm; in the base, the shaft, the capital, of a pillar; and in the length, the breadth, the height, of a room. Some proportion is also required in different things intimately connected, as betwixt a dwelling-house, the garden, and the stables. But we require no proportion among things slightly connected, as betwixt the table a man writes on and the dog that follows him. Proportion and uniformity never coincide: things perfectly similar are uniform; but proportion is never applied to them: the four sides and angles of a square are equal and perfectly uniform; but we say not that they are proportional. Thus, proportion always implies inequality or difference; but then it implies it to a certain degree only: the most agreeable proportion resembles a *maximum* in mathematics; a greater or less inequality or difference is less agreeable.

27. Order regards various particulars. First, in tracing or surveying objects, we are directed by a sense of order: we conceive it to be more orderly, that we should pass from a principle to its accessories and from a whole to its parts, than in the contrary direction. Next, with respect to the position of things, a sense of order directs us to place together things intimately connected. Thirdly, in placing things that have no natural connection, that order appears the most perfect, where the particulars are made to bear the strongest relation to each other that position can give them. Thus parallelism is the strongest relation that position can bestow upon straight lines. If they be so placed as by production to intersect each other, the relation is less perfect. A large body in the middle and two equal bodies of less size, one on each side, is an order that produces the strongest relation the bodies are susceptible of by position. The relation

betwixt the two equal bodies would be stronger by juxtaposition; but they would not both have the same relation to the third.

28. The beauty or agreeableness of an object, as it enters into the original perception, enters also into the secondary perception or idea. An idea of imagination is also agreeable; though in a lower degree than an idea of memory, where the objects are of the same kind. But this defect in the ideas of imagination is abundantly supply'd by their greatness and variety. For the imagination acting without control, can fabricate ideas of finer visible objects, of more noble and heroic actions, of greater wickedness, of more surprising events, than ever in fact existed. And by communicating these ideas in words, painting, sculpture, &c. the influence of the imagination is not less extensive than great.

29. In the nature of every man, there is somewhat original, that serves to distinguish him from others, that tends to form a character, and, with the concurrence of external accidents, to make him meek or fiery, candid or deceitful, resolute or timorous, chearful or morose. This original bent is termed *disposition*. Which must be distinguished from a *principle*: no original bent obtains the latter appellation, but what belongs to the whole species. A principle makes part of the common nature of man: a disposition makes part of the nature of this or that man. A *propensity* comprehends both; for it signifies indifferently either a principle or a disposition.

30. *Affection*, signifying a settled bent of mind toward a particular being or thing, occupies a middle place betwixt propensity on the one hand, and passion on the other. A propensity being original, must exist before any opportunity be offered to exert it: affection can never be original; because, having a special relation to a particular object, it cannot exist till the object be presented. Again, passion depends on the presence of the object, in idea at least, if not in reality: when the idea vanishes, the passion vanishes with it. Affection, on the contrary, once settled on a person, is a lasting connection; and, like other connections, subsists even when we do not think of it. A familiar example will clear the whole. There may be in the mind a propensity to gratitude, which, through want of an object, happens never to be exerted, and which therefore is never discovered even by the person who has it. Another who has the same propensity, meets with a kindly office that makes him

grateful to his benefactor: an intimate connection is formed betwixt them, termed *affection*; which, like other connections, has a permanent existence, though not always in view. The affection, for the most part, lies dormant, till an opportunity offer of exerting it: in this circumstance, it is converted into the passion of gratitude; and the opportunity is greedily seized for testifying gratitude in the most complete manner.

31. *Aversion*, I think, must be opposed to affection, and not to desire, as it commonly is. We have an affection for one person; we have an aversion to another: the former disposes us to do good to its object, the latter to do ill.

32. What is a sentiment? It is not a perception; for a perception signifies our consciousness of external objects. It is not consciousness of an internal action; such as thinking, suspending thought, inclining, resolving, willing, &c. Neither is it a conception of relation amongst objects or of their differences: a conception of this kind, is termed *opinion*. The term *sentiment* is appropriated to those thoughts that are suggested by a passion or emotion.

33. *Attention* is that state of mind which prepares a man to receive impressions. According to the degree of attention, objects make a stronger or weaker impression[3]. In an indolent state, or in a reverie, objects make but a slight impression; far from what they make when they command our attention. In a train of perceptions, no single object makes such a figure as it would do single and apart: for when the attention is divided among many objects, no single object is intitled to a large share. Hence the stillness of night contributes to terror, there being nothing to divert the attention.

> *Horror ubique animos, simul ipsa silentia terrent.*
>
> —*Æneid.* 2

---

[3]. Bacon, in his Natural History, makes the following observations. Sounds are meliorated by the intension of the sense, where the common sense is collected most to the particular sense of hearing, and the sight suspended. Therefore sounds are sweeter, as well as greater, in the night than in the day; and I suppose they are sweeter to blind men than to others: and it is manifest, that between sleeping and waking, when all the senses are bound and suspended, music is far sweeter than when one is fully waking.

ZARA: Silence and solitude are ev'ry where!
 Through all the gloomy ways and iron doors
 That hither lead, nor human face nor voice
 Is seen or heard. A dreadful din was wont
 To grate the sense, when enter'd here, from groans
 And howls of slaves condemn'd, from clink of chains,
 And crash of rusty bars and creeking hinges:
 And ever and anon the sight was dash'd
 With frightful faces and the meagre looks
 Of grim and ghastly executioners.
 Yet more this stillness terrifies my soul
 Than did that scene of complicated horrors.

—Mourning Bride, act 5. sc. 8

And hence it is, that an object seen at the termination of a confined view, is more agreeable than when seen in a group with the surrounding objects.

The crow doth sing as sweetly as the lark
When neither is attended; and, I think,
The nightingale, if she should sing by day,
When ev'ry goose is cackling, would be thought
No better a musician than the wren.

—Merchant of Venice

34. In matters of slight importance, attention, in a great measure, is directed by will; and for that reason, it is our own fault if trifling objects make any deep impression. Had we power equally to with-hold our attention from matters of importance, we might be proof against any deep impression. But our power fails us here: an interesting object seizes and fixes the attention beyond the possibility of control; and while our attention is thus forcibly attached by one object, others may solicit for admittance; but in vain, for they will not be regarded. Thus a small misfortune is scarce felt in presence of a greater:

LEAR: Thou think'st 'tis much, that this contentious storm
 Invades us to the skin; so 'tis to thee;
 But where the greater malady is fix'd,

> The lesser is scarce felt. Thou'd'st shun a bear;
> But if thy flight lay tow'rd the roaring sea,
> Thou'd'st meet the bear i' th' mouth. When the mind's free,
> The body's delicate: the tempest in my mind
> Doth from my senses take all feeling else,
> Save what beats there.
>
> —*King Lear, act 3. sc. 5*

35. *Genus*, *species*, *modification*, are terms invented to distinguish beings from each other. Individuals are distinguished by their qualities: a large class of individuals enjoying qualities in common, is termed a *genus*: a subdivision of such class is termed a *species*. Again, that circumstance which distinguisheth one genus, one species, or even one individual, from another, is termed a *modification*: the same particular that is termed a *property* or *quality* when considered as belonging to an individual or a class of individuals, is termed a *modification* when considered as distinguishing the individual or the class from another. A black skin and soft curled hair, are properties of a negro: the same circumstances considered as marks that distinguish a negro from a man of a different species, are denominated *modifications*.

36. Objects of sight, being complex, are distinguishable into the several particulars that enter into the composition: these objects are all of them coloured; and they all have length, breadth, and thickness. When I behold a spreading oak, I distinguish in this object, size, figure, colour, and sometimes motion: viewing a flowing river, I distinguish colour, figure, and constant motion: a dye has colour, black spots, six plain surfaces, all equal and uniform. The objects of touch, have all of them extension. Some of them are felt rough, some smooth: some of them are hard, some soft. With respect to the other senses, some of their objects are simple, some complex: a sound, a taste, a smell, may be so simple as not to be distinguishable into any parts: others are perceived to be compounded of different sounds, different tastes, and different smells.

37. The eye at one look can take in a number of objects, as of trees in a field, or men in a crowd: as these objects are distinct from each other, each having a separate and independent existence, they are distinguishable in the mind as well as in reality; and there is nothing more easy, than to

abstract from some and to confine our contemplation to others. A large oak with its spreading branches, fixes our attention upon itself, and abstracts us from the shrubs that surround it. In the same manner, with respect to compounded sounds, tastes, or smells, we can fix our thoughts upon anyone of the component parts, abstracting our attention from the rest. But the power of abstraction is not confined to objects that are separable in reality as well as mentally: it also takes place where there can be no real separation. The size, the figure, the colour, of a tree, are inseparably connected, and cannot exist independent of each other: the same of length, breadth, and thickness: and yet we can mentally confine our observations to one of these, neglecting or abstracting from the rest. Here abstraction takes place where there cannot be a real separation.

38. This power of abstraction is of great utility. A carpenter considers a log of wood, with regard to hardness, firmness, colour, and texture: a philosopher, neglectting these properties, makes the log undergo a chymical analysis; and examines its taste, its smell, and its component principles: the geometrician confines his reasoning to the figure, the length, breadth, and thickness. In general, every artist, abstracting from all other properties, confines his observations to those which have a more immediate connection with his profession.

39. Hence clearly appears the meaning of an *abstract term*, and *abstract idea*. If in viewing an object, we can abstract from some of its parts or properties, and attach ourselves to others; there must be the same facility, when we recall this object to the mind in idea. This leads directly to the definition of an abstract idea, *viz.* "A partial view of a complex object, limited to one or more of the component parts or properties, laying aside or abstracting from others." A word that denotes an abstract idea, is called an *abstract term*.

40. The power of abstraction is bestowed upon man, for the purposes solely of reasoning. It tends greatly to the facility as well as clearness of any process of reasoning, that, withdrawing from every other circumstance, we can confine our attention to the single property we desire to investigate.

41. Abstract ideas, may, I think, be distinguished into three different kinds, all equally subservient to the reasoning faculty. Individuals

appear to have no end; and did we not possess the faculty of distributing them into classes, the mind would be lost in an endless variety, and no progress be made in knowledge. It is by the faculty of abstraction that we distribute beings into *genera* and *species*: finding a number of individuals connected by certain qualities common to all, we give a name to these individuals considered as thus connected; which name, by gathering them together into one class, serves in a curt manner to express the whole of these individuals as distinct from others. Thus the word *animal* serves to denote every being which hath self-motion; and the words *man*, *horse*, *lion*, &c. answer similar purposes. This is the first and most common sort of abstraction; and it is of the most extensive use, by enabling us to comprehend in our reasoning whole kinds and sorts, instead of individuals without end. The next sort of abstract ideas and terms comprehends a number of individual objects considered as connected by some occasional relation. A great number of persons collected together in one place, without any other relation but merely that of contiguity, are denominated *a crowd*: in forming this term, we abstract from sex, from age, from condition, from dress, &c. A number of persons connected by being subjected to the same laws and to the same government, are termed *a nation*; and a number of men subjected to the same military command, are termed *an army*. A third sort of abstraction is, where a single property or part, which may be common to many individuals, is selected to be the subject of our contemplation; for example, whiteness, heat, beauty, length, roundness, head, arm.

42. Abstract terms are a happy invention: it is by their means chiefly, that the particulars which we make the subject of our reasoning, are brought into close union, and separated from all others however naturally connected. Without the aid of such terms, the mind could never be kept steady to its proper subject, but would perpetually be in hazard of assuming foreign circumstances or neglecting what are essential. In a word, a general term denotes in a curt manner certain objects occasionally combined. We can, without the aid of language, compare real objects by intuition, when these objects are present; and, when absent, we can compare them by means of the ideas we have of them: but when we advance farther, and attempt to make inferences, and draw conclusions, we always employ abstract terms, even in thinking. It would be as difficult to reason without them, as to perform operations in algebra without signs: for there is scarce any reasoning

without some degree of abstraction; and we cannot abstract to purpose without making use of general terms. Hence it follows, that without language man would scarce be a rational being.

43. The same thing, in different respects, has different names. With respect to certain qualities, it is termed a *substance*; with respect to other qualities, a *body*; and with respect to qualities of all sorts, a *subject*: it is termed a *passive subject* with respect to an action exerted upon it; an *object* with respect: to a percipient; a *cause* with respect to the effect it produces; and an *effect* with respect to its cause.

Finis

A Note About the Author

Henry Home, Lord Kames (1696–1782) was a Scottish judge, philosopher, and agriculturalist. Born at Kames House in Berwickshire, Home was educated by a private tutor until the age of 16. In 1712, he was apprenticed to a lawyer in Edinburgh. Called to the Scottish bar in 1724, he gained a reputation as a legal scholar and leading philosopher of the Scottish Enlightenment. In addition to his legal work, for which he was named Lord Kames in 1752, Home was involved with the manufacture of linen in Scotland as a prominent shareholder and director of the British Linen Company. Much of his writing is focused on property and the historical development of human society, making him an important early figure in anthropology and sociology. His book *Elements of Criticism* (1762) has been designated a landmark text in the development of the academic discipline of English literature. Home was a founding member of the Philosophical Society of Edinburgh and a patron to David Hume, Adam Smith, and James Boswell.

A Note from the Publisher

Spanning many genres, from non-fiction essays to literature classics to children's books and lyric poetry, Mint Edition books showcase the master works of our time in a modern new package. The text is freshly typeset, is clean and easy to read, and features a new note about the author in each volume. Many books also include exclusive new introductory material. Every book boasts a striking new cover, which makes it as appropriate for collecting as it is for gift giving. Mint Edition books are only printed when a reader orders them, so natural resources are not wasted. We're proud that our books are never manufactured in excess and exist only in the exact quantity they need to be read and enjoyed.

Discover more of your favorite classics with Bookfinity™.

- Track your reading with custom book lists.
- Get great book recommendations for your personalized Reader Type.
- Add reviews for your favorite books.
- AND MUCH MORE!

Visit **bookfinity.com** and take the fun Reader Type quiz to get started.

Enjoy our classic and modern companion pairings!

Bookfinity is a registered trademark of Ingram Book Group LLC. © 2023 Bookfinity. All rights reserved.

www.ingramcontent.com/pod-product-compliance
Lightning Source LLC
Chambersburg PA
CBHW031417150426
43191CB00006B/307